opposing viewpoints

SOURCES

america's economy

opposing viewpoints

america's economy

vol. 1

David L. Bender, *Publisher*
Bruno Leone, *Executive Editor*
M. Teresa O'Neill, *Senior Editor*
Bonnie Szumski, *Senior Editor*
Susan Bursell, *Editor*
Lynn Hall, *Editor*
Janelle Rohr, *Editor*
Julie Bach, *Assistant Editor*
Ken Iosso, *Editorial Assistant*
Karin Swisher, *Editorial Assistant*

Bernard S. Bachrach, Ph.D., *Consulting Editor*
Professor of History
University of Minnesota, Minneapolis

greenhaven press, inc.

577 Shoreview Park Road
St. Paul, MN 55126

"Congress shall make no law . . . abridging the freedom of speech, or of the press."

first amendment to the US Constitution

contents

Male/Female Economics

Welfare

foreword

"It is better to debate a question without settling it than to settle a question without debating it."

Joseph Joubert (1754-1824)

The purpose of Opposing Viewpoints SOURCES is to present balanced, and often difficult to find, opposing points of view on complex and sensitive issues.

Probably the best way to become informed is to analyze the positions of those who are regarded as experts and well studied on issues. It is important to consider every variety of opinion in an attempt to determine the truth. Opinions from the mainstream of society should be examined. But also important are opinions that are considered radical, reactionary, or minority as well as those stigmatized by some other uncomplimentary label. An important lesson of history is the eventual acceptance of many unpopular and even despised opinions. The ideas of Socrates, Jesus, and Galileo are good examples of this.

Readers will approach this anthology with their own opinions on the issues debated within it. However, to have a good grasp of one's own viewpoint, it is necessary to understand the arguments of those with whom one disagrees. It can be said that those who do not completely understand their adversary's point of view do not fully understand their own.

A persuasive case for considering opposing viewpoints has been presented by John Stuart Mill in his work *On Liberty*. When examining controversial issues it may be helpful to reflect on his suggestion:

> The only way in which a human being can make some approach to knowing the whole of a subject, is by hearing what can be said about it by persons of every variety of opinion, and studying all modes in which it can be looked at by every character of mind. No wise man ever acquired his wisdom in any mode but this.

Analyzing Sources of Information

Opposing Viewpoints SOURCES includes diverse materials taken from magazines, journals, books, and newspapers, as well as statements and position papers from a wide range of individuals, organizations and governments. This broad spectrum of sources helps to develop patterns of thinking which are open to the consideration of a variety of opinions.

Pitfalls to Avoid

A pitfall to avoid in considering opposing points of view is that of regarding one's own opinion as being common sense and the most rational stance and the point of view of others as being only opinion and naturally wrong. It may be that another's opinion is correct and one's own is in error.

Another pitfall to avoid is that of closing one's mind to the opinions of those with whom one disagrees. The best way to approach a dialogue is to make one's primary purpose that of understanding the mind and arguments of the other person and not that of enlightening him or her with one's own solutions. More can be learned by listening than speaking.

It is my hope that after reading this anthology the reader will have a deeper understanding of the issues debated and will appreciate the complexity of even seemingly simple issues on which good and honest people disagree. This awareness is particularly important in a democratic society such as ours where people enter into public debate to determine the common good. Those with whom one disagrees should not necessarily be regarded as enemies, but perhaps simply as people who suggest different paths to a common goal.

The Format of SOURCES

In this anthology, carefully chosen opposing viewpoints are purposely placed back to back to create a running debate; each viewpoint is preceded by a short quotation that best expresses the author's main argument. This format instantly plunges the reader into the midst of a controversial issue and greatly aids that reader in mastering the basic skill of recognizing an author's point of view. In addition, the table of contents gives a brief description of each viewpoint, allowing the reader to identify quickly the point of view for which he or she is searching.

Each section of this anthology debates an issue, and the sections build on one another so that the anthology as a whole debates a larger issue. By using this step-by-step, section-by-section approach to understanding separate facets of a topic, the reader will have a solid background upon which to base his or her opinons. Each year a supplement of twenty-five opposing viewpoints will be added to this anthology, enabling the reader to keep abreast of annual developments.

This volume of Opposing Viewpoints SOURCES does not advocate a particular point of view. Quite the contrary! The very nature of the anthology leaves it to the reader to formulate the opinions he or she finds most suitable. My purpose as publisher is to see that this is made possible by offering a wide range of viewpoints that are fairly presented.

David L. Bender
Publisher

introduction

"Every major idea of economics can
be simply expressed."

Leonard Silk

Editor's note: To aid the readers' understanding of economic theory and technical terms used throughout the articles in this anthology, the editors include here an excellent and basic overview of the American economy written by Leonard Silk. Mr. Silk is the economics columnist for The New York Times, *a former senior fellow of the Brookings Institution and chairman of the editorial board of* Business Week. *He is the recipient of a number of awards and the author of many books which emphasize understanding the science of economics for beginners.*

Every major idea of economics can be simply expressed. . . .

The abstract language and theories of economics have made many a person feel that this subject is just too difficult and too dull to be worth the effort. Alas, this is true for most laymen of a great deal of economic literature, as it is of the literature of physical sciences and social sciences.

But the importance of economics to people in their daily lives—in the "ordinary business of life," as Alfred Marshall put it—is too great for economics to be brushed aside as either irrelevant or too difficult. Economics does not have to be dull. Applied to the real problems of your life, and every one else's life, it can be compelling, exciting . . . and useful.

Today a bewildering array of economic problems cries out for solution. Some are grouped around issues of economic stability—inflation and unemployment; others around the growth of productivity and real income resulting from investment, research, technological progress, and improving human knowledge and skills; others around the growth of population, the scarcity of

Leonard Silk, *Economics in Plain English,* New York: Simon & Schuster, 1978, 1986. Copyright © 1986 by Leonard Silk. Reprinted by permission of SIMON & SCHUSTER, Inc.

resources, the persistence of poverty. At the same time, there remain the grand issues of order and freedom, the role of markets and the state, the design and redesign of the institutions of capitalism and socialism, and the struggle to build viable political-economic systems in the poverty-racked and debt-ridden countries of the Third World. Overall, there is the problem of how to build a stable and expanding international economic order. . . .

The Economy Changes

The physicist deals with events in a closed system—one not subject to influences or disturbances from outside. The physicist investigating the properties of matter can ignore such outside disturbances as national elections, changes in social moods, conflicts between nations, the ups and downs of business, or anything else outside his abstract version of reality.

The economist, however, is concerned with events in an open system—a system subject to all the outside disturbances the physicist can exclude.

Not every scientist can employ a system as closed and "pure" as that of the theoretical physicist. When a natural scientist is compelled to work in an open system, he is likely to be as uncertain in his findings and predictions as the economist. For instance, to predict next year's weather, the meteorologist, an open-system scientist, would need extremely detailed knowledge of present conditions all around the globe (since a small local deviation can cause an ever-expanding influence), information about the state of the sun (to predict changes in heat and corpuscular radiation), data from inside the earth (to predict volcanic eruptions and spread dust screens through the atmosphere). Further, the accurate long-range weather forecaster would need to be able to predict economic and political events (such as coal strikes or wars or nuclear tests; even a carelessly thrown match could cause deforestation and change rainfall and climate).

The economist is in the same open boat as the weatherman—or perhaps a worse one. . . .

Can the key concepts of economics be simply stated? Let's try.

Resources

Anything that can be employed to produce economic goods or provide services—such as arable land, oil, natural gas, minerals, forests, waterfalls and all other kinds of natural resources; human beings with their various strengths, skills, talents, and brains; plant, equipment, dams, generators, telephone systems, airports, airplanes, and all other forms of capital goods; mathematics, logic, science, technology, and other forms of human knowledge, some of which are embodied in machines, some in the minds of people, and some stored in libraries, computers, etc.

Resources are *necessarily* used in the production of goods—or, as economists love to say in one of their hoariest jokes, "There is no such thing as a free lunch," or TINSTAAFL. Of course, strictly speaking, there *is* such a thing as a free lunch—not just manna from heaven, but mother's milk, apples that fall on your head, berries beside the road, plankton (if you happen to be a whale), the pleasures of the sun in the morning and the moon at night, running brooks, fresh breezes, the oceans, the atmosphere, love. Some of these free goods become economic goods as civilization advances. But it is well to remember that both free goods and economic goods are capable of satisfying. . . .

Human Wants

These are both physical and psychic, and usually both together. Food satisfies a physical want, but caviar at $500 a pound obviously does a lot more than supply calories; so do our clothes, houses, cars, furniture, not to mention our books, films, sessions with psychoanalysts, lawyers, tennis coaches. Even doing nothing—leisure—fulfills a psychic want. Doing nothing may become the greatest aspiration of some people, those who aspire to the leisure class.

Scarcity

The gap between human wants and the means of satisfying them.

The age of scarcity is not ending, as John Kenneth Galbraith suggested two decades ago in *The Affluent Society*. On the contrary, because of rapid economic growth and the drain on nonrenewable natural resources, scarcity may be increasing. To be sure, one might end scarcity by reducing human wants rather than by trying endlessly to increase output. But, thrusting aside the "limits to growth" issue, the economist sees scarcity around him everywhere, every day, in little things as well as big—in the strain on family budgets and government budgets, in

people's conflicting wants for more income and less work.

Scarcity is really what economics is all about. Scarcity and choice.

Choice

To economize is to choose. Each individual must choose how best to satisfy his wants by allocating his limited time and energy to different uses and by distributing his income among the goods and services he wants to buy.

Each business organization must choose how to allocate its limited capital, labor, natural resources, management, and knowledge to achieve its objectives, including profits, growth, and the satisfying of public and governmental pressures.

Each nation must decide how limited resources can best be used to satisfy both the present and future needs and desires of its people—or of their leaders (not necessarily the same needs and desires). At a high level of generality, each nation can be said to have the same problems of deciding what goods to produce, how to produce them, who shall get them, and how much production and employment there will be both now and in the future.

Whether the problem of choice confronts the individual, a business organization or a nation, solving the problem will involve some cost.

Opportunity Cost

What you give up, in making one thing, by not making something else.

Since resources (with the sole exception of knowledge in certain forms) are finite and scarce, you can ordinarily satisfy one want only by not satisfying another want. If you use a field to grow oats, you can't use it at the same time to grow beans. If you use a day to produce thing A, you can't use it to make thing B. Time itself is limited. The opportunity cost of devoting a given amount of resources to national defense, for example, is not devoting those resources to social welfare—or vice versa. Thus, societies must make "trade-offs"— between guns and butter, energy and the environment, production of more goods versus more leisure, and so on, whenever resources are limited. So must individuals and businesses.

Cost-Benefit Analysis

An evaluation of what you spend or sacrifice in relation to what you get. This should be the basis on which you make choices and trade-offs.

If benefits exceed costs, a particular use of resources makes sense, though not as much sense as some other use where the benefits would exceed the costs by even more. This principle holds for all economic decisions, whoever makes them and however the decisions are made, whether by a single decision maker or by the interaction of many decision makers in a market.

Marginalism and Equilibrium

Most economic decisions are about a bit more of this or a bit less of that; we choose "at the margin." Consumers don't decide to give up meat altogether, if meat prices go up, but to buy a bit less of it, and substitute a bit more fish for meat. A businessman doesn't decide to get rid of all his workers if wages go up more than productivity, but he may decide to trim his work force and substitute machinery for workers in his effort to maintain or increase his profits. And, within a nation or the world economy, shifts go on all the time at the margin, with some workers and producers shifting from one line of production to another, with one nation expanding its output of electronics and cutting its output of textiles, and another exporting more of its foodstuffs and importing more of its oil.

All these shifts at the margin are conceived by economists as tending toward a state of "equilibrium," in which the consumer is satisfied with his pattern of consumption and sees no advantage in further change, the businessman has done what he could in response to higher wages or other costs and pressures, and the nations have ceased sorting out their division of labor and are ready to settle for the existing market structure. Of course, no such state of general equilibrium exists or has ever existed; life is change, imbalance, readjustment. Nevertheless, the concept of equilibrium has some usefulness for the economist in indicating the direction of change, and how the current problems of choice may be resolved before new disturbances occur.

Economic System

The setup in any nation that determines how resources will be used; what goods and what services will be produced; who will get them, and whether and how much the economy's capability of producing goods will grow.

A "command" system is one in which the government makes all those major decisions. A "market" system is one in which many firms and individuals, casting their "dollar votes" in the marketplace and interacting with each other, determine the answers. "Mixed" economic systems contain both "command" and "market" elements. Democratic socialism is such a mixture, with emphasis on public goods and social control of business. Communism is basically a command system, capitalism basically a market system, but in all advanced industrial societies (such as the Soviet Union and the United States) each system contains an admixture of the other. Purists within each system—hard-line Stalinists in the Soviet Union, libertarians in the United States—would like, to the extent possible, to get rid of the disparate elements of the other system. Purists often feel highly emotional or even religious about expelling what they regard as the alien "command" or "market," capitalist or socialist elements, as the case may be.

The Profit System

Those who think they understand it are constantly berating those who they think don't.

Profits are essential to capitalism. No business can survive without some. But that is not to say that any given level of profits is economically necessary or desirable. Competition is supposed to regulate the rate of profit of any firm or industry. Profits may be very high for some industry for a period of time because of growing demand or technological breakthroughs, and the high profits are supposed to attract new resources to expand production in that industry. But profits in that industry may stay high because of the existence of monopoly or oligopoly and the difficulty of entry by new firms.

Profits help provide capital for business investment in plant and equipment. Businessmen can also raise funds by borrowing at banks and from other savers through new stock or bond issues, but it helps firms to have some profits to show if they ever expect to repeat the process of borrowing.

In 1977 corporate profits after taxes amounted to 6.7 percent of national income—much less than most people believe. Several polls have found that the public generally thinks that corporate profits amount to one-third or more of national income.

Economic Incentives

Businessmen regard profits as the elixir of life and are inclined to treat them reverently. They grow furious with those whom they accuse of regarding profits as a dirty word. Profits, they say, are the incentive for creativity and efficiency. Profits are the preserver of liberty. Lemuel Boulware, a retired vice-president of General Electric Company and a titan of tough bargaining with labor unions, said, "Profit, property, and freedom are inseparable. . . . Profit benefits the nonowners much more than it does the owners of a business. Profit is even the poor man's best friend. It is the greatest engine of human betterment ever devised by man."

But non-true believers ask whether greater corporate profits and social welfare necessarily coincide. If particular companies' pursuit of greater profits means the rapid exhaustion of a scarce resource (such as soil or minerals), society may suffer, they say. Similarly, they add, the search for greater profits may influence foreign policy in dangerous or wasteful ways (as by maximizing arms sales to the Middle East or swelling the production of military hardware for national use or storage for future use).

In short, the cost-benefit ratio of individual firms, as measured by profits, does not necessarily correspond to the cost-benefit ratios for the nation or the world as a whole. The sum of optimal, profit-maximizing decisions by firms may or may not be the best decision for the society as a whole.

The toughest part of national and global decision making is measuring true costs and benefits; the same resources can be shifted to many different uses, and some costs (like that of pollution) are hard to calculate. It is also difficult to measure potential benefits, such as those of clean air, better-educated minds, a richer cultural scene or peace itself (within cities or between nations).

Practically speaking, even if one has a good idea of the national or global cost-benefit ratios and seeks to shift resources to better uses, it may be hard to get the people who control those resources to shift them or allow them to be shifted—because of habits or vested interests. A particular company or region doesn't always want to give up its defense orders; a labor union doesn't want to see jobs moved to another region or country where the benefits might be larger for the society as a whole, but not for the individual union and its members.

Those who habitually praise the free-enterprise, profit, or market system don't like to submit to the discipline of the market when it affects their own interests adversely, even if only in the short run.

Markets

Minisystems (or microsystems—their study is called microeconomics) in which particular goods and services are exchanged at a price, with the traders free to sell or not sell what they have for what they want.

Communist systems have markets (such as the markets for vodka or mandolins or underwear, as well as black or illegal markets) but the state plans and coordinates the (legal) markets. Capitalist systems are coordinated mainly be changing prices, costs, and profits.

Interdependence

In capitalist systems, all markets are interdependent, with money, goods, and services flowing from market to market, from consumers to producers to workers, and so on, around and around in a "circular" way. Money flows one way and goods and services flow the other, in an ever-continuing series of voluntary exchanges. The exchanges are voluntary because each party sees an advantage to himself or herself in the trade; thus, exchange is not what mathematicians call a zero-sum game (1 gainer + 1 loser = 0) but a positive-sum game in which both buyer and seller consider themselves winners—although one may win more than the other. But if any rational buyer or seller considers himself a net loser by an exchange, the exchange will not take place. Of course, people can be gypped—but they do not know that at the time

they make the deal, or they will not make it. And some people may regret having to sell something they own at a loss or buy something at a price far above what they had intended; but if they go ahead, it is presumably because it would cost them even more if they did not.

Division of Labor

These interlinked ideas explain why voluntary exchange, with benefits to both buyers and sellers, takes place. Specialization—the concentration of a producer (individual, business, or nation) on a narrower range of production than all the things it consumes—occurs because it results in greater efficiency; hence, the same resources can be used to produce more goods in total—so that there will be a bigger pie for the different specializers to divide up if they exchange shares of what each has produced with one another.

Each producer has a "comparative advantage" in doing what it does best—and trading for the rest. Just as a highly paid lawyer should not waste his time typing his own briefs (even if he is a better typist than his secretary) or a highly paid doctor should not paint his own house (even if he is a better and faster painter than any he can hire), a nation should concentrate on what it can do best, given its limited resources.

Critics of this argument contend, however, that free trade is a game stacked against labor or against poorer nations. Many labor unions in advanced countries claim that free trade undermines wage standards and shifts jobs to low-wage countries; they reject the counterargument of free-trade advocates that a rise in total productivity and output will increase the workers' share of a bigger pie, insisting that many workers thrown out of their old jobs cannot or will not move to the industries with "comparative advantage." Those who recognize that there is reality to this claim often propose that government should help the immediate sufferers from free trade to "adjust" by providing subsidies to help them move or to train them for new jobs; in effect, the beneficiaries of free trade ought to "bribe" the victims, and thereby share the benefits with them.

Poor countries also contend that rich, industrial countries have profited unduly and unfairly from free trade. The prices of industrial goods produced by the rich countries, they say, are fixed by powerful industries, while the prices of their own raw materials and minerals are set in highly competitive world markets to their disadvantage. The developing countries assert that their dependence on foreign markets makes their own economic development hazardous: a shift in world market prices can cripple their growth and worsen the misery and hunger of their people, who at best live at the edge of survival. . . .

Markets

All economics is divided into two major parts:

Microeconomics (micro=small): The part concerned with the behavior of people and organizations in particular markets; and

Macroeconomics (macro=great): The part concerned with the operation of a nation's economy as a whole.

We look at microeconomics, the study of particular markets, of which the two most fundamental concepts are *supply* and *demand*.

Supply

The varying amounts of any good that its producers or owners are willing to offer at different prices. To the economist supply is not a point (a fixed amount) but a curve that relates quantity to price.

In the case of supply, price and quantity are ordinary positively correlated; higher prices call forth increased supplies. Some suppliers are "price takers"; they must accept as given the price for their product that is set in the market. Among price takers are the producers of corn and wheat, leather and hides, coal and concrete, alcohol and ammonia, bricks and lime—products which are relatively homogeneous and which have many producers, so that it is easy for customers to substitute the output of one producer for that of another.

But some producers, called "price searchers," have a greater measure of control over a market and look for customers willing to pay the prices they set. Price searchers include local builders or merchants or candy concessionaires in a movie theater who can raise their prices above what outside competitors charge—because their customers find it inconvenient or more costly (including time and transportation costs) to go elsewhere. Some price searchers are big producers, like General Motors or the Aluminum Corporation of America, who are dominant forces in a wide market. And some are producers of highly specialized and desirable goods, such as Gucci shoes, Steuben glass, IBM computers, particular books, films, pharmaceuticals, musical instruments, etc.

Producers of different goods have varying degrees of "elasticity of supply"—the additional quantity they are willing to offer at higher prices. A few products have zero-elasticity of supply; there is only one Hope diamond, and no matter how much anyone is willing to pay, there will never be more than one Hope diamond—or one Mona Lisa, one Acropolis, one Marlon Brando. The market can bid the price of them skyhigh without increasing the supply.

But few goods are unique. Some are extremely elastic in their supply; you can get as many extra paper clips, cans of dog food, stockings, or copies of a best-selling book as you like, with little or no increase in price, or even a reduction in price over time.

Supplies of most goods are more elastic in the long run than in the short, because it takes time for producers to expand their plant for making more of the product to meet increasing demand. Many goods will fall in price as the volume of production increases, due to "economies of scale" resulting from better technology, savings on materials, lower fixed costs, etc.; this has been the case with radio and TV sets, ball-point pens, calculators, computers, and chickens.

The general public and most politicians underestimate the elasticity of supply; they don't seem to believe, for example, that higher prices will bring forth more oil, or that increased supplies will keep oil prices from going through the roof. Nor do they believe that lifting rent controls in New York will bring more housing—including existing housing—on the market.

Price is determined by the interaction of supply and . . .

Demand

The quantity of any good that would be bought at different prices. Generally speaking, the higher the price of anything, the less of it will be demanded.

One's desire for a good is not the same as one's demand for it. Desire has to be backed by money and a willingness to spend the money to become demand. When the price of a good falls, a person may or may not actually buy more of it, depending on what he thinks an extra unit of that good is worth "at the margin"—on what economists call its "marginal utility."

Characteristically, goods have "diminishing marginal utility"—that is, the more you have of any particular good, the less you are willing to pay for an additional unit of it. If you have one auto, a second car may be worth considerably less to you, and a third may be worth far less than the cost of owning and operating one more car. A few products may seem to possess "increasing marginal utility," so that the more you get, the more you want—like eating pistachio nuts or drinking beer or smoking cigarettes. But sooner or later, diminishing marginal utility appears to set in. Even a billionaire may find that he has no appetite for that seventh villa, that third yacht, or that sixth wife. An exception may be drugs like heroin, on which somebody is "hooked." But these are pathological cases. Avid collectors of art, stamps, or rare books may also be slightly pathological—their appetites grow with consumption, rather than diminish.

Normally consumers, rich, poor, or middle class, vary their consumption patterns in response to prices going up or down for two basic reasons:

Using more of a now less expensive product and less of a more expensive one. If gasoline prices and taxes on "gas-guzzling monsters" go up, we may substitute smaller cars for larger ones, extra miles of commuting by bus for commuting in our own cars, or even apartments in town for houses in the suburbs or exurbs. One might even substitute status-enhancing clothes or jewelry for status-enhancing cars.

Shoppers routinely substitute cheaper chicken for dearer veal, Tide for Bold (or vice versa), etc., juggling new market prices and marginal utilities endlessly.

The Income Effect

The effect of a price increase or decrease on the real income of a consumer. A price increase causes one's real income to decline, a price cut makes it rise.

With a price *decrease*, the consumer has more money to spend either on that good or on other goods. Ordinarily, a price cut on a particular good makes it seem like a bargain, and that pleasant experience often leads us to buy more of it. Similarly, a price *increase* is experienced as unpleasant, and usually causes us to buy less of it—unless, as we noted in the case of Giffen's Paradox, the income effect of a price increase is such that one must consume more of the "inferior good" (potatoes or spaghetti or bread) whose prices have risen, as a substitute for the "superior goods" (steak or lobster or entertainment) which one can no longer afford.

The substitution and income effects, taken together, determine the elasticity of demand for any product. The demand for coffee, wine, oil, and food products (taken collectively, not individually) is relatively *inelastic;* producers who realize this often try to restrict supply in order to get or keep their prices up; the Arab oil embargo of 1973 was a perfect demonstration of how, in the face of highly inelastic demand, oil producers were able to restrict supply and greatly raise prices. Wine growers in France and milk producers in Wisconsin have been known to spill their products on the ground in order to keep prices up, in the face of inelastic demand. Their aim is to keep a small increase in supply from causing a huge drop in price—and in their own incomes.

The Price Mechanism

Markets come into equilibrium at the price at which supply (the quality offered) equals demand (the quantity demanded).

Sellers are satisfied (in the sense that they are selling all they want to sell at that price, and would not want to sell more at a lower price) and all buyers are satisfied (in the sense that they are buying all they want at that price and would not want more at a higher price).

Market prices may move up or down (or remain the same) in response to a host of factors causing shifts in supply (the whole supply curve) or demand (the whole demand curve) or both together.

Bad weather makes prices go up—not just the prices of agricultural products, but of a great many other goods, ranging from steel to nightgowns, because of interruptions of production, breakdowns in transportation, power failures, etc.

Changes in technology cause shifts in supply curves; a more efficient way of making transistors brings down the prices of calculators, computers, radios, television sets, record players, recorders. Increases in the scale of production, as we have seen, often bring down certain product prices.

Shrinking oil and mineral reserves contract supply, and prices move up. "Diseconomies" resulting from shrinking scales of production, as when the market for handmade pocketbooks, horsedrawn carriages, grandfather clocks, custom tailoring, and handmade furniture contracts, push up the prices of such products not only absolutely, but relatively far above what they were in the old days, when skilled labor was cheaper and more abundant.

Similarly, many factors can cause demand curves to swing up or down—booms or busts in the national economy, affecting the incomes of consumers; changes in taste—a President may increase the national taste for chamber music or hominy grits, a popular singer may increase (or decrease) the taste for orange juice; changes in "joint demand"—a fall-off in movie attendance may shrink demand for popcorn, a rise in interest in skiing may increase the demand for liniment and orthopedic surgery; changes in fashion—the Hamptons may be in, Newport may be out; changes in the seasons, changes in military threats, changes in the livability or stench and danger of cities, changes in the public mood toward hope or despair, excitement or boredom—in brief, changes.

The price mechanism sensitively catches and reacts to all such changes. If equilibrium prices of particular goods move up, more will be produced—because benefits to producers will tend to exceed costs by a wider margin—and human and material resources will tend to shift to those uses.

If equilibrium prices of other goods move down, less of them will be produced, as the cost-benefit ratio for producers is squeezed, and resources shift away to other uses, where the cost-benefit ratios (measured by profits) are higher.

Similarly, consumers will drop out of a market (or buy less in it) as their own cost-benefit ratio declines with a rising price of a particular product. Conversely, they will buy more of a product when their cost-benefit ratio improves.

This is how a market economy allocates its goods and services; the price mechanism constantly flickers out millions and millions of signals. These bits of precisely articulated information help producers to decide what to produce and consumers what to consume, in order to make more money or increase their satisfactions.

Income Distribution

The price mechanism also is the prime determinant of how income is distributed in a market economy—since income is the return to resources owners (including workers, who own and sell their own labor), as determined in the marketplace. You don't have to like it. But whether you do or not, it is the supply and demand of particular goods and services in the marketplace (backed up by the force of law protecting individual ownership rights) that determine that some rock singer makes a million dollars a year and some professor of microbiology makes thirty thousand dollars and some textile worker seven thousand dollars and some luckless people nothing (unless they get unemployment compensation or welfare).

In the United States, the government takes a hand in changing the distribution of income. It taxes money away from some and transfers it to others. Its purported aim (as through the progressive income tax) is to take relatively more from the rich and (through public education, health, housing, and other programs as well as transfers) give relatively more to the poor. In fact, however, much that government does transfers funds to the middle class or even the rich; for instance, state colleges and universities benefit the middle class or rich much more than they do the poor, and so do Federal housing plans, urban redevelopment programs, highway programs, subsidies for airports and private airplanes, grants for research and the arts, and some programs to preserve wildlife and the woods (where the rich and middle class go, rarely the poor). This does not make such government programs necessarily wrong; the programs may be inherently desirable—and beneficial in the long run also to the poor (if, for example, medical progress is fostered by research grants to the already well-off, or if subsidies to the development of solar energy ultimately protect the jobs and increase the living standards of the poor as well). Virtually every organized group in the society, from oil drillers to doctors to lawyers to farmers to workers to bankers to college professors to defense producers to old people to welfare recipients seeks to use the Federal government to increase its share of national income for allegedly worthy reasons.

But it is the operation of the market that fundamentally determines the distribution of income, although the role in government has grown increasingly important in shaping patterns. While government in the United States has not imposed an upper ceiling on individual incomes, it has put a rough floor under the lowest incomes. No one need starve or lack clothing, shelter, or health care—if he or she knows how to get help, which is a considerable *if.*

It is not only through government that various private groups attempt to alter the distribution of income in their favor. Discrimination against minority workers or women increases the take of male white workers, and some unions, whether openly or covertly, favor such discrimination. Management groups or university faculties may do (and in the past have done) the same. Government, through the equal-opportunity laws, tries to correct such discrimination.

The chief way that private groups seek to increase their share of income is by augmenting their monopoly power in the market.

Monopoly

A market structure in which there is complete control by one seller of the production or sale of a product or service. Those who praise monopoly say it permits strong firms to do research, be nice to their workers and benefit society. Those who damn it say it milks consumers and leads to excessively concentrated political as well as economic power.

Competition

The opposite of monopoly—a market in which many suppliers contend for sales and many consumers contend for available goods. Competition is considered a good way of keeping suppliers on their toes and passing benefits along to consumers. The foes of competition always insist that they are trying to prevent "cutthroat" competition—stores that underprice "unfairly," osteopathic physicians who take clients away from M.D.'s, foreign producers who "dump" their goods at prices below costs, gypsy taxi drivers who are breaking the fee structure of licensed cabs and allegedly taking bread out of the mouths of the children of legitimate cab drivers, etc. The simple rule is: Monopolists hate competition.

Monopolistic Competition

The halfway house between monopoly and competition; monopolistic competition is where things are in most major American industries.

The question is how concentrated an industry must be before its market power is to be deemed injurious to the public interest. Alternatively, when can an industry be regarded as "workably" competitive? The antitrust authorities and the courts are supposed to sort out that difficult issue. They tackle it hesitantly, torn between the goals of efficiency and equity, a fundamental conflict within a mixed economy.

Efficiency Versus Equity

Lovers of the market system say its glory is its efficiency; it gives the most output for any given set of resources. But critics contend that markets are not necessarily "fair" (they may reward the greedy or tricky, not the good or even the socially valuable). And, add the critics, market prices do not take account of the undesirable social effects of production—such "externalities" as filth, contamination of water and air, urban congestion, ruin of land (as from strip mining), or the depletion of natural resources. Nor, they say, does the market price provide a reward for *favorable* externalities, such as housing that improves the whole community, or the growth of skills and knowledge that results from a company's research and training programs, so that such effects are underproduced relative to social need.

Markets are criticized for distributing income unequally and arbitrarily; excessively large rewards go, say the critics, to those who got to a country first—and their heirs. The critics contend that in advanced capitalist economies markets are dominated by producers and stacked against consumer interests.

The defenders of capitalism sometimes concede that markets are imperfect, but they say that other systems are marred by complete domination of consumers by producers. In Communist countries, the state is the sole monopolist and the sole check on its own powers. . . .

A command system has difficulty in distributing rewards and providing economic incentives for the host of small daily actions that add up to good service and attention to consumer needs and tastes. Can Orders of Lenin or good-conduct medals do the job for the hosts of salespeople and producers involved? Awarding the medals is, after all, a command function that doesn't change the system. Can *fear* be as efficient as the desire for personal gain and the daily pressures of the marketplace? Not likely.

Private Goods and Public Goods

Critics of capitalism assert, however, that it is loaded in favor of such "private" goods as autos, soap, deodorants, watches, refrigerators, clothing, etc., and against "public goods," such as public television, public beaches, concert halls, museums, symphony orchestras, ballets, parks, hospitals, medical services, public schools, or decent homes for the aged. Private goods are favored by the market system, say its critics, because they are easier to produce, package, sell—and make a profit on.

But champions of the market system say private goods are what customers really want. Given a free choice, they assert, people always prefer to spend their own money on whatever they prefer, rather than pay higher taxes and have the government spend it for them, allegedly in their own best interests.

The critics respond that people have been "brainwashed" by advertising, and corrupted by the all-pervasive commercial culture and by their desires for status and the attributes of material success. Public goods are slighted by market systems, say the critics, because they are hard to sell to individual customers. Since everyone shares public goods, each individual thinks, "If I don't pay for my small share (of a park, a school system, or public TV) it won't matter much. I won't get less of it. Let somebody else pay."

But the champions of capitalism maintain that Communist societies don't do any better on public goods than do capitalist societies; if anything, they say, the Communists are less sensitive to pollution and environmental considerations, less efficient in providing public services to citizens, because they are more secretive, less democratic, less subject to being cast out by the electorate. Indeed, public goods in totalitarian societies are evaluated as to whether they will enhance the power and prolong the regime of the political authorities and the bureaucracy, not whether they serve the interests of ordinary people. . . .

The Challenge of Economics

Some danger exists that economics—a limited field but one with some significant achievements behind it—will drown prematurely in a sea of related disciplines and philosophical speculations before it has adequately solved some of its own traditional problems, such as how simultaneously to achieve full employment and price, stability, and how to put together a stable, essentially free, and expanding world economy.

Yet it seems to me that efforts to solve even those traditional economic problems cannot be hampered, but only advanced, by a deeper understanding of many matters that lie beyond the boundaries of conventional economics.

Business Does Have Social Responsibility

Robert Almeder

In order to create a climate more favorable for corporate activity, International Telephone and Telegraph allegedly contributed large sums of money to "destabilize" the duly elected government of Chile. Even though advised by the scientific community that the practice is lethal, major chemical companies reportedly continue to dump large amounts of carcinogens into the water supply of various areas and, at the same time, lobby to prevent legislation against such practices. General Motors Corporation, other automobile manufacturers, and Firestone Tire and Rubber Corporation have frequently defended themselves against the charge that they knowingly and willingly marketed a product that, owing to defective design, had been reliably predicted to kill a certain percentage of its users and, moreover, refused to recall promptly the product even when government agencies documented the large incidence of death as a result of the defective product. Finally, people often say that numerous advertising companies happily accept, and earnestly solicit, accounts to advertise cigarettes knowing full well that as a direct result of their advertising activities a certain number of people will die considerably prematurely and painfully. We need not concern ourselves with whether these and other similar charges are true because our concern here is with what might count as a justification for such corporate conduct were it to occur. There can be no question that such behavior is frequently legal. The question is whether corporate behavior should be constrained by nonlegal or moral considerations. As things presently stand, it seems to be a dogma of contemporary capitalism that the sole responsibility of business is to make as much money as is legally possible. But

the question is whether this view is rationally defensible.

Sometimes, although not very frequently, corporate executives will admit to the sort of behavior depicted above and then proceed proximately to justify such behavior in the name of their responsibility to the shareholders or owners (if the shareholders are not the owners) to make as much profit as is legally possible. Thereafter, less proximately and more generally, they will proceed to urge the more general utilitarian point that the increase in profit engendered by such corporate behavior begets such an unquestionable overall good for society that the behavior in question is morally acceptable if not quite praiseworthy. More specifically, the justification in question can, and usually does, take two forms.

Justifying Unethical Practices

The first and most common form of justification consists in urging that, as long as one's corporate behavior is not illegal, the behavior will be morally acceptable because the sole purpose of being in business is to make a profit; and the rules of the marketplace are somewhat different from those in other places and must be followed if one is to make a profit. Moreover, proponents of this view hasten to add that, as Adam Smith has claimed, the greatest good for society is achieved not by corporations seeking to act morally, or with a sense of social responsibility in their pursuit of profit, but rather by each corporation seeking to maximize its own profit, unregulated in that endeavor except by the laws of supply and demand along with whatever other laws are inherent to the competition process. Smith's view, that there is an invisible hand, as it were, directing an economy governed solely by the profit motive to the greatest good for society, is still the dominant motivation and justification for those who would want an economy unregulated by any moral

Robert Almeder, "Morality in the Marketplace," *Business & Society*, Winter 1980. Reprinted with permission.

concern that would, or could, tend to decrease profits for some *alleged* social or moral good.

Milton Friedman, for example, has frequently asserted that the sole moral responsibility of business is to make as much profit as is legally possible; and by that he means to suggest that attempts to regulate or restrain the pursuit of profit in accordance with what some people believe to be socially desirable ends are in fact *subversive* of the common good since the greatest good for the greatest number is achieved by an economy maximally competitive and unregulated by moral rules in its pursuit of profit. So, on Friedman's view, the greatest good for society is achieved by corporations acting legally, but with no further regard for what may be morally desirable; and this view begets the paradox that, *in business* the greatest good for society can be achieved only by acting without regard for morality. Moreover, adoption of this position constitutes a fairly conscious commitment to the view that while one's personal life may well need governance by moral considerations, when pursuing profit, it is necessary that one's corporate behavior be unregulated by any moral concern other than that of making as much money as is legally possible; curiously enough, it is only in this way that society achieves the greatest good. So viewed, it is not difficult to see how a corporate executive could consistently adopt rigorous standards of morality in his or her personal life and yet feel quite comfortable in abandoning those standards in the pursuit of profit. . . .

"Being socially responsible in ways that go beyond legal profit-making is by no means a dubious luxury for the capitalist in today's world."

The second way of justifying, or defending, corporate practices that may appear morally questionable consists in urging that even if corporations were to take seriously the idea of limiting profits because of a desire to be moral or more responsible to social needs, then corporations would be involved in the unwholesome business of selecting and implementing moral values that may not be shared by a large number of people. Besides, there is the overwhelming question of whether there can be any nonquestionable moral values or noncontroversial list of social priorities for corporations to adopt. After all, if ethical relativism is true, or if ethical nihilism is true (and philosophers can be counted upon to argue for both positions), then it would be fairly silly of corporations to limit profits for what may be a quite

dubious reason, namely, for being moral, when there are no clear grounds for doing it, and when it is not too clear what would count for doing it. In short, business corporations could argue (as Friedman has done) that corporate actions in behalf of society's interests would require of corporations an ability to clearly determine and rank in noncontroversial ways the major needs of society; and it would not appear that this could be done successfully.

Perhaps another, and somewhat easier, way of formulating this second argument consists in urging that because philosophers generally fail to agree on what are the proper moral rules (if any), as well as on whether we should be moral, it would be imprudent to sacrifice a clear profit for a dubious or controversial moral gain. To authorize such a sacrifice would be to abandon a clear responsibility for one that is unclear or questionable.

If there are any other basic ways of justifying the sort of corporate behavior noted at the outset, I cannot imagine what they might be. So, let us examine these two modes of justification. In doing this, I hope to show that neither argument is sound and, moreover, that corporate behavior of the sort in question is clearly immoral if anything is immoral— and if nothing is immoral, then such corporate behavior is clearly contrary to the long-term interest of a corporation. In the end, we will reflect on ways to prevent such behavior, and on what is philosophically implied by corporate willingness to act in clearly immoral ways.

Proving the Opposition Wrong

Essentially, the first argument is that the greatest good for the greatest number will be, and can only be, achieved by corporations acting legally but unregulated by any moral concern in the pursuit of profit. As we saw earlier, the evidence for this argument rests on a fairly classical and unquestioning acceptance of Adam Smith's view that society achieves a greater good when each person is allowed to pursue her or his own self-interested end than when each person's pursuit of self-interested ends is regulated in some way or another by moral rules or concern. . . .

However, there is nothing inevitable about the greatest good occurring in an unregulated economy. Indeed, we have good inductive evidence from the age of the Robber Barons that unless the profit motive is regulated in various ways (by statute or otherwise) untold social evil can (and some say *will*) occur because of the natural tendency of the system to place ever-increasing sums of money in ever-decreasing numbers of hands. If all this is so, then so much the worse for all philosophical attempts to justify what would appear to be morally questionable corporate behavior on the grounds that corporate behavior, unregulated by moral concern, is necessarily or even probably productive of the greatest good for the greatest number. Moreover, a rule utilitarian would not be very hard pressed to show the many unsavory implications to society as a whole if society were to take seriously a rule to the effect that, provided only that one acts legally, it is morally permissible to do whatever one wants to do to achieve a profit. . . .

The second argument cited above asserts that even if we were to grant, for the sake of argument, that corporations have social responsibilities beyond that of making as much money as is legally possible for the shareholders, there would be no noncontroversial way for corporations to discover just what these responsibilities are in the order of their importance. . . .

For one thing, this argument unduly exaggerates our potential for moral disagreement. Admittedly, there might well be important disagreements among corporations (just as there could be among philosophers) as to a priority ranking of major social needs; but that does not mean that most of us could not, or would not, agree that certain things ought not be done in the name of profit even when there is no law prohibiting such acts. There will always be a few who would do anything for a profit; but that is hardly a good argument in favor of their having the moral right to do so rather than a good argument that they refuse to be moral. . . .

A Clear Moral Responsibility

In addition to the fact that the only two plausible arguments favoring the Friedman doctrine are unsatisfactory, a strong case can be made for the claim that corporations *do* have a clear and noncontroversial moral responsibility not to design or implement, for reasons of profit, policies that they know, or have good reason to believe, will kill or otherwise seriously injure innocent persons affected by those policies. Moreover, we have said nothing about wage discrimination, sexism, discrimination in hiring, price fixing, price gouging, questionable but not unlawful competition, or other similar practices that some will think businesses should avoid by virtue of responsibility to society. My main concern has been to show that since we all agree that murder for money is generally wrong, and since there is no discernible difference between that and certain corporate policies that are not in fact illegal, then these corporate practices are clearly immoral (that is, they ought not to be done) and incapable of being morally justified by appeal to the Friedman doctrine since that doctrine does not admit of adequate evidential support. In itself, it is sad that this argument needs to be made and, if it were not for what appears to be a fairly strong commitment within the business community to the Friedman doctrine in the name of the unquestionable success of the free enterprise system, the argument would not need to be stated.

The fact that such practices do exist—designed and implemented by corporate managers who, for all intents and purposes, appear to be upright members of the moral community—only heightens the need for effective social prevention. Presumably, of course, any company willing to put human lives into the profit and loss column is not likely to respond to moral censure. Accordingly, I submit that perhaps the most effective way to deal with the problem of preventing such corporate behavior would consist in structuring legislation such that senior corporate managers who knowingly concur in practices of the sort listed above can effectively be tried, at their own expense, for murder, rather than censured and fined a sum to be paid out of corporate profits. This may seem a somewhat extreme or unrealistic proposal. However, it seems more unrealistic to think that aggressively competitive corporations will respond to what is morally necessary if failure to do so could be very or even minimally profitable. In short, unless we take strong and appropriate steps to prevent such practices, society will be reinforcing a destructive mode of behavior that is maximally disrespectful of human life, just as society will be reinforcing a value system that so emphasizes monetary gain as a standard of human success that murder for profit could be a corporate policy if the penalty for being caught at it were not too dear.

"Corporations do have a clear and noncontroversial moral responsibility not to design or implement, for reasons of profit, policies that they know, or have good reason to believe, will kill or otherwise seriously injure innocent persons affected by those policies."

In the long run, of course, corporate and individual willingness to do what is clearly immoral for the sake of monetary gain is a patent commitment to a certain view about the nature of human happiness and success, a view that needs to be placed in the balance with Aristotle's reasoned argument and reflections to the effect that money and all that it brings is a means to an end, and not the sort of end in itself that will justify acting immorally to attain it. What that beautiful end is and why being moral allows us to achieve it, may well be the most rewarding and profitable subject a human being can think about. Properly understood and placed in perspective, Aristotle's view on the nature and attainment of human happiness could go a long way toward alleviating the temptation to kill for money.

In the meantime, any ardent supporter of the capitalistic system will want to see the system thrive and flourish; and this it cannot do if it invites and demands government regulation in the name of public interest. A *strong* ideological commitment to what I have described above as the Friedman doctrine is counterproductive and not in anyone's long-range interest because it is most likely to beget an ever-increasing regulatory climate. The only way to avoid such encroaching regulation is to find ways to move the business community into the long-term view of what is in its interest, and effect ways of both determining and responding to social needs before society moves to regulate business to that end. To so move the business community is to ask business to regulate its own modes of competition in ways that may seem very difficult to achieve. Indeed, if what I have been suggesting is correct, the only kind of enduring capitalism is humane capitalism, one that is at least as socially responsible as society needs. By the same token, contrary to what is sometimes felt in the business community, the Friedman doctrine, ardently adopted for the dubious reasons generally given, will most likely undermine capitalism and motivate an economic socialism by assuring an erosive regulatory climate in a society that expects the business community to be socially responsible in ways that go beyond just making legal profits.

The Survival of Capitalism

In sum, being socially responsible in ways that go beyond legal profit-making is by no means a dubious luxury for the capitalist in today's world. It is a necessity if capitalism is to survive at all; and, presumably, we shall all profit with the survival of a vibrant capitalism. If anything, then, rigid adherence to the Friedman doctrine is not only philosophically unjustified, and unjustifiable, it is also unprofitable in the long run, and therefore, downright subversive of the long-term common good. Unfortunately, taking the long-run view is difficult for everyone. After all, for each of us, tomorrow may not come. But living for today only does not seem to make much sense either, if that deprives us of any reasonable and happy tomorrow. Living for the future may not be the healthiest thing to do; but do it we must, if we have good reason to think that we will have a future. The trick is to provide for the future without living in it, and that just requires being moral.

Robert Almeder is a professor of philosophy at Georgia State University.

"In his capacity as a corporate executive, the manager is the agent of the individuals who own the corporation . . . and his primary responsibility is to them."

Business Does Not Have Social Responsibility

Milton Friedman

When I hear businessmen speak eloquently about the "social responsibilities of business in a free-enterprise system," I am reminded of the wonderful line about a Frenchman who discovered at the age of 70 that he had been speaking prose all his life. The businessmen believe that they are defending free enterprise when they declaim that business is not concerned "merely" with profit but also with promoting desirable "social" ends; that business has a "social conscience" and takes seriously its responsibilities for providing employment, eliminating discrimination, avoiding pollution and whatever else may be the catchwords of the contemporary crop of reformers. In fact they are—or would be if they or anyone else took them seriously—preaching pure and unadulterated socialism. Businessmen who talk this way are unwitting puppets of the intellectual forces that have been undermining the basis of a free society these past decades.

The discussions of the "social responsibilities of business" are notable for their analytical looseness and lack of rigor. What does it mean to say that "business" has responsibilities? Only people can have responsibilities. A corporation is an artificial person and in this sense may have artificial responsibilities, but "business" as a whole cannot be said to have responsibilities, even in this vague sense. The first step toward clarity in examining the doctrine of the social responsibility of business is to ask precisely what it implies for whom.

Presumably, the individuals who are to be responsible are businessmen, which means individual proprietors or corporate executives. Most of the discussion of social responsibility is directed at corporations, so in what follows I shall mostly neglect the individual proprietor and speak of corporate executives.

In a free enterprise, private-property system, a corporate executive is an employe of the owners of the business. He has direct responsibility to his employers. That responsibility is to conduct business in accordance with their desires, which generally will be to make as much money as possible while conforming to the basic rules of the society, both those embodied in law and those embodied in ethical custom. Of course, in some cases his employers may have a different objective. A group of persons might establish a corporation for an eleemosynary purpose—for example, a hospital or a school. The manager of such a corporation will not have money profit as his objective but the rendering of certain services.

Manager's Primary Responsibility

In either case, the key point is that, in his capacity as a corporate executive, the manager is the agent of the individuals who own the corporation or establish the eleemosynary institution, and his primary responsibility is to them. . . .

Of course, the corporate executive is also a person in his own right. As a person, he may have many other responsibilities that he recognizes or assumes voluntarily—to his family, his conscience, his feelings of charity, his church, his clubs, his city, his country. He may feel impelled by these responsibilities to devote part of his income to causes he regards as worthy, to refuse to work for particular corporations, even to leave his job, for example, to join his country's armed forces. If we wish, we may refer to some of these responsibilities as "social responsibilities." But in these respects he is acting as a principal, not an agent; he is spending his own money or time or energy, not the money of his employers or the time or energy he has contracted to devote to their purposes. If these are "social

Milton Friedman, "The Social Responsibility of Business Is to Increase Its Profits," *The New York Times*, September 13, 1970. Copyright © 1970 by The New York Times Company. Reprinted by permission.

responsibilities," they are the social responsibilities of individuals, not of business.

What does it mean to say that the corporate executive has a "social responsibility" in his capacity as businessman? If this statement is not pure rhetoric, it must mean that he is to act in some way that is not in the interest of his employers. For example, that he is to refrain from increasing the price of the product in order to contribute to the social objective of preventing inflation, even though a price increase would be in the best interests of the corporation. Or that he is to make expenditures on reducing pollution beyond the amount that is in the best interests of the corporation or that is required by law in order to contribute to the social objective of improving the environment. Or that, at the expense of corporate profits, he is to hire "hard-core" unemployed instead of better-qualified available workmen to contribute to the social objective of reducing poverty.

In each of these cases, the corporate executive would be spending someone else's money for a general social interest. Insofar as his actions in accord with his "social responsibility" reduce returns to stockholders, he is spending their money. Insofar as his actions raise the price to customers, he is spending the customers' money. Insofar as his actions lower the wages of some employes, he is spending their money. . . .

Unanswered Questions

On the grounds of consequences, can the corporate executive in fact discharge his alleged "social responsibilities"? On the one hand, suppose he could get away with spending the stockholders' or customers' or employes' money. How is he to know how to spend it? He is told that he must contribute to fighting inflation. How is he to know what action of his will contribute to that end? He is presumably an expert in running his company—in producing a product or selling it or financing it. But nothing about his selection makes him an expert on inflation. Will holding down the price of his product reduce inflationary pressure? Or, by leaving more spending power in the hands of his customers, simply divert it elsewhere? Or, by forcing him to produce less because of the low price, will it simply contribute to shortages? Even if he could answer these questions, how much cost is he justified in imposing on his stockholders, customers and employes for this social purpose? What is his appropriate share and what is the appropriate share of others?

And, whether he wants to or not, can he get away with spending his stockholders', customers' or employes' money? Will not the stockholders fire him? (Either the present ones or those who take over when his actions in the name of social responsibility have reduced the corporation's profits and the price of its stock.) His customers and his employes can

desert him for other products and employers less scrupulous in exercising their social responsibilities. . . .

Many a reader who has followed the argument this far may be tempted to remonstrate that it is all well and good to speak of Government's having the responsibility to impose taxes and determine expenditures for such "social" purposes as controlling pollution or training the hard-core unemployed, but that the problems are too urgent to wait on the slow course of political processes, that the exercise of social responsibility by businessmen is a quicker and surer way to solve pressing current problems.

"In practice the doctrine of social responsibility is frequently a cloak for actions that are justified on other grounds rather than a reason for those actions."

Aside from the question of fact—I share Adam Smith's skepticism about the benefits that can be expected from "those who affected to trade for the public good"—this argument must be rejected on grounds of principle. What it amounts to is an assertion that those who favor the taxes and expenditures in question have failed to persuade a majority of their fellow citizens to be of like mind and that they are seeking to attain by undemocratic procedures what they cannot attain by democratic procedures. In a free society, it is hard for "good" people to do "good," but that is a small price to pay for making it hard for "evil" people to do "evil," especially since one man's good is another's evil. . . .

A Fraudulent Cloak

Of course, in practice the doctrine of social responsibility is frequently a cloak for actions that are justified on other grounds rather than a reason for those actions.

To illustrate, it may well be in the long-run interest of a corporation that is a major employer in a small community to devote resources to providing amenities to that community or to improving its government. That may make it easier to attract desirable employes, it may reduce the wage bill or lessen losses from pilferage and sabotage or have other worthwhile effects. Or it may be that, given the laws about the deductibility of corporate charitable contributions, the stockholders can contribute more to charities they favor by having the corporation make the gift than by doing it themselves, since they can in that way contribute an amount that would otherwise have been paid as corporate taxes.

In each of these—and many similar—cases, there is a strong temptation to rationalize these actions as an exercise of "social responsibility." In the present climate of opinion, with its widespread aversion to "capitalism," "profits," the "soulless corporation" and so on, this is one way for a corporation to generate good will as a by-product of expenditures that are entirely justified in its own self-interest.

It would be inconsistent of me to call on corporate executives to refrain from this hypocritical window-dressing because it harms the foundations of a free society. That would be to call on them to exercise "social responsibility"! If our institutions, and the attitudes of the public, make it in their self-interest to cloak their actions in this way, I cannot summon much indignation to denounce them. At the same time, I can express admiration for those individual proprietors or owners of closely held corporations or stockholders of more broadly held corporations who disdain such tactics as approaching fraud.

Maintaining a Market System

Whether blameworthy or not, the use of the cloak of social responsibility, and the nonsense spoken in its name by influential and prestigious businessmen, does clearly harm the foundations of a free society. I have been impressed time and again by the schizophrenic character of many businessmen. They are capable of being extremely far-sighted and clear-headed in matters that are internal to their businesses. They are incredibly short-sighted and muddle-headed in matters that are outside their businesses but affect the possible survival of business in general. This short-sightedness is strikingly exemplified in the calls from many businessmen for wage and price guidelines or controls or income policies. There is nothing that could do more in a brief period to destroy a market system and replace it by a centrally controlled system than effective governmental control of prices and wages. . . .

"There is one and only one social responsibility to business—to use its resources and engage in activities designed to increase its profits."

The political principle that underlies the market mechanism is unanimity. In an ideal free market resting on private property, no individual can coerce any other, all cooperation is voluntary, all parties to such cooperation benefit or they need not participate. There are no "social" values, no "social" responsibilities in any sense other than the shared values and responsibilities of individuals. Society is a collection of individuals and of the various groups they voluntarily form.

The political principle that underlies the political mechanism is conformity. The individual must serve a more general social interest—whether that be determined by a church or a dictator or a majority. The individual may have a vote and a say in what is to be done, but if he is overruled, he must conform. It is appropriate for some to require others to contribute to a general social purpose whether they wish to or not.

Unfortunately, unanimity is not always feasible. There are some respects in which conformity appears unavoidable, so I do not see how one can avoid the use of the political mechanism altogether.

But the doctrine of "social responsibility" taken seriously would extend the scope of the political mechanism to every human activity. It does not differ in philosophy from the most explicitly collectivist doctrine. It differs only by professing to believe that collectivist ends can be attained without collectivist means. That is why, in my book *Capitalism and Freedom*, I have called it a "fundamentally subversive doctrine" in a free society, and have said that in such a society, "there is one and only one social responsibility to business—to use its resources and engage in activities designed to increase its profits so long as it stays within the rules of the game, which is to say, engages in open and free competition without deception or fraud."

Milton Friedman is a Nobel laureate economist, presidential advisor, and the author of numerous books, including Capitalism and Freedom.

"Unlawful business behavior . . . occurs with disturbing frequency."

Corporate Ethics Are Nonexistent

Mark Green and John F. Berry

Corporate illegality usually escapes major media attention—until its tawdry existence is rediscovered in a spate of shocked headlines, as though it were a new form of Legionnaires' disease. Such was the case . . . when an apparent corporate crime wave dominated the front pages. Some prominent examples:

Paul Thayer, former chair of LTV, is sentenced to four years in jail for perjuring himself to a Federal commission over insider trading activities. E.F. Hutton confesses to engaging in a multi-billion-dollar check-kiting scheme. General Electric admits it has defrauded the Pentagon by passing on bogus costs. The First National Bank of Boston owns up to violating the Bank Secrecy Act because it failed to report $1.22 billion in large cash transactions, some of which, according to the Justice Department, involved laundering drug money. Cartier is accused of tax fraud by the New York Attorney General's Office, and General Dynamics is charged with contractor fraud by the House Oversight and Investigations Subcommittee.

Rash of Corporate Crime

Will this . . . rash of corporate illegality elicit the same public outrage as street crime? Unlikely. The Reagan Administration talks about white-collar crime as often as it does Chilean oppression, while the media plays the acquiescent bystander. The criminologists downplay it. In the introduction to his influential book *Thinking About Crime*, James Q. Wilson writes that the public is correct in fearing crime in the streets more than crime in the suites because "economic violators don't make difficult or impossible the maintenance of basic human communities." As *The Wall Street Journal* editorialized a decade ago, "It isn't very helpful to

Mark Green and John F. Berry, "White-Collar Crime Is Big Business," *The Nation*, June 8, 1985. *The Nation Magazine,* Nation Associates Incorporated © 1985.

suggest that white-collar crime is a more serious threat . . . than predatory street crime, which inspires fear right across the board."

While the suffering exacted by violent crime should not be deprecated, it is also true that the loss of lives and dollars from unsafe products, pollution and price fixing greatly exceeds that from all the Saturday night specials in America. Exactly how extensive and expensive is unlawful business behavior? The answer is that it occurs with disturbing frequency. Four-fifths of the respondents to a 1961 reader survey by *The Harvard Business Review* thought that certain practices in their industry were unethical. Two decades later, four in ten businessmen and -women told a Gallup Poll that a superior had requested that they do something unethical; one in ten said they were asked to engage in unlawful conduct. In a monumental study of Federal court actions brought against the largest U.S. companies in 1975 and 1976, Marshall Clinnard and Peter Yeager found that 60 percent had had at least one action brought against them, and that 42 percent had had multiple charges. A 1982 survey in the conservative *U.S. News & World Report* concluded, "Of America's 500 largest corporations, 115 have been convicted in the last decade of at least one major crime or have paid civil penalties for serious misbehavior. Among the 25 biggest firms . . . the rate of documented misbehavior has been even higher."

Those statistics indicate that the recent headlines are less spectacular aberrations than revealing examples. What they do not reveal, however, is the cost. Corporate malfeasance is a tax of several billion dollars a year which cheats consumers and undermines the integrity of the business system. Let us itemize the bill:

When J. Paul McGrath became head of the Justice Department's Antitrust Division in late 1983, he announced that "there is a lot of price fixing out there that doesn't get detected." Indeed, in a survey of 110 presidents of Fortune 1000 companies conducted by one of the co-authors in 1971, 60 percent agreed with the general proposition that "many [companies] . . . price-fix."

Price fixing raises the cost of goods and services and it is a criminal offense. Federal antitrust authorities have successfully prosecuted companies in several industries with measurable benefits to consumers, as two examples show:

Since the Federal Trade Commission won a price-fixing case against Levi Strauss in 1978, purchasers have saved over $225 million on lower-priced Levi's jeans—about $2 less per pair—and on the lower-priced jeans of competitors.

Between 1979 and 1983, Federal prosecutors in twenty states broke a highway contractors' bid-rigging conspiracy. They obtained 400 convictions leading to 141 jail sentences and $50 million in fines. After the 1979 indictments, roadbuilding costs in Georgia fell about 20 percent. With the breakup of this cartel, the average number of bidders for Federal highway construction jobs grew from three to five.

What is the price of price fixing? One antitrust analyst concluded that, on the average, price fixing "inflates prices by some 25 percent or more above the non-collusive or competitive level." Economists' estimates for the annual cost of restraints on the market—price fixing as well as oligopoly and monopoly power—range from $32 billion (F.M. Scherer) to $265.2 billion (Keith Cowling and Dennis Mueller).

The Price of Pollution

Profit considerations encourage companies to pollute the environment. Free waste disposal, to be sure, cuts production costs to the firm, but only because residents, workers and other companies involuntarily pick up the tab in the form of diseases, higher health care premiums, increased mortality rates, decreased property values, higher repair costs and stunted economic growth. These "externalities," as economists call them, are a kind of transfer payment imposed by private managers on unsuspecting citizens.

Take air pollution, for example. According to a 1979 Environmental Protection Agency study, a reduction by 60 percent of the amount of sulfates and particulates released into the atmosphere by industry would produce health benefits every year worth $33.5 billion to $74 billion.

As for the water pollution "bill" for 1983, 82 percent of the companies that discharge wastes failed to comply with E.P.A. regulations regarding dumping into waterways. One group of researchers estimated that water pollution imposed $10.1 billion in damages annually—60 percent of which related to lowered property values and the restriction of recreational activities.

The toll of hazardous chemical wastes—including radioactive materials, heavy metals, asbestos, acids, synthetic and organic chemicals—is perhaps the highest of all. More than 226 million tons of hazardous wastes are generated annually—a ton for every person in the United States—and 80 percent of the firms disposing of this waste dump it into the environment illegally. According to the E.P.A., there are 32,000 toxic-waste dumps around the United States leaching chemicals into the soil under neighboring communities. The Office of Technology Assessment estimates that the cost of cleaning up those sites may be as high as $100 billion.

"Corporate malfeasance is a tax of several billion dollars a year which cheats consumers and undermines the integrity of the business system."

One long-term legacy of pollution is an increased incidence of cancer, though experts disagree about the extent of the correlation. There's a consensus that at least 7 to 10 percent of the annual 450,000 cancer deaths are caused by artificial chemicals—some 45,000 deaths a year. Since fifteen to forty years can elapse between the exposure and the cancer—and since most of the 53,000 commercial chemicals haven't been tested for health hazards—scientists and health officials worry that cancer rates may soon climb.

The Price of Discrimination

"A mind is a terrible thing to waste," says the advertisement for the United Negro College Fund. So is the talent of an employee, especially when it is wasted for the reason alluded to in the ad: discrimination. Racial and gender discrimination not only perpetuate inequality, they are also inefficient. Wasting employees' talents means that they never develop their personal potential and the economy never reaches its productive potential.

Blacks, on the average, earn 63 percent of what whites do and have an unemployment rate double that of whites. According to documents revealed in a 1983 civil suit in Alabama, some businesses refuse to open manufacturing facilities in counties with large black populations because blacks are thought more likely to join unions and less skilled than whites. A study by the Congressional Research Service found that in 1978 discrimination cost nonwhites $37.6 billion in lost jobs or inequitable salaries.

Women don't fare much better. A full-time working woman typically earns 64 percent of what a man with an equivalent position earns, a differential that endures despite decades of equal-pay laws. "A substantial chunk of the wage gap is simply due to discrimination," concluded Nancy Rhytina of the Bureau of Labor Statistics, after a study of full-time pay scales in ninety-one occupations. Based on this and on comparable-worth settlements in several cities, gender discrimination costs women $81.2 billion a year.

The Price of Payoffs

The suicide in 1975 of Eli Black, chief executive officer of United Brands, touched off a series of investigations that revealed what former S.E.C. chair Ray Garrett Jr. called a "corporate Watergate": "bribery, influence-peddling, and corruption on a scale I never dreamed existed." Under pressure from the S.E.C., some 500 U.S. firms admitted to at least $1 billion in foreign payoffs. According to an inquiry conducted by the commission, top management knew of or directed the payments in at least half of all disclosed cases.

Since the passage of the 1977 Foreign Corrupt Practices Act, the incidence of foreign bribery has dropped, though apparently it has not been eliminated. In 1984 the Justice Department investigated the Bechtel Group for bid rigging and illegal payments in South Korea. A Korean chauffeur reportedly told the Internal Revenue Service that on several occasions he delivered thousands of dollars in cash from Bechtel consultants to a South Korean utility that was awarding contracts for the construction of a nuclear plant.

What about domestic bribery? An ethic of corruption abroad can infect decisions at home; after all, the same management makes both judgments.

"Corporate illegality is a several-hundred-billion-dollar albatross around the economy's neck."

With millions of dollars riding on the decision of one procurement officer, some companies regard illegal bribes of several thousands of dollars to these officials as sound investments. In December 1983, the former chief executive officer and chair of Frigitemp pleaded guilty in Federal court to charges of conspiring to pay $2.7 million to General Dynamics executives to win subcontracts for the construction of natural-gas tankers. According to Jules Kroll, a New York City consultant specializing in procurement, "Graft by purchasing agents is considered a way of life in industries as unrelated as entertainment, car equipment rentals, apparel, printing, construction, retailing and many manufacturing industries."

Based on a 1977 estimate from the American Management Association, commercial bribery and kickbacks range from $3.5 billion to $10 billion a year, costs passed on to consumers in the price of goods and services.

The Price of Occupational Hazards

Each year some 6,000 workers—largely construction workers, steel workers, electricians, loggers and ditch diggers—are killed in industrial accidents. Five million more are injured, and 6.6 percent of those require hospital care. The National Institute for Occupational Safety and Health (NIOSH) has estimated that exposure to deadly chemicals and other toxic materials in the workplace causes 100,000 deaths anually and 390,000 cases of disease.

What is the economic toll of this human suffering? For occupational injuries in 1978, the bill came to $23 billion in lost wages, medical expenses, insurance claims and productivity delays. Management can't be blamed for all of this—just most of it. One study found that unsafe working conditions are responsible for 60 percent of on-the-job accidents.

The cost of occupational diseases is even higher. A Department of Labor study indicates that the tab for treating all such illnesses would be between $30 billion and $50 billion a year. According to a 1981 NIOSH risk assessment, under Federal health and safety regulations, 25 percent of all those working with asbestos—or 508,000 workers—will die of asbestosis.

The Price of Product Defects

In the past decade, courts, agencies, public health groups and the press have exposed instances of product defects where it appeared that the manufacturer knew about the life-threatening danger. In the best known case, a design defect caused some Ford Pintos to burst into flames when their gas tanks were ruptured in low-speed, rear-end collisions. As a result, according to one investigative report, 500 to 900 people lost their lives. Internal memorandums from the Ford Motor Company show that the firm knew of the danger and refused to install a $10 shield around the gas tank because the total fleet-wide cost would exceed the probable costs of an occasional law suit.

The waste of lives and dollars from product-related injuries led to the creation of the Consumer Product Safety Commission in 1973. The agency helped slow down the rate of certain accidents, but it is poorly funded, statutorily weak and does not have the resources to track down all hazardous products. According to a report in the *National Journal*, dangerous or misused products result in 28,000 deaths and 130,000 serious injuries each year. Safety Commissioner Stuart Statler estimates that product-related deaths and injuries caused by products under his agency's jurisdiction total $10 billion annually.

Automobile accidents due to defective design or parts add another $9 billion (one-quarter of the $36 billion annual death and injury toll from auto accidents), according to Joan Claybrook, former head of the National Highway Traffic and Safety Administration.

The Price of Employee Theft

The problem of crime committed not *by* business but *against* business is very much on corporations' minds. Based on the variety and cost of this "enemy within"—the theft by employees of merchandise, supplies, cash and, with the help of computers, information—it should be.

The huge bill from employee theft is paid for either in lower shareholder dividends or in higher consumer prices. A study in 1977 by the American Management Association concluded that nonviolent crimes against business cost $30 billion to $40 billion annually. The U.S. Chamber of Commerce cites one insurance company report that says, "At least 30 percent of all business failures each year are the result of employee dishonesty." An analysis by Price-Waterhouse in 1984 attributes half of the shrinkage of retailing inventory to employee theft (the rest goes to shoplifting and poor paperwork).

The Price of Financial Fraud

Business people and firms profit from a broad range of creative financial schemes involving deceptions or violations of regulatory standards. In April 1984, *The Wall Street Journal* blew the whistle on one of its own writers for allegedly leaking items from upcoming columns to investors. That was only the most publicized example of a swelling number of insider-trading costs (*Business Week* calls it an "epidemic"). Forty-four people were formally charged with illegal insider trading in the two years prior to *The Journal's* revelation—one-third of all the cases the S.E.C. has handled in its thirty-five-year history. Other prominent cases include Paul Thayer and Thomas Reed, a national security aide under Reagan. The S.E.C. charged Reed with using inside information to convert a $3,000 stock option into a $427,000 gain.

Unfortunately, sharing privileged information appears to be an irresistible temptation to insiders who want to make enormous profits at no risk—especially because the number of hostile tender offers has ballooned in the past few years. According to a report in the *Journal of Finance*, "approximately half of the market reaction to impending takeovers occurs before the public announcement date."

In 1978, the Department of Energy set out to recover what it said was $10 billion worth of overcharges and pricing violations by U.S. petroleum companies, such as firms labeling old oil as new to charge higher prices. Five years later, the Reagan Administration reduced the amount of the alleged overcharge to $4 billion and drastically cut back the resources devoted to those cases. Nevertheless, in 1983 a Federal judge ordered Exxon to refund customers $1.5 billion.

Illegal financial transactions in the banking system have also caused considerable damage. A 1984 House Government Operations Committee study showed that embezzlement, excessive loans to insiders, and other wrongdoings figured in three-fifths of the seventy-five Federal bank failures between 1980 and 1983.

"The loss of lives and dollars from unsafe products, pollution and price fixing greatly exceeds that from all the Saturday night specials in America."

Corporate illegality is a several-hundred-billion-dollar albatross around the economy's neck. It lowers productivity, inhibits innovation, boosts prices, misallocates resources, increases injuries and causes deaths. Not only does it squander economic growth and transfer costs from producers to consumers, it also sabotages the trust that binds businesses and consumers together in a competitive market economy.

Mark Green is president of the Democracy Project, a public policy institute in New York City. John F. Berry, previously with The Washington Post, *is managing editor of* Management Report *on ESPN cable network.*

"In spite of all these negative headlines . . . the premise that the image of business . . . is on the decline is not supported."

Corporate Ethics Are Improving

Reginald H. Jones

Delivered to the Arthur W. Page Society, Ponte Bedra, Florida, September 23, 1985.

For the past 15 years I've been telling every audience that would listen to me that the greatest asset of any corporation is its public franchise—that the corporation would exist only so long as the public was satisfied with its performance. It was a humbling experience to learn that I had not advanced a novel concept. Well before my time, Mr. [Arthur] Page had said, ''. . . all business in a democratic country begins with public permission and exists by public approval.''

From the perspective of about 50 years in business, I must say that I've seen the reputation of business take an awful beating *more* than three times. Each time, there were serious observers who feared (or hoped) that the corporation as we know it was going to lose its public franchise and be swallowed up by some form of government ownership or control. The critics have always been with us.

In my college days, it was the President himself, Franklin Roosevelt, pounding away at what he called ''robber barons'' and ''economic royalists.''

Then in the late 1930s we had a ferocious attack on ''the merchants of death''—the defense companies that just as quickly became the wonderful ''arsenal of democracy'' when we got into World War II.

After the war, there was a renewal of the attack on big business, this time centered in academia. Some of you may remember the key books of the time: Holly White's *The Organization Man,* Wright Mills' *The Power Elite,* Professor Galbraith's *The Affluent Society,* Vance Packard's *The Hidden Persuaders,* and many, many other campus favorites.

By 1965, American business had given the nation

Reginald H. Jones, address delivered to the Arthur W. Page Society, September 23, 1985.

two decades of growth and prosperity such as it had never known. For this we were rewarded with a campus revolution against capitalism. Business recruiters offering good jobs were attacked and driven off the campus. As many of you know, it took a pretty tough hide for a businessman to serve as a trustee for his alma mater. This was an attack that was to have lasting effects, for those students of the 1960s became the legislative aides in the Congress and State Houses of the 1970s.

An Important Lesson

It was brought home to me during a dinner conversation with Alan Greenspan just after he left Washington, where he had served as chairman of the Council of Economic Advisors. I asked Alan, ''What do you think was the most important lesson you learned in Washington?'' Without a moment's hesitation, he said: ''Reg, it's this: All legislation originates in academia.''

By the 1970s, Ralph Nader had brought the lawyers into the act. He institutionalized the attack on big business by way of so-called ''public interest groups.'' Mr. Nader was unsafe at any speed, but he drove the environmental movement and the public safety issues up to terrific momentum, and let loose a tangle of regulations and lawsuits that almost strangled the U.S. economy. Politicians were quick to jump on that careening bandwagon, and not for the first time, business executives found themselves substantially without defenders in Washington and the state capitals.

So business has taken some hard licks in the past 50 years. As recently as 1976, Robert Heilbroner could write another of his lugubrious epics, this one entitled *Business Civilization in Decline.*

But the so-called ''fat cats'' seemed to have nine lives. Each time private enterprise seemed about to go under, it bobbed back up again. Whether we can say business rallied, or just admit that events saved us, the system that Michael Novak calls "democratic capitalism" has proved to be remarkably resilient.

So here we are in the 1980s. Which way are we headed? Is the reputation of business going down for the umpteenth time?

There are plenty of reasons for concern.

Just look at the headlines. E.F. Hutton kiting checks. Runs on banks in Ohio, Maryland and elsewhere. So far this year, 80 banks have failed—more than in any year since the Great Depression. Prominent bankers and financiers behind bars—and this is in the staid old banking business.

Or consider the impact of the daily news stories about takeover battles. "Greenmail!" "Poison pills!" "Junk bonds!" "Golden parachutes!" What does the public think of the corporate raiders, out to make a bundle not by offering new products or services, but simply through financial manipulation? They may be heroes to the speculators hoping to catch some of the loose change that falls out of their latest lunge at an unwary target, but they can't help but make business people look like a greedy, money-mad lot.

Consider the defense companies, those sturdy high-tech defenders of our liberties—now charged with fraud and found guilty of gross overcharges: the $400 screwdrivers and the $800 toilet seats. Great companies like General Dynamics and General Electric were temporarily forbidden even to do any further business with the Defense Department until they got their houses in order.

One thing the public does expect of business is that it will pay its fair share of taxes. So when it is reported that many major corporations, and most defense companies, pay no federal income taxes at all, nobody wants to hear the explanations. Even the President finds it useful to inveigh about "loopholes," though he called them "investment incentives" when he put them into his tax bill in 1981.

Meanwhile there are always the disasters: an unprecedented string of airline crashes; food products withdrawn because of contamination; the Tylenol mystery and the asbestos cases; and the terrible tragedy of Bhopal, India, followed by frightening echoes in West Virginia. No matter how well the public relations responsibilities are handled, it's almost impossible for any company to come out of these situations smelling like a rose—though it's been done on a few occasions.

Business Is Booming

And yet, in spite of all these clearly negative headlines and events, the premise that the image of business, *per se*, is on the decline is not supported by the current data.

Just take a look at the results of recent surveys on the reputation of business. These surveys can vary, depending on how the questions are worded. It's always smart to sprinkle the findings with a little salt before you swallow them.

Nevertheless, I was surprised to find that business and industry are evidently held in the same high esteem as the church and the police, with favorable ratings from 86 percent of the respondents in a Roper Report of March, 1985.

At the other end of the scale, only 49 percent of the public in the same survey have a favorable opinion of labor unions. The court system rates only· 52 percent favorable. Congress and the Supreme Court and the schools and the medical care system are in the 66 percent area. Even the press and TV fail to match the attitudes toward business, with about 77 percent favorable.

"We have better . . . and more enlightened business executives."

This friendliness toward business in general may not extend to business in particular. But 86 percent feeling favorable toward business is in sharp contrast to the troubled '60s and '70s, when all institutions were under attack and business leaders were near the bottom of the list in *any* rating of favorability or public trust.

What's happened? Why the improved image? Why is business seen in a more favorable light today than just five or 10 years ago?

Maybe we have better, more sophisticated public relations people and more enlightened business executives. I'm sure we do. We couldn't have gone through so many attacks from so many angles without learning *something*. But there are other factors.

Some of the reasons for the present friendly attitudes toward business are these—and I think they are worth exploring:

For one thing, there has been a pendulum swing back in favor of market economics, patriotism and traditional values. Believe me, there is a rhythm to these things. Perhaps it's the challenge-and-response phenomenon that intrigued Arnold Toynbee, or the action-reaction beloved of the physicists. Whatever the mechanism, the pendulum has swung back in favor of the private sector. For how long? That's another question.

We also have a popular President who is generally sympathetic toward business and market economics, and a Congress that is much less inclined toward business-bashing than in years past.

Perhaps most importantly of all, we have had a few years of good times, with over 100 million employed, low inflation and rising personal disposable income. Experience tells us that attitudes toward business basically rise and fall with the economic cycle.

But there are other factors. Economic journalism has grown immensely in the last few years, and it's reaching a larger audience. Just look at the development of the financial section of *The New York Times*. Reflect on the fact that the *Wall Street Journal* reaches 6.8 million people every working day. And now we have business and financial reports on TV.

All this has helped, but we have much yet to do on the economic-education front. Last fall the Hearst Corporation published survey reports showing that, while 86 percent of the respondents knew the legal minimum wage, 76 percent didn't even know what the Dow Jones Average represents. Only 16 percent knew that corporate after-tax profits average less than 10 percent. Too often our communications preach to the choir and deal in such abstractions as gross national product and current account balances.

There has also been a real turnaround in academia. During my active years in General Electric, I visited campuses whenever I could fit them into the schedule. Then in the first three years of my retirement, I went to at least two different colleges or universities every single month during the school terms. This has provided me with a comprehensive overview of the changes that have occurred in both students and faculties over the past 15 years.

Capitalism Is In

I'm pleased to report that capitalism is in, and socialism is out. The structural economists have been routed by new knowledge. Today the kids don't want to overthrow the system. They do want to see some changes to satisfy their ethical concepts; but they want to work within the system, not against it.

"Business and industry are evidently held in the same high esteem as the church and the police."

And perhaps we also have to give some of the credit to Japan, Inc. There is now widespread public recognition that we face very tough foreign competition. There is a danger that this could turn into a wildfire of protectionism. But the old automatic antagonism between management and its employees has cooled off considerably. The public and the workers increasingly appreciate that we'll have to work together to keep our businesses healthy, to keep jobs available and to keep the economy rolling along.

We've also witnessed a rebirth of the entrepreneurial spirit in America, and a renewed interest in the Horatio Alger mythology. Two million copies of Lee Iacocca's autobiography are read. Tom Peters makes millions huckstering platitudes we've heard for generations. George Gilder in his *Spirit of Enterprise* captured the mood when he wrote: "While the entitled children ache at the burden of laboring nine to five, the entrepreneurs rise before dawn and work happily from five to nine."

And maybe, just maybe, some of our hard work in the 1970s—the investments in anti-pollution equipment, the efforts to improve product safety, the drive to mend fences in Washington, the willingness to speak up and to recognize our social responsibilities—maybe these efforts are paying off.

Improving the Corporate Reputation

Business today *is* more conscious of its public relations than it used to be.

So for many reasons, including the growing sophistication of our public relations practitioners, we meet at a time when the reputation of business is somewhat reassuring. But I needn't remind you of the perennial perils of complacency.

Maybe the oil industry deserves its little breather after a decade of hard knocks from everybody. It's good to see more widespread public support for the auto industry after its unrelieved troubles of the past 10 years. But you know very well that today's peacock is tomorrow's feather duster.

The chemical industry seemed finally to have worked out a *modus vivendi* with the environmentalists when Union Carbide's troubles reawakened all the latent fears of the doomsday crowd.

Wherever there is fear, there is also dissatisfaction and potential hatred for those seen to be the cause. Airline passengers are nervous. Bank depositers are nervous. Even the golden boys of Silicon Valley are nervous as the shakeout hits the semiconductor and computer companies. Lots of workers are nervous about whether business executives are going to handle their jobs responsibly, with due consideration for their serious personal concerns.

And if (or rather, when) the economy turns down, and even bigger layoffs become necessary without offsets in services industries, and inflation starts sending prices up again—well, that's when we move back into stormy waters.

How can we sustain the reputation of business and lay up a little insurance against the troubles that seem inevitably to come creeping up on us? It's not only a job for the public relations department. It is even more a job for the CEO, who is finally responsible for whatever happens to the company. It is here that he needs public relations counsel and support.

The principles of Arthur Page are as applicable as they ever were. "Tell the truth. Prove it with actions. Listen to the customer. Manage for tomorrow. Conduct public relations as if the whole company depends on it. Remain calm, patient and good-humored."

To these simple and effective principles of Arthur Page, with some temerity, I would add a few more thoughts for the modern business executive and his public relations counsellors.

There was a time when the CEO could sit in his office and concentrate on the internal affairs of the company. If his public relations people communicated with the public and the customers in the modest and truthful manner urged by Mr. Page, and took care of the press, he really did not need to concern himself with these matters very much.

But the world has changed.

Government More Intrusive

Not only have the critics of business become much more adept at creating issues, but they have learned how to use the courts and the media to make their views prevail. Government has become a much more intrusive factor in the economy. In fact, the economy has been politicized, the public policy—by way of regulation, legislation and the courts—esentially determines the climate in which business operates.

If the economic or regulatory climate is too oppressive, no amount of internal shuffling of resources is going to make the business successful. Nobody makes much money in a recession. Nobody has new jobs to offer when tax policy is loaded against capital investment. Nobody can take long-term business risks if the government has allowed inflation to get out of hand. And if the courts decide that your company has to be broken up—well, ask AT&T. It's public policy that determines the climate in which business either thrives or fights for its life.

In 1962, Alfred Chandler wrote on the subject of strategy and structure. He divided strategy into four separate areas of concern.

"Not only have critics of business become more adept at creating issues, but they have learned how to use the courts and the media."

At the lowest level, there is *functional* strategy, at that time dealing largely with one function, manufacturing.

Next, there is *business* strategy, integrating all functions of the business.

Thirdly, there is *corporate* strategy, which is required when a corporation has several businesses and, so, is decentralized.

And finally, there is *enterprise*, strategy, or fitting the corporation into the body politic. This involves the external environment—legal, political and social—and considers the interaction among stakeholders.

Just this year, Ned Bowman of the Wharton School asked 26 CEOs to tell him their major concerns or worries. He analyzed their replies by Chandler's categories. Fifty-six were matters of corporate strategy, as you might expect. But 23 were issues of enterprise strategy. Business and functional strategy concerns were really minimal at the CEO level.

CEOs and a Healthy Business Climate

And that is why today's executives can no longer afford to leave public policy in the hands of the lawyers and pundits and politicians. Whether they want to or not, today's CEOs have to step out into the arena of public policy and make their views known. They must become, to some extent, public figures—open to public judgment, and sometimes to willful abuse, but doing their best to establish public policies that will keep the economy strong and healthy, and their own company thriving. My beloved friend, John deButts of AT&T, put it best when he said CEOs have to "Meet the Press" and "Face the Nation."

To succeed in this essentially political assignment, CEOs are going to need strong, reliable support from their public relations people. They're going to need help in building contacts with the media, with academia, with regulators and legislators, and with anybody who can help their views prevail. They're going to need help in taking the public pulse and keeping up with the mercurial shifts of political alliances as issues develop. They're going to need help in communications.

But most of all, they're going to need help in developing solid, persuasive company positions on the issues that affect the business—and a strategy to win public support. In other words, public issues management.

That is the kind of work that brings public affairs people into the policy-making process. It's the aspect of public relations that I think deserves highest priority and surely offers the greatest opportunity for personal advancement and service to any company—as well as the country.

Reginald H. Jones is Chairman Emeritus of General Electric Company.

"The proper social responsibility of business is to . . . turn a social problem into economic opportunity."

Businesses Can Be Both Profitable and Ethical

Peter F. Drucker

In the early years of this century, two Americans—independently and, in all probability, without knowing of each other—were among the first businessmen in the world's history to initiate major community reforms. Andrew Carnegie preached and financed the free public library. Julius Rosenwald fathered the county farm-agent system and adopted the infant 4-H Clubs. Carnegie was already retired from business and one of the world's richest men. Rosenwald, who had recently bought a near-bankrupt mail-order firm called Sears, Roebuck & Co., was only beginning to build both his business and his fortune.

Both men were radical innovators. Successful businessmen up to their time, beginning with the Florentine Medicis in the 15th century, had aimed at becoming aristocrats. Carnegie and Rosenwald became social reformers. The monuments that earlier businessmen had erected for themselves were cultural: museums, opera houses, universities. . . . Carnegie and Rosenwald instead built communities and citizens—their performance, capacity, and productivity.

But there the similarity ends. The two held basically different philosophies. Carnegie . . . shouted his from the housetops: The sole purpose of being rich is to be a philanthropist. God, Carnegie asserted, wants us to do well so that we can do good. Rosenwald—modest, publicity-shy, unassuming—never preached; but his deeds spoke louder than his words. "You have to be able to do good to do well," was Julius Rosenwald's credo—and, I believe, a far more radical one than that of the anarchist steelmaster from Pittsburgh. Carnegie believed in the social responsibility of wealth. Rosenwald believed in the social responsibility of

Peter F. Drucker, "Doing Good Makes Cents," *Reason*, November 1985. From Brooks, Liebman, and Schelling's PUBLIC-PRIVATE PARTNERSHIP: NEW OPPORTUNITIES FOR MEETING SOCIAL NEEDS, Copyright 1984, the American Academy of Arts and Sciences. Reprinted with permission from Ballinger Publishing Company.

business.

Rosenwald deeply believed in the need to develop the competence, productivity, and income of what was then still a desperately poor and backward American farmer whose skill and productivity were well below that of the competent farmers of western Europe. . . . Rosenwald saw the need to make effective the enormous funds of scientific farming knowledge and farming skills that decades of systematic study of agronomy and farm marketing had brought together. In 1900 or 1910, these were still largely theory rather than practice and inaccessible to all but a tiny minority of large and wealthy agriculturalists.

Rosenwald's motives clearly were "philanthropic," that is, the love of his fellow men. But he also saw—as no businessman, American or European, had seen before—that Sears, Roebuck's prosperity depended on the prosperity of its customer, the farmer, which in turn depended on the farmer's skill, productivity, and competence. . . .

Do Good to Do Well

In its view of "social responsibility," much of American business and the American public still follow Carnegie. They accept as he did that wealth and economic power entail responsibility for the community. They may not share his vision of the rich man as social reformer, but they accept, at least in theory, Carnegie's assertion that doing well commits one to doing good. . . .

But, in the years to come, the most needed and the most effective—perhaps the only truly effective—approach to social responsibility will increasingly be that exemplified by Rosenwald. Only if business, and especially American business, learns that to do well it has to do good, can we hope to tackle the major social challenges facing developed societies today. Government, the agency to which the generations after Carnegie and Rosenwald increasingly came to look for the solution to social problems, cannot tackle these challenges. They can be solved only if seen and treated as opportunities. And the economic realities ahead are such that social needs can be financed increasingly only if their solution generates capital—that is, generates a profit. This, governments cannot do. But it is precisely what business is being paid for.

Why shouldn't government do these tasks and tackle these problems? . . .

One reason is surely that government is doing far too many things. By itself, a social program accomplishes nothing except the expenditure of money. To have any impact at all, such a program requires above all the hard work and dedication of a small number of first-rate people. First-rate people are always in short supply. There may be enough for a very few social programs at any one time.

But government is also congenitally unsuited to the time dimensions of social programs. Government needs immediate results—especially in a democracy where every other year is an election year. It took 80 years before America's program of agricultural education and research began to revolutionize American farming and farm productivity. It took 20 years before every American at work was covered by Social Security. Would the American electorate have waited 20, let alone 80, years before seeing major results from President Johnson's "War on Poverty"? And yet we know that learning has a long lead time before it shows massive results. Individuals, not classes, learn; and there has to be built up, one by one, a large stock of individuals who have learned, who serve as examples, as multipliers, as leaders, and who give encouragement.

Making Matters Worse

Paradoxically, government, which finds it hard to start small and to be patient, finds it even harder to abandon. Every program immediately creates its own constituency, if only the people who are employed by it. It is easy, all too easy, for modern government to give. It is all but impossible for it to take away. The rule for failures is therefore not to bury them but to redouble the budget and to divert to them the able person who might, if employed on more-promising opportunities, produce results.

Furthermore, it is all but impossible for government to experiment. Everything it now does has to be nationwide from the start, and everything has to be finite. But that, in anything new, is a guarantee of failure. It is surely no coincidence that practically all successful New Deal programs had been "piloted" as small-scale experiments in states and cities over the preceding 20 years. The two total New Deal failures, the NRA and the WPA, were also the only genuine inventions without prior experiment at the state or local level. . . .

The increasing inability of government to "do"—to

tackle effectively the social needs of contemporary developed society—creates a major opportunity for nongovernmental institutions, and especially for the most flexible and most diverse of nongovernmental institutions, business. Increasingly, even in countries organized on what are proclaimed to be "socialist" principles, we will have to reprivatize, turning activities over to profitmaking businesses or to nongovernmental, nonprofit institutions (which are equally "private"). We will, in other words, have to create conditions under which a task is outlined by government and under which the means to perform the task are provided for either by government or by "third-party payors," but under which the actual performance of a task is done by nongovernmental institutions, especially business, and is done locally and on a competitive basis.

> "Only if business . . . learns that to do well it has to do good, can we hope to tackle the major social challenges facing developed societies today."

A good example is the American communication system, in which the tasks done exclusively 50 years ago by the post office are now increasingly carried out by a host of agencies competing with each other and with the Postal Service. Quite clearly garbage removal, health care, and many other services will become reprivatized in such a way that the service itself is grounded in public policy and law (if only through tax advantages), while the performance is the task of competitive private business enterprises.

This, rather than the traditional "mixed economy," is likely to be the true mixed economy of the future. It will consist of three parts rather than of the two that the economist talks about traditionally. There will be a private sector, in which government limits itself to protection against fraud, extreme exploitation, collusion, unsafe working conditions, deprivation of civil rights, and so on. There will be a true public sector—for example, defense (excluding procurement) or justice, in which government will both specify the job and do it. And there will be a mixed sector—the best example I know is the American hospital system. It is primarily a private system. Nonprofit community hospitals, church-affiliated hospitals, and proprietary for-profit hospitals, are increasingly organized in large and growing chains. All then compete for patients, yet most of their income is public money—whether it comes direct from the government via the tax system or through compulsory private health insurance plans. Another example is defense procurement.

In most of the present discussion of the social responsibility of business it is assumed, if only by implication, that making a profit is fundamentally incompatible with social responsibility or is at least irrelevant to it. Business is asked to do things because it earns, or seems to earn, a "profit," which enables it to do "good" even if it does not obligate it to do so. In most discussions of social responsibility, business is seen as the rich man who should, if only for the good of his soul, give alms to the less fortunate.

> *"Carnegie believed in the social responsibility of wealth. Rosenwald believed in the social responsibility of business."*

"To do good in order to do well"—that is, to convert social needs and problems into profitable business opportunities—is rarely considered by today's advocates of social responsibility—even by those, such as Milton Friedman, who deny that business has any social responsibility. Most of the people who discuss social responsibility, including its opponents, would be exceedingly suspicious of any business that asserted . . . that it is the purpose of business to do well by doing good. To those hostile to business, who believe that profit is a rip-off, this would appear the grossest hypocrisy. But even to those who are pro-business and who then, as Andrew Carnegie, demand that business, the rich man, give alms and become a philanthropist, doing good in order to do well would not be acceptable. It would convert what is seen as virtue into self-interest. And for those who counsel business to stick to its last and to leave social problems and issues to the proper authorities, which in fact means to government, the self-interest of business and the public good are seen as two quite separate spheres. But in the next decade it will become increasingly important to stress that business can discharge its social responsibilities only if it converts them into self-interest, into business opportunities.

Creating Jobs

The first social responsibility of business in the next decade will be one not mentioned in the discussions of the social responsibilities of business today. It is the increasingly important responsibility for creating the capital that alone can finance tomorrow's jobs. In fact, the oldest and perhaps the only truly valid definition of economic progress is the shift to jobs requiring more capital investment per worker. The demand for capital formation will be as great as the demand was a hundred years ago when today's modern industries emerged, and when capital investment per worker over 20 or 30 short years at least tripled and probably quadrupled. And there will be equal need for a "surplus" to pay for the research and development needed when technology, as well as the world economy and society, is rapidly changing. . . .

The first social responsibility of business is, then, to make enough profit to cover the costs of the future. If this social responsibility is not met, no other social responsibility can be met. Decaying businesses in a decaying economy are unlikely to be good neighbors, good employers, or socially responsible in any way. When the demand for capital grows rapidly, surplus business revenues available for noneconomic purposes, especially for philanthropy, cannot possibly go up. They are almost certain to shrink.

Naturally this argument will not satisfy those who believe that today's businessman should become the successor to yesterday's prince—a delusion to which businessmen unfortunately are only too susceptible. But princes were able to be benefactors because they first took it away—mostly, of course, from the poor.

There are also those, again especially among businessmen, who believe that to convert problems into business opportunities is prosaic and not particularly romantic. They see business as the dragon slayer—and themselves as St. Georges on white chargers. But the proper social responsibility of business is to *tame* the dragon: to turn a social problem into economic opportunity and economic benefit, into productive capacity, into human competence, into well-paid jobs, and into wealth.

Peter F. Drucker is Clarke Professor of Social Science and Management at the Claremont Graduate School, Claremont, California. He is the author of several books on business ethics including The Peter Principle.

"Corporate crime . . . is as much a part of the free enterprise system as buying cheap and selling dear."

Businesses Are Concerned Solely with Profit

Matthew Rothschild

The Wall Street Journal, the daily blotter of corporate crime, is bulging with accounts of transgression, E.F. Hutton's check-kiting scheme being only the most sensational. Exxon was slapped with a $2 billion fine for bilking consumers and the Government; Eli Lilly pleaded guilty to twenty-five counts of failing to inform the Government of the fatal effects of the company's anti-arthritis drug Oraflex, and a host of other companies had to cash in their get-out-of-jail-free cards.

"There's a whole lot of rascality going on," says Michael Barrett, staff director and chief counsel of the House Energy and Commerce subcommittee on oversight and investigations. One Government attorney, who requested anonymity, speculates that "the incidence of corporate crime is 100 times what the authorities ever hear about."

This spate of misconduct brings into focus a self-evident but long-denied fact about the business world: Corporate crime is no aberration; it is as much a part of the free enterprise system as buying cheap and selling dear. What counts is turning a buck—any which way you can. The bottom line is, after all, the bottom line.

Lie, cheat, steal, and kill—these are the commandments of capitalism, obeyed by the Robber Barons of the Nineteenth Century just as they are by the Harvard MBAs of the Twentieth. But not all corporate criminals are evil people; more often than not, they are pillars of the community. How do individuals who lead exemplary lives of private virtue succumb to depravity once they enter the corporate suites? What pressures are brought to bear on the otherwise upright individual who becomes a middle manager or senior executive? And having crossed the ethical divide, how do these corporate officers sleep at night?

"It's a very complex porridge," says Ralph Nader. Corporate crime "becomes part of the culture. It's like watching the cook in the restaurant. The first day on the job, you're surprised when an egg falls on the floor and you see the cook put it back in the skillet, but after you see him do it day after day, you think it's normal."

John Kenneth Galbraith says "bureaucratic regimentation, overwhelmingly," leads corporate officers to a life of crime. "The ultimate objective is profit, no question about it, but on the level of the individuals, it's the bureaucratic impulse."

Corporate incentives to perform, coupled with bureaucratic pressures to conform, turn the boardrooms into incubators of crime. Once enmeshed in the system, the individual participants conjure up a whole variety of defense mechanisms to shield themselves from the implications of their actions.

Just Plain Greed

I think it's just greed," says Jay Magnuson, the Cook County, Illinois, prosecutor who this year won murder convictions against the president and two other officers of Film Recovery Systems, Inc., after a Polish immigrant died of the cyanide fumes he inhaled while working at the company. "They knew the dangers. They discussed putting in safety features but they didn't want to spend the money."

Such cupidity occurs not just in small, fly-by-night operations but in the giant *Fortune* 500 companies as well. "No matter how successful they are," says Diane Vaughan, Boston College sociologist and author of *Controlling Unlawful Organizational Behavior*, "in order to keep their position and their status, these companies experience the same pressures" to commit crime.

A.H. Robins with its Dalkon Shield and Ford Motor Company with its Pinto come readily to

Matthew Rothschild, "No Place for Scruples," *The Progressive*, November 1985. Reprinted by permission from *The Progressive*, 409 East Main Street, Madison, WI 53703. Copyright © 1985, The Progressive, Inc.

mind. "Financial considerations" impelled Ford to keep Pintos on the market even though the company knew the cars exploded when hit from the back, says Michael A. Cosentino, a prosecutor in Elkhart, Indiana, who unsuccessfully sued Ford on three counts of reckless homicide in 1980. "A study was done as to what it would cost to fix the car as opposed to the cost of collisions and personal injuries," Cosentino says. "The study indicated it was more beneficial not to do anything about it."

Not all businesses come up with such candid cost/benefit analyses, but the same message often percolates down from senior management. "If the person at the top creates an atmosphere of profit at any cost, you can have a corrupt institutional ethic," says Mark Green, president of the Democracy Project and co-author of *The Challenge of Hidden Profits.*

This obsessive concern for profit typifies many corporations. "The market ethic says if it's profitable, it's probably OK," comments Ken Goodpaster, associate professor at Harvard Business School. "That is what Adam Smith really told us about capitalism: Profit is the best safeguard of the public good. Some corporations have that built into their mindset, and that can lead people to behave in unethical ways."

Even in corporations that don't conflate morality with profit, the fundamental imperatives of business—to make money, fast—can breed corruption. "What you have coming at middle managers on a continual basis is profit performance," says Gary Edwards, executive director of the Ethics Responsibility Center in Washington D.C. The culture of most corporations dictates that the people who get promoted "are the people who meet and exceed the profit projections for the quarter. That's a powerful message to middle managers."

Credit to the Criminal

With everything—salaries, bonuses, promotions, careers—geared toward the short term, the incentive to cut corners mounts with the pressure to perform. And often those who cut the corners win the cheese. "The sharpies get promoted because they produce a little bit more," says Barrett of the House Energy and Commerce staff. "And at the top level, the executives don't want to know. They're making money; they're doing better than their competitors."

"Eventually, you're going to have people in the organization whose consciences are asleep because the corporation has weeded out all whose consciences were awake," says Goodpaster of Harvard. "That's how corruption spreads."

This system can rot every rung of the corporate ladder as the cheaters get promoted and the individuals who harbor scruples fall by the wayside. "At every step of management, the ethical standards

of the lowest prevail," says Miles Lord, who presided at one of the A.H. Robins Dalkon Shield trials and is now in private law practice in Minneapolis. "The incentives corporations give force employees to do such things. It's the system itself: No one in a corporation is free to act according to his own best conscience. Even the president of the corporation is a victim."

Like other company employees, chief executive officers have their careers hitched to the short-term profit, especially in our time, when corporate raiders can swoop in and pluck any faltering firm. And the high brass adds its own impetus to unseemly behavior.

"Lie, cheat, steal, and kill—these are the commandments of capitalism."

"These fellows at the very top are not free from pressures, but the pressure is considerably more subtle," says Roger Tuttle, who represented A.H. Robins and acknowledged under oath that the company had destroyed documents relating to the Dalkon Shield. "These guys who rise to the top, most are hard-driving, egocentric, A types," explains Tuttle, now a law professor at Oral Roberts University. "They want the corporation to be profitable, and they want to be thought of as good managers. There is a certain—perish the thought— God-like quality of being head of a corporation. They think, 'Because I say so and because where I am, it's therefore right and ought to be obeyed.'"

Once the chief executive officer gives the word, the whole company swings into action. "There's nobody inside the corporation who can say, 'Hey, come clean,'" Nader points out. "It all goes up vertically, all with incentives not to do the right thing."

The Evil Nature of Bureaucracy

To some extent, corporate crime derives not from any characteristic peculiar to the profit-making enterprise but from the nature of bureaucracy itself. Like governments and universities, modern businesses bear all the earmarks of Max Weber's loathsome discovery: Such organizations require that you check your morals at the door.

"It's a problem of bureaucracy in general," says Christopher Stone, law professor at the University of Southern California.

Basic to any bureaucracy is the diffusion of responsibility among hundreds of individuals, myriad organizational structures, and semi-autonomous specialties. "You have to understand how a large corporation thinks," says prosecutor Cosentino. "No one man is responsible—there are committees, boards, panels. It becomes the thinking of a corporation, not an individual.''

''When you are responsible for the consequences of your actions, you act responsibly,'' Mark Green adds. ''But from nine to five, a lot of managers lose their identity in the collective vat that is the corporation. When you're just one hand that yanks the chain, you feel you are not responsible. You say, ''Well, the lawyers will catch it, the engineers will catch it, the accountants will catch it, the CEO [chief executive officer] will catch it.'' When so many share a part in the decision, it absolves any one of them of a sense of responsibility.''

Freed from the yoke of moral accountability, individuals harness themselves to the goals of the bureaucracy, whatever those goals may be. ''The environment within an organization provides competing claims,'' says Professor Stone. ''The most immediate claim is loyalty.''

Bovine obedience to the group prevails. ''You go along,'' Galbraith notes, ''and if you don't, you become an outsider.''

The bureaucratic pressure to conform is almost irresistible. ''It's a rare individual who stands up to a group and says, 'You people are all wrong,' '' comments former Robins attorney Tuttle. ''When the group arrives at an objective, you have this pressure multiplied by the number of people in the group.''

What's more, the person's identity becomes so wrapped up with the group that morality all but disappears. ''Personal prestige and reputation, as well as economic well-being, rise and fall with the well-being of the organization,'' says Boston College's Vaughan. ''When push comes to shove, the values and rewards become more important to them than the threat of being punished or the fear of what their family is going to say.''

''Corporate incentives to perform, coupled with bureaucratic pressures to conform, turn the boardrooms into incubators of crime.''

Tuttle, who also represented Exxon, adds another common reason why people go along: ''There is this tendency to please the boss—whether it's Ma and Dad at home, the teacher in grade school, the chancellor of a university, the head of a company, or the President of the country. All of us like to get pats on the back from the ultimate power structure.''

When a corporation commits a serious crime, especially one that causes death, individual officers within the corporation—despite the cushioning of bureaucracy—still face a personal crisis: Their self-image as ethical human beings stands under attack. To protect themselves, they marshal curious psychological defenses.

The first trench is not acknowledging the connection between the corporate product and the harmful result. ''They come up with a whole series of denials of evidence,'' says Dr. Sidney Wolfe, director of Public Citizen's Health Research Group. ''They don't confront themselves with what they're doing.''

Once the connection is irrefutable (and corporations will pay lawyers millions of dollars to find loopholes through which to wriggle), executives tend to pass the buck. ''They deny knowledge,'' says Miles Lord. ''They turn their backs. They pretend they don't know.''

This, anyway, is what they say publicly. But privately, the conflict may still rage. To calm it, they engage in elaborate self-deception. ''The basic principle is that they learn to talk about crime as if it isn't crime,'' says Don Cressey, criminologist at the University of California at Santa Barbara. ''They find some way to talk to themselves about crime without thinking of themselves as criminals.''

Fine Distinctions

''There's a very fine line between a clever business deal and a criminal activity,'' Vaughan says. ''They don't think of it as crime. They think of it as solving a business problem.''

They seem to manifest what Dr. Robert Jay Lifton, professor of psychiatry and psychology at City University of New York's John Jay College of Criminal Justice, calls ''psychic numbing—the diminished capacity to feel.'' Lifton, who has studied Nazi war criminals, says ''a split between knowledge and feeling'' can occur. ''One may know certain things but the emotional component can be suppressed through other influences—goals for which this knowledge is disturbing, unacceptable, or threatening. This knowledge can't be absorbed by the self in any fashion.''

Business analysts who have examined the issue of corporate crime find such a phenomenon taking place. ''There is a disengagement of normal ethical standards from business life,'' says Gary Edwards of the Ethics Responsibility Center. ''The senior people become schizophrenic about it. It's a moral schizophrenia: You tell yourself that to succeed in business you need to follow different rules of behavior. So there's pressure to compartmentalize, to do all the right things in your family and community life, but to disengage your moral sensibilities in business.''

Ken Goodpaster of Harvard also observes this tendency but puts it in slightly different terms. ''What you have sometimes,'' says Goodpaster, ''is a situation where the moral values of the individual will come into conflict with the mores and mindset of the corporation and will cause that individual to become anesthetized—to put the individual mindset on hold and take on the mindset of the corporation."

Being in a corporation "would encourage misconduct in anyone," Vaughan says. "It's inherent in the position itself. The problem does not lie with the individual, but with the organization and its structure."

A River of Crime

Under the Reagan Administration, corporate crime has come into its own. The floodgates are open, and businesses are taking every advantage.

"It seems to me it's increasing," says Mike Barrett of the House Energy and Commerce staff. "With fewer Government investigators, there's a catch-me-if-you-can attitude."

And with the Justice Department's failure to prosecute any individuals in the E.F. Hutton case, corporate criminals are laughing all the way to the bank, for Reagan has validated their own self-justifications.

"There's great encouragement in the new Reagan-Meese design in letting actual criminals off," Galbraith says. "It's a very agreeable arrangement, as it exempts individuals from wrongdoing."

Amidst all the felonious activity, corporate America still tries to gloss its image. One company buys television advertisements to puff the virtues of the "entrepreneur," and another boasts of "making money the old-fashioned way." The Committee for Economic Development, a business-dominated group, publishes a report blaming America's schools for failing to foster honesty.

But the make-up artists can't cover all the warts. According to a . . . CBS-*New York Times* poll, 55 percent of Americans believe that most corporate executives are dishonest and that corporate criminals get off virtually scot-free. They perceive what has eluded the textbooks for two centuries: that Adam Smith's invisible hand wears a black glove.

Matthew Rothschild is an associate editor of The Progressive *magazine.*

"Private business showed savings of 37 to 96 percent over government costs."

Privatization Saves Taxpayers Money

Peter A. Holmes

In Phoenix, a small, private company handles landfill operations at a saving of more than $1 million a year to the city. In Imperial Beach, Calif., volunteers need only $12,000 a year in taxpayers' money to run a city-owned recreation center.

Management of parking enforcement for 70 cities, including Philadelphia and Washington, is provided by Datacom Systems Corporation. A subsidiary of Pan American World Airways runs the busy Westchester County, N.Y., airport.

Frustrated by its inability to collect delinquent loans from students, business people, farmers and others who have borrowed from the U.S. Treasury, the federal government has turned to private debt-collection agencies to recover some of the $21 billion overdue on loan repayments.

Boston University has offered to run the long-troubled public school system in its home city. An increasing number of private delivery services are challenging the U.S. Postal Service's monopoly on first-class mail.

Privatization Trend

Those developments are representative of an intensifying and highly significant privatization trend in government at all levels across the nation, a trend that has a double benefit for business. The prospect of reduced taxes is one of privatization's major advantages to business. The other is the direct opportunities it offers to provide, at a profit, services now performed by government employees.

An added impetus for companies seeking opportunities via the privatization route is the public's overwhelming support for the concept. In fact, there is a substantial segment that would carry privatization to lengths not generally envisioned by the present supporters of the movement.

Peter A. Holmes, "Taking Public Services Private." Reprinted by permission from NATION'S BUSINESS, August 1985. Copyright 1985, U.S. Chamber of Commerce.

Nearly 20 percent of the respondents in a poll conducted by the Roper Organization responded affirmatively when asked if it would be a good idea for government to contract with private industry for management of the nation's armed forces. And 22 percent said it would be a good idea to let private business run local law enforcement operations. While there are no serious suggestions that private business run the Pentagon or take over crime investigations, the privatization movement is ‚ becoming an important aspect of the American scene.

John Naisbitt, author of the best-seller *Megatrends* and an authority on national trends, says that privatization "is sweeping the country" and that public support for it is evidence of profound change.

Rethinking the Welfare State

"Privatization," Naisbitt explains, "is part of the process of rethinking the welfare state. Society is searching for new ways of delivering services because of our collective sense of efficiency. The entrepreneur, not the bureaucrat, is the hero of society. While we can't be sure how it will all turn out, privatization will be part of the emerging post-welfare state."

Stuart Butler, a privatization expert for the Heritage Foundation, puts it this way:

"The reason that privatization . . . has aroused such interest recently is that it seems to offer a solution to the problem that confronts many politicians seeking to reduce government spending. The anger of someone denied a government service is always greater than the gratitude of a taxpayer when savings are made. By providing the option of a similar, or even superior, service from the private sector at less cost to the taxpayer, privatization allows the legislator the chance of satisfying both constituencies at once."

Frank Sellers, director of the Business Alliance on

Government Competition, based at the U.S. Chamber of Commerce, adds: "The private sector is simply seeking the chance to compete with government-performed activities. Business is used to taking its chances in the marketplace, whereas government has become inefficient because it is a monopoly. What the executive and legislative branches of government sometimes lose sight of is that the federal government should make use of every opportunity to service its citizens at the least possible cost, while performing necessary services."

Reducing Costs

A study by Ecodata, Inc., supports the view that privatization can lower costs. The New York research firm compared costs of eight services when provided in eight cities by local government and by the private sector. The services: street sweeping, janitorial operations, refuse collection, payroll administration, traffic signal maintenance, repairs to asphalt surfaces, tree-trimming and lawn care.

Private business showed savings of 37 to 96 percent over government costs in seven of the eight services. The cities did better only in handling payrolls.

Today's surge of privatization began at the local level, largely as a result of the tax revolt that developed in the mid-1970s. The most highly publicized manifestation of that revolt was California's referendum on Proposition 13, which put sharp limits on local governments' power to increase real estate taxes.

"Society is searching for new ways of delivering services because of our collective sense of efficiency."

The tax revolt erupted in many other parts of the nation in various forms. And even in the absence of referenda, many governments came under strong pressure to economize. The powerful combination of runaway inflation and sharp economic downturn in the late 1970s, plus major cuts in federal aid to states, were all factors.

An overview of the broad range of privatization efforts spotlights Phoenix as one of the nation's leading laboratories for programs involving the private sector in government services. Visitors from communities throughout the country stream into the Arizona city to learn how Phoenix has put privatization to work for its taxpayers. Private firms there operate the bus system, collect trash, sweep the streets, maintain traffic lights and street lights, tow and store illegally parked cars, operate municipal parking lots, run the landfill and maintain grounds of public buildings.

City Auditor James Flanagan says the city saves $2.3 million a year on 17 services provided by private contractors. It saves an additional $3 million, he says, in costs that are avoided because city departments are required to bid against private contractors for the right to perform many municipal services.

Cost Accounting

This forces the government agencies to seek every operating economy. Flanagan says the city has as many as 30 people doing cost accounting. Both the city's public works department and private contractors, for example, submit sealed bids on five-year contracts awarded for trash collection. At any given time, trash collection might be performed in two service districts by a private firm and in two by the city department, all on the basis of low bids.

Raymond L. Meyer, an operations supervisor for Waste Management of Phoenix, Inc., says his company can pick up trash at less cost than the city because of its management skills and business experience. The Phoenix company is a unit of Chicago-based Waste Management, Inc., and Meyer says: "As a national company, the resources available to us are a lot more than what the public sector has."

Nationwide, Waste Management has contracts with 432 cities, another measure of the spread of privatization.

On the other hand, Phoenix Public Works Director Ronald W. Jensen says his department has learned a lot about cost analysis of rubbish collection since a private firm won the first competition for a contract in 1978. The department failed in the next four bidding competitions but finally won a contract for itself last year, when it came in $1 million under the next lowest bidder.

Competitive Mode

Jensen explains the turnaround: "Our people are really in a competitive mode. We have cut our costs way back because we have learned from the experience of private contractors. We have the unions convinced about the need to improve productivity."

Jensen's department is unionized, as is much of the city government.

The city once assigned three men to a collection truck. Now one driver drives the truck and operates a mechanical arm that lifts specially designed 30-gallon plastic receptacles, dumping their contents into the truck.

And instead of using regular police officers for security and crowd control at its civic center and other city-owned buildings, Phoenix contracts that service to Anderson Agency, Inc., a local firm founded in 1977. Don Hesselbrock, the company's marketing director, says lower costs are not the only benefit the city receives from its private security force. "Our men are trained to prevent things from happening, while police officers are trained to stop crimes in progress or solve them after they have happened," he says.

Anderson uses part-time guards at many of the more than 150 events held annually at the municipal civic center, enabling the city to avoid use of highly trained police officers.

Mass transit is another area of major savings through the Phoenix privatization program. The American Transit Corporation, based in St. Louis, manages and operates the bus system for Phoenix, as it does for 20 other cities. Robert Hocken, general manager of the Phoenix system, says: "We run a tight organization. Every employee gives us a return on our money. Somehow, we don't miss those big bureaucracies the public sector has."

What kind of economies are involved? City and transit company figures show that private operation of the system saves the taxpayers an eye-popping 62 percent over what it would cost the city to provide the service. That figure holds even though the city determines the quality of service, sets the bus routes and owns most of the buses.

Southwest of town, alongside the dry bed of the Salt River, Oakland Scavenger Company runs one of two city landfills. The economy-minded family business has added 3½ years to the landfill's life. Its contract contains incentives for packing the most trash into the smallest space, deferring the point at which the landfill's capacity will be exhausted. City Auditor Flanagan says the arrangement with Oakland Scavenger saves the city $1.3 million a year in direct costs, and the maximum use of available space provides a bonus in terms of deferred costs of developing a new landfill miles away.

Both the city and its contractors are highly pleased with the results of privatization in terms of cost reductions on the one hand and business opportunities on the other. But the arrangement has not been totally free of problems.

Lessons Learned

Mayor Terry Goddard recalls, "They got their pencils a little too sharp at one company that could not uphold their contract." The bankruptcy of a trash collection company that was not adequately capitalized taught the city to insist on bigger bonds and to pay more attention to contractors' financial resources, Goddard says.

While the government of a large city like Phoenix offers many opportunities for privatization, the movement is growing among smaller communities, also. Imperial Beach, a mostly residential city of 25,000 in Southern California, was one of many California communities faced with a sharp decline in revenues as a result of Proposition 13. Since 1981, it has cut its work force 65 percent. City Manager

Sherman Stenberg explains:

"It was out of dire necessity. Four years ago, we were concerned that Imperial Beach would have to declare bankruptcy. Proposition 13 cut property taxes by 60 percent—$600,000."

How did the community keep functioning? For one thing, it turned its emergency medical service responsibilities over to Schaefer's Ambulance Service, a San Diego firm that has contracts with 16 other communities.

An agreement was reached with the nonprofit Boys and Girls Club of America, Inc., to take over operation of the community recreation center. The city pays the club $1,000 a month to cover its wage and equipment costs, which are minimal. Residents volunteer large amounts of time and equipment to the recreation program.

"Business is used to taking its chances in the marketplace, whereas government has become inefficient because it is a monopoly."

A private company provides local bus service. Trash is collected by a firm that uses the same automated system that Phoenix does.

An outside engineer replaced a city employee in the job of designing public works projects. Maintenance in three city parks has been contracted out to private gardeners.

Contracting Out

In another step, the city abolished its police department and contracted with the San Diego County Sheriff's Department for law enforcement services. Though this is not privatization, it is allied to it—part of the trend in which communities are going outside their own governmental establishments when they can obtain services for less.

Imperial Beach has a total of 47 contracts with private companies, nonprofit organizations and other area governments. The city manager says he is on to lookout for additional opportunities to shift services to the private sector.

Other examples of success in privatization can be found throughout the country. Gainesville, Fla., contracts with private companies for management and maintenance of city-owned vehicles. A private contractor runs the fire department in Scottsdale, Ariz. Business people are forming a limited partnership to build, own and operate a major water-storage facility for a metropolitan Washington regional government authority.

More than a dozen companies operate airport control towers or have taken over the entire management of smaller airports. Robert Poole, president of the Reason Foundation, points out that a private contractor took over operation of the Farmington, N.M., airport tower for $99,000 a year; the Federal Aviation Administration had been spending $287,000 there.

Poole's California-based foundation was formed six years ago to promote private sector options for government services.

In New York City, badge-wearing employees of a private company patrol streets in search of cars with outstanding parking tickets. Computer terminals on the dashboards of these marshals' vehicles provide registration numbers of scofflaws' cars. The marshals, who work on a fee basis, are authorized to settle the unpaid account with a vehicle's owner, tow the vehicle away or immobilize it.

The project was launched primarily to track down owners of out-of-state vehicles that had been ticketed in the city. More than 17,000 such cars were spotted last year, and the city received $4.5 million that otherwise might not have been paid. This year, in-state vehicles with unpaid tickets have also been targeted.

Federal Privatization

There is also a strong trend toward privatization at the federal level, but the entire issue is much more complex when it comes to Washington. The twin pressures of budget cutbacks and Reagan administration philosophy work on behalf of shifting government functions to the private sector, but bureaucratic inertia and self-interest work in many ways against it.

For example, the President's Council of Economic Advisers suggested that the government get out of the business of allocating landing rights at airports and let the airlines buy and sell them. But the Federal Aviation Administration appears cool to the idea. And the FAA is sitting on a proposal backed by the council to hire private air traffic controllers at larger airports.

One stumbling block to privatization at the federal level is the Service Contracting Act, which controls wages that must be paid by private companies under federal contract. The act works against the type of savings on personnel costs private companies can achieve in privatization at the nonfederal level.

It can be done, however, even in Washington. D.K. Associates, of Rockville, Md., provides printing, graphic administration, word processing and other services to the FAA, National Aeronautics and Space Administration and Defense Department under 14 separate contracts. Total billings range from $4 million to $5 million annually.

Jerry Kessenich, vice president of the six-year-old company, recalls audio-visual services that had been provided by 88 government employees at Lowry Air Force Base. "In our first year of operation we did 165 percent of what the government said we should

expect," Kessenich says, adding it was done with only 35 people. "And within two years, we were able to cut that down to 29 people and still maintain the higher work load."

He noted that his firm bid $750,000 for the Lowry job, which the Air Force had proposed to do itself for $1.4 million. Says Kessenich: "We made a handsome profit on that contract and provided much more service than the government ever did."

A-76 Contracts

D.K. Associates estimates that 70 percent of its work comes from what, in federal jargon, are termed A-76 contracts. A-76 refers to a government directive requiring cost analysis of federal services to determine whether they can be performed at lower cost in the private sector.

Most federal departments are under orders from the Office of Management and Budget to survey their costs for 14 commercial-type activities: data processing and transcription, training, audio-visual services, food service, facilities maintenance, mailing and filing, architectural and engineering services, library operation, laundry, warehousing, vehicle maintenance, accounts management and loan processing.

Arlene Triplett, an associate OMB administrator, says the surveys will identify cost differences among government agencies in providing those services and show how some agencies are able to provide them more economically than others.

As a result, Triplett notes, the agencies would be in a better position to submit competitive bids against private contractors.

Over the next three years, OMB plans to review jobs of 115,000 government workers in commercial-type activities. Based on experience with similar reviews in the past, work done by 60,000 of them could end up in private firms.

"Government is like a gas. It expands to spend the money available. Your gut tells you right off the bat that there has to be a more efficient way."

Butler of the Heritage Foundation, a Washington-based, private think tank that has had a strong influence on the Reagan administration, suggests that the work of entire bureaucracies, such as the Health Care Financing Administration, be contracted out to the private sector as part of an overall strategy to eliminate the federal deficit.

The OMB review system is flawed, Butler says, because it is being conducted by individuals who are themselves government employees without strong incentives to turn activities over to the private sector. He suggests that an outside group with no stake in the current system would be more aggressive in pursuing privatization.

Such a group, Butler adds, could be modeled along the lines of the Grace Commission, which recommended ways to cut federal spending.

Voucher System

Meanwhile, the Reagan administration is leaning toward various forms of privatization that would include the voucher system for a number of social services. Recipients of those services would not receive them through normal government-agency channels but would be given vouchers for specified amounts of money. They could use the vouchers to obtain the services from sources of their choice—public or private.

"The fact today is that government . . . is involved in hundreds, if not thousands, of business activities in which it has no real comparative advantage and no basic reason for being involved."

There is strong support within the administration, for example, for a system under which vouchers would be issued to all school-age children and could be used at the discretion of the child's parents as payments to public or private schools. The funds public schools received through the voucher system would replace the current program of direct federal aid to such schools.

While both advocates and critics of the voucher approach view it as a radical proposal, the GI Bill that paid college education costs of millions of military veterans over the past 40 years is actually a massive voucher plan. In addition to education, public housing is one of the principal areas in which use of vouchers is recommended.

Opposition of the National Education Association, the most powerful of the lobbies fighting to preserve the status quo in public education funding, has been the principal roadblock to implementation of any voucher plans. Another major labor organization unhappy with the concept of privatization is the American Federation of State, County and Municipal Employees. That union's ranks could diminish in direct proportion to the spread of privatization at those levels of government.

Alice Grindstaff, an AFSCME economist, says that contracting government services to the private sector is the result of bad management in government agencies.

"Let's avoid the whole situation," she says. "We can provide the services more efficiently through better labor-management cooperation."

Grindstaff argues that contracts with private firms may contain pitfalls for government officials. The pitfalls include, she says, hidden and unexpected costs, favoritism by government officials toward certain private firms, poorly drawn contracts, contract irregularities such as bid-rigging, risk of contractor bankruptcy and public loss of control of what taxes go for.

Business View

But businesses see the issue far differently. Many are positioning themselves to take advantage of the market opportunities resulting from privatization. One is Combustion Engineering, Inc., of Stamford, Conn., a boiler manufacturer facing declining sales in the electricity-generating industry. The company has established an urban systems and services division to use its construction and management skills in three municipal service areas with strong potential for privatization: conversion of refuse to energy, water treatment and mass transit.

Dudley C. Mecum, president of the division, expresses confidence that Combustion Engineering can operate more economically and efficiently than government in providing such services: "Government has not had the discipline of the bottom line. Government is like a gas. It expands to spend the money available. Your gut tells you right off the bat that there has to be a more efficient way."

Mecum predicts resource recovery will be a $20 billion market over the next 15 years, and mass transit will constitute a $26 billion market over the same period. He reports that his company is now negotiating with Detroit, San Francisco and a half-dozen other cities to construct and operate municipal waste-recovery plants.

E.S. Savas, a professor of management at Bernard Baruch College in New York, who launched studies of privatization as an assistant secretary of Housing and Urban Development, says that "the evidence in favor of privatization is becoming overwhelming."

Detroit's city government, he says, discovered it cost $26 to process a $15 parking ticket and contracted the work out to a private firm—whereupon the cost dropped to $1.80.

The growing acceptance of privatization is also illustrated by the circumstances surrounding the renewed offer of Boston University to run the Boston public school system. John Silber, president of the university, recalls that the suggestion produced only an amused reaction when he first made it four years ago.

"Now," he says, "nobody is laughing." The reason for the changed response can be found in the recent history of what was once one of the nation's best public school systems.

Enrollment dropped from 100,000 to 47,000 in 11 years amidst bitter controversy over integration. The per-pupil spending rate of $7,000 is one of the highest in the nation, but Scholastic Aptitude Test scores are below those of the state, region and nation.

Silber, who won national attention as an outspoken conservative who rescued Boston University from near-insolvency, blames political interference and patronage for the city school system's problems. He has proposed that his university take over the system under a five-year contract, hire a superintendent and bring in financial, personnel and management experts. The university would be paid on the basis of cost reductions. Over time, Silber promises increased enrollment and improved test scores.

While the proposal presses the outer limits of what is generally considered the potential of privatization, growing public concern over the quality of public education might eventually lead taxpayers to conclude that the private sector does have a role in that field.

No Reason for Government Involvement

For the present, discussions of privatization will center on the view expressed by experts like the Reason Foundation's Robert Poole:

"The fact today is that government—local, state and federal—is involved in hundreds, if not thousands, of business activities in which it has no real comparative advantage and no basic reason for being involved."

Peter A. Holmes is a senior editor of Nation's Business.

"Many [state and city governments] have learned too late that what looked like a bargain proved to be an added drain on the public treasury."

Privatization Costs Taxpayers Money

American Federation of State, County and Municipal Employees

California contractor Paul Fitzhenry certainly deserved high marks for candor. In 1981, he submitted a bid to handle the city of Fresno's janitorial services for $70,825 a year. Because the city was paying $236,000 to 17 public employees to do the same work, Fitzhenry's bid looked like a real bargain.

[American Federation of State, County and Municipal Employees] AFSCME and other labor unions objected, however, and when the matter went before the City Council, a different picture emerged.

Fitzhenry acknowledged that he had made a very low bid in order to win the initial contract and said it would certainly cost the city more when the contract came up for a renewal a year later. How much more he didn't say.

He also revealed that he used persons who had other full-time jobs and who would be working for him only part-time at lower wages. Thus it was likely that the quality of work would not be as good. And the proposed contract contained a major loophole: it did not cover overtime or any extra chores such as rug shampooing and steam cleaning.

On top of all this, Darrell Pennington, Fresno's general services director, reported that when the city had used a private janitorial service a few years earlier, the work was so bad that the job had to be turned back to public employees. So the city decided to continue using public employees, based on all the evidence.

The Fresno case is a telling example of the hidden costs of contracting out. As in so many other cases, a contractor deliberately bid low in order to win the contract with the intention of raising the price after the city has become dependent on his services. What

AFSCME, *Passing the Bucks: The Contracting Out of Public Services.* Washington, DC: American Federation of State, County, and Municipal Employees, 1984. Reprinted with permission.

was different in Fresno is that the contractor acknowledged doing exactly that—beforehand.

Fresno was fortunate to have all the facts at hand before it decided on contracting out a service. Other states and communities across the nation haven't been so lucky; many have learned too late that what looked like a bargain proved to be an added drain on the public treasury.

Contracting's Hidden Costs

There are many reasons why contracting out often does not save money for state and local governments.

Beyond the obvious additional cost of profits for the contractors, there are many hidden costs to the government signing the contract. In comparing in-house with contracted operations, local and state governments often fail to consider such costs as contract preparation, administration and monitoring, and the expense of renegotiating the contract with the same or other contractors. They frequently overlook the fact that contractors often have free use of government facilities, equipment, and materials. They also often fail to consider potential costs that may not be apparent at the time a contract is signed. For example, many public managers have found that when a contractor is not performing satisfactorily, they have had to use in-house crews to correct the problem. Also, contractors have sometimes gone bankrupt or had other problems, leaving a government in the lurch until the situation is resolved.

Another factor that is often overlooked is the cost of having public supervisors or employees train contractor work crews; if training is not provided, productivity suffers, and if it is provided, the public staff's effort can become significant in terms of cost and time away from other responsibilities. Similarly, in contract operations with high turnover, such as janitorial and security services, there also is the hidden cost of either government managers' or the contractor's time spent breaking in new employees; in addition, high turnover reduces efficiency and productivity.

Drawing up the contract itself has another cost pitfall: public administrators find it extremely difficult to include every contingency. For contractors, if something isn't down on paper, it is outside the contract; thus, any unexpected situation means an extra charge to government.

Hidden charges also crop up in specialized consulting contracts. There are far too many examples of firms' preparing expensive studies and reports which public agencies later regard as worthless. The entire cost of such contracts is wasted money.

"In comparing in-house with contracted operations, local and state governments often fail to consider such costs as contract preparation, administration and monitoring, and the expense of renegotiating the contract."

There may in fact be short-term savings in some contracted-out services, but it is always essential to look at the long-term balance sheet. As the Fresno case illustrates, short-term savings turn into long-term losses when a contractor deliberately buys in on a contract and then, after a government has become dependent on outside services, jacks up the price on contract renewal time.

Many contracts contain clauses that allow contractors to increase charges in subsequent years or permit them to recover cost overruns for unforeseen situations. Once again, short-term savings can turn into long-term losses for a government. In addition, while some contracts are for a fixed price, others repay all the contractor's expenses. Too often, governments are overcharged or billed for expenses unrelated to contract performance under the guise of "overhead." A good auditing system can sometimes discover these overcharges, but many more go undetected.

Laying Off Public Employees

Contracting out sometimes involves laying off public employees who previously performed the service, but this, too, entails costs. Laid-off public employees are entitled to unemployment compensation paid by the employer. Some laid-off workers, because of their economic circumstances, may also qualify for various public welfare programs. Layoffs also reduce a jurisdiction's tax revenues for the simple reason that people without jobs rarely earn taxable income and don't buy as

many items on which sales taxes are charged. These are all additional hidden costs.

Another hard-to-calculate hidden cost of contracting out is its effect on the morale of the remaining public workers. For example, if a local government's public works department contracts out one of its services and lays off employees, other departmental employees inevitably worry that their jobs are on the line. Studies by the U.S. General Accounting Office have shown that federal workers faced with the threat of layoffs are less productive than those with job security. Threatened workers, whether public or private, spend much time discussing their future, trading rumors, looking for other job possibilities and just plain worrying about what happens if they get the axe. This distraction cuts productivity—and represents another potential hidden cost of contracting out.

More Hidden Costs

Many of these hidden costs were spelled out in a study published in October 1978 by Dr. Leonard Greenhalgh, assistant professor of business administration at Dartmouth College. The study showed that for every $1,000,000 supposedly saved by New York State government in laying off employees, there were $613,000 in associated costs, reducing the "savings" to $387,000.

The study was based on the proposition that 100 state employees, earning an average of $10,000 per year, were being laid off and were not being replaced. Among the major hidden costs of such a layoff program, Greenhalgh wrote, would be lost productivity, unemployment insurance, administration of the layoffs and lost state income tax revenues.

Greenhalgh noted that layoffs such as this are a surefire way to win newspaper stories saying that the state is "saving" big money, but, as his statistics show, it just isn't so. In instituting layoff programs, Greenhalgh wrote, "costly side effects . . . have not been fully counted" by the state "and are thus not fully heeded in the state's decision-making."

In the area of lost productivity alone—a $268,000 cost item—Greenhalgh interviewed state workers and union management officials and found that when there is a threat of layoffs, employees do not work as hard. "This may not necessarily be the result of anger or bitterness toward the employer," Greenhalgh wrote, but "may just as easily be the result of preoccupation and depression." This, he said, has "an economic impact on the state . . . often in areas that are not measurable, such as quality of care."

Greenhalgh's study published by the Civil Service Employees Association—New York State Continuity of Employment Committee, did not address itself to the issue of employee layoffs caused by contracting out. When the costs of using private-sector workers paid by a contractor to replace public workers are added into the equation, there would certainly be a net loss to the state with contracting out.

The Rochester Trash Case

Examples also abound of the failure of contractors to hold down the cost of government services or to do a job at less cost than public employees.

Public administrators in Rochester, New York, proved that when competent public management was combined with a productivity-minded public employee workforce, the city could collect trash 20 to 35 percent cheaper than contractors. The municipality was able to trim its 1979-1980 cost of residential collection from $8,667,100 to $6,263,200 in 1980-1981, the lowest cost for trash collection in ten years.

The city's ability to maintain a high level of service and to cut costs prompted James E. Malone, Rochester's commissioner of environmental services and assistant city manager, to say: "There simply is no reason—except bad management—that prevents a city from providing extremely cost-effective refuse collection service."

How was Rochester able to do it? Under a system instituted in 1978, Rochester had been charging residential customers $50 a year. But the city found out that provision of service cost about $115 a year per customer—a $65 loss. With expenses increasing, the city decided to look into contracting out.

At the time, neighboring communities with contracted systems were charging residential customers between $98 and $122 per year for once-a week curbside collections. Based on a previous contracting-out proposal in 1977, it appeared that Rochester could get a contractor to do the job for just under $100 per household—less than the $115 per household it was costing the city.

Different Qualities of Service

On further analysis, however, Rochester officials found that city crews had been making backyard pickups, without a limit on the number of cans, while contractors accepted only curbside pickups, often limiting the number of cans—which, from the citizens' standpoint, meant a reduced level of service. Also, city crews routinely picked up bulk refuse at curbside—a service for which most contractors charge extra.

City officials were also concerned about the future of the 250 sanitation workers. A contractor might hire some, but others would go on the unemployment rolls. Because its sanitation workers were also used for snow removal, the city realized that if they were laid off, it would then have to depend also on contractors for snow removal—and thereby increase the city's costs for that service. City officials also saw difficulties in preparing a contract that would include everything that was handled by

the public work force; they felt it would be difficult for a contractor "to respond economically to a specification calling for collection of 'everything.'"

As Malone and City Manager Peter A. Korn later wrote, even under a contracted operation "the city still would be faced with problems of inspection, of responding to complaints, of enforcing the sanitation code, and of supervising the contractor's work, making it impossible for the city to 'get out of the business' entirely even if a performance contract were eventually signed."

Korn and Malone said that, for a number of reasons, "the city should be able to operate at a lower cost than a private operator . . . . The city does not pay federal excise taxes or local sales taxes. This means substantial savings in the purchase of equipment, fuel, and other materials that, together, constitute a large part of the cost of operation." In addition, "the city does not have to make a profit [and] finally, the city is able to borrow money at considerably lower cost than can private operators."

The City's Plan

City officials came up with a plan which involved the use of new vehicles which would permit two-member, instead of three-member, crews. The new equipment enabled the smaller crew to collect 87½ percent of the quantity a three-member crew could collect.

Because going to two-member crews would mean a 12½ percent decline in productivity per crew, the city's next step was to update and redesign routes to provide for more efficient collection. Using computer modeling, the city cut back the number of routes from 47 to 43.

"Examples also abound of the failure of contractors to hold down the cost of government services or to do a job at less cost than public employees."

AFSCME Local 1635, which represented the refuse workers, did not like the prospect of its members losing their jobs, but instead of a confrontation, city and union officials sat down at the bargaining table and worked out what Korn and Malone termed "a creative and responsible labor agreement unique in Rochester's history." Under the agreement, the city pledged not to contract out trash collection—a move which would have cost more than 250 city employees their jobs. Also, the city agreed to place all refuse workers displaced by the new system in other city jobs, with retraining provided when necessary; this meant no city employee would lose his or her job. Anyone required to take a lower-level job would not suffer a pay reduction. Also, the city agreed to pay the two-member crews at higher rates than the old crews, in recognition of the increased work involved.

From the public's standpoint, the quality of trash collection service was maintained at a reasonable price of $72 a year. From the city's standpoint, the cost of collection per residence was reduced from $115 to about $83 per year. From the union's standpoint, its members kept their jobs. The Rochester example demonstrates how public management and public employees can work together to devise a program that saves the city money, that ensures that residents get quality services, and that maintains an experienced and dedicated public work force.

Public Cheaper than Private

Local governments around the country have also found that public trash collection, properly managed, is cheaper than a contractor-run operation. In the mid-1970s, public administrators in Cape Girardeau, Missouri, discovered that many of its residents could not afford the $36 per year for trash collection charged by a contracting firm. The rate was expected to increase shortly by another $18 or $19, and this meant that still more people would be unable to afford the service. Besides charging individual residences, the private collector was also collecting $14,000 per month from the city. With the cost of the service rising for both the city government and its residents, and with a potential health problem because 4,000 of the city's 10,000 households had no collections at all, the city decided to take over the service. The city determined it could provide curbside pickup, free of charge, to all residents and save money. Six years later, the community was still receiving trash pickups as a public service.

Salem, New Hampshire, also learned about contracting out the hard way. In looking at its snow removal operations, which included both in-house and contractor crews, town officials concluded it was cheaper to cut back on contractor use and to pay town employees overtime to handle more of the work. The change came after a major blizzard in 1978 when the town's public workers complained to Salem selectmen that the total snow removal cost of $32,057 was too high because of excessive reliance on the contract crews. In a later blizzard that winter, the town paid contractors $10,900 less than for the first blizzard and relied more heavily on its own employees—and saved more than $8,300 as a result.

Troy, New York, discovered that work could be done more cheaply by public crews. In 1980, alarmed by "astonishingly rapid cost increases" in street reconstruction and heavy maintenance contracts, Troy officials determined that if the city purchased a better and more efficient asphalt paver and relied more heavily on city crews, it could

reduce its road-paving costs significantly.

After the in-house program was in place, City Manager John Buckley estimated that the city saved about $160,000 in paving alleys and secondary streets. Public Works Commissioner Thomas Murley said that "with the new machine, we'll be able to do a lot more paving and a better job." The men are enthused about it. They used to say, 'Let us have a big machine. We can do a good job.' So we fought for that machine. And let me be honest, it was a tough battle." In recent years, the city has worked toward relying entirely on its own crews for road paving.

New York City Learns a Lesson

New York City officials also have learned that contracting out can be an expensive proposition. For example, New York City's Human Resources Administration (HRA), acting on the recommendation of AFSCME District Council 37, undertook periodic reviews of the cost and quality of contracted work. The agency found that a number of custodial and printing contracts which it had had for years were far more costly than in-house work.

Some custodial and printing contracts which were costing the city $1.1 million a year could be performed by city employees at a cost of $525,000—which included wages, fringe benefits and materials—less than half the cost of the contracts. The city took over the work in July 1982, producing not only big dollar savings but other benefits as well.

"In 1980, . . . Chicago's city government paid private firms $3.5 million to maintain and to collect coins from parking meters—a figure that was more than four times the $814,000 paid by the city of Los Angeles for comparable service."

As the agency's executive deputy administrator for management, Melvyn Hester, observed: "We have greater administrative control. We train and supervise the workers and get better quality work as a result. If there's a problem, we can get it corrected. Anyone who has ever dealt with a balky private contractor knows that this is a plus. In addition, we have greater flexibility. [City] workers can cover a different location if needed. You can't do that with an outside crew." In every way, he said, the switch in-house away from contractors "represents an improvement in our productivity." The annual saving was expected to be nearly $300,000, and the department reported the quality of work greatly improved.

New York City's decision to bring custodial and printing work in-house was the result of a study by HRA contracts by District Council 37. The study concluded that more than half of the work involved in the custodial contracts could be done at a lower cost by city employees. Research and Negotiations Director Al Viani states: "While we still haven't accomplished all we intend to there, HRA has certainly taken a positive attitude about it. The result is that they're saving a lot of money."

"Too often, state and local governments find themselves in a position akin to that of a hapless shopper who pays more for something than it is worth, doesn't get the quality promised, and then ultimately has to pay even more to get what he or she hoped to obtain in the first place."

Although the HRA seemed to have learned the lesson that money can be saved by performing work in-house, another New York City government agency, the Transit Authority, hadn't gotten the message. In 1982, the agency's five-year capital improvement plan called for contracting out almost half of its engineering work—this despite an AFSCME study which showed potential savings of $53 million over the five-period if all or most of the work were performed in-house.

The Fiasco in Baltimore

The City of Baltimore also has had a distressing— and costly—experience with contracting out. In March 1982, the city dismissed Facility Management, Inc., a subsidiary of the Hyatt Management Corporation, as the manager for the city's Civic Center, Convention Center and Convention Bureau. City officials contended that the contractor had run up deficits as high as $800,000 in its management of the three facilities, that its books were a "shambles," that it had tried to "hide" serious financial problems in the records, and that it was way overdue in paying many creditors.

The worst of those problems occurred at the Convention Center. According to Douglas S. Tawney, who was appointed by the city as director of the facilities, and Guy Tamberino, the centers' new comptroller, Facility Management left behind a tangled financial mess. The two men said they had found boxes of unpaid bills, with unsigned checks attached, some of them dating back almost one year, and they had uncovered some $211,000 in checks that had been written to cover the two centers' bills

but which had never been to creditors. Tamberino said he had found one bill for $11,000, sent in November 1980, in a stack of papers on an office desk. The city determined that Facility Management had underestimated the year's utility bill for the facilities by $400,000 and also discovered that, while many bills were going unpaid, Facility Management officials were investing the $250,000 allocations the city was paying in high-interest, six-day notes at a bank.

The terminated contract was to have extended into 1983. The city filed suit against Facility Management, alleging mismanagement and breach of contract. In an out-of-court settlement, the firm agreed to turn back to the city some $800,000 in operating funds that had been advanced to it, and the city said it would pay Facility Management $100,000 in management fees claimed by the firm.

The Issue of Responsibility

Other cities have also found contracting out to be expensive and inappropriate. In Cleveland during the early 1980s, an 89-member task force of specialists from private industry, working for the city full-time at their companies' expense for 12 weeks, took a hard-nosed look at the city's books and its management operations. Normally, business officials would have a built-in bias in favor of contracting out, but his panel, appointed by Mayor George V. Voinovich, concluded that the city could save $1 million a year by handling data processing with public employees rather than by contracting it out.

Regarding the delivery of public services, Frederick B. Unger, community affairs director for the Eaton Corporation, headquartered in Cleveland, spoke for many of the panel members in saying: "We pay taxes to do these things."

Cleveland attorney Thomas E. Wagner, who had previously served as city law director for Mayor Voinovich, echoed Unger's statement. "The basic function of government is to deliver basic city services, and the city has the responsibility for doing that," said Wagner. "In the process, it can receive assistance from the private sector, but the primary obligation rests with the public sector."

Voinovich said it could be proper for a city to use the private sector to "provide the expertise" to get a city department running smoothly but that it would be inappropriate to have "the private sector come in and run a city department."

Chicago's Solid-Gold Parking Meters

In 1980, the *Chicago Tribune* reported that Chicago's city government paid private firms $3.5 million to maintain and to collect coins from parking meters—a figure that was more than four times the $814,000 paid by the city of Los Angeles for comparable service. One of the parking meter contracts was with a firm operated by a close friend of the husband of then-Mayor Jane Byrne. Los Angeles, with 26,920 meters, had an annual maintenance cost of $30.24 per meter, compared with Chicago's average cost of $98.71 for 35,100 meters.

One of the contracts, with the First National Bank of Chicago to count the money collected from the meters, was for $479,941—plus the unspecified cost of city employees assigned to watch the counting; in Los Angeles, public employees did the same work for $264,000. In 1979, the Chicago contractor charged the city $2,112,787 to inspect, maintain, and lock the meters; Los Angeles accomplished the same work, using 14 city employees and one supervisor for $500,000.

Milwaukee's Best Shot

In Milwaukee, Wisconsin, in late 1982, AFSCME District Council 48 blocked, at least for the time being, an attempt by the Milwaukee County Department of Parks, Recreation and Culture to contract for the operation of the county's Lincoln and Oakwood golf courses with Kemper Sports Management, Inc. An AFSCME analysis showed that the two golf courses had produced a total of $121,466 in net revenue for the county in 1981, but that under the Kemper management proposal there would be just $53,867 in net revenue for the county—a decrease of almost $70,000. In addition, AFSCME pointed out the county would continue to pay for all equipment and building repairs of more than $200; this meant that local taxpayers would be "in effect, subsidizing the contractor in its profit-making venture." As AFSCME analysts further noted, given the increasing revenue-producing ability of the county's golf courses, "it seems senseless to switch horses in midstream now that the going is good." Accepting the AFSCME argument that contracting out would be more expensive, the county's parks committee shelved the proposal.

One-Star Service with a Four-Star Bill

In another area of contracting, many institutions have found it expensive to use private food services. In 1978, a Milwaukee County, Wisconsin, government study committee visited public hospitals and heard much criticism by hospital officials of contracted food-service programs.

According to a committee memorandum, Dee Wilden, an experienced food service manager at St. Mary's Hospital, was "categorically and resolutely opposed to contracting for dietary services." Wilden told the investigators that "food vendors underestimate the cost to the hospitals for their services and then compromise quality in order to approximate their estimated budget." When contractors take over food services, Wilden said, "in two years the quality drops and the expense escalates to the point where most hospitals have terminated the incumbent vendors and awarded the contract to another." Still other hospitals have, after bad experiences with food service contractors, returned the service to in-house personnel, Wilden said. He also complained that contractors' statistical record-keeping is so poor that the hospitals find it "extremely difficult to develop any meaningful cost analysis."

At Northwest General Hospital, the panel found that the institution had not renewed a one-year food services contract with ARA Services, Inc., in the mid-1970s because ARA was charging more per meal than had the previous in-house system. Despite repeated prodding by hospital officials, the firm did not provide required budgetary information. During the last two months of ARA's contract, hospital officials said, the cost per meal was $3.09. More than three years later, despite inflation, the hospital's in-house system had cut food costs 25 percent—to $2.30 per meal. . . .

The Bottom Line: Let the Buyer Beware

These examples of excessive or unnecessary costs of contracting out are by no means isolated. Numerous examples of other types of contracting problems also have significant cost implications. For instance, contract-related corruption—payoffs, kickbacks, price-fixing, no-bid contracts, the use of contracts as patronage for cronies and political supporters—not only undermines the integrity of state and local government, but also adds substantial unnecessary costs to the delivery of public services.

"Contract-related corruption . . . not only undermines the integrity of state and local government, but also adds substantial unnecessary costs to the delivery of public services."

Too often, state and local governments find themselves in a position akin to that of a hapless shopper who pays more for something than it is worth, doesn't get the quality promised, and then ultimately has to pay even more to get what he or she hoped to obtain the first place. In the area of contracting out, *caveat emptor*—let the buyer beware—is the governing ethic.

AFSCME, part of the AFL-CIO, is the national union of state, county, and municipal governments employees.

*"Sale of . . . power production
facilities . . . would provide the Federal
Government with substantial benefits."*

viewpoint 9

Selling Some Federal Assets
Would Aid the Federal Budget

President's Private Sector Survey on Cost Control

The concept of privatization in the Federal
Government is a relatively new concept, even
though it has been applied successfully at the state
and local levels. . . .

Privatization, in a literal sense, means to turn over
an activity, or part of an activity, currently
performed by the Federal Government to a non-
Federal entity. It is an option for implementing
Government programs and policies, allowing the
Government to *provide* services without *producing*
them. Privatization seeks to increase the
Government's efficiency by:

- better utilizing its scarce resources;
- fulfilling its responsibilities at a cost savings;
- putting the private sector to work for the U.S.
  taxpayer; and
- allowing management to reap the benefit of
  success and carry the responsibility of failure.

Privatization does not recommend an abdication of
Government services, but presents a more cost-
effective way for the Government to deploy its
limited resources. The Task Force's primary goal was
to provide a model for Government decision-makers
to review past and future program management
practices and to offer privatization as a means
toward this end.

Largest Conglomerate

With a fiscal year 1983 operating budget of
approximately $850 billion, the Federal Government
is the largest conglomerate in the world. It is the:

- largest power producer;
- largest insurer, lender, and borrower;
- largest hospital system operator;
- largest landowner and tenant;
- largest holder of grazing land and timberland;

- largest owner of grain; and
- largest warehouse operator, shipowner, and
  truck fleet operator.

The Government expanded to its present size
because of the assumption that it is the only capable
producer of the services it needs to provide to its
citizens. For example, once the Government decided
to provide the military with the benefit of less
expensive food, it chose to implement this service by
establishing a complete retail grocery system. In the
1860s, this may have been the Government's only
option, but today this duplication of private sector
services decreases the efficiency of the retail grocery
for the military because management of the
commissaries lacks the driving forces of marketplace
competition. The Government, by directly producing
the commissary service, creates a separate,
uncompetitive market with no pressure to control
costs. . . .

Can the Federal Government *provide* services and
yet not actually *produce* those services itself, while
retaining ultimate responsibility and utilizing more
efficiently its limited resources by better capitalizing
on the competition of the open market? . . .

Power Marketing Administrations

[Specifically] should the Federal Government sell
all or part of its electric generation and transmission
facilities currently utilized by the Power Marketing
Administrations (PMAs)? In addition, should the
Federal Government begin to implement a user fee
system for the use of the falling water that generates
electricity at Federal multipurpose dams?

Proceeds from the sale of its hydroelectric
generation and transmission facilities should yield
the Federal Government $25 billion over five years.
In addition, in the sixth year after all the assets are
sold, reduction in net outlays for capital investment
and interest subsidies, plus the collection of user
fees and interest earned on the cash flow, would

President's Private Sector Survey on Cost Control, ''Report on
Privatization,'' Spring/Fall 1983.

produce over $5 billion in savings and revenue for the Federal Government. The three-year impact would total $19,836.5 million, including $3,205.0 million in reduced interest, user charges of $1,301.5 million, reduced costs of $330 million, and revenue accelerations of $15 billion.

Background

Shortly after the turn of the century, the Federal Government undertook a comprehensive water resource management program encompassing the construction and operation of both single and multipurpose dams and reservoirs in a number of river basins across the nation. The program implemented by the Army Corps of Engineers (COE) emphasized navigation and flood control projects, whereas irrigation projects were constructed by the Bureau of Reclamation in the Department of Interior. Over the years, 123 water resource projects were constructed which, in addition to their principal purposes, provide municipal and industrial water supplies, recreation facilities, fish and wildlife habitat, pollution and salinity control, and where economically feasible hydroelectric power. The Federal Government's physical assets, including the dams used to generate this hydroelectric power and the transmission lines used to wheel electric power to market, are but a small portion of its total investment represented in these multipurpose water resource projects. . . .

In the past, the Federal Government chose to finance and operate hydroelectric power operations at its own multipurpose dams. In its mission to market surplus hydroelectric power, the Federal Government engaged in a commercial enterprise more typically conducted by local, public or private organizations.

It is the conclusion of this Task Force that local public or private organizations could finance and operate hydroelectric power generation at Federal multipurpose dams. Further, because the direct marginal cost of generating this electricity is expected to be less expensive than alternative power generation, a reasonable user fee could be charged to the purchasers by the Federal Government to help offset some of the cost of building and maintaining the remainder of the multipurpose project which created the potential for hydroelectric power for the benefit of preference power consumers.

Financial management—it is the conclusion of this Task Force that PMAs are not meeting their financial performance obligations. The current PMA financial problems result from the continued use of project repayment schedules based on assumptions that have consistently generated less revenue than required to cover all operating costs, including interest expense and amortization of the Federal investment in accordance with sound business principles. Revenues are projected on the basis of

hydrological conditions that may not coincide with actual experience on hydroelectric output. In addition, PMAs are not constrained by general business practices with respect to additional future capital investments. Cash deficits before debt repayment to the Federal Government will likely continue to increase, thereby continuing to increase the Federal investment at the cost of many for the benefit of preference customers.

"The Government expanded to its present size because of the assumption that it is the only capable producer of the services it needs to provide to its citizens."

These rate setting practices produce results that cannot be reconciled with traditional financial statements and which prevent any *current measure* of accountability. Sound business principles demand current accountability for a portion of future liabilities. Rather than pay off an equal portion of the capital investment each year, the BPA repayment study shows capital repayments of $3 billion through 2014 and $20 billion by 2033. If current financial practices are continued, a vast majority of the Federal capital repayment will always be in the last half of the repayment schedules.

PMA ratemaking procedures have been under fire from both non-Federal and Federal observers (including some PMA officials themselves) for at least 20 years. In 1962, BPA—by far the largest of the five—unilaterally abandoned its policy of scheduled amortization of Federal investments on the grounds that a rate increase "would seriously impair economic growth of the region, and must be avoided if at all possible."

Valuable Assets Can Be Sold

The Federal hydroelectric power generating and transmission equipment represent valuable assets which can and should be sold. . . . Sale of PMA power production facilities to any of the potential purchasers would provide the Federal Government with substantial benefits, including elimination of current operating deficits, new capital additions and receipt of the lump sum sale price. However, the benefits to the Federal Government and to the economy as a whole vary depending upon the type of purchaser. . . .

Possibly the greatest benefits to the Federal Government would result from the sale of PMA power production facilities to IOUs [independently operated utilities] or private industry. Not only would the Federal Government be relieved of the operating losses associated with PMA facilities and receive a lump sum purchase price, but any private firms' earnings on such assets would be taxable. In addition, private firm ownership of PMA power production facilities would subject those facilities to the full range of state and local income and property taxes, eliminating any need for local impact assistance from Federal sources.

Recommendations

The Federal Government should begin immediately an orderly process of disengagement from participating in the commercial enterprise of electric power marketing. A Presidential advisory committee should be created to promote the sale of *all* electric generating and transmitting assets operated by COE, Bureau of Reclamation, and the five PMAs, in a manner which maximizes the return to the Federal Treasury. These assets, subdivided into logical business units, should be sold over a five-year period to qualified bidders offering the highest price. . . .

"The Federal hydro electric power generating and transmission equipment represent valuable assets which can and should be sold."

All future hydroelectric power development should be financed from non-Federal sources. Where funds have been appropriated and construction has begun, the advisory committee should determine if the asset under construction can be sold, and if not, look for a means of ceasing all project construction until a buyer or developer can be found. . . .

Savings and Impact Analysis

The savings to the Federal Treasury from selling the generating and transmission assets utilized by the five PMAs results from the future savings on Federal interest subsidies, annual Federal capital investments, the profit on the sale of the assets and interest earned on these funds. The assumptions used to generate the Federal savings resulting from the sale of these assets are as follows:

- The assets that generate and transmit power sold by the five PMAs would be sold for $25 billion over a five-year period in equal increments.
- The average Federal cost of capital over the five-year period will be assumed to be 10 percent.
- The Federal Government has increased its net investment in PMA assets by $500 to $600 million per year over the last three years. This savings analysis assumes that the Federal Government would continue to invest $550 million annually if the PMAs were not sold. Further, this annual net investment will be reduced by 20 percent per year as the PMA assets are sold over the five-year time

frame.
- The Federal Government will collect $393 million per year in user fees for falling water at Federal multipurpose dams. (For conservatism, no escalation of user fee rates was included in this analysis except for an inflationary adjustment of 10 percent.)

The Federal Treasury would benefit by a total of $42.1 billion over the six-year period by selling the assets currently utilized by the five PMAs. In addition, the Federal Treasury will continue to benefit by more than $4 billion annually resulting from the interest earned on cumulative funds returned to the Treasury, the elimination of annual capital investments, and the revenue generated by user fees.

The President's Private Sector Survey on Cost Control, often called the Grace Commission, was established by President Ronald Reagan and headed by Peter J. Grace. Its purpose was to evaluate numerous areas of government expenditure and to make recommendations on reducing them. This viewpoint is taken from one of the Commission's reports, "Report on Privatization," which explored the possibilities of transferring some of the government's services out of federal hands and into the private sector. The excerpt presented here deals with only one of the many areas covered by the report.

"Can private interests, solely concerned with profit, run a program that benefits a large portion of society in such a manner as to continue its beneficent purpose?"

viewpoint **10**

Selling Some Federal Assets Would Only Benefit Profiteers

Daily World, Hobart Rowen and Folger Addison

Editor's note: The following viewpoint consists of three parts: Part I is from the Daily World*; part II is by Hobart Rowen; and part III is by Folger Addison.*

I

In the powerhouse of Grand Coulee Dam, a billboard-sized meter clicks off the dollar value of the power from its mighty generators. Building these dams cost taxpayers billions of dollars, but as the meter proves, we have been repaid many times over.

Entire regions were electrified and industrialized. Irrigated deserts bloomed. Flooding and soil erosion were brought under control. No capitalist could have built these projects. It required the capital and human resources of the public sector.

Beginning with the Tennessee Valley Authority, these projects proved what can be achieved through public ownership. Indeed, the lesson of TVA should not be lost on jobless steelworkers, who might now be at full production if we had a publicly owned "Steel Authority" under democratic control.

Instead, President Reagan proposes . . . the giveaway to corporate profiteers of the Bonneville Power Administration and three other hydro complexes. This goes hand in hand with his scheme to "privatize" the Federal Housing Administration; and to hand over to oil, timber and mining interests the 800 million acres owned by the federal government. Reagan will use the loot from selling our national heritage to buy more bombs and missiles.

Public ownership of all the power utilities in the U.S. is an issue whose time has come. Even businessmen, long the greatest foes of public ownership, are concluding that the only way around

Daily World, "Giving Away Our Resources," December 27, 1985.

Hobart Rowen, "Toppling the Myths About Privatizing," *The Minneapolis Star and Tribune,* February 9, 1986, published originally in *The Washington Post.* © The Washington Post.

Folger Addison, "Bankers Would Be Big Winners in 'Privatization' Plan," *The Spotlight,* April 7, 1986.

the utility ripoff is to put this critical industry in the hands of the public. A movement for the public takeover of Long Island Lighting Company in Suffolk, New York, is organized by a local builder, who puts his case this way: "This is not a left-wing or kookie solution to the problem . . . It's a businessman's solution."

Our nation's natural and manmade resources are not Reagan's to sell. Congress must be compelled to save what is rightfully ours from the corporate thieves.

II

The Reagan administration's plan to sell off federal assets to help reduce budget deficits is a wicked deception: It is another effort, like Gramm-Rudman, to avoid tough decisions.

Under the heading of "privatization," the Reagan budget calls for selling the Bonneville and three other regional power administrations; the Naval Petroleum Reserves at Elk Hills; National Weather Service satellites, and other miscellaneous goodies that would yield about $7 billion in fiscal 1987 and $10.5 billion in fiscal 1988.

About half of these totals would come from abandonment of new public-housing projects in favor of "vouchers," prepaid hunting licenses for poor families to find and rent housing on the private market.

Just picture the nation's builders rushing out to build low-cost units for the poor, the elderly and the handicapped. "It's the biggest boom for slumlords I can imagine," snorted Michael Sumichrast, the respected chief economist of the National Association of Home Builders.

We are being asked to pay homage to the Reagan ideology, which centers on a shrinking role for the federal government. Underlying this ideology is the assumption that a private company can always do business more efficiently than the government. That must be real news to the General Dynamics Corp., and other defense contractors whose overruns add up to the multibillions; to the many hundreds of banks and savings-and-loan institutions that have gone bust or been bailed out by the federal government; and to Arrow Air, the small private airline which carried 248 U.S. servicemen to their death last December near Gander, Newfoundland.

The Pentagon, trying to save a few dollars, contracted out their return trip from the Middle East, instead of flying them back in military planes. After a routine investigation, the Pentagon has extended Arrow's contract. Performance, said a Pentagon spokesman with a straight face, was satisfactory. I wonder how the families of the 248 feel about that.

How long must we accept the myth that the public sector is inefficient and the private sector efficient? This is not a black-and-white issue. The inefficiency of government bureaucracies can be staggering. But the record in the private-sector bureaucracies can be equally bad. Look at how the American auto industry has screwed up in its effort to match foreign manufacturers.

No Impact on Deficit

The reason that people worry about the deficit is that it takes money from the private sector that otherwise would create jobs. So what do you do when you sell government assets? As Northwestern University Professor Robert Eisner points out, you take money from the private sector in just the same way you would if you were selling bonds or T-bills. In other words, in selling off these assets to make the budget accounting sheets look more acceptable, the Reagan administration hasn't changed the economic impact of the deficit at all.

Eisner wrote in a Washington Post article that sluffing off assets to reduce the deficit is "as bizarre as suggesting that a family sell its $100,000 home to make its $50,000 mortgage disappear.

"The federal government's assets are creating wealth for the nation. When the government builds an airport, for example, it is creating wealth for the airlines, and the passengers who use the airlines to do business. That is not bad for the country."

It's reasonable, I suppose, to ask what sort of commercial-type operations are being performed by government that the private sector could do equally well. Garbage collection may well be something that private companies can do better than municipal governments.

On the federal side, production of electric power may be an example of a function that now ought to be turned over to private hands, even though the government got into the power business originally because private companies didn't want to risk their money generating electricity for rural areas.

But if it makes sense to sell Bonneville—despite

the enormous negative impact on the Northwest that will come once a private buyer boosts the subsidized Bonneville rates—it should be for the reason that the subsidy can no longer be justified, and not to make a quick dent in the federal deficit.

Above all, it is time to quit denigrating the public sector. It may not be fashionable any more, but let me risk reminding President Reagan that the public welfare is more important than private profit.

III

Despite the resounding rejection of his first attempt to unload government assets, President Ronald Reagan is proposing to do the same thing again, only this time on a far greater scale.

Now the president has the excuse that the Gramm-Rudman budget cutting measure mandates putting government assets and functions on the auction block, in order to meet the strict budget deficit targets over the next five years.

In all of the hullabaloo favoring "privatization," no one mentions that the only ones to profit would be the bankers, who would create the money and collect the interest to finance the huge schemes. Any benefit to the consumer would be less than the increased costs brought on by the huge debt these schemes create.

"Congress must be compelled to save what is rightfully ours from the corporate thieves."

Privatization is favored by the banks and their spokesmen for that reason. As far as consumers go, it is a glittering fraud.

Targeted for "sale to the public" with bank loans making it possible are such government properties as the Naval Petroleum Reserve, the Tennessee Valley Authority, the government's interest in the U.S. Postal Service, federal loans to students and the Federal Housing Administration with its multibillion-dollar home mortgage portfolio.

The government-owned freight railroad system Conrail, as well as the two federally owned airports, Washington National and Washington Dulles, are currently in the process of being sold.

Privatization, the drive by the Reagan administration to divest the federal government of assets and functions and give them to the private sector, is proceeding apace. . . .

This is the second time Reagan has proposed a massive selloff of government properties. The president proposed the sale of "unneeded" government assets in 1982, claiming that the government could raise $9 billion in three years from the proceeds.

The plan called for the sale of tracts of land in the national forest system, scrublands in the arid Western states, military lands located in Hawaii on Waikiki Beach and the National Weather Service's satellites, from which are obtained data to predict the weather and track potentially life-threatening storms.

The plan met with such stiff resistance that the president was forced to back off. Negative reaction to the plan came from both parties in Congress, as well as from a broad range of private citizens.

"The federal government's assets are creating wealth for the nation."

The government holds about $250 billion in loans. These loans range from student loans to rural electrification loans to the mortgages held by FHA to small business loans handled by the Small Business Administration. Since this latter program has been targeted for elimination, these loans would probably be the first to be sold off.

The administration is also eyeing the transfer of the construction and operation of Veterans Administration hospitals to private firms. And it is considering allowing private companies to conduct non-emergency rescues at sea, currently handled mostly by the Coast Guard. (The Coast Guard has begun charging for non-emergency rescue missions.)

Government agencies are also contracting out more and more of their functions to private businesses, particularly such functions as data processing, recordkeeping, accounting, and administrative and clerical functions.

Global Phenomenon

Privatization is not strictly an American phenomenon. Partly through the encouragement and inducement of the Reagan administration, many other nations in the Third World are following the lead of the president.

The Agency for International Development, an American taxpayer-funded foreign aid program, has issued directives to its missions in 40 countries to begin discussions with governments on ways to privatize certain sectors of their economies. AID has set a goal of at least two privatization activities to be completed by the end of 1987.

The World Bank, another U.S. taxpayer-funded entity, has also been encouraging privatization and making funds available for the transfer of government-owned industries and functions to the private sector.

The World Bank has even, in many countries, made privatization a condition for the granting of new loans.

In Europe, privatization is also booming. The best example of this is Great Britain, which, under Conservative Prime Minister Margaret Thatcher, the British government has sold off $28 billion worth of government assets and industries, and is proceeding along this course at a rate of $5 billion a year, helping to raise short-term cash for Britain's struggling economy, especially hard hit by the recent drastic drop in crude oil prices.

Argentina is also engaging in wholesale privatization, Argentine Under Secretary of Finance Juan Sommer recently announced that his country will soon sell off its petrochemical and steel companies to the private sector. This would have the effect of transferring much of Argentina's publicly held foreign debt, which now totals $48 billion, to the private sector.

There is more to the concept of privatization than simply selling off government assets. Other moves considered to be part and parcel of privatization include the following: contracting out government services; granting private companies permission to compete with state-owned monopolies and imposing user fees for government services.

The concept of privatization is eagerly pushed by the "conservative think tanks" that have gained enormous influence within the Reagan administration. The Heritage Foundation, one of the most powerful of these think tanks, recently issued a report containing a plan to halve the 1987 deficit. The recommendation was simple: Sell off 30 government programs.

The plan included the sale of the FHA, which the president is seriously considering, the sale of Amtrak (the government-owned passenger rail system) to railroad employees, and a scheme whereby the management of the national park system would be turned over to environmentalist groups on contract to the government.

Heritage Foundation officials said they would have preferred to recommend that most of the government programs mentioned in their report be simply eliminated, but that privatization was seen as more "politically feasible."

Chief Problem

There are many problems with privatization, chief among which is a philosophical one: Can private interests, solely concerned with profit, run a program that benefits a large portion of society in such a manner as to continue its beneficent purpose?

For example, the government-run electric utilities produce and market hydroelectric power at a substantial discount, yet still manage to turn a profit.

The government owns five power marketing authorities, which include 123 electric generating and transmission stations, as well as 622 substations. The Bonneville Power Administration sells power in the Western states at a rate of 0.5 cent per kilowatt hour. In comparison, the national average cost of power generated by the private sector is 4.8 cents.

Although the government would realize a one-time profit of as much as $16 billion from the sale of the government-owned electric utilities, it would also dry up the revenue produced from these utilities, which are returned to the U.S. treasury.

Not so readily toted up is the cost to the consumers of government-generated power. Farms and businesses that depend on this cheap power to maintain competitiveness in the face of cheap imports will suffer immensely from this added cost of doing business.

Home consumers of electric power will also face another rise in the cost of maintaining a house, possibly large enough to put home ownership further out of reach for the millions of workers who are struggling to save enough to partake of this portion of the American dream.

"In all of the hullabaloo favoring 'privatization,' no one mentions that the only ones to profit would be the bankers."

What is so philosophically repellent about the government owning and managing vital public services, such as utilities and railroads, that conservatives rush to dispose of them whenever they feel the climate is right for such a move? This is a question asked by many who see no harm, and much good, in placing vital public services in the hands of the government and out of the hands of profit-oriented private interests.

Break Up Monopolies

Conservatives, libertarians and anarchists believe, to varying degrees, that government is inherently bad, and that the less government there is, the better off the people will be. This is not always true, as is proved by the increased standard of living brought about by the breakup of the monopolies of the late 18th and early 19th centuries.

The monopolies centering around the railroads, steel, oil, meat processing etc. dictated prices and strangled competition, free from government interference. It wasn't until government entered the picture and broke up the trusts—government intervention—that prices fell, competition thrived and Americans began to enjoy an increased standard of living.

There is also another serious issue involved in privatization. Part of the problem facing our economy now stems from the merger mania being experienced among all the larger companies, who are buying one another out at an unprecedented rate. This has led to the expenditure of billions of dollars,

with no new plants, facilities or jobs being created.

What is worse is that many of the buyouts are debt financed; that is, the corporate raider attempting a buyout issues so-called "junk bonds" to raise the cash needed to complete the transaction.

The selloff of government assets will have much the same result. Although billions of dollars will be spent to effect the transfer from public to private sector, no new jobs, facilities or plants will be created. In short, no new wealth will be created out of an enormous investment.

The Daily World *is the official newspaper of the US Communist Party. Hobart Rowen is the Economics editor for the* Washington Post. *Folger Addison wrote this viewpoint for* The Spotlight, *a very independent, weekly newspaper which focuses on "criminal politics" and economic issues.*

"In many cases, . . . the federal government has made great strides toward removing or at least reducing dangers that affect us all."

Regulation Improves the Public Safety

David Bollier and Joan Claybrook

When Jonas Salk discovered a vaccine for polio, the news was welcomed by *The New York Times* as "one of the greatest triumphs in the history of medicine." The serum's widespread use lowered the incidence of polio from 21,000 cases in 1952 to fewer than 900 in 1962. Thanks to Salk, proclaimed the cover of *Time* magazine, "generations will grow up free."

Salk's considerable achievement drew praise because it was the work of one easily identifiable hero against a disease that was widely known and feared. We are not so quick to support great potential strides in public health when they are made by the federal government and when they take on not bacterial but man-made killers. In 1984, for example, the Environmental Protection Agency proposed a new rule to reduce the amount of lead in regular gasoline. The rule, which went into effect in March 1985, will protect an estimated 50,000 children from brain damage due to airborne lead. But because those responsible for this regulation were anonymous bureaucrats, and because the hazard being fought was not an identifiable "disease," there were no brass bands—only a quick blip on the evening news.

Regulators have not always been quick to respond to health and safety hazards, and when they have, the results often have been disappointing. In many cases, however, the federal government has made great strides toward removing or at least reducing dangers that affect us all. These success stories have gone unsung, particularly in the present conservative climate, where it has become fashionable to denounce all regulation as inherently meddlesome. With a president in office who has shown himself unabashedly hostile to regulation and a Congress

entering the tight-fisted era of Gramm-Rudman, it's worth considering instances where federal regulators, no less than Dr. Salk, have saved American lives. Herewith, we submit seven regulations that have made a difference.

Safe Drugs: Pre-Market Testing

There's a reason why you cannot buy "Hamlin's Wizard Oil" or "Warner's Safe Cure for Diabetes" at your corner drug store. Nearly 50 years ago, the Food and Drug Administration determined that these once-popular "medicines" were worthless and banned their sale. Ever since, consumers have been spared costly frauds and, more importantly, serious illness, drug addiction, blindness, and death caused by quack medicines.

In 1938, 100 people, many of them children, experienced slow, agonizing deaths from a special elixir used to treat streptococcal infection. The next year Congress gave the FDA authority to review and approve drugs before they go on the market. The FDA now requires the pharmaceutical companies to perform rigorous tests, the results of which the FDA scientists review. Although drug companies often complain about the lengthy process, the FDA's drug approval system has saved thousands of lives and prevented millions of adverse drug reactions.

Between 1959 and 1961, for example, approximately 10,000 babies in more than 20 countries were born with serious deformities because their mothers had taken a sedative, thalidomide, during pregnancy. American women who obtained the medicine from Canada and Europe or participated in investigational tests were affected as well. A skeptical FDA medical officer withheld full approval, preventing tens of thousands of birth defects in the U.S. The FDA has screened out other medications that have caused deaths and injuries overseas. For example, it refused to approve isoproterenol inhalers—used to relieve asthma—

David Bollier and Joan Claybrook, "Regulations that Work," *The Washington Monthly*, April 1986. Reprinted with permission.

which caused the death of 3,500 children in England and Wales in the 1960s. It also banned Stalinon, an ineffective treatment for boils that killed more than a hundred patients in a small French town in 1954, and Aminorex, an appetite suppressant marketed in Europe, which caused an epidemic of primary pulmonary hypertension and 26 deaths.

Safe Food: Slaughterhouse Inspections

The serious problems with meat slaughterhouses and packinghouses first came to public attention in the early 1900s when Upton Sinclair's muckraking novel, *The Jungle*, and subsequent congressional hearings revealed revolting conditions: filth on meat, standing water that could breed disease, inadequate toilet facilities for workers, and meat-borne diseases. Much of the burden for preventing such conditions falls on the Department of Agriculture (USDA) slaughterhouse inspection program. First, the department must approve the blueprints of a new plant to ensure that it meets sanitation standards. Water supplies, for example, must be safe from contamination, and slaughterhouses no longer may have wooden floors, which can rot, spawning disease. USDA inspectors check cattle, sheep, swine, goats, and other livestock for diseases that may be difficult to detect after slaughter, like rabies and listeriosis. For the slaughter, the USDA stipulates methods that are both sanitary and humane. Don Houston, administrator of the Food Safety and Inspection Service, notes, "We have very specific procedures that a company must follow to make sure that manure is not released on the carcass. For certain cuts, you have to tie off certain body orifices, etc." To be sure that the standards are adhered to, USDA inspects carcasses after the slaughter.

"In barely a decade, . . . the EPA has made dramatic progress in cleaning up the air."

Data on diseased carcasses is collected daily and fed into the USDA's Livestock Disease Reporting System, which monitors disease patterns and checks how thoroughly inspections are being performed. With this specific information, inspectors can identify diseases that are confined to certain parts of the country or breeds of livestock. . . .

Clean Air: Industrial Pollution

Before the 1970 Clean Air Act, American industry dismissed air pollution as either negligible or the inevitable price of progress. "Particulates"—better known as smoke, soot, and invisible dust—poured into the air, aggravating asthma and heart disease and carrying carcinogens, toxic gases, and heavy metals into people's respiratory systems. Electric

utilities burned high-sulfur coal and oil; owners of apartment buildings vented incinerator smoke into the open skies; factories, refineries, printing plants, and other industrial enterprises had become so accustomed to pollution-prone production methods that the prospect of cleaning up the air seemed unlikely.

In barely a decade, though, the EPA has made dramatic progress in cleaning up the air. The particulate levels in Birmingham, Alabama, for example, were more than double the primary health standard in 1972. By mid-1976, annual emissions from stationary sources had dropped 83 percent, from 155,000 tons to 26,000 tons. Sulfur dioxide levels in Washington, D.C. are now half their 1960 levels and the pulp and paper mills of New Hampshire and Maine pour less than one-tenth of the particulates into the air than they did prior to 1970.

Reducing Air Pollution

The EPA has three tools for reducing air pollution. The "new source performance standards" require that a new factory have the most modern pollution control devices. As new plants with stricter controls gradually replace old ones with less effective, obsolete controls, a region's air quality improves over time. The EPA established industry-by-industry standards, but in 1982 the Reagan administration removed 12 types of industries from the list of those needing regulation.

The "emissions offsets" require that if a company in an already highly polluted area is opening a new facility that will increase the pollution, it has to reduce pollution within its existing facility or convince another polluter to reduce its output. Thus, when General Motors proposed a new assembly plant in Oklahoma City, it, with the help of local officials, paid local oil companies to reduce their pollution emissions. The offset policy successfully allows polluters to establish a market price for "pollution rights." Air pollution has become a commodity that companies can buy, sell, trade, and even bank, and businesses have an incentive to efficiently meet the EPA's pollution standards. The Reagan administration, however, has drastically weakened the offset program. By making some changes within the regulations, the administration has enabled companies to get away with increasing the pollution level a certain amount and not having to use state-of-the-art pollution control technology.

The third tool is the EPA's "prevention of significant deterioration" program, which keeps industries that dislike strict cleanup requirements in one state from relocating to cleaner regions of the country and start polluting there. The EPA requires industries to abide by especially tough pollution standards in areas without major pollution problems.

Lead can cause irreversible brain damage, kidney

problems, anemia, mental retardation, seizures, and even death. Children are especially vulnerable, particularly those from poor families, who are more exposed to peeling paint and automobile pollution. (They are also likelier to suffer from poor nutrition, which aggravates the effects of lead poisoning.) Lead poisoning kills several hundred children each year and causes learning deficiencies in thousands more.

Because lead is a multi-source pollutant—it is transmitted through the air and in food, paint, and soil—the federal government's response has had to take several forms. With prodding by the FDA, food manufacturers voluntarily have reduced the amount of lead in metal containers or have switched to glass containers when possible. The FDA has put special emphasis on packaging foods for babies and young children in lead-free containers. As a result, there was an approximately 40 percent decrease in the amount of lead in canned foods from 1977 through 1982.

The fight against lead in paint has been a mixed success. On the one hand, the Lead-Based Paint Poisoning Prevention Act of 1971 has reduced the lead content of new paint products to .06 percent. (During the 1950s the lead content of house paint was as high as 60 percent.) On the other hand, 28 million buildings remain with walls covered by lead-based paint. The act directed a federal effort to reduce lead hazards in existing buildings, but this has been hampered by scientific uncertainties, limited funding, and the magnitude of the problem. Environmental Action reports that more than one half of the 61 cities that had lead testing programs in 1981 have had their funding reduced and 14 cities have eliminated their programs.

It is in the battle against airborne lead that regulators have been most successful. Airborne lead has been the easiest to control because 80 percent originates from one source—motor vehicle exhaust. For decades, auto emissions contained lead because gasoline refiners found it a cheap, simple way to boost the octane of lowgrade fuels to prevent engine knocking. Lead probably would have remained the octane-booster of choice if Congress hadn't decided to clean up the nation's air. When it was discovered that only a few tankfuls of leaded gasoline could ruin the most promising emission-control device—the catalytic converter—it was clear that lead would have to be controlled. So, starting in 1975, when new cars were required to be equipped with catalytic converters, refiners were forced to invest in technology to produce high-octane gasoline without lead. By 1984 only 45 percent of the gasoline sold in the nation was leaded. Under current law, this figure is expected to drop to 18 percent by 1990, as pre-1975 cars are retired from use.

But the EPA wasn't interested just in protecting its catalytic converters; it also was concerned about reducing the amount of lead in the air. So in 1973 the agency initiated regulations requiring a progressive reduction in the lead content of "regular" (leaded) gasoline as well. By March 1985 the EPA had set the acceptable level of lead in regular gasoline at 0.1 gram per gallon—down from 2.2 grams per gallon prior to 1973. The agency has proposed regulations banning all lead in gasoline in 1988; the true test of its commitment to reducing lead content is whether it issues the final regulation. This would help prevent more than 1,000 strokes and 5,000 heart attacks among those who suffer from high blood pressure.

"The switch to unleaded gasoline . . . [has] made the air safer to breathe."

While lead exposure remains a serious health problem, the switch to unleaded gasoline and the reduction of lead content in regular gasoline have made the air safer to breathe, especially in urban areas. In a study conducted between 1976 and 1980, the Centers for Disease Control found a remarkable 36.7 percent decline in the overall mean blood-lead level in the U.S. population.

One other benefit: cars that run on unleaded gasoline can run three to five times longer without an oil change. A 1984 EPA study estimated that reduction of lead to 0.1 gram per gallon could save car owners as much as $660 million annually in auto maintenance costs.

Clean Water: Technology Standards

By the late 1960s it had become apparent that existing environmental laws had not prevented rampant abuse of the nation's waters. The food, textile, paper, chemical, coal, oil, rubber, metals, machinery, and transportation industries were spewing out an estimated 25 trillion gallons of waste water each year. In one notorious case, the Reserve Mining Company of northern Minnesota was dumping an average of 67,000 tons of iron ore tailings into Lake Superior daily.

Galvanized by the glare of public attention and concern, Congress in 1972 approved amendments to the Federal Water Pollution Control Act that fundamentally changed the way the government regulates water pollution. Previously, states had set water quality standards for individual bodies of water. Although logical in theory, in practice that approach resulted only in protracted battles over the definition of standards and little progress. The 1972 amendments cut through this regulatory Gordian knot by establishing uniform, technology-based standards. The amendments authorized construction of sewage treatment plants and required industry to use the "best practicable technology" to control pollution and to apply to local environmental agencies for dumping permits.

Less than a decade later, dramatic improvements were visible throughout the country. Lake Erie, once considered dead, now attracts hundreds of thousands of fishermen each year. The Detroit River also had been considered a dead river after years of absorbing sewage, chemicals, oil, acid, garbage, and paper sludge. A quarter-inch film of oil covered much of the shoreline and large greaseballs frequently washed ashore. By 1975, the discharge of oil and grease into the river was reduced an estimated 82 percent from 1963 levels. In all, from 1972 to 1977 the regulations reduced industrial discharge of six major pollutants by 69 percent or more.

Workplace Safety: Asbestos

Prior to the 1970 creation of the Occupational Safety and Health Administration (OSHA), government and industry contended that they held little responsibility for the 14,000 workers who were killed and the two million who were disabled in industrial accidents every year. OSHA changed that, issuing regulations under the belief that companies have a responsibility to remove unreasonable workplace hazards.

Among the most significant OSHA regulations are those limiting worker exposure to asbestos. Airborne asbestos fibers can cause cancer and asbestosis, a lung disease that resembles emphysema. Because asbestos was unregulated until 1972, an estimated 8,200 to 9,700 workers will die each year during the rest of this century from asbestos-related cancers.

In 1972, in response to overwhelming medical evidence and a petition from the AFL-CIO, OSHA limited asbestos dust levels in the workplace to two million fibers per cubic meter. A study issued in 1975 showed that the regulation was saving hundreds, and perhaps thousands, of lives each year. Unfortunately another study showed that a cancer risk continued at levels as low as 100,000 fibers per cubic meter.

The Reagan administration was uninterested in toughening the asbestos standards until the EPA scandals of 1983 focused attention on its environmental record. In 1984, one standard was proposed but then struck down in court. OSHA has since proposed a new, permanent standard of 200,000 fibers per cubic meter. If this limit goes into effect and is properly enforced, thousands of workers will be spared an unnecessary cancer risk. Even the weak asbestos standards in effect, however, probably will not be well enforced if the administration's past OSHA record is any indication. A 1984 study showed that OSHA's inspection record had improved since the early days of the administration, but there are still serious gaps. . . . Follow-up inspections, for examples, were down 87

percent from the Carter administration and penalties for serious health and safety violations had declined 33 percent.

Vinyl chloride and a related resin, polyvinyl chloride, both found in plastics, can cause liver cancer. In 1972 about 10,000 workers were routinely exposed to vinyl chloride, while the emissions from the plants endangered those who lived within a five-mile radius. The general public was exposed to vinyl chloride, through plastic bottles, plastic wrap, hair spray, insecticides, and disinfectants.

In 1972, again responding to a petition from the AFL-CIO (and one from the United Rubber Workers), OSHA reduced the permissible exposure level of vinyl chloride from 500 parts to one part per million. The affected companies protested that the regulation would cost them $90 billion and that thousands of workers would be thrown out of work. In fact, the changes required ended up costing only $300 milion and no jobs were lost. And the technology developed to comply with the standard actually improved productivity. One study predicted that there would be 2,000 fewer cancer deaths in the last quarter of this century as a result of the regulation. . . .

"Consumers strongly support specific types of regulation."

The Reagan administration has launched a full-scale attack on health and safety protections that save lives and prevent injuries. Often the administration's approach has been to revoke these regulations on the grounds that there are less costly solutions. The ascendency of the economic paradigm in assessing federal regulation tends to obliterate the memory of why regulations are needed in the first place. It seeks to substitute a specious economic test for a distinctly moral criterion for regulation—prevention of human and environmental harm.

While conservative critics of regulation might review this notion of regulation as quaint and uninformed, it is the underlying reason why public support for specific regulatory programs remains so strong. . . . Consumers strongly support specific types of regulation. . . . Virtually no support is found for rolling back or dismantling consumer protection regulation.

Journalist David Bollier and activist Joan Claybrook are the authors of Freedom from Harm, *the book from which this viewpoint was adapted.*

"Deregulation has been a golden opportunity both for imaginative entrepreneurs and for their customers. The entire American economy has benefited."

viewpoint 12

Deregulation Improves the Economy

B. Robert Okun

The United States is now entering the second decade of a public policy revolution that is contributing substantially to America's current prosperity. In a total reversal of corporatist policies dating to the New Deal and, in the case of railroad regulation, to the 1880s, the federal government has been getting out of the business of sanctioning and enforcing cartels in such industries as airlines, trucking, railroads, telecommunications, and energy. The result of this deregulation has been to lower prices, improve customer service and choice, hasten technological change in the previously cartelized industries, and to bolster the competitiveness and efficiency of the American economy as a whole.

The deregulation revolution began under President Ford, accelerated under President Carter, and is continuing at an irregular pace under President Reagan. It has been truly bipartisan in sponsorship, and has been supported by three White Houses and five Congresses. Senator Edward M. Kennedy cooperated with Ford Administration officials in championing airline deregulation. Senators Howard Cannon, a Democrat, and Robert Packwood, a Republican, played important roles in deregulating trucking. The academic groundwork was prepared by economists spanning the political spectrum—from Harvard Law School as well as the University of Chicago, from the American Enterprise Institute and Brookings alike.

Roots of Deregulation

One of the first experiments in deregulation came in 1968 when the Federal Communications Commission (F.C.C.) allowed limited competition against AT&T in the sale of non-Bell system terminal equipment. The F.C.C. continued to open up more and more telecommunications services to

competititon during the mid-to-late 1970s. And in 1980, it permitted AT&T, through a separate subsidiary, to market enhanced services such as its advanced communications system on an unregulated basis.

The most significant transportation deregulation took place during the Carter Administration, when the Civil Aeronautics Board (C.A.B.) and the Interstate Commerce Commission (I.C.C.) began to repeal the rules that set prices, allocated markets, and restricted the entry of new competitors into the airline, trucking, and railroad industries. In 1977, the C.A.B. allowed the first certification of a new airline for interstate travel since the 1940s; it had previously blocked entry by 79 straight applicants. By 1985, the C.A.B. was totally out of business. Today airline entry, fares, and route structure are almost completely unrestricted, though airline safety and access to airport gates are still tightly regulated by the Federal Aviation Administration.

During the Reagan Administration, the F.C.C. has substantially deregulated television and radio broadcasting and computer-related telecom- munications services; it has also taken steps necessary to implement the divestiture of AT&T ordered by Federal District Judge Harold Greene in 1982. One of President Reagan's first steps in office was to immediately lift the oil price controls and allocation quotas that had been instituted by President Nixon and were gradually being phased out under President Carter. And in the face of Congressional opposition, especially from mid- western and northeastern legislators, he has been steadily whittling away at the convoluted regulatory apparatus governing the pricing and distribution of natural gas.

The industries experiencing this deregulation have been thoroughly shaken up, with the result that their efficiency and ability to respond quickly to changing technologies and customer preferences have

"Let Markets Be Markets," by B. Robert Okun is reprinted from *Policy Review* Issue No. 35 (or Winter 1986). *Policy Review* is a publication of The Heritage Foundation, 214 Massachusetts Ave, NE, Washington, DC 20002.

substantially improved. Brash new competitors have revolutionized the transportation and communications industries—from People Express and New York Air in airlines, to Overnight Transportation Company and A-P-A Transport in trucking, to MCI and GTE in long-distance calling and Rolm in telephone switchboards. Obsolete plants and equipment, such as inefficient oil refineries, have had to be closed. And labor productivity has soared, particularly in transportation, as downward cost pressures have forced changes in inefficient work rules and inflexible labor contracts.

The process has been painful for many established companies that depend on regulation for guaranteed markets. Some business giants such as Braniff and Continental Airlines have gone bankrupt or near-bankrupt. Dozens of trucking companies have gone out of business. But deregulation has been a golden opportunity both for imaginative entrepreneurs and for their customers. The entire American economy has benefited from lower costs of freight, communications, and energy.

The Price Is Right

Dire predictions that costs would rise after deregulation have been refuted in industry after industry. In 1977, for example, Senator George McGovern entered into the *Congressional Record* a statement by Donald Moran, vice president for sales and traffic at North Central Airlines:

> Competition would prompt reduced fares at first, but then fares would return to what they are now because cut-rate competition will have put everyone else out of business. Small carriers will disappear. Big airlines will get bigger. There wouldn't be more competition. There would be less.

What happened was just the opposite. Between 1980 and 1985, 76 major new carriers and 203 commuter lines such as Ransome and Henson entered the industry. Other local service carriers such as USAir and Piedmont were suddenly free to extend their networks. The result was more competition than ever before, with fare wars and massive discounting often initiated by the new entrants. Majors and new competitors alike could survive only by carrying fewer empty seats, making more efficient use of their airplanes, and boosting worker productivity. United and Western Airlines, for example, use their planes 10.5 hours per day, compared with 8.5 hours before deregulation. Airline pilots have had to give up their insistence on three pilots in cockpits designed for two, and the average size of crews per aircraft has declined since 1979 without any sacrifice in service.

Thanks to competition, these improvements in efficiency have been translated into savings for consumers. By 1984, according to the C.A.B., American travellers had saved $3.5 billion on air fares since deregulation. Though short-haul fares between smaller cities rose considerably, the declines in long-distance fares between large cities were even greater. Today travellers can fly from coast to coast for $79. Thomas Moore, currently a member of the Council of Economic Advisers, calculates that the average per-mile airline fare fell by 8.5 percent in real terms between 1976 and 1982, even though the inflation-adjusted costs of air travel (primarily fuel and capital) rose by 15 percent in the same period.

Energy Efficiency

Critics of deregulation were also wrong in energy markets. When President Reagan decontrolled prices for crude oil and refined petroleum products in January 1981, Edwin Rothschild, director of the Energy Action Education Foundation, predicted that rising oil prices would add one percentage point to the rate of inflation. Senator Howard Metzenbaum was even gloomier: "I believe we will see $1.50 gas this spring and maybe before. And it is just a matter of time until the oil companies and their associates, the OPEC nations, will be driving gasoline pump prices up to $2 a gallon."

Fortunately for American consumers, these predictions proved false. Prices did rise initially. But the average price per gallon of leaded gasoline has fallen from $1.31 in 1981 to $1.10. The price of crude oil has fallen 20 percent in real terms and continues to decline. The reason is simple. The removal of allocation quotas and the lifting of strict price controls on oil produced by "older" wells, led to an increase in domestic oil exploration and production. Meanwhile, higher prices throughout the world had led both to energy conservation and new oil discoveries and hence to a worldwide glut that progressively lowered prices. After deregulation, U.S. energy producers and consumers were for the first time able to respond quickly to changing market conditions around the world.

"Thanks to competition, these improvements in efficiency have been translated into savings for consumers."

The partial decontrol of natural gas, limited to about half of domestic gas supplies, has similarly led to lower prices in defiance of alarmist prophecies. In July 1984, the Citizen/Labor Energy Coalition predicted that real gas prices at the wellhead would rise by five percent in 1985, as the result of the lifting of controls on some gas in January 1985. The Interstate Natural Gas Association of America made a comparable forecast in December 1984.

By March 1985, however, the price paid to producers by interstate pipelines had fallen seven percent in real terms from 1984 levels, and is expected to fall another 10 cents per million cubic feet. In November 1985, the American Gas Association estimated that increased competition among producers and pipelines would reduce gas bills by 8.3 percent over last year.

Keep on Trucking

Some of the most dramatic savings from deregulation have come in trucking, where tariffs must still be filed with the I.C.C. but substantial discounts are now permitted, and truckers have much greater route flexibility for most commodities. In many instances, trucking companies need no longer return from their destinations with empty trailers. No longer must a hauler prove that it will not harm existing firms when it wants to serve a new route. New competitors—the I.C.C. has authorized 31,000 new carriers over the past five years—are taking full advantage of technologies that are dramatically lowering distribution costs: containers that fit on the back of flatbed trucks, fuel-efficient engines, and on-board computers.

"Deregulation has been so advantageous to Americans that other countries are beginning to follow the U.S. lead."

Thanks to these changes, the average shippers' discount in trucking since 1980 has been 20 percent off tariff, and discounts are frequently as high as 40 percent. Lever Brothers, the giant consumer goods firm, estimates that its shipping costs have declined by 10 percent in real terms since 1980. And the Intermodal Transportation Association estimates that the American economy is saving between $40 billion and $50 billion a year in logistics and distribution costs as the result of transportation deregulation, as well as improvements in handling inventory.

Telephone Technology

Communications costs, which had already been falling as the result of advances in microwave, satellite, and digital switching technology, fell even more rapidly after deregulation. AT&T lowered its long-distance telephone rates by six percent in 1984, its largest decrease in 14 years. Another 5.7 percent reduction followed in June 1985. Price pressure is coming from competitors such as MCI, Sprint, Allnet, and ITT, which are selling long-distance service at prices 12 to 20 percent under AT&T.

Prices for local phone service have been rising as a result of the delayed impact of the inflation of the late 1970s and several pre-divestiture rulings by the F.C.C., which were designed to move the United States toward more cost-based telephone service.

However, the residential telephone flat rate for local service still averages $14 a month in urban areas and $10 a month in the suburbs. And for the American economy as a whole, the advantages of competition in long-distance calling and switchboard equipment are dramatic. Americans today can buy wireless telephones, or obtain such features as customized dialing, call holding, and call conferencing. According to the National Telecommunications and Information Administration, the communications costs for a major New York City bank, Irving Trust, have been rising less than three percent annually in the last two years, compared with 15 percent before deregulation.

Railroads are the one deregulated industry where prices have risen. Indeed, without the flexibility to charge higher rates that was granted by the Staggers Rail Act of 1980, a number of railroads probably would have gone bankrupt. But even here, though there are claims of unfairness by some coal shippers and electric utilities, railroads have not raised their prices dramatically. Bureau of Labor Statistics data indicate that rail rates increases, adjusted for inflation, averaged one half of one percent per year from 1980 to 1984, after deregulation, compared with 3.3 percent from 1976 to 1980. Clearly competition from other modes of transportation—trucks, air freight, and pipelines—diminishes the possibility of monopoly practices by railroads in transporting most commodities.

Victory for the Free Market

The decontrol of prices and market entry is consistent with strict enforcement of safety standards, and in fact the safety performance of deregulated industries has been impressive. From 1979 through 1984, 138 Americans died in commercial airline crashes, compared with 206 fatalities from 1974 through 1978, prior to deregulation. Alarms have been raised, however, about the tragic increase in domestic air traffic accidents in 1985—243 through October. Transportation Secretary Elizabeth Dole is planning to add nearly 1,000 inspectors over the next several years in an effort to make sure that the tragedies of 1985 are not repeated.

Decartelization is also consistent with the goal of universal service. Over 10 I.C.C. studies over the past three years indicate that truck service to small communities is at least as extensive as before deregulation. "Lifeline" telephone service at reduced rates has been made available for eligible low-income households. Before divestiture, over 90 percent of American households enjoyed telephone service; the percentage is as high today. And though major airlines have dropped service to 74 communities since deregulation, the total number of departures from these communities rose by 26 percent by 1984 as regional and commuter airlines came in to take advantage of market opportunities.

Deregulation has been so advantageous to Americans that other countries are beginning to follow the U.S. lead. Canada is aggressively decontrolling oil and natural gas prices. Last year, Great Britain denationalized its telephone system, as institutional investors and the general public were permitted to buy stock in British Telecom. Although the telephone system is still a monopoly, strict regulations governing the supply, installation, and maintenance of end-user equipment have been relaxed. Modern digital switches have been installed, fiber optics has been introduced, and the average Briton can now choose from a variety of new products such as cordless phones and computer networks.

Japan's businesses are putting strong pressure on their government to privatize the Nippon Telegraph and Telephone Company, and to allow more competition in long-distance services and data processing networks. The Japanese businesses want communications costs as low as their American competitors. There is similarly growing pressure in Europe to deregulate airline fares that cost about twice as much per mile as in the United States.

Economic deregulation is the first major victory of free market economics in American public policy, and it sets an important precedent. Since the New Deal, economic advances in the United States have been equated with bold government initiatives. The spectacular benefits of deregulation have shown the progress that can come from reducing government's role rather than enlarging it. By liberating price controls and permitting competition, the deregulation revolution has allowed entrepreneurs to find the most profitable ways of serving customers.

Tax cuts have been given much of the credit for the Reagan economic boom that has led to 10 million new jobs for Americans over the last three years. But much of the credit also belongs to a quieter 10-year-old revolution known as deregulation.

B. Robert Okun is executive director of the House Republican Research Committee.

"The time has come for us to put that [bankers'] capital, that [bankers'] expertise, to work so that banking can give the consumer . . . the best deal."

Banking Deregulation Benefits Consumers

Bill Prince

Banking is built on confidence. The confidence that you have in your bank, or your banks, or your banker. That's confidence that causes you to put your funds on deposit in those banks. The confidence that you have in the fact that the industry will continue, will be there when you need it to borrow money or to earn maximum returns on your deposit dollars. But even with that confidence today, there are more questions about the banking industry than we have ever had in at least the last 50 years. Questions about its direction, and, in fact, about its stability. And that's the reason that I'm here to talk to you about deregulation of banking; what I describe as banking in transition.

Airline Deregulation

But before I do that, I'd like to talk to you about the deregulation of another industry, the passenger airline industry. Not just for comparison but rather for contrast.

One U.S. policy expert observed several years ago that the lesson of history is that there *are* no lessons in history. There may be many striking similarities between any two developments or events, but under the surface, the differences between the two are always much greater than the similarities. The worst mistake a policy-maker can make is to focus on the similarities while ignoring the differences; to focus on what is happening today and to try to mold that into what happened yesterday. I believe the same holds true for any public policy question.

You're well aware that not long ago we had, in this country, an airline industry that was heavily regulated. An agency of the Federal government made all of the important decisions for it: routes, rates, you name it. The airline industry had a market

Bill Prince, speech delivered to the Rotary Club of New York City, January 19, 1984.

that was large and largely profitable. Although the industry was heavily regulated, the airlines did compete, one with another. And that wasn't easy because each of them offered essentially one and the same product. They could pack a bunch of people into a big metal tube with wings and fly from here to there. From the marketing point of view, each airline had to instill in the consumer's mind that more value was being offered for its product than was offered by the product of its competitor.

Now, since they could not compete with fares, they began competing with frills; who served the best food, who got the baggage unloaded fastest, and, in some instances, who had the best movies.

The government claimed that this system was justified, that this system of regulation was working because it ensured that every community with an airport had more than ample airline service. When it came to handing out routes, the Federal government would put them into packages. If you had a highly profitable series of routes, then you had to take one unprofitable route. And, because every community that was served by an airline was also served by a Congressman, this particular type of regulation made sense in Washington.

Hidden Costs of Frills and Subsidies

Then, in the 1970's, a very remarkable thing happened. People suddenly realized that there was no such thing as a free lunch, even on an airline. Someone was bearing the hidden cost for the frills and subsidies of the system. That someone was the consumer. Those people who believed that they were paying for more than they were getting began to complain and the politicians listened. Suddenly, the airlines were given the flexibility to choose where they could fly, where they wanted to fly, where they didn't have to fly. Suddenly, they were given the ability to set their own fares. Suddenly, the airline executives were faced with a very big, big problem. The plain truth was that the industry still had only one product to sell. Fifty years of government regulation had locked it into flying people from here to there; other than price, there was no way that they could enhance the value of their product, so price competition became the name of the game. And, of course, it became a very deadly game for some of the airlines. You're familiar with so many of the results of those problems.

"Because of price deregulation today, you pay for what you get and you get what you pay for."

If I had been an airline executive when deregulation occurred, I honestly do not know what I would have done, because basically, they had very few alternatives. Fortunately, I'm not an airline executive, I'm a banker. So let's look at the deregulatory world that the bankers face today to see if *we* have any alternatives.

At one time the Federal government told the airlines what routes to fly and at one time, the government told the bankers what kind of savings instruments they could offer. At one time a Federal agency set the rates for the airline industry. At one time, Federal regulators told bankers what interest rates to pay depositors.

Who Benefits from Deregulation?

Those times are gone for bankers, as well as for the airlines. And for the most part, so are the frills that the banks used to offer—premiums, toasters, free checking accounts and so on.

Because of price deregulation today, you pay for what you get and you get what you pay for. Who has benefited from this deregulation? Quite obviously, the winner is the consumer who now earns market rates on their deposit dollars. But market rates are not the only change, it's only a small part of the commercial and consumer benefits from deregulation. The availability of earning interest on deposit accounts has made the greatest contribution to the depositor. As an example, in the year 1950, ninety percent of all funds on deposit in banks was non-interest bearing. Banks were paying interest on ten percent of their deposits. The average interest rate paid in the year 1950 on the ten percent of funds on time deposits was 0.84 percent. The average cost, the average interest cost of all their deposit dollars, was eight one-hundreths of one percent. In 1980, thirty-seven percent of all the funds on deposit were in non-interest bearing accounts. In other words, sixty-three percent of the deposits were now earning interest. Today,

approximately fifteen percent, perhaps a little under fifteen percent, of all bank deposits are interest free. In other words, in the range of eighty-five percent of all funds on deposit in banks, are now earning the depositor interest.

Over time, the deregulation will continue to narrow the difference between what we bankers pay for money as deposits and what we receive for it as loans. It would appear that this process will squeeze earnings in the same way that rate cutting hit the airlines. But actually, it doesn't have to happen that way because there's a very important difference between banking and airlines. They're limited to one highly defined product and with the exception of making it cheaper, they have little potential for enhancing it. Banking offers basic financial service; all the basic financial services that the consumer wants, needs or demands. The way to pay for things, that's the product that we offer whether that be in the form of a check, or savings, or a loan and this service can be enhanced in many ways. Ways that are limited only by the imagination and that are limited by the restrictions of the Federal government. In other words, while airlines are basically at the end of deregulation, banking is at the point where further deregulation will allow us to expand our product line to offer new financial services and new packages of service.

Now, consumers will not be the only beneficiaries of a more competitive environment. I talked earlier about the lessons of history. The similarities, the dissimilarities. The lessons of history have taught us that the marketplace exerts its will on the delivery of financial services—a recent lesson that was taught to us by money market activity, money market funds and money market savings.

Attracting Customers

If a perceived need can be met by a new competitor or in another location, customers have shown the necessary sophistication to 1), be aware of the new options that are available, and 2), to take advantage of it by moving their business. Consequently, those delivery systems that offer the widest array of services and those geographic areas which permit the most service flexibility, will most successfully attract the customers' businesses. The bank of the future should be able to put together investment packages that offer a balance of convenience, earning potential, safety and tax advantages. In other words, a one-stop financial service center.

Changes used to be discussed in some long-term evolutionary time frame. But in this age of technology, change manifests itself more quickly as a revolution in the way we do things.

Our goal is to force a link between changes in technology and changes in consumer attitudes, between changes in consumer financial needs and changes in government regulation. Bankers *can* serve all the financial needs of the public and banking *can* avoid the earning squeeze that paying the customer at market rate for his deposit dollars would bring if deregulation continues. It would benefit, again, the consumer.

No one can doubt that the deposit regulation of the past several years has benefited the consumer almost immeasurably. The whole point of banking deregulation, from here on, is to give bankers the flexibility to offer even more customized financial services. Services that the public wants. A good illustration of what I'm talking about is happening right now. Several months ago regulators gave banks the green light to offer discount brokerage service. Today, these services are offered by over 1,000 banks. It's convenient, it's low cost and it can be tied in to a federally insured deposit account. Buy orders can be paid from this account, proceeds from sales can be channeled into this account; brokerage and banking at the same institution, the best of two worlds. Discount brokerage is obviously only a very small part of the financial services market, but it shows the big potential that bankers have for meeting the customers' and consumers' financial needs.

At this time banks are prohibited from meeting many of the needs that are perceived in the marketplace, by laws that were passed way back in the 1930s. Quite obviously, the world has changed a great deal since then. The needs and wants of the people of this country have changed a great deal since then. In 1933, a subsidiary of a bank held the controlling interest in a travel agency with the name of American Express. Congress forced the bank to give up that travel agency in 1934. Today, American Express is a bank and a securities company and it's still a travel agency.

Put Bankers' Expertise to Work

Legislation that is currently pending in Congress would allow banking organizations to perform many of the new financial services for their customers. The most important things about all the new services in the legislation, is that banking already has the capital necessary to support those services; the traditional financial expertise of the banker. The time has come for us to put that capital, that expertise, to work so that banking can give the consumer not just a new deal, not just a fair deal, but what we think is the best deal.

There are a number of additional things that we could talk about in addition to deregulation. International debts, bank failures, home computer banking; a lot of things that perhaps might be on your mind or your neighbor's mind, but time does not permit us to go into a great deal of detail. But I would like to say one thing about bank failures that's on a lot of people's minds, it's in the

newspapers almost daily, and I would like to put into perspective some of the things that you've been hearing and reading, and talk about some of your fears.

In 1983, there were forty-eight bank failures. Now that's the most number of bank failures in any year since 1934 the greatest number of bank failures in any one year—ranks third. The perspective of that, during the year of 1983—remember, forty-eight bank failures—there were 439 new banks opened. In 1982, there were forty-two bank failures. The perspective in that year, there were 375 new banks opened, so the banking industry is still in very good condition.

"The lessons of history have taught us that increased competition generates additional economic activity and creates jobs."

Talking about the things that are on a lot of our minds—international debts, bank failures—I ought to refer to a speech that I heard way back in 1970, given by New York's own Walter Wriston. He spoke to a bankers' group in Fort Worth, Texas. I have to classify that speech as probably one of the greatest speeches that I ever heard. Perhaps, one of the reasons was that it talked very little about banking. Its title, a very unlikely title for a business group, for a banking group, "Every Battle is not Armageddon." The thrust of his speech was that communicators of the world pass home the message, day after day, that every problem has become critical, every battle is Armageddon and every crisis may be mankind's last chance to survive. Mr. Wriston said that the people, that those people that are saying that, are guilty of intellectual overkill.

Today, banking is engaged in a competitive struggle of awesome dimension. Banking is struggling with world debt problems, domestic loan problems, government deficits—so many economic ills— including bank failures. And when we're having those economic ills, bank failures, part of that, are inevitable. The message here, though, that should be remembered, is that every battle is *not* Armaggedon. *This* battle is not Armageddon. Banking *will* survive to serve you.

Bill Prince is the Chairman of the Board and Chief Executive Officer of The First City National Bank in Lutkin, Texas.

"Deregulation of banking is potentially dangerous—not only for the institutions that might get caught up in turbulent markets for financial services, but for the nation."

Banking Deregulation Threatens the Economic System

Robert A. Bennett

Not very long ago, banks were perceived as public utilities and their stocks were viewed as safe and sound investments. But that image has changed dramatically as banks, in recent years, have rushed helter-skelter into previously undreamed-of fields— and into a new banking era.

The primary goal of top managers in the nation's banks is no longer to keep their heads soberly above water and to lend only to those who are virtually risk-free. Today, as the banks leap into new markets and thrash about trying to maximize profits, they are begging people to borrow larger and larger amounts at interest rates that are freer than ever before to rise and fall. There are banks today selling insurance, stocks and even cut-rate merchandise. And the industry is banging on the doors of Congress and state legislatures for freedom to plunge even further into new businesses. There are nonbanks—brokerage firms, retailers and furniture stores—fighting for a bigger piece of the consumer banking market.

It's all happening in a national environment of dizzying deregulation that has transformed competition in trucking, airlines, communications— and banking. But in many minds, banking is fundamentally different from other industries that have been exposed to the cold winds of the marketplace. Deregulation of banking is potentially dangerous—not only for the institutions that might get caught up in turbulent markets for financial services, but for the nation.

Dangerous Discipline of Bankruptcy

The ultimate discipline of the marketplace in a deregulated world is the threat of bankruptcy. But big banks—which provide the financial

underpinnings of the national economy—are too important to be allowed to collapse. Public policy has for decades affirmed this doctrine by keeping banks from going far afield into other businesses and by propping them up when they get in trouble.

Though the wave of deregulation is too new to have produced major gaffes yet by profit-driven banks, the changes have raised fears in some quarters about the future. "When you encourage the entrepreneurial drive of the banks," said Henry Kaufman, an economist and managing director of Salomon Brothers, "the only way that drive can be disciplined is by allowing banks that have behaved improperly to fail. This is a key issue. Are we willing as a society to have major institutions that hold savings and temporary funds fail so that the proper discipline can be exerted on them?"

Mr. Kaufman, whose firm is a direct competitor of the commercial banks in some areas, may have a biased view. But others in more neutral positions share some of his major concerns. Paul A. Volcker, chairman of the Federal Reserve Board, is perhaps the most prominent. He has been in the forefront of a call for a pause in the rush to deregulation so that the country can figure out what it wants its banking system to be. Both men are alarmed at the piecemeal fashion in which changes are being made in the financial system before an overall blueprint for change has been established.

Though little heed has so far been paid to Mr. Volcker's call, a major public policy debate about the future of banking has begun bubbling to the surface in Washington, in academia and on Wall Street. A few diehard free-marketeers argue that the virtues of marketplace efficiency so clearly overwhelm the risks from bank failure that deregulation should go all the way to freedom for the banks—including the freedom to fail.

But the major debate emerging is between those like Mr. Volcker and Mr. Kaufman who think that the process of bank deregulation should proceed in a more orderly fashion so that the emerging financial structure can be carefully designed to meet the nation's basic needs, and others, like Walter B. Wriston of Citicorp and William M. Isaac of the Federal Deposit Insurance Corporation, who want to sweep away the remaining cobwebs of regulation quickly to open the banks and nonbanks to even grander competition.

"Move Forward or Die"

According to Mr. Wriston, banking regulations have traditionally lagged behind reality. Explaining his passion for breaking down old restraints on bank operations, he once said, "My experience has been you either move forward or you die—it's true in biology."

Mr. Wriston was a pioneer, but now most bankers seem to agree with him about the need to push aggressively for new powers. "Bankers want to be protected but yet they want a lot of freedom," said George M. Salem, a bank-stock analyst at A.G. Becker Paribas Inc.

Banks as Arm of Government

For decades, banks have operated under a tacit quid pro quo with the United States Government. They have agreed to certain limits on their operations in return for certain privileges, protections and the Government's ultimate backing of their liabilities. Banks are lenders of last resort to American industry—and the Federal Reserve Board is the lender of last resort to them. Banks are the vehicles through which the central bank channels monetary policy. It is through the banks that the Government often deals with major economic crises, ranging from the quadrupling of oil prices in 1973 to the 1980 silver debacle that threatened to topple major securities firms.

In quiet and subtle ways, the Government also often works through the major banks to implement aspects of foreign policy. Some years ago, for example, when the State Department wanted to help the Polish Government, Washington quietly had the Commodity Credit Corporation guarantee commercial bank loans to Poland. And in the last year or so, when the big banks ran into trouble as a result of the heavy lending to third world countries—which has been encouraged by the Government—the Government once again rushed to their aid. The Treasury, through its Exchange Stabilization Fund, loaned billions of dollars to such countries as Mexico and Brazil to keep them afloat, and the regulators in Washington even bent some rules so that the private banks could participate in complicated programs to reschedule these countries' huge debts.

The unique position of the banking system in the United States is mirrored abroad. Few nations, even the most liberal on matters of foreign investment, would allow their largest banks to be taken over by foreigners. And many major nations, such as France and Italy, have nationalized their banking systems.

In large part, the special position of banks stems from the awesome power they have in controlling vast amounts of capital. For that reason, most democracies, including the United States, have taken pains to assure that those powers are not abused, and that banks do not show favoritism to one potential borrower over another. That is a major reason that United States laws have prohibited banks from engaging in most other businesses.

Today, however, with the deregulation craze in full swing, many of the truisms of the past are being ignored. As a result of dramatic technological advances that have made it practical to provide banking services through toll-free phone calls, the mail and automated teller machines, many nonbanks have begun to enter banking. And, in some cases, because they are not fettered by costly, high-overhead branch structures, they can beat the banks at their own game.

Risky Ventures

At the same time, banks are going ahead willy-nilly, finding loopholes in state and Federal laws that allow them to enter new, and sometimes riskier, activities.

Only last week, the Bank of America, the nation's largest bank, announced that it would begin offering insurance in its California branches, although currently it is illegal for banks to engage in most types of insurance activities. The bank's strategy: placing another company's agents in the bank's branches to sell the insurance.

"You can't have a system where the banks are free to take as much risk as they choose and then dump the losses on the taxpayer."

New York-based Citicorp, the country's biggest bank holding company, which has been gobbling up savings and loans around the country, is operating a convention center in Westchester County and offering customers a discount shopping service. Chemical Bank, another New York-based financial giant, has published a catalogue offering cut-rate merchandise to its customers. And banks across the country have begun selling stocks, a practice that until recently was considered a violation of the 1933 Glass-Steagall Act, which suddenly is being interpreted differently.

As the banks extend their reach into new markets, their new competitors are looking over the fence, too, in the other direction, combing the law books for new ways to make profits from consumer banking services. Indeed, Sears, Roebuck & Company, the nation's biggest retailer, today earns roughly as much money from financial services as from selling merchandise, and its top management is on the prowl for 51 more banks to add to its sole savings and loan in California.

Not only Sears, but many businesses that once were quite distinct from banks have begun to look remarkably like them. Money market mutual funds, most of which are operated by securities firms, take deposits and even allow their customers to write checks. Even supermarkets and gas stations are installing automatic teller machines.

"We've had periods when banking was relatively free of regulation. Those periods were characterized by one crisis after another."

While all this has transpired, the attention of policy makers in Washington and in state capitals has been focused for the most part on narrow questions: Should banks be allowed to cross state lines? Should they be allowed to underwrite corporate securities? Should they be allowed into insurance? Should deposits in money market mutual funds, the banks' arch rivals, be insured by the Federal Government? Should securities firms, insurance companies and others be allowed to buy banks?

What's required now, said Charles M. Williams, George Gund Professor of Banking at Harvard Business School, is a "more focused discussion of what kind of banking system we need. It strikes me that, to answer the question of what powers a bank should have, there is a plaintive cry to determine just what banking is."

Consumer Protection

One thing seems clear: If policymakers continue to believe the nation's major banks and their depositors should be protected by such Government-supported institutions as the F.D.I.C. and the Federal Reserve, there must be some form of regulation in effect to temper the banks' activities. William R. Cline, a senior fellow at the Institute for International Economics in Washington, explained: "The counterpart of Government insurance is some degree of Government regulation because, if the Government merely provides safeguards, it would tend to create excessive risk-taking by the banks. The central question is where one strikes the proper balance between differing levels of regulation."

In trying to explain the role of the banking system,

Mr. Volcker recently told a Congressional committee that "our point of departure is the basic proposition that banks, and depository institutions generally, continue to perform a unique and critical role in the financial system and the economy—as operators of the payments system, as custodians of the bulk of liquid savings, as key and impartial suppliers of short-term credit, and as the link between monetary policy and the economy.

"This unique role," he said, "implies continuing governmental concerns about the stability and impartiality of these institutions—concerns that are reflected in the Federal 'safety net' long provided by the discount window and by deposit insurance, by regulatory protection against undue risk, and by policies to discourage conflicts of interest and undue concentration of banking resources."

On the broad issues, Mr. Volcker's arguments elicited some sympathy at recent hearings from Jake Garn, the Utah Republican who heads the Senate Banking Committee. And Mr. Volcker said that he agrees with many elements of a bill Mr. Garn has submitted that would substantially expand the powers of the banks.

But there also have been important areas of disagreement. Last year, for example, Mr. Garn responded negatively when Mr. Volcker sought legislation to close, temporarily at least, a loophole that allowed nonbanking companies to acquire banks and run them as strictly consumer-banking organizations. Even other Federal regulators reacted cooly to Mr. Volcker's pleas, although eventually they agreed to a moratorium. But that came late in the game and did not apply to applications for such "nonbank banks" that already had been received by regulators. In fact, . . . the Comptroller of the Currency approved a pending application for such a ban that had been submitted by the FMR Corporation, which operates the Fidelity Group of mutual funds. Unlike money market funds that take consumers' money and issue checks, these new nonbank banks are insured by the F.D.I.C. Others that have received such consumer bank licenses include the American Express Company, the J.C. Penney Company, the Dreyfus Corporation, the Beneficial Company, the Parker Pen Company and Western Family Inc., a chain of furniture stores in the West.

In the emerging debate over the future of American banking, Alan Meltzer, a monetarist economist at the Carnegie-Mellon Institute in Pittsburgh, stands to one side. He says banks should be fully subject to market pressures and even the biggest should be allowed to fail.

"You can't have deregulation without people accepting the risk," he said. "There has to be understanding that if banks get into trouble, they have to pay the consequences. You can't have a system where the banks are free to take as much risk as they choose and then dump the losses on the taxpayer."

The role of the Federal Reserve, according to Mr. Meltzer, should be to avoid a chain reaction if a major bank were to fail. If such a failure were to cause a run on banks, the Fed should lend money to banks that run short of cash, but such loans should be made at penalty rates and should be backed with top-quality collateral, he said.

Within the high reaches of Government, Mr. Isaac of the F.D.I.C. comes closest to agreeing with Mr. Meltzer's free-market philosophy.

"During much of the last 50 years we have relied excessively on Government and not enough on market forces," Mr. Isaac said. "That has been done at great cost."

And Mr. Isaac advocates some fairly radical moves to impose "market discipline" on the banking system. Currently, all banks insured by the F.D.I.C. pay the same rates on their insurance premiums. But Mr. Isaac would vary the premium according to the agency's estimate of the riskiness of a particular bank's activities.

He also advocates asking big depositors to "share the risk" with the F.D.I.C. The agency has often in recent years merged a failing bank or savings bank into a stronger one as a way of avoiding outright bankruptcy. This tactic usually is possible only if the F.D.I.C. agrees to make up any losses passed along to the new institution. Under Mr. Issac's scheme, big depositors—those with more than $100,000 in the problem bank—would be required to share some of the loss with the F.D.I.C.

Necessary Government Involvement

But even Mr. Isaac argues that the Government must play a role in banking. "There's always going to be a fair amount of Government involvement in banking compared with any other business because banking is so central to the workings of the economy," Mr. Isaac said. "We've had periods when banking was relatively free of regulation. Those periods were characterized by one crisis after another. It's not realistic to think that Government will ignore banking: what we're talking about is balance." In much of the 19th century, when banking regulation was virtually nonexistent, financial panics and bank failures were commonplace.

Mr. Kaufman of Salomon Brothers, thinks the Isaac strategy would sweep away too much regulation. He contends that banks and Government are inseparable and that it's dangerous to give banks too much leeway. "You are dealing with one of the most powerful ingredients within a society," Mr. Kaufman said.

For their part, most bankers say they have little choice but to move into new fields. They claim that they have lost much of their traditional business to nonbanking companies.

It began, they say, in the 1960s, when big corporations started lending directly to one another through the so-called commercial paper market. This reduced the major source of big banks' deposit and loan business. And still more business was lost as the result of the development of the "Eurodollar" market in London, where corporations could shop for cheap loans and high deposit rates from banks around the world.

These pressures on their corporate business caused many large banks to increase their dealings with consumers. But there too, banks have run into stiff competition from nonbanks. In fact, until banks were allowed to pay market-oriented interest rates at the end of 1982, the unregulated money market mutual funds had drawn almost $200 billion in deposits from the banking system. But the change also raised the cost of funds to the banks, and this has caused many to stretch further for profits.

"There's always going to be a fair amount of Government involvement in banking compared with . . . other businesses."

According to many economists, the far higher rates banks must now pay for consumer deposits has contributed importantly to the higher interest-rate levels that now prevail nationwide.

Some bankers are deeply unhappy about the changes. "I accept that concept of a special role, of the uniqueness of a deposit-taking privilege," said John R. Petty, chairman of the Marine Midland Bank and former Assistant Secretary of the Treasury in the Johnson and Nixon Administrations. "But something happened on the way to the farm. Some years back that uniqueness disappeared. Had the regulators and Government been resolute in preserving it, the whole view of the banks in the community and deregulation would have taken a different course."

"I find it inconceivable that anybody could walk the cat back," lamented Mr. Petty.

Robert A. Bennett wrote this viewpoint for The New York Times.

"Whether inspired by panic over losing control or by sheer political opportunism, the regulatory impulse is wrong and must be resisted."

viewpoint 15

Telephone Deregulation Is Essential in a Free Economy

Robert W. Poole Jr.

Editor's note: The following viewpoint consists of two editorials by Robert W. Poole Jr. on the subject of deregulation.

I

Decade after decade, populist politicians and consumer advocates attacked Ma Bell, railing against the evils of the phone monopoly. Today, their victory is nearly complete, thanks to a decade of deregulatory moves by the Federal Communications Commission (FCC) and a seven-year Justice Department antitrust case. But just as the hated monopoly is finally expiring, a rump protest in Congress threatens to undo much that the deregulators have wrought. Ironically, the protestors are. . . the populists and consumer advocates!

What's happened is a failure to think through what competition—the only alternative to monopoly—really means. For most of this century, plain old telephone service was all there was, and it was provided by monopoly firms, most of them part of the Bell System (AT&T). To promote "universal service," both the regulators and the companies supported a whole system of subsidies. Long-distance users were systematically overcharged to subsidize local customers; and long-distance rates were averaged, so that high-traffic routes subsidized low-traffic ones.

Costly Subsidies

That, of course, is *one* way to run a telephone system. But it's a costly one, both in the arrogance of a monopoly provided and in the inefficiency bred by subsidies and lack of competition. As new technologies came along in the 1960s, competitors began chipping away at the monopoly's edges. First the FCC legalized "foreign attachments"—non-Bell

phones, answering machines, PBXs, etc. Later it began allowing firms like the pioneering MCI to offer discount long-distance services. By the late 70s, the monopoly was in shreds.

Consumers have benefited enormously from these changes. Today you can purchase your own cordless, memory-dialing, privacy-screening telephone from any of dozens of firms, saving a fortune over leasing (forever) from Ma Bell. And you can choose from a variety of long-distance companies, at rates as much as 50 percent lower than Bell's. Lower rates and all-digital links have enabled businesses to take full advantage of the computer revolution, transmitting huge volumes of data, often as a substitute for costly travel.

Controversial Access Charge

The breakup of AT&T is simply the culmination of these trends. With long-distance service increasingly digital and competitive, it made no sense for Bell to be stuck forever with artificially high long-distance rates to subsidize local users. So as part of the breakup that is spinning off local Bell companies, the FCC wants to allow the new (long distance) AT&T to price competitively. To make up for the loss of subsidy at the local level, the FCC would allow the locals to charge an additional flat monthly fee—called an "access charge"—on the grounds that customers should pay for the local line that gives them access to the long-distance network.

It is this "access charge," and the resulting increase in the local portion of phone bills, that has aroused the populists in Congress. Yet once the FCC allowed companies like MCI to begin competing in long-distance eight years ago, it was *inevitable* that long-distance charges would no longer be able to subsidize local service—and therefore that local rates would have to go up. Yet it is only now, when the horse has long since galloped out of the barn, that the politicos are trying to slam the door.

The would-be reregulators realize what a bind their inattention has put them in. They cannot simply forbid the local access charges and require that AT&T continue to subsidize the local companies. That would drive more long-distance users to the new competitors. So they want to tax *all* long-distance users, on a per-minute basis, to raise funds for local subsidies. But that will only prompt more large business users to build their own private systems to bypass the common carriers altogether. So the pols want to tax bypass systems, too. In other words, if you develop, at your own expense, a microwave/satellite cross-country telecommunications system, you will still have to pay a tax so that Joe Smith can get cheap phone service at his weekend cabin in the Rockies. And this is being advocated in the name of fairness!

"A continuation of monopoly and cross-subsidization would have precluded today's robust, dynamic telecommunications free-for-all, which is giving us a system that is, more than ever, the envy of all the world."

What lies behind such measures is the wrong-headed idea that telephone service is a right and some people must be forced to provide it for others. The opposite idea is that telephone service, like other goods, is a matter of choice—and that those who choose to live in low-demand, high-cost areas should be free to make that choice *and pay the price.* This is the principle we've accepted in deregulating airlines, trucks, and buses. It's working well, providing large cost savings and more choices of service for most users and only modest cost increases or reductions in service for small numbers of users. The same will be true for telecommunications.

We are just at the beginning of a revolution in telecommunications spawned by advancing technology. . . . The advent of cellular radio networks, microwave links, fiber-optic circuits, two-way cable, "intelligent" phones, and home computer terminals opens the door to a host of services whose exact forms we can only imagine. Which of these will be provided by local cable companies? Which by local phone companies? Which by radio common carriers? *Nobody knows.*

Regulation Is Wrong

But those who would reassert regulatory control are making one huge assumption: that regulators know better than competing firms and consumers who should develop which technology and how each should be marketed and priced. Whether inspired by panic over losing control or by sheer political opportunism, the regulatory impulse is wrong and must be resisted.

It is wrong because it seeks to undo a decade of progress toward user-pays telecommunications. It is wrong because it risks holding back an explosion of new and beneficial services. But most of all it is wrong because it would substitute *force* for *choice.* Deregulating telecommunications is not merely sensible; it's also the right thing to do.

II

Chances are you've heard your share of telephone horror stories—*el cheapo* phones that break down, sharply rising local phone bills, not knowing whom to call when something goes wrong.

And no doubt you've heard these familiar laments, repeated at least monthly in newspaper editorials and columns: "We had the finest telephone system in the world. Why did they have to go and break it up?" and "If it ain't broke, why fix it?"

But the charge that today's rapidly changing telecommunications system is the result of the court-imposed breakup of AT&T is simply wrong. Two driving forces—the microchip revolution and 18 years of telephone deregulation—made a system much like today's virtually inevitable.

The microchip made possible vast improvements in telecommunications: switching systems that are computers rather than mechanical monsters, desktop computers that can communicate cross-country, a huge expansion in the availability of radio frequencies for mobile telephones (using computerized "cellular" systems). These changes made the arbitrary but long-standing legal separation between the computer business and the telephone business obsolete—unless we were to be denied all the benefits of the new technologies. But there was no way that existing political realities (that is, the antitrust laws) would permit this huge business to be handed to a monopoly Bell system.

Chipping Away at Monopoly

In parallel with the microchip revolution, competitors were already chipping away at Ma Bell's monopoly. Way back in 1968, a company named Carterphone won a court case which permitted telephone users to hook its equipment up to Ma Bell's lines. Soon thereafter, an upstart named MCI won its first of many legal battles to compete with Bell in providing long-distance service. Once competition in equipment and service was legalized, the old structure and cross-subsidized pricing were doomed.

There are two ways to price telephone services. One is to charge high rates to high-demand, easy-to-serve users and use some of the resulting high profits to subsidize low-demand, hard-to-serve users.

This is the *cross-subsidies* model. The only way the high-demand users will sit still for it is if they're given no choice. That's exactly the position they'd been in ever since about 1913, when AT&T's Theodore Vail sold America's politicians the idea that phone service is a "natural monopoly" that should be provided by one huge regulated monolith.

The other alternative is *cost-based* pricing—what generally results when competition is allowed. When, for example, MCI and Sprint and other firms compete for the easy-to-serve long-distance customers, the competition drives prices down closer to the (relatively low) costs of providing that service, leaving no extra profits to subsidize, say, rural users. So the latter have to be charged rates much closer to the real (higher) cost of serving them. Try as you might to mix the two systems, it simply can't be done. Competition, once permitted, dries up the revenues needed to cross-subsidize higher-cost users.

Inevitable Changes

So *regardless* of whether or not AT&T had been broken up by a federal court order in 1982, we would today be seeing long-distance rates coming down, local bills (especially rural bills) going up, and such new forms of "user-pays" as charges for directory assistance and paying by the minute for local calls. And there is no real possibility of going back to the old, monopoly system. With the costs of "bypass" technologies such as satellite dishes and local fiber-optic loops continuing to plummet, more and more business users will be able to avoid using those portions of the phone system that attempt to charge the kinds of non-competitive prices needed to continue cross-subsidization.

All well and good, you may say, but what's in it for me? Why wasn't I better off before, with "the world's finest telephone system"?

Benefits to Consumer

Well, to begin with, take note of the huge variety of telephone equipment you can now buy from anyone—phones with built-in answering machines, portable phones, cellular mobile phones. You also have a choice of long-distance companies, at highly competitive rates. And coming soon will be all-digital service for accessing your favorite computer data service or bulletin board, and a whole host of shopping and information services available from either your local cable company or the local phone company, in heated competition.

At work, your firm is benefiting from unprecedented competition in equipment and services: PBX prices that have declined 30 percent over the past three years, a 50 percent drop since 1981 in the cost of key systems (small versions of PBXs), and central-office switching costs that have declined by 7-10 percent a year since 1980.

What this means for the American economy is

seldom appreciated. Economist Michael Borrus of the Berkeley Roundtable on the International Economy points out that lower costs due to deregulation have led to US telecommunications usage per capita nearly twice as great as Japan's and two and a half times that of Europe. In fact, all the basic arteries of our society, through which flow goods (transportation), money (financial system), and information (telecommunications), are being opened up to competition (and thus lower prices and innovation). Japan and parts of Europe are far behind in this regard—France and West Germany don't permit *any* telecommunications competition.

"Lower costs due to deregulation have led to US telecommunications usage per capita nearly twice as great as Japan's and two and a half times that of Europe."

In short, although we did have a telephone system that "worked," a continuation of monopoly and cross-subsidization would have precluded today's robust, dynamic telecommunications free-for-all, which is giving us a system that is, more than ever, the envy of all the world.

Robert W. Poole Jr. is the editor-in-chief of Reason, *a monthly magazine supporting "free minds and free markets."*

viewpoint **16**

Telephone Deregulation Harms the Consumer

Gregg Easterbrook

My phones aren't working properly. Last year I could have made one call to an evil, bloated monopoly, and they would have been fixed promptly at no charge. This year C&P Telephone told me I might have defective "customer premises equipment"—the phones themselves—which is no longer C&P's problem. A serviceman would be sent only after the phones had been checked. (Pardon me, Captain Yossarian.) So I called AT&T Information Systems, from which one of my phones is leased, and was told I'd have to transport the suspect C.P.E. to a Phone Center Store myself. Or I could mail it in at my own expense, and they would send a replacement—er, well—eventually. (By the way, you can't order phones over the phone. Thousands of businesses offer fingers-do-the-walking telephone shopping, but AT&T requires you to go to a Phone Center Store in person.) Unless the defect is in my other phone, which was purchased from ITT. Since the warranty on my ITT model expired approximately as I was opening the box, I might as well buy a new one, which would cost about the same as getting the old one (which may or may not be broken) repaired. So . . . once I invest $49.95 (I like the sturdy kind of phone you can slam down after someone refuses to talk to you) and an entire day of driving around town, C&P Telephone will send a serviceman to see why my calls aren't getting through—for $55 an hour.

Isn't it wonderful how they broke up Ma Bell to help the consumer?

And think of the money I'm saving! My basic phone service, which was about $8 a month till recently, is now about $13: if C&P's latest rate request is granted, my bill will rise to about $28 a month. Plus a $1 federal "access charge" due in

June. Plus fifty cents a hit for long distance directory information, once free. Ma Bell interstate rates, in turn, have fallen 6.1 percent since divestiture. To come out ahead all I have to do is make $344.25 worth of long distance calls per month.

Subsidizing the Little Guy

Five years ago the idea that 1984 would produce a wave of nostalgia for the phone company would have seemed as inconceivable as an oil glut. When Ma Bell was around, all we could do was complain about her: the phone company was a cultural synonym for arrogance, incompetence, and abuse of the little guy. Consumer activists scarcely could pronounce the name AT&T without asperity. Yet AT&T was supplying indisputably the best and cheapest telephone service in the world. In Japan a residential phone installation could cost $800; in France the waiting period for extension lines ran about two years; in no other country except Canada was instant access to dial tones taken for granted. And now, rid of Ma Bell, we finally begin to see what had been right under our noses: that the evil monopoly had been systematically manipulating telephone rates for the purpose of subsidizing the little guy and soaking the well to do.

"Before divestiture we had an industry where no company could get rich, because profits were controlled at a fair level, and a regulatory premise that every American ought to get a telephone as a gift from the tooth fairy," says Charles Wholstetter, chairman of the board of Continental Telecom, a $2 billion consortium which owns rural telephone companies, communication satellites, and similar ventures. "This system produced telephone reliability, and placed all the financial strains on those who could best afford to pay. Would you please tell me why that was so horrible we had to break it up?"

From its beginnings until roughly the 1960s, AT&T

had what economists call a "natural monopoly." There was no sensible alternative to copper wires for telephone transmissions; having many companies build competing networks would have been an extravagant waste of capital. AT&T also had an unnatural monopoly obtained through regulatory hanky-panky—the exclusive right of its subsidiary, Western Electric, to manufacture telephone equipment.

In exchange for monopoly status, AT&T had been subject to regulation. When the Federal Communications Commission [F.C.C.] was founded in 1934, it pressed for a rate structure under which most of the cost of equipment used jointly by local and long distance callers would be assigned to the long distance rates. Assigning costs was a toss-up anyway; since household wire can be used for local or interstate calls interchangeably, what share of the expense "belongs" to which type of call?

Soaking the Rich

Ma Bell went along with the arrangement. Having a full monopoly, it didn't care who was subsidizing whom so long as the net contained profit. Of equal importance, the company viewed low residential rates as essential to its goal of getting the entire country hooked up. Today nearly everyone has a phone, but during the first half of the century, AT&T was not at all certain it would be able to see its idea of a phone in every pot. (In 1940 only 37 percent of households had phones.) Forcing well-heeled users to pay most of the freight would also subsidize installation so that individuals joining the system would not need cash up front. "Rates were deliberately and openly designed to achieve the goal of universal service," Charles Brown, chairman of AT&T, has said. "These effects were disbelieved or ignored until recently." Brown estimates that just before the breakup on January 1, 1984, residential service on average cost the phone company $26 a month, far more than the average local rate.

"Now, rid of Ma Bell, we finally begin to see what had been right under our noses: that the evil monopoly had been systematically manipulating telephone rates for the purpose of subsidizing the little guy and soaking the well to do."

Big-business customers weren't wild about the idea of subsidizing you and me. But what else could they do? Until the 1960s, their only alternative was burying zillions of miles of copper wire. Communication satellites and microwave transmissions changed that. Suddenly a large customer could afford to "bypass," building its own long distance network which would not be burdened by subsidies to local rates.

Blocking Competition

At the same time equipment manufacturers were beginning to voice objections to Western Electric's sweetheart deal. Every attempt by independents to make phone gear, no matter how peripheral, was attacked by phalanxes of Bell lawyers. Once Bell went to court to block manufacture of a little plastic cup one was supposed to slip over the mouthpiece for private conversations in a crowded office, saying it threatened no less than the integrity of the entire Bell system. During the 1960s Bell lawyers increasingly based their arguments on technicalities and loopholes. It became clear that Bell manufacturing divisions were fat and smug, clinging to basic product designs as though they had been handed down by Moses. AT&T's major project innovation of the period was the Princess phone.

Thus it was pressure within the business community, not from consumers, which began AT&T's downfall. In 1968 the F.C.C. ruled that independent manufacturers could make phone equipment, and that firms like MCI could wholesale the new transmission technologies. AT&T responded by giving MCI a ridiculous run-around.... In 1974 Gerald Ford's Justice Department filed the antitrust suit that ultimately led to divestiture.

Victory in Defeat

Ma Bell settled the 1974 suit out of court. The ease with which AT&T gave in, and its Cheshire Cat grin upon emerging from "defeat," should have sounded warning klaxons. Bell agreed to sell off local operating companies like C&P; most, though not all, had belonged to the monopoly, the main exception being rural systems of the type owned by Continental Telecom. Operating companies would be regrouped under seven new regional holding companies. The regionals would handle local service and remain regulated; AT&T would become a manufacturer and long distance carrier, competing with MCI and others.

The residential subsidy was essentially eliminated. C&P, for example, got $748 million back from toll calls in 1983, but anticipates only $592 million in toll revenues [in 1985]. Ma Bell's battle cry was that it needed a "level playing field" relative to other interstate carriers. Always spared the subsidy, firms such as MCI and GTE had been getting a free ride, accounting for most of their price advantage; they were assessed only for "traffic sensitive" outlays—that portion of local equipment that would not be required if interstate calls didn't exist. One solution to this would have been to make MCI and GTE contribute to residential costs. Instead the opposite approach of not making AT&T pay either was adopted.

During settlement talks AT&T was able to portray itself as the aggrieved party, missing no opportunity to point out that divestiture was somebody else's idea. In truth, several AT&T factions had been panting to be thrown in the divestiture briar patch. Bell market analysts accurately foresaw that the coming digital explosion would open up many new categories of business. Trouble was, the same antitrust exemptions that forbade other companies for competing against Bell also forbade Bell from entering fields not related to phone service—with its guaranteed rates of return and ease of access to credit, AT&T might have smashed smaller companies in home appliances or breakfast cereal, and so on. Bell made the freedom to act like a regular manufacturer part of its price for consenting to divestiture; AT&T personal computers are now on the market.

Congress, as usual, didn't catch on until long after it was too late to do anything. Little happened in the months immediately following the settlement, when action might have had some impact. Only as the formal divestiture date approached did Congress start huffing and puffing.

At a joint House-Senate hearing in July 1983, numerous members of Congress made ringing speeches about how the breakup would clobber their constituents. Even Barry Goldwater called the breakup "potentially the worst thing that has ever happened to our national interest," but when Brown of AT&T was asked if divestiture could still be blocked, he coolly replied, "That ship has sailed."

Contested Access Charge

Ultimately Congress did nothing about divestiture, focusing instead on the F.C.C.'s "access charge" plan. The agency, supposedly the major actor in phone regulation, had not been consulted on the biggest phone decision of all time; some rookies from the Justice Department got all the action, and the F.C.C. was angry. Moreover, terms of the settlement set up U.S. District Court Judge Harold Greene as a kind of super-referee of communications theory—exactly what the chairman of the F.C.C. is supposed to be. Yearning to restore its authority, the F.C.C. started cooking up extra schemes of its own. Congress, in turn, since it controls the F.C.C. but not Judge Greene, zeroed in on access charges as a place to seem to do something dramatic without having to take on any of the major players.

The F.C.C. under Chairman Mark Fowler—a communications lawyer who won his position primarily on the strength of friendship with Charles Z. Wick—first decided to impose an access charge of $2 per month per residential phone, rising to about $4 per month by 1990. This charge would be for the privilege of paying still more; individuals will be assessed whether they made long distance calls or

not. Since 1 in 6 households place no long distance calls in a typical month, and only 4 percent place more than $25 worth, almost everyone will end up a loser on the access charge alone—to say nothing of higher local rates, where the real money is. Even most businesses will end up behind on the charge alone, since 87 percent have long distance bills under $50. (Business access charges are somewhat higher; business local rates are also rising.) In a letter to Congress, the chief of the F.C.C.'s common carrier bureau, Jack D. Smith, cheerfully explained that since the local rates were in the process of tripling, added consumer costs from access fees would be small by comparison.

"The regionals for their parts are getting ideas about metamorphism into tiny AT&Ts."

Access fees are intended to supplement local operating companies' lost subsidies by shifting more cost away from businesses which are in a position to bypass, onto individuals who are not. Each additional bypass would cause local rates to rise even further. In New York City just 5 percent of the New York Tel's customers account for 70 percent of its revenues. It appears that unless divestiture is altered by Congress, access fees are a necessary evil; having tasted a new system designed to serve their interests for a change, the big boys are not going to turn back the clock voluntarily.

Potential for Consumer Disaster

Consumer groups now opposing access fees are being penny-wise and pound foolish, because in the deregulated environment, forcing down local monthly bills through political pressure will backfire. Over the long term a potential for consumer disaster exists as the price of bypass equipment falls enough that medium-sized companies, not just the Fortune 500, can afford it.

Congress postponed . . . and leaned on the F.C.C. to reduce the initial fee to $1: but it dodged the much more meaningful issue of local rates. In the wake of the settlement, C&P asked for a 130 percent residential rate increase in the District of Columbia, and 28 percent in Maryland; Southwestern Bell asked a 204 percent for Texas, Mountain Bell asked 201 percent for New Mexico, Pacific Telesis for a $1.36 billion total increase for California, including a 10 percent "rate surcharge." Though the new local operating companies have little choice but to increase rates—given the reduction in long distance income—they are relying on public confusion about deregulation to try to win very large rate boosts before the smoke clears.

So far the regionals have been acutely conscious of not cutting off service to poor or rural customers, since outrage over cutoffs might be the only factor that could galvanize Congress into action. A variety of plans involving "lifeline" phones and rural assistance funds seems likely to ensure that telephone ownership will remain nearly universal: the poor will still have phones, they just won't be able to use them. Message-unit billing policies, in which the consumer gets "dial-tone-service" (a phone number) at a small fee and pays per minute for local calls, are really devices to reduce rate shock—keeping the official cost of having a phone low while greatly increasing the cost of using that phone. Either way the working poor and the middle class are going to get soaked.

Power-Hungry Baby Bells

Meanwhile, mysteriously, the promised huge cuts in residential long distance rates have not materialized. At divestiture the traffic-sensitive fees, which all long distance carriers paid, were increased. This means that while AT&T (freed from the subsidy) now pays less to local loops, MCI and the rest pay more. Discounts at the cut-rate carriers have fallen to as small as 5 percent. MCI recently raised some prices, and it did so in the old Trust Your Mother fashion via a tiny box in its newsletter labeled "Rate Adjustment."

"This new technology could have evolved without slam-bam divestiture."

The regionals for their parts are getting ideas about metamorphism into tiny AT&Ts. U.S. West has gone into the real estate business. Bell Atlantic wants in to cable TV operations, and Ameritech is sprouting into a full-scale conglomerate with amazing speed. Headquartered in Illinois, Ameritech already has operations in states where it owns no phone companies. James Bauer, president of Ameritech's development division, told me the company aspires to offer "information transportation." Ameritech is involved in shared tenant services (allowing large office buildings to lease complete packages of phone service and switchboards), corporate financing, venture capital projects, and a "least-cost routing" computer that switches a business's long distance calls to whatever carrier offers the best price that day. Since long distance transmission is a fungible commodity—what do you care who carries your call?—switchers may soon render everybody's rates exactly the same.

There can be no doubt that that competition has breathed life into a once sluggish business. The regionals have begun laying fiber-optic cable which will carry more information than copper, enabling computers to communicate with each other at much greater speeds. The system is being converted from the original electromechanical principle to digital transmission, which will also help machines talk to each other. (And this may render obsolete all those phones consumers have been buying in the last few years to save money, including the lovely decorator models with the speaker in the beak of a simulated wood grain duck decoy.) Battery-powered cellular mobile phones already enable someone walking down the street in Chicago to direct-dial Tokyo, and similar wonders are in the works.

Yet this new technology could have evolved without slam-blam divestiture. The pace of change would have been slower, but since present changes are coming faster than regulators or consumers can stay on top of them that might not have been so bad. AT&T can launch satellites too: and if it's true, as some contend, that new technologies will eventually make interstate calls extremely cheap, there's no reason why AT&T could not have switched to the new equipment, cut its costs and continued to profit while charging lower prices. (Bear in mind, when promised that large rate increases today will mean great bonanzas at an unspecified later time, that power companies promised electricity "too cheap to meter" if only customers would front the cost of nuclear plants.)

Benefits to Businesses

More important, in addition to almost all the new costs falling on the average householder, so far almost all the new benefits are flowing to big businesses and the wealthy who make frequent use of data transmission and similar services. And now there is no one with final responsibility for making the overall system work. Personal computer buyers quickly discover that the manuals for unit, printer, and software are written as if the other parts of the system didn't exist; and if something goes wrong with the only item users actually benefit from—having the whole computer work together—each component manufacturer says the other is to blame. Now it'll be the same for the phones, where all users really care about is whether the system works, not who made each part. As the new telephone firms try to blame each other for systemwide problems, and focus their attention on glamor fields like "information transportation," what will become of local service?

Divestiture may be well out to sea, but there are steps that could be taken to restore the old system's advantages while retaining the new one's innovative spirit. Congress could re-impose the residential subsidy and make it apply to all long-distance carriers, while either forbidding businesses to bypass or requiring those that do to pay fees approximating toll charges. The regionals complain that such legislation would be unenforceable, although they give no persuasive reason why: having cowed Congress they want to keep it cowed, and so far are succeeding.

Meanwhile, the F.C.C. wants further tinkering in the name of doctrinal purity. Fowler has suggested removing rate-of-return restrictions on AT&T altogether, and making further changes that would shift more costs to individuals. It is interesting to note that after the zeppelin-lifting volumes of hot air the Reagan Administration has pumped about "user fees," the one place it is actually following through is the one place where user fees would hurt the poor and help the rich.

Is it an exaggeration for Goldwater to invoke the national interest? Possibly not. As Senator Bob Packwood of Oregon, another Republican, points out, "For the better part of 200 years, this country has had a policy of attempting to make transportation and communications available to everybody." Strictly from a market perspective, it's inefficient to build roads in Montana or phone lines in Nebraska, because greater numbers could be served at lower costs elsewhere. Yet building an American physical framework available to anyone, anywhere increases national unity and opens the door to the future. If the standards of the AT&T deregulation had been applied to road construction, Packwood notes, "There would be parts of this country that would have no highways."

Reducing Shared Inspiration

Another national interest being lost in the shuffle is Bell Laboratories, whose scientists invented the transistor and over the years have averaged nearly one patent per day. Bell Labs had two marvelous features. First, since research was financed from a stable revenue base, it was able to hire the sort of slightly wacky mad-genius types who make for breakthroughs and turn them loose on projects with no immediate payoff. Second, because the underwriting was quasi-public, Bell Lab patents were available to all, including entrepreneurs who needed information from basic research but couldn't possibly finance their own block-long laboratory complexes. In fact, such companies, taking abstract ideas from Bell Labs and adapting them to market conditions, inspired much of the current telecommunications revolution. A better combination of public benefit and private initiative is hard to imagine. Now Bell patents are proprietary, and the labs are shifting toward short-term applied research. Of course, some new scientific force may arise to replace Bell Labs; it had no monopoly on thought. But it also wasn't broken. Why did we break it up?

Gregg Easterbrook is a staff writer for The Atlantic.

"The Airline Deregulation Act has dramatically achieved its primary objective of helping consumers by cutting airline prices without cutting service."

Airline Deregulation Keeps Prices Low

Simon Lazarus & Clarence B. Carson

Editor's note: The following viewpoint is taken from two articles favoring airline deregulation. Part I is by Simon Lazarus, Part II by Clarence B. Carson.

I

With Braniff Airways bankrupt, Continental Air Lines in reorganization and Eastern Airlines, among other carriers, considered near the brink, airline employees' unions are urging repeal of the Airline Deregulation Act of 1978. Their concerns deserve serious attention, but re-regulation is not the answer.

Tossing aside the benefits that the Airline Deregulation Act has brought to consumers, the industry and to employees as well would be a classic case of throwing the baby out with the bath water.

Consider, first, the fact that the Airline Deregulation Act has dramatically achieved its primary objective of helping consumers by cutting airline prices without cutting service.

The real minimum cost of a round-trip coast-to-coast ticket is now less than 40 percent of its pre-deregulation level in 1974, when the Civil Aeronautics Board [C.A.B.] first began to loosen regulatory controls. Adjusted for inflation, the 1974 round-trip ticket costing $360 would today cost more than $1,000. Across the board, real-price levels are down by about one-fifth. Choosing the cheapest flight may seem complicated, but for most of us it sure beats having no choice at all.

Nor have these gains for big city travelers come at the expense of cuts in service to small communities. Commuter airlines have more than made up for losses of trunk carrier jet service. In 72 communities formerly served by jets, a recent C.A.B. staff study showed, there was a 30 percent increase in service

between 1978 and 1981. A new generation of highly efficient commuter aircraft, equipped with 30 to 50 seats and prop-jet engines, is providing more as well as cheaper flights to passengers from these communities.

Before anyone jumps to rebuild a regulatory shelter for the weaker airlines, it would be prudent to consider the public reaction to price increases that would make air travel once again, as it was before deregulation, affordable mainly to business travelers and the well-to-do.

Reinstituting regulation might make the going easier for some inefficient airlines, but it would not guarantee them immortality. After all, Eastern, currently considered precarious, was equally so throughout the 1970's. In 1974, Eastern, held up as an exemplar of regulated inefficiency, was reported to have 13 times as many executives as its chief competitor, Delta Air Lines.

Deregulation and Employees

As competition forces the older carriers to trim their ranks and to increase productivity, it is understandable that many of their employees look back with nostalgia to the pre-1978 period. But deregulation has not adversely affected overall employment levels in the industry. Quite the contrary. According to the C.A.B., employment by the trunk carriers in 1982 was 263,108—down slightly from the 265,777 registered in 1977. But this small drop was more than offset by the jump in employment of 13,157 among local service carriers that occurred during the same period. The expansion of these smaller carriers is directly traceable to the competitive opportunities opened by deregulation.

Taking aim at a broad program that is yielding such benefits—simply to address the genuine but narrow transition problems of employees of certain high-cost airlines—makes no sense.

Employees, in all industries, do have a legitimate

stake in assuring that the scope and pace of their adjustment to changes in the competitive environment should be fixed voluntarily, through collective bargaining under the national labor laws. . . .

"Airlines functioning behind a protective shield become flabby."

Recent accords at Eastern and at Western Airlines indicate that the collective-bargaining process is up to the challenge of accommodating the transition. To the extent that additional Federal intervention is required, the place to start would seem to be the labor protection provisions of the Airline Deregulation Act itself. These give displaced employees hiring preference with other airlines and also provide for Federal monthly assistance and relocation payments. Curiously, airline employees' unions have not made it a major priority to direct public attention to the fact that the compensation provisions have never been funded.

In view of the trauma of fuel-price escalation and the recent deep recession, what is most striking about the post-regulation industry is its relative overall health, not its weak spots. Scrapping deregulation would not banish the industry's real problems, but would create a great many more.

II

Competition is often heartily applauded in general and avidly avoided in particular. When I taught in schools and colleges I could see clearly the desirability of teacher licensing and tenure. After all, we can't have just anybody teaching our children, can we? And teachers must have security in their jobs without fear or favor. Right? Of course, few of us are above clothing selfish interests in the attractive mantle of the welfare of mankind. Even now, I could make a good case, I think, why writers should not be exposed to the rigors of competition. After all, why should those of us who are well qualified and adept at writing have to compete with every "low life" who can fashion a sentence? We should be made economically secure from the whims of editors and the low taste of readers by licensing, government restrictions on entry to the field, and hefty subsidies. Right? So each of us tends to think, and governments have acted with alacrity to accommodate many of us.

There is nothing new in these general tendencies, but what makes it current is the present hassle over airline deregulation.

Some of the major airlines are in deep trouble. Continental has gone into court to declare bankruptcy and protect the airline from its creditors.

Others have lost oodles of money lately, and their cash income persistently fails to match the outgo. Some have outspokenly blamed their troubles on high labor costs. Union leaders, on the other hand, blame the financial difficulties of the companies on deregulation. Company leaders have not rushed to join this clamor, but some of them, the officers of Delta, for example, opposed deregulation from the outset. In any case, it is reasonable to expect that all the hoary arguments for protecting and regulating an industry will be rehearsed once again in the coming weeks and months.

Before getting into these, however, it might be well to settle what is under discussion here. Deregulation deals mainly with fares, service, and routes. It does not involve traffic control, safety, or health regulations. Another point that should be made here is that the airline business is not "a natural monopoly" if there is such a thing. No airline does or can own the airspace for flying, and none does, to my knowledge, own any airport, though it might be possible to do so.

What airlines do, as a rule, is fly airplanes carrying passengers and freight from one airport to another and maintain various personnel and auxiliary facilities in support of this operation. There is no more reason, on the face of it, for protecting them from competition than preventing competition among grocery stores. Both perform useful services: grocery stores offer food and drink for sale; airlines offer transportation for sale. Both are commercial undertakings, and both serve the general public. There is one more reason in the nature of the undertaking why one should be more likely to be profitable than the other. True, airlines operate on schedules, and may have airplanes flying without a capacity load. Grocery stores, too, ordinarily operate on schedules, and their business may vary during the hours they are open.

No Guarantees

Indeed, there are no guarantees that any competitive business will be profitable. Some ventures are profitable; many fail for one reason or another. Hundreds of service stations and grocery stores go out of business annually. Even a great chain of department stores, such as W.T. Grant, can find it necessary to close down permanently. Granted, it was a dramatic event when Braniff, a major international airline, closed down operations and idled its brightly painted planes. But that was as much a part of the saga of American business as any of numerous successes.

It is easy to be philosophical about other people's failures, of course, but that is not my point. My point is that businesses are risky; the counterpoint to profits are losses. Moreover, it is the very possibility of failure that spurs businesses to serve customers effectively. It is also the possibility of failure that leads us to try so hard to avoid competition. Airlines with protected routes, fares that are established by a government regulatory agency, and competition reduced to genteel advertising aimed at promoting customer identification with the varnish of a particular airplane, feel themselves secure. This sense of security has often been augmented by government subsidies.

Regulation Encourages Laziness

The trouble with such a situation is that airlines functioning behind a protective shield become flabby. They tend to be operated for the advantage and profit or prestige of the company and its employees. Routes are set up for the convenience of the company. Passengers in Birmingham may have to fly to Atlanta to catch a plane for New Orleans; those in Columbia may have to go to Atlanta to fly to Washington. Companies with a supposed insulation against failure tend to yield to union demands for ever higher wages. Such companies tend to buy the latest and most expensive airplanes and seek prestigious international routes.

Competition bursts the bubble. New airplanes in particular areas provide non-stop service to long-neglected communities, go to the market for employees, and generally are not saddled with costs and inefficiencies which accumulated in the halcyon days of regulation. In short, competition tends to force businesses to serve customers, to bring lower prices and better service, and to induce companies to hold down costs in order to make profits. It tends to weed out those who cannot or will not do these things. There is no substitute for competition to accomplish such results.

Simon Lazarus is a lawyer who handled regulatory issues on the White House Domestic Policy Staff between 1977 and 1981. Clarence B. Carson writes about economic issues for The Review of the NEWS, *a weekly conservative news journal.*

"We are concerned lest. . . safety becomes one of the extras sacrificed by . . . airlines in order to either lower fares or increase profits."

Airline Deregulation Endangers Safety

Henry A. Duffy

In little more than a decade, America has deregulated three of our economy's most vital industries—transportation, telecommunications, and finance. Although the differences between the industries are nearly as great as the ways they have been affected by deregulation, one outcome is common to all three—the wide open, competitive atmosphere that accompanies deregulation thrust each of the industries into a turbulent transition period.

This turbulence has been both positive and negative. Deregulation in the financial markets, for example, has created new ways for people to save and invest their money, but has had the result of diverting investors away from productive, capital investment. Deregulation in the airline and bus industries has brought cheaper fares to selected larger markets, higher fares to others, and cut out smaller, less popular markets altogether. Changes in telecommunications laws and the break-up of AT&T brought cheaper long-distance phone rates, but the cost of local service has skyrocketed.

Illusory Benefits

The airline industry, whose health is vital not only to our nation's commerce and trade, but to our society's mobility, is in the throes of change that threatens its very existence. Supporters of deregulation point to some cheaper fares and the entry of new carriers to the market as signs of the success of deregulation. Unfortunately, whatever positive change we have seen up to this point may be illusory.

The cutthroat fare wars and below-cost pricing which have pervaded this industry are not healthy competition. While we are currently experiencing a respite in the fare wars, it could be only the calm

Henry A. Duffy, "Deregulating Safety," *USA Today*, July 1984. Copyright 1984 by The Society for the Advancement of Education.

before the storm as carrier after carrier announces that, while it won't drop the first shoe, it is prepared to match fare cuts by others. Fare wars are a cancer, eating away at the bone and muscle of a healthy airline industry—our exemplary safety record.

The industry's outstanding safety record comes as a result of commitment to an *additional* margin of safety by the airlines and their employees. This added margin of safety was achieved by exceeding, not just meeting, the minimum safety standards established by the Federal Aviation Administration (FAA).

We are concerned lest this margin of safety becomes one of the extras sacrificed by "no-frills" airlines in order to either lower fares or increase profits. Kenneth S. Hunt, FAA director of flight operations, echoes a similar concern. "Those who just barely meet the minimum standards don't stay in business very long," he warns.

Absolutely crucial to the maintenance of air safety are the well-trained, responsible professionals— pilots, mechanics, engineers, flight attendants, and all the rest—whose lives are dedicated to air transportation. Maintaining safety also requires fully equipped training facilities and maintenance centers, safety programs, reliable aircraft, and responsible work rules.

The latest technology will get you nowhere unless you have well-trained mechanics to check and double check before a plane goes in the air; unless you have an adequate number of FAA inspectors to insure safety; and, ultimately, unless you have highly skilled pilots, like the Eastern L-1011 crew that guided it to safety after all the engines failed over water.

This is the human element of safety that is often overlooked by airline managers making cost-benefit decisions to reduce operating costs. This industry must remain committed to paying the price of an extra margin of safety, because highly trained employees, redundant systems, and modern technology are not inexpensive.

However, the cutthroat competition of deregulation puts many airlines under immense financial strain, and may call into question their ability to maintain the extra margin of safety. Since 1978, 26 airlines have declared bankruptcy or ceased operations (eight in the past year alone), and industry losses have totalled more than $1,500,000,000. Even the current upward swing by some airlines is offset by the shaky financial future of some industry majors.

In the aggressive and uncertain deregulated environment, how long will it be before an airline manager's commitment to the additional margin of safety could waver under the continued cost pressures? Some would argue it already has.

When Continental Airlines declared bankruptcy under Chapter 11 on Sept. 24, 1983, thousands of the most experienced pilots, mechanics, and flight attendants struck the company in protest of the airline's refusal to honor its collective bargaining contracts. With many of its best employees on the picket line, the "New Continental" continued to operate under emergency rules with one-third of its normal manpower—mostly quickly promoted junior officers and newly hired personnel.

The results? A "New Continental" pilot completely missed the runway while landing in Denver on Nov. 9, 1983. This pilot had been hastily promoted from co-pilot less than six weeks before. Fortunately, the taxiway where he landed was free of ground equipment and aircraft, so no one was injured in the incident.

Ill-Advised Rush

Nevertheless, the question must be raised: Was that pilot ready to take over the captain's seat, or was the move an ill-advised rush by Continental in order to turn a profit? The issue of hasty upgrading of pilots had caused Continental's Senior Director of Flying, Capt. W.S. Laughlin, Jr., to resign in protest only three weeks before. In his letter of resignation, he warned the "New Continental":

> Let me caution you on using contract pilots and/or upgrading Continental Airlines pilots too quickly. There are many routes that take experience and knowledge to be operated in an efficient, safe and professional manner.

Upon landing at New York's LaGuardia Airport on Dec. 28, 1983, a "New Continental" aircraft crumpled its fuselage. Not only did the pilots not enter the incident into their log, the plane continued to fly revenue passengers for three days before an American Airlines tower official questioned the use of the damaged craft. The plane was then wrapped to cover its wrinkles and flown to Los Angeles, where it remained in a high-security hangar. At the time of this writing, the FAA was reluctant to comment on this incident, pending further investigation.

The disastrous accident at Washington National Airport in January, 1982, involved an aggressive airline born of deregulation and a captain with little more than three years' experience with the company. He had been moved up to captain in less than two years, and had a total of only 2,300 hours in jet transports. Only 34 years old, the pilot had little experience in the severe weather common to East Coast winters. The National Transportation Safety Board, which was responsible for investigating the accident, was highly critical of both the captain's judgment and experience. Again, one must ask: Was safety or profit the top priority in the decision to promote that man to captain in less than two years?

Costly, Essential Pilot Training

The captain of a DC-10 manages a 296-ton, $25,000,000 piece of machinery that travels at eight miles a minute in three dimensions. The process of training someone to do that job and providing for the continued safety of his passengers is neither quick nor easy—and it should not be unduly accelerated in the name of profit.

The average newly hired pilot in an airline under contract with the Air Line Pilots Association (ALPA) comes with a minimum of 2,500-3,000 hours of flight time—often from a military background. Nearly every incoming pilot has a college degree; many have master's degrees.

Starting as a second officer (flight engineer in a three-seat cockpit) or first officer (co-pilot in smaller aircraft with two-seat cockpits) at a pay rate of as little as $15,000, the pilot will work anywhere from 10 to 20 years to gain enough seniority to upgrade to captain. During the early years of his tenure, the pilot will be subjected to furloughs in response to the ebb and flow of the crewing requirements of his airline.

"Fare wars are a cancer, eating away at the bone and muscle of a healthy airline industry—our exemplary safety record."

This pilot is paying his dues. Most importantly, he is gaining experience and honing his skills and judgment under the tutelage of a senior, highly qualified captain. During this time, he will probably accumulate an additional 5,000-10,000 hours of flight time.

In addition to his normal workload, a pilot must attend frequent refresher courses and spend considerable time studying the latest methods and technology. In order to maintain his pilot's license, he must also pass an annual proficiency check by the FAA and must pass a rigorous physical examination every six months. Pilots who suffer an illness considered minor in another profession may be grounded, thereby losing their livelihood.

Following this extensive preparation period, the pilot must successfully complete three to four months of intensive training and testing, designed to peak his skill and enable him to handle a whole catalog of emergencies. This intensive training is also intended to screen out those who are marginal or below-average. Finally, after passing both the company's and the FAA's "captain's checks" and flying under the direct supervision of a check captain for 25-50 hours, the pilot is certified to become a captain and assume the responsibility that goes along with it.

"In the aggressive and uncertain deregulated environment, how long will it be before an airline manager's commitment to the additional margin of safety could waver under the continued cost pressures?"

The thorough training of a highly skilled pilot requires a healthy investment of time and money—on the part of the pilot, the company, and the FAA. Still, it is an investment which we must continue to make if we are to maintain the safest air transportation system in the world. Many of the new entrant carriers lack both the essentials of time and money. They are impatient and impetuous, because deregulation allows them to rush into business practically overnight. As a pilot with 30 years' experience, I can assure you that, as a traveler, you don't want to fly with an impatient, impetuous upstart.

Effects of Discounted Fares

There are other, more subtle results of a financially strained airline industry. For example, today's heavily discounted fares result from problems of excess capacity and cash flow. Deregulation has spawned many new airlines, and thus created an abundance of seating capacity. Unfortunately, capacity continues to grow without attracting a corresponding increase in passengers. Excess capacity is wasteful, and someone has to pay for the cost of all the empty seats.

Cash flow problems cause airlines to cut fares to below cost to generate full passenger loads and more immediate dollars to pay bills. This fact could result in airline managers attempting to pressure pilots—most especially those pilots not protected by an ALPA contract—to operate aircraft against their prudent professional judgment. After all, the thinking goes, if the airline is hurting financially,

then it certainly doesn't need the extra expense of grounding an aircraft for repairs.

This subtle pressure could lead to a revival of the 1930's practice known as "pilot pushing," where airlines literally demanded pilots to fly in marginal conditions for cost reasons. The airlines ALPA members fly for know better than to take us on regarding this issue, but what of the unorganized airlines? Who protects their pilots from disciplinary actions when they question whether is is safe to take off or land? Concern for those pilots is one thing; it is quite another when you realize that you and I and every other airline traveler share the skies with them.

Low Profits Limit Improvements

Although the human element is the most important, it is by no means the only area which requires both a commitment to safety and financial stability. Financially strapped airlines can not afford the installation of equipment and technology that have demonstrated they can improve safety. The technology exists for collision-avoidance systems; the cash to buy them does not.

If we are to live up to our commitment to the safest air transportation system in the world, we must make certain the industry is economically able to support the cost of meeting that extra margin of safety. Having racked up over $1,500,000,000 in losses in five years, today's airline industry is not.

Economics and safety simply can not be separated. The Congress recognized the vital importance to safety of a financially healthy airline industry way back in 1937, when it was first considering regulation of what was a chaotic, unprofitable, and essentially unregulated aviation industry. At that time, the Senate said:

> It should not be necessary to point out that a profitable operation is necessary for safety. It is bad enough for ordinary corporations to be harassed by losses, but in the case of an air vehicle, when safety depends on extensive equipment, there must be ample funds or the ships must be grounded.

In recent testimony before a Senate subcommittee, James Danaher, director of the National Transportation Safety Board's Bureau of Technology, raised a similar, 1983-version of that warning flag. Citing the commuter airlines' "tendency to overlook and short circuit" Federal safety provisions, he warned that cost-cutting and corner-cutting could jeopardize air safety.

Safety and Confidence

Three airlines have ceased operations in the last year for safety reasons. Air Illinois voluntarily quit service after an accident in which 10 people were killed. The FAA investigated the adequacy of the airline's maintenance procedures and its operational procedures. The FAA also ordered Global International Airways and Guy America to cease operations for safety violations. In the airline industry, where consumer confidence is vital to its existence and success, any reduction in safety has the potential to send the entire industry into a tailspin.

In addition to the constant cost pressure on the airlines, the FAA's safety function has been affected in a very direct and visible way by deregulation. Although the number of carriers has nearly doubled since deregulation in 1978, the number of FAA inspectors responsible for monitoring the new airlines has been cut by 20%. Due to the manpower shortage, general aviation inspectors are now being used to monitor commercial air carriers. This is akin to allowing a general practitioner to take over the chores of a brain surgeon.

"As pilots, we are apprehensive and concerned about the disturbing trends in the airline industry."

The Civil Aeronautics Board (CAB) is responsible for certifying new carriers before they begin to fly. This involves a thorough examination of the prospective airline's financial condition, managerial skills, and disposition to comply with Federal safety regulations. These duties, already pared back by deregulation, will fall completely by the wayside when the CAB goes out of existence at the end of [1985].

Protecting Consumers

Also unclear is the future of CAB's consumer protection duties. Issues such as smoking sections, overbooking, or charter regulations have come under the purview of the CAB, but are not specifically to be transferred to any particular agency, if they are to be continued at all. Without an overbooking rule, for example, it is not unreasonable to expect airlines to greatly reduce or restrict compensation to "bumped" passengers.

The FAA already seems to be attempting to abdicate its responsibility for consumer protection. In response to a 1981 petition by the Aviation Consumer Action Project asking that the FAA require airlines to carry more fully equipped medical kits aboard airlines, the FAA claimed that it had no authority to require carriers to install the extra equipment. Recently, however, an appeals court ordered the FAA to own up to its responsibility to review the petition on its merits.

As pilots, we are apprehensive and concerned about the disturbing trends in the airline industry. Having dedicated our entire lives to aviation and creating a safe airline industry, we feel betrayed by the actions of several deregulators, such as "inflation

fighter" Alfred Kahn, the former CAB chairman, who is credited with initiating deregulation.

After his short stint with the Federal government, Kahn took to the private sector, where he is now on the board of directors of New York Air, a company spawned by Kahn's deregulation effort. He is joined on the board of New York Air by the former general counsel of the CAB, Philip Bakes. Not coincidentally, the president and chief executive officer of New York Air is Michael Levine, a former top aid to Kahn at the CAB.

Even some of the most ardent early supporters of deregulation now sing a different tune. John Robson, the pro-deregulation chairman of the CAB during the Ford Administration, admitted in an interview with *Fortune* magazine:

> Let's not kid ourselves. Fred Kahn (CAB Chair) and I had a window of about four years, when we had stable fuel prices, a growing economy, widespread discontent with government regulation and strong White House backing. I guarantee you, if Congress were voting on airline deregulation today, it wouldn't pass.

Senate Minority Leader Robert C. Byrd (D. W.Va). expressed similar sentiments: "I wish I had the chance again—I would vote against it."

Renewed Commitment to Safety Needed

To remedy the present situation, we do not advocate a return to the previous regulated airline industry. We have consistently recommended that pricing guidelines be established to prevent fare wars and predatory and discriminatory pricing policies. Having failed to convince Congress of that need, we insist on the renewed commitment on the part of the Congress and the FAA to the maintenance of safe airways.

The twin-headed monster—burgeoning losses caused by deregulation, coupled with government cutbacks in essential manpower devoted to safety—could bring the nation's airline industry to its knees. Clearly, this was not the intent of Congress, and it should not sit idly by while one of the nation's most vital industries destroys itself.

Henry A. Duffy is chief executive officer of the Air Line Pilots Association, Washington, DC.

"The [deregulation] legislation removes outdated and inefficient regulatory procedures . . . and frees licensees of unnecessary government participation in their affairs."

viewpoint**19**

Broadcast Regulation Is No Longer Needed

Robert E. Lee

From a statement accompanying his testimony supporting Senate bill 270 which proposed deregulation measures for radio broadcasting.

The Commission believes this legislation achieves significant public interest objectives and paves the way for even greater public benefits in the provision of telecommunications service. The [Federal Communications] Commission supports the bill.

S.270 confers statutory approval upon the Commission's own recent deregulation efforts and proposes statutory changes that will aid greatly the Commission's efforts to further deregulate broadcast communications. We strongly support the bill's provision establishing indefinite radio station license terms and providing the Commission the discretion to grant certain broadcast applications based on a system of random selection. Our studies have shown that periodic review of radio licenses, essentially to evaluate programming performance, is not necessary where marketplace forces are already providing incentives for stations to perform in the public interest. Random selection, replacing comparative hearings, would eliminate a process that, while well intentioned, has evolved into a regulatory nightmare. Comparative hearings result in unconscionable delays in the initiation of new service and enormous monetary costs with little apparent public benefit. We recommend that the bill be enlarged to permit random selection in all Commission licensing efforts.

The Commission also makes suggestions with respect to parts of the proposal and seeks further clarification of others. For example, the Commission believes some restriction should be imposed on the age of allegations in a petition to revoke. Five- or ten-year television license terms also are suggested. And, an apparent inconsistency is noted between the

proscription on requiring certain programing, on one hand, and license adherence to the Fairness Doctrine, on the other.

In sum, the Commission believes the legislation removes outdated and inefficient regulatory procedures, enhances the government's ability to expeditiously authorize new service, and frees radio licensees of unnecessary government participation in their affairs. The Commission is confident that these benefits will be achieved while the public continues to receive a diverse radio broadcast service fully responsive to its interests. Moreover, these benefits will produce substantial savings in private, government, and public dollars.

As you know, the FCC recently took substantial deregulatory steps in the area of broadcast radio. These actions were based on our recognition that as a result of many changes in this dynamic industry the public interest would be better served in the absence of certain Commission rules and procedures. There remain several areas where further deregulation is warranted. But, action in these areas is, or may be, beyond the Commission's statutory authority. The Commission is therefore pleased to see this legislative initiative, and it supports it.

Areas of Deregulation

The FCC's recent deregulatory actions cover four areas: nonentertainment programing, ascertainment requirements, commercialization, and logging requirements. While we retain a generalized obligation for licensees to offer programing responsive to community issues, current percentage guidelines for nonentertainment programing are eliminated. In recognition that individual stations do not operate in a vacuum, licensees are allowed to consider the service offered by competing stations when determining which community issues to address. In this manner, we are allowing licensees maximum flexibility to be responsive to their public

Robert E. Lee, testimony before the Senate Committee on Commerce, Science, and Transportation, February 26, 1981.

while maintaining each station's individual obligation to address community issues.

We are also eliminating formal ascertainment procedures, which have developed into a costly and inefficient exercise that does not necessarily result in programing responsive to the public. In place of the formal ascertainment procedures, licensees must maintain in their public files a list of five to ten community issues that they addressed in their programing in the past year with an enumeration of examples of such programing and how they determined their public's concern for those issues.

The Commission is also eliminating its guidelines on levels of commercialization, leaving it to the operation of marketplace forces to determine the appropriate amounts of commercial time. We believe this will have little impact on overall commercialization levels, but it will allow licensees who face unique circumstances to experiment.

Finally, we are eliminating the program log keeping requirement, which has imposed an enormous paperwork burden on licensees without providing commensurate benefits to the public.

We have taken these actions based on a thorough review of a vast record, which included a detailed staff analysis, over 20,000 public comments, and a two-day panel of distinguished experts with diverse viewpoints. I would like to highlight several key factors that helped provide the basis of our decision.

Growth of Radio Broadcasting

Radio broadcasting has grown dramatically since 1934, when fewer than 600 stations served the nation. Today, there are nearly 9,000 AM and FM radio stations in the United States. Approximately 19 additional stations go on the air each month. FM service, once a struggling stepchild, has attained competitive parity with AM service. Concurrent with this growth in the number of stations has been a growth in program diversity—in nonentertainment as well as entertainment formats. Specialized networks, such as the National Black Network and the National Spanish Radio Network, have developed. Also, noncommercial radio has blossomed. National Public Radio affiliates can now reach approximately 60 percent of American households with their daily diet of public affairs programing.

Most Americans now have available a wide array of entertainment and nonentertainment radio programing. This is an exciting development, but it should not be surprising. It is a natural consequence of the maturation of broadcast radio. As the number of radio stations has grown, licensees have found it increasingly attractive to program for specialized audiences rather than to seek a fractionalized share of the middle-of-the-road audience. Increasingly sophisticated advertisers have accelerated this trend by recognizing the advantages of targeting their commercial messages. At the same time, new means

of program distribution have spurred the development of the aforementioned specialized networks and thus have helped link specialized audiences across the country.

In light of changes in the industry's competitive complexion, technical advances in program distribution, and shifts in consumer demand, a full review of our radio broadcast regulations were appropriate to determine whether Commission rules were still relevant. The question presented was whether these developments were sufficient to ensure service in the public interest without inordinate government intervention.

More Public Service than Required

Our staff collected and analyzed a huge mass of data. They found that most radio stations provide news and public affairs programing far in excess of our percentage processing guidelines. To determine whether licensees provide such programing in response to public demand or simply as an "insurance policy" against loss of license, the staff investigated when in the broadcast day that programing was aired. They found that news programing is broadcast more often during drive time, which is radio's prime time, than during other hours; that is, news programing is most frequent during morning and evening rush hours when radio listenership and advertising rates are at their peak. Based on the comments received in the rulemaking, the staff concluded that stations generally try to offer their most popular programing when the potential audience is greatest in order to attract the largest possible audience and, thus, the greatest possible advertising revenues. If news programing were not popular, our staff reasoned, stations would only put it on to meet Commission percentage guidelines and would do so primarily at off-peak hours when the potential audience is small. This proved not to be the case. It is clear from the data that news programing is highly popular and will continue to be demanded—and provided—absent Commission rules.

"Most radio stations provide news and public affairs programing far in excess of our percentage processing guidelines."

Public affairs programing appears to be less popular. However, certain market incentives exist even for the provision of public affairs programing. In very large markets, where there are many competitors and hence where stations have tended to specialize, there were often several stations that had sizeable public affairs schedules—presumably appealing to a specialized audience that prefers such programing. In very small markets, where radio stations often are the only local media outlet, public affairs programing often comprised a sizeable share of program time. In addition to news and public affairs programing, radio stations provided sizeable amounts of other nonentertainment programing, including agricultural and religious broadcasts. In other words, the data collected by the staff provided strong evidence that radio markets have developed to the point where Commission guidelines for nonentertainment programing are largely irrelevant to the quantity of programing actually broadcast.

"Radio markets have developed to the point where Commission guidelines for nonentertainment programing are largely irrelevant to the quantity of programing actually broadcast."

The empirical evidence concerning commercialization was even more striking. Although Commission processing standards allow for 18 minutes of commercial messages per hour, and up to 20 minutes for 10 percent of the hours, stations rarely approached those levels of commercialization. In fact, only about 10 percent of the stations in our sample had even 1 hour in which they aired 18 minutes or more of commercials. Most stations never broadcast as much as 15 minutes of commercials per hour. The conclusion in our Report and Order is that market forces, not Commission guidelines, set commercialization levels. In large markets, the existence of many competing stations limits any individual licensee's ability to overcommercialize. In small markets, there is often too little demand by merchants for commercial time or too much competitive pressure on licensees from distant signals to allow these stations to air high levels of commercials. Also, advertisers in markets of all sizes prefer to have their messages aired free of the clutter of other commercials.

Developments reported in the trade press since our action on the radio deregulation Report and Order substantiate the data. A recent article in *Advertising Age* indicates that many advertisers, especially large advertisers, would be upset if stations were to increase their levels of commercialization and create clutter in a deregulated environment. According to several of these advertisers, they would react to such an eventuality by moving their messages to other stations. Clearly, market forces exist to limit air time devoted to commercials.

The basic rationale for our deregulation action is that radio broadcasting has developed into a competitive industry in which natural market forces are more effective than Commission regulation in inducing licensees to act in the public interest. These market forces, which reflect the public's tastes, interests, and desires, are the reason why radio programing is responsive to the public interest and why today most Americans can receive a large number of radio signals offering a wide variety of entertainment and nonentertainment programs. These same forces justify your legislative initiative which would limit the Commission's impact on the programing decisions of radio broadcasters.

The Commission's deregulatory action was limited in scope, partially due to the constraints of the Communications Act as interpreted by the Commission and the courts over the years. There is considerable room for legislative clarification of the public interest standard and for further deregulation. On the whole, we applaud the steps you are taking here.

Seeking Best Service to Public

The Commission's primary function is the authorization of service. We all seek the best possible service to the public. If the authorization process is inefficient, unwieldy, and slow, as it unfortunately is at this time, the public is deprived of service, the Commission's resources are wasted, and the taxpayers are deprived of the full value of their tax dollars. We therefore are especially encouraged by the sections of this bill that would provide us greater flexibility to streamline the authorization process, and our suggestions for modifications or additions largely address this issue.

The first part of S. 270 proposes the Act be amended to provide indefinite license terms for radio broadcast stations. In the past, the Commission has favored only license term extension. I believe, however, a good case can also be made for indefinite terms, particularly in light of the prohibitions on Commission intervention in programing matters set forth in S. 270.

Periodic review is primarily aimed at evaluating licensee programing performance. Our recent extensive review of radio programing indicates, however, that the overwhelming majority of stations far exceed the minimum criteria established to demonstrate satisfactory performance in the public interest in both nonentertainment and commercial programing. Further, it appears from our data that this satisfactory performance is due more to marketplace incentives than to Commission regulation.

Marketplace Provides Motivation

It has been argued that periodic license review motivates licensees to be responsive to the public since it provides a formal focal point for judging a licensee's performance. That is, it provides a vehicle for organized community groups to seek what they believe to be responsive programing. However, as radio competition has increased and as stations have become more specialized, the marketplace itself has provided that motivation much more effectively. Quite simply, licensees must be responsive or they will lose their audience. Thus, indefinite license terms are appropriate in the current competitive radio markets.

What limited value the periodic review process may have as a means of oversight or spur to greater performance is far outweighed by the burden the process imposes upon the licensees, the Commission and, in the end, the public, for it is the public that pays the price of keeping the administrative machinery in place to ferret out the occasional poor performer. Uncovering an occasional malefactor does not seem to justify continued periodic review of all radio licensees.

"If the [Commission's] authorizing process is inefficient, unwieldy, and slow, as it unfortunately is at this time, the public is deprived of service."

The second part of the Bill proposes significant changes in radio station comparative licensing procedures. The present statute requires an administrative hearing where more than one qualified applicant has applied for a particular available frequency. The proposed legislation would permit a Commission choice among these applicants through a system of random selection. Since there would be no license term for radio stations, thus eliminating comparative renewal situations, this procedure would apply to applicants for new stations only. I support this proposal. The present comparative process, while well intentioned, has evolved into a monster. In the search for the best qualified applicant, we have lost sight of the overall goal—service to the public. The procedure produces unconscionable delays in instituting new service and enormous monetary costs to those seeking licenses, with little apparent public benefit. These delays and costs themselves present substantial barriers to entry into broadcasting.

Benefits of Deregulation

The third part of S. 270 pertains to "radio deregulation." This language is intended, in part, to codify the deregulatory efforts taken by the Commission earlier this year. I, of course, welcome it. Despite the Commission's recent deregulation action, legislation in this area would be extremely beneficial. Our authority to deregulate has already been challenged in court, and we anticipate several years of litigation. Explicit statutory authority for our

actions would put an end to these challenges and would allow the public to enjoy the benefits of deregulation sooner.

I am also pleased to see that this bill would prohibit the Commission from requiring radio station adherance to a particular program format. As you may know, this issue has generated substantial litigation before the Commission and the courts. In fact, the issue was recently argued before the Supreme Court and a decision is expected at any time. The Commission firmly believes that regulation in this area is not only unnecessary but also a serious intrusion upon basic licensee programming discretion. Even if we prevail in the Supreme Court, the statutory restriction proposed here would put the matter to rest for good.

In conclusion, I think S. 270 represents a good legislative initiative. It will remove outdated and inefficient regulatory procedures, enhance the government's ability to expeditiously authorize new service, and free radio licensees of unnecessary government participation in their affairs. These benefits, moreover, will be accompanied by substantial savings in public funds which can be diverted to other more productive uses. We are confident that these benefits will be achieved under circumstances clearly indicating that the public will receive a diverse radio broadcast service fully responsive to their interests.

At the time he presented this testimony, Robert E. Lee was the Acting Chairman of the Federal Communications Commission.

"Freeing radio from its obligations as a public trustee [of the airways] and leaving it to be dominated by so-called marketplace forces is too dangerous to our national interest to be tolerated."

Broadcast Deregulation Harms the Public

Everett Parker, Justin J. Finger, & Pluria W. Marshall

Editor's Note: The following viewpoint consists of excerpts from three statements testifying against radio broadcast deregulation. Part I is taken from testimony of the Reverend Everett Parker, Director of Communication of the United Church of Christ; Part II is from testimony by Justin J. Finger, National Civil Rights Director of the Anti-Defamation League (ADL) of B'nai Brith. Part III is from testimony by Pluria W. Marshall, Chairman of the National Black Media Coalition.

I

From the standpoint of the public welfare, radio is the communications medium we depend upon most. It is virtually ubiquitous. For local service, radio is more important than is television, especially in times of crisis. Radio provides an outlet for the views of racial and cultural minorities, for the airing of local issues and for exposure of local talent.

Our system of radio station assignments is based upon the concept of service to particular communities of license. It is designed to protect and foster the cultural diversity that makes the United States an interesting, vital place in which to live.

General David Sarnoff gave one of the clearest definitions of the function of radio:

"The local broadcasting station has established itself as a permanent factor in the broadcasting picture. It has a distinct function to perform and interests to serve. Like the local newspaper . . . the local broadcasting station can and does give expression to community interests."

Without this dedication of radio to localism, a different assignment process would have evolved. A few powerful stations—or, today, a satellite—could easily blanket the country with standardized formats at great savings in spectrum space.

It is fashionable to claim—without the slightest

Everett Parker, Justin J. Finger, and Pluria W. Marshall, testimony before the Subcommittee on Communications of the Senate Committee on Commerce, Science, and Transportation. Presented on February 26, March 23, and February 27, 1981, respectively.

shred of evidence—that marketplace forces will fulfill the program needs of listeners. In fact, radio stations are so limited in outreach and so widely distributed that they are not truly competitive.

Some 2,000 communities have only one radio station. It is only in great metropolitan areas that we have a relatively large number of stations, and most of them specialize, rather than compete.

Also, stations licensed to serve nearby communities generally prefer to program from the entire metropolitan area.

Now there is no one from New Jersey on this panel, but many radio stations in New Jersey are marketed to advertisers as New York or Philadelphia stations. New Jersey has no VHF outlets. S. 270 would eliminate radio coverage of New Jersey's local news, issues, campaigns, and public service announcements.

The American people are not just hapless consumers to be delivered to broadcasters and their advertisers for their mutual enrichment. The people own the airwaves. The broadcasters are trustees. Legitimate use of a frequency requires the broadcaster to provide local residents with formats and programs that fulfill their perceived needs.

People value their right to service from radio stations and of access to the air very much; so much so that more than 20,000 civic, religious, educational, cultural and professional organizations filed formal comments with the FCC opposing the Commission's proposals to deregulate radio. . . .

Obligation to Community Needs

The obligation to ascertain community needs goes back at least as far as the Radio Act of 1927. This duty is implicit in the basic obligation to the public interest. Broadcasters have made a farce of ascertainment by demanding overcomplicated rules that require them to talk to specific, easily reached, familiar community figures designated by the FCC.

We favor the elimination of the FCC's formal ascertainment requirements and the substitution of broadcaster-initiated means for determining community needs. A station whose license is challenged should be prepared to demonstrate it knew of community needs and that its programs responded to such needs. Licensees should be especially familiar with the needs of the less favored elements in the community, the poor, racial minorities, the aged, children, and they should be required to demonstrate the methods by which they became familiar with such needs.

In summary, we oppose any reduction of opportunities for local self-expression and for service to local needs. . . .

We recommend specific financial commitments for local service, time standards for local public service announcements and clearly defined policies for carriage of local news. We oppose the substitution of a gambling device such as lotteries for sober judgment in the award of licenses. Minority-owned applicants are favored now. S. 270's lotteries would end this simple fairness to those excluded in the past.

We believe community service should continue to be based on documented efforts to identify community needs, particularly the needs of less favored groups. We insist that accountability is a basic requirement of trusteeship and that records of broadcast service must be maintained.

People are willing to have regulations that are onerous or outmoded modified, but not at the price of their well being. Freeing radio from its obligations as a public trustee and leaving it to be dominated by so-called marketplace forces, as S. 270 would do, is too dangerous to our national interest to be tolerated.

II

In the words of its sponsor, S. 270 is "one of a series of bills" that will be introduced to "accomplish the statutory deregulation of radio.". . .

The bill would free licensees of any requirement to "provide news, public affairs, locally produced or any other programs"; it would preclude requirements that licensees "adhere to a particular programming format" or "maintain program logs"; and it would also eliminate the requirements that licensees "ascertain the problems, needs and interests to its service area."

Marketplace Inadequate Protection

The underlying premise of this deregulation effort is that marketplace forces will be adequate to protect the public interest. This assumption is questionable at best. Instead of benefiting the listener and improving broadcast service, the legislation is calculated to protect the broadcaster. Deregulation may be appropriate in other industries where the

benefits of competition and a relatively free marketplace inure to the consuming public. However, here deregulation would subordinate the public interest to the broadcaster's interest. As the Supreme Court said in *Red Lion Broadcasting v. FCC*, broadcast licensees are public trustees. ". . . given the privilege of using scarce radio frequencies as proxies for the entire community. It is the right of the viewers and listeners, not the right of the broadcasters, which is paramount."

Of particular concern to the ADL is the provision in S. 270 for virtually perpetual radio licenses. Presently, the burden on those contesting a renewal is already a substantial one; licenses are rarely prevented from being renewed. However, the proposed legislation will make an already advantaged position all but impregnable. By eliminating the renewal requirement, the bill eliminates the licensee's obligation to give his periodic accounting of service to the public which owns the air waves, and which has entrusted this precious resource to the licensee in a custodial capacity. The bill, by setting up indefinite licenses subject to revocation in only limited circumstances and under a severely abbreviated 60-day statute of limitations, effectively insulates those broadcasters who misuse and abuse their public trust from any challenge to their licenses.

"The forces of the marketplace will not be sufficient to assure that the public interest will be served by the communications industry."

Another major concern of the ADL is the elimination of the requirement that licensees provide public service time. Over the years, ADL and others have used such time to broadcast messages which combat prejudice and bigotry and which reinforce America's democratic principles.

For the listening public, radio is a primary source of information about other people and their points of view. Under FCC provisions in force for nearly half a century, the public was relatively assured that its diverse interests would be served. Religious and ethnic communities had access to air time to broadcast and inform others about their particular concerns.

However, under this legislation there would, for the first time, be a statutory prohibition against any requirements that licensees provide public access to the airwaves. This prohibition may serve the interests of advertisers and station owners as they see them. However, in our judgment it would create a dramatic turn away from serving the "public interest, convenience and necessity," the standard under which licenses have always been and even under this bill will continue to be granted.

In fact, by prohibiting the FCC from considering any predetermined performance criteria or other guidelines respecting programming, the bill eliminates any objective standards or tests by which to judge a licensee's claim of serving the interests and the needs of the listening public in his broadcast area. Without any ascertainment requirement, how does the FCC insure that the community needs are known to and being met by the licensee? Without program logs or any format requirements, how does the FCC guarantee that a licensee serves the public interest? Without any regular license renewals, how do public interest groups like ADL successfully oppose licensees who misuse and abuse their public trust?

"[With deregulation] only persons who are most attractive to advertisers will be targeted for program service."

We believe that the forces of the marketplace will not be sufficient to assure that the public interest will be served by the communications industry. Rather, Congress should continue to insure that the public has access to the airwaves and that the public interest standard for broadcasting is retained in a meaningful way.

III

Deregulation now would work serious inequities on those least served by broadcasting today—I am speaking of Black American and other minority groups who are grossly underrepresented in employment, program service and ownership of radio and television stations.

Obviously there are more radio stations now than there were a generation ago, when you and I were young men growing up before the age of television. However, the number of stations has not kept pace with the growth of the population in the past decade, or with the growing diversity of the population—20 percent of which is now non-white. There are more stations, but each station must serve more people and a wider spectrum of human needs.

This growing scarcity is reflected in the growth of the sale price of stations, which far outpaces the rate of inflation. Only three initial licenses for radio stations have ever been issued to Blacks. The other Black-owned stations, representing about 1 percent of all stations, were bought from whites at prices the initial owners obviously did not have to pay for the spectrum space.

What would happen if radio stations were no longer required to ascertain community needs and serve all segments of the population? What will happen is cream-skimming—only persons who are most attractive to advertisers will be targeted for program service by the strongest stations. Minorities and the poor will be served only by a few specialized ethnic stations, usually with weak signals and inferior facilities, if at all. We will have de facto segregation of the airwaves.

Arbitron surveys consistently reveal that more than half of Black radio listening is to Black-oriented or jazz radio stations. Thus, the fact that only one or two (or, more frequently, zero) stations in a community have this format places upon these stations an enormous public service responsibility, a responsibility which would become that much greater if other stations are declared to have no responsibility to their Black listeners.

Furthermore, the owners of Black-oriented stations are not, in most cases, millionaires, nor are they always angels. Like other broadcasters, they may succumb to the human temptation to place profit before public service. The human cost is staggering—millions of Black children with radios at their ears, hearing "shake your booty, get down, get down" and not a word about getting an education and preparing for a career. It means millions of Black men and women unable to turn to their radio stations to learn about better housing, health care services and job training.

Public Service Essential

The Federal Radio Commission, in its 1928 Annual Report, declared that radio stations which do nothing but play music waste the spectrum, since the same service is available from a Victrola. Fifty-three years later, that statement still makes sense. The industry asserts that public service will continue even without regulatory oversight, but we see licensees of Black-oriented stations—Black and white—cutting back on news, public affairs and public service. Some have openly declared their intention to eliminate news and public affairs if they can get away with it. The result would be disastrous for Black America. We can ill afford to lose what little service we have.

Everett Parker, Justin J. Finger, and Pluria W. Marshall all testified against Senate bill 270 which proposed deregulation of radio broadcasting.

"Gold is honest money because it is impossible for governments to create it."

The US Should Return to the Gold Standard

Ron Paul and Lewis Lehrman

The economic shortcomings of the past were due to abuse of the gold standard, not to the standard itself. Men and governments have failed in the past; gold has not. The rule of law has been challenged by the rule of men throughout history, and this will continue. But the rule of law and the sovereignty of the people are much more likely to prevail with gold than with paper. For many economic reasons it is critical that the rule of law and gold win the great debate on monetary policy. . . .

Common Objections to Gold

In any debate about the gold standard, certain objections are repeatedly raised by opponents of monetary freedom, even though those objections have been refuted many times before. Some of these objections are:

1) There is not enough gold;
2) The Soviet Union and South Africa, since they are the principal producers of gold, would benefit from our creation of a gold standard;
3) The gold standard causes panics and crashes;
4) The gold standard causes inflation;
5) Gold is subject to undesirable speculative influences.

The first objection, there isn't enough gold, is based upon a misunderstanding of a gold standard. It assumes that the present exchange ratio (or a lower ratio) between a weight of gold and a greenback is the exchange ratio that must prevail in a gold standard. Such obviously is not the case. Doubling the exchange ratio, for example, doubles the money supply. Lower prices under a gold standard eliminate the necessity for such large sums. One can buy a suit that costs 400 paper dollars with 20 gold dollars.

In 1979, there were a total of 35,000 metric tons of

Ron Paul and Lewis Lehrman, *The Case for Gold: Minority Report of the U.S. Gold Commission*, Washington, DC: The Cato Institute, 1982. Reprinted with permission of the Cato Institute, 224 Second St., SE, Washington, DC 20003.

gold in central banks and non-Communist government treasuries alone. The United States government, officially holding 264 million ounces (8,227 tons), owns about one-fourth of that total. The best estimate on the total amount of gold in the world is three billion ounces, meaning that about one-third of the world's gold is held by governments and central banks, and two-thirds by private persons. Far from being a dearth of gold, there are enormous amounts in existence. Gold, unlike most commodities, remains in existence. It is not burned or consumed, and the amounts actually lost are insignificant when compared to the amounts now in public and private possession.

The second objection, concerning the Soviet Union and South Africa, is equally groundless. These nations, as the world's largest producers of gold, have profited handsomely from the massive increase in gold prices in the past 10 years. Such increases do not occur under a gold standard.

Soviet Gold in Perspective

Recently a newsmagazine reported that "the Soviet Union holds an estimated 60 million ounces of gold and has unmined reserves of perhaps 250 million ounces more. At today's prices that would give the Soviets a $146 billion stranglehold on western economies." But let us put these figures in perspective. Below is a table showing the gold holdings of major central banks.

Official Gold Holdings
September 30, 1979
(tons)

United States	8,227
Canada	657
Austria	657
Belgium	1,063
France	2,546
German Federal Republic	2,961

Italy	2,074
Japan	754
Netherlands	1,367
Portugal	689
South Africa	374
Switzerland	2,590
U.K.	584
OPEC	1,207
Other Asia	607
Other Europe	1,209
Other Middle East	461
Other Western Hemisphere	654
Rest of World	320
Unspecified	113
Total	29,110
IMF	3,217
European Monetary Cooperation Fund	2,664

This table, taken from the *Annual Bullion Review 1980* of Samuel Montagu & Co., is based on IMF statistics.

The Soviet Union's alleged 60 million ounces is less than 1,900 tons, less than one-fourth of the U.S. official gold holdings. Even the alleged 250 million ounces of "unmined reserves" are less than the United States has in Fort Knox and our other bullion depositories. . . .

In 1976, the Soviets exported 412 tons, 1.2 percent of the governmental holdings of the non-Communist world. Assuming they could export at this rate continuously—a very doubtful assumption—it would take them almost a century just to match current official holdings. If one includes private holdings, the percentage drops to about one-half of one percent, and the time required extends to more than two centuries. The fear of the Soviet Union and South Africa either dumping or withholding gold and thereby wrecking a gold standard by altering significantly the purchasing power of gold is baseless. The only reasons sales by such governments now influence the market is that official holdings are immobilized and the value of the paper dollar fluctuates violently. Were we to institute a gold standard, those holdings would once again enter the market. We should stop giving such windfalls to the Soviets and South Africans as they have enjoyed during the last 10 years. The real fear should be the massive increase in the money supply caused by the Federal Reserve in the last 10 years and the probability of still further massive inflation. The red herring of external shock destroying a gold standard is designed to distract one's attention from the threat of internal shock caused by the Federal Reserve.

The third objection, that the gold standard causes panics and crashes, is also false. The extensive examination of the monetary history of the United States during the 19th century demonstrated that it was not the gold standard, but government

intervention in the banking systems, that caused the problems. The legal prohibition of branch and interstate banking prevented the prompt and convenient clearing of notes issued by those banks. Frequent suspensions of specie payments were special privileges extended to the banks by the government. Fractional reserves, wildcat banking, the National Banking System, and the issuance of greenbacks all contributed to the instability experienced during the 19th century.

"It was not the gold standard, but government intervention in the banking systems that caused the problems."

But even with these interventions, as long as the dollar was defined as a weight of gold, the benevolent influences of the gold standard were felt. Chapter Two of the [Gold] Commission's report indicates that the problems of the 19th century were due to abuses and lapses of the gold standard, not the standard itself. . . .

Inflation and Gold

The fourth objection, that the gold standard causes inflation, can also easily be disposed of. Economist Dr. Alan Reynolds, in his appearance before the Commission, did so:

> When the 1968—1980 period is compared with the "purest" gold standard, 1879—1914, it is not at all clear that even short-term price stability was superior in recent years. Average changes in consumer prices were zero under gold, over 7% under paper; . . .
>
> Long-term interest rates were much lower and more stable under any form of gold standard than in recent years, and annual price changes were typically smaller. James Hoehn of the Federal Reserve Bank of Dallas concludes that, "Short-run monetary stability is no better today than it was in the gold standard period. This result is surprising and difficult to explain in view of the greater present day stability of the banking system.". . .

Now that the market for long-term bonds has been destroyed by 10 years of paper money and the United States has experienced its worst price inflation in its national history, it is difficult to take seriously the charge that the gold standard causes inflation.

Dr. Roy Jastram, in his seminal work *The Golden Constant*, presents the statistical evidence that gold provides protection against inflation and actually results in gently falling prices. Such gentle falls in turn cause increases in the real wages of workers. . . .

In 1833, the index of wholesale commodity prices in the U.S. was 75.3. In 1933, just prior to our going off the domestic gold standard, the index of wholesale commodity prices in the U.S. was 76.2: a change in 100 years of nine-tenths of one percent. The index of wholesale commodity prices in 1971 was 255.4. Today, the index is 657.8. For 100 years on the gold standard wholesale prices rose only nine-tenths of one percent. In the last 10 years of paper money they have gone up 259 percent.

Gold and Speculation

The final objection to the gold standard, that gold is subject to speculative influence and therefore too unstable to be used as a standard for anything, is also spurious. During the past decade, gold has become a major hedge against inflation. The run-up in gold prices from $35 to $850 per ounce came as a result of fears about the value of paper currencies and developing international crises. This speculation—actually a seeking of protection from the continual devaluation of paper currencies—has markedly accelerated in recent years. Not only is the decline of the paper dollar causing larger investments in gold coins, but also in real estate, collectibles of all types, and any other good that promises to retain its value. The Commodity Exchange reports that there are now over 100 different futures contracts offered by the nation's 11 exchanges. Since 1975, 42 new futures contracts have been introduced, and 37 proposed contracts are currently pending government approval. This enormous growth in speculation has occurred during the last 10 years. People who object to gold because it is speculative confuse cause and effect. Were we on a gold standard, there would be no speculation in gold at all. Gold is currently an object of "speculation" precisely because we have an irredeemable paper money system and people are trying to protect themselves from it. The real speculation is in the anticipation of the further depreciation of the dollar.

"Gold provides protection against inflation and actually results in gently falling prices."

All these objections to gold cannot shake the overwhelming historical and theoretical arguments for a gold standard. But there are other arguments for gold as well. We will now take them up in turn.

Money and the Constitution

In addition to the compelling economic case for the gold standard, a case buttressed by both historical and theoretical arguments, there is a compelling argument based on the Constitution. The present monetary arrangements of the United States are unconstitutional—even anticonstitutional—from top to bottom.

The Constitution actually says very little about what sort of monetary system the United States ought to have, but what it does say is unmistakably clear. Article I, section 8, clause 2 provides: "The Congress shall have power . . . to borrow money on the credit of the United States . . . [clause 5:] to coin money, regulate the value thereof, and of foreign coin, and fix the standards of weights and measures . . . [and clause 6:] to provide for the punishment of counterfeiting the securities and current coin of the United States. . . ." Further, Article I, section 10, clause 1 provides: "No state shall . . . coin money; emit bills of credit; [or] make anything but gold and silver coin a tender in payment of debts. . . ."

When the Founding Fathers wrote the Constitution in the summer of 1787, they had fresh in their minds the debacle of the paper money printed and issued by the Continental Congress during the Revolutionary War. The paper notes, "Continentals" as they were called, eventually fell to virtually zero percent of their original value because they were not redeemed in either silver or gold. They were "greenbacks" and were the first of three major experiments with "greenbacks" that this nation has conducted. The Continental greenback failed miserably, giving rise to the popular phrase "not worth a Continental."

A Hatred of Paper Money

Consequently, when the Constitutional Convention met in 1787, the opposition to paper money was strong. George Mason, a delegate from Virginia, stated that he had a "mortal hatred to paper money." Delegate Oliver Ellsworth from Connecticut thought the Convention "a favorable moment to shut and bar the door against paper money." James Wilson, a delegate from Pennsylvania, argued: "It will have a more salutary influence on the credit of the United States to remove the possibility of paper money." Delegate Pierce Butler from South Carolina pointed out that paper was not a legal tender in any country of Europe and that it ought not be made one in the United States. John Langdon of New Hampshire said that he would rather reject the whole Constitution than allow the federal government the power to issue paper money. On the final vote on the issue, nine states opposed granting the federal government power to issue paper money, and only two favored granting such power.

The framers of the Constitution made their intention clear by the use of the word "coin" rather than the word "print," or the phrase "emit bills of credit." Thomas M. Cooley's *Principles of Constitutional Law* elaborates on this point: "To coin money is to stamp pieces of metal for use as a medium of exchange in commerce according to fixed standards of value."

Congress was given the exclusive power (as far as governments are concerned) to coin money; the states were explicitly prohibited from doing so. Furthermore, the states were explicitly forbidden from making anything but gold and silver coin a tender in payment of debt, while the federal government was not granted the power of making anything legal tender.

In his explanation of the Constitutional provisions on money, James Madison, in *Federalist* No. 44, referred to the "pestilent effects of paper money on the necessary confidence between man and man, on the necessary confidence in the public councils, on the industry and morals of the people, and on the character of republican government." His intention, and the intention of the other founders, was to avoid precisely the sort of paper money system that has prevailed for the past 10 years.

"The present monetary arrangements of the United States are unconstitutional—even anticonstitutional—from top to bottom."

This intention was well understood throughout the 19th century, and was denied only when the Supreme Court found it expedient to do so. For example, Daniel Webster wrote:

> If we understand, by currency, the legal money of the country, and that which constitutes a lawful tender for debts, and is the statute measure of value, then undoubtedly, nothing is included but gold and silver. Most unquestionably, *there is no legal tender, and there can be no legal tender in this country under the authority of this government or any other, but gold and silver,* either the coinage of our mints or foreign coins at rates regulated by Congress. *This is a constitutional principle, perfectly plain and of the very highest importance.* The states are expressly prohibited from making anything but gold and silver a tender in payment of debts, and although no such expressed prohibition is applied to Congress, yet as Congress has no power granted to it in this respect but to coin money and to regulate the value of foreign coins, *it clearly has no power to substitute paper or anything else for coin* as a tender in payment of debts in a discharge of contracts. . . .

> The legal tender, therefore, the constitutional standard of value, is established and cannot be overthrown. *To overthrow it would shake the whole system.* (Emphasis added.) . . .

Today's paper money system, issued by a coercive banking monopoly, has no basis in the Constitution. It is precisely the sort of government institution— one far more clever than the bumbling efforts of Charles I to confiscate wealth—that can forcibly exact financial support from the people without their consent. As such, it is a form of taxation without representation, and a denial of the hard fought and won principle of consent before payment of

taxes. . . .

Gold is honest money because it is impossible for governments to create it. New money can only come about by productive effort and not by political and financial chicanery. Inflation is theft and literally steals wealth from one group for the benefit of another. It is possible to have an increase in the supply of gold, but the historical record is clear that all great inflations occur with paper currency. But an increase in the supply of gold—presuming that it is not accomplished through theft—is quite different from an increase in the supply of irredeemable paper currency. The latter is a creature of politics; the former is a result of productive labor, both mental and physical. Gold is wealth; it is not just exchangeable for wealth. Today's notes are not wealth. They are claims on wealth that the owners of wealth must accept as payment.

No wealth is created by paper money creation; only shifts of wealth occur, and these shifts, although significant and anticipated by some, cannot always be foreseen. They are tantamount to theft in that the assets gained are unearned. The victims of inflation suffer through no fault of their own. The beneficiaries of the inflation are not necessarily the culprits in the transfer of wealth; the policymakers who cause the inflation are.

Legally increasing the money supply is just as immoral as the counterfeiter who illegally prints money. The new paper money has value only because it steals its "value" from the existing stock of paper money. (This is not true of gold, however. New issues of paper money are necessarily parasitic; they depend on their similarity to existing money for their worth. But gold does not. It carries its own credentials.) Inflation of paper money is one way wealth can be taken against another's wishes without an obvious confrontation; it is a form of embezzlement. After a while, the theft will be reflected in the depreciation of money and the higher prices that must be paid. The guilty are difficult to identify due to the cleverness of the theft. They are never punished because of the legality of their actions. Eventually, though, as the paper money becomes more and more worthless, the "legalized counterfeiting" becomes obvious to everyone. Anger and frustration over the theft results and is justified, but it is frequently misdirected and may even lead to a further aggrandizement of governmental power.

Role of Government

Ideally, the role of government in a sound monetary system is minimal. Its purpose should be to guarantee a currency and assure that it cannot be debased. The role would be similar whether it is protecting a government gold standard or private monies. Neither the government nor private issuers of money can be permitted to defraud the people by depreciating the currency. The honesty and integrity of the money should be based on a contract; the government's only role should be to see that violators of the contract are punished. Depreciating the currency by increasing the supply and diluting its value is comparable to the farmer who dilutes his milk with water yet sells it for whole milk. We prosecute the farmer, but not the Federal Reserve Open Market Committee. Those who must pay the high prices from the inflation are like those who must drink the diluted milk and suffer from its "debased" content. . . .

Throughout history, rulers have used inflation to steal from the people and pursue unpopular policies, welfarism, and foreign military adventurism. Likewise throughout history the authorities who have inflated have resorted to blaming innocent citizens, who try to protect themselves from the government-caused inflation. Such citizens are castigated as "speculators" out of ignorance, as well as from a deliberate desire to escape deserved blame.

Gold money is always rejected by those who advocate significant government intervention in the economy. Gold holds in check the government's tendency to accumulate power over the economy. Paper money is a device by which the unpopular programs of government intervention, whether civilian or military, foreign or domestic, can be financed without the tax increases that would surely precipitate massive resistance by the people. . . . Paper money is political money with the politician in charge; gold is free-market money with the people in charge.

John Locke argued for the gold standard the same way he argued for the moral right to own property. To him the right to own and exchange gold was a civil liberty equal in importance to the liberty to speak, write, and practice one's own religion. Free people always choose to trade their goods or services for a marketable commodity. Money is the most marketable of all commodities, and gold the best of all money. Gold has become money by a moral commitment to free choice and honest trade, not by government edict. Locke claimed the right to own property was never given to the individual by society, but that government was established to ensure integrity in contracts and honest money, not to be the principal source of broken contracts or the instigators of a depreciating currency. Gold is not money because government says it is: It is money because the people have chosen to use it in a free country.

Threat to Freedom

Eliminating honest money—commodity money defined precisely by weight—is a threat to freedom itself. It sets the stage for serious economic difficulties and interferes with the humanitarian goal of a high standard of living for everyone, a standard which result from a free market and a sound monetary standard. . . . As the economy deteriorates in countries that have inflated and forced to go through recession and depressions, international tensions build. Protectionism (tariffs) and militant nationalism generally develop and contribute to conditions that precipitate armed conflict. The immorality of inflation is closely linked to the immorality of preventable and aggressive wars.

Money, when it is a result of moral commitment to honesty and integrity, will be trusted. Trustworthy money is required in a moral society. This requires *all* paper money and paper certificates to be convertible into something of real worth. Throughout history, money has repeatedly failed to maintain trust due to unwise actions of governments whose responsibility was to protect that trust, not destroy it. Without trust in money gained by a moral commitment to integrity, a productive economy is impossible. Inflation premiums built into the interest rates cannot be significantly altered by minor manipulations in the growth rate of the supply of money, nor by the painful decreases in the demand for money brought on by a weak economy. Only trust in the money can remove the inflation premium from our current financial transactions.

"Paper money is political money with the politician in charge; gold is free-market money with the people in charge."

Trust is only restored when every citizen is guaranteed convertibility of money substitutes into tangible money at will. False promises and hopes cannot substitute for a moral commitment of society to honest money—ingrained in the law and not alterable by the whims of any man. The rule of moral law must replace the power of man in order for sound money to circulate once again. Ignoring morality in attempts to stop inflation and restore the country's economic health guarantees failure. A moral commitment to honest money guarantees success.

Congressman Ron Paul is a member of the Committee on Banking, Finance, and Urban Affairs and a member of the Subcommittee on Coinage. Lewis Lehrman was a corporate executive and is the editor of Money and the Coming World Order. *He is founder of the Lehrman Institute, a public policy research foundation in New York City.*

viewpoint 22

The US Should Remain on a Dollar Standard

Edward M. Bernstein

The persistent inflation and the inability of the United States to restore monetary stability has led to proposals to return to the gold standard. Bills have been introduced in the Congress to establish a gold coin standard and a flexible gold standard based on an adjustable price for gold. More important, Public Law 96-389, authorizing the increase of the U.S. quota in the International Monetary Fund, provides for the establishment of a Commission of 15 members under the chairmanship of the Secretary of the Treasury with the following duty:

> The Commission shall conduct a study to assess and make recommendations with regard to the policy of the U.S. Government concerning the role of gold in the domestic and international monetary systems and shall transmit to Congress a report containing its findings and recommendations not later than one year after the date of enactment of this Act.

The interest in returning to a gold standard reflects the view that if the creation of money were limited, the inflation would stop for lack of the monetary fuel that powers it. Much of the support for a return to the gold standard, however, is based on an idealized view of the 100 years of the classical gold standard as an age of unparalleled monetary stability and economic progress. The fact is that under the gold standard prices rose and fell for 20 to 30 years at a time so that the history of prices in that period was one of alternate inflation and deflation. . . .

Can the Gold Standard Be Restored?

It is always possible to establish a gold standard if a country is willing to accept the restraints that this entails and the economic consequences that may ensue. The minimum tests of a gold standard are (1) the maintenance of the equal value of the currency and gold by the monetary authorities through the

purchase and sale of gold freely at a fixed price; and (2) limitation of the money supply through gold reserve requirements, including the obligation to reduce the money supply when there is a diminution of the gold reserves. As a practical matter, a gold standard can function properly only as part of an international monetary system. Otherwise, sudden changes in the supply of or demand for gold would fall entirely on one country, as it did on the United States after 1934. Purchases and sales of gold by the monetary authorities at a variable free market price do not constitute a gold standard. Such transactions are merely another form of intervention in the exchange market and another type of open market operation.

Those who advocate a return to the gold standard assume that it would be possible to select some price of gold that would enable the monetary authorities to maintain the equivalence of gold and currency without being drained of their gold reserves or being swamped by a backflow of gold from hoarders, investors, and speculators. The change in the price of gold since 1973, and particularly its volatility, should make one skeptical of this possibility. It was possible to maintain the equivalence of the value of money and gold for generations under the classical gold standard because the allocation of private monetary assets to gold and money had been adapted to the traditional monetary price in the course of centuries. Changes in the preference for gold relative to money were small and took place gradually, but the monetary authorities could keep gold and money equally attractive in the long run by allowing commodity prices to rise or fall with changes in the cost of producing gold and in the short run by changing interest rates which raised or lowered the opportunity cost of holding gold instead of money.

As the price of gold has ranged between $226 an ounce and $850 an ounce in the past two years, it is

Edward M. Bernstein, "Is a Return to the Gold Standard Feasible?" Testimony included in "Report to Congress of the Commission of the Role of Gold in the Domestic and International Monetary Systems," March 1982.

not possible to say now at what price the monetary authorities could expect to maintain the equivalence of gold and money under stable monetary conditions. If gold were an ordinary commodity, with production and consumption usually about equal, apart from relatively small changes in stocks, it would be possible to estimate what the price would be if supply and demand were at trend levels. In the long run, the price would have to reflect the cost of production and demand would be adjusted to the relative price of gold and other commodities. The supply of and demand for gold does not fit this pattern. Production accounted for about 59 per cent of the supply in 1976-79 and consumption in the arts and industry accounted for 70 per cent of the private absorption of gold. The price has fluctuated sharply in this period without any apparent relation to changes in production or in the absorption of gold in the arts and industry.

"The value of gold cannot be determined in the same way as the value of other assets."

The present price of gold and the fluctuations . . . were brought about by the demand of hoarders, investors and speculators. Their demand is for holding gold as an asset, but the value of gold cannot be determined in the same way as the value of other assets. It is possible to estimate the value of such typical assets as stocks and bonds because they are income-earning assets. Their value is determined by discounting the future flow of earnings, and for bonds also the return of principal, at current interest rates. One may err in projecting the flow of earnings and the security of the principal of a bond, or the appropriate interest rate at which the flows should be discounted, but the method of evaluation is clear. Even the value of underdeveloped land can be estimated by discounting the projected flow of earnings, although there is greater uncertainty about the earnings. As gold is not an income earning asset, it cannot be valued that way. Its sole return to the owner is through a rise in price. What makes the price of gold $670 an ounce today is that buyers expect the price to be about $760 an ounce a year from now.

Gold Value Related to Politics

The view that the price of gold will increase at a rate in excess of the interest rate assumes that the present price is justified by economic conditions and that the inflation will accelerate. The inflation of itself does not justify the enormous increase in the price of gold to its present level. At $670 an ounce, the purchasing power of gold as measured by the

U.S. wholesale price index (290.8 in September 1980 on a 1957-59 base) is nearly three times as high as at the two previous peaks—in 1896 when the index was 25.4 and the price of gold was $20.67 an ounce, and in 1934 when the index was 41.0 and the price of gold was $35 an ounce. The recent rise in the price of gold was not in response to the acceleration of inflation but to the political situation in Iran and Afghanistan. Without saying that world peace was an essential element of the classical gold standard, it is a fact that the political disorder in the world adds to the difficulty of maintaining the equivalence of gold and currency at a fixed price.

If the monetary authorities were to establish a gold standard now with the price at close to the present free market price a deterioration of the political situation could cause an enormous outflow of gold and a sharp contraction of the money supply, even if the economic situation should become more stable. On the other hand, if reasonable price stability were restored and the political situation improved, the monetary authorities could be confronted with an enormous backflow of gold which would necessitate an expansion in the money supply. From the floating of the dollar in 1973 to 1979, investors and speculators increased their holdings in the form of bullion by about 66 million ounces and hoarders increased their holdings in the form of coins, facsimile coins, medals and medallions by about 55 million ounces. A large part of these holdings, particularly those of investors and speculators, could be sold to the monetary authorities if the gold standard were restored and price stability achieved. It is worth noting that they reduced their holdings by about 16 million ounces in 1969-72 after their huge purchases in 1967-68.

Difficulty of Maintaining Gold Standard

It would also be very difficult to maintain the gold standard if it were restored. Under a gold standard, the increase of the money supply is limited by the increase in the gold reserves. Assuming that confidence in currencies were restored so relatively little of the supply would be absorbed by hoarders, investors and speculators, the growth of the monetary stock of gold would depend on newly-mined production, net sales of the Communist countries, and the consumption of the arts and industry. The production of gold outside the Communist countries reached a peak of 41 million ounces in 1970, fell to 31 million ounces in 1975, and has remained at that level since then. The decline was almost all in South African production, although output of other areas was also down slightly. The smaller output of South Africa may be partly due to real factors, but it is mainly due to the policy of mining and milling lower grades of ore as the price of gold increases. In the first eight months of 1980, South African production was 3.6 per cent less than in 1979 and some of the output was added to reserves instead of being sold in the free market.

Sales by the Communist countries, nearly all by the Soviet Union, were very large in 1972-79. These sales are for the purpose of acquiring foreign exchange to finance imports from the West. [But] sales are highly volatile, fluctuating directly with the Soviet balance of payments deficit and inversely with the price of gold. . . . In any case, the gold sales of the Soviet Union are highly variable and cannot be regarded as a reliable source for additions to the monetary stock of gold.

Even if hoarding, investing and speculation were to fall to the moderate levels of the early 1960s, the supply of gold that could be added to the monetary stock would be very small. The absorption of gold in the arts and industry has exceeded newly-mined gold by 20 per cent in 1976-79, although some of the gold purchased by fabricators may have gone into inventories. This occurred in spite of a large reduction is such use of gold in 1979 because of the high price and the slowdown in some industrial countries. Perhaps, if a gold standard with a fixed price of gold were restored, the gold producing countries might increase their output. But unless there were an adequate, steady, and assured growth of the monetary stock of gold, it would not be possible for a gold standard system to function effectively.

The Existing Stock of Gold

The existing stock of monetary gold, apart from the holdings of the Communist countries, is over 1.13 billion ounces, including holdings of the international monetary institutions. Most countries carry these reserves at an average market value over a preceding period, although the United States still values its holdings at the old monetary price of $42.22 an ounce. No large country has monetized its gold reserves at the present price. These gold holdings constitute a huge reservoir of assets that would free the international monetary system from dependence on additions to the monetary stock for the growth of the monetary base. Countries could monetize their gold holdings at a regular rate to assure the monetary growth that they regard as necessary. Sales of gold could also be made out of these gold holdings without the necessity of deflating the money supply, and purchases of gold could be added to these gold holdings if they were financed by sales of Treasury bills without inflating the money supply. However, if the monetary authorities followed such policies, making the money supply independent of the increase or decrease in the gold reserves, it could not be said that the country was on the gold standard.

The bills introduced in the Senate (S. 3181) and the House of Representatives (H.R. 7874) would establish gold convertibility of the dollar or a gold coinage immediately or within a few months. This attitude of urgency in establishing a kind of gold standard is reminiscent of the debate on the resumption of specie payments after the Civil War. Some people thought it would be prudent to accumulate a larger gold reserve and to reduce the amount of greenbacks in circulation before undertaking specie payments. Others, among them Chief Justice Chase, who had been Secretary of the Treasury during the wartime inflation, believed that no delay was necessary, that "the way to resume is to resume." Inherent in this approach is the assumption that if inter-convertibility of gold and dollars were established at some price previously determined in the New York market, purchases of gold from or sales of gold to the Federal Reserve Banks would by themselves adjust the money supply to an amount appropriate to the monetary price of gold. That could entail a large contraction of the money supply through Federal Reserve sales of gold or an excessive expansion of the money supply through Federal Reserve purchases of gold. It would be ironic if the restoration of the gold standard were itself to have a seriously destabilizing effect on the money supply. Actually, it is questionable whether the monetary system contemplated in the bills referred to above could be regarded as a gold standard in the usual meaning of this term.

"Even if hoarding, investing and speculation were to fall to the moderate levels of the early 1960s, the supply of gold that could be added to the monetary stock would be very small."

The gold standard is not an end in itself but a means of achieving certain objectives. The first is to restore and maintain a reasonably high degree of stability of prices and costs. This cannot be achieved automatically by establishing gold convertibility of the dollar. It requires greater budgetary discipline, a more cautious monetary policy, and the limitation of the increase of incomes to the increase of productivity. The second objective is to achieve greater stability of exchange rates. Initially, the target could be to maintain the average foreign exchange value of the dollar within a moderately broad range relative to the other currencies in a unit of Special Drawing Rights—the D-mark, sterling, the French franc, and the yen. Ultimately the dollar would have to be stable in terms of each of these currencies. That would necessitate keeping down the inflation to the same rate as in the most stable industrial country and giving greater consideration to the behavior of the exchange rate in formulating monetary policy. These are the conditions that would have to be established before the United States could safely return to a gold standard. If the United States could achieve such a degree of price and exchange stability, there would be no need for a gold standard.

Edward M. Bernstein prepared this paper for a hearing on the feasibility of a return to the gold standard held by the Subcommittee on Mines and Mining of the Interior Affairs Committee of the House of Representatives. It was also presented as testimony to the Gold Commission which in 1984 recommended to Congress that the US retain the dollar standard.

The US Should Change to a Competitive Money Standard

G.A. Selgin

There is today much frustration, not to say cynicism, regarding the operation of our monetary system. Theorists from all quarters agree that, in recent years especially, the Federal Reserve has seriously mismanaged the money supply. Some believe that the authorities have been inept; others think they are dishonest. And yet a third group regards the institution itself as incapable even in principle of fulfilling its self-assigned function. Probably the truth is a combination of these three views.

Whatever its foundation, the prevailing mood has bred numerous proposals for radical reform. All have in common the aim of reducing the influence of Federal Reserve officials over money, prices, and interest rates. Discussion centers less and less on such concepts as "scientific control" and "fine tuning." It is well enough, the proposals imply, if the Fed can merely be prevented from engaging in any more mischief.

Broadly, the proposals are of two kinds: those that would enforce a strict, constitutionally mandated rule governing the growth of Federal Reserve dollars ("base" or "high-powered" money), and those that would abolish the present monetary arrangement entirely, replacing it with one based on competitively supplied monies.

Despite the extent of dissatisfaction with the present system, such proposals have not found favor among politicians or even among most academics. Many of the latter fear that a rigid base-money rule, while perhaps providing a generally stable monetary "framework," would not allow the money supply sufficient flexibility and responsiveness to changing circumstances. A complete abandonment of the present monetary standard in favor of a competitive

supply of money is seen as an altogether too drastic measure that would lead, especially during the transition period, to more rather than less overall monetary instability and chaos. Even authors sympathetic to both goals—creating a stable monetary framework and eliminating government intervention—regard the two as incompatible in practice.

A Third Alternative

There is substance to these criticisms. And yet, although each of the radical reforms mentioned may be unsatisfactory if adopted independently, they may be combined to form a third alternative that would be neither defective nor disruptive—one that could achieve monetary stability while simultaneously eliminating all government interference.

Specifically, this third alternative calls for freezing the monetary base, thus removing the Federal Reserve from the business of money production, *after* restoring the right of commercial banks to issue their own notes, redeemable on demand in Federal Reserve dollars. Thus, commercial banks would be able to issue fractional-reserve demand liabilities not solely by offering checkable deposits, but also by offering alternative paper instruments suitable for meeting the public's currency needs. This arrangement would allow Federal Reserve dollars to be used exclusively as bank reserves for settling interbank clearings, and not (except in insignificant amounts) as pocket and till money by the public.

Athough the proposal outlined here may seem revolutionary, it is not, resembling in some respects the pre-Federal Reserve arrangement that functioned from 1863 to 1913. However, at least part of the time, the pre-Federal Reserve system (the National Banking System) operated on a gold standard, whereas the present proposal assumes a continuation of the current paper-dollar standard. More significantly, the National Banking System suffered

G.A. Selgin, "The Case for Free Banking: Then and Now," *Cato Institute Policy Analysis*, No. 60, October 21, 1985. Reprinted with permission from the Cato Institute, 224 Second St., SE, Washington, DC 20003.

from serious regulatory defects that the present proposal avoids. To place this proposal in perspective, a review of the history of the National Banking System is in order, revealing how the defects of that system might easily have been cured through deregulation instead of the establishment of a central bank.

Banking Before the Civil War

In the decades just before the Civil War, there was no central bank: the charter of the Second Bank of the United States, which in some ways had functioned as a central bank, had expired in 1837. Nevertheless, banking was far from being an unregulated industry. Each state and territory had its own regulations. For instance, the territory of Wisconsin, formed in 1836, outlawed note-issuing banks altogether, as did Iowa, Oregon, Arkansas, and Texas upon being admitted to statehood. Elsewhere the number of banks was limited by legislative charter. In addition, there were laws prohibiting branching, prescribing reserve requirements, and regulating the type of investments and loans banks could (or had to) make. . . .

_____

"By 1861, . . . unregulated competition in banking . . . had done more to secure sound money than all the regulations and restrictions imposed."

_____

During this period, banks operated on a gold standard, and since currency issue was not monopolized, many banks issued their own redeemable notes, just as banks today provide their customers with checking-account balances. In the first half of the nineteenth century, notes outnumbered demand deposits and were the most important form of bank liabilities. The bond-deposit regulations required a bank to secure its note issues with government bonds, including bonds of the state in which it was incorporated. Typically, a bank desiring to issue $90 in notes would first have to purchase $100 (face value) of specified state bonds, which it would then deposit with the state comptroller in exchange for certified currency. In this system, bond collateral was held to be more liquid and secure than other interest-earning assets. . . .

By 1861, the evidence suggests, unregulated competition in banking, like that in New England, had done more to secure sound money than all the regulations and restrictions imposed throughout the rest of the country. This contrast might even have been observed by some officials in Washington at the time. But the Civil War had just begun, and Washington had priorities other than sound money

when it set about to redesign the nation's banking system.

The Civil War brought four major pieces of monetary legislation: the legal-tender laws, in 1862; the National Banking Act, in 1863; an act outlawing private coinage, in 1864; and an act imposing a prohibitive 10 percent tax on state-bank note issues, in 1865. The combined effect of the last three acts was to place the entire currency supply under federal jurisdiction. Together with the legal-tender laws, these acts comprised a program for securing means other than direct taxation to pay for the war against the South.

"Greenbacks" Issued

The legal-tender laws contributed to this program by authorizing the Treasury to issue "greenbacks," putting the nation on a fiat standard. The National Banking Act allowed the establishment of federally chartered note-issuing banks, the notes of which had to be secured by deposits of federal securities. This bond-deposit requirement, borrowed from the misnamed antebellum "free banking" laws, was designed to create a forced market for federal debt: for every $90 of notes they issued, national banks had to purchase $100 (face value) in government bonds, to be deposited for safekeeping with the federal comptroller of the currency. In addition, the 10 percent tax on state-bank note issues assured that state banks would no longer deprive the federal government of potential revenue from bond sales to their nationally chartered rivals.

Thus, by 1866 the currency supply consisted entirely of greenbacks, the availability of which was fixed by statute, and of bond-secured national-bank notes, the availability of which depended upon the cost to the national banks of purchasing eligible government bonds on the open market.

Obviously, a fixed greenback supply could not adjust to changes in the public's demand for currency, as, for example, when the public wished to convert bank-deposit holdings into pocket and till money. Furthermore, reliance upon a fixed greenback supply for meeting increased currency demands would have serious consequences because greenbacks, unlike competitively issued bank notes, were a form of base money. When held by banks, they formed a part of bank reserves, useful in the settlement of clearing balances and therefore useful as a basis for loan expansion. Thus, their ebb and flow—in and out of circulation—would mean constant, unwarranted fluctuations in system reserves and, hence, in the total supply of bank money.

Had their issue been unrestricted, national-bank notes might have provided an adequate alternative to greenbacks as a means of fulfilling the public's demand for currency. However, under the bond-deposit requirements, banks became unwilling to secure notes in response to public demand. Rather, the supply of national-bank notes tended to follow the supply of bond collateral: the supply of bond collateral determined both the absolute limits of note issue and its profitability. The absurdity of this arrangement may be seen in the fact that retirement of the national debt would have resulted in complete elimination of national bank currency. . . .

Free-Market Responses

Prior to 1871, the expansion of the national debt assured an adequate supply of national-bank currency. But that year marked the beginning of a long period of debt contraction. The Treasury was running a surplus, which it used to buy up and retire government bonds. As the supply of federal securities declined, their market values increased, and the national banks found it increasingly difficult and costly to acquire the collateral needed for new note issues. These circumstances precluded secular growth of the currency supply and prevented cyclical increases in demand from being met, except by payment of high-powered reserve media that had to come largely from New York.

Here, then, was the setting for the great "money panics" of 1873, 1884, 1893, and 1907. Each of these severe crises coincided with the height of the harvest season, in October, when it was usual for large amounts of currency to be withdrawn from interior banks to finance the movement of crops. They were the only financial disturbances to interrupt what was otherwise a period of unmatched economic growth and prosperity—and they would never have occurred except for unwise government regulations that restricted banks' powers of note issue.

Hampered by regulations, the banks at first responded to heightened currency demands simply by reducing their extensions of credit. They took this step partly in response to lost reserves and partly because the demand for currency would fall along with a decrease in the banks' total liabilities. Such reductions resulted in great hardship for would-be borrowers, who suddenly found even routine requests denied. In more serious cases, banks resorted to the drastic policy of "restriction of payments": deposit holders were no longer allowed to convert their balances into currency. This policy had the unfortunate consequence of encouraging the public to hoard outstanding currency even when its outstanding supply might have exceeded trade requirements. Over time, deposit holders learned to anticipate currency shortages, so that the slightest indications of stringency were enough to set off large-scale runs and hoarding panics.

The marketplace showed great ingenuity in dealing with the money panics. In northern states, Canadian bank notes, not burdened by bond-deposit requirements, appeared in circulation. Private

clearinghouse associations issued temporary "clearing-house loan certificates" and "clearinghouse certificates." The former were used as supplements for gold in interbank settlements and as emergency reserves so that suspensions could be avoided; the latter were issued in small denominations to satisfy the currency needs of the public. Although these certificates violated the provisions of the National Banking Act and hence were illegal, they were so instrumental in overcoming the crises that regulators turned a blind eye toward them.

"In many communities, checks of well-known individuals and firms . . . were issued in small, round denominations and passed from hand to hand until they were black with endorsements."

In many communities, checks of well-known individuals and firms, including payroll checks, were issued in small, round denominations and passed from hand to hand until they were black with endorsements. Banks issued cashiers' checks and negotiable certificates of deposit, also in small, round denominations. These were further means of evading the bond-deposit laws. In the last of the great pre-Federal Reserve "currency panics" in 1907, no less than $334 million of such emergency currency, and probably a great deal more, was issued by banks, bank clearinghouses, and businesses all over the country. As a result, the extent of bankruptcies and other economic destruction that occurred during the panics was greatly reduced. In contrast, government regulations, besides causing the crises in the first place, only got in the way of free-market emergency measures.

Early Proposals for Reform

Although often sincere, many early reformers of the monetary system simply failed to recognize restrictions on note issue as the fundamental cause of the banking crises. Observing the scarcity of credit and the numerous bank failures, they concluded that banks had been negligent in holding reserves. Thus, bank-note inelasticity was misinterpreted as inelasticity in the supply of reserves. The result was widespread agitation for augmentation of the reserve base. The Silverites called for the monetization of silver, and the Greenback party emerged, favoring new issues of U.S. notes. But most popular, particularly with economists, were proposals calling for a special central reserve agency that would provide emergency reserves during periods of crisis. Such proposals were the basis for the Federal Reserve Act.

The Federal Reserve System was, in fact, a most unsatisfactory solution to the problems of the national banks. Through its administration of what soon became a monopolized note supply, the Fed indeed had unlimited capacity to satisfy the public's currency demands. But it could do much more than that: Fed issues not needed in circulation could augment the reserves of commercial banks, sponsoring a multiplication of commercial-bank liabilities. This vast capacity for inflation was absent in the plural note-issue system set up by the National Banking Act, under which no single bank could uniformly increase the reserves of all other banks.

The responsible solution to the problems that plagued the national banks was not the *monopolization* of the currency supply—which opened the way to vast inflation, especially after the abandonment of the gold standard—but its *deregulation.* The most severe problem, that of currency shortage, would have disappeared with the repeal of the bond-deposit laws. Repeal would have placed note issue on an equal footing with the granting (and acceptance) of deposit accounts, and banks would have been able to issue notes up to the full extent of deposit-customer requirements. Bank reserves would thereby have been insulated from changes in currency demand. Of course, this reform would still have left much scope for further deregulation, of which a repeal of the prohibition on inter- and intra-state branching would have been especially beneficial. But even by itself, revocation of the bond-deposit laws would have been superior to the Federal Reserve "solution."

Competitive Note Issue

We have come a long way since 1913. The last of the national bank notes were retired from circulation in 1935, and the currency supply has remained monopolized ever since. In 1933 the first steps were taken to suspend gold convertibility and to make Federal Reserve dollars a fiat standard. This process was completed in 1971. The Fed has long ceased to be regarded—or to act—as an agency designed to intervene only during "emergencies." It now assumes responsibilities that include nothing less than comprehensive control of all money and credit markets—control that it was never able to responsibly exercise even on a smaller scale.

Yet the fundamental options today are no different from those in 1913. True, base money is now government supplied, and the momentum behind the present fiat-dollar standard is a compelling argument for its retention. But that does not mean the Fed should retain its power to *manipulate* the supply of standard money. Nor, furthermore, is there anything about the present system that would make a return to competitive note issue undesirable. Indeed, such a return—without the unwise regulations that

condemned the National Banking System—is the key reform needed to make removal of the Federal Reserve possible without serious negative consequences.

To see why this reform is so important, consider the consequences of freezing the monetary base without first allowing commercial banks to participate in note issue, as in the latest monetary reform proposal of Milton Friedman. For Friedman, a monetary freeze is a desirable prelude to other reforms that would eventually include allowing banks to issue currency. . . .

"The responsible solution to the problems that plagued the national banks was not the monopolization *of the currency supply . . . but its deregulation."*

Friedman predicts that a freeze in the monetary base without competitive note issue would still allow desired changes in the multiplier (the ratio of outstanding currency and demand deposits to base money) reflecting the demand of individuals for monetary assets. Deregulation in combination with "financial innovation" would, according to Friedman, guarantee adequate stability.

But what means does Friedman's reform provide for satisfying changes in the public's demand for currency, that is, the demand for pocket and till money? How could this demand—which changes both cyclically and secularly—be satisfied during the interval between the freezing of the monetary base and private-bank issue of circulating paper? It could be satisfied only through changes in the apportionment of base money between banks (which hold it as reserves) and the public (which uses it in pockets and tills).

The preceding review of the events of the National Banking System era provides some clues as to the probable consequences of this arrangement: when the public's demand for currency increases, reserves will be withdrawn, and a contraction of credit must follow. Suppose the reserve ratio (the reciprocal of the money-multiplier) is 10 percent. Then a withdrawal of $1,000 in base money will necessitate a $9,000 contraction of credit additional to the $1,000 contraction involved in the original withdrawal transaction. The total contraction of liabilities would therefore be $10,000—a very significant change arising from a much smaller change in how the public prefers to hold its money. Ideally, the latter type of change ought to be accommodated without the former.

The result is no better when the public's demand

for currency falls, assuming that the currency in circulation includes some base money. In that case, the redundant base money flows back to the banks, where it becomes the basis for inflationary credit expansion. In short, as long as the currency needs of the public are subject to change, a frozen monetary base cannot be consistent with nominal-income and price stability. To put it another way, Friedman's proposed reform would lead to a repetition of some of the same problems encountered in the old National Banking System. To correct this defect in Friedman's proposal, the schedule for reform must be reversed: commercial banks should be allowed to issue paper currency, especially notes redeemable in base dollars, *before* the monetary base is frozen. Then they could independently accommodate positive and negative changes in the public's demand for hand-to-hand money. Note issue by commercial banks would prevent fluctuations in currency demand from having an undesirable influence on bank reserves and lending power.

A Practical Proposal for Reform

A reasonable starting point for implementing the reform outlined above would be to remove such archaic and obviously unnecessary regulations as statutory reserve requirements and restrictions on regional and nationwide branch banking. The majority of nations with developed banking industries have had no need for such regulations, evidence enough that their elimination in the United States would not have grave consequences. In fact, branch banking has significant advantages—both macroeconomic and microeconomic—over unit banking, and its absence is probably the major cause of the frequent collapse of American banks. As for statutory reserve requirements, they serve no purpose other than to act as a kind of tax on bank credit. Furthermore, their existence restricts the ability of banks to accommodate changes in the public's willingness to hold bank liabilities. If the monetary base is frozen, this restrictive effect is absolute.

"Consider the consequences of freezing the monetary base without first allowing commercial banks to participate in note issue."

While these deregulations are in progress, Congress should proceed to restore to all commercial banks the right to issue redeemable demand notes unrestricted by any bond-deposit requirements. This reform would not in any way complicate the task facing the Federal Reserve Board. Indeed, its only effect would be to reduce somewhat, perhaps

entirely, the Fed's need to take account of fluctuations in the public's currency needs when adjusting the money supply: the multiplier would become more stable and predictable to the extent that bank notes were employed to satisfy temporary changes in currency demand. Over time, the banks would establish the reliability of their issues—which, incidentally, need not be considered any less trustworthy by the public than traveler's checks.

Making the Public Comfortable

Obviously, in order for competitive note issue to achieve the desired result of entirely displacing base money from circulation, the public must feel comfortable with, or at least indifferent about, using bank notes instead of base money as currency. This might be a problem. It would be easier to switch from metallic base money, which is obviously a less convenient currency medium than bank notes redeemable in it. There is no similar advantage to using paper bank notes instead of equally convenient paper base dollars. Nevertheless, imaginative innovations could probably induce the public to prefer bank notes. These innovations would fall into two categories: those that would make base dollars less desirable as pocket and till money, and those that would enhance the desirability of bank notes.

As regards the first category, the existing base-money medium could be replaced by paper units of somewhat larger physical size, fitting less easily into existing wallets and tills; bank notes, conversely, could be made the size of present dollar bills. The appearance of base dollars could also be altered in other ways, for instance, by having them engraved in red ink. In this form, they might seem even less familiar to currency users than the newly available bank notes. Finally, base dollars could be made available only in less convenient denominations. Two-dollar bills would be ideal, since they already have an established reputation for undesirability. Banks, of course, could be allowed to issue whatever note denominations they discovered to be most desired by their customers.

Two possibilities come to mind for the second category. First, banks could stock their automatic teller machines exclusively with notes, and bank tellers could be instructed to give notes to depositors who desire currency, unless base dollars are specifically requested. Of course, such practices would be consistent with the maximization of bank profits, so that no special measures would be needed to encourage them. As a second possibility, banks might conduct weekly lottery drawings and offer prize money to those possessing notes with winning serial numbers. In practice, the drawings would be no more objectionable than similar lotteries now held by several daily newspapers. They would make notes more appealing to the public, and they would constitute an indirect way of paying interest to note holders, just as interest is paid on some checkable deposits.

A combination of measures such as these would almost certainly lead to near-complete displacement of base dollars from circulation. Once this stage was reached—say, once 5 percent or less of bank deposits and currency in circulation consisted of base dollars—a date could be chosen on which the supply of base money would be permanently frozen. When this date arrived, outstanding Federal Reserve deposit credits would be converted into paper dollars, and banks that held deposits with the Fed would receive their balances in cash. At this point as well the Federal Reserve System would cease its money-creation activities. Its clearing function could be privatized, as it had been before 1913, and the frozen stock of base dollars could be "warehoused" by private clearinghouse associations. Dollar "certificates" or clearinghouse account entries could be used to settle interbank clearings, saving the dollar supply from wear and tear. Only a small amount of base dollars would actually be held by individual banks for satisfying rare customer requests. In the case of a "run" on base dollars, a bank in distress could receive assistance from its more liquid branches or from other banks acting through the clearing agency. . . .

"The existing base-money medium could be replaced by paper units of somewhat larger physical size."

This proposal undoubtedly raises more questions than can be answered in a brief policy study. . . . The purpose here has been to suggest the essential role of free banking in reforming the present monetary system. The reform strategy outlined here is both practicable and desirable, achieving the two goals of stability and complete freedom from government intervention that have up to now been regarded as incompatible. The most important question that remains to be answered is whether policymakers will abandon their present "monetary frustration" and embrace free banking, or whether they will miss this opportunity—the way they missed it in 1913.

G.A. Selgin is assistant professor of economics at George Mason University.

*"The President's proposals would reduce
. . . inequities and distortions."*

Reagan's Tax Proposal Is Fair

Edward Yorio

On May 29, 1985, President Reagan sent Congress a tax program designed, in his words, to achieve "fairness, growth, and simplicity." The program's immediate precursor, a Treasury Department Report ordered by the President in his 1984 State of the Union address, had been released shortly after the 1984 national elections. Although the President's proposals and the Treasury Report differ in important details, both endorse the six principal criteria of sound federal income tax policy: simplicity and practicality, equality, fairness, neutrality, economic growth, and adequacy. . . .

Adequacy and Fairness

The basic thrust of the President's Tax Proposals is simple and straightforward. First, rates of taxation for individuals and corporations would be substantially reduced. Second, numerous exclusions, deductions, and other tax preferences would be either restricted or eliminated. Taken together, the proposals, when fully effective, are intended to raise virtually the same amount of revenue as current law. The proposals are also designed to require each income class to contribute the same percentage of total revenues as is being contributed by that class under current law with the exception of the poor, who will pay a much smaller percentage. If the President's proposals are in fact essentially revenue neutral and neutral among income classes, they would satisfy the adequacy and fairness criteria of federal income tax policy on the assumption that the amount of revenue currently raised by the income tax and the existing distribution of the tax burden are appropriate. . . .

Doubts have been expressed, however, about whether the proposals are indeed revenue neutral and neutral among income classes. Congressional

leaders and at least one economist have contended, for example, that the proposals will result in a revenue shortfall because the Administration has not taken into account how taxpayers might alter their behavior in order to pay lower taxes. Others have argued that the proposals give very wealthy taxpayers a greater tax reduction than other taxpayers or that middle-income taxpayers, specifically two-earner couples, will receive a smaller tax cut than other individual taxpayers. Moreover, the proposals deliberately increase the level of progressivity between middle income and poor taxpayers by providing a somewhat greater percentage reduction of tax for the latter.

These objections, even if valid, do not appear to be fatal to the President's program. To begin with, the greater percentage reduction for taxpayers below the poverty line results from a decision to exempt these taxpayers from the federal income tax by increasing the personal exemption, the zero bracket amount, and the earned income credit. These proposals can be justified on three grounds. First, they would simplify greatly the administration of the tax by removing numerous individuals from the tax rolls and by reducing the number of taxpayers who will itemize their personal deductions. Second, removing taxpayers below the poverty line from the tax rolls arguably makes the tax system more fair by exempting those taxpayers with the least ability to pay. Third, the exemption of poor taxpayers from income tax liability somewhat counteracts the extreme regressivity of the Social Security tax, the other major levy currently imposed by the federal government on the earnings of poor taxpayers.

The charge that the President's proposals would produce a revenue shortfall can be addressed, if it is correct, by revising the program somewhat to ensure revenue neutrality. Similarly, the excessive advantage that the very rich seem to derive from the proposals can virtually be eliminated by the simple expedient

Edward Yorio, "The President's Tax Proposals: A Major Step In the Right Direction," *Fordham Law Review*, May 1985. Reprinted with permission of the *Fordham Law Review*.

of retaining—rather than reducing—the current tax of taxation on realized long-term capital gains. Lastly, the alleged bias against two-earner couples in the President's proposals can be alleviated by changing the tax treatment of child-care expenses or by providing some other tax relief for two-earner couples. With these or similar changes to which the Administration is reported to be receptive, the goals of revenue neutrality and neutrality among income classes will be met and the criteria of adequacy and fairness satisfied. . . .

Simplicity and Practicality

Although the President's proposals complicate the tax system for certain individual taxpayers, the proposals generally serve the criterion of simplicity and practicality extremely well. To begin with, the proposals will reduce both the number of taxpayers required to file tax returns and the number who will itemize their personal deductions. Consequently, the costs of taxpayer compliance and of government administration of the law will be lower. Equally important, the reduction in marginal tax rates is likely to limit the incentive of certain taxpayers to engage tax planners to minimize their tax liability. Tax planning will also be discouraged by the simultaneous elimination or reduction in the benefits flowing from participation in some important tax shelters. Reducing the incentive to plan and the benefits of planning will save transaction costs of planning, compliance, and administration generated under current law. Moreover, as certain taxpayers are weaned from tax avoidance, the perception of other taxpayers about the fairness of the system will improve. . . .

"The basic thrust of the President's Tax Proposals is simple and straightforward."

Other, more subtle changes will also make the income tax simpler and more practical for individual taxpayers. Under current law, for example, numerous tax issues require an investigation of all the facts and circumstances surrounding a contested transaction to determine the taxpayer's tax liability. Income tax rules that require analysis of many facts are costly and inefficient. Recognizing this problem, the President's proposals repeal or modify several provisions of current law that employ a multifactor test to determine tax liability. The proposals would also simplify current law by replacing a host of different requirements for nondiscrimination in fringe benefit plans with a generally uniform nondiscrimination rule. . . .

The major omission of the proposals with respect to simplicity and practicality lies in the President's decision to retain a partial deduction for realized

long-term capital gains. Because the capital gains deduction may be the most complicating provision of the Code affecting individual taxpayers, it generates considerable transaction costs in planning and administration. Thus, failure to repeal the deduction would be a major defeat for tax simplification. Moreover, the proposal to permit individual taxpayers . . . to elect to index for inflation on the basis of capital assets sold in a particular taxable year would both complicate the tax system and create additional opportunities for tax avoidance.

Equality and Neutrality

Since the criteria of equality and neutrality are complementary, the President's proposals will be measured against both criteria simultaneously as the proposals affect exclusions from gross income . . . income-splitting, . . . and tax-shelters.

Under the President's proposals, a number of items excluded from gross income under current law will be wholly or partially taxed. Some of the inclusions will make the tax system more equitable by taxing recipients of previously excluded income like taxpayers whose income does not benefit from the exclusion. Other inclusions will improve both the equity and neutrality of the tax system. The proposal to tax unemployment compensation and disability compensation payments, for example, will eliminate a tax advantage to single taxpayers under current law and will result ultimately in a truer reflection of production costs in industries with high injury or layoff rates. . . .

The major defect in the President's proposals regarding exclusions from gross income results from the failure to tax aggressively the plethora of fringe benefits that are exempt under current law. Because of differences in bargaining leverage among taxpayers, exemption of certain fringe benefits produces discrepancies in the tax liability of otherwise similarly situated taxpayers. Moreover, economic distortions result when the exemption of a fringe benefit induces employers to compensate employees through the fringe benefit rather than in cash. As a result, demand for resources devoted to producing the fringe benefit increases and the price of the fringe benefit is artifically higher than it would be under a neutral tax system.

Because the arguments on grounds of equity and neutrality for taxing fringe benefits like other income are strong, the Treasury Report to the President (not surprisingly) recommended the repeal or restriction of a host of currently exempt benefits. Unfortunately, the President's proposals reject all but four of the Treasury Department's recommendations. . . .

For income tax purposes, individual members of the family, other than husband and wife, are treated as separate taxable entities. Viewing the family as a set of discrete taxpayers often diverges from a reality in which members of the family act as an economic unit, sharing resources and assuming mutual responsibilities. This divergence between the income tax world and the real world inspires efforts to reduce taxes by shifting income from members of the family with high income to members with low income or to trusts. Because of personal exemptions and the zero bracket amount and, most importantly, because of the progressive rate structure, successful attempts to shift income often produce considerable tax savings. Because the incentive to shift the income arises from the treatment of individuals and trusts as separate taxable entities, elimination of the incentive would require that the income and deduction of family members be aggregated for income purposes. But difficulties in determining exactly which income and deductions should be attributed to the family group have probably deterred lawmakers, at least until now, from enacting an aggregation rule.

Income Tax Savings

Income-splitting exacts a heavy toll. The incentive to shift income among taxpayers leads to a large amount of tax planning and generates significant transaction costs. Moreover, significant inequities exist because opportunities for income-splitting are greater for propertied taxpayers than for wage-earners. Lastly, economic distortions may result whenever taxpayers are induced to transfer property to their children or to trusts not because the transferee values the property more highly, but simply because the transfer will result in income tax savings.

The President's proposals would reduce these inequities and distortions in two primary ways. First, unearned income of children under fourteen years of age that is "attributable to property received from their parents" would generally be taxed to the children but at the marginal tax rate of their parents. For this purpose, a child's unearned income will be presumed to be attributable to property received from a parent unless the child can meet a strict burden of proving the contrary. Second, the income of so-called Clifford trusts, which is currently taxed at the marginal rate of the trust or of its beneficiaries, would generally be taxed to the trust but at the marginal tax rate of the grantor if the grantor is still alive. These proposals, if enacted, would reduce the income tax incentive to transfer property to minor children or to trusts because the income generated by the property would continue to be taxed at the parent's or grantor's marginal tax rate. Consequently, many of the inequities and distortions of income-splitting under current law would be eliminated. . . .

The President's tax proposals contain a number of recommendations designed to reduce the benefits of tax shelters. The investment tax credit and a number of energy tax credits would be repealed. Because the immediate tax benefits of these credits are available only to investment in certain property, repeal of the credits is likely to improve the overall neutrality of the tax system. The Administration has recommended, in addition, that recovery periods for depreciation purposes be extended slightly to reflect actual economic depreciation a bit more closely. The Administration would also require certain preproduction costs that are immediately deductible under current law to be capitalized instead for income tax purposes.

"The President's proposals . . . would improve the equity and neutrality of the tax system."

In addition to these proposals designed to strip certain tax shelters of their federal advantage, the Administration has made several proposals to limit opportunities to convert ordinary income deductions into tax-preferred income. The deduction of a taxpayer's share of the interest expense of a limited partnership, for example, would be subject to certain limitations. On the income side, depreciable property and certain other property would be denied the benefits of capital gains treatment. Percentage depletion, one of the linchpins of energy tax shelters, would be phased out over a five-year period. . . . Finally, the tax benefits from leveraging through nonrecourse financing would be reduced by the President's proposal to subject real estate investments to current law limiting the loss a taxpayer may deduct from investments other than real estate to the amount the taxpayer has at risk in the investment.

The effect of these proposals and of the reduction in marginal tax rates is likely to dim the luster of many popular tax shelters. For that reason, the President's proposals, if enacted, would improve the equity and neutrality of the tax system. But the President has missed a few major opportunities to curtail the activities of tax shelters even further by rejecting a number of recommendations contained in the Treasury Report. Repeal of the capital gains deduction, for example, would eliminate an important mechanism for converting ordinary income deductions into tax-preferred income. Requiring the intangible drilling costs of oil and gas wells to be capitalized, which the Treasury Department recommended, would eliminate one of the most important deferral advantages currently tolerated by the Code. Eliminating that preference and subjecting all minerals, including oil and gas, to total repeal of percentage depletion would improve the equity of the tax system and ensure that market forces—rather than tax subsidies—would determine the allocation of resources in the development of alternative sources of energy.

A Step in the Right Direction

This article has focused primarily on the effect of the President's proposals on individual taxpayers. . . . From the standpoint of personal taxation, the proposals would eliminate or reduce many of the complexities, inequities, and distortions caused by current law. Although the program is not ideal, its deficiencies generally result not from the changes actually proposed, but from the President's unwillingness to support the even more dramatic recommendations of the Treasury Report. Perhaps the President was concerned about the risks of suddenly eliminating many important tax incentives. Or perhaps his program represents the limits of what is now politically feasible. If not, Congress should improve on the program in ways suggested by this article.

The danger, however, is that Congress will be swayed instead by the pleas of interested parties— the real estate industry, the coal industry, municipal unions, state and local public officials, and others— to restore tax advantages that would be excised by the President's program. If so, a major opportunity for significant reform of personal income taxation will have been lost. It is better, in general, to take a step in the right direction than not to move at all.

Edward Yorio is a professor of law at Fordham University School of Law.

"The Reagan plan is worth at least forty times as much to rich people as it is to people in the middle."

Reagan's Tax Proposal Is Unfair

Bernard D. Nossiter

President Reagan's Tax Proposals for Fairness, Growth and Simplicity are a radical assault on the progressive income tax, a knee in the groin for workers and a windfall for those whose income derives from speculation in stocks and bonds. It is eminently fair to the very rich, provides genuine relief for the very poor and is so complex that the Commissioner of Internal Revenue has said he will need more help to administer it.

"Our tax system has come to be un-American," Reagan declared, but for all its flaws, the system is in the American grain. Its fourteen brackets reflect an elemental notion of justice: the higher a person's income, the more he or she should pay, relatively and absolutely, to support the expenses of government. The first income tax, established by Woodrow Wilson in 1913, embodied the principle. Those with incomes between $4,000 and $20,000 paid 1 percent; those between $20,000 and $50,000 paid 2 percent; and so on up to 6 percent on incomes of more than $500,000.

A Giant Step—Backward

Reagan's plan, in his own words, is "a giant step toward an ideal system," presumably a single rate for all. He compresses the fourteen brackets into three, lopping off three at the bottom and bringing down the top rate, for incomes over $70,000, from 50 percent to 35 percent—a generous slice of 30 percent. A single rate, however, is regressive: like a sales tax, it imposes the same percentage burden on rich and poor. . . . Reagan is not likely to be around long enough to see his ideal system realized, but a successor Bush regime could carry on the crusade.

Tax reformers less cynical than Reagan make fairness their primary objective. Those with the same income should pay the same tax regardless of how they earned their money. The Reagan proposal does not do this. Citizens who draw paychecks would pay more, proportionately, than those whose income derives from oil and gas wells, real estate shelters and capital gains.

The President's most generous gift to his well-heeled supporters is the privileged taxation of capital gains, the income from the sale of assets like shares of stock. Half of this income would go untaxed, meaning those in the top bracket would give up only 17.5 percent of their gain. This is a pleasant bonus, better than the current capital-gains rate of 20 percent. It would provide an added incentive for T. Boone Pickens and other raiders who make their money by frightening corporate executives with the loss of their perquisites. Pickens now keeps $40 million of the $50 million that raided executives pay him to go away. Under Reagan's system, he would keep $41.25 million. To be sure, he would have to hold his shares six months. More modest shareholders who sell old Exxon paper or old I.B.M. paper would benefit similarly, if on a smaller scale. These schemes, of course, would be open to any worker who had the cash.

Two-Faced About Oil

The President is two-faced about oil. He plans to strip the industry of its egregious depletion allowance but preserve its far more valuable benefits from intangible drilling costs. Those are the expenses of readying a site for drilling, everything except the cost of the drill itself. In normal business practice, this equipment would be written off over the ten or more years of its useful life; the oil industry, however, can write them off in one year, as if they were ordinary business expenses for postage stamps, files or salaries. The Treasury Department estimates this device will save the industry more than $8 billion a year in taxes.

At the other end of the scale, the Administration

Bernard D. Nossiter, "Reagan's Tax Package Unwrapped," *The Nation*, August 3/10, 1985. *The Nation Magazine*, Nation Associates Incorporated © 1985.

boasts that it will take $2.5 million families near the poverty line off the tax rolls. Although the government has played fast and loose with many figures, there is reason to believe that the Reagan measure would come close to bringing the impoverished back to where they were in 1978, before higher Social Security taxes and inflation swelled their tax burden. The President, however, has chosen a Reaganite way to lower taxes for the poor. He raises by a little the bottom income slice that is exempt from taxes and almost doubles the deduction all taxpayers can take for dependents. Thus, the corporate executive who makes $300,000 a year and has a wife and two children could lop off from his taxable income the same $8,000 as the single mother in Harlem who has a low-paying job and three children. Reagan also increases an earned-income credit for the working poor. Still, even according to Reagan, barely one family in four earning less than $10,000 would receive a tax cut; one in twenty-five would suffer an increase. On the other hand, nearly three in four earning $200,000 or more would enjoy lower taxes.

Torturing the Middle Class

In contrast with his treatment of these two special classes—the very rich and the very poor—Reagan has devised some ingenious torments for salaried workers. Now unemployment pay and compensation for those injured on the job are largely tax free (jobless benefits over $18,000 are taxed). Such payments are clearly income, but society says that because jobless or disabled workers endure unusual stress and pain, they should not pay. They may be struggling to meet mortgages or finance costly medical care.

According to Reagan's philosophy, however, benefit payments are disincentives, encouraging people not to work. Under his plan, those benefits would be taxed like any other income—except the income Pickens or the Rockefellers make. As a miner with black lung disease coughs for the last time, Reagan would leave him one consoling thought: his funeral benefits would not be taxed.

For businesses, expenses incurred to produce income are deductible. Reagan proposes to curtail similar privileges for workers, creating a new category of disprivileged income. Union dues, work clothes, the cost of schooling to upgrade a skill, would be deductible only after the first 1 percent of a worker's income is subtracted. Thus, a worker earning $35,000 could not deduct the first $350 of these expenses.

Health benefits provided by an employer to workers are also not taxed now. But Reagan regards them as income in kind. His scheme taxes the first $300 of any family's benefits, the first $120 of a single worker's. He sweeps impartially into his net the medical insurance provided to the $200,000-a-

year lawyer and the $15,000-a-year garment worker.

Taxes, the President says, should "reflect and support our deeper values and highest aspirations." One of his, quite evidently, is to take women out of the job market and put them back in the home, rearing children, cooking, attending the church of their choice. To that end, he would do two things: restore the marriage penalty and reduce tax savings for less-well-off employed mothers who pay someone to tend their children. The marriage penalty is an anomaly of graduated rates. The combined income of a husband and wife puts them in a higher bracket than if they were living in sin, filing separate returns. To overcome this disadvantage, current law allows the couple to deduct up to $3,000. Reagan would like to abolish that.

He has run into formidable trouble, however. Bob Packwood, Republican chair of the Senate Finance Committee, has raised some objections. The Treasury Department did not realize (or did not want to know) that the loss of this deduction would turn tax cuts into tax increases for many median-income earners in Oregon, New York and other states with high budgets. The department's statisticians had carefully drawn up analyses of the median-income family in all fifty states, showing that everyone would pay lower taxes under the Reagan plan. Unfortunately, those calculations were based on families with one income earner. Since a majority of husbands and wives in this bracket work, the analyses were useless.

"Reagan's Tax Proposals . . . are . . . a knee in the groin for workers."

Much of the media debate has dealt with Reagan's proposal to end deductions for state and local taxes. The purpose of that provision, aside from raising cash to pay for other giveaways, is to force states to slash their budgets for schools, welfare, public housing and other things Reagan doesn't like. There is something to Reagan's argument that the current provision compels low-taxed Oklahomans to subsidize indirectly high-taxed New Yorkers—just as New Yorkers subsidize Oklahoma's oil wells. If Federal grants replaced the revenues the states would lose after they cut their taxes, and if a tax reform bill was passed that would close all escape hatches for the rich and their corporations, removing the provision could be justified. Since neither seems likely, it is not.

Aiding the Rich

To make his worker "reforms" palatable, Reagan's scheme reduces taxes modestly for many people. Its three brackets trim rates for all income classes; the increased personal exemptions and the expanded slice free of all taxes finish the job. Taken together, these measures outweigh the lost deductions at least for some. But how much each income group gains is unclear. In a striking departure from past practice, the Treasury Department offered only percentage estimates, which are misleading, rather than the absolute dollar amounts. Thanks to the admirable Center on Budget and Policy Priorities, a foundation-supported research group in Washington, some independent calculations are available: those with incomes under $10,000 will get an average cut of $104; between $20,000 and $30,000, $149; between $30,000 and $50,000, $211; over $200,000, $9,254. Therefore, the Reagan plan is worth at least forty times as much to rich people as it is to people in the middle.

"Reagan has devised some ingenious torments for salaried workers."

For business, the proposal closes some of the more blatant loopholes but leaves enough of them open to require taxpayers to list their "preference" income, or money derived from loopholes. Most intriguing and most arcane is the treatment of depreciation. Every prudent firm must put aside funds to replace worn-out or obsolete machines, plants and buildings. This is a reasonable deductible business expense. From a common sense and an economist's point of view, a firm should be allowed to deduct during a tool's useful life a sum equal to the cost of replacing it.

But Reagan has gone this one better. His 1981 measure gave firms fast write-offs, enabling them to deduct far more than replacement costs and at a pace much quicker than that of useful life. That has helped Lockheed, General Electric, other arms merchants and large corporations earn billions in profits and still escape all taxes. The new proposal retains fast write-offs but at a somewhat slower rate. That is no small boon. The proposal would save corporations at least $176 billion over the next five years compared to write-offs at an economic rate tied to the useful life of a tool or plant.

Giving With One Hand

Corporate bliss is not unalloyed, though. Reagan would wipe out the investment credit, a splendid subsidy which allows firms to subtract from putative tax bills up to 10 percent of the cost of any machine. That makes up a big part of the tax-free privileges of many giants. But what the President takes away, he quickly restores, at least for his corporate friends: their national tax rate would drop from 46 percent to 33 percent.

The perpetuation of fast write-offs, like the

windfall for capital gains, is defended as a stimulant to economic growth, marshaling capital and spurring investment to lead the economy onward and upward. No doubt, tax privileges will produce some marginal investment that would not otherwise be made. But in the end, individuals and corporations invest in anticipation of future demand. Growth is better obtained by insuring a rising level of demand and marshaling tax, spending and monetary policies to employ idle resources. At full employment, the pressure of demand will call forth investment. Tax gimmicks are an inferior method for achieving the desired goal.

Reagan, of course, rejects this argument. In the short run, he seeks to cut the taxes paid by his friends and the corporations they control. In the long run, he seeks to rewrite history, converting the traditional progressive income tax into a blunt, regressive instrument that strikes hardest at those who work for his friends.

Bernard D. Nossiter is a veteran journalist who is completing a study of US North-South economic conflict.

*"Simplicity, clarity and evenhandedness
are characteristics of the flat rate [tax]."*

The Flat Rate Tax
Would Be Just

Robert W. Lee

The official mission of the Internal Revenue
Service, according to the *United States Government
Manual*, "is to encourage and achieve the highest
possible degree of voluntary compliance with the tax
laws and regulations and to conduct itself so as to
warrant the highest degree of public confidence in
the integrity and efficiency of the Service."

There was a time, not too long ago, when efforts
of the I.R.S. to maintain those standards were
relatively uncomplicated and successful. Prior to
World War II, Representative Bob Livingston (R.-
Louisiana) reminds us, "paying taxes was considered
almost a sign of distinction. Relatively few citizens
had high enough incomes to be taxed, the rates were
low and the tax code was simple. Taxes weren't too
much trouble, and people were happy to contribute
to their government. It was a sign of "having made
it."

A Snarled Hodgepodge

The times, needless to say, have changed. Today's
federal tax code, rather than serving as a blueprint
for equitably raising funds to finance legitimate and
constitutional functions, has (in Congressman
Livingston's words) degenerated into "a snarled
hodgepodge of varying rates, exemptions, credits,
deductions and complexities that only a few highly
paid tax experts can begin to understand." Indeed,
"Congress has turned the tax code into a vehicle for
social engineering and political favoritism" by
tinkering with and twisting the tax system "to
satisfy the gripes and self-pleadings of every special
interest that can howl loud enough to be politically
heard."

The Congressman is right, of course. Burgeoning
taxes, accompanied by the increasing complexity of
the tax code and the roughshod manner in which it

"The Flat-Rate Tax and Other Needed U.S. Tax Reform" Robert W. Lee first
appeared in the April, 1984 issue of *American Opinion* (Belmont, MA 02178)
and the excerpts used are reprinted by permission of the publisher. All
rights reserved.

is enforced by the I.R.S., have all but destroyed the
remaining vestiges of the respect which Americans
are said to have once held for our system of
taxation. It should hardly be a surprise that a "tax
rebellion" has sprung up in recent years, and is
growing, or that the "rebels" (as the I.R.S. itself
reluctantly admits) are gaining in social
respectability.

Former I.R.S. Commissioner Donald Alexander told
a Congressional Committee not long ago: "The only
way we can keep them [*American taxpayers*] honest
and paying their taxes is to keep them afraid." The
ominous implications of that statement are
consistent with reports we have . . . received from
professional tax accountants indicating that the I.R.S.
is preparing to crack down more ruthlessly than ever
in an attempt to coerce citizen compliance with our
"voluntary" tax apparatus.

Major Overhaul

A major overhaul is essential. And soon. Basic
structural and administrative reforms and imperative
if the increasingly hostile Hatfield-McCoy
relationship between taxpayers and the government
is to be cooled and pacified. *Structurally*, it is time to
replace the graduated income tax (and its plethora of
economically unsound credits, deductions, and other
loopholes) with a relatively modest flat-rate income
tax applied to an income base broadened by
elimination of the loopholes. . . .

Flat-Rate Alternative

According to national polls, the American people
favor an income-tax system that is simple,
understandable, and fair. Which is apparently why
they rank our present graduated ("progressive")
system as the very worst tax of all.

In contrast, simplicity, clarity, and evenhandedness are characteristics of the flat-rate
("proportional") tax which is now widely considered

to be the most politically viable of the responsible alternatives to the increasingly unacceptable *status quo*. One of the most important and encouraging developments on the American scene in many years is the extent to which citizens of varying political persuasions, from Republican and Democratic to "Liberal" and Conservative, are rallying behind the flat-rate concept. Typical is the observation of Representative Leon Panetta (D.-California), whose "Liberal" credentials are confirmed by his lowly Conservative Index rating of only seven percent during the present Congress. Panetta says:

"The present Internal Revenue Code is riddled with countless exemptions, credits, exclusions, and hidden loopholes. The primary reason for this increasing complexity is the continuing use of the code for achieving societal goals that are unrelated to the raising of revenue. . . .In addition, the system encourages taxpayers to direct resources toward investments which have no economic or productive value other than reducing their tax burden." And Congressman Panetta further notes that these "terribly complex laws have led to the growth of an Internal Revenue Service bureaucracy . . . which is forced by the ambiguity of the laws to establish arbitrary rules and regulations in order to carry out its enforcement responsibilities.". . .

Representative Panetta is one of a number of Congressmen who have introduced flat-rate tax proposals. As might be expected during the early stages of the debate on such an important issue, there is as yet no consensus on what shape a final bill should take. The measures already pending would, for instance, establish a tax rate of ten, or fourteen, or nineteen percent. In some instances, *all* deductions and credits would be eliminated, while in others, deductions for such items as religious contributions and catastrophic medical expenses would still be allowed. The bills introduced to date would allow a generous *exemption*, to preclude the poor from paying taxes below a certain level of income.

Inherent Superiority

As early as 1962, economist Milton Friedman proposed a flat-rate income tax, but it was not until the advent of the Reagan Administration in 1981 that the concept was taken seriously by the political and intellectual communities. Since that time, there has been an explosion of serious literature analyzing the issue. While the eventual outcome may be uncertain at this stage, there is no question but that the flat-rate tax has a fighting chance, or that its prospects for eventual passage will steadily improve as more Americans become aware of its *inherent* superiority to the Marxist "progressive" approach. Consider, for instance, the matter of complexity.

The current tax laws are so complicated that not even the I.R.S. itself is able to render consistently

reliable advice. Ralph Nader's Tax Reform Research Group ran a test some years ago which entailed submission of tax data for a non-existent couple with one child to twenty-two I.R.S. offices around the country. The result was astonishing: Each office came up with a different result, ranging from a refund of $811.96 to an underpayment of $52.14. Similarly, when a House Subcommittee called seventeen I.R.S. taxpayer assistance offices, it received thirty-two wrong answers to 124 common tax questions prepared by the Library of Congress. It has been officially estimated that the I.R.S. fouls up, to one degree or another, approximately seventy-five percent of the itemized-deduction returns it prepares for taxpayers who come to it for help.

"It is time to replace the graduated income tax . . . with a relatively modest flat-rate income tax."

The federal income tax went into effect on March 1, 1913, with a two-page Form 1040 accompanied by another two pages of instructions. The tax affected only 357,515 citizens (four-tenths of one percent of the population had to file returns), most of whom paid one percent or less. The top bracket was seven percent, a rate far below our *lowest* bracket today. And today's top bracket is more than seven times what it was at the start.

With a flat-rate tax, calculations would be sufficiently simple to fit on a form no larger than a postcard!

Reduced Costs

And what about cost? In its first year, administration of the 24-page list of income-tax regulations was handled by 4,200 I.R.S. employees at a cost of $800,000. But by 1983, some 85,000 I.R.S. operatives were employed, at an expense of nearly $3 billion, to enforce more than five thousand pages of tax regulations. And the I.R.S. budget is just the beginning, for it is estimated that the public expends over *six hundred million hours* filling out the hundreds of required federal tax forms. In addition, there is the approximately $1 billion paid to commercial tax preparers by citizens too baffled to attempt the task themselves. Also, there is the significant expense of maintaining and storing records and receipts for years, just in case they are needed for verification during a tax audit. "To summarize," authors Robert E. Hall and Alvin Rabushka inform us, "taxpayers bear some $9 to $10 billion in real costs for preparing and verifying their taxes, above and beyond what they actually pay in taxes."

Adoption of a flat-rate taxing system would

decrease the I.R.S. workload to the point where an Internal Revenue Service budget cut of fifty percent or more would be justified. The need for professional assistance when toting up one's tax bill would drop precipitously. The investment of personal time by the average taxpayer would likely be cut from many hours to a few minutes. And, storage space now given to receipts (other than those for business expenses) could be devoted to storing jams and jellies, since there would be no deductions for which receipts would be required.

Return to Free Market

Perhaps the single most important result of a switch to a flat-rate income tax would be the elimination of the graduated aspect of the present system. By eliminating deductions, credits, and other loopholes, economic decisions would once again be made on the basis of Free Market considerations, rather than what impact a decision will have on one's tax obligation. The billions of dollars now malinvested in tax-avoidance schemes (such as tax-shelter ratholes) would instead be drawn to those areas of the economy where they would be most productive. There would be no need to "index" tax tables to counteract the evil of "bracket creep," as there would be no higher brackets into which to creep. And, charitable donations would be free to flow to the most deserving recipients, rather than be enticed toward entities crowned with government-authorized "tax exempt" status.

"There are a number of important features inherent in the very nature of this tax . . . that argue strongly for acceptance."

That last business has puzzled your reporter for years. How did we ever get snookered into accepting the bizarre idea that government is qualified, and should be given the authority, to decide what is or is not a proper recipient of private charity? The authority to grant or withhold or cancel tax-exempt status involves a subtle coercive influence which can cause an organization to "go easy" with any criticism it might be inclined to make of policies or personnel favored by an incumbent Administration rather than risk losing its exemption. A number of organizations ostensibly formed to oppose collectivism and Big Government have been neutralized by concern about losing their tax-exempt status. On the other hand, some exempt organizations and institutions have been outspoken in opposing certain government policies and have as a result faced constant and expensive harassment over the exemption issue.

The flat-rate tax would solve this problem by removing government-imposed incentives favoring one recipient over another.

A Vote for the Flat Tax

The eventual nature of a flat-rate system, including the acutal rate which is imposed, will be a congressional decision heavily influenced by input from the constituents of every Senator and Representative. Keeping the rate low at the start, and thereafter, will depend on the vigor with which Americans act in their own interest. . . .

Our brief review of the potential of the flat-rate tax is far from exhaustive, but it should make clear that there are a number of important features inherent in the very nature of this tax, and which are largely unrelated to the exact rate of the tax, that argue strongly for acceptance. While the opposition of special interests benefiting from the existing loophole system may be substantial, it can be overcome once enough Americans realize the positive long-range implications of the flat-rate tax for the political and economic welfare of our nation and, therefore, its citizens.

Robert W. Lee, a former corporation president, is a contributing editor for The Review of the News, *where his "From the Hopper" and "A Capital Report" columns appear regularly.*

"The flat tax is a wolf in sheep's clothing."

The Flat Rate Tax Would Be Unjust

Floyd K. Haskell and Ronald D. Pasquariello

A flat-tax fever has struck Washington in the past few years. The flat tax is like a boomerang. No matter how many times you throw it away, it keeps coming back, often in slightly different forms.

In its simplest form, a flat tax is a tax with just one rate. Instead of the 12 different rates on the present tax schedule, ranging from 12 percent to 50 percent, it would have just one, applicable to all taxpayers. That single rate might be 20 percent, or any figure between 10 and 25 percent, if one is to judge from the numerous flat-tax proposals floating around Capitol Hill.

Though it only really caught on in the past two years, the idea was proposed by the Chicago University economist Milton Friedman in the 1960's. Never really taken seriously politically, it lay dormant for a number of years, but was given new life by the Reagan Administration. Between May and June of 1982, Treasury Secretary Donald T. Regan named the flat tax fairest of all, Budget Director David Stockman promised (but reneged) to make it part of the 1984 budget, President Reagan pronounced it very tempting, and Edward Meese said any progressive tax is immoral. Simultaneously other Administration officials were telling a different story. Treasury Department's Assistant Secretary for Tax Policy John E. Chapton, for example, warned that a flat tax would reduce the tax burden of high-income taxpayers and increase the burden on many low-income people. Notwithstanding that advice, by September 1982 there were nine flat-tax proposals before Congress, and almost every major finance committee held hearings on the concept.

Five arguments, used in various guises, are usually given to justify the switch from progressive to flat income taxation. This first has to do with simplicity.

Floyd K. Haskell and Ronald D. Pasquariello, ''A Flat Tax or a Fair Tax?'' *America*, December 29, 1984. Reprinted with permission of America Press, Inc. 106 West 56th Street, New York, NY 10019. © 1984 All rights reserved.

This is by far the strongest argument favoring the change. Our present tax system is so complex that it has generated a corps of specialists in the public and private sectors whose primary job is to sort out and interpret provisions of the tax code. The code's complexity has overwhelmed the average taxpayer with a multitude of forms and procedures that make compliance all but impossible. The flat tax of a single rate and no exemptions is, on the other hand, sometimes called the postcard tax, because that is all that would be needed in the simplest system to file one's tax return.

Controlling Inflation

The second argument has to do with inflation. Under the current progressive-tax system, inflation-induced increases in income push individuals into higher brackets. For most taxpayers the increase in tax liability is greater than their real increase in income. A flat-rate would eliminate bracket creep. With only one rate, inflation would not push taxpayers into higher tax brackets.

In the third place, the marriage penalty would be eliminated. Married people would not be penalized for filing a joint return because the flat rate would be the same on both individual and joint returns.

A fourth reason given to favor the flat tax is that it would end the preferential treatment of most types of income and hence improve horizontal equity. Horizontal equity demands that the tax system tax individuals in similar positions equally. Under the current system, exemptions and deductions allow this principle to be violated, since what is an allowable deduction for one person may not apply to another. A homeowner, for example, can take advantage of the home mortgage interest rate deduction while a renter in otherwise similar circumstances could not.

Improved economic efficiency is the fifth argument. Under the present system, deductions, credits, exemptions and other preferential tax treatment are incentives to artificially shelter income from taxation. Investors either time the realization of their capital gains to periods when they are in lower brackets (after retirement, for example), or invest in artificially constructed tax shelters (llama ranches, deep sea treasure hunts, spaghetti westerns, etc.). Both these factors represent the largest part of what may be the fastest growing industry—tax avoidance—in the country. Both of them distort the efficient allocation of our economic resources. The simplicity of a flat tax would promote better compliance and help prevent the loss of tax revenues through artificial means.

Trade-Off Simplicity

Interestingly, each of these arguments for a flat tax can be answered by modifications in the present progressive system. Simplicity, horizontal equity and economic efficiency can be achieved in one fell swoop by eliminating all loopholes; inflation can be dealt with by indexing the tax schedule; and the marriage penalty can be handled by a simple formula.

Most policymakers know this. What, then, accounts for the apparent popularity of the flat tax? Reading between the lines, it seems to have to do with one of two things. Liberal tax reformers are frustrated with their inability to bring about real tax reform and see the flat tax as a way to brush away all inequities in one legislative pirouette. Conservatives, arguing that more money in the hands of the well-to-do is the best thing for the country, see it as a necessary support for trickle-down economics, which turns out to be a spectator sport for most Americans but the very rich.

But what are we trading off for simplicity?

The current individual income tax is progressive. A flat tax is not; it is proportional. Flattening means squeezing out the progressivity of the tax system. The average effective rate under the present system projected for 1984 rises from about 5 percent for incomes from $5,000 to $10,000 to about 25 percent for those with incomes above $200,000. No flat-rate would replicate this degree of progressivity. Since the flat-tax rate would probably be between 15 percent and 20 percent, those high-income taxpayers who now pay average rates above these levels would get tax cuts, and those currently paying less would get a sizeable tax increase. The rich would get a tax break, and the lower and middle classes would be left holding the bag.

Built-In Inequity

The question now becomes: Is it justifiable to shift the tax burden further from the rich to middle- and low-income taxpayers in the name of simplicity?

Flat-tax proposal framers recognize this built-in inequity. They try to deal with it by allowing some deductions (most often for home mortgage interest and charitable contributions), by increasing the personal exemption, by exempting low-income persons from all taxes and by imposing several tax rates. All these do is reduce the degree of unfairness in an inherently unfair system. While low-income workers would be exempted from paying higher taxes, the middle-income earners would be penalized.

Justice and fairness require that those who make large amounts should pay a higher rate of tax on income. It seems totally unfair for persons who earn $15,000 and $150,000 to pay the same rate.

Suppose the flat rate were 20 percent, with no exemptions, deductions, credits. On $15,000, Mr. Ashley's household of four would pay $3,000 to the Internal Revenue Service. Mr. Bentley's four would pay $30,000 on his income of $150,000. There seems to be a patina of fairness to these figures. But now look at what is left to each family. Mr. Ashley has $13,000 to support his family for a year; Mr. Bentley has $130,000. Is that fair?

"The rich would get a tax break, and the lower and middle classes would be left holding the bag."

The flat tax is a proportional tax. While progressive taxes apply a higher rate as income increases, proportional taxes apply the same rate to all taxpayers. Proportional taxes are never fair, because a low-income person has to pay a greater share of his or her income on basic necessities than a well-to-do person. (The 80 percent of taxpayers, who can earn less than $30,000 per year, spend between 60 and 70 percent of their budgets on the basic necessities—food, housing, energy, medical care.) In addition, from that salary must come the price of clothing, education, a modicum of leisure, transportation, skill acquisition, etc. Each dollar taken in tax inflicts more hardship on a person of low income than on a person of high income.

Rich Should Pay More

Another argument against a proportional tax is simply that the well-to-do having a greater ability-to-pay should pay more.

Those who are concerned about the distribution of wealth in this country need to worry about the flat tax. The tax system is the only mechanism we have for redistributing income. Our present Federal tax system does so minimally, because of the exceptions allowed by law. A flat tax would not redistribute income at all. The before-tax and after-tax distribution of income would be exactly the same because the tax would extract the same share from each taxpayer.

Not all flat-tax rate proposals are for a single rate. Some proposals are called flat taxes, but would have a scale of rates—15 percent, 20 percent and 25 percent, for example. These proposals only muddy the waters. Varying rates are of the essence of progressivity. It is not the progressivity of our present system that causes our difficulties, but the exceptions. The real answer to our tax inequities is to restore the tax base, that is, to eliminate tax loopholes and simplify, but not eliminate, the progressive rate scale.

"Those who are concerned about the distribution of wealth in this country need to worry about the flat tax."

So let the taxpayer beware. The flat tax is a wolf in sheep's clothing. Simplification of the tax system and flat rates are completely separate issues. Closing loopholes can be effected with or without flat rates. If it is desirable to close loopholes, and it is, in order to reduce tax rates and inequities, that can be done without the massive shift to a flat-tax rate. The decision about the flat tax is not just about advantages of one tax over another, but about the relationship between taxes and redistribution. Flat-tax proposals divert attention from the graver issues at hand. Just as one can imagine a flat-rate tax with few or no inequities, so one can imagine a progressive-tax system with none.

Floyd K. Haskell is a former Democratic senator from Colorado and chairman of the Taxpayers Committee. Ronald D. Pasquariello is a senior fellow in urban policy at the Center for Theology and Public Policy in Washington, DC.

Improve the Present Tax System

Ronald D. Pasquariello

It's tax time again. Every household in America has already heard from the friendly people at the Internal Revenue Service. . . .

It's also tax time in another sense. One more hour of reckoning is upon the nation. During the past three years, we have multiplied the deficit three- and fourfold, from $66 billion at its highest under President Ford to more than $200 billion—and growing—in the Reagan administration. Pressure is now on the president to increase taxes to minimize the burden of future deficits. And the president is, unfortunately, in the eyes of conservative and liberal economists, resisting that pressure.

There is no doubt about it: we need a tax increase to pay for the failed supply-side policies of the current administration. But the issue is deeper than that. We need drastic tax reform.

Nothing is bright deep in the heart of taxes. The tax system is a dense jungle of injustices, of threats to the construction of a decent social and communal life.

Domination of the Rich

On close examination, the American tax system turns out to be an incredible system of social domination and exploitation. It mediates the domination of the rich over the poor. It obstructs the work of *shalom*, concern for the welfare of the whole community, in favor of the advantage of the rich. If the wealthy forced the poor or middle class to give them a substantial part of their earnings directly, the injustice would be obvious, and morally sensitive people would react quickly. The effect of government tax programs is precisely that, but, unfortunately, there seems to be little reaction.

In analyzing distributional policies, one must look at both sides of the coin: who pays and who gets.

Taxes are the revenue (paying) side of the federal budget. Americans find certain programs necessary for the well-being of the nation. Taxes pay for those programs. In budgetary matters, Christian altruism has been myopic. Much effective effort has been focused on the distribution of benefits, such as food stamps, welfare, housing and Medicaid. Little has been done to check on who is paying for these programs.

It is our only real mechanism for the redistribution of wealth, but the tax system fails the test of distributive justice. If the before-tax distribution of shares of income and wealth in the society is unjust, then the tax system ought to be the mechanism to make the after-tax distribution just. At best, it leaves the distribution of wealth untouched.

In reality, the poor and middle class pay for life in these United States. And because the system is regressive—the richer a person gets, the lower a percentage of income he or she pays in taxes—the poor and middle class pay more than their share.

Elements of distributive justice are built into the system. By tradition, and common sense, Americans are to be taxed according to their ability to pay. Progressive taxation, that people should pay a higher share of taxes the higher their income, is the shape this principle usually takes. Progressive taxation is a myth. It simply does not exist in the aggregate, though certain portions of the system are progressive.

Listing the Injustices

Below are some of the problems with the system that make it unjust. One may be surprised to find Reagan's tax policies not prominently listed. This is not to say his policies do not belong there. They do. But Reagan's tax programs have only aggressively taken advantage of the system's bias toward the rich. They are better off because of his tax policies, though the tax system has always served them well.

Ronald D. Pasquariello, "A 'Jungle of Injustices': U.S. Tax System Stands in Need of Overhaul," *National Catholic Reporter*, February 17, 1984. Reprinted by permission of the author and the National Catholic Reporter, P.O. Box 419281, Kansas City, MO 64141.

—The system taxes income, not wealth. This is one of the principal inequities in the system. It taxes income heavily and wealth—real estate, corporate stock, business assets, government bonds—hardly at all. The assets of wealth are underreported and favorably taxed. According to a Treasury Department study, net capital (wealth) income in the economy was $305.5 billion in 1980. Only one-third of this was reported on the individual income tax returns. The average marginal tax rate on all capital income was about 10 per cent.

Income tax is a misnomer. Our system is primarily a wage and salary tax. All but 10 per cent of the total income of about 95 per cent of Americans is from wages and salaries. These are fully taxed at ordinary income rates. The millionaires in the 1978 tax returns had only 16 per cent of their income from wages or salaries. The higher your income, the smaller a factor wages and salaries are in your total wealth.

"On close examination, the American tax system turns out to be an incredible system of social domination and exploitation."

More than 60 per cent of the personal income tax is on wages and salaries. Estimates put the total burden of the tax system on wages and salaries at more than 70 per cent.

Wealth can be taxed more heavily. The arguments against taxing it are ideologically, not empirically, founded. Instead, wealth is treated favorably. Moreover, the tax code even distinguishes among the rich. Those with capital income among the rich are treated most favorably.

Inadequate Distribution of Wealth

—Taxes do not alter the distribution of wealth. We are very aware of concentrations of wealth in other countries, particularly in Latin America. If polled, most Americans would probably deny the existence of such concentrations at home. And little research material is available on the topic.

Yet, in America in 1970: the top 20 per cent of all families had 76 per cent of all wealth; the top five per cent of all families had 40 per cent of the wealth; the top one per cent owned 25 per cent of the wealth; and the top .3 per cent was shown (in 1972) to have 15 per cent of the personal net wealth.

Despite our feeble attempts at progressivity, studies of the tax system indicate that the distribution of wealth before and after taxes is hardly altered. Wealth remains untouched. The top fifth, the bottom fifth and the middle three-fifths of the population hold onto the same share of wealth before or after taxes.

The ability-to-pay principle is undermined. The rich take more out of the society and make more demands on the society than the non-rich, but they do not pay their fair share for those benefits.

Unfair Personal Income Taxes

—Personal income taxes, particularly in the upper brackets, are not as high as they appear to be. In 1980, the top nominal rate (the rate on the books) was still 70 per cent (it is now 50 per cent). Someone in that bracket in 1980 should have paid about 57 per cent in taxes. The top rate actually paid was 34 per cent.

This means that, by taking advantage of the exemptions allowed by the tax code, Americans in the top tax brackets were able to reduce their tax burden up to 20 per cent. Using 1966 data, one tax analyst determined that the top one per cent of income earners paid only 18 per cent in income taxes.

The bulge is in the middle. In terms of taxes actually paid, middle income earners pay higher taxes than those below them and the super rich. The personal income tax, the most progressive element in the federal tax system, is only slightly progressive. As you get to the top, it becomes regressive (top income earners pay a smaller share of their income in taxes than those with less income).

Regressive Payroll Tax

—The payroll tax is blatantly regressive. General agreement about the tax system exists here. No one denies that the payroll tax takes more from the non-rich than from the rich.

It is levied only on wage income, which is one reason it is regressive. It does not touch income from capital, which becomes more significant as one moves up the income scale.

The payroll tax is also regressive because it is a flat tax on wages and salaries up to a certain maximum. In 1982, it was 6.7 per cent on the first $32,000 of wages. If you made $10,000 or $32,000, you paid 6.7 per cent of your income in payroll taxes. If you made $100,000, you paid 2.1 per cent. At $500,000, you only paid .4 per cent. Most of the income of high-salaried people is excluded.

The result is that the tax is greatest on the middle class and least on the rich. Social Security rates most drastically affect those in the $20,000 to $50,000 income bracket and have the least effect on those with incomes greater than $100,000.

Disappearing Corporation Taxes

—Corporation taxes—taxes on net profits—are disappearing. They have a different tax structure than personal taxes. They are progressive because the owners of corporate stock tend to be the rich or well-to-do. These facts are becoming increasingly irrelevant because this tax is gradually disappearing.

The tax on corporations' net profits in the years before World War II often produced more revenue than the individual income tax or any other tax. After the war, it fell into second place, behind the individual income tax. In the late 1960s, it was overtaken by payroll taxes. During World War II, it provided more than 20 per cent of total government revenues. Today, it provides less than six per cent.

Insignificant Estate and Gift Taxes

—Estate and gift taxes are being eliminated. These taxes, though small, were considered progressive because they fell mainly on the rich, that is, those who had wealth to pass on. Estate and gift taxes have never been a significant part of our tax structure.

Reagan, in what was perhaps a gesture symbolic of his tax policies, pushed through Congress in 1981 a tax bill that essentially abolished these taxes for nearly all Americans. This perpetuates inequality and the concentration of wealth by preserving large fortunes intact.

Besides a concentration of wealth, a concentration of tax savings exists in our society. Tax savings accrue mainly to people with large incomes. According to a Treasury Department study, about 25 per cent of the tax savings in 1974 went to the wealthiest 1.2 per cent of taxpayers. The 160,000 richest taxpayers saved $7.3 billion in taxes—an average of $45,625 each. They saved more than three times the median income in that year.

Most Americans know them as loopholes, deductions, credits, exemptions. The technical term is ''tax expenditures.'' It is a bit confusing, but accurate. Taxes are ways of collecting money. Expenditures are ways of spending money. A tax expenditure is a way of spending money by not collecting it.

Increasing Bias

This bias of the tax system has increased dramatically. The tax loss caused by favorable tax exemptions was only $36.6 billion in 1967. That loss was more than $295 billion in 1983.

Tax expenditures are only for the rich or well-to-do. Tax deductions for individuals provide no benefits to the 69 per cent of taxpayers who do not file itemized returns. Some tax expenditure facts for 1981 are: 74 per cent of the benefits from the mortgage interest deduction went to 19 per cent of taxpayers; 94.1 per cent of the benefits from the exclusion of interest on state and local bonds went to the most affluent taxpayers; 63.5 per cent of the capital gains exclusion benefits the wealthiest taxpayers.

The individual income tax is a hodgepodge of horizontal inequities. It makes sense in economic ethics that people in similar economic circumstances should be treated similarly. This is called horizontal equity. If two people have the same income and the same family circumstances, it is reasonable that they should pay the same amount of taxes.

The system, however, does not work that way. Because of exclusions and deductions, taxpayers with essentially similar incomes end up paying quite different amounts of tax.

Two suburban families, living side by side, with the same number of children of the same age, with total family incomes of $50,000, could be paying taxes that differ by a few thousand dollars. This could happen if one family owned their house and the other rented—the renter could not take advantage of the mortgage interest deduction. Or it could happen if the income of one family was exclusively from wages and salaries, and the income of the other was from wages and capital income. It could also occur if both made the same salary, but one invested part of it to take advantage of certain tax expenditures and the other did not.

An Unfair System

This tax system is unfair. It is unfair because:

—It is unnecessarily complex. Traditionally, a law that is too complex for those upon whom it imposes itself is considered immoral. Our tax laws are such, individually and in the aggregate.

—It increases the tax burden on the poor and middle class. The government must raise money to support its programs. Because of the regressivity in the system, the poor and middle class are paying higher taxes than they would. The government must raise its rates to get enough money to meet its obligations. If only the tax expenditures were eliminated, everyone's tax rates could be reduced by up to one-third, according to some estimates.

"It is our only real mechanism for the redistribution of wealth, but the tax system fails the test of distributive justice."

—It favors the rich. The failure of the tax system to redistribute wealth deprives the disadvantaged of their economic rights. It also allows wealth to be concentrated in the hands of the few. Concentrations of wealth mean concentrations of economic power. And concentrations of economic power lead to great degrees of control of political power. Isn't it, after all, the well-endowed lobbies and the large political campaign contributions that carry the most clout in Washington?

—It is unjustly designed. It is filled with special provisions that favor one segment of the population.

—It does not redistribute income. One needs to remember that it is the only instrument for redistributing income in our society. It is obvious that the before-tax distribution of wealth in the society is unjust, because few control most of the wealth while many lack basic necessities. The system does not alter that distribution of wealth. It dips into wealth as a sieve into water. The before- and after-tax distribution of wealth is the same.

Unnecessary Injustice

None of this is necessary. The usual arguments in favor of tax exemptions and non-progressivity have to do with economic growth. Under the rubric of "capital formation," some tax lobbyists and economists say the special tax provisions and the non-progressivity of the system are needed to foster economic growth.

According to this ideology, the most effective way to stimulate investment is to lighten the tax load on wealthy investors. "Capital formation" should be a red flag to most Americans. Baldly, it means the tax system should be skewed to the advantage of the rich. It is one more Trojan horse for trickle-down economics. But fairness in the system does not have to be sacrificed to economic efficiency.

"The personal income tax, the most progressive element in the federal tax system, is only slightly progressive."

We can have growth with equity. Other industrial countries have demonstrated the possibilities. Ultimately, our rate of investment (of capital formation) depends on a number of factors. There is no simple correlation between tax levels and exemptions and the fraction of total output that society sets aside to invest.

The tax system needs no special provisions. It could be a simple progressive system that would collect all the revenues the government needs to meet its budgetary obligations. All Americans would pay acccording to a progressive scale on their total income. What is now a tax expenditure can become a budgetary outlay, with this advantage: budgetary outlays would be subject to closer scrutiny and greater control.

The debate about the tax system has become one of quantity more than quality. It makes the maximation of profit and wealth more important than the human needs of all people in our society. From a moral and ethical perspective, it should do the reverse.

Ronald D. Pasquariello is senior fellow in urban policy at the Center for Theology and Public Policy. He is the author of Faith, Justice and Our Nation's Budget.

"Most Americans do not realize they have no income that can be legally taxed under our income tax laws."

Eliminate the Income Tax

Irwin Schiff

For over seventy years the Federal government has been illegally collecting income taxes and . . . the courts (if not Congress) know it. Federal judges allow property to be illegally confiscated and knowingly send innocent people to jail in order to intimidate an uninformed public and to aid the IRS in illegally enforcing Federal tax law. The reason the public can be duped and intimidated is because it *does not know the law or even the legal meaning of income.* Most Americans do not realize they have *no income that can be legally taxed under our income tax laws.* . . .

In essence, history has repeated itself and America now finds itself in the same circumstances as Thirteenth Century Egypt. In the Twelfth Century, slaves known as Mamelukes (literally "owned men") were brought to Egypt to serve as soldiers to the Sultan. In 1250 they overthrew the government they were supposed to serve, installed one of their own as Sultan and ruled Egypt for the next two hundred and fifty years. America has essentially the same problem.

The Federal government was created (with limited power) by the people of America in order to protect their unalienable rights to life, liberty, and property. Federal employees were recruited and sent to Washington to administer the laws commensurate with this limited grant of power. Initially, these employees were conceived as servants of the people; however, as the Mamelukes before them, the Federal bureaucracy has now illegally installed itself as the master while the people have become their servants.

In order to manage this, America's Mamelukes had to destroy the very document designed to limit their power and keep them in check. This was largely achieved by those assigned the role of "judges." In

addition, the key ingredient in the expansion and preservation of Mameluke control of America has been their success in installing and *illegally* enforcing the income tax.

Many Americans are now united in a struggle to depose American Mamelukes and to retrieve and reestablish both the document and the freedoms they have destroyed. The days of Mameluke control of America are numbered. More and more Americans are learning to recognize our Mamelukes for the usurpers they are. They are learning how to successfully fight them. . . . The faster we get rid of our Mameluke masters and their illegal income tax the better off we will all be.

Not only is the battle to free America from Mameluke control exciting, it will also allow you to have *more money to spend while enjoying life, your new-found liberty, and your increased ability to pursue your own happiness.* According to the April, 1983 issue of *Life* magazine some 20,000,000 working Americans have stopped filing income tax returns—WE NOW HAVE THE MAMELUKES ON THE RUN! . . .

Wages Belong to Government

It is ridiculous for an American writer to have to argue that the wages of American workers belong to them, but the country is now run in a way that suggests that such wages belong to the government. If a worker has absolutely no control over his wages, can he be said to own them? And if workers do not own their wages, who does? The party who controls their disposition and use does. If the government can send out form letters with mimeographed signatures and receive as much of a worker's pay as it wants— *despite the worker's sworn statement that no such amounts are owed*—then it is obviously the government that controls, and thus owns, those wages; and if the government owns a worker's wages (i.e., his productivity) it reduces the worker to the ranks of a slave. There is absolutely no doubt

Irwin Schiff, *The Great Income Tax Hoax*. Hamden, CT: Freedom Books, 1985. Reprinted with the author's permission.

that the Federal government, through the use of illusionary "legal" procedures, has, in reality, transformed American workers into slaves of the "state." Those who wish to dismiss this charge as utter nonsense simply do not understand the nature of slavery because they automatically associate slavery with chains and whips. Based upon such an image my analogy might appear irresponsible and far-fetched, but the basic difference between a slave and a free man is that a free man *owns* his labor and a slave does not. If someone or something has the power to take the fruits of your labor and you are legally powerless to do anything about it, then you are, in effect, being held in abject slavery. Many people have been left with literally nothing (even slaves have to be fed, clothed, and housed) after the government "requested" that their employers deduct money from their wages and send it to the government in payment of

1. alleged back taxes due;
2. $500 "fines" (for various "offenses" for which no hearings were ever held and for which no court verdicts were ever rendered); and
3. current taxes (for which it is alleged that false claims were made by the worker).

When an American worker explains that anywhere from one-third to all of his paycheck is going to the government to pay taxes, fines, and penalties that, by law he could not possibly owe, how can anyone say that such an individual is not a "slave of the state?"

Government Violates the Law

Tax "laws" were written to be constitutional, but the government violates those "laws" while implementing the tax. For example, the W-4 form itself is an acknowledgement that American workers own their wages just as they own the money in their wallets, the food in their lunch pails, or the cars they drive to work. Employers cannot arbitrarily take this property (wages) and send it to a third party (even the Federal government) without permission. An employee gives his employer *permission* by submitting a W-4 form to the employer indicating various withholding allowances which represent the employee's willingness to have an amount withheld from his pay. If an employee chooses not to "allow" such withholding, he has the legal right to do so by claiming "exempt." It is up to the worker to decide his own tax status and what to "allow" the employer to do with *his* money. Without a court order only the worker has the legal right to determine who gets his wages—and *if he does not have this right he does not own his wages.* . . .

Many Americans believe that without an income tax the country will collapse. The fact is our economy is in very serious danger of doing that *because of* the income tax! We have a current year

trade deficit of over $123.3 billion (which is constantly growing) and more than $200 billion Federal deficit. Our politicians simply lack the backbone to make the necessary political decisions because of the pressure that is generated by special interest groups that always resist the real choices that must be made. The only thing we can count on our spineless politicians to do is allow the nation to drift into bankruptcy.

The Federal government, whose real debt is over $10 trillion, not the puny $1.3 trillion it fraudulently reports—or more than $50,000 for every American—is already bankrupt and there is nothing anyone can do to make it worse. The government's repudiation of this debt will either come now or later and the sooner it comes the better off the country will ultimately be because the longer it is allowed to grow the worse the situation and its adjustment will be. Current deficits in excess of $200 billion alone will be adding $20 billion in interest charges to the following year's budget. In fact, the total interest on the debt is the largest single item in the Federal budget. The Reagan Administration tells us that America had a prosperous year in 1984. If we cannot even come close to balancing the budget in a prosperous year, what will the deficit be in a bad one? If we do not balance the budget in a good year, does anyone really believe that our politicians are serious about *ever* balancing it?

"Tax 'laws' were written to be constitutional, but the government violates those 'laws' while implementing the tax."

On February 4, 1985, President Reagan unveiled his $973.7 billion budget for 1986. It allocated 29 percent for "National defense" and 5 percent for "All other Federal operations," plus 41 percent for "Direct benefit payments to individuals" and 10 percent for "Grants to states and other localities." This means that only 34 percent of Federal expenditures for 1986 will be used for *legitimate constitutional purposes*, while 51 percent will be allocated for *expenditures not authorized in the Constitution*—making 51 percent of the proposed Federal budget illegal!

These figures, however, only represent 85 percent of Federal spending. The remaining 15 percent is allocated *to pay interest on the national debt!* Incredibly, therefore, in 1986 Washington wastrels will spend *three times as much on interest as they plan to spend on running the entire Federal government* (apart from the Defense Department). . . .

The fact that neither the politicians nor most of the American people face is that there can be no balanced budget, no reduction of the national debt, and no sound economy until the Congress turns back to the Federal government its constitutional functions and takes away the unconstitutional encroachments on the rights of the states and the people. The Constitution set very rigorous limits on how and where the Federal government could act. Every dollar spent had to be earmarked for such matters as the national defense, the maintenance of law and order, and other specified activities for the general welfare. And general welfare was narrowly defined, excluding subsidies to identified groups in the population such as farmers, businessmen, college professors, or those who believe that the government "owes" them a living.

"The constitution set even more rigorous limits on the Federal government's power to tax, though that part of our basic law has been forgotten."

Multibillions are spent each year on agriculture and agri-business—and the more the government spends, the worse becomes the plight of the farmer. In order to mute the opposition to special-interest government, the Congress creates tax shelters which aggrandize the rich and impoverish the economy. The government takes from those who produce the sweat of their labors and lavishly bestows it on a small minority. No nation can prosper if it moves down this primrose path, nor can it survive. The way to Hell, we are told, is paved with good intentions—and so is the way to national extinction. Even the neo-socialist governments of Western Europe are beginning to understand this!

The constitution set even more rigorous limits on the Federal government's power to tax, though that part of our basic law has been forgotten. The Founding Fathers realized that direct taxation, even at its most restrained, is a form of extortion. The Supreme Court, in the days when the justices read the Constitution and not the works of Harvard professors, recognized this. This, of course, was before politicians had adopted the rule of "tax and tax, spend and spend, elect and elect." Except in emergencies, such as those created by wars, the government financed itself by indirect, or excise taxes—which I have shown gave the taxpayer the right of choice. One of the major causes of the War of the Revolution was taxation, and the American people and their political leaders never really forgot this until the New Deal and World War II. Then, to make the rising income tax "less painful" the withholding tax was introduced as unconstitutional a way of extorting money (without either a liability or an assessment) as the country has ever seen.

To impose this form of systematic extortion, the Federal government, the Congress, and the "courts" have had to scrap almost every one of the ten amendments in the Bill of Rights. . . . Due process, the right not to be compelled to be a witness against one's self, the protection against unlawful searches and seizure, even free speech—as I have amply demonstrated—have been tossed out the window by tax laws and tax regulations capriciously enforced.

Surrendering the Government

And for what? If the Federal government operated within its constitutional restraints, the excise taxes which supported it through most of the nation's history would be sufficient. There would be no need to surrender the government and the nation to the Mamelukes who are interested not in the general welfare but in the preservation of their power. This country grew from a scattering of states along the Eastern seaboard into a superpower without an inquisitorial system of income taxes. Free Americans produced for themselves the highest standard of living in history, and gave the world a haven for the politically and economically oppressed.

Is the American Dream to become a nightmare? Not if the American people realize that the issue is simple: Either we have a Bill of Rights or we have an inquisitorial and self-defeating income tax. We cannot have both. The question for the American people is, "Which will it be?"

Irwin Schiff is a well-known critic of all governmentally imposed taxes, including social security.

"Any tax [reform] . . . that does not include abolition of the corporate tax really does not deserve the name."

Reduce Corporate Taxes

Bruce Bartlett

Taxation of corporations is among the most complex issues in the field of taxation. It is uncertain, for example, who pays the corporate income tax or whether there is justification for levying it. Professor Arnold Harberger of the University of Chicago, a leading authority on the corporate tax, argues that it lacks any economic rationale whatever. Nevertheless the tax remains a major source of revenue for governments at all levels and periodically draws the ire of tax reformers, who feel that corporations are not paying their "fair share" of taxes—based on a naive and incorrect assumption that, if corporations paid more, other Americans would pay less. Some of this flawed thinking even finds its way into the Treasury Department's recent tax reform proposals. Though recommending a lower marginal tax rate for corporations, the Treasury would end so many deductions that the corporate tax burden in fact would increase.

Discussion of the corporate income tax is clouded by confusion and poor economic analysis. Notes Professor George F. Break of the University of California at Berkeley: "Perhaps no issue in public policy illustrates more clearly people's preference for clinging to simplistic images . . . than does that of the corporation income tax." If these misunderstandings about the nature of taxation lead to a further increase in the corporate tax burden, the economic impact could be severe. Administration officials and legislators thus should not be seeking ways to increase the corporate share of taxation. They should be moving toward abolishing the separate corporate income tax and fully integrating it into the individual income tax system. Such a step would recognize that ultimately it is always people who pay

taxes. And further, shifting the entire corporate burden to the income tax would mean that richer Americans would pay most of these taxes, now classed as corporate but being passed on, in large part, in the form of lost output and higher prices for all Americans.

How Much Tax Do Corporations Pay?

Perhaps the most vocal advocate of higher taxes on corporations is Robert S. McIntyre of Citizens for Tax Justice, a Naderite group, who has written widely on the subject. He mainly examines corporate annual reports or other sources and tabulates the number of companies paying little or no tax. From this he claims that corporations are undertaxed.

McIntyre and his colleagues appeal to the emotions of the overburdened individual taxpayer, easily angered by the suggestion that big business is somehow evading taxation. On numerous occasions, the Treasury Department has attempted to set the record straight, but to little avail. A 1977 study by Treasury economist Seymour Feikowsky, for example, exlained that simply taking the figure for federal income taxes paid from a corporate income statement and comparing it with the firm's income before tax indicates very little. "In almost every case," notes Feikowsky, "the ratio thus computed tells little or nothing about the taxability of the corporation's income." He points out that a number of factors determine the effective corporate tax rate. Among them:

1) Both foreign and domestic tax and income items must be accounted for. Many corporations that appear to pay little U.S. tax pay huge taxes to foreign governments on their foreign operations. U.S. tax law allows companies a credit against U.S. taxes for foreign taxes in order to avoid unreasonable double taxation on the same income.

2) The accounting rules for determining income for

Bruce Bartlett, "The Federal Tax Debate: How Much Should Corportions Pay?" *Backgrounder*, January 8, 1985. Reprinted by permission from The Heritage Foundation.

financial reporting purposes are not the same as those used for tax accounting purposes. In general, reported income is larger than taxable income. While this has no effect on the taxability of corporate income, it tends to make the effective corporate tax rate reported on financial statements appear lower than it really is.

3) Allowances must be made for capital "consumption," that is, equipment worn out during the production process, because this represents a cost to the company. Moreover, depreciation and depletion schedules used for financial reporting and income tax accounting are different.

4) At the corporate and Treasury levels, current year tax accounts are ambiguous measures of the tax attributable to the income of that year. Corporations often have to file amended tax forms for earlier years to use carry-back losses or other items for tax purposes. Firms may have refunds carried forward from previous years, which may make the company's current year tax liability appear much lower at first glance than it really is. . . .

The Case For Repeal

Common myth says that the corporate tax is paid by corporations. It is not. Taxes can only be paid by people, not paper organizations. Ultimately people shoulder the burden of any tax. But in the case of the corporate tax, no one is quite certain which people. Some studies suggest that it is entirely paid by the stockholders—the owners of the corporation—while others suggest that substantial portions of the tax ultimately are paid by the firm's employees and the purchasers of its products in the form of lower wages and higher prices. One thing is very certain, however. All the resources used to pay corporate taxes ultimately must come out of the pockets of individual Americans.

"All the resources used to pay corporate taxes ultimately must come out of the pockets of individual Americans."

Regardless of the share of the corporate tax paid by shareholders, moreover, corporate income is taxed twice: once at the corporate level and again when corporate profits are paid out as dividends. With a maximum corporate tax rate of 46 percent and a maximum individual tax rate of 50 percent, the marginal tax rate on corporate income can be as high as 73 percent.

There is a consensus among economists that the U.S. tax burden on capital is excessive. By making it less attractive to own corporate stock, such taxes force companies increasingly to borrow in order to raise capital. In 1968, corporate equities composed

over 35 percent of household financial assets; now they make up only about 18 percent. Companies thus become more vulnerable in economic downturns, because interest payments must be paid regardless of whether there are profits, whereas dividends need not. In Japan, where companies raise far more capital through borrowing than American firms do, bankruptcy rates are four to five times higher.

Even more important, small firms just starting up generally must raise their capital through equity, because the risk in making such loans is too great for banks. The more difficult the tax code makes it for companies to raise capital through sales of stock, the more difficult it is for new firms to become established. Of course, other taxes—particularly the capital gains tax—also discourage investments in new firms. This is the reason that the 1978 and 1981 cuts in the maximum marginal tax rate on long-term capital gains have triggered a three-fold increase in new issues of corporate common stock and a three-fold increase in trading volume on the New York Stock Exchange. Thanks to these tax cuts, equity capital is much easier to raise today than it was just a few years ago, helping to spur today's high-tech boom.

Wreaking Havoc

The corporate tax wreaks havoc with the U.S. economy. It misallocates capital, diverts corporate behavior from more efficient activities, and imposes an excessive tax burden on capital. This leads to fewer jobs and lower standards of living than if the corporate income tax did not exist. Economist Arnold Harberger calculates the corporate tax's cost to the economy at 0.5 percent of national income. Gregory Ballentine of the University of Florida (currently chief economist for the Office of Management and Budget) puts it at 25 percent of all revenues actually collected by the corporate tax. For these and other reasons, many economists now advocate abolishing the corporate tax.

Liberal Support for Abolition

The case for abolishing the corporate income tax has been accepted by many liberals. In 1977, for example, Americans for Democratic Action, an old-line liberal group, endorsed the following resolution at its annual convention:

> The corporate income tax should be abolished. All corporate income—regardless of whether it is or is not actually paid to the shareholder—should be allocated to individual shareholders and these shareholders should pay tax on this income at their own personal income tax rates. Such a proposal would mean that poor and rich shareholders would pay taxes on their corporate income at rates appropriate to their circumstances. Large shareholders would pay more taxes than they now pay; small shareholders would pay less taxes than they now pay.

Liberal economist Lester Thurow of the Massachusetts Institute of Technology also wants to end the corporate income tax. In his 1980 book, *The Zero-Sum Society*, he argues that:

> The corporate income tax should be abolished regardless of whether you are a conservative or a liberal. Based on our principles of taxation, the corporate income tax is both unfair and inefficient. In a country with a progressive personal income tax, every taxpayer with the same income should pay the same tax (horizontal equity), and the effective tax rate should rise in accordance with whatever degree of progressivity has been established by the political process (vertical equity). The corporate income tax violates both of these canons of equity. Consider the earnings that are retained in the corporation on behalf of the individual shareholder. Low income shareholders with personal-tax rates below the corporate rate of 46 percent are being taxed too much on their share of corporate income. To the low-income shareholder the corporate income tax is unjustly high. Conversely, high-income shareholders with personal-tax rates above 46 percent are being taxed too little on their share of corporate income. To the high-income shareholder the corporate income tax is a tax shelter or tax loophole. As a consequence, vertical equity is being violated. Horizontal equity is also being violated, since two individuals with exactly the same income will pay different taxes, depending upon the extent to which their income comes from corporate sources.

Among leading newspapers, *The New York Times* has endorsed abolition.

Benefits of Repeal

A recent econometric study suggests that merging the corporate tax with the personal income tax could have enormous benefits. Static efficiency gains, that is, immediate increases in output thanks to the more rational taxation of income, would amount to $12 billion more per year in national income (1983 dollars). Abolition would also generate economic activity, resulting in an increase in long-term real economic growth of almost one percent. If this had been instituted in 1973, it would have translated into as much as a $500 billion increase in national wealth; and if this wealth had been reinvested and new income generated, the improvement would have yielded about $1 trillion by today.

Those who favor eliminating the double tax on corporate profits by abolishing the corporate tax do not always agree on how to do it. For example, some experts suggest that dividends received by individuals should be tax-free, while others suggest it would be better to allow corporations simply to deduct all dividends paid from their taxable income as a business expense. Others believe there should be a different tax rate on dividends and on retained earnings, while some would keep the current tax structure but give shareholders credit for their pro-rata share of the corporate income tax paid.

Each method has problems in terms of its impact on different income classes and on corporate

behavior. For example, there is concern that allowing dividends to be deducted would encourage firms to pay out excessive amounts of dividends, rather than using earnings for expansion. This is typical of the practical problems with every method. And although such problems are important, they should not distract policy makers from the fundamental goal of eliminating the corporate income tax. The technical problems can be dealt with as long as the goal is understood.

"Merging the corporate tax with the personal income tax could have enormous benefits."

Despite the strong arguments for abolishing the corporate tax, neither of the two major congressional tax reform proposals—Kemp-Kasten or Bradley-Gephardt—nor the recent Treasury proposal have much to offer on the subject. Each would lower the top statutory tax rate on corporations, but would retain the basic corporate tax structure, which is really the root of the problem. Recent research indicates that the elimination of various tax incentives for corporations, such as the Investment Tax Credit and accelerated depreciation, while continuing to retain the corporate tax, even at lower rates, would slow the economy. Economists at Washington University in St. Louis, for instance, estimate that the Kemp-Kasten "FAST" tax proposal would raise the cost of capital 7.7 percent and reduce the real stock of equipment 6.2 percent by 1989. The Bradley-Gephardt "FAIR" tax proposal, on the other hand, would increase the cost of capital 12.7 percent and reduce the real stock of equipment 8.1 percent by 1989.

The deficiencies of existing proposals should not dissuade reformers from moving forward with steps to reduce the impact of the corporate income tax. It only means that more care should be taken to design a tax reform program that recognizes that "fixing" the corporate tax structure is not enough—it needs to be abolished. . . .

Conclusion

While, at first glance, it might appear that abolition of the corporate tax would benefit the rich, there is no evidence for this. For one thing, one-third of all corporate stockholders have incomes below $25,000 per year. For another, all consumers will benefit from lower prices charged by firms after their taxes fall. In fact, economist Joseph Pechman of the Brookings Institution has concluded that the corporate tax is actually regressive—imposing higher rates on the poor than on the rich. He estimates that in 1975 the corporate tax burden on households with the lowest 5 percent of income was 9.7 percent—but only 3.2 percent on the top one percent. Over one-third of all corporate stock, moreover, is managed by financial institutions, such as pension funds and insurance companies, on behalf of working people. So the corporate tax hits the savings of these middle- and lower-income Americans.

A reduction in taxes that improves corporate profitability would be of greatest benefit to average Americans. And, of course, all Americans would benefit from higher economic growth, more jobs, and a better standard of living. Any tax ''reform,'' therefore, that does not include abolition of the corporate tax really does not deserve the name.

Bruce Bartlett is a John M. Olin Fellow at The Heritage Foundation.

Do Not Reduce Corporate Taxes

Dollars & Sense

In December 1985 the White House drove a nail into the coffin of its own supply-side economics. The administration found itself supporting tax reform legislation that rolled back the tax breaks for business that had been the centerpiece of Reagan's supply-side tax cuts of 1981.

Supply-side gospel was in the soul of most of official Washington in 1981. Congress readily accepted the administration's contention that taxes on business were hurting the U.S. economy. The supply-siders argued that tax cuts which lowered the cost of capital to business would spur investment in new factories and equipment, increase workers' productivity, and create new jobs.

Two provisions in Reagan's Economic Recovery and Tax Act of 1981 pushed the level of tax relief to businesses to new heights. First, the investment tax credit was increased to allow companies to deduct 10% of the cost of new capital investment from their tax bill. In addition, rapid depreciation schedules were introduced into the tax code which allowed corporations to write off investments in plant and equipment from their taxes over five years instead of 15 years.

Five years and some $200 billion of tax cuts later, there is little evidence that these supply-side tax incentives worked. Real business investment increased by an average of 3.2% annually during the first Reagan term—a far cry from the 11% initially predicted by former Reagan budget director David Stockman.

The 1981 tax cuts didn't spur an investment boom but they did create a new phenomenon in the business world: the "zero-tax corporation." Between 1981 and 1984, 129 of the largest nonfinancial corporations paid no federal taxes in at least one of

those years. Fifty of these corporations paid no taxes whatsoever during this time and most actually received rebates for taxes paid in previous years.

Reagan's tax cuts also decreased the total corporate contribution to U.S. Treasury coffers. In 1978, corporate income taxes accounted for 15% of all federal receipts; by 1985, corporate contributions had dropped to only 8%.

The tax cut largesse heaped upon highly profitable corporations like Dow Chemical and General Electric created a political backlash against the Reagan business tax incentives. Though Dow earned $972 million in profits from 1981-84, its tax rate was *negative* (-18.5%)—meaning it actually received $180 million in refunds from the federal government for taxes paid in previous years.

Said one Democratic Congressman, "If you want to know who killed the investment tax credit, the answer is General Electric." GE earned $6 billion between 1981 and 1983 but was able to use corporate tax incentives to eliminate its federal tax liability and collect tax rebates of $283 million.

Numerous other instances of profitable zero-tax corporations (many of them defense contractors) proved to be more than members of Congress could stomach politically. The 1985 tax reform bill passed by the House eliminates the investment tax credit entirely, establishes a minimum corporate tax rate, and scales back accelerated depreciation by about one-third.

Money for Nothing

There is little evidence to indicate that the manufacturing corporations that benefited most from the Reagan tax incentives subsequently increased their investment spending. A survey of corporate behaviour by *Citizens for Tax Justice* (CTJ), a coalition of unions and citizens, found just the opposite: corporations with the biggest tax breaks actually cut back their investment spending.

Dollars & Sense, "What Do Corporations Really Want?" May 1986. Reprinted with permission from Dollars & Sense, 38 Union Square, Somerville, MA 02143.

The CTJ survey included 259 of the largest nonfinancial corporations accounting for half of all pretax domestic profits in the U.S. Forty-four of these companies paid no federal taxes between 1981 and 1984 on their $54 billion of domestic profits, and some received tax rebates from the government, to the tune of $2 billion.

Yet as a group these no-tax companies cut capital spending by 4% between 1981-84 and reduced employment by 6%. The four corporations with the largest net refunds — Boeing, Dow Chemical, ITT, and Tenneco — cut their combined investment by 30% and employment by 19%.

Overall, the survey found no correlation between tax incentives and improved capital spending or job creation. The 103 corporations in the survey which cut investment were taxed at a rate of 16.3%. At the same time, the 156 companies in the survey that increased investment spending between 1981 and 1984 paid an average tax rate of 17.5%.

"Income has been redistributed upward to corporations and their shareholders."

In fact, the 43 highest-taxed companies in the survey, with an average tax rate of 37%, boosted their capital spending by an average of 21%, and added 4% more workers to their payrolls.

If the zero-tax companies were hesitant to buy new plant and equipment, it wasn't because they lacked the cash, but rather chose to spend it on other things. Corporate cash flow jumped 23% in 1983, and 17% in 1984. Between 1981 and 1984, dividend payments to stockholders of the zero-tax corporations were up 22%. A random sample of these companies showed that compensation for chief executive officers jumped 54%.

U.S. corporations pursued a number of other activities during this period. The total dollar value of corporate mergers tripled between 1980 and 1984, reaching $200 billion in 1985. And it is estimated that corporate funds allocated to stock repurchase programs (to fend off hostile takeovers and boost shareholder earnings) jumped fivefold between 1983 and 1984.

Cars and Computers

Though the major manufacturing corporations apparently have not been spending on capital investment, the overall level of investment in the economy did recover as the economy grew after the recession. Investment spending declined by 40-50% in 1982 and 1983 from its 1981 level because of the deep recession, and did not show an increase until the fourth quarter of 1984. But by 1985 investment levels had recovered. Nonresidential fixed investment (which includes business spending for producers'

durable goods and structures) was 30% above the level in 1979 (an appropriate comparison insofar as the economy was growing in both years).

Most of the recent growth in investment spending in the U.S. economy is not related to manufacturing capacity or equipment. Investment patterns now tend to be driven by the needs of a "post-industrial" economy. Business is spending less on new factories and industrial equipment and more on office buildings, hotels, autos for business use, and high tech products — chiefly computers and other office equipment, and communications gear.

Much of the 20% real increase in spending for producers' durable goods (business spending for equipment and machinery) between 1979 and 1984 is accounted for in two categories. Investment in cars for business use jumped by 67%, and business spending on "high tech products" (which includes computing, accounting, and office machines; communications equipment; and instruments) rose by 75%. . . .

Similar trends held for investment in structures. Spending for commercial structures (office buildings, retail) and hotels jumped by about 50% (in real terms) between 1979 and 1984. At the same time investment in industrial and farm structures dropped by 25% and 50% respectively.

This drop in investment in the manufacturing sector is not surprising given the excess capacity in the economy. Only 80% of manufacturing capacity was being used in February 1986. Many manufacturers have more plant and equipment than they can now use, and so have little incentive to build new factories. Given the relatively high unemployment rate, manufacturers can also draw on a large pool of labor to expand output with existing equipment, rather than commit to new capital investment.

Sluggish overall growth in the economy also hinders capital spending. GNP increased by a meager 2.2% in 1985, and the signals are mixed about the future course of the economy. In such an uncertain environment, business is more likely to take a wait-and-see attitude toward investment spending.

It is not surprising that tax incentives have not been able to overcome these obstacles to investment growth. Tax cuts don't spur investment; they do redistribute income. In this instance income has been redistributed upward to corporations and their shareholders. The redistribution of income to the wealthy does little to strengthen overall demand in the economy. Yet it is demand, not lower corporate taxes, which is probably the most important incentive for new business investment.

Dollars & Sense is a monthly publication that focuses on domestic and international economics.

"Step back from the political brink . . . and look at the deficits with [a] scientific eye."

Budget Deficits: An Overview

Frank C. Wykoff

The 1983 federal budget deficit was $195 billion. By 1989, according to the Congressional Budget Office, the deficits will reach $326 billion. The prediction is contingent on sustained real economic growth of 4% per year. CBO warns that with slower growth the 1989 deficit could reach $390 billion.

The deficit is not the accumulated debt from past years of budget imbalance; it is the current flow of red ink—the yearly difference between expenditures and revenues. The prospects for a yearly flow of deficits on the order of $200 to $300 billion may be compared to the entire debt accumulated during World War II. The federal debt was less than $200 billion at the end of World War II.

President Reagan's economic advisers predict that without corrective legislation the "cumulative budget deficits would be more than $1,100 billion over the next six years." In terms of sheer magnitude, our peace-time economy has never experienced such red ink.

David Stockman, ex-director of the Office of Management and the Budget, and Martin Feldstein, chairman of the President's Council of Economic Advisers, find current deficit levels unacceptable. Feldstein and his staff were so appalled at the implications of current budget realities that they refused in February 1984 to forecast the economy in their "Report to The President" without the explicit assumption that the deficits would be corrected. Among other things, they flatly advocate tax increases. Stockman hopes for a political ground swell to pressure budgetary responsibility.

Economists . . . from liberals Joseph Pechman at Brookings and Lawrence Klein at Wharton to conservatives Herbert Stein at the American Enterprise Institute and Milton Friedman at the Hoover Institute . . . believe that current budget policy is intolerable. Only a few fringe supply siders disagree. Indeed the figures are stunning. . . . It is clear that some changes in how we do federal business will have to be undertaken soon.

Objective Analysis

Let's step back from the political brink for a moment and look at the deficits with the scientific eye of the astrophysicist studying Jupiter. Just as the scientist has no emotional attachment to the chemical content of Jupiter's atmosphere, let's study the deficit issue without emotion. Detaching our emotions from the issue may sound simple. It is, in practice, quite difficult. . . . Every policy decision regarding the deficit involves highly emotional and value-laden choices: cut defense, reduce food stamps, raise business taxes, cut medical care to the aged.

What caused the deficits to be so large in the first place? What can be done about them? Is rapid economic growth a feasible solution, or will we have to make structural changes in budget policy? What does it mean to say deficits are "big"? Will they lead to economic collapse or hyperinflation? Act like a foreign journalist studying America's government; pretend that you're interested but uninvolved.

Budget Categories

Like any family, firm, or institution, the federal government has a budget. Whenever expenditures exceed tax revenues, borrowing occurs and the government runs a deficit. Laymen like to compare the federal budget to their own family finance. This comparison is misleading because, unlike an individual, the government does not have a fixed life. A better analogy is a large corporation because corporations also have no fixed life. The corporation and the government need never retire their debt because they have no fixed life.

However, the firm's prospects must grow with its debt issue if it is to remain solvent. Who would lend

Frank C. Wykoff, "What Journalists Should Know About Budget Deficits," *The Journalist*, Spring 1984. Reprinted with permission from the Foundation for American Communications.

money to a firm if its debt obligations were growing faster than the firm's prospects? The government's ability to pay its obligations is dependent on the growth potential of the economy at large. Thus if the interest bill on the debt grows faster than the economy, then potential lenders may begin to question the government's ability to pay. No one is currently suggesting that the deficit issue is that serious.

Let's study the deficit by looking at the two sides of the government budget: expenditures and revenues.

Expenditures

Economists distinguish three types of expenditure items:

(1) "Government expenditures on goods and services" are expenditures for which the government receives a currently produced good or service. Included in this category are purchases of physical goods, such as missile systems, typewriters and highways, and purchases of labor effort, such as soldiers' services, engineers' services, and judges' services. The biggest single item in this category is defense spending, which consumed 26% of total federal outlays in 1983.

"It is clear that some changes in how we do federal business will have to be undertaken soon."

---

(2) "Transfer payments" are expenditures for which no good or service is received by the government. The biggest item here is income maintenance programs: 43.3% of the 1983 budget. Two thirds of these expenditures are for social security and Medicare. Other transfers include Aid to Families with Dependent Children, Medicaid for the poor, unemployment compensation and agricultural subsidies.

(3) Interest payments on the federal debt: The accumulated sum of net deficits in the past is the current stock of debt. The federal government is obliged to pay interest on this debt. This interest payment, over 11% of the budget, was a non-trivial $90 billion in 1983. (Interest is paid to those who hold U.S. government securities and include corporations, financial institutions, the Federal Reserve and individuals.)

Revenues

The revenue side of the federal budget contains three principal sources of taxes: (1) personal income taxes [in 1983] contributed $288.9 billion, or 48% of tax revenues. (2) Payroll taxes, the generic term for social security contributions, provided $209 billion,

35% of tax revenues. (3) Corporation income taxes contributed $37 billion, 6% of Federal revenues. The remaining 11% came from other taxes and fees, such as estate and gift taxes, customs duties and so forth.

We can now write a constraint which the federal budget must always obey:

Borrowing =
(expenditures + transfers + interest)
minus
(income taxes + payroll taxes
+ corporate taxes + other taxes)

We see that the deficit will increase when any expenditure, transfer, or interest item increases or when any revenue item falls. While this may seem trite, it illustrates that one can attribute the cause of the deficits to any spending item which one feels is too large or to any revenue item which one feels is too small.

Thus, to ask "What is the cause of the deficit?" is to ask for a value-laden answer rather than for an analytical response. Economists, wearing hats of politicians, will attribute the deficit to items they don't like: too much defense, overly rapid growth in medical services and so on. The disinterested journalist should not accept these value-laden opinions as scientific analysis.

At the same time we can see that the big ticket items are going to have to be altered if we are to reduce the $200 billion deficit. Thus we cannot assume that defense, income security and taxes are immune from a serious review of the budget.

Historical Perspective

We can look to historical trends in budget policy to learn how we got into this permanent budget imbalance mode. *Figure 1* contains three pie charts which illustrate the allocation of Federal spending by major category in 1960, 1980 and projected for 1987 according to the 1982 Economic Report of the President.

Over the twenty-year interval from 1960 to 1980, defense spending fell from 48% to 21.5% of the budget, while social payments increased from 26% to 49%. The lower defense budget reflected a cooling of the cold war arms race and the decline in post-Vietnam defense allocations. The greater social spending was associated principally with the Johnson Great Society programs. The greatest expansion by far in all social programs was for social security, which reflected both an increase in the number of eligible aged Americans and improved social benefits and Medicare support.

The 1987 figures indicate the priorities of President Reagan, since these projections are based on administration budget proposals. Most dramatic is the reversal of the downward trend in defense spending from 21.5% of the budget to 35%. Equally important is maintenance of social support spending at the relative levels of 1980. Thus, the two major

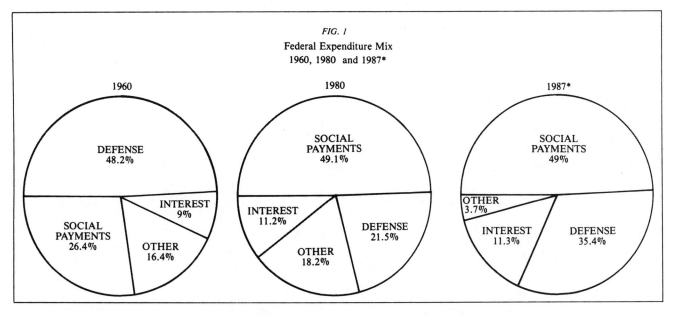

FIG. 1
Federal Expenditure Mix
1960, 1980 and 1987*

1960

DEFENSE
48.2%

INTEREST
9%

SOCIAL
PAYMENTS
26.4%

OTHER
16.4%

1980

SOCIAL
PAYMENTS
49.1%

INTEREST
11.2%

DEFENSE
21.5%

OTHER
18.2%

1987*

SOCIAL
PAYMENTS
49%

OTHER
3.7%

INTEREST
11.3%

DEFENSE
35.4%

Source: Economic Report of the President, February, 1982.

*The 1987 figures are projections.

spending categories which have either grown dramatically in the past twenty years or which are projected to grow dramatically in the next five years are social security and defense spending. Can we seriously expect significant budget cuts if we protect these two items?

Revenues sources have also undergone important changes over the years. *Figure 2* contains two pie charts which illustrate the trend from 1950 to 1980 in federal revenue sources.

In 1950, personal income taxes were the main source of federal revenues, 38%. The corporate income tax contributed 25% and payroll taxes 10%. The 1980 pie chart indicates two striking trends in the composition of federal taxes over the thirty years since 1950: (1) the corporate tax fell from 25% to 13% and (2) payroll taxes increased from less than 10% to more than 30%. Since 1980, the corporation income tax has fallen to 6% of federal revenues. Under existing law, the corporation income tax can

be expected to evaporate. The personal tax rate cuts which received so much press attention will merely have kept personal tax revenues on pace with the overall level of tax receipts.

Growing Deficits

Given the trends for increased social and defense spending coupled with a shrinking corporate income tax, growing deficits should not surprise us. Let's review the record. *Figure 3* plots the ratio of the federal debt to GNP from the end of World War II to the present. Note that until recently this ratio was declining. Even though we continually ran deficits, our economy was outstripping the accumulated debt. While the absolute size of the debt was growing because we were adding new deficits almost every year, it was growing much slower than the economy.

Because GNP, a measure of our ability to pay interest on the debt, was growing more rapidly than the debt itself and because it was incurred mainly to fight World War II, we didn't worry about it too

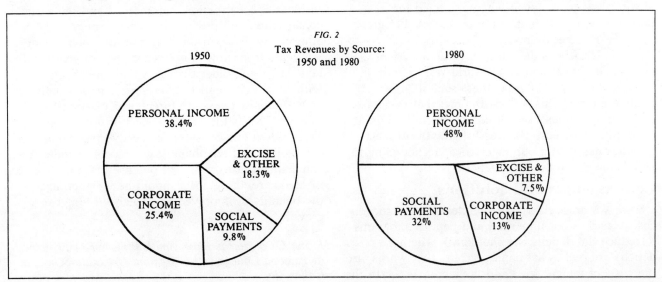

FIG. 2
Tax Revenues by Source:
1950 and 1980

1950

PERSONAL INCOME
38.4%

EXCISE
& OTHER
18.3%

CORPORATE
INCOME
25.4%

SOCIAL
PAYMENTS
9.8%

1980

PERSONAL
INCOME
48%

EXCISE &
OTHER
7.5%

SOCIAL
PAYMENTS
32%

CORPORATE
INCOME
13%

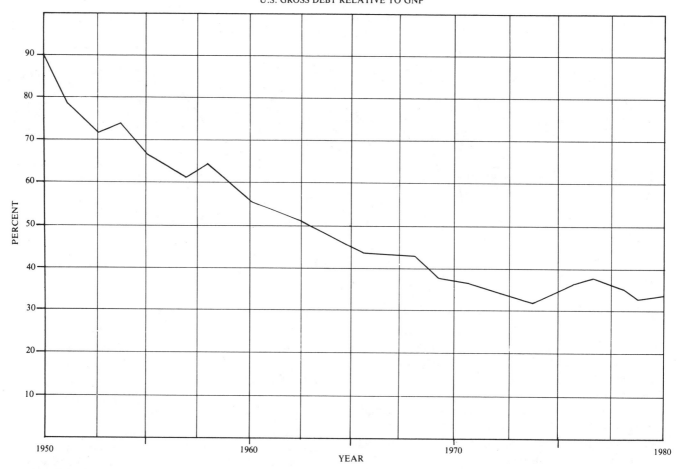

FIG. 3
U.S. GROSS DEBT RELATIVE TO GNP

much. Deficits have fluctuated within a range of 3% of GNP over the past 25 years. We ran only two surpluses in that quarter century in 1965 and 1969.

History discloses that deficits are by no means new. Why do we act so shocked at current deficit projections? Basically, the new deficits differ from historical deficits in three important respects: (1) they are peacetime deficits which will persist regardless of economic performance, (2) in absolute dollar magnitude, the new deficits are very large by historical standards even when corrected for inflation, and (3) deficits are now expected to grow faster than the economy.

By the late 1980s deficits will be about 7% of GNP every year. Since the end of World War II, only in 1968, a war year, did we witness such a large relative budget. This reflects the fact that these are ''structural deficits,'' which unlike ''cyclical deficits'' cannot be resolved by successful growth. At least growth rates within our experience are not going to be adequate to reduce the deficits.

Consequences and Solutions

Since we must either raise unpleasant and socially costly taxes or cut important and popular programs to reduce the deficits, we should ask whether deficits are really that damaging. In other words, are the costs of budget costs and tax increases worth the

benefits? While economists argue about the consequences of deficits, two points are widely shared: (1) deficits, by themselves, will not choke off a cyclical recovery. Deficits are cyclically expansionary, not contractionary. (2) Federal borrowing competes with private borrowers and thus the real cost to the private sector of borrowing is larger with deficits than without them. Any clear supply and demand thinking will confirm this effect.

Eventually, deficit spending will squeeze residential construction, commercial and industrial construction and production of machinery and equipment. Thus, in the long run, perhaps five or ten years from now, our stock of capital goods will be smaller and older than it would have been without deficit finance. Therefore, our productivity and competitiveness are threatened by deficit finance. This is the principal cost of deficit finance. Thus, when one considers corrective measures such as gasoline and telephone taxes, repeal of indexation, value-added taxes, a slower defense buildup or a cut in Medicare, those costs should be weighed against the benefits of improved and balanced long-run growth.

Frank C. Wykoff is Elden Smith Professor of Economics at Pomona College and Claremont Graduate School in California.

"It is . . . truly frightening to think of the people . . . who don't believe that the deficit is a problem."

The Budget Deficit Is a Grave Threat

Fred Shaw

I guess everyone . . . has seen the television show "The Six Million Dollar Man." In the tradition of prime-time TV, it is exciting and a lot of fun. Today, I'm going to give you my "Four Million Dollar Speech."

I hope it will excite your interest and concern, but I don't think you will find it to be a lot a fun.

You see, it will cost the federal government an estimated $100 billion simply to pay interest on the national debt this year. This is about $190,000 each and every minute of the year.

At that rate, in the time I will spend speaking today—a little over 20 minutes—the federal government will run up another $4 million or so in interest due.

Four million dollars.

Even to a banker, that's a lot of money.

As a banker, I view money and credit differently from the way most people do.

Because of my profession, I take the long view. To the banker, money is more than wealth—it is also the means to produce more wealth. Bankers always see money and credit as investments intended to pay off down the line.

Let's Pretend

I want to take the opportunity to give you the commerical banker's perspective on the federal budget and on the deficits that it is producing.

Now we all know that federal budget deficits must somehow be financed. To do this the government can simply increase the amount of dollars in circulation or it can borrow money.

Pretend for a moment that I am the only banker in the country. Were the government to ask me as a banker for a loan to finance the entire federal deficit at the level it is forecast to run over the next few years, I would have to consider very closely whether to make the loan or not.

In making judgements about credit, a banker looks at five factors, which we call the five C's: character, capacity, capital, collateral, and condition.

Judging the government's application by these criteria, I as a banker would conclude that: the government doesn't default on its loans; therefore, it passes the test of character, as longs as the government can tax, it has the capacity to repay; the capital and the collateral are there, because they are the nation itself, *but* both the long-term condition of the economy and the financial condition of the government would give me reason to pause.

Look at the results such a loan would have.

What are we trying to achieve with economic policy?

Ideally, we want a stable economy with low inflation, low unemployment, and strong growth. The last year has seen our economy develop nicely along these lines.

But I am afraid that if large federal budget deficits are allowed to continue, they would make the continued achievement and long-term maintenance of these goals difficult, if not altogether impossible.

Indeed, if these deficits are not soon curtailed, the chances increase that our economy will be plunged right back into recession; interest rates will soar; inflation will rise with a vengeance and double digit unemployment will return.

Quite simply, we must recognize and confront the federal budget problem *now*, or we may seriously jeopardize the standard of living for all of us in the long run.

According to preliminary forecasts by the non-partisan Congressional Budget Office, under the government's current taxing and spending policies the deficit will continue to grow for the foreseeable future. The deficit for 1984 [was] estimated at $185 billion, for 1986, it will be $197 billion; and by 1989,

Fred Shaw, delivered before the Downtown Lion's Club in Memphis, TN, on February 22, 1984.

it is estimated at a staggering $280 billion.

Of course, deficit estimates depend on the economic assumptions used and are tricky to make. But the important point here is, no matter which assumptions one uses, the deficit is already too high, and it will continue to rise.

The deficit problem really has two parts—magnitude and time.

Our annual deficits and the total debt we have established are so enormous that they are difficult for most people to comprehend.

I would like to take a moment to try to put the amounts into perspective.

Defining a Billion

To spend a billion dollars, a shopper would have to spend a hundred dollars a minute—each and every minute—for 19 years.

A billion seconds ago America was still reeling from the surprise attack on Pearl Harbor.

A billion minutes ago, Christ was still living.

A billion hours ago, man had not appeared on earth.

A billion federal budget dollars ago was only yesterday.

We now use the figure of $200 billion as the benchmark for deficits.

Just what is $200 billion?

Look at $200 billion in this way. If you had $200 billion worth of freshly printed $1 bills and you stacked these bills one on top of the other, your stack, when completed, would be more than 14,000 miles high and would weigh approximately 4 billion pounds.

So much for $200 billion.

Remember, this is just one's year's worth of debt. We have amassed a *total* debt in excess of $1.3 trillion. Let's try to get a handle on this one-trillion-plus dollar national debt by looking at what a trillion is.

"If these deficits are not soon curtailed, the chances increase that our economy will be plunged right back into recession."

If you divided one trillion dollars among every man, women and child in the U.S., every individual would get approximately $4,400.

One trillion dollars in single dollar bills would cover 3,931 square miles, an area almost four hundred times the size of Washington, D.C. Placed end to end, they would stretch around the world 1,800 times.

In 1982 prices, one trillion dollars would buy more than 172 million new automobiles and more than 18 million new homes.

Remember, though, that our national debt is actually 1.3 trillion dollars.

As for the time component, for the last 30 years Congress has consistently expanded the size of the federal budget.

Like an adolescent who has just discovered credit cards, the lawmakers have just as consistently spent beyond our means.

In 1970, the entire federal budget was $200 billion and that year we had a $2.8 billion deficit.

In 1983, the federal budget exceeded $800 billion and we had a deficit of about $200 billion. Our current deficit exceeds the total amount of money spent by the government just 13 years earlier!

If the government in Washington continues its present course, it is truly frightening to think what might happen in the next thirteen years.

Myths of the Deficit

It is also frightening to think of the people—our families, friends, colleagues, neighbors—who don't believe that the deficit is a problem. Besides the difficulty of comprehending the numbers involved, there are myths in this country that blind people to the threat the federal deficit represents.

John Kennedy once said, "The great enemy of the truth is very often not the lie—deliberate, contrived and dishonest—but the myth—persistent, persuasive and unrealistic."

The truth is that the federal deficits must be reduced or we will all suffer, but two pervasive myths concerning deficits must be dispelled before serious efforts can be made at reducing them.

The first myth is that the deficit is somehow a short-term glitch: that it has really only been with us for the last couple of years and can easily be eradicated by a robust economic recovery.

The fact is, however, that the deficits we are now faced with have been structurally embedded into the economy. Since 1961, the federal government has experienced 22 deficits and just one surplus. Even under the most optimistic of growth scenarios—unless major changes are made—we will be facing deficits at least until the end of this decade and probably beyond that.

Does the Deficit Matter?

The second budget myth is that the deficit really does not matter. While we know it is out there, it really does not touch on our everyday affairs. And besides, when figured as a percentage of the Gross National Product or the total amount of debt outstanding, the deficit doesn't look that large.

Such thinking is not only terribly misleading, it is downright dangerous.

Mammoth deficits do affect our everyday lives—they help determine how many Americans are working, how much the value of their dollar is eroded by inflation and how difficult it is for businesses and consumers to get credit.

As a banker accustomed to taking the long view—that is, looking at money and credit as an investment—allow me to explain how the deficit affects the everyday lives of every American.

The important question is not how large the deficit is compared to the Gross National Product or total outstanding debt. The important question is how much net new savings the federal government will absorb trying to finance the deficit and how much will be left over for private investment in plant and equipment, research, technology and consumer goods.

Investment, in other words, which is essential if our economy is to keep moving and our standard of living is to be maintained.

Traditionally, the federal government has used about one-quarter of our national savings pool.

If deficits continue at their current high level, this figure will be closer to one-half to two-thirds of that pool—year after year.

The obvious result of this course is that interest rates are pushed higher and higher, since there is greater competition for the same amount of capital. Think about that the next time you or someone you know wants to purchase a car or a home.

Putting Off the Day of Reckoning

It has been said that our nation pays the debts of the last generation by issuing bonds payable to the next generation. This is like using a giant chain letter to pass along the day of reckoning from one generation to the next, thankful that we were able to avoid dealing with it. What we are really doing is straining future generations with a sea of red ink.

Furthermore, we not only owe our debt to future generations, we owe a substantial part of it—as much as 30 percent, according to some estimates—to overseas interests who purchase federal securities as an investment. I think it is all well and good for anyone who wants to invest in America to do so—but what happens if one morning they wake up and decide not to do so anymore? What happens then?

I do want to point out here that in modern economic theory, the budget does not have to be balanced every year.

In a recession, such as the one we just went through, a deficit may provide a cushioning effect—in part because slack production means there is less overall competition for funds.

But as the economy picks up, as it has this last year, demand for funds begins to rise and the deficit begins to have a negative drag. The greater the deficit, the greater the drag. Period.

As an alternative to borrowing, the federal government may decide to finance its deficits by creating more money. Then we will suffer from inflation. In the classic economic definition, we will

have more dollars chasing the same amount of goods.

Take a moment to recall how bad our inflation was just four years ago.

In 1980, we had an inflation rate in excess of 20 percent. Twenty percent annual inflation means that in addition to the normal income tax you pay the government, you also pay a 20-cent-on-the-dollar "penalty tax."

When inflation is on the rise, no one has any incentives to save or invest. Industry becomes starved for capital, savers watch their nest eggs disappear and recession returns to the horizon. In addition, interest rates rise.

"We must recognize and confront the federal budget problem now, or we may seriously jeopardize the standard of living for all of us."

That's right. Whichever course the government takes to finance its deficit—borrowing, creating money or a mix of the two—interest rates rise.

And rising interest rates bring higher unemployment in their wake.

For example, high interest rates cause our dollar to gain value in comparison to foreign currencies. Since 1980, the dollar has appreciated by 50 percent against the money of other nations. As a result, American goods and services became extremely expensive in foreign markets. Exports were lost, and trade deficits resulted ($65 billion last year alone).

In the abstract, these figures may not seem all that important. You might think they are gathered simply to keep an economist busy or to fill the appendix of yet another government report.

But the fact is, every billion dollars worth of American exports creates 25,000 American jobs. And since 1978, more than 80 percent—or almost 5 million—new manufacturing jobs in the U.S. were export-related. Chances are good that the livelihood of someone you know depends in some fashion on American exports.

Reduce Federal Spending

I have gone into such detail and depth today to underscore the fact that the only way we are going to extricate ourselves from this deficit mess is to significantly reduce overall government spending. Budget reductions must be made to maintain the four goals of economic policy: stability, growth, continued low inflation and low unemployment. All types of government spending should be candidates for reduction.

Federal spending falls into four general areas: defense, direct benefit payments for individuals known as entitlements; interest on debt; and a mish-mash group called non-defense discretionary expenditures, which includes most federal departments, such as Treasury, Labor and Commerce. This last group makes up about 14 percent of the entire federal budget.

Of course, Congress appropriates the money that runs the government, but much of that money must first be requested by the federal bureaucracy.

The late Leonard Reed, a writer and former bureaucrat himself, has given probably the best description of how the bureaucracy views its role in the federal budget process.

"No activity in a government agency is given as high a priority as securing and enlarging its budget," he once wrote. "Bureaucrats almost invariably believe in the function their agency exists to perform, whether it is providing information to farmers or preserving the national forests. A new bureaucracy, the darling of the Administration that establishes it, has a missionary zeal about its function. As the bureaucracy ages, it loses glamour and finds itself expending an increasing share of its energy on obtaining funds.

"Since there is a certain logic to the proposition that without money an agency can't function," Reed concluded, "the bureaucrat . . . finds nothing wrong with spending more and more of his time and attention aiding the quest for more money, much of which is now added to support the large money-raising apparatus that has grown up in the agency."

One of the more notorious results of this evolution is Washington's end-of-the-year spending spree. In the weeks before the September 30 deadline, it is harvest time for consultants and contractors as each agency tries to use up all its appropriated funds so that it won't appear to have been overbudgeted.

I don't need to go into the details of horror stories on federal agency expenditures. We've heard them so often that they have become familiar. I can only hope that this familiarity will breed contempt—contempt for the practice of putting narrow bureaucratic interest above the interest of the public.

Since defense and direct benefit payments for individuals made up about 71 percent of government expenditures last year, it is obvious that these areas must be examined closely. The entitlement programs—programs like Medicare and Medicaid, veterans' benefits and the like—can only be changed by changing the underlying laws which entitles people to benefits. Unless the laws are changed, this category will continue to make up almost half of the budget.

Learning Unselfish Discipline

Fortunately, since we live in a democracy we can deal with the deficits—but it is going to take a large degree of unselfish discipline.

Democracies are deficit prone exactly because it is far more pleasant to raise spending than to reduce it. As can be expected, the Santa Clauses get re-elected and the Scrooges get rejected.

We all know how easy it is to add an extra item to our budget—to expand our wish list. But try to delete an item from the government budget—whether it be a dam or a highway, a military base or a new type of tank—and the special interests will cry out in wounded anguish.

"If a national debt is excessive, it becomes a national curse."

But the funny thing is, you and I make up the special interests. Take a minute to think about whether you receive some sort of government benefit.

—Are you a farmer earning thousands of dollars for not planting a crop?

—Are you a small businessman taking advantage of government loans?

—Are you a parent with a child in college who receives a government subsidized loan?

The list could go on and on. The important point is that we have got to realize that we cannot reduce the deficit unless and until we ourselves as individuals make some sacrifice.

As a banker familiar with the political process, I fear that future attempts to deal with the entitlement problem will run the danger of ending up like the recent compromise on funding the largest entitlement of all—Social Security.

True, the compromise was a step in the right direction, but it did not go far enough and did not solve the problem of the long-run viability of the system. There was too much emphasis on increases in taxes rather than reductions in benefits. More work needs to be done on reducing the growth of benefits in the long run.

Taxes: Not the Answer

Since I've brought up that great bugaboo—taxes—I should explain how banking economists view the issue.

Taxation affects more than the balance sheet of a government—indeed it has long been recognized that taxes may have a negative effect on the long-run health of the economy. The power to tax is truly the power to destroy. Furthermore, in the context of the deficit, tax increases may fail to reduce the deficits by shifting the political focus away from the need to reduce expenditures.

Let me give you a recent example.

Not too many months ago, Congress approved a $98.3 billion tax hike bill. For every $1 of tax increase mandated by this bill, we were supposed to see $3 in corresponding spending reductions. The legislation was hailed as a great fiscal achievement.

But we have yet to see the spending reductions which we were promised, and, furthermore, economists tell us that this legislation has a negative impact on the prospects for long-term economic growth by decreasing incentives to invest.

Taxes are not the answer to the deficit crisis.

The Impact of the Deficit

In conclusion, I would like to again stress that we cannot expect to solve the deficit crisis until we appreciate how it affects the quality of our lives.

More than 200 years ago, Alexander Hamilton wrote that a national debt, if it is not excessive, will be to us a national blessing. Riding his train of thought a little further down the line, *if* a national debt is excessive, it becomes a national curse. Our national debt threatens to be the cause of great harm to all Americans. It has already turned us all—you, me, every American alive plus all those who will be born for years to come—into history's largest debtor class.

When Hamilton was alive, individuals who could not pay their debts were thown into debtors' prison.

Our accumulated deficits are slowly but surely incarcerating our entire population in what soon may become an inescapable debtors' prison. The walls of this prison are not made of brick, concrete and steel. Instead, they are composed of high interest rates, inflation, unemployment and sluggish investment.

"Our accumulated deficits are . . . incarcerating our entire population in what soon may become an inescapable debtors' prison."

Our key to escape may be found by reducing these deficits through discipline in the spending process.

For that key to work, however, we must start to turn it around now.

We must begin to make it clear to our elected representatives that we will no longer tolerate the buy-now-pay-whenever spending binges which got us into this deficit mess. And, we must begin to support and work for candidates who have pledged to put a lid on government spending wherever it originates.

But remember, this course will also require some degree of sacrifice from all of us. Each of us must be willing to forego some little "goodie" the government has provided—whether it be an increase in a benefit check, a tax loophole or whatever. We are the ones who are going to have to act if we ever hope to see the deficit logjam broken.

Let's do it now . . . before it is too late.

Fred Shaw is a banking advisor for the American Bankers Association and president of the Union National Bank & Trust Company in Elgin, Illinois.

"Today's conventional fears about those big bad deficits amount to little more than mass paranoia."

The Budget Deficit Is Not a Threat

Harold B. Ehrlich

Virtually all of the economic statistics reported recently have seemed favorable—in one way or another. Industrial production showed gains, as did retail sales. Total employment rose, while unemployment declined. Inventories rose, but not excessively in relation to the strong pattern of final sales seen in 1983. Inflation continued to run at modest rates. All in all, the economy demonstrated further improvement, and, crucially, at a *sustainable* pace, with no signs of "overheating" anywhere in sight.

Nonetheless, shrill warnings about the dire consequences of Federal budget and U.S. trade deficits have emanated from governmental, corporate, and financial leaders alike. People seem fearful that this combination of red ink flowing both from Washington and from our foreign business dealings somehow would cripple the recovery, rekindle inflation, or cause some other calamity. Thus, despite the favorable manner in which the economic environment has been shaping up, there have been proposals to raise taxes and to institute other measures designed to close these financial gaps.

A Healthy America

At the moment, economic conditions in America could hardly be much better—despite some troublesome exceptions. For example, retail sales have continued to improve, but at diminishing rates compared with the torrid pace seen last fall. Similarly, industrial production has continued to climb, but, again, at a diminishing rate. On the whole, neither manufacturers, wholesalers, nor retailers have accumulated excess inventories. By the same token, few among these groups of businessmen have overbuilt physical facilities to any extent.

Harold B. Ehrlich, "Who's Afraid of the Big Bad Deficit?" *USA Today*, May 1984. Copyright 1984 by The Society for the Advancement of Education.

Above all, costs have not risen appreciably, and productivity has improved considerably. Therefore, profits and cash flow have soared, in many cases to record levels.

At the same time, conditions in the jobs market have also improved impressively. More people are employed than ever before; the average number of hours worked each week has risen markedly; wage rates have lifted (although not run away); and unemployment has diminished, even though it is still great. Thus, aggregate personal income—particularly after taxes—has been climbing steadily, continuing month after month to set new records for the postwar period. Aided by gains in stocks, bonds, and real estate prices, personal wealth has also reached new highs. With all of this prosperity at hand, and with inflation truly low by the standards of recent years, consumers obviously feel good enough about their position to boost their buying actions as well as their intentions for the future.

Similarly, corporate earnings, cash flow, and new order rates have remained so strong that capital expenditures for new plant and equipment now are programmed to rise more than nine per cent in "real" (inflation-adjusted) terms for 1984 over 1983. Moreover, much of this new spending is slated for equipment designed to promote both output and productivity, without adding greatly to floor space. Thus, it would appear that the usual cycle of plant expansion and inventory accumulation has not even begun, which means that the U.S. economy still has plenty of room for further growth before developing significant strains.

Admittedly, conditions are still depressed in a number of "heartland" areas and industries. However, in many other places and businesses, particularly in the computer and related fields, things are literally booming. Looking ahead, it is hard to visualize what barriers would stop this upsurge, granting that the *rate* of gain may well be somewhat slower for a while as compared with the heady advance of 1983. After all, the vast majority of people and companies alike are earning good money, have substantial borrowing capacity, and there is plenty of credit available. Besides, continued growth of military spending should provide additional sustenance for the overall economic expansion.

Keep in mind that the favorable environment which exists in the U.S. today has emerged *despite* the persistence of high interest rates (particularly in "real" terms), despite record Federal deficits (that were *unexpected*), even despite America's massive and growing deficiency in foreign trade. Think how good things could really become in the event that one or more of these global problems appeared on its way to resolution. Considering how much conditions have improved in the face of such substantial adversities, why should people be so afraid of those big bad deficits?

Real and Imagined Fears

To begin with, it is conceivable that the Federal Reserve, the Administration, or even Congress could initiate inappropriate countermeasures designed to close the budgetary gap—either in the coming months or, more likely, shortly after the presidential election—if only because so many influential people are pressing for such actions. For instance, in a speech to the Mortgage Bankers Association of America on Jan. 12, [1984] Federal Reserve Board member Lyle Gramley stated that present Federal deficits pose "a very serious threat to the economy and to the financial markets." He went on to imply that, unless this fiscal thrust were curbed, interest rates were likely to climb high enough to choke off the recovery. Speaking to a group of prominent businessmen in Florida on the very next day, Fed chairman Paul Volcker conveyed much the same message.

Among the denizens of the investment and banking communities, the impact of large deficits upon the economy as well as the markets is the subject of daily discussion. A recent nationwide survey of top leaders from a wide variety of other industries showed that they also viewed continuing large deficits as far and away the nation's most serious and pressing economic problem. Martin Feldstein, chairman of the President's Council of Economic Advisors, apparently feels so fervently about the need to close the deficit, and quickly, that he has been willing to risk his prestigious job by publicly voicing this conviction in apparent conflict with White House policy.

However, even Pres. Reagan now seems to think the issue sufficiently pressing to consider appointing a special commission charged with conducting a study and making recommendations. (Fortunately, sadly, or amusingly—depending upon one's point of view—the findings of this commission would not be issued until early 1985, well after the election.) These days, even at social gatherings, the deficit seems to generate much hand-wringing and heated conversations.

Granting that these concerns may be muddled and miguided, nonetheless, they have been responsible in part for interest rates being higher than indicated by reasonable analysis. In addition, much of this misunderstanding about the derivation, financing, and economic impact of the deficit may prompt untimely tax increases, unnecessarily large or otherwise inappropriate expenditure reductions, even excessively restrictive monetary policies. Thus, the real problem with the present deficit is not so much the realities of what it is all about, but the *perceptions* of it, which—even though faulty—can exert material pressures upon both financial market prices and governmental activities.

The Deficit Takes the Blame

It is a fact that a great many influential people truly believe big deficits cause inflation, recessions, "crowding out" of private investment, high interest rates, low profits—and, who knows, maybe even halitosis or lung cancer! It can be argued that none of these notions are *necessarily* accurate, that the economic impact of governmental deficits depend upon many other factors operating at the same time. These include the state of employment and capacity utilization, the thrust of private-sector demand, the total availability of credit, the manner in which the deficit was generated, the means by which it was financed, and—perhaps above all—its size and *direction* relative to the size and direction of the Gross National Product.

"The real problem with the present deficit is not so much the realities of what it is all about, but the perceptions of it."

Studies by a number of noted economists have reached similar conclusions, findings that generally have contradicted the conventional wisdom about deficits. For example, there seems little evidence to support the widely accepted contention that large deficits usually cause high interest rates. To the contrary, in fact, the data tend to show a converse correlation. In addition, deficits do not seem to exhibit much relationship with interest rates, inflation, or the course of monetary policy. If anything, examinations of history have suggested that tax increases designed to reduce the deficits have tended to cause *higher*, rather than lower, interest rates! Finally, there seems to be no factual support for the belief that government financial requirements resulting from big deficits tend to "crowd out" private borrowing and investment.

Fear Will Subside

In any event, today's fears about the consequences of budgetary imbalance should subside in time, not because people may suddenly experience some great enlightenment, but because the magnitude of future deficits probably will prove much lower than expected at present. Moreover, the gap should be closing. First of all, the expenditure side of the equation should continue to run below present projections, as has been happening for some time now, because the costs of goods and services—*i.e.*, rates of inflation—have been overestimated in the official budget. . . .

"Today's fears about the consequences of budgetary imbalance should subside in time . . . because the magnitude of future deficits probably will prove much lower than expected."

Secondly, in contrast to the overestimation of government spending, Treasury tax receipts have been greater than expected, because the recovery has been more substantial than had been forecast, particularly for personal income and corporate profits. So, for the first two months of the fiscal year, revenues jumped some 11% above the same period of last year—this despite the cut in tax rates which took effect last July [1984]. Finally, Federal revenues should get another boost from the recent hike in the Social Security levy, from other tax increases passed as part of the 1982 Tax Equity and Fiscal Responsibility Act, and from the fact that both individual and business incomes are really rocketing upward now.

The combination of this surge in receipts, but only modest increase in spending, has caused the deficit decline already. Specifically, for the first two months of [1984], the budgetary gap ran at a rate of little more than $160,000,000,000, well down from the $195,000,000,000 recorded for last year, and even short of the $180,000,000,000 projected for all of this fiscal year. Moreover, given the way things are going now, we should not be surprised to see the deficit for fiscal 1984 come under $160,000,000,000 and possibly even as low as $150,000,000,000.

Given such an outcome, the Federal deficit would be running at a rate of around four per cent of the Gross National Product, down from approximately six per cent of GNP for fiscal 1983. Above all, the deficit's *relationship* to GNP would be diminishing because the direction of the deficit would be downward, while the direction of the GNP would be still strongly upward.

Looking ahead . . . we can visualize the deficit narrowing to a range of $125-$140,000,000,000, even without any increments in tax rates—admittedly, a questionable assumption for next year. Thus, given no major alterations in either taxation or spending programs, the Federal deficit could be running less than three per cent of U.S. Gross National Product. . . .

In addition, state and local governments in *aggregate* are now racking up a substantial surplus, in contrast to the large deficits recorded in past years. Specifically, for the period ended Dec. 31, 1983, the revenues of all state and local governments exceeded their expenditures by some $52,000,000,000, and it looks like another surplus of perhaps as much as $65,000,000,000 could be recorded for calendar year 1984. Adding these positive figures to the Federal government's negative ones would produce an over-all national deficit of approximately four per cent of GNP for 1983, and between two and two and one-half per cent of GNP for 1984. Thus, on an aggregate national basis, the governmental fiscal deficiency is declining (without any active new measures) at an even faster rate—relative to GNP—than at the Federal level alone.

These rates and trends do not portend much danger of collision between the financing requirements of the public and private sectors, certainly not with corporate cash flow burgeoning. Keep in mind that the Treasury has been raising huge and increasing sums of new money for some time now, without any concomitant "crowding out" of private borrowers from the marketplace. Individual as well as business loan demands have been accommodated well, despite the competition for funds from governmental agencies, and despite the "snug" monetary policy which has been maintained by the Federal Reserve. Interest rates have even declined in the bargain! Certainly, Federal budgetary requirements have not by any means stymied private capital investment, which rose in 1983 and is slated to increase even more rapidly.

Looking ahead, public financing should subside shortly, fortunately, just when borrowing by people and companies could increase. Given continued low inflation, the Federal Reserve should maintain at least a "neutral" monetary stance, and may even relax its posture somewhat. From this point of view, we can see no reason for interest rates to rise much, and they should decline once people begin to understand that today's conventional fears about those big bad deficits amount to little more than mass paranoia.

Harold B. Ehrlich is chairman of the board of the investment firm Bernstein-Macaulay, Inc. in New York City.

"Forecasters are no more reliable than fortune tellers or astrologers."

The Deficit's Threat Cannot Be Determined

Thomas M. Humbert

As Congress convenes to discuss impending federal deficits, gloomy forecasts are treated almost with the reverence once given to pronouncements from Mount Olympus. Lawmakers rushing to offer proposals—usually tax increases—to bridge the budget gap seldom pause even for a moment to question the predictions of the economic soothsayers.

Yet a review of the "science" of economic projections indicates that such forecasters are no more reliable than fortune tellers or astrologers. Government predictions of deficits, in particular, are often wide of the mark. At the beginning of each year, the Office of Management and Budget (OMB) estimates the budget deficit and other economic aggregates for the fiscal year beginning nine months later. OMB's yearly budget deficit projections have on average erred by 254 percent of the estimated deficit between 1971 and 1983. OMB has come within 50 percent of the actual deficit only five times in the last thirteen years. Moreover, OMB's errors are as likely to underestimate deficits as overestimate them.

Example: The President's FY 1983 Federal Budget, prepared by OMB, *under*estimated the active deficit by over $100 billion—a 100 percent forecasting error; OMB later *over*estimated the same deficit in a forecast issued just two months before the end of the fiscal year—by $14.4 billion. . . .

Dismal Record

Given this dismal track record, how much should policy making be based on OMB's estimates of the deficit? Not much—particularly when presumed deficits become the rationale for massive tax increases. . . . OMB's past deficit errors have tended to follow the economic cycle closely. In recoveries,

actual deficits typically have been smaller than OMB predicted. OMB forecasting errors also have tended to grow as the recoveries advanced.

Why does OMB miss the mark? The major reason is the inherent difficulty confronting any forecaster trying to predict the economic cycle, particularly changes in such crucial variables as Gross National Product (GNP), unemployment, and inflation (CPI). OMB's yearly GNP estimates erred an average of 36 percent between 1977 and 1981. Its forecasts of percentage changes in CPI erred by an average of 130 percent between 1976 and 1982, and its annual estimates of percentage changes in unemployment erred by over 50 percent in the same period. Even a small change in these fundamental economic assumptions can have massive effects on budget deficits. A 2 percentage point sustained increase in the rate of economic growth, for example, would reduce the cumulative FY 1984-1987 budget deficit by $440 billion, or one-half of its current projected level.

The OMB is not the only forecaster to miss consistently, so errors cannot be blamed on politics or overoptimism among White House economists. A survey of leading private sector forecasters, whose clients pay for accurate information, shows that they miscalculated the timing of the economic recovery and missed the 1982 GNP growth by as much as 4 percentage points, or $120 billion in some cases. The bipartisan Congressional Budget Office (CBO) also miscalculated the 1982 deficit by $80 billion—a whopping 80 percent error.

Impossible to Predict

The problem is not with the forecasters, but with the inherent impossibility of predicting even a few months in advance the performance of a volatile $3 trillion economy. To generate accurate economic projections, forecasters would need perfect foresight of the economic cycle, business and consumer

Thomas M. Humbert, "Understanding the Federal Deficit, Part I: How Forecasters Get It Wrong," *Backgrounder*, January 27, 1984. Reprinted with permission from The Heritage Foundation.

psychology, the impact of upcoming government taxes, the effects of budget and monetary policy, foreign shocks such as the OPEC oil price runup, and such events as natural disasters and wars. Even then, the forecasters would face the sticky task of translating these factors into government revenue and expenditure figures.

In order that the public be protected from policies based on flimsy forecasts, every congressional initiative or Administration budget request based on an economic forecast should be accompanied by the track record of the forecasting agency. In this way Americans could judge how much credence to place in the predictions underpinning the legislation being passed in their name.

In short, no forecaster can be expected to model accurately the activities and daily decisions of millions of economic actors. Human behavior, unlike natural phenomena, cannot be fully quantified. This is because human beings have free will and freedom of choice, and are never entirely predictable. Given these inherent limitations, economic policy should not be guided by forecasts, especially in turbulent times, but by fundamental principles designed to create a stable climate for long-term economic growth. If Congress cannot read the future, it should not keep trying to make a mid-course correction whenever a new prediction is released. It should chart a course of tax, regulatory, and spending policies to encourage risk-taking and reward work— and stick to it.

Influence on Economic Policy

Economic forecasting plays a fundamental role in economic policy making. While official government forecasters claim that their long-range assumptions are not intended as precise forecasts of economic conditions, it is nonetheless true that these budget assumptions, as well as private sector forecasts, are used to justify economic policy initiatives of critical importance. In particular, forecasts of enormous budget deficits "as far as the eye can see" have fueled the movement pressing President Reagan to back major tax increases.

OMB's record of predicting budget deficits and other economic aggregates is distressing. Each January, OMB issues a forecast in the *Budget of the United States Government* for the fiscal year beginning the following October. OMB also updates this budget forecast in the *Mid-Session Review*, published around July each year. . . .

Underlying Problems

The underlying problem with deficit forecasting is that economists cannot measure the deficit directly. The deficit is the difference between two very large numbers: estimated government outlays and receipts. A small percentage change in either of these two massive numbers can have a large impact on the residual government deficit. Just a 2 percent increase in government revenues, and a similar decrease in government outlays, for example, could change the budget deficit by $30 billion.

There are a number of reasons why government and private forecasts alike have been wide of the mark in estimating federal revenues and outlays.
Economic Cycles

No forecaster has been able to predict the economic cycle with consistency. Yet even a small change in the underlying assumptions about GNP, inflation, and interest rates can have a dramatic effect on budget deficit forecasts.

Economic growth—The economic growth rate has enormous consequences for the budget deficit. During periods of rapid expansion, business profits, wages, interest, and dividend income surge while the Treasury gains new tax revenues generated from these sources. Greater economic growth, meanwhile, reduces government expenditures, since more jobs mean less unemployment compensation, welfare, and other social spending. As such, the deficit is cut from two directions.

"Errors are as likely to underestimate deficits as overestimate them."

The most powerful way to cut the deficit is by economic growth. According to CBO calculations, a 2 percentage point sustained increase in economic growth would reduce the cumulative deficit by $440 billion. . . . If the economic forecasts underestimated growth by such a degree, that alone would reduce upcoming budget deficit projections by as much as one-half.

Inflation—Inflation directly affects federal spending and revenues. Inflation boosts nominal corporate profits, personal incomes, payrolls, and sales and therefore increases tax collections—particularly as people are pushed into higher income tax brackets. (Beginning in 1985, however, indexation of brackets will reduce these inflation-induced tax revenues.) Federal spending also increases due to inflation, because many government programs, including Medicare, Social Security, and federal pay, increase with inflation. . . .

Interest rates—The $1.4 trillion government debt has made interest expense one of the largest and fastest growing items in the federal budget, skyrocketing to nearly $130 billion in FY 1983. Unanticipated fluctuations in interest rates can have significant effects on the accuracy of federal budget forecasts. . . .

Unemployment—A falling unemployment rate reduces unemployment compensation expenditures and other social welfare spending. Increased employment expands the tax base and therefore sharply increases tax revenues. . . .

Complexities in Revenue and Outlay Estimates

Even if the economic cycle could be gauged accurately, the forecaster must convert the resulting economic assumptions into revenue and outlay estimates. To do this, he must try to unravel the complexities of spending patterns, the timing of income tax payments, the use of tax deductions and shelters, the utilization of government programs, and many other factors. Errors made in these elements are compounded in the final revenue and outlay forecasts and then magnified in his deficit projection.

Legislative Changes

Forecasts assume certain legislative changes in tax and budget policy. But even the most seasoned political pundits rarely predict accurately what Congress and the President will do.

Other Surprises

There are many other unexpected events that may trigger a different deficit than that projected by economists. A natural disaster, such as a drought or a bad winter, can drastically alter government outlays and consumer spending patterns and have a significant effect on the deficit.

OMB Is Not Alone

OMB is not the only agency or organization to have trouble in developing accurate forecasts. Some critics say OMB's forecasts naturally are inaccurate because politics clouds its decision making. Others charge that administrations are inherently less competent or motivated than the private sector or the Congressional Budget Office. A recent review of both private sector and CBO forecasts, however, reveals that poor performance is not an OMB monopoly. . . .

"[The] record of predicting budget deficits and other economic aggregates is distressing."

The poor record of all forecasters—private as well as government—holds important implications for current public policy:

1) Congress should not place more confidence in forecasters than their record justifies—especially in the case of projections of the economy four or five years hence. Policymakers should be extremely reluctant to use highly speculative forecasts to justify fundamental and far-reaching economic policy changes.

2) Given the inherent limitations of forecasting, policymakers should rethink the case for tax increases based on the current gloomy budget deficit

forecasts. There is no reason to suppose that these forecasts will be any more accurate than those in previous years—while it is certain that tax increases could choke off the recovery.

3) "Fine-tuning" the economy, national industrial plans, and efforts to smooth out the business cycle require accurate forecasting of economic trends and aggregates. Firm statistics simply do not exist, so such detailed policies are doomed to failure. Indeed, they even can destabilize the economy, given that errors in forecasting closely follow the business cycle. "Countercyclical" economic policies based on erroneous forecasts actually could magnify swings in the economy, providing excessive stimulus in recoveries and too much restraint in recessions. Rather than providing policymakers with information to counterbalance the economic cycle, forecasting actually tends to intensify economic fluctuations. . . .

4) Accompanying every government budget should be a prominent disclaimer that economic assumptions are only careful guesses, not a scientifically reliable forecast of the likely outcome. Indeed, when policy initiatives and budgets are based on official forecasts, the Administration and congressional committees should be required to make public the track record of the forecasting agency during the previous ten years, so that the public might award the projections proper credence.

5) Since forecasts are unreliable, solid economic principles should become the basis for economic policy. Such policy should lay a stable foundation for long-term growth and not be adjusted on a yearly basis to anticipate flimsy predictions of future economic conditions. Congress and the Federal Reserve System should continue to move toward a tax system that rewards risk and effort, a regulatory system that removes barriers to enterprise, a spending reduction policy that shrinks the public sector, and a monetary policy that provides for stable and low money growth.

More Heat than Light

Government and private sector forecasts generate more heat than light. The naive confidence placed in economic forecasts by economists and policymakers alike is hardly warranted by the record. Official deficit forecasts for only one year have erred on average 254 percent a year over the last thirteen years. Even private sector firms, which earn their living from forecasting, are inaccurate in predicting the future. A forecast of two, three, four, and five years ahead is rarely closer to reality than a look into a crystal ball.

Would planning the economy, manipulating aggregate demand, and pursuing fashionable cure-alls such as industrial policy seem so desirable if the sorry forecast record were more widely known? Would economists and policymakers push for the large tax increases now being debated if they realized the massive range of errors inherent in any deficit prediction? The flawed record of forecasting certainly should cause economic advisors and lawmakers to use forecasts in a far more cautious and tentative manner.

"Policymakers should be extremely reluctant to use highly speculative forecasts to justify fundamental and far-reaching economic policy changes."

But what should economic policymakers use as a guide if the science of prediction is so crude and unreliable? Perhaps they should recognize that the first step to wisdom is to recognize the obvious limitations in any sort of prediction and act accordingly. If Congress cannot predict the size of the federal deficit, or any other key variable, it should not try to persuade the American people to accept frequent policy changes to fit the latest economic forecasts. It should move instead to establish a broad, long-term tax and monetary framework, based on the lessons of economic history, and leave the guessing game to the gamblers on Wall Street.

Thomas M. Humbert is a senior policy analyst and Walker Fellow in economics for The Heritage Foundation, a conservative think-tank in Washington.

The Deficit Is Caused by Excessive Government Spending

Melville J. Ulmer

Years ago there was a famous boxer known as Falling Phil Scott who won a remarkable series of bouts, while barely landing a blow, by rising from the canvas, clutching his groin, and screaming "Foul!" Thinking of Falling Phil, an anti-hero in my boyhood, I think of the Democratic party. Dropped to the political canvas, . . . it now claims victory. The grounds? It seems that the public has been unfairly mesmerized by the dazzle of the present President's TV personality. Under that spell Americans were rendered purblind to the imperishable aspirations for which his opponents loyally stand. So, unabashedly in the role of victor, the dominant left wing of the Democratic party now seeks to realize the two paramount goals solemnly engraved in the 1984 party platform. The first is to add Central America to the list of the bauble blithely awarded to the Soviet Union in the past: Vietnam, Laos, Cambodia, Mozambique, Ethiopia, and South Yemen. That one I leave to the President, with heartiest best wishes. The second is to stimulate and extend the welfare state with a vigorous injection of new taxes drawn from business and the "rich." With Walter Mondale's public reception still fresh in mind, even the party's run-of-the-mill politicians agree that this one must be pursued with circumlocutory prudence.

Focusing on the Deficit

The Democratic stratagem for achieving this cardinal economic objective centers on the federal deficit. Practically everyone agrees that the deficit is a problem, though the reasons advanced often collide in confusion. At any rate, Democrats—and throughout I mean the party's powerful ultra-liberal wing—know the answer. It is disclosed in the glee with which their intellectual leaders greeted "Treasury I"—the department's initial version of a

tax reform program, later withdrawn in embarrassment. Before the ink was dry on the Treasury's document, Joseph Pechman gushed in the *Washington Post* over its ingenious merits, which included a hefty hike in business taxes amounting to 25 percent in the first year of operation and 36 percent later. Pechman is the veteran tax expert of the Brookings Institution, a long famous safe house for Democratic economists displaced by Republican administrations. Michael Kinsley of the *New Republic* followed closely, enthralled by the enlightened shift of the tax burden from "labor" to "capital." But these and the similar effusions that followed are just suggestive signs. The ultimate goals are far more ambitious, reaching back to the golden dreams of the last Democratic presidential convention with strong echoes from the one that nominated George McGovern.

Perils of the Deficit

The basic tactic currently devised is to hammer incessantly at the menace of the federal deficit, a safe enough butt since no matter what action is taken it's not likely to disappear soon. As Pechman recently pronounced with customary literary flair, the prospective deficits are from $200 to $300 billion or higher annually "as far as the eye can see." Unless, of course, "appropriate" actions are taken. Now if nondefense spending can be effectively blocked, as Tip O'Neill and his comrades in alms promise, only two courses will remain open: a severe boost in taxes and an assault on defense. Meanwhile, government handouts, special interest coddling, industrial meddling, and pork barrel gorging can go on unabated. Net result: the 1984 Democratic platform resurrected and in action! But before confronting such possibilities, a few words are in order about the peril of the deficit. Just what does it do?

The fears, ironically, come from Pechman, Walter

Melville J. Ulmer, "Open Secrets of the Deficit," *The American Spectator*, July 1985. Reprinted with special permission of King Features Syndicate, Inc.

Heller, James Tobin, and other Keynesians who for decades have been proclaiming that deficit spending was the route to prosperity. Today their views of the damage of the deficit, present or prospective, coincide with that of the Democratic left, along with scattered middle-of-the-roaders, in what may be termed the liberal or conventional theory. The unique part of their reasoning is not that it leads to an urgent need for balancing the budget, a consummation that all but a few mentally deficient homeless would applaud. The unique element is a corollary that achieving the balance is in itself more important than how it is done. This opens the door to their own judicious preferences already identified: higher taxes along with a shriveled defense.

The Liberal Theory

The liberal theory of the deficit's menace appears in two segments, one focusing on domestic repercussions, and the other on international economic relations. The latter starts with the now familiar proposition that federal borrowing to finance the deficit "crowds out" private demands for credit. It supposedly does so by raising the cost of capital—the interest rate—thereby blocking private investment. In turn, the high interest rate attracts funds from abroad, boosting the value of the dollar—since to invest here, foreigners must *buy* dollars. Ultimately, the inflated dollar reduces U.S. exports (which become more expensive for foreigners), and increases U.S. imports (which become cheaper for us). The unpleasant effect has been the spreading unemployment observed in industries like steel, autos, and textiles.

Popular though it is, this view is not fully consistent with the facts. There has been no progressive rise in interest rates; instead, they dropped sharply from 1981 to 1983, rose a bit in mid-1984, and have been drifting lower since, even while the deficit steadily mounted. The reason for this overall drop is the success story of our business recovery. Corporations managed to finance their capital needs primarily through ample retained profits rather than borrowing. Nor was there any perceptible crowding out. Indeed, investment rose vigorously, leading the business expansion through 1983 and 1984 while employment, relative to the adult population, ascended to an all-time peak—a tribute to lower tax rates and improved incentives generally. True, the value of the dollar advanced with an unfortunate impact on some exporting industries, but that can be explained as well by a second version of recent events.

A Second Explanation

This more verifiable explanation states that the high value of the dollar stems directly from the prosperity of the American economy, especially relative to the dragging industrial activity through most of Western Europe. A general perception of the USA as the world's safest and most profitable haven for investment drew funds from abroad, rather than a mere elevation of interest rates. At least as important, the same perception induced American business to cut its own annual investments in foreign countries in favor of those at home. Our flow of private capital abroad dropped from $108 billion in 1982 to $43 billion in 1983 and $12 billion in 1984. Since this sharply diminished flow reduced the supply of dollars in international markets, it was sufficient in itself to put upward pressure on the dollar's value. Hence, in this rival view, the role of the deficit in impairing our international balance of trade is minimized. Major responsibility would be assigned elsewhere—say, in the self-impoverishing domestic policies of Western Europe and the predatory trade practices of nearly all our trading partners.

Missing the Mark

We turn now to the conventional liberal interpretation of the deficit's impact on our domestic economy aside from international trade, which is true as far as it goes, even platitudinous, and therefore more significant for what it omits than for what it says. For example, its disciples point out that a growing deficit means that government is placing more and more funds in the income stream than it is taking out. That's a conventional thought if ever there was one—indeed true by definition. Just as conventional, and as impervious to contradiction, is the observation that *sooner or later* this process will generate inflation. Also, *given enough time*, the Treasury's incessant borrowing will raise the market rate of interest. Finally, and inevitably, as the national debt ascends, so do its interest obligations, which must be met by taxpayers. All true, all consistent with the textbooks, and yet the argument misses a central point. It places excessive emphasis on financial entities and too little on the fundamental *material* effects of the government budget.

"Stiffly higher taxes . . . would . . . yield in the end a greater deficit than ever before."

To appreciate that, ask yourself what would happen if the present deficit, arising as it has, were financed fully by taxation, placing the budget in balance. No inflation, right? Maybe lower interest rates. But what else?

Basically, an enlarging deficit enables government to grasp an ever greater command over private physical resources. This is the *real* crowding out.

And it achieves this goal by the blunt means of inflation, even though, under present circumstances, that simply keeps prices higher than they otherwise would be. When government buys ever greater amounts of the nation's supply of labor and other resources, it gets them by outbidding the private sector, and it can borrow or even create money to gets its way. But this last observation demonstrates that those who call for a boost in taxes—the devious Democrats as well as some ''moderate'' Republicans—are merely surrendering to the persistent onslaught of government. Federal expenditures crowd out private expenditures, and *taxes crowd out private incomes*. The second simply certifies the first.

''There is, then, no alternative . . . other than to chop public outlays ruthlessly.''

At best, matching rising public outlays with higher taxes—balancing the budget—succeeds in financing government's growth without inflation. ''At best'' is a warning. Because far more likely, the stiffly higher taxes involved would obliterate private investment, induce the biggest recession of the postwar era, touch off a sickening collapse in budgetary revenue, and yield in the end a greater deficit than ever before. For what it's worth, there would be one consolation. Every plank in the Democratic platform would be realized: a larger role for government, a squeeze on business, a bureaucratic ''industrial policy,'' and enough retraining programs and handouts to fulfill a social worker's loftiest dreams.

Blame Public Spending

What to do? A glance at the federal budget over the last several years is instructive . . . .

The principal message of these data is that responsibility for the deficit's explosion over the last several years must be placed squarely on public spending. Revenue rose quite exuberantly from 1980 to 1984, by a solid 29 percent, considerably more than the advance of population and the price level combined. In other words, *real* receipts per capita rose significantly. But barely anything reasonable in the way of taxes could have matched government outlays, which climbed by 44 percent. Nor, liberal protestations to the contrary, can ''defense'' be identified as the villain of the piece, although waste is as inexcusable here as elsewhere in government. *Non*-defense expenditures accounted for three-fourths of the total and rose by 37 percent in the four-year period considered. In the face of so huge and generalized an advance, to balance the budget by ''enhancing'' revenue would require a 50 percent increase in *both* individual and corporation income taxes.

Would that be enough to reproduce the toboggan slide of 1920-32? Quite possibly, were we mad enough to hold our chins out to take it. Such grotesqueries aside, it's worth noting that even now, federal, state, and local taxes together absorb 40 percent of our total annual earnings, as measured in the Commerce Department's national income. That's not a figure that liberal economists like to acknowledge without the pressure of thumbscrews. Especially in international comparisons, their tendency is to treat the federal level as *all* government.

No Alternative

Getting back to the figures, one may look with some pride at the spectacular boost in revenue in 1984, reflecting the strength of the business recovery and the power of growth as a force in limiting the deficit. Limiting yes, but not a sufficient force to halt its expansion, much less to reverse it. The officially estimated figures for 1985 demonstrate that with the deficit's renewed upward draft, despite the Administration's optimistic forecast of business activity, an even mild recession in the period . . . would deepen the problem severely. There is, then, no alternative to the liberal pincer movement of government's continued expansion, coupled with killing taxes, other than to chop public outlays ruthlessly.

Of course, to stifle hyperanxious cries on the left, we quickly acknowledge the need to continue aid for the truly needy. But that's not the point of this analysis. Rather, it is that, for healthy survival, we must slice through the labyrinth of subsidies, giveaways, pork barrel back-scratching, special interest favors, useless or less useful ''programs'' that now crowds our budget, not excluding a thorough reform of the entire welfare system. In addition, steely-eyed efficiency experts should be turned loose all over government, with the Grace Commission report in hand.

Turn the Rascals Out

It cannot honestly be expected that all this will materialize very soon with our two Houses of Congress populated as they are. Nor with so much of the media howling as they do, in leftist cant. Therefore, the first order of business is to turn the rascals out as quickly as possible. Until then, expect budgetary compromises, and for the good of the country, let's hope that meanwhile conservative voices will resound at least as forcefully as those from the other side.

Melville J. Ulmer is professor of economics at the University of Maryland. He has authored several books and has been an economic consultant to both Republican and Democratic administrations.

"The current deficit is primarily a result of Reagan's tax policies."

The Deficit Is Caused by Inadequate Taxation

Dollars & Sense

The enactment of Gramm-Rudman constitutes a significant step toward the time-honored (not to say hackneyed) conservative goal of balancing the federal budget. It also represents the culmination of a drastic—and dangerous—departure from the strategies conservatives have traditionally pursued.

Prior to 1980, conservatives generally argued that the federal government would have to cut spending before it could cut taxes. They used the possibility of future tax cuts as a bribe to persuade Congress to reduce domestic outlays. Everyone's tax burden could be lightened, they insisted, if only "wasteful" government expenditures like Social Security, education, and welfare could be eliminated.

Reagan has stood this conservative approach on its head. By cutting taxes and increasing military spending, the Reagan administration has spawned an atmosphere of crisis surrounding the deficit, which it has used to bludgeon Congress into cutting spending on other domestic programs. The attack on these programs is making it more and more difficult for the government to sustain its traditional functions.

Need for Progressive Tax Policies

According to conservatives, the free market operates best with little intervention from the state—whether in the form of taxes, regulation, or government spending. Yet state intervention is necessary in order to moderate and compensate for many of the inherent irrationalities of capitalism.

Through progressive tax policies and welfare programs, the government can redistribute income downward, reducing political tensions. It can use fiscal policy to offset cyclical downturns and prevent severe recessions. Thus the state plays a critical role in mediating—if not resolving—conflicts engendered within the system.

In addition, there are certain things the private market cannot or will not do which are necessary for a viable economy. The government must perform the tasks of developing infrastructure for transportation and communication, protecting the environment, educating the workforce, and so on.

Blame It on Tax Cuts

The current deficit is primarily a result of Reagan's tax policies, and only secondarily the product of excessive government spending. The 23% income tax cut that he initiated in 1981 has cost the government roughly $100 billion a year in lost revenue, while military spending has increased by $30 billion a year over the same period.

Yet Reagan has chosen to define the deficit as a domestic spending crisis, rather than as a problem of lost taxes. In his view, the government's role in the economy must be pared down to a level which can be supported at the current level of revenue.

Unwilling to take the political risks of raising taxes or reducing military spending, liberals leapt onto the Gramm-Rudman bandwagon last fall. By accepting a measure that elevates the reduction of the deficit to the level of top national priority, they have allowed conservatives to set the agenda for the role of government in the economy.

Gramm-Rudman: A Diversion

The initial version of Gramm-Rudman—the Balanced Budget and Emergency Deficit Control Act of 1985—was introduced in the Senate as an amendment to a bill to raise the federal debt ceiling from $1.8 trillion to $2 trillion. Senate Republicans wanted to find a way to divert public attention from the fact that the huge national debt is largely the result of Reagan's own policies. Reagan's budget deficits have averaged $175 billion per year, reaching a record high of $220 billion in 1985. (The largest pre-Reagan deficit was $68 billion in 1980.)

The Republicans put their heads together and

Dollars & Sense, "Deficit Deja Vu," March 1986. Reprinted with permission from Dollars & Sense, 38 Union Square, Somerville, MA 02143.

came up with what sponsor Warren Rudman (R.-NH) blithely called "a bad idea whose time has come." The proposed amendment specified maximum budget deficits for each fiscal year between 1987 and 1991. Each year, $36 billion was to be chopped off the deficit, causing it to fall from $144 billion in 1987 to zero in 1991. For political reasons, social security was exempted from any automatic spending reductions, but with this exception the President was to be given broad discretion as to where to make the cuts. Conveniently, the Senate proposal delayed the enactment of spending cuts until after the November 1986 elections.

Once approved by the Senate, the amendment moved to the Democrat-controlled House. The Democrats made a number of positive alterations, but the overall thrust stayed the same. Aid to Families with Dependent Children (AFDC), Supplemental Security Income (SSI), Medicaid, child nutrition, and food stamps joined Social Security in being exempted from automatic spending cuts. Furthermore, half of the cuts were required to come from the Defense Department.

In addition, presidential discretion as to where to make the cuts was reduced. The final version stated that if Congress and the President failed to reach an agreement on some combination of these measures to meet the deficit target, automatic cuts in domestic and military spending would go into effect. Finally, the Democrats also insisted that the $11.7 billion in deficit reductions be made by March 1986, and that the 1987 cuts be voted in as of October 1.

Tailoring Reduction to Tax Policies

Just how large are the deficit reductions required by Gramm-Rudman? Even under the best of circumstances, the amount will be substantial. The Congressional Budget Office has made two sets of projections to help estimate the amount of money that will have to be cut from the federal budget in order to meet the Gramm Rudman targets based on current spending and taxing policies.

The "steady growth" projections assume a constant 3.5% rate of GNP growth through 1991. This is tantamount to assuming that the current recovery will last about twice as long as the average U.S. postwar expansion. If we accept the steady-growth hypothesis, in 1989 the government will have to spend $60 billion less than it did this year. The more plausible low growth estimates assume that there will be a mild recession starting in mid-1986 and ending in late 1987. Under the low-growth scenario, the deficit will have to be cut by $184 billion.

While the bill mandates shrinking the size of government, it also makes it nearly impossible for the government to spur economic growth. Furthermore, by eliminating fiscal policy as a tool for moderating the effect of recessions, Gramm-

Rudman will surely hamstring the government's ability to provide an "automatic stabilizer" for the economy.

Normally, when unemployment rises, government spending on unemployment insurance and related programs goes up. Tax collections fall, since income has fallen. Generally, for every 1% increase in unemployment, the federal deficit jumps by roughly $40 billion. But by providing income to the unemployed, government spending props up demand—which in turn fuels a recovery. As workers are rehired, government expenditures drop and tax revenue rises until the deficit is reduced.

Under Gramm-Rudman, a downturn would still lead to an increase in the deficit for that year. To meet the deficit target for the following year, that year's deficit cut would have to be still larger. So, just as a recession begins, the government would have to lower its spending and/or increase taxes. Either action would reduce consumer income and lead to lower consumer spending—further deepening the recession.

Escape Clause

While recessions have the valuable function of lowering labor costs and disciplining the labor force, even the most ardent capitalist does not look forward to a severe and prolonged depression. Consequently, Gramm-Rudman comes equipped with a "recession escape clause." If the Department of Commerce produces statistics indicating that economic growth in the two most recently reported quarters has been less than one percent, the majority leaders of both Houses must introduce resolutions that suspend the deficit ceilings for two fiscal years. But unless the resolutions are approved by majorities in both the House and the Senate, the deficit ceilings would remain in effect.

"Reagan has chosen to define the deficit as a domestic spending crisis, rather than as a problem of lost taxes."

Anticipating recessions poses even greater problems. The bill requires Congress to consider the repeal of the deficit ceilings if either the Congressional Budget Office or the Office of Management and the Budget predicts a recession in the coming year. Unfortunately, the government has managed to consistently avoid predicting the onset of *any* recession in the past ten years. Hence, it seems likely that the government will wind up pursuing contractionary fiscal policies for the next five years, regardless of the state of the economy.

The crisis mentality over the federal deficit has also increased the pressure to raise taxes. Members of both political parties now publicly argue that the passage of Gramm-Rudman has made tax hikes inevitable. But Reagan continues to insist that raising taxes is "not an option." Instead, he has seized the opportunity to push for tax reform—consolidating tax brackets, closing loopholes, and eliminating some deductions. This move will do nothing to increase the amount of revenue raised through taxes. But what it will accomplish is the elimination of tax policy as a tool for adjusting the distribution of income.

"The huge national debt is largely the result of Reagan's own [tax] policies."

Lower taxes and a simplified tax system could limit the role of local as well as federal government. . . . Reagan has pushed for eliminating the federal income-tax deduction for state and local tax payments. This would force high-tax states like New York and Massachusetts to cut back on their spending.

If public pressure to raise taxes does prevail, Reagan is most likely to accede to the taxes which are least progressive, such as the value-added tax or oil import fees. A White House official described the latter as popular with Reagan because "it's a tax that's not a tax." These are taxes on consumption, rather than income, and since poor people spend a larger proportion of their incomes on consumption, they are disproportionately affected.

Undermining Tax Policy

Thus the two traditional functions of the tax system—to redistribute income and to provide revenue for the legitimate functions of government —are being undermined. Even the attempt to raise revenue through other means is aimed at reducing the role of the government in the economy. For example, the Reagan administration is plugging the sale of government assets as a way to raise federal revenue. Reagan is hoping to sell off the Bonneville Power Administration, and may also call for the sale of part of the government's $245 billion loan portfolio to private investors.

Such sales would do nothing to change the government's long-term revenue situation. Nor would the sale of government loans really reduce net federal borrowing from the private sector. The total amount of private capital tied up in projects determined by the government would stay the same. On the other hand, they would bring the Reagan administration closer to its goal of abolishing government operations that compete, however indirectly, with private profit-making.

Deficits have been with us more or less steadily since the 1920s. If the deficit were really the

problem, raising taxes would be a reasonable solution. But Reagan is pushing a not-so-hidden agenda. He has vowed to meet the 1991 Gramm-Rudman deficit target while allowing the Pentagon to indulge in 3% real spending growth. And it looks like he'll have his way, since no one is likely to pose an effective challenge to the Reagan agenda: even when Congress had a chance to vote a 5% cut in the military last October, it refused to do so.

The Reagan budget proposal for 1987 targets some two dozen domestic programs. The Legal Services Corporation, Urban Development Action Grants, the Small Business Administration, and mass transit subsidies will all be subject to cuts. The Department of Transportation expects to lose $400 million that might have gone to building and repairing bridges and highways. The Education Department has anounced that it may have to cut off aid to 68,000 middle-income students.

No matter what capitalists say, government is not a disposable item. Eliminating the public sector will have the eventual result of exposing the inadequacies of the capitalist economy and exacerbating the conflicts generated in the system. Nonetheless, working people have a long and difficult struggle ahead to win back the social and economic gains rolled back by Reagan.

Dollars & Sense *is an economic journal offering interpretations of current economic events from a socialist perspective.*

Reagan's Budget Policies Have Improved the Economy

Ronald Reagan

The major economic objectives of my Administration from its beginning have been strong, sustainable, noninflationary economic growth and expanding economic opportunities for all Americans. To achieve these goals, we have pursued policies that are in the long-term best interest of the Nation.

The benefits of this approach are now clear. The economy has entered . . . a robust expansion that has dramatically increased opportunities for all Americans. Millions of new jobs have been created. Investment opportunities have increased. Standards of living have risen. Moreover, this success has been accomplished without rekindling inflation.

Committed to Growth

We are committed to continuing and extending policies that encourage the private investment and innovation that are the foundation of this expansion. We continue to resist unnecessary increases in government spending and unwarranted interference in private markets. Sustained, strong economic growth depends critically on allowing the market system to function as freely as possible. Free markets provide proper incentives to work, save, and invest, and they ensure that the interests of consumers are served.

These basic principles were embodied in our 1981 Program for Economic Recovery and reaffirmed in the second-term Program for Growth and Opportunity. These programs do not offer "quick fixes" but rely on the inherent ability of the free market system to allocate resources efficiently and to generate economic prosperity. The fundamental responsibility of the Federal Government should be to provide a stable environment within which people can make economic decisions, not to make those decisions for them. To this end, our initial program

involved four essential elements:
- Restrain the growth of Federal spending,
- Reduce personal and business taxes,
- Reduce regulatory excesses, and
- Encourage stable and moderate monetary growth.

Successful Policies

The success of our policies is now apparent. Even though economic growth slowed a bit in 1985 compared with its strong performance in 1983 and 1984, the expansion has nonetheless proceeded at an encouraging pace. It is already . . . longer in duration than the average peacetime expansion since World War II. If the expansion continues as expected . . . it will be the third longest in the postwar period.

This expansion has been characterized by unusually strong real business investment in plant and equipment due to our successful attack on inflation and to our tax policy, which stimulated investment. Real business investment has contributed nearly twice as much to real gross national product (GNP) growth in this expansion as it typically has in previous postwar expansions; as a share of real GNP, it is higher than at any other time in the postwar period. Stronger U.S. investment means not only a stronger economy today, but also higher productivity and the potential for faster growth in the future.

Strong employment growth is another outstanding feature of this recovery. Since the end of the last recession in November 1982, the U.S. economy has employed more than 9 million new workers. Futhermore, the unemployment rate fell from 10.6 percent in November 1982 to 6.9 percent in December 1985. Despite this dramatic improvement, however, we will not be satisfied until all American workers can find jobs at wages commensurate with their skills.

When we initiated our Program for Economic Recovery, we were confident that a resourceful,

Ronald Reagan, *Economic Report of the President*, Washington, DC: United States Government Printing Office, February 1986.

flexible economy, unencumbered by excessive governmental intervention, would create jobs. At the same time, we believed that restrained monetary growth would reduce inflation. Our optimism was justified. The rate of inflation is now less than one-third of the rate in 1980. During this expansion, inflation has maintained its lowest level in more than a decade despite the tremendous employment growth that the economy has generated. Reflecting in part the reduction in inflation, interest rates—especially long-term rates—have declined throughout 1985 and by the end of the year were at their lowest levels in 6 years.

"The success of our policies is now apparent."

Our success in reducing inflation came as a surprise to some. As inflation rose in the 1970s, some businesses and individuals incurred debt in order to purchase assets, expecting the income generated by these assets to rise with inflation while the real burden of servicing the debt decreased. With the decline in inflation, the real burden of debt servicing rose and the income generated by many assets fell. This combination of events has strained some U.S. financial institutions. Falling farm incomes have hampered the ability of some farmers to pay interest on their debt. Similarly, many less developed countries have had difficulty repaying loans from U.S. financial institutions. The stress that the undesirable rise in inflation and its desirable but unexpectedly rapid decline have imposed on the U.S. financial system emphasizes the importance of achieving and maintaining long-term price stability.

America's optimism concerning continued growth in economic opportunities is shared by businesses and individuals throughout the world. The United States has been and remains one of the few major immigrant-receiving countries, reflecting in part the economy's ability to generate economic opportunities. During the current expansion, profitable investment opportunities in the United States have also attracted foreign capital, helping to finance the rapid growth in investment. The inflow of foreign capital indicates a strong economy. As other nations continue to move toward market-oriented policies and reduce excessive government spending, taxation, and structural rigidities, they too will generate increased investment opportunities, resulting in increased growth and stronger currencies as more capital flows into their economies.

Many factors point to continuation of the current expansion. Economic conditions . . . are expected to improve further. Monetary growth . . . has been sufficient to accommodate growth in the economy.

The leading economic indicators have risen in 11 of the past 12 months. Inventories are relatively low, and as sales continue to expand, production should increase to replenish depleted inventories. Interest rates have continued their decline, promising to spur additional capital spending. Furthermore, the warning signals that typically precede the end of expansions have not been observed. Thus, we feel confident that the current expansion will continue. . . .

We expect increased growth in real GNP of 4 percent in 1986, continuing throughout 1987 and 1988 and declining gradually in 1989-91 as the economy approaches its long-run real growth trend. Given the monetary and exchange rate developments during the past year, we anticipate a slight rise in inflation in 1986-87. However, if the Federal Reserve reaffirms its resolve to achieve price stability, a goal that I support without reservation, the downturn in inflation should resume in later years.

Changing events, including erratic monetary and fiscal policies, can bring any expansion to an abrupt and unexpected halt. Our projections for the longer term are premised on the assumption that stable economic policies will foster continued economic growth and will also provide the needed flexibility for the economy to respond to external disturbances. Our policy goals reflect this commitment to economic stability as the key contribution to sustained growth, stable prices, declining interest rates, and falling unemployment. The American people have a right to expect such results and, with the cooperation of the Congress and the Federal Reserve, we expect to continue to deliver them.

Limited Government

In formulating our program for healthy and continued economic expansion, we recognized the limited role that government properly plays. The Federal Government cannot provide prosperity or generate economic growth; it can only encourage private initiative, innovation, and entrepreneurial activity that produce economic opportunities. An overly active government actually hinders economic progress. Federal spending absorbs resources, many of which could be better used by the private sector. Excessive taxation distorts relative prices and relative rates of return. By arbitrarily reallocating resources, it inhibits the economy's ability to grow. Thus, the best way for government to promote economic growth is to provide a foundation of stable, predictable economic policies, and then to stand back and let the creative potential of the American people flourish.

The Federal Government has several definite responsibilities that my Administration continues to uphold. The first is to provide an adequate national defense. World peace and security require the United States, as the leader of the free world, to demonstrate its willingness and ability to defend its own national security and to contribute to the defense of its allies.

Decline in Poverty

Furthermore, we will not ignore the less fortunate in this society. My Administration continues to provide an appropriate safety net to aid those individuals who need help. At the same time, we have worked to develop a strong, vibrant, opportunity-generating economy that can offer meaningful jobs to all who are able to work. The economic expansion has done much more to reduce poverty than any government transfer program. The significant decline in the percentage of the population in poverty in 1984 reflects both the success of our programs and the strength of the economy. Moreover, tax reform will benefit the working poor. My proposed tax reforms eliminate the Federal income tax burden of most working poor.

Finally, even though we believe that markets generally allocate resources most efficiently, there are a few special cases, such as air and water pollution, in which the market mechanism alone may be inadequate. In these instances, government intervention is necessary, but even here, it should be based on market principles. For example, the Environmental Protection Agency has approved arrangements that enable firms to earn credits for reducing emissions below the required limit, which they can sell to other firms facing higher costs of emission control. In this way, environmental quality is maintained and improved while the costs of compliance decline.

Reducing the Deficit

Fulfillment of these limited responsibilities, however, does not require the level or the rate of growth of Federal spending that the Nation has been experiencing. In spite of our efforts, spending remains excessive and has been the primary cause of the large budget deficit. Tax rate cuts did not generate this deficit; in fact, current tax receipts are as large a share of GNP as they were in the late 1970s, even after the reduction in tax rates that we initiated in 1981. The key to resolving the Federal budget deficit is to restrain unneeded spending. Spending, not the deficit, is the true indicator of the cost of government, because it measures the total economic resources diverted from the private sector. Excessive spending affects the economy in deleterious ways regardless of whether it is financed through taxation, borrowing, or even inflation. Private capital formation is reduced, resources are inefficiently allocated, and economic growth is slowed.

I applaud and support the . . . Balanced Budget and Emergency Deficit Control Act of 1985, known

commonly as Gramm-Rudman-Hollings, as a way to work with the Congress to reduce Federal spending and the deficit. I intend to submit budgets in each of the coming years that satisfy the act's deficit targets, not by sacrificing the programs essential to the Nation, but by reforming or eliminating those programs that are ineffective or nonessential. I reject the notion of increased taxes. Higher taxes would only encourage more Federal spending and limit the economy's ability to grow.

Gramm-Rudman-Hollings accomplishes only part of our long-term objective of Federal fiscal responsibility. Properly applied, it will produce a balanced budget by 1991, but it does not guarantee a continued balanced budget thereafter. We must now direct our attention to a constitutional amendment providing for a permanently balanced budget. Together, these two measures will provide an orderly transition to a balanced budget, restrain future spending, and ensure that future fiscal decisions are prudent and responsive to the national interests. Accordingly, I continue to support strongly and to urge the adoption of a balanced-budget constitutional amendment. I also seek legislation that would authorize the President to veto individual line items in appropriations measures. Such authority is essential to ensure that only effective and essential government programs are funded.

Reform Taxes

Over the years, successive modifications of the Federal tax code have resulted in a complex tax system that contains many loopholes and artificially encourages some types of activities at the expense of others. Furthermore, the inflation of the 1970s distorted the overall pattern of capital taxation and pushed personal incomes into ever-higher tax brackets, discouraging saving and investment. Our actions to reduce tax rates have corrected many of these distortions and inequities. Individual income tax rates have been reduced and indexed to the inflation rate; effective tax rates on new investments have been lowered substantially. Still, more must be done.

"America's optimism concerning continued growth in economic opportunities is shared by businesses and individuals throughout the world."

In May 1985, I submitted to the Congress a comprehensive reform of the tax code to make it simpler, fairer, and more conducive to economic growth. I proposed reducing marginal tax rates for individuals and businesses, broadening the tax base by eliminating the majority of existing loopholes, taxing different activities consistently so that resources are allocated on the basis of economic merit and not tax considerations, and compensating for or eliminating much of the remaining influence of inflation on effective tax rates on capital. Just before it recessed, the House of Representatives passed a tax reform bill that incorporated some of these principles. Despite substantive differences between my proposal and the House bill, I urged its passage to move the legislative process forward. We will now work with the Senate to generate a fair and simple tax code that is truly pro-family, pro-jobs, and pro-growth. . . .

My Administration recognizes the responsibility of the Federal Government to promote economic growth and individual opportunity through policies that lead to maximum employment, production, and purchasing power. We intend to maintain this course with policies that continue to promote strong, sustainable, noninflationary growth and provide expanding economic opportunities for all. We shall continue to resist additional government involvement as a solution to short-term problems. Such involvement has been unsuccessful in the past and ultimately becomes part of the problem rather than part of the solution. With the cooperation and support of the Congress and the independent agencies, we will pursue the appropriate policies necessary to sustain the current expansion and to stabilize prices.

Ronald Reagan, President of the United States, campaigned on promises to improve the economy.

"The promised harvest of plenty failed to materialize."

Reagan's Budget Policies Are Destroying the Economy

The Center for Popular Economics

The new economic orthodoxy promised a miracle and delivered a debacle:

—the supply-siders promised lower taxes without government deficits and without cuts in needed government services. They delivered tax cuts and wound up with record-setting government deficits despite taking the axe to domestic social programs;

—the monetarists promised a surgical strike against inflation with few casualties and a swift victory—a kind of economic equivalent of the Grenada invasion. They ended up presiding over the recession they had created—the most severe in the post-war era. The operation looked much like the Philadelphia police department's slash and burn approach to the dissident group MOVE.

A False Victory

The costs of the debacle are only now becoming apparent. The impression that Reaganomics is working may be attributable to the President's own popularity and persuasion powers. But it also results from the fact that both the U.S. government and the economy as a whole have gone deeply into debt, masking the severity of the failure, delaying the day of reckoning, and allowing the President—assisted by the myopia of sympathetic economic commentators—to proclaim victory.

When a family or a business tries a new course of action and ends up after some years, deeply and unexpectedly in hock to the future, we tend to conclude that they made a mistake. We think it is reasonable to apply this elementary reasoning to the track record of the new orthodoxy.

The heyday of orthodox economic policy under the tutelage of Paul Volcker and Ronald Reagan has taken place under adverse circumstances not entirely

of its own making. Since the mid 1960s signs of weakness in basic economic structure and performance have been accumulating. The after-tax rate of return on corporate capital—the capitalist's eye view of the economic health of the economy—peaked two decades ago, and has languished since. Growth rates of output have also been failing over the long term, not only in the U.S. but in other industrial and developing countries as well. While the U.S. and world economy have continued to endure the ups and downs of cyclical recession and recovery, the long downward secular trend has been the primary backdrop for domestic economic policies.

The Misery Index

When Ronald Reagan kicked off his first presidential election campaign in 1979, the U.S. economy was in serious trouble. Inflation was running at 13% a year. The unemployment rate was 5.8%. And the so-called Misery Index—the sum of the unemployment rate and the inflation rate—was the highest it had been in the entire post-war period.

Beset by low productivity growth, spiralling oil prices and declining international competitiveness, Jimmy Carter had given up on his strategy for dealing with problems of the American economy. With the help of G. William Miller, then Chairman of the Federal Reserve, Carter's approach was to run a loose monetary policy and a tight budget policy. The easy credit policies of the Fed resulted in generally lower interest rates in the U.S., and this encouraged people with money to desert the dollar in favor of currencies that carried higher interest rates. This caused the dollar to fall *vis-a-vis* U.S. competitors. . . .

As the dollar's value sank with inflation, large banks and corporations holding dollars in 1978 and 1979 began to panic. By the summer of 1979, a major sell-off of the dollar occurred and a full-

The Center for Popular Economics, *Economic Report of the People.* Boston, MA: South End Press, 1986. Reprinted by permission of the author and South End Press, Institute for Social & Cultural Change, 116 St. Botolph St., Boston, MA 02115.

fledged currency crisis broke out. Miller resigned and Carter appointed Paul Volcker as chairman of the Fed. Carter hoped that Volcker, a banker's banker, could restore the world's confidence in the dollar and American banks. Almost immediately, Volcker's Federal Reserve System raised interest rates to break the inflationary spiral and dollar depreciation. In the process, the fed sparked a sharp recession just prior to the 1980 election.

Volcker's appointment, in short, meant the abandonment of the Carter strategy, and soon thereafter, of Jimmy Carter. In combination—but not always in cooperation—Volcker and Reagan fashioned a new economic strategy which promised to find a non-inflationary solution to the U.S. economy's problems.

Double Debt Crisis

It did not work. They beat inflation. But they did not reverse the long-run structural decline of the U.S. economy. Instead, conservative economics generated a double debt crisis of government budget and foreign trade deficits. To pay for these deficits, the U.S. government is now billions of dollars in debt. This money will have to be repaid eventually, with interest.

The objective of conservative economics was to restore profitability, international competitiveness, and sustained economic growth without inflation. This was no easy task. To try and accomplish it, the Federal Reserve and the Reagan administration combined well-worn recipes into a novel concoction.

Monetarism, the first ingredient, came from the Federal Reserve System's classic cook book. In its most recent guise, monetarism is an academic and rather technical doctrine which advocates close control over the money supply. Milton Friedman is the best known economist associated with this view. But historically, monetarism has been an intellectual disguise for the kind of policy which central banks often seem to like most: tight money and high interest rates. . . .

Monetarism's Backfire

Capitalist economies run on profits and the U.S. economy is no exception. So the key to understanding why monetarism backfired is to analyze its effect on profits.

By increasing the cost and decreasing the availability of credit and recessing the economy, the Federal Reserve's high interest rate policy threatened rather than bolstered profits. Businesses welcomed their increased bargaining power with labor; but with high unemployment it became harder to sell products.

As a result, monetarism shifted the problems of the U.S. economy from banks and other financial institutions onto families trying to make ends meet and onto manufacturing corporations.

If high unemployment forced workers to take significant wage cuts, then firms could increase their profit margins, even without having to raise prices. However, profits depend not only on the amount of profits made on each good sold, but they also depend on how many goods the firm can sell. By recessing the economy, high interest rates reduced the amount firms could sell.

Enter Supply-Side

Enter Ronald Reagan and his administration's supply-side solution, the second ingredient of conservative economics. "Supply-side economics" rejected the somber trade-offs of monetarism; it was a plan for reducing inflation and increasing corporate profits at the same time.

"Conservative economics generated a double debt crisis of government budget and foreign trade deficits."

If the idea behind the Federal Reserve's monetarist policies was to lower inflation by restricting the *demand* for goods, the idea behind "supply-side" economics was to reduce inflation by increasing the *supply* of goods. The key to increasing supply was to increase corporate incentives to produce by increasing business profitability.

It made a lot of sense to focus on boosting supply rather than holding back demand. But the supply-side remedies turned out to be simply the latest revision of a perennial theme of economic orthodoxy: the government as culprit.

Blaming Government

As Reagan saw it, bad government policies were at the root of declining U.S. production and profits:

> The most important cause of our economic problems has been the government itself. . . . In particular, excessive government spending and overly accommodative monetary policies have combined to give us a climate of continuing inflation. That inflation itself has helped to sap our present growth. . . . High marginal-tax rates on business and individuals discourage work, innovation and the investment necessary to improve productivity and long-run growth.

Moreover, the Reagan administration argued that by helping support citizens who did not have jobs, the spending policies of the "welfare state" had undermined workers' willingness to work hard on production lines or accept jobs with low wages. As a result, Reagan argued, productivity on the shop floor had suffered and firms were forced to pay "excessive" wages to get workers to work. Lower productivity and higher wages, in turn, had increased costs. If these costs are not passed on as higher prices, they lower corporate profits. If they are passed on, they lead to more inflation. In either case, according to the administration, the "welfare state" was the culprit.

Given this diagnosis, Reagan's administration embarked on a carrot and stick "supply-side" policy of tax spending and regulatory changes to reduce the "welfare state," encourage work, innovation, saving and the investment necessary to improve productivity and long-run growth.

Tax Cuts for the Wealthy

On the tax side, the Reagan administration cut taxes for working and wealthy individuals. The idea was that the wealthy would save their tax cuts which, in turn, would make more funds available for investment. The ideology of tax cuts for workers was necessary to justify the tax cuts for the wealthy. The Reagan administration hoped that people would invest these increased tax savings into U.S. corporations.

The administration also cut taxes for corporations to increase their after-tax profits. In return, they thought corporations would increase their investment.

The third ingredient of conservative economics was a massive increase in military spending. Military spending increases profits for military contractors quite directly. More importantly, military spending provides the military muscle necessary to protect U.S. economic "interests" abroad.

"Conservative economics has generated one of the largest government budget deficits in peacetime history."

Thus conservative economics combined tight money, "supply-side economics," and massive increases in military expenditures in a strategy aimed at reducing inflation for financial institutions, increasing after-tax income for the wealthy, and boosting profits for business. In return, the wealthy would save more, and business would invest more. Economic growth would follow, "trickling down" its benefits to everybody.

Collapse and Recession

The competitive edge of U.S. business did not revive; it collapsed. The economy did not boom; it lapsed into a record setting recession.

By raising real interest rates, monetarism succeeded in driving up the value of the dollar, putting workers and unions on the defensive. But the promised harvest of plenty failed to materialize.

Every important economic indicator except inflation reveals continuing economic deterioration under conservative economics. To forestall pointless debate and to avoid complex statistical manipulation,

our data do not focus on any given year, nor do we emphasize the depth and length of the 1980-82 recession while ignoring the strength of the ensuing recovery or *vice versa*. Rather, we focus on average performance of the economy over a whole business cycle, which is the fairest means of evaluating our 6-year (1979-1985) experience with economic orthodoxy in action. Choosing the business cycle eliminates distortions that would result from comparing, for example, a recession year with a boom year.

We define a completed cycle as the entire period from one business cycle peak to another. We define the peak of a business cycle as the year when the unemployment rate hits a cyclical low. According to this measure 1979 was a peak and . . . 1985 [was] as well. We have thus identified the years 1979 to 1985 as a completed business cycle, one which coincides with the reign of the new economic orthodoxy.

Low Growth

Besides generating record rates of unemployment, between 1980 and 1985 conservative economics produced the lowest average rate of growth of real GNP of any cycle in the post-war period. Conservative economics did not restore U.S. international competitiveness. Instead the merchandise trade deficit, as a share of GNP, *doubled* from .8% between 1974 and 1979 to 1.9% between 1980 and 1985.

A look at business cycle peaks rather than averages offers another view of the relative performance of conservative economics. In 1985, unemployment was higher than it had been at any cycle peak since the Great Depression. Inflation fighting was the clear winner, falling to the lowest rate for a peak year since 1959. And in 1984, the economy grew at an overall rate of 6.8%. . . .

The economy's rebound from the 1980-82 doldrums in 1984 helped to re-elect Ronald Reagan and breathe new life into conservative economics.

Economic growth, which averaged 6.8% in real terms in 1984, has since slowed dramatically to 3.3% in the 3rd quarter of 1985. But the stellar 1984 upswing, particularly in the context of the continuing long-term deterioration in economic performance, appears to be a puzzle. The answer, however, is simple: the policies of conservative economics looked good in 1984 because the U.S. economy was living on borrowed time.

Mortgaging Our Future

Rather than laying the foundation for sustained economic growth, conservative economics has generated one of the largest government budget deficits in peacetime history and a massive trade deficit. Generating a double debt crisis, conservative economics is mortgaging our future.

The common view of the budget deficit is that it is

an unmitigated evil because it raises interest rates, reducing investment and driving up the value of the dollar. However, the evidence suggests that the deficit has had little effect on interest rates.

Indeed, recent large budget deficits, by increasing demand for goods and services, are probably responsible for much of the economic recovery from 1982 to 1985.

The trade deficit is also a cloud with a silver lining. Though widely regarded as the bane of our economic existence, the trade deficit has allowed the U.S. economy to live beyond its means, thus cushioning the fall in living standards and obscuring the failures of conservative economics. Between 1980 and 1984, the United States imported $275 billion more than it exported. This meant the U.S. was able to spend $275 billion more than it made. Indeed, the trade deficit was nearly 3% of U.S. GNP in 1984. . . .

Short-Run Advantages

Being able to spend more than one produces has short-run advantages. For those who do not work in import-competing and export-competing industries, trade deficits can mean more for less. If the value of imports had equalled the value of exports between 1980 and 1984, U.S. national income—and therefore spending—would have been reduced by the value of the trade deficit. For example, the United States would have had to get by with $275 billion less in new plants and equipment, or housing, or health care. Or the government would have had to spend $275 billion less on arms.

But this opportunity to live beyond our means has been bought on borrowed time. Even the most obvious success of conservative economics, a dramatic reduction in inflation, has been partly acquired on borrowed time.

"Ronald Reagan has locked up the prize for the Penury Index."

According to a number of estimates, around a third of the reduction in inflation has been due to the effects of the appreciating dollar. When the dollar falls—as it will eventually, either slowly or in a panic—prices of imported goods will rise and inflation will be reignited. When we repay our foreign debts the price dampening process will work in reverse: we will pay later for the relative price stability bought now.

And repaying our external debts means the U.S. will have to produce more than we consume and invest domestically. Writing in June 1985, National Bureau of Economic Research economist Jeffrey Sachs concludes:

. . . exchange depreciation has reduced U.S. inflation by as much as three percentage points as of 1985. Given the strong likelihood of a depreciation of the dollar, those inflation gains will likely be lost, or more than lost in the future.

Even paying the interest and profits on U.S. debt to other countries is already putting a mounting strain on the economy.

The Penury Index

Jimmy Carter may have won the prize for the Misery Index—the sum of inflation and unemployment; but Ronald Reagan has locked up the prize for the Penury Index, the percentage of gross national product that the country pays in profit and interest to foreigners every year. The Penury Index tripled between 1970-1973 and 1980-1984.

Moreover, the U.S. has run such large deficits abroad that, in 1985, the United States became a net debtor country. *We have borrowed more from foreigners than they have from us* for the first time since the First World War.

But borrowing isn't necessarily detrimental to economic well-being. Whether borrowed money enriches or impoverishes depends on how it is spent. In fact, borrowing is a good idea if the borrowed resources are invested in productive activities that yield higher returns than the interest which must be paid on the loan. In that case, the loan can be repaid with interest and money is still left to spare. If the money is squandered, on the other hand, all that remains is a debt which will absorb future resources.

Have conservative economic policies led to sufficient productive investment to make the debts worthwhile? Or have these policies mortgaged our future?

Measuring Productive Investment

To answer, we must estimate the amount of productive investment in our economy. This must include more than investment in plant and equipment by firms. It must also include money that corporations, households, and federal, state and local governments invest in research and development, in material and cultural infrastructure, and in preserving the natural environment.

We have calculated such a measure: we call it TIME—the Total Investment Measure. TIME attempts to measure the total social productive investment in the U.S. economy. It estimates the resources allocated for the future.

TIME includes non-defense government spending on investment goods; total spending on non-defense research and development by businesses, government and universities; total spending on education; state and local government capital spending, which is primarily infrastructure spending; and private non-residential net fixed investment.

If the share of TIME in national income is going

up at the same rate as debt, then the economy is apparently investing its borrowings wisely, that is, in productive activities which can help pay off the borrowing.

If the share of TIME is not rising at the same rate as the debt, however, then it is likely the loans are being wasted and future generations will have to bear the price.

Failure of Conservative Economics

And indeed, TIME or social investment is falling while U.S. borrowing from foreigners is rising. This means that unless social investment can become dramatically more productive dollar-for-dollar, conservative economics has indeed mortgaged our future.

While research and development expenditures are increasing as a percent of GNP, federal and, more importantly, state and local spending on non-defense capital infrastructure is declining. Expenditure on education as a share of GNP is declining as well, as is net fixed investment.

The Total Investment Measure (TIME) also includes expenditures on environmental protection. As one might expect, these expenditures, as a percentage of GNP, have decreased under the reign of conservative economics. Annual data compiled by McGraw-Hill show a steady decline in corporate expenditures for air and water pollution as a percent of GNP since 1979 (with a slight increase in 1984). The averages for this period also indicate that business expenditures for environmental protection during the reign of conservative economics were the lowest since the late 1960s.

Rather than using the opportunity of the budget deficit and the trade deficit to invest borrowed funds productively for the future, conservative economics has pursued policies which waste this borrowed money. We—and our children and their children— will have to pay the price.

The Center for Popular Economics brings together economists from public interest, community, women's, labor, religious, and third world groups for the purpose of effecting economic changes.

"A close examination of . . . the crisis prediction . . . reveals the forecast to be, at best, premature, and at worst, a convenient fiction popularized by those now benefitting from [it]."

The "Crisis" Is Fabricated

Jon Osborne

We face global financial ruin from an "international debt crisis," the authors of countless recent books and articles warn us. They tell us why the crisis exists and, typically, how to avoid the disaster that it is ushering in. But a close examination of both the logic behind the crisis prediction and the evidence submitted to support it reveals the forecast to be, at best, premature, and at worst, a convenient fiction popularized by those now benefitting from the political results of its general acceptance.

Weak arguments and scarce evidence have, of course, never discouraged government action, so in November 1983 Congress approved an administration plan to grant the International Monetary Fund (IMF) an additional $8.4 billion, if not to actually solve the anticipated crisis, to at least frighten the bogeyman away for the time being. The sad irony of this tale is that the very measures that Congress [took] to remedy this doubtful crisis will only make its advent more likely.

Beneficiaries Promote "Crisis"

First to warn us of the possibility of an international debt crisis were the banks that made loans to foreign governments—loans now thought to be vulnerable to default—and the various governments that received those loans. And those same parties are also the principal beneficiaries of present government efforts here and abroad to insure this debt by subsidizing its repayment. Their authoritative voices warned of a financial collapse, and a press ever eager to exaggerate disaster echoed the doomful pronouncements. Thus egged on, governments of net lender countries moved to shield indirectly, by way of IMF subsidies, their domestic banks from the risks naturally associated with

Jon Osborne, "Paper Crisis." Reprinted, with permission, from the May 1984 issue of *Reason* magazine. Copyright © 1984 by the REASON Foundation, 2716 Ocean Park Blvd., Suite 1062, Santa Monica, CA 90405.

international debt. The international banks want the subsidies as a means of costlessly increasing the security of their international loans. The debtor governments want the subsidies as a new source of income. Both benefit from these subsidies and therefore both claim that a crisis exists; but what is the basis of this assertion and how have these various interests been able to convince so many of its validity?

The mechanics of the crisis, as foreseen by its "victims" and their unwitting allies in the press, are deceptively simple: As a debtor government progressively borrows more money, the cost of servicing its debt rises proportionately. Because the borrowed funds are not always invested in productive ways, however, they frequently do not generate sufficient income to cover the interest cost associated with borrowing. The interest cost must therefore be paid out of the general-income sources of the debtor government. But as the total cost of servicing the debt rises in proportion to its sum, it becomes an increasing strain on the budget of the debtor government. As a debtor government accumulates more foreign debt, it reaches a point at which it can no longer cover out of general revenue the servicing costs of all of its unproductive debt. The government then defaults. The lending banks suffer losses as a result, sending financial shock waves throughout their native countries and the rest of the world. This is the theory.

The evidence supporting this theory is that government-held debt is rising, as a matter of record, at a seemingly astonishing rate and many heavily indebted governments are, also as a matter of record, claiming increasing difficulty in servicing their debt. The three debtors most vociferous in their claims of hardship are also the three largest debtors: Argentina, Brazil, and Mexico. And in *nominal* terms the growth rate of their debt *is* staggering (see chart 1). From 1972 to 1981 these countries' combined debt grew at an average annual compounded rate of 26 percent; by 1981 their combined debt was about eight times what it had been in 1972. Two of these three countries, Argentina and Mexico, have already been forced to suspend servicing payments temporarily at one time or another due to an apparent shortage of funds. The crisis it would seem, is already here.

Real Terms Less Frightening

But however conclusive these facts may seem, they are compelling only because they are incomplete. In *real* terms, the rate of increase in the combined debt of these countries is not as impressive, and in fact their total debt grew at a rate only one-tenth as fast between 1978 and 1981 as between 1972 and 1978; clearly the rate of growth of these countries' national debt is slowing dramatically (see chart 2). And even where the absolute levels of debt commitments are already so high, an increase in publicly held debt does not necessarily mean an increase in the probability of default. According to the theory, it is the decreasing ratio of government income to servicing costs of government debt that is supposed to bring on collapse. So if a govenment's income is rising at a rate faster than or equal to the rate of increase in servicing costs, the danger of default may actually be diminishing.

This, in fact, is the case in the three countries

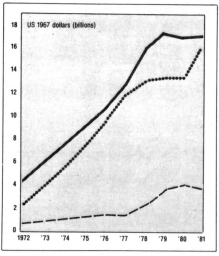

2
Public and publicly guaranteed debt

Measured in constant dollars, the rate of growth of these countries' national debt is slowing dramatically.

Brazil ▬▬▬
Mexico •••••••••••••
Argentina ▬ ▬ ▬

being examined. The ratio of debt (the source of servicing costs) to gross national product (GNP)—the total value of a nation's output of goods and services (the source of government income)—has declined or leveled off in each of these countries since 1978 (see chart 3). The same story can be told in terms of world debt. Its real value has not increased markedly since 1978, and world debt as a percentage of GNP is in decline (see charts). If the reason for the anticipated mass default is that the serving costs of accumulated debt are becoming an increasing strain on debtor governments, we have nothing to fear. A level of strain higher than we are now experiencing has already been tested without incident.

"In real *terms, the rate of increase in the combined debt of these countries is not as impressive."*

But there is another, even more fundamental level on which the case for the international debt crisis fails: it fails at the theoretical level. It assumes that the unavoidable outcome of a failure of a foreign government to generate sufficient income to service its debt is default, and it thereby ignores the very definition of debt. *Debt is a claim on assets, not on income.* The prediction that debtor governments may someday be unable to service their loans out of current *income* may well be true, but that is not the only factor relevant to the determination of whether those governments will have the ability to repay their debt. When an individual fails to meet the agreed-to payments on his loans, the assets in his possession are assigned to his creditors. One does not simply default and walk away with nothing more than a bad credit rating. Similarly, when a government encounters difficulty in servicing its debt out of income, it ought properly to liquidate

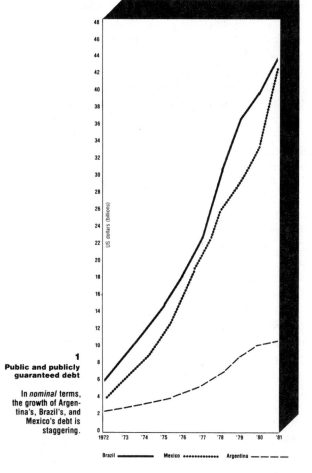

1
Public and publicly guaranteed debt

In *nominal* terms, the growth of Argentina's, Brazil's, and Mexico's debt is staggering.

US dollars (billions)

Brazil ▬▬▬   Mexico •••••••••••••   Argentina ▬ ▬ ▬

assets in its possession in order to compensate its creditors.

Much of the government-owned asset base in debtor countries is, after all, a product of the very funds that were borrowed: foreign governments typically have vast amounts of nationalized assets at their disposal. Among the 500 largest foreign-owned companies, *Fortune* magazine recently listed four government-owned Brazilian companies, with total stockholders equity of about $12 billion; two government-owned Mexican companies, with total stockholders equity of about $23 billion; and two government-owned Chilean companies, with total stockholders equity of about $2.5 billion. And though each of these governments owns literally tens or hundreds of additional companies and millions of acres of land, the abovementioned companies alone have enough equity to cover 25 percent of Brazil's debt to foreign banks, 53 percent of Mexico's and 33 percent of Chile's. (Note, too, that I have valued these companies at book value, usually only a fraction of the actual market value of a viable company.)

"Default for these governments is not a necessity—it is a matter of choice."

The people of these countries are poor, but their governments are not. If there is going to be a problem, then, it will not be one of ability to repay the loans but of *willingness*. Most of the funds loaned by banks to debtor governments were invested in government-owned industry and business projects—

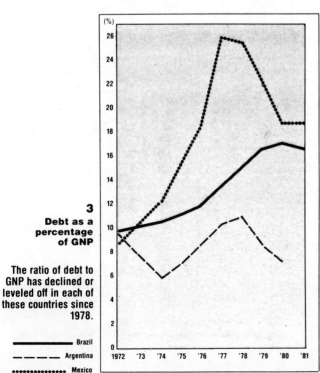

3
Debt as a percentage of GNP

The ratio of debt to GNP has declined or leveled off in each of these countries since 1978.

——— Brazil
– – – Argentina
••••••• Mexico

the money has not disappeared.

Whether the insecurity of international debt is due to genuine economic problems in debtor countries or whether it is simply due to a reluctance on the part of debtor governments to honor otherwise unenforceable agreements, crisis-theory proponents might respond to my observations, the fact remains that default by a number of debtor governments is a real possibility. But as was demonstrated above, default for these governments is *not* a necessity—it is a matter of choice, and the inclination to default is not a new problem. It is one that has been successfully resolved by a mechanism already in place.

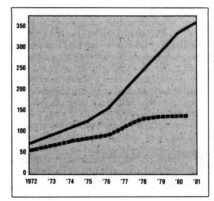

4
Public and publicly guaranteed international debt (total)

The real value of world debt, as measured in constant dollars, has not increased markedly since 1978.

US DOLLARS (BILLIONS) ———
US 1967 DOLLARS (BILLIONS) ▪▪▪▪▪▪▪▪

There is a natural reluctance on the part of debtors to service or repay their debt. Some outside incentive must therefore be given to the debtor to comply according to agreement. Within states, that incentive is usually the threat of legal recourse. Between states, at least in the world of international public finance, that incentive is the fear that foreign investment will be discouraged if contracts are not honored and debts repaid. Companies and banks that lose assets to a foreign government because the government fails to honor its agreements will also lose confidence in the government, and the nation's economy generally, as profitable objects of investment. And because foreign investment is such an important factor in promoting the growth of poorer countries, no rational debtor government would like to see such investment in its country discouraged. There are, therefore, incentives already in place to encourage service and repayment of international debt. Were such incentives not already at work, the crisis would have come and gone long ago as debtor governments would have defaulted on their debt years ago instead of continuing to service it.

The Crisis Will Not Happen

As orginally forseen, then, the crisis will not happen. Taken as a whole, the developing countries of the world are fully capable of servicing and repaying their foreign debt. But a debacle of a different sort—in which the IMF, with taxpayers' money, will bail out more and more defaulting foreign governments—has now been made possible by Congress's recent efforts to avert the supposed financial ruin by subsidizing its would-be victims. As noted above, debtor governments are faced with a delicate balance of incentives and disincentives to repay their debt. And historically, governments have generally serviced their debts according to agreement. But IMF subsidies, recently made available to debtor governments apparently likely to default, will upset this balance; for such subsidization is a signal to other debtor governments, previously not expected to default, that if they only prove themselves sufficiently irresponsible, the IMF will reward them.

If at one time it was thought that a crisis could arise because one or two governments appeared likely to default, the crisis is now more likely, not less. The remaining debtor governments may be so emboldened by the success of their neighbors in receiving subsidies that they too may opt for the easy way out.

It is too late to reverse our decision to subsidize the IMF and, in turn, its beneficiaries. Now we can only hope that decision will not create a real crisis where once there was none.

Jon Osborne has an MBA in finance and accounting and has worked for the Midwest Stock Exchange.

The Crisis Threatens World Economic Stability

Charles Krauthammer

According to [filmmaker Alfred] Hitchcock, when you are pursued through dark alleys and sinister corridors and finally make it to the safety of your room, you lean up against the door as you close it quietly behind you, sigh in relief, and turn on the light. Then comes the voice ("I thought you'd never get here") from the man sitting comfortably behind your desk and pointing a gun at your face.

Escape from OPEC, the top grossing story of the '70s, [was] a slower paced and less thrilling adventure, but it [had] the same ironic climax. On the tenth anniversary of the first OPEC offensive, as the West [patted] itself on the back and [heaved] a sigh of relief that the oil crisis [was] over, it [found] itself looking down the barrel of an even deadlier threat: the debt crisis. The story now being told of the last decade is how inflation, recession, and energy efficiency paid the oil bill. The story that hasn't been told, because cameras have an easier time covering gas lines than bank boardrooms, is how a huge part of the bill was never paid; it was mortgaged. Now the debt has matured. The real story of the last decade is how one nightmare was transformed, piece by piece, into another: OPEC into ODEC, the Organization of Debt Exporting Countries, a club that as yet dares not speak its name, but whose desperation and potential for disruption threatens to bring down the world financial system.

Paying the Oil Bill

The oil bill of the '70s was paid in four ways. The first two, and the ones we remember best, were forms of economic pain. You can't drain more than $1 trillion out of Western economies without inflicting some. First came inflation—a generalized tax, largely hidden, fairly equitable, and popular

Charles Krauthammer, "From OPEC to ODEC," *The New Republic,* November 28, 1983. Reprinted by permission of THE NEW REPUBLIC, © 1983, The New Republic.

with politicians because it lets them hide behind nominally increasing incomes. But after the second oil shock of 1979-80, when inflation reached 20 percent, the U.S. government applied the monetary brakes and precipitated the deepest world economic contraction since the Great Depression. The second shock was paid off principally by workers in the form of unemployment.

A third way the bill was handled, the one we celebrate, was through ingenuity. Western industry achieved in a decade an astonishing 31 percent increase in energy efficiency which hugely reduced demand . . . and then price. This mode of payment carried with it a largely hidden cost: an inevitable, though temporary, loss of productivity (felt most deeply in the highly mechanized "smokestack" industries), since energy-fueled machinery is inherently more productive than human labor.

And that seemed to do it. The oil crisis was solved. Even the . . . heat-up of the Iran-Iraq war, which threatens to close the Strait of Hormuz, through which eight million barrels of oil pass each day, has sent barely a ripple through the spot oil market. . . .

Now, just when we thought it was safe to return to our economic house, we find a small time bomb waiting for us. It's called the debt crisis. To hear talk of it, one would imagine that it was created ex nihilo by malevolent bankers or gerry-built by a committee of Latin American finance ministers. In fact, it is principally a little gift from OPEC. It is the last remaining—and best-disguised—installment on the enormous excise tax OPEC imposed on the rest of the world over the last ten years. The problem with this part of the tax is that it was never really paid. The oil bill was handled one final way: debt, third world debt.

The oil-poor countries of the third world had to pay a total of $350 billion for their imported oil in the decade after 1973. They didn't have it, so they borrowed it. The banks were eager to lend the money. They were awash with huge petrodollar deposits and dizzy with the wisdom that you couldn't lose on a "sovereign risk" loan. They fell over themselves lending to anybody with a flag and a U.N. seat. Debt of the non-OPEC third world countries (call them ODEC, debt exporters) increased by $480 billion in that decade. (The calculation is made by William Cline in his excellent study *International Debt and the Stability of the World Economy*.) Some of that money went to consumer subsidies, some to real development projects; most was forked over to oil producers. They reinvested back in the banks, which could then lend it again to hapless ODEC, this time to pay interest on the original loans.

"Recycling" Debt

It looks like three-card monte. Bankers call it "recycling." Recycling was the magic which produced a neat solution to two problems: OPEC's inability to spend its export earnings (a skill now mastered—by 1982 OPEC's annual current account balance was near zero); and ODEC's inability to pay for its imports. It couldn't last, and it didn't.

Things began to unravel after the second oil shock of 1979-80. Western goverments checked inflation by throwing the world economy into recession. One effect was that third world debtors found the traditional markets for their exports depressed, and thus did not have the earnings to pay the interest on their debts. At the same time, Western countries adopted tight money policies also to restrain inflation. That made interest rates on new loans higher than that of the old loans ODEC was trying to pay off. The debt burden increased, now at higher rates. And as inflation dropped, debtor countries could no longer pay off their loans in cheap, soft dollars. The dollar hardened, real interest rates reached historic highs, and exports plummeted: the big third world debtors began experiencing what the experts call disruptions of debt servicing. Around two-thirds of ODEC debt is now experiencing "disruption." Two years ago $2.6 billion of debt was formally rescheduled. This year it will reach $90 billion.

> *"If you owe the bank a thousand dollars and can't pay, it's your problem; if you owe the banks $300 billion . . . and can't pay, the banks are in trouble."*

The catastrophe was coming into sight. As long as the debtor countries can borrow enough new funds to pay back interest on their old loans, the recycling merry-go-round can continue to spin. But as soon as

large debtors begin to stumble and declare themselves unable to keep up with interest payments, recycling threatens to slow down and stop. Creditors get worried. Some, the least exposed, stop throwing good money after bad. Debtors can't get enough new loans to service old ones. If nothing is done, the debtors default. And then what?

It's the old adage: if you owe the bank a thousand dollars and can't pay, it's your problem; if you owe the banks $300 billion (which is what ODEC owes) and can't pay, the banks are in trouble. They are in trouble. Consider that the largest U.S. bank, Citibank, has a capital of $6 billion, and the largest nine U.S. banks together have a capital of about $28 billion. Citibank's loans just to Brazil amount to 75 percent of Citibank's capital. The nine banks alone have lent ODEC countries $64 billion, or more than twice their total net worth. A simple moratorium of, say, one year's interest and principal payments from Latin American debtors would not only wipe out all the profits of the big banks, it would devour much of their capital. With a huge loss of capital, they would have to reduce lending greatly (they lend at a ratio of about 20 to 1 against capital). Loans dry up, the debtors can't borrow, the merry-go-round stops. And if just Brazil, Mexico, and Argentina decided to repudiate their debts altogether, the nine largest U.S. banks would be wiped out.

Wishing the Banks Ill

There is good reason to want to see the banks go under, if only for their stupidity and greed. If OPEC had had to lend its third world brothers the $350 billions needed to pay for oil, the debt problem would be OPEC's, and what it couldn't collect would be written off as extortion money never paid. But of course OPEC wouldn't lend to such poor risks. So the banks did, taking OPEC's money (much of it deposited short-term), lending it (much of it long-term) to third world countries, and taking a handsome spread for themselves. Now they've discovered that the loans are unrepayable. And their problem is that when Kuwait makes a withdrawal, the banks have to pay; when the banks recall a loan or demand interest payments, Brazil can call a rescheduling conference.

Another reason to wish the banks ill is their, shall we say, insouciance. Donald Platten, chairman and chief executive officer of Chemical Bank since 1973, was recently asked, "Do you believe you might have erred in thrusting Chemical more deeply into the international arena?" Answer: "Not at all. New York is a port city whose influence ranges throughout the world. A bank like ours must be a big player in international banking if we want to have import in line with our size." Import, mind you. Question: "But don't you think that the banks might have gone too far in foreign lending?" Answer: "I have never worried that the international banking system would collapse as a result of the current problems. It's too unacceptable to allow that to happen." The unpleasant fact for those who would like to requisition Platten's house, limo, and shirt as part payment on the billions of his depositors' money he lent abroad and will never see again, is that he's right. It can't be allowed to happen.

Default Can't Be Allowed

Why? Because if the merry-go-round stops, the debtors default, and the banks collapse—no one is quite sure what combination of hyperinflation and contraction would result from frantic attempts of central banks to make up the losses (by printing money). All we know for sure is that governments could not just stand by and watch as lending ceased, trade ground to a halt, and the world economy settled into a depression. It's not a pretty picture, and the banks know it. That's why they remain serene.

Governments, on the other hand, are getting nervous. Rather than face the prospect of massive reconstruction in the case of collapse, they are acting now. The central banks, the International Monetary Fund, and other public agencies are pumping money to keep the loans alive. Mexico got through one crisis last year thanks to a rescue operation engineered by the U.S. Treasury. Brazil will get through next year with an $11 billion I.M.F. package. Dozens more debtors are lined up at the I.M.F. window for relief.

Just about everyone is unhappy with this arrangement. The political right is enraged at the idea of giving away taxpayers' money to ingrates who vote against us in the U.N. The irony is that the I.M.F. is probably the most effective neocolonialist instrument the modern world has yet devised. When it lends to a country, it imposes strict conditions: austerity, import restrictions, cuts in subsidies for food and other staples, etc. Then it supervises the borrower government to make sure its conditions are met. That kind of control used to be enforced by Gurkhas. What used to be Whitehall's work is now carried out by international bureaucrats who like to trade stories (in private) about the debtor countries they "run."

The IMF and Involuntary Lending

The banks are upset, too, because the I.M.F. won't let them off the hook. It keeps them lending in situations they are now trying to escape. It is genteelly called "involuntary lending": the I.M.F. says that it will not lend a penny more to, say, Brazil unless the banks match the I.M.F. loan with new loans of their own. (It's the international equivalent of matching grants at a PBS [public television] fundraiser.)

Western banks and governments are equally unhappy about sending new loans abroad to pay for

old ones, but what is the alternative? A general collapse would engulf Western economies. But even the contained default of an individual debtor country poses great risks. The extreme hardship that would result could lead to civil strife and political radicalization—and the biggest borrowers are in Latin America. That's why the Reagan Administration is trying to get Congress to approve an . . . increase in the U.S. contribution to the I.M.F.

"Overwhelmed by the burden of debt service and chafing under stringent I.M.F. 'conditionality,' [debtor countries] are rapidly developing the economic and political incentives to default."

It might turn out to be throwing good money after bad, but there is little choice. The hope is that as the industrial countries come out of the recession, they will begin importing more from the third world, and thus stimulate third world exports and earnings; and as interest rates decline and third world economies rebound from the current world recession (historically their recovery lags behind that of the industrial countries), the debt burden will stabilize at tolerable levels.

Developing Incentives to Default

Western interest lies in muddling through and hoping. The rub is with the debtor countries. They have less reason to hope, and even more reason to be unhappy with muddling through. Overwhelmed by the burden of debt service and chafing under stringent I.M.F. "conditionality," they are rapidly developing the economic and political incentives to default. The purely economic incentive for default classically comes into play at the point where interest payments exceed net borrowing. As long as a country can borrow more than it pays out in interest, it has an economic incentive to continue the relationship. That was the case for the last decade. For example, in 1975 non-oil developing countries received three times as much in borrowing as they paid out in interest. In 1982, however, for the first time interest payments exceeded borrowing. ODEC paid out $59 billion in interest and could cover it with only $57 billion of new loans.

And I.M.F. conditions for these new loans have added political incentive to repudiate the debt burden. In Argentina, the official who negotiated an I.M.F. loan agreement in New York was arrested (for jeopardizing the sovereignty of the nation) upon his return home. In Brazil, where the I.M.F. required that the government reduce wage indexing from more than 100 percent of inflation to 80 percent, the popular governor of the state of Rio de Janeiro, Leonel Brizola, declared that "the demands of the I.M.F. are a provocation to the Brazilian people," and called for a ten-year moratorium on interest payments. The I.M.F. has a worse name than the C.I.A. Graffiti has appeared in Brazil demanding "I.M.F. Out," and the leader of the general strike in Sao Paolo blamed "the whole problem" in Brazil on "the foreign debt and the impositions of the I.M.F."

So why not default? Because Brazil and Argentina and other debtors know what's happened to the economies of the only two countries to have repudiated their debt in the last twenty-five years, Cuba and North Korea. If you repudiate the debt you give up access to future capital. Without access even to short-term capital, international trade becomes exceedingly difficult since you have to pay for imports right away and you won't be paid for exports for months after they are delivered. You also run the risk of economic reprisals that go beyond denial of capital: seizure of assets, embargoes, and the like.

Threat of a Debtor's Cartel

But there is a way out. What if all the debtor countries got together and repudiated their debts collectively? Why not a debtor's cartel, a true Organization of Debt Exporting Countries? That hasn't happened yet because the larger, healthier debtors do not want to jeopardize their current credit ratings by issuing threats that associate them with their poorer ODEC brothers. But as the situation of the better off and larger debtors progressively worsens, the temptation will grow.

The first rumbles are already being heard. The Organization of American States convened a meeting in September to discuss the "external financing" problem "in the face of the extreme gravity of the liquidity crisis confronting the developing countries in the region." The [Organization of American States] O.A.S. Executive Secretary for Economic and Social Affairs declared that "the special conference has not been convoked in order to discuss the formation of a 'Debtors Club,' collective negotiations, or other proposals of this type." An interesting denial. He was calling instead for reasonable people to reason together reasonably.

With an unspoken threat to help things along. Would a threat of general default by a true ODEC be taken seriously? Isn't it suicidal? Yes, but it is mutual suicide. And like all threats to bring on mutual suicide (brandishing, say, nuclear or oil weapons), its purpose is not to bring on the apocalypse, but to establish a relationship of equality between two otherwise unequal adversaries. An ODEC ultimatum would be designed to concentrate Western minds on the wisdom of easing the debt burden. It would undoubtedly be accompanied by calls for reasoned negotiations for softened terms, trade concessions,

and other ways to shift more of the burden to the creditor countries.

For years under the banner of the New World Economic Order [N.W.E.O.] the third world has been demanding a redistribution of the world's wealth, a demand the West has scorned. The irony is that while the third world was complaining about Western stinginess, private lenders were quietly executing the greatest transfer of resources from rich to poor nations in history. The question now is: How much will have to be returned?

Carrying a Big Stick

The point of an ODEC is to alter the terms of those negotiations by bringing a tire iron to the table. The model is OPEC. While N.W.E.O. advocates pleaded impotently for Western attention, OPEC showed the world how to get it. Indeed, OPEC's success inspired the heady demands for a N.W.E.O., but not every poor country could find oil. It has now found a fairly good substitute. Through the magic of recycling, oil has been turned to paper— and the tire iron has been passed from OPEC to the poorest victims of its past success.

Charles Krauthammer is editor of The New Republic *and a prominent writer on political topics.*

viewpoint 42

The Crisis Is an
Opportunity for the US

Jackson Diehl

The United States today has the greatest opportunity to build a partnership with Latin America's biggest countries since John F. Kennedy's Alliance for Progress. Eight South American nations are now governed by democratic administrations that have proved both more moderate and more politically stable than their failed predecessors of the 1960s and '70s.

Yet none of these moderate leaders has managed to establish steady economic growth or assure the long-term payment of his country's debts. Five South American countries are suffering from inflation rates measured in hundreds— or thousands—of percentage points. And all are desperate for dollars to save their countries' economies and their regimes.

"The United States is in the position to play an important role in the consolidation of pro-western democracies," says Enbiqee Vanoli, a leader of Argentina's governing Radical Civic Union. "But a failure to understand our situation could have very serious consequences."

At stake in the continent is the most extensive movement toward democracy since the late 1950s, when elected governments were the rule and Venezuela and Colombia established what are now South America's only long-standing civilian regimes. Since 1979, Ecuador, Peru, Bolivia, Argentina, Uruguay and Brazil have all shaken off military governments that had lasted from seven to 21 years.

Many American policy makers hope the politics of this movement could become a model for the trouble spots of Central America, Africa and Asia.

Revitalizing Respect for Civil Liberties

Across the area, the new democratic administrations have been led by centrists who have managed to revitalize respect for civil liberties and

Jackson Diehl, "Debt-Ridden South America: Lands of Opportunity for the US," *The Washington Post National Weekly Edition*, August 26, 1985. © The Washington Post.

consensus politics for the first time since the 1960s, when the influence of Fidel Castro and Che Guevara spread through the region.

Peruvian President Fernando Belaunde has embodied the process. Recovering from a 1968 leftist military "revolution" that overturned his democratic government, he won re-election when Peru returned to democracy in 1980 and served out a full five-year term. Last month he became the first elected Peruvian president to turn over power to an elected successor in more than 60 years.

In Argentina, Uruguay and Brazil, where centrist politicians have also prevailed over populists and leftists, terrorist and guerrilla movements that once numbered membership in the thousands have disappeared or renounced violence, and public sympathy for them, once widespread, has vanished.

"Anybody who walks around with a gun now is finished politically," said editor James Neilson of the Buenos Aires Herald. "That's a very new development."

Deeply marked by the violence and intolerance of the last two decades, the new class of South American leaders has been preoccupied with avoiding the factional and ideological excesses that led to the coups of the 1970s. This spirit of reform has been the primary content of their platforms and the source of their electoral appeal.

In Argentina, for example, President Raul Alfonsin was virtually indistinguishable from the rival, favored, Peronist candidate on economic policy in the 1983 election. But Alfonsin won an overwhelming victory by promising to respect civil liberties, correct abuses of human rights and prevent the internal violence that ravaged the country under the Peronist government of the 1970s.

What has hamstrung the governments of Alfonsin, Belaunde, former president Osvaldo Hurtado of Ecuador and Hernan Siles Zuazo of Bolivia is that this political renovation has not been accompanied by a fresh approach to severe structural economic problems.

Economic conditions have changed drastically since the civilian political parties of these leaders were last in government in the 1960s. That decade was one of rising export prices, strong foreign investment and rapid growth throughout Latin America.

In the last five years, trade with industrialized countries has rapidly deteriorated as prices for Latin America's traditional exports—copper, silver and grain, for example—have plummeted. Meanwhile, flows of capital from banks and other investors have dried up as governments have not been able to manage the staggering sums of money they borrowed in the 1970s for development projects that are now recognized as ill-advised. International interest rates have risen, multiplying the burden of debt payments. As a result, every South American country now has loans that can be paid only by reorienting economic activity toward trade at the expense of internal prosperity.

"The dangerous thing, in U.S. terms, is that this search for economic solutions has caused a shift away from the 'centrists' of the Latin American political spectrum."

The challenge of finding a new formula for growth under these adverse conditions is the implicit mandate of the new governments. For it was economic failure, rather than political considerations, that led to the downfall of the military rulers.

Only after the economy had crashed in Argentina, Uruguay, Brazil and Bolivia, and only after the Peruvian military's socialist experiment failed, were a decisive majority of those countries willing to rally behind the political liberalism offered by politicians like Belaunde, Alfonsin and the late Tancredo Neves in Brazil.

Nevertheless, these leaders' preoccupation with strengthening civil rights, decentralizing decision-making and "professionalizing" corrupt armies—the product of their own bitter experiences—has in many cases prevented them from recognizing or accepting the new economic challenge.

Brink of Default

In Peru, Belaunde took office with an energetic program to strengthen civil liberties. But in economic policy, the veteran leader simply picked up where he had been interrupted in 1968, seeking growth through massive government investment in infrastructure and frontier development.

When the foreign debt crisis reached Peru in 1982, Belaunde proved unable to respond, insistently continuing his investment program. The result has been an economic collapse that has brought Peru to the brink of default on the $12 billion it owes abroad. Belaude's successor, Alan Garcia, has announced that his country will limit its debt payments to 10 percent of export earnings in the coming year.

In Argentina, Alfonsin entered office in December 1983 with a program for sweeping political reforms. Treatment of the country's soaring inflation and debt was a secondary priority, and the expansionist policy that finally took shape during 1984 was nearly identical to that applied by the Radical Civic Union's previous government in the mid-1960s.

While Alfonsin's approach led Argentina to the brink of hyperinflation, an even greater economic disaster was underway in neighboring Bolivia. There, Siles Zuazo was forced to renounce the last year of his term after overseeing the collapse of production, a virtual default on the foreign debt and the explosion of inflation to a percentage figure calculated in the tens of thousands.

Even when civilian leaders have given priority to economic restructuring, their willingness to act has been limited by their acute consciousness of the political polarization of the past. Almost every South American president has echoed new Brazilian President Jose Sarney's argument that measures imposing economic hardship on the public threaten the existence of a new democracy.

Such concerns at times appear more rooted in the conflicts of the 1960s than in the overwhelming centrist consensus reflected in the elections of the 1980s. "The fear for political stability becomes self-defeating, because if you worry about it too much you end up not taking any action," says Roberto Cortes Conde, an Argentine historian. "The point should be to prove that democratic governments are capable of taking the hard steps."

While these political limitations have helped prolong the region's internal imbalances, the strategy of western governments and the IMF for managing foreign debts has also failed to provide a clear way out.

IMF Austerity

Three years of austere adjustment programs overseen by the IMF have improved trade earnings in several South American countries. But they have been ineffective in controlling inflation or reigniting foreign investment and economic growth.

The dangerous thing, in U.S. terms, is that this search for economic solutions has caused a shift away from the "centrists" of the Latin American political spectrum—those that stress civil rights, tolerance of opposition and a results-oriented, pragmatic approach to policy, open to compromise.

In Ecuador's [1984] election, . . . for example, Hurtado was replaced by Leon Febres-Cordero. Hurtado's main focus was a scrupulous rebuilding of democratic institutions—his respect for the constitution, the courts and the congress carried the fervor of the professor of political science that he was. Febres-Cordero, by contrast, is from the right of Ecuador's political spectrum. He is attempting to implement a strongly free-market economic program that seems to favor the interests of big business and large landowners, and he has been accused of seeking to subvert the constitution in the process.

In Peru, Belaunde has turned over power to Garcia's APRA party. Garcia has taken the radical position of rejecting the very principle of International Monetary Fund intervention in the economics of his country and has said he will refuse to accept any of its recovery plans.

Early in August, elections to replace Siles Zuazo in Bolivia returned a plurality for Hugo Banzer, a retired general who ruled the country as dictator in the '70s.

Argentina's Alfonsin, meanwhile, has set aside his political and military reforms to launch his drastic austerity program marked by a wage-and-price freeze and the introduction of a new currency.

Increased US Role

The ineffectiveness of multilateral solutions, whether proposed by the IMF or by the 11-nation Cartagena group of Latin debtors, has led to the increased role of the United States in the region. Brazil, Peru, Argentina and even Chile have all come to depend on the Reagan administration for emergency loans or political support with banks and the IMF in the last two years, and now look to Washington in proposing long-term solutions to the debt problem.

Not since Washington terminated arms sales to the major South American countries in disputes over nationalization, nuclear power and human rights in the 1960s and '70s have U.S. leaders has such an opportunity to exert economic and political influence in the region.

For the Reagan administration, the potential benefits of such cooperation can be glimpsed in the close consultations between Argentine and U.S. economic officials on Argentina's new anti-inflation plan. Buenos Aires conspicuously has moderated its promotion of a Latin American debtors' group and its criticism of U.S. policy in Central America.

In Brazil, U.S. support in debt-financing arrangements has been accompanied by a renewal of cooperation in military and scientific affairs. In Chile, the prospect of American opposition to a new financing arrangement recently helped prompt Gen. Augusto Pinochet to lift a state of seige.

The risks of the new situation, however, may be equally great. Peru's failure to win stronger U.S.

economic help under Belaunde's administration has helped inspire the more militant position of Garcia, whose rhetoric toward the Reagan administration has frequently been hostile.

Most of Latin America's democratic leaders continue to warn that the United States must act more aggressively to help resolve the continent's economic crisis, or face the loss of the continent's rare embrace of moderate democratic politics.

"Most of Latin America's democratic leaders continue to warn that the United States must act more aggressively to help resolve the continent's economic crisis."

In simplest terms, that means more U.S. dollars—more investment in Latin American industries, more favorable terms for Latin America's exports to the United States and, above all, more help paying off the banks.

"If the United States isn't willing to understand the reality of our problems," Garcia warned several months before his election, "it could be confronted with a hostile bloc of governments in South America."

Jackson Diehl is a staff writer for The Washington Post.

"Aid policies can be reshaped . . . [to] encourage participatory development."

The Developed Nations Must Aid the Debtor Nations

The Debt Crisis Network

There can be no durable solution to the debt crisis that does not address the staggering poverty of the majority in most debtor nations. Without an improvement in their welfare, the world economy as a whole will never be healthy or stable. Nor can the crisis be resolved as long as:

- countries' debt burdens are growing faster than their economies;
- IMF medicine further debilitates the patient, rather than offering assistance to meet specific economic problems and development needs;
- policy responses to the debt crisis adversely affect the living standards of workers, farmers, and others in the developed world; and
- an inordinate amount of power in the international financial system remains in private hands, outside the domain of public concerns.

We propose an alternative framework for solutions . . . that:

- in the *short-term*, alleviates the debt burden of the least developed nations, and redefines rigid IMF conditionality toward more developmental forms of adjustment for all developing countries;
- in the *medium-term*, offers a package for debt relief; new criteria for bilateral aid, and outlines regulations for private banks; and
- in the *longer-term*, reverts a more democratic IMF to a more modest role of providing short-term balance of payments support in a reformed international financial system. . . .

Short-Term Measures

For short-term alleviation of the suffering of the most vulnerable groups in the developing world, it is useful to distinguish three groups of developing countries with different needs and requiring

different treatment.

The United Nations has identified 36 countries which, by its criteria, are the "least developed" in the world. Most are currently suffering food crises affecting large portions of their populations, and are badly in need of immediate debt relief. These 36 countries collectively owe only $26.2 billion (1982), only 2.9 percent of Third World debt, and most of it is owed to government sources. In order to save tens of thousands of lives, Western governments should follow the lead of those Scandinavian governments that have transformed outstanding debt to some of these countries into grants. New credit should be made on easier terms to ease the immediate suffering. Western banks could carry out a similar debt forgiveness with only a minor impact on earnings.

Safeguards have been proposed to insure that debt cancellation is not followed by the same borrowing practices that created the crisis at the expense of development. The West German Green Party, for example, suggests that interest and principal write-offs be paid (in local currencies) by debtor countries into a national development fund managed by non-governmental organizations (e.g. farmer's associations, unions, consumer groups, women's groups). The fund would finance self-reliant development projects which aim to satisfy basic needs.

A second group includes those few countries where government disregard for the development conditions of the country and the basic needs of the majority is so blatant that the world community advocates a total halt to all new loans to their governments. At present, broad consensus exists on South Africa, and there is a growing consensus on Chile, Zaire, the Philippines, and Guatemala, and elsewhere. Emphasis should be placed on channeling assistance to non-governmental groups in these countries.

The Debt Crisis Network, *From Debt to Development: Alternatives to the International Debt Crisis.* Washington, DC: Institute for Policy Studies/Transnational Institute, 1985. Reprinted with permission.

A third group includes the majority of developing countries, which fall between the first two categories. The U.S. executive director to the IMF (and to the World Bank with respect to non-project lending) should support a new developmental version of conditionality for these nations that would guide the use of resources to assure that they do not go down the drain like so much of the money lent during the 1970s. In particular, before voting in favor of a loan, the U.S. executive director should be satisfied that:

- the country has provided a development plan tailored to its specific resource base, infrastructure, development goals, and problems. The plan must have economic targets that are feasible, unlike the majority of IMF plans for debtor countries in 1984, which were violated soon after going into effect.
- the U.S. executive director to the Fund, in accordance with U.S. law (PL96-369 of 1980), should only vote for those loans where the plan submitted adequately provides for: creating safe, healthy, and environmentally sound jobs; narrowing the gap in wealth and income between rich and poor; and advancing health, housing, education, and other basic human needs.
- two other considerations, not designated by the 1980 law, should be added. First, the economic plan should specify measures to redress the severe impact of the debt on vulnerable groups, particularly women and children. Second, the plan should demonstrate that natural resources (forest, wetlands, agricultural lands) are conserved and managed for sustainable development.
- the plan must demonstrate the ability of the country to repay the loan and to continue servicing its debt, as long as service payments do not exceed 20 percent of the country's export earnings. Even these payments should be seen as short-term; in the medium-term, a more thorough debt cancellation and loss sharing plan is proposed.

All letters of intent to the IMF should also spell out the projected impact of economic adjustment policies on jobs, wealth distribution, and basic needs. The secrecy surrounding these programs should also be eliminated. Adjustment programs and IMF loans are supposed to be in the interest of developing country recipients, and taxpayers from all over the world pay for the loans. The IMF should therefore make public the contents of adjustment programs.

Medium-Term Measures

In the medium-term, the United States should adopt policies which discourage the kind of lending that fueled the debt crisis and should address ways to decrease the overall level of debt. It can do this primarily through bilateral lending policies and banking legislation. First, however, it needs to address the central issue of debt relief and loss sharing.

"U.S. aid policies have tended to exacerbate the debt crisis."

None of the above measures significantly reduces the $895 billion Third World debt looming over the entire system. Politically, this larger question is unlikely to be seriously addressed in an international forum before the next major recession in the United States and world economy. When that occurs, we should be ready to launch proposals for bankers, government officials, and representatives of non-governmental organizations—under the auspices of the United Nations—to bring to the table. They should include:

- proposals to convert parts of official debt (i.e. debt to government institutions) and parts of the private debt into grants;
- proposals for a multi-year moratorium on debt servicing of both public and private debt and a significant extension of periods for consolidating and repaying the remaining overdue debt service over the longer-term; and
- proposals to repay some of the debt "in kind." One such form of repayment that might be explored is the preparation of packages of "services" such as conservation of species (genetic) diversity in biological reserves and national parks.

Just as the current patchwork approach to solutions involves losses borne largely by poor and working peoples, so too will these proposals involve large losses as portions of the debt are written off. Negotiations among banks, developed country governments and developing country governments will be necessary to work out how losses will be shared among the three groupings. Public pressure will be essential to insure that the taxpayers' contribution to the loss sharing is compensated with an increase in public authority over the nation's banking system.

Bilateral Aid

U.S. aid policies have tended to exacerbate the debt crisis. U.S. loans have generally been channeled into export-oriented projects compatible with the overall growth philosophy of the IMF and World Bank. This export-led model has depended upon heavy borrowing from abroad.

An overhaul of U.S. aid policies can be reshaped along the following guidelines that encourage participatory development.

Aid should be channeled to institutions that encourage greater self-reliance in developing countries and among the poorer majorities. U.S. assistance should support, not discourage, developing country efforts to diversify economic activities away from reliance on trade toward those that provide employment opportunities in areas that benefit the local population. Such activities might include: public works projects that renew ecosystems or develop needed infrastructure with minimal reliance on imports, and projects that enhance food production for local consumption. These include measures to insure more equitable land distribution; a greater focus on the needs of small, subsistence farmers (particularly women) and agricultural laborers; and a shift from export-oriented and large agribusiness production to staple food production.

Democratically managed rural credit organizations could be encouraged that support expanded agricultural processing, packaging, storage, marketing and transportation. Small-scale skills could also be given priority, particularly those which generate employment for women.

Aid policies should support better representation and involvement of the poor in economic decisions and development activities affecting their lives. The poor need to participate in defining the problem as well as in project design, implementation and evaluation. Many Third World governments and economic institutions do not represent poor and working people; in these countries, it is essential that the United States develop much greater sensitivity to local conditions so that it can channel its aid to those organizations which do. This is one avenue whereby poor people can gain a louder voice in policies which affect them. U.S. aid policies can encourage more democratic decision-making structures by funding community development projects and cooperatives run by workers and peasants themselves.

"Development and basic human needs criteria should form the basis for U.S. policy decisions."

Reduce military and security-related assistance and raise development assistance. Security assistance is often a direct response to the need by certain Third World governments to repress unrest among the population, unrest often fueled by austerity borne of the debt crisis. The needs of the people would obviously be better met if much of the amount spent on military aid was instead spent on long-term economic development. What does it mean for U.S. economic relations with the rest of the world that "security assistance" accounts for 69 percent of

foreign aid authorizations in the 1986 budget, compared to 55 percent in 1981? In most cases the answer is simple: more debt and more repression.

End use of U.S. aid for political and domestic economic aims. Often, aid is used to further U.S. financial and direct investment in the developing world or is tied to the purchase of U.S. goods and services. The United States has also politicized multilateral aid agencies such as the World Bank by diverting resources from countries whose political or economic systems do not meet U.S. approval. Instead, development and basic human needs criteria should form the basis for U.S. policy decisions within multilateral financial institutions.

Oppose linking aid to a country's acceptance of IMF conditions. Such linkage renders U.S. bilateral aid subject to the inappropriate, harmful conditions pushed by the IMF.

Policy Toward Banks

Banks have added to the crisis in recent years by charging high interest rates on new loans that have essentially been used to service old loans. Banks could be pressed to write off, or convert into grants, interest payment arrears accumulated as a result of recent rate increases. Congressman Charles Schumer and economist Alfred Watkins have calculated that 70-80 percent of the new loans to many of the largest debtors since 1979 have been used to pay interest on old loans, and hence have had nothing to do with development. To reverse this practice, they have proposed that: "banks should be forbidden to report profits on any foreign loans on which the banks are lending borrowers the money to pay interest. This will not only reduce the rewards for loaning money to pay back loans; it will also give banks an incentive to lower their interest rates to levels that debtor nations can pay without taking out new loans."

Other legislative measures toward banks that would help ease repayment burdens include requirements on banks to cap loans renegotiation fees and interest rates charged to the poorest countries, as originally proposed by Schumer in 1983.

Longer-Term Measures

In the longer term, once the immediate crisis is over, we would urge that a reformed and democratized IMF be reduced to a far more modest task of coordinating the foreign exchange policies of its members and of responding to their truly short-term liquidity needs. Or, as clearly spelled out in the Fund's Articles of Agreement, "to make financial resources available to members, on a temporary basis and with adequate safeguards, to permit them to correct payments imbalances without resorting to measures destructive of national and internationsal prosperity." Indeed, the prosperity clause is certainly violated in current IMF "austerity" packages.

This overall alternative should be pursued in conjunction with proposals to change certain related facets of U.S. macro-economic policy, particularly in the fields of: fiscal and monetary policy, trade, transnational corporations, and agriculture. . . .

None of these measures will be accepted without substantial public education and political struggle. Such a struggle can only occur if there are local, regional and national debates on these issues by an informed citizenry. The debate over the debt crisis has far too long been confined to the ranks of bankers, government officials, and a small coterie of economists. Representatives from religious and civil rights organizations, unions, hunger and development groups, the women's movement, environmental agencies, community groups, and others must enter into the fray. Silence from their ranks will only perpetuate debt, poverty, and underdevelopment. Education, debate, and political action are the ingredients of a more humane and democratic alternative.

The Debt Crisis Network grew out of a gathering of representatives of religious organizations, unions, environmental organizations, researchers, and other citizen groups which shared a mutual commitment to social justice and to just, equitable, and long-term solutions to the debt crisis.

"Above all else, [foreign aid] keeps in power third world governments that would otherwise perish of their own incompetence and unpopularity."

viewpoint **44**

The Developed Nations Use Aid as a Tool of Imperialism

Cheryl Payer

"The Monkey's Paw" is a classic horror story about an amulet with the power to grant three wishes to its owner. There is a gruesome twist: each wish comes true, but in such a grotesque fashion as to be a catastrophe for the wisher.

The moral of the story is especially relevant to progressives today who are trying to influence the actions of a government dominated by reactionaries: you must be very careful what you campaign for, because you might get it, or parts of it, twisted into forms which suit your opponents' cause rather then your own.

The proposals presented by John Cavanagh and the Debt Crisis Network (DCN) are dismaying because they are not progressive but regressive. At its best, and most utopian, the vision is of a benign form of imperialism. At worst, if well-intentioned grassroots activists take it seriously, it could revive the hopes of the bankers and the Reagan administration for a taxpayer-financed aid bailout which would keep the serious imperialists funded for a few more years.

Cavanagh and the DCN present essentially two major responses to the debt crisis: debt forgiveness and more aid. Let us examine each of these in turn.

Problems with Debt Collection

Asking for debt relief is like pushing an open door. It is almost universally recognized that the debtor countries cannot pay even the current interest on their debts; the banks and the U.S. government have been doing little more than providing debt relief since the crisis broke in 1982. Cavanagh's piece gives the misleading impression that the debtor countries are servicing their debts and obeying austerity programs imposed by the IMF. They are not.

Cheryl Payer, "The Case Against Debt Relief," *Dollars & Sense*, December 1985. Reprinted by permission of Dollars & Sense, 38 Union Square, Somerville, MA 02143.

Virtually all of the Latin American debtor countries have either fallen behind on their debt payments, or pay part of the interest with money borrowed from the IMF and their bank creditors for that purpose. Cavanagh applauds Peru's new initiative to limit debt service payments to "only" 10% of next year's export income—but Peru paid nothing in 1984!

Not long ago countries were careful to keep repayments to the International Monetary Fund up to date, because the Fund was the key to money from other creditors. Now the IMF itself has a serious debt collection crisis, because countries don't see it in their interest to repay IMF loans when they have to use their own money instead of borrowed funds. Newspaper accounts indicate that a number of African countries have not been paying their debts to the IMF.

Equally serious, the IMF's attempts to impose its austerity programs on third world debtors are in a public shambles. Mexico, which had long been the model debtor from the banks' point of view, was declared out of compliance with its IMF program just before the earthquake struck; Brazil and Peru have both announced that they will not seek new IMF agreements to replace the ones they have broken. In Argentina, for the first time, an austerity program designed by a debtor nation was rubber-stamped by the IMF.

Austerity Programs Can't Be Enforced

There is austerity in the third world, to be sure; the credit-dependent economies are suffering severe withdrawal pains after the borrowing and spending binge of the 1970s. And the poor suffer the most. It does not follow, however, that the poor will be granted any relief if debts are forgiven or turned into grants. The poor also suffered when the credit was flowing freely: income distribution *worsened* in many countries, including Brazil and the Philippines, during the very years that capital inflows were at their highest.

Poor people in third world countries can only benefit from either economic growth or debt repudiation if their government cares enough to attempt the difficult and politically risky path of redistributing income. And nonrevolutionary governments will only care to attempt this if the people use their power, through ballots, strikes, or riots, to persuade the government it would be *more* risky to ignore their demands.

It is clear that something like this is beginning to happen all over Latin America in the wake of the debt crisis. IMF austerity programs cannot be enforced because poor and working people refuse to tolerate them, because even regressive governments like that of Mexico find the political costs of such programs too high, and *because the IMF no longer can bribe governments with the huge sums of money needed to make such austerity palatable.*

"My own hope is that repressive and undemocratic elites throughout the third world will be destabilized by the drying up of funds which have rewarded and supported them in the past."

This is why the proposals of Cavanagh and the DCN are regressive, despite the good intentions of the authors. Because of the debt crisis, military governments have been rolled back in several of the largest countries of South America, labor unions have regained legality and legitimacy, and governments are thumbing their noses at the IMF. One key prop of the imperialist system—the inflow of aid and credit—has collapsed from the weight of its own contradictions.

The only thing which can save imperialism from at least partial collapse these days is the injection of enormous sums of new money linked to "conditionality" of the old type. The dilemma of Wall Street and the Reagan administration is their lack of ideas on where to find such enormous sums. The taxpayers are in revolt, as illustrated by the near success of attempts to block the IMF quota increase in Congress two years ago. This highlights another serious defect of the Debt Crisis Network proposals.

The Aid Trap

Cavanagh says nothing about where the "aid" he proposes would come from (aside from a suggestion that military and security-related assistance should be reduced, which I would endorse.) There is only one answer: from the taxpayers of the United States and of other developed countries. If taxes came only out of millionaires' pockets we might be complacent

about this prospect, but they don't; they come from the poor and working people of our country. If aid really helped poor people in debtor countries we might feel that it is progressive to ask our working classes to make the sacrifice. The whole history of aid programs tells us otherwise.

Indeed, the saddest aspect of the Cavanagh proposal is that it ignores the large body of literature which indicates in damning detail just what a regressive role so-called foreign aid played in almost every recipient country in the post-war era. Numerous studies have shown that foreign aid serves several functions: it finances unsaleable First World exports, it buys political advantage for the creditor country, it provides the only incentive for acceptance of IMF austerity programs, it destroys agricultural and industrial production in the "aided" country. Above all else, it keeps in power third world governments that would otherwise perish of their own incompetence and unpopularity. The one thing that foreign aid does *not* do is alleviate poverty.

Cavanagh, of course, is thinking of quite a different type of aid; he recommends encouraging "participatory development," "democratically managed rural credit organizations," and so forth. But it is flatly impossible, a contradiction in terms, to imagine that foreign aid can promote "greater self-reliance," "projects that enhance food production for local consumption," or "needed infrastructure with minimal reliance on imports." Foreign aid can *only* pay for imports and can only reinforce import and trade dependence. The case of Tanzania is Exhibit A here. Eighteen years ago, President Nyerere declared a desire for self-reliance in the Arusha declaration. "Nice" countries and non-governmental organizations hastened to send aid in support of self-reliance. Today, the country is pathetically and paralyzingly import-dependent. Creditors can aid self-reliance only by cutting off credit.

Cavanagh's advocacy of a "reformed and democratized IMF" and "a new developmental version of conditionality" is troubling. He doesn't specify how it would be democratized—as he himself notes, many of its third world member governments do not represent all of their peoples. Nor is it clear who in the world would fund it if they couldn't also control the way the money was disbursed. He also refrains from suggesting who has the wisdom (and arrogance) to decide what "developmental" conditionality would look like.

Starting at Home

I agree with Cavanagh that, for all its grave defects, Congress remains the last bastion of representative democracy in this nation. We should cherish, defend, and above all *use* it to the limit of our powers. But citizens' pressure on Congess is an extremely blunt instrument, as the fate of the 1980

IMF-human rights legislation cited by Cavanagh illustrates. Citizens' pressure can be felt most immediately, and most effectively, by telling the administration what it *can't* do, by refusing to authorize money for it.

Which governments in the Western hemisphere come closest to providing the sort of participatory, humane development which Cavanagh and his associates prefer? I would suggest that Cuba and Nicaragua are making the sincerest efforts in that direction. Yet the first gets no U.S. aid, and U.S. taxpayers' money has been appropriated for the purpose of destroying the second.

There are a lot of positive things progressives can accomplish through Congress, and they will save taxpayers' money rather than adding to the burden. We can cut off aid to the contras, to the Philippines, to Chile. We can refuse to bail out the government of South Africa in its current financial crisis. But until we are able to elect more progressive leaders, we have no business authorizing the leaders we do have to spend our dollars on developmental aid. When aid to the Nicaraguan contras can be called "humanitarian," progressives should not provide moral support to any kind of aid program. The best thing we can do is insist that our government, which poisons everything it touches in foreign relations, *stand back and keep its mitts off.*

Reduction Is Essential

It is not only necessary but highly desirable, from the standpoint of the future independence and welfare of indebted countries, that they adjust to the new reality: huge capital inflows like those of the 1970s are no longer available to their governments. Let me make it clear that I am not in favor of forcing any country to pay these unmanageable and illegitimate debts. I am saying they don't need debt relief, *because they are quite capable of seizing it for themselves.* The big question is how they will handle the absolutely necessary, inevitable, and painful readjustment of living standards required by the new post-credit situation of the 1980s.

Today the new money is simply not available in the massive amounts needed to replicate the old-style bailouts; therefore, repudiation (in one form or another) is inevitable. If repudiation is carried out by new governments which truly have the interests of poor people at heart, it will be a very positive step. If debt relief comes as a gift from the banks or the creditor governments, it will not be progressive, because they will be doing it to save their own hegemony (and their markets). The people at the bottom won't benefit, and the governments of the borrowing countries won't have learned anything. Such a resolution can only mean that the whole process will start up again, with yet another, larger debt crisis in the future.

My own hope is that repressive and undemocratic elites throughout the third world will be destabilized by the drying up of funds which have rewarded and supported them in the past, and that they will be succeeded by more popular and humane governments. Such governments will probably find it imperative to repudiate the debts of the old regime. It will be the duty of progressive people to oppose destructive intervention—military and financial—by our own leaders against such governments. This, rather than debt relief or new fixes of foreign capital, is the most precious gift we can give them to show our solidarity.

Cheryl Payer is the author of The Debt Trap *and* The World Bank: A Critical Analysis.

"There must be greater emphasis on both market-oriented economic policies to foster growth and adequate financing to support it."

viewpoint **45**

The Baker Proposal to End World Debt

James A. Baker III

It is essential that we begin the process of strengthening our international debt strategy.

Three years ago the international financial community developed a flexible, cooperative, case-by-case strategy to address the debt problem and lay the basis for growth in the debtor nations. In three years:

—Aggregate current account deficits in developing countries have been sharply reduced from $104 billion in 1982 to $44 billion this year.

—Growth in developing countries has been restored to about 4 percent, compared to less than 2 percent in 1982.

—This growth has been fueled by sharp increases in developing nations' exports, including a 21 percent increase in their exports to the United States last year.

These developments reflect improved growth and sharply lower interest rates in the industrial nations, as well as adoption of improved policies within most debtor countries. These policies have been given important support by reschedulings and rollovers amounting to approximately $210 billion, and by net new commercial bank lending.

The international financial institutions have also played an important role in the progress that has been achieved. The IMF in particular has very capably played a leadership role, providing guidance on policies and temporary balance of payments financing, both of which have catalyzed commercial bank flows.

Despite this progress, some serious problems have developed. A number of principal debtor countries have recently experienced setbacks in their efforts to improve their economic situations, particularly with regard to inflation and fiscal imbalances,

James A. Baker III, in a speech before the joint annual meeting of the International Monetary Fund and the World Bank on October 8, 1985 in Seoul, Korea.

undercutting prospects for sustained growth. Bank lending to debtor nations has been declining, with very little net new lending anticipated this year. The sense of increasing reluctance among banks to participate in new money and debt rescheduling packages has introduced serious uncertainties for borrowers, in some cases making it more difficult for them to pursue economic reforms.

These problems need to be addressed, promptly and effectively, by building upon the international debt strategy in order to improve the prospects for growth in the debtor countries. This is an enterprise which will require, above all, that we work together and that we each strengthen our commitment to progress.

Solving the Debt Problem

If the debt problem is to be solved, there must be a "Program for Sustained Growth," incorporating three essential and mutually reinforcing elements:

• First and foremost, the adoption by principal debtor countries of comprehensive macroeconomic and structural policies, supported by the international financial institutions, to promote growth and balance of payments adjustment, and to reduce inflation.

• Second, a continued central role for the IMF, in conjunction with increased and more effective structural adjustment lending by the multilateral development banks (MDBs), both in support of the adoption by principal debtors of market-oriented policies for growth.

• Third, increased lending by the private banks in support of comprehensive economic adjustment programs.

I want to emphasize that the United States does not support a departure from the case-by-case debt strategy we adopted three years ago. This approach has served us well; we should continue to follow it. It recognizes the inescapable fact that the particular circumstances of each country are different. Its main components, fundamental adjustment measures within the debtor nations and conditionality in conjunction with lending, remain essential to the restoration of external balance and longer-term growth.

We need to build upon the current strategy to strengthen its ability to foster growth. There must be greater emphasis on both market-oriented economic policies to foster growth and adequate financing to support it.

Growth-Dependent Lending

In essence, what I am suggesting is that adequate financing can be made available through a combination of private creditors and multilateral institutions working cooperatively, but only where there are reasonable prospects that growth will occur. This will depend upon the adoption of proper economic policies by the developing countries. Financing can only be prudently made available when and as effective policies to promote economic efficiency, competitiveness and productivity—the true foundations of growth—are put in place. We cannot afford to repeat the mistakes of the past. Adjustment must continue. Adjustment programs must be agreed before additional funds are made available, and should be implemented as those funds are disbursed.

"Financing can only be prudently made available when and as effective policies to promote economic efficiency, competitiveness and productivity—the true foundations of growth—are put in place."

These efforts should be mutually reinforcing. Sound policies in the principal debtor countries will not only promote growth, but will also stimulate the needed private bank lending. And it will be important that these policies be supported by the IMF, complemented by the MDBs. These institutions can help encourage and catalyze both needed policies and financing.

In today's highly interdependent world economy, efforts at economic isolationism are doomed to failure. Countries which are not prepared to undertake basic adjustments and work within the framework of the case-by-case debt strategy, cooperating with the international financial institutions, cannot expect to benefit from this three-point program. Additional lending will not occur. Efforts by any country to "go it alone" are likely to seriously damage its prospects for future growth.

I would like to elaborate on the actions that will be required by each participant in this three-point program.

Change in the Principal Debtors

The essence of the need for structural change in the principal debtors is captured in two quotations I would like to share with you.
First:

> "The only way to overcome our economic crisis is to tackle at their root the structural problems of our economy to make it more efficient and productive." (President de la Madrid of Mexico)

And second:

> "Economic growth will have solid foundations only if we reestablish trust and stimulate private enterprise, which must be the flagship of our economic development . . . We will promote authentic institutional change in the economic sector." (President Sarney of Brazil)

These are not the words of a U.S. Secretary of the Treasury. They are statements made in July [1985] by the Presidents of Mexico and Brazil. I believe they reflect a growing sentiment in Latin America.

It is essential that the heavily indebted, middle income developing countries do their part to implement and maintain sound policies. Indeed, without such policies, needed financing cannot be expected to materialize. Policy and financing are not substitutes but essential complements.

For those countries which have implemented measures to address the imbalances in their economies, a more comprehensive set of policies can now be put in place, which promises longer term benefits from stronger growth, higher standards of living, lower inflation, and more flexible and productive economies. These must not only include macroeconomic policies, but also other medium and longer term supply-side policies to promote growth.

We believe that such institutional and structural policies should include:

—increased reliance on the private sector, and less reliance on government, to help increase employment, production and efficiency;

—supply-side actions to mobilize domestic savings and facilitate efficient investment, both domestic and foreign, by means of tax reform, labor market reform and development of financial markets; and

—market-opening measures to encourage foreign direct investment and capital inflows, as well as to liberalize trade, including the reduction of export subsidies.

Strengthening Larger Policies

This broader approach does not mean that policy areas that have been the focus of efforts to date—in particular fiscal, monetary, and exchange rate policies—can receive less attention. Indeed, macroeconomic policies have been central to efforts to date and must be strengthened to achieve greater progress. These policies should consist of:

—market-oriented exchange rate, interest rate, wage and pricing policies to promote greater economic efficiency and responsiveness to growth and employment opportunities; and

—sound monetary and fiscal policies focused on reducing domestic imbalances and inflation and on freeing up resources for the private sector.

The cornerstone of sustained growth must be greater domestic savings, and investment of those savings at home. Macroeconomic and structural policies which improve economic efficiency, mobilize domestic resources, and provide incentives to work, save, and invest domestically will create the favorable economic environment necessary for this to occur. Such an environment is also critical to attract supplemental foreign savings.

As a practical matter, it is unrealistic to call upon the support of voluntary lending from abroad, whether public or private, when domestic funds are moving in the other direction. Capital flight must be reversed if there is to be any real prospect of additional funding, whether debt or equity. If a country's own citizens have no confidence in its economic system, how can others?

There are essentially two kinds of capital inflows: loans and equity investments. Foreign borrowings have to be repaid—with interest. Equity investment, on the other hand, has a degree of permanence and is not debt-creating. Moreover, it can have a compounding effect on growth, bring innovation and technology, and help to keep capital at home.

We believe that the debtor nations must be willing to commit themselves to these policies for growth in order that the other elements of a strengthened debt strategy can come into place.

Enhancing Effectiveness

The international financial institutions must also play an important role in strengthening the debt strategy to promote growth. However, we must recognize that the international financial institutions cannot have sufficient resources to meet the debtor nations' financing needs all by themselves. An approach which assumes that the IMF and the World Bank are the sole answer to debt problems is simply a non-starter. For most developing countries other sources must play a more important role. These include private sector borrowing, increased export earnings, foreign equity investment, and repatriation of capital which has fled abroad. All these routes should be pursued. . . .

The international banking community has played an important role during the past three years. I am, however, concerned about the decline in net bank lending to debtor nations over the past year and a half, particularly those nations which are making progress. All of us can appreciate the commercial banks' concerns, but we believe these concerns would dissipate if the banks were confident that the new lending is in support of policies for growth in the developing nations.

If creditor governments, in an age of budget austerity, are to be called upon to support increases in multilateral development bank lending to the debtor nations, and if the recipient nations are asked to adopt sound economic policies for growth to avoid wasting that financing, then there must also be a commitment by the banking community—a commitment to help the global community make the necessary transition to stronger growth.

"We believe that the debtor nations must be willing to commit themselves to these policies for growth."

Our assessment of the commitment required by the banks to the entire group of heavily indebted, middle income developing countries would be net new lending in the range of $20 billion for the next three years. In addition, it would be necessary that countries now receiving adequate financing from banks on a voluntary basis continue to do so, provided they maintain sound policies.

I would like to see the banking community make a pledge to provide these amounts of new lending and make it publicly, provided the debtor countries also make similar growth-oriented policy commitments as their part of the cooperative effort. Such financing could be used to meet both short-term financing and longer-term investment needs in the developing countries, and would be available, provided debtors took action and multilateral institutions also did their part.

We would welcome suggestions from the banking community about arrangements which could be developed in order to ensure that adequate financing to support growth is available. . . .

Conclusion

In conclusion, much has been accomplished in the past few years in addressing the pressing economic problems of the early 1980s and preparing the foundation for future global growth. We must now join together to consolidate our progress in building stronger economies for the future.

Sound policies and growth in the industrial world can provide a solid foundation for strengthening and adapting the current international debt strategy. Let us not lose the present opportunity. I have proposed a three-point "Program for Sustained Growth" to provide renewed impetus for resolving the debt problem. We must not deceive ourselves. There are no easy solutions, and none of us can escape our responsibilities.

The principal debtor nations must make the hard policy decisions to restructure their economies. The commercial banks must provide adequate resources to support these efforts. The MDBs must increase the efficiency and volume of their lending.

> "The principal debtor nations must make the hard policy decisions to restructure their economies."

Moving from proposal to implementation will be a demanding exercise and cannot be accomplished overnight. As we adapt our strategy, we must continue to look to the IMF as the catalyst for new financial flows. And with these new flows will come new hope.

We will be building on the efforts of the past. The needs are clearly recognized by borrowers and creditors alike. Fundamentally, there is no disparity of interest among our nations. We have a common interest in growth—sustained growth that rests on productivity, innovation and investment. Let us begin our efforts now.

James A. Baker III is Secretary of the Treasury of the United States.

"The trouble with the Baker Initiative is that there has been insufficient consideration . . . of how to execute this strategy."

viewpoint 46

The Proposal Is Inadequate

Bruce Bartlett

At the October 1985 meeting of the World Bank and the International Monetary Fund [IMF] in Seoul, U.S. Treasury Secretary James A. Baker, III unveiled a plan for dealing with the continuing Third World debt problem. His plan involves an additional $20 billion loan to the Third World countries by private banks and increased lending by multilateral development banks (MDBs) as well, in return for the recipients' adoption of market-oriented economic policies. Baker's proposals for Third World governments include:

- Increased reliance on the private sector, and less reliance on government, to increase employment, production, and efficiency.
- Supply-side actions to mobilize domestic savings and facilitate efficient domestic and foreign investment by means of tax reform, labor market reform, and development of financial markets.
- Market-opening measures, including the reduction of export subsidies, to encourage foreign direct investment and capital inflows, as well as to liberalize trade.

The theory is that, if Third World nations were to dismantle state enterprises, abandon regulatory interference with the market, cut taxes and government spending, and in general, establish free markets, growth and exports would be stimulated, generating the cash to repay not only the new loans but the old ones as well.

In theory this is a good plan. Initiatives providing long-term solutions to the debt problem are badly needed. Third World nations, moreover, must do something to increase the growth that will not ensue from the interventionist policies that have characterized their economic policies for more than a generation. They must adopt free market policies

Bruce Bartlett, "The Promises and Pitfalls of Baker's Third World Debt Plan," *Backgrounder*, December 19, 1985. Reprinted by permission of The Heritage Foundation.

and cut back government interference with the economy. Offering Third World nations the "carrot" of additional aid in return for adopting better economic policies makes sense.

Pitfalls of the Baker Plan

The trouble with the Baker Initiative is that there has been insufficient consideration at the Treasury Department of how to execute this strategy and how to avoid its potential pitfalls. Indeed, it appears that Treasury officials strongly resisted promoting market-oriented policies in the Third World. Treasury apparently relented only when Republicans on the House Appropriations Committee threatened to block MDB contributions unless U.S. representatives to these institutions were instructed to demand more market-oriented policies. Only after Congressman David Obey (D-WI), chairman of the House Appropriations Subcommittee on Foreign Operations, refused to support the Administration's budget requests for the MDBs without the backing of House Republicans did Treasury instruct its representatives at the IMF and the World Bank to insist that new aid be dependent on the adoption of free market policies by recipient countries.

Treasury Assistant Secretary David Mulford outlined the following objectives in an April 1985 memorandum to the U.S. executive directors of the World Bank and International Monetary Fund:

1) Use tax policies to encourage savings and investment in support of growth and economic stability. Such policies could encompass overall reductions in income taxes, reductions in marginal tax rates, adjustment of tax systems in light of inflation, the impact of taxation on the misallocation of resources, changes in the structure of commodity or excise taxes, and changes in tax expenditures (deductions or credits).

2) Liberalize foreign trade to facilitate exports and to remove import restrictions. These measures could

include reduction or elimination of export taxes, development of nontraditional exports, creation of free trade zones, and deregulation of foreign exchange controls to encourage productive activity in which the country has a clear comparative advantage.

3) Promote pricing policies reflecting market forces to foster efficient allocation of resources. Such steps could include decontrol of agriculture prices, termination of price controls on industrial products, and lifting ceilings on interest rates.

4) Facilitate appropriate foreign investment. This could include simplification and liberalization of laws regarding foreign investment, active promotion of joint venture activities, and extending the same treatment to foreign investors.

5) Support private sector-oriented growth, encourage privatization, and discourage, where appropriate, direct government activity in the economy.

The strategy outlined in Mulford's memorandum is welcome, but long overdue. Yet Treasury must take care that it does not make the Third World debt situation worse than it now is. There is a danger, for instance, that new loans by private banks to Third World countries will simply expose banks further to the dangers of default. The new private bank loans, moreover, if made in response to Secretary Baker's initiative, might carry an implicit U.S. government guarantee. Although such a guarantee would not exist legally, it might well exist in a political sense, requiring a U.S. bailout in the event of default.

And there is also the danger, of course, of Third World countries botching their market-oriented strategy. Prodding a nation to reverse decades-old extensive government interference in its economy is by no means easy. Special interests strongly will resist the loss of jobs, income, and privileges. True liberalization and decentralization of economic power threaten a ruling elite far more than do IMF "austerity" measures, which may lead to greater centralization.

Political Obstacles

It may, indeed, be politically impossible for Third World countries to do all that needs to be done. Third World countries, moreover, historically have resisted advice from Western nations and development institutions, dismissing it as paternalism smacking of neocolonialism. And of course, many Third World countries lack government administrators and a business class familiar with the operation of a free market. Mistakes, therefore, inevitably will be made even by the most well-intentioned Third World leaders, thus endangering the success of the overall plan.

The lack of capital in the Third World will be a problem even with the Baker initiative's additional $20 billion. Even if this were not a problem, many

Third World states are not capable of absorbing large amounts of capital and using it efficiently. The financial and other institutions necessary to allocate capital efficiently, on projects of genuine economic value, simply do not exist. Thus past loans have tended to be made through the government. This has caused an enormous waste of resources, as funds have been channeled into projects favored by political interests rather than economic considerations. It also has tended to increase the concentration of government power, which in turn discourages the development of market institutions. If future loans continue to go directly to central governments, foreign direct investment will be discouraged and scarce resources wasted with little benefit to developing nations.

A Permanent Solution

Despite these possible pitfalls, the Baker Initiative could offer some hope of unraveling the problems posed by the huge Third World debt. To do so, however, the Treasury must be committed firmly to free market expansion in the Third World and insist on compliance with its conditions.

"[The] Treasury [Department] must take care that it does not make the Third World debt situation worse than it now is."

So far, the Treasury has been unwilling to use its leverage to force the World Bank and other MDBs to insist on a free market strategy. It now has an excellent opportunity to do so, for the U.S. is negotiating a general capital increase for the World Bank and other MDBs. In this, Washington should be pushing the types of measures outlined in a June 28, 1985, letter to Secretary Baker from Congressmen Jack Kemp (R-NY), Mickey Edwards (R-OK), Jerry Lewis (R—CA), and John Porter (R-IL). These include:

1) Reform of concessional lending. Maturities on MDB loans need to be cut to 25 years (from over 50 years, in some cases, now) and interest charges raised to 6 percent, from rates as low as 0.5 percent. "Soft" loans should be gradually phased out and countries forced to borrow on more stringent terms.
2) Increased private sector emphasis. MDB loans need to be directed toward the private sector and away from the public sector.
3) Economic conditionality. MDB lending should be targeted toward those countries that have made free market, pro-growth policy reforms.

In the past, the Treasury has presented the Congress with requests for general capital increases for the MDBs as *faits accomplis*, saying that the U.S. is obligated to appropriate such funds because they are the product of international negotiations. This year, for the first time, congressional leaders have made their demands prior to the start of negotiations and threatened to block MDB appropriations unless reforms are made. Therefore, there is no excuse for the Administration to fail to make part of its negotiating strategy the reforms outlined in the June 28 letter.

"A successful Baker Initiative must devise a mechanism allowing the U.S. banks to write down their bad loans."

U.S. banks know that they have made many bad loans to Third World countries, which ultimately will not be repaid, threatening not merely their profits but their very solvency. They understandably thus encourage foreign aid from Western nations and MDBs, which would provide Third World nations with the capital and foreign exchange to continue making loan repayments and prevent the day when these loans must be written off. Predictably, these banks may see the Baker proposal as another opportunity to relieve themselves of their liabilities.

If their goal were to unload their foreign debts, why, then, would they even consider lending another $20 billion as Secretary Baker advocates? There appear to be three reasons. The first is the hope that the federal government would implicitly guarantee such loans. Second is a desire to expand the number of banks with Third World exposure to increase the political pressure for an ultimate bailout. And lastly there is an understanding that there will be a major capital increase for the World Bank over the next few years—perhaps as much as $80 billion, of which the U.S. would kick in $20 billion. In effect, this increased capital could be used to repay private bank loans. Indeed, there is even evidence that important government officials, such as Federal Reserve chairman Paul Volcker, endorse this strategy, feeling that a shift of Third World default risk from private banks to MDBs is necessary and desirable.

Write-Down Bad Loans

As such, a successful Baker Initiative must devise a mechanism allowing the U.S. banks to write down their bad loans. This cannot be done all at once because it would literally wipe out—on paper anyway—the capital reserves of many large banks, plunging them into technical insolvency and bankruptcy. At that point, their deposits would all become government liabilities through the Federal Deposit Insurance Corporation. Such a policy, therefore, would make no sense.

A better solution would be the development of a secondary market for Third World loans, which would allow the banks to recover some of their principal. This would assume a willingness on the part of debtor countries to trade equity in their productive assets for loan forgiveness. For example, many Third World governments own business enterprises or shares in such enterprises that could be applied to outstanding debts. The benefit to debtor countries would be settlement of their debts on better terms—say 50 cents on the dollar. It would, in short, operate much like an ordinary bankruptcy proceeding, where debtors are relieved of their debts in return for liquidation of their assets.

Barriers to this could be U.S. government regulations, such as the Glass-Steagall Act, which prevents banks from owning equity, and accounting conventions, which may force banks into technical insolvency, even though their actual financial position may be improving, by removing from their books loans that never would be repaid. Bank stock prices probably already incorporate the knowledge that many Third World loans will have to be written off eventually and discount future earnings accordingly. Indeed, to the extent that banks are able to settle on such loans at more than the market currently thinks possible, the result would be an increase in bank stock prices.

Conclusion

The problems can be overcome, however, by a Reagan Administration commitment to deal with the Third World debt problem permanently. This would entail removing the governmental barriers to growth in Third World countries and instituting procedures for an orderly write-down of bad loans, rather than putting off the problem with more loans and running the risk of an ultimate bailout of the private banks. . . .

The Administration is to be commended for recognizing the seriousness of the Third World debt problem and offering a substantive proposal for dealing with it that relies on free markets and economic growth, rather than bailouts. However, there seems to be too little emphasis on important details and an apparent overemphasis on the interests of the MDBs and the private banks, with the danger that this proposal could become a bailout, or at least be ineffective.

Bruce Bartlett is John M. Olin Fellow at The Heritage Foundation.

"If United States policies in international trade remain unaltered, the prospects for the domestic fiber, fabric and apparel industry and its 2 million employees are bleak."

Restricting Foreign Imports Would Aid the US Garment Industry

Fiber, Fabric, and Apparel Coalition for Trade (FFACT)

The United States, once the merchandiser to the world, is being reduced to a consumer nation, importing a record $123 billion more in goods in 1984 than American industry was able to sell abroad.

It is a trend that threatens the economy, social fabric and security of the nation. Millions of families face dislocation and financial ruin. Entire industries essential to national self-sufficiency and defense are disappearing.

Virtually every major industry is affected by imports. Commerce Department figures show a negative trade balance in 15 of 20 major manufacturing areas it tracks.

Steel and automobiles are highly visible examples; yet, a much larger industry, the fiber, textile and apparel complex is now foundering under the weight of a rapidly increasing import burden.

Perhaps because the industry is such a day-to-day part of our lives; perhaps because it is so decentralized in terms of both ownership and often geography; perhaps because its factories are more often located in rural areas and do not evoke the familiar smokestack image of steel and oil; perhaps for all of these reasons, America's fiber, textile and apparel industry is the forgotten giant of the American economy—and the forgotten victim of imports.

The textile industry alone accounts for $45 billion of our Gross National Product—more than basic metals, more than automobiles or petroleum refining or aerospace.

The textile and apparel industry employs 2 million (one in every ten manufacturing jobs and more than steel and automobiles, combined) in facilities spread across 48 of the 50 states—and another two million work in support and allied industries.

Fiber, Fabric, and Apparel Coalition for Trade, "Failed U.S. Trade Policies Threaten a Basic, American Industry," published by FFACT, March 14, 1985. Reprinted with permission.

Over the last two decades, the textile industry alone has spent, on average, a billion dollars a year on new plants and equipment, including a record $1.7 billion in 1984. It has become the most modern—and most productive—textile industry in the world, yet import penetration continues to grow at a record pace. Coming on the heels of a 25 percent jump in 1983, import growth surged again in 1984 by an astonishing 32 percent.

In 1984, apparel imports captured half the U.S. market and in some categories have captured 80 percent of the market.

Altering the Fabric of Society

If the trend continues, a certainty if current import policies are left unchanged, the American fiber, textile and apparel industry will simply cease to exist by the early 1990s. It is a trend that could alter the very fabric of America. . . .

The textile and apparel industries are basic to all nations. Every developing country views the building of a textile industry as being in its national interest, not only to meet domestic demand, but as a means of generating foreign exchange.

Since initial capital requirements in apparel production, and to a lesser degree, textile manufacturing, can be relatively lower than in other industries, and since the more labor-intensive nature of the industry puts large numbers of people into the mainstream of the economy, this industry is particulary appealing to countries with scarce capital and abundant, cheap labor that are just beginning the development process.

The result is that many economic decisions—such as where, when and to what extent to expand production—are made for non-economic reasons such as national pride and the political need to maintain high employment at any cost.

For this reason, the industry has traditionally existed in virtually every country in the world. Also, the global industry has been, and is today, characterized by a whole host of direct and indirect government subsidies, by high tariff barriers, by customs and licensing barriers, by import quotas and by outright import prohibitions.

Also, the fiber, textile and apparel industry is subject to an unusually long-standing and complex international trade management process. . . .

"The fact of the matter is that U.S. companies must compete against foreign governments . . . or partnerships between foreign firms and their governments."

The U.S. industry is being steadily devastated:
- U.S. textile and apparel imports have doubled since 1980.
- Total imports of cotton, wool, man-made fiber mill products and apparel have increased by 123 percent in 10 years.
- Import growth at 25 percent in 1983 and 32 percent in 1984 is causing massive layoffs, plant closings, business failures and community hardship.
- The Big Five, accounting for 53 percent of U.S. textile and apparel imports, prevent the other 141 countries from participating meaningfully in the U.S. market.

Free Trade and Reality

The highly competitive nature of the U.S. fiber, textile and apparel industry has always served it and the nation well. The events of the past few years only bear that out. Capital investment has been extraordinary and productivity has increased. Both of these factors would contribute to a reasonably good financial outlook for surviving firms were it not for the prospect of growing penetration of the U.S. market by foreign competitors.

If these competitors were simply foreign companies, a case could be made that the American firms were simply not up to the challenge and have not earned the right to ask for relief.

The fact of the matter is that U.S. companies must compete against foreign governments (China, for example) or partnerships between foreign firms and their governments (Japan, Incorporated).

MITI, Japan's legendary Ministry of International Trade and Industry, serves as a model for many developing countries to provide the combination of capital formation, subsidies, tax relief, import restrictions and long-term commitment to "compete" in the global marketplace.

The government of China, unburdened by any notion of a private sector, provides the national commitment, 16-cent-per-hour wages and subsidies to create an industry at any cost.

Meanwhile, our government maintains a philosophically worthy, but woefully outdated commitment to free trade in a world where free trade is a myth. The reality is a world where managed trade is the norm, and blatant combinations of export subsidies and import restrictions are the wave of the future. Other myths are common:

MYTH: The strong dollar is the real culprit. As the dollar weakens, so will pressures on the industry.

REALITY: The strong dollar has only made imports more profitable for importers. The long-term trend is growing import penetration, strong dollar or not. The development policies of major exporters are based on the long-view of capturing the U.S. market. Besides, there is no evidence the strong dollar, which has already caused irreparable damage through plant closings, is about to weaken.

MYTH: Foreign nations would retaliate if we were to impose import restrictions.

REALITY: We are now subjected to constant "retaliation" from foreign nations which are already excluding or strictly limiting U.S. exports. The European Economic Community, to protect its industries, set strict limits on imports of textiles without adverse effect. China and its vast market, once the major concern of those who feared retaliation, is now a net exporter of cotton and is near becoming a net exporter of grain and China, like most other countries, buys where it gets the best price. We already have a net negative trade balance of $60 billion with the Big Five alone. It is difficult to imagine "retaliation" could make things much worse.

MYTH: Restricting imports will raise consumer prices.

REALITY: The lower basic cost of imported goods is not the whole story. There is considerable evidence that any "savings" on imported goods merely result in higher markups for retailers, not reduced prices for consumers. The best evidence of this is that retail prices are continuing at a high level, despite the strong dollar, which should have resulted in lower prices for consumers.

Import Monopoly

The long-term benefit to the consumer of unrestrained imports is also in doubt. Within hours of the last U.S. velveteen manufacturer being driven out of business by massive imports, Japan announced a substantial increase in its prices for the same fabric. The high price of silk has long reflected an import monopoly and consumer prices are soaring in the import dominated footwear market.

It is increasingly apparent that if the American fiber textile and apparel industry is to survive, the United States government must send a clear message to the rest of the world that it is U.S. policy to conduct trade on an "in-kind" basis. If free trade is ever again to become a viable working philosophy of international commerce, this may well be the only method of achieving it.

The Outlook

If United States policies in international trade remain unaltered, the prospects for the domestic fiber, fabric and apparel industry and its 2 million employees are bleak. In the short term, if import penetration of U.S. markets continues, hundreds of thousands more workers will be laid off or more likely terminated because of plant closings.

In the long term (five to ten years), the giant American textile complex, as one industry executive put it, could be reduced to a tiny boutique industry, producing only miniscule quantities of high-quality, high-style goods.

U.S. cotton producers—whose most dependable customers are U.S. textile mills—will see their domestic markets nearly wiped out in just four years if textile imports continue at current rates.

Wool growing, off 75 percent from post-World War II levels, has no export market at all, which means that every imported wool fabric or article of apparel adds to the trade deficit and depresses the price of domestic raw wool.

Arguments that laid-off workers can be retrained or can move to areas where jobs are available (if there are, in fact, such areas) simply do not mesh with reality. A study at one plant in the Southeast showed that 70 percent of laid-off employees are now working at the federal minimum wage—two dollars an hour lower than the textile plant's minimum.

No amount of retraining can handle the huge numbers of layoffs facing textile and apparel workers and retraining assumes the availability of jobs.

Further, since many textile and apparel jobs go to individuals whose families are employed in other local industries including agriculture, moving "to where the jobs are" simply isn't feasible. A large percentage of the employees in the textile and apparel complex are women and minorities—far more than any other manufacturing industry.

The only "growth" industry capable of absorbing these workers is the service sector, where wages almost invariably run at the federal minimum or slightly above. At best, if current policies continue, we will have imported a lower standard of living for the majority of workers and their families. At worst, they face the prospect of placing an added burden on American taxpayers.

In addition, large numbers of workers in support industries which build textile machinery and agricultural equipment, transport the goods or produce fiber for textiles, face layoffs or termination as well.

Dozens of communities across the nation and a number of states will see their economies and their tax bases eroded or destroyed if the current trends in textile imports are not turned around.

- When Riegel Textiles closed down its Ware Shoals, S.C. plant in November 1984, 900 jobs in a town of 1,900 population were lost despite an extensive modernization program and substantial layoffs two years before. The company paid 60 percent of the town's property taxes and owned the city water system.
- In the six months since the Old Fort (N.C.) Finishing Co. stopped production after beginning a multi-million dollar modernization program, the community has lost more than the 500 jobs that were terminated. A supermarket, a tire distributorship and three other businesses have closed down.
- In Greer, SC, when the Victor yarn mill shut down leaving 320 unemployed, there was some good news. The J.P. Stevens Co. decided to move 300 additional workers to its accounting, computer and customer service operation at the same location. The bad news was that only a handful of the laid-off workers were qualified for the new white-collar jobs at the facility.

"It is almost universally conceded that the enormous trade deficit is devastating the American economy, and, if allowed to continue unchecked, will erode America's position of leadership."

- In Cumberland, MD, 200 laid-off clothing workers, many of them life-long residents of the area, learned at a workshop that moving away from the area might well be their only option for finding work.

These closings came in the wake of the huge import surges of 1983 and 1984. In 1984, there were at least 61 textile plant closings in North and South Carolina alone.

An Equitable Solution

It is almost universally conceded that the enormous trade deficit is devastating the American economy and, if allowed to continue unchecked, will erode America's position of leadership in the global economy.

Trade agreements now in place have failed to produce the results envisioned, although stringent enforcement of the MFA might produce some positive benefits. However, this administration is following in the footsteps of its predecessors by ignoring the thrust of the agreements in pursuit of other foreign policy ends.

A viable alternative is the enactment of legislation to require specific action that preserves America's commitments to an enhanced global economy, but not at the expense of a vital domestic industry.

The legislation should reduce the level of import penetration of fiber, textile and apparel products from major exporting countries to permit a fairer market share for developing countries. It should also reduce the overall growth rate of these imported products so that they do not exceed the long-term growth of the U.S. market for such goods.

"The legislation should reduce the level of import penetration of fiber, textile and apparel products from major exporting countries."

Effective legislation would recognize the value of reasonable quantities of imports as being healthy not only to the global economy, but to the domestic economy, as a competitive force. Such legislation would satisfy both the announced policy objectives of the United States and create a domestic climate conducive to the continuing health of a basic American industry.

Without such legislation, the fiber, textile and apparel industry and the millions of workers that depend on it for a livelihood face a bleak future that could cause irreparable damage to the American economy as a whole.

FFACT is a garment industry organization that supports limiting imports to protect US industry.

"The most effective way of dealing with the rising tide of imports is not to try to dam up foreign trade."

Reducing Foreign Imports Would Not Aid US Industry

Murray L. Weidenbaum

Every day we read and hear about companies and their employees who are so hard hit by the flood of imports. What is the evidence? The truth is far less dramatic than the overblown charges. Let me cite six key examples.

Myth #1. Japan is the problem. If only they opened their markets to our products . . . It is surely true that Japan maintains an intricate variety of obstacles to imports that compete with its own products and that its government reduces those obstacles only in response to our constant pressure. Furthermore, our trade deficit with Japan—$33 billion in 1984—is far greater than our trade deficit with any other country. Yet, even if Japan did no foreign trade at all, the United States would still be experiencing a historically high excess of imports over exports. Without Japan, our total current account or trade deficit in 1984 would have been $69 billion—$11 billion more than the previous year's record breaker.

Meanwhile, our traditional export surplus with Western Europe has turned into a trade deficit, standing at $13 billion in 1984. Our trade accounts with Canada and Mexico are likewise in the red—$20 billion and $6 billion respectively last year. In fact, the United States has a trade deficit with almost every nation in the non-communist world. Hence, it is silly to say in effect that everyone is out of step except us. We in the United States must be doing something basically wrong.

US and Free Trade

Myth #2. The United States is an island of free trade in a world of protectionism. It would help to clear the air if we would acknowledge that not all of our actions are angelic. We have created many obstacles to inhibit imports into the United States. "Buy American" statutes give preference to domestic

Murray L. Weidenbaum, "Foreign Trade and the U.S. Economy: Dispelling the Myths," *Cato Policy Report*, January/February 1986. Reprinted with permission of the Cato Institute, 224 Second St., SE, Washington, DC 20003.

producers in government procurement. American flag vessels must be used to ship at least one-half of the commodities financed with U.S. foreign aid. Agricultural laws limit imports of sugar, beef, dairy products, and mandarin oranges.

Despite all the talk about being the only country that practices free trade, only 30 percent of our imports are now allowed in without paying a tariff—down from 54 percent in 1950. Numerous non-tariff barriers are imposed by federal, state, county, and municipal governments. For example, local construction codes are a popular device to keep out foreign-produced building supplies.

Myth #3. Imports are dragging down the American economy, depressing employment especially in manufacturing. In reality, the rapid rise in employment in the United States in recent years is the envy of the rest of the world. Total U.S. civilian employment has increased from 98.8 million in 1978 to 107.2 million today. That 8.4 million rise far exceeds the increase in Japan and Western Europe combined.

Then again, we hear so much about the decline in U.S. manufacturing. But I'll let you in on a well-kept secret. Industrial production reached an all-time peak in 1984, when the Federal Reserve's index averaged 122. 1985 is on a high plateau, averaging 124 since January. Moreover, manufacturing's share of the real gross domestic product has held steady for the last 30 years—at about 25 percent. Indeed, services have loomed larger than goods production in the United States at least since 1929, which is as far back as the national income accounts go.

In addition, the total number of manufacturing jobs has fluctuated in the vicinity of 19 million since 1970. This is not booming growth, but it is certainly a far cry from the supposed decline and fall of U.S. manufacturing that we hear so much about. My colleague at the Center for the Study of American Business, Richard McKenzie, is doing research that shows that the total employment of production workers in the United States is continuing to rise. The fastest growing opportunities for production workers are occurring in the service industry. Manufacturers are performing fewer activities in-house and are contracting out more to suppliers, many of whom are classified as part of the service sector. The total employment of production workers rose from 47 million in 1975 to 62 million in July 1985.

The Myth of Protecting Jobs

Myth #5. Protection is the way to save jobs. Wrong again. Protectionist actions increase the cost of producing goods and services in the United States, reducing the competitiveness of American products. A recent study by Arthur Denzau at the Center for the Study of American Business shows that if the United States had imposed a 15 percent import quota on steel in 1984, as the steel industry sought, 26,000 steel-worker jobs could have been saved—but at the cost of 93,000 jobs in the steel-using industries. Higher prices for protected domestic steel would have made American automobile and durable-goods producers less competitive.

Protectionism is the most inefficient welfare program ever designed. A government spending program in which the benefits delivered to recipients amounted to only 50 to 60 percent of the cost would be criticized as shamefully wasteful. But in the case of protectionism, the typical increase in prices paid by American consumers far exceeds the total wages of the jobs that are "saved." In the case of footwear quotas, the ratio of costs to benefits was 9 to 1; in the case of steel and autos, 4 to 1. Protectionism is a politician's delight because it delivers visible benefits to the protected parties while imposing the costs as a hidden tax on the public.

Myth #6. Workers in import-affected industries deserve to be treated more generously than other employees. I know of no reason why workers in industries facing serious international competition should be viewed as more meritorious than, say, defense workers who lose their jobs when government contracts are completed or cancelled. After all, the line of causation from the government's budget deficits to the high-priced dollar to rising imports to reduced employment is far more indirect than the link between a government decision to close a military facility and the resultant economic hardship.

Don't Dam Up Foreign Trade

The most effective way of dealing with the rising tide of imports is not to try to dam up foreign trade. It is to increase the competitiveness of American industry. I would like to suggest five positive approaches to foreign trade policy that would help American business compete.

1. Reduce the budget deficit. Although the linkages are complex and indirect, financing a string of $200 billion deficits has raised real interest rates substantially, and that, in turn, has attracted large amounts of foreign capital. The substantial inflow of foreign money has increased the demand for dollars and has resulted in a major appreciation of the dollar. The high relative value of the dollar has made it easier for foreign companies to compete against American companies.

2. Gear tax reform to enhance productivity and competitiveness. Most tax reform proposals to date ignore the repercussions on international trade. The industries hardest hit by imports are those whose tax burdens would rise the most under the various tax proposals submitted by Messrs. Bradley, Gephardt, Kemp, Kasten, Regan, Reagan and Rostenkowski.

This is not the time to elevate the development of an ideal tax system to the top of the roster of public issues. Tax policy must continue emphasizing incentives for the items important to enhancing our international competitiveness: saving, investment, and research and development.

3. Renew the regulatory reform effort. The costs of producing goods and services in the United States can be decreased by launching another effort to reduce government regulation of business. Studies of U.S. and Western European regulation show that we impose much higher economic costs in achieving similar social benefits. Closer attention to the tremendous burdens imposed by EPA, OSHA, and other regulatory agencies would help restore industrial competitiveness.

4. Reduce U.S. barriers to U.S. exports. About one-half of our trade deficit with Japan could be eliminated if Congress rescinded the bans on the export of timber and oil. Also, restraints on the export of strategic goods should be administered with common sense. It does not contribute to national security to prevent American companies from selling items overseas that are readily available from foreign competitors.

"Protectionist actions increase the cost of producing goods and services in the United States, reducing the competitiveness of American products."

5. American business and labor must face the challenge of increasing their productivity. We cannot blame our poor production practices on foreigners. The answer is not to prop up industries with import restrictions or government subsidies or to try to prevent businesses by law from closing or "running away." Labor and management in each company needs to face the challenge of enhancing their competitiveness. Protectionism is counterproductive because it lessens the pressure on management and labor to lower costs and improve quality. The painful fact is that foreign competition is a most effective spur to greater productivity.

Fundamentally, free trade is a consumer issue because the consumer bears the burden of protectionism. Why are consumer organizations mute on the subject of protectionism?

I'll conclude by quoting my favorite advocate of free trade, Lee Iacocca. In defending new joint-production arrangements with foreign companies, Iacocca bluntly observes: "If you don't go to to the lowest-cost source, you're an idiot." But supposedly that is true only for business. When consumers follow Lee's advice, they are attacked for being unpatriotic.

Murray L. Weidenbaum, former chairman of the president's Council of Economic Advisers, is director of the Center for the Study of American Business at Washington University of St. Louis.

"It is absurd to let foreign mercantilist enterprise overrun U.S. industry in the name of free trade."

US Industry Needs Trade Protection

Robert Kuttner

In the firmament of American ideological convictions, no star burns brighter than the bipartisan devotion to free trade. The President's 1983 Economic Report, to no one's surprise, sternly admonished would-be protectionists. An editorial in *The New York Times*, midway through an otherwise sensibly Keynesian argument, paused to add ritually, "Protectionism might mean a few more jobs for American auto workers, but it would depress the living standards of hundreds of millions of consumers and workers, here and abroad." . . .

The standard trade war story goes like this: recession has prompted a spate of jingoistic and self-defeating demands to fence out superior foreign goods. These demands typically emanate from overpaid workers, loser industries, and their political toadies. Protectionism will breed stagnation, retaliation, and worldwide depression. Remember Smoot-Hawley! . . .

Comparative Advantage

Recall for a moment the classic theory of comparative advantage. As the English economist David Ricardo explained it in 1817, if you are more efficient at making wine and I am better at weaving cloth, then it would be silly for each of us to produce both goods. Far better to do what each does best, and to trade the excess. Obviously then, barriers to trade defeat potential efficiency gains. Add some algebra, and this is how trade theory continues to be taught today.

To bring Ricardo's homely illustration up to date, the economically sound way to deal with the Japanese menace is simply to buy their entire cornucopia—the cheaper the better. If they are superior at making autos, TVs, tape recorders, cameras, steel, machine tools, baseballs,

semiconductors, computers, and other peculiarly Oriental products, it is irrational to shelter our own benighted industries. Far more sensible to buy their goods, let the bracing tonic of competition shake America from it torpor, and wait for the market to reveal our niche in the international division of labor.

But this formulation fails to describe the global economy as it actually works. The classical theory of free trade was based on what economists call "factor endowments"—a nation's natural advantages in climate, minerals, arable land, or plentiful labor. The theory doesn't fit a world of learning curves, economies of scale and floating exchange rates. And it certainly doesn't deal with the fact that much "comparative advantage" today is created not by markets but by government action. If Boeing got a head start on the 707 from multibillion-dollar military contracts, is that a sin against free trade? Well, sort of. If the European Airbus responds with subsidized loans, is that worse? If only Western Electric (a U.S. supplier) can produce for Bell, is that protection? If Japan uses public capital, research subsidies, and market-sharing cartels to launch a highly competitive semiconductor industry, is *that* protection? Maybe so, maybe not.

Equal Efficiency

Just fifty years ago, [John Maynard] Keynes, having dissented from the nineteenth-century theory of free markets, began wondering about free trade as well. In a 1933 essay in the *Yale Review* called "National Self-Sufficiency," he noted that "most modern processes of mass production can be performed in most countries and climates with almost equal efficiency." He wondered whether the putative efficiencies of trade necessarily justified the loss of national autonomy. Today nearly half of world trade is conducted between units of multinational corporations. As Keynes predicted, most basic

Robert Kuttner, "The Trade Fallacy," *The New Republic*, March 28, 1983. Reprinted by permission of THE NEW REPUBLIC, © 1983, The New Republic, 1983.

products (such as steel, plastics, microprocessors, textiles, and machine tools) can be manufactured almost anywhere, but by labor forces with vastly differing prevailing wages.

With dozens of countries trying to emulate Japan, the trend is toward worldwide excess capacity, shortened useful life of capital equipment, and downward pressure on wages. For in a world where technology is highly mobile and interchangeable, there is a real risk that comparative advantage comes to be defined as whose work force will work for the lowest wage.

"What we consider nontariff barriers are the essence of other nations' economic development strategies."

In such a world, it is possible for industries to grow nominally more productive while the national economy grows poorer. How can that be? The factor left out of the simple Ricardo equation is idle capacity. If America's autos (or steel tubes, or machine tools) are manufactured more productively than a decade ago but less productively than in Japan (or Korea, or Brazil), and if we practice what we preach about open trade, then an immense share of U.S. purchasing power will go to provide jobs overseas. A growing segment of our productive resources will lie idle. American manufacturers, detecting soft markets and falling profits, will decline to invest. Steelmakers will buy oil companies. Consumer access to superior foreign products will not necessarily compensate for the decline in real income and the idle resources. Nor is there any guarantee that the new industrial countries will use their burgeoning income from American sales to buy American capital equipment (or computers, or even coal), for they are all striving to develop their own advanced, diversified economies.

Free Trade Revered

Against this background of tidal change in the global economy, the conventional reverence for "free trade" is just not helpful. As an economic paradigm, it denies us a realistic appraisal of second bests. As a political principle, it leads liberals into a disastrous logic in which the main obstacle to a strong American economy is decent living standards for the American work force. Worst of all, a simple-minded devotion to textbook free trade in a world of mercantilism assures that the form of protection we inevitably get will be purely defensive, and will not lead to constructive change in the protected industry.

The seductive fallacy that pervades the hand-wringing about protectionism is the premise that free trade is the norm and that successful foreign exporters must be playing by the rules. Even so canny a critic of political economy as Michael Kinsley wrote . . . that "Very few American workers have lost their jobs because of unfair foreign trade practices, and it is demagogic for [Walter] Mondale and company to suggest otherwise." But what is an unfair trade practice? The Common Market just filed a complaint alleging that the entire Japanese industrial system is one great unfair trade practice!

GATT Treaty

To the extent that the rules of liberal trade are codified, they repose in the General Agreement on Tariffs and Trade (stay awake, this will be brief). The GATT is one of those multilateral institutions created in the American image just after World War II, a splendid historical moment when we could commend free trade to our allies the way the biggest kid on the block calls for a fair fight.

The basic GATT treaty, ratified in 1947, requires that all member nations get the same tariff treatment (the "most favored nation" doctrine), and that tariffs, in theory at least, are the only permissible form of barrier. Governments are supposed to treat foreign goods exactly the same as domestic ones: no subsidies, tax preferences, cheap loans to home industries; no quotas, preferential procurement, or inspection gimmicks to exclude foreign ones. Nor can producers sell below cost (dumping) in foreign markets.

Since 1947 there have been seven "rounds" of multilateral negotiations under GATT auspices, which have sharply reduced prevailing tariffs. In the last series of negotiations, the so-called Tokyo round, the United States pressed unsuccessfully for reductions in "non-tariff barriers." Not surprisingly, this campaign failed, for what we consider nontariff barriers are the essence of other nations' economic development strategies.

Lacks Enforcement

Moreover, the GATT lacks an enforcement mechanism. If an alleged treaty violation is confirmed, the complaining country has the right to impose countervailing duties. But this action itself invites further retaliation and is usually decided on political, not legal, grounds. For example, when the European Airbus consortium cracked the U.S. market with a billion-dollar sale to Eastern Airlines, the deal included loans far below market rates, an unequivocal violation of the GATT regime. But the United States, torn between alienating Boeing—or alienating Eastern and half of Europe—did nothing.

Nor does the United States quite live up to its own saintly standards in trade. Probably the most famous recent example is the 1971 Domestic International Sales Corporation Law, which gives tax advantages to American exporters. The Common Market filed a GATT complaint against the patent tax favoritism;

the GATT upheld it; and nothing else happened. The law is still on the books. We also periodically pressure trading partners to adopt voluntary import quotas; we export billions of dollars worth of subsidized farm products. And for years the Europeans have complained that Pentagon spending on research and development is a hidden subsidy to the United States aerospace industry.

In classical free trade theory, the only permissible candidate for temporary protection is the "infant industry." But Japan and its imitators, not unreasonably, treat every emerging technology as an infant industry. Japan uses a highly sheltered domestic market as a laboratory, and as a shield behind which to launch one export winner after another. Seemingly, Japan should be paying a heavy price for its protectionism as its industry stagnates. Poor Japan! This is not the place for a detailed recapitulation of Japan, Inc., but keep in mind some essentials:

Sheltered Growth

The Japanese government, in close collaboration with industry, targets sectors for development. It doesn't try to pick winners blindfolded; it creates them. It offers special equity loans, which need be repaid only if the venture turns a profit. It lends public capital through the Japan Development Bank, which signals private bankers to let funds flow. Where our government offers tax deductions to all businesses as an entitlement, Japan taxes ordinary business profits at stiff rates and saves its tax subsidies for targeted ventures. The government sometimes buys back outdated capital equipment to create markets for newer capital.

The famed Ministry of International Trade and Industry has pursued this essential strategy for better then twenty years, keeping foreign borrowers out of cheap Japanese capital markets, letting in foreign investors only on very restricted terms, moving Japan up the product ladder from cheap labor intensive goods in the 1950s to autos and steel in the 1960s, consumer electronics in the early 1970s, and computers, semiconductors, optical fibers, and just about everything else by 1980. The Japanese government also waives antimonopoly laws for development cartels, and organizes recession cartels when overcapacity is a problem. MITI encourages fierce domestic competition before winnowing the field down to a few export champions.

Free-trade purists and neoprotectionists alike can readily agree that America should bargain harder for reciprocal access to Japanese markets, but that would solve only a small part of the Japan problem. The other elements of Japan's brilliantly successful mercantilism—the development loans, the incubation of supply with state-seeded demand, the cartels— constitute a fundamentally different strategy of economic development, which happens to be

attractive to much of the world. It is not likely to be banished from international commerce by American appeals to the GATT or the sainted memory of David Ricardo.

Converting Sin into Virtue

The Japanese not only sin against the rules of market economics. They convert sin into productive virtue. By our own highest standards, they must be doing something right. The evident success of the Japanese model and the worldwide rush to emulate it create both a diplomatic crisis for American trade negotiators and a deeper ideological crisis for the free trade regime. As Berkeley professors John Zysman and Steven Cohen observed in a careful study for the Congressional Joint Economic Committee [in] . . . December [1982], America, as the main defender of the GATT philosophy, now faces an acute policy dilemma: "how to sustain the open trade system and promote the competitive position of American industry" at the same time.

Unfortunately, the dilemma is compounded by our ideological blinders. Americans believe so fervently in free markets, especially in trade, that we shun interventionist measures until an industry is in deep trouble. Then we build it half a bridge.

"Japan uses a highly sheltered domestic market as a laboratory."

There is no better example of the lethal combination of protectionism plus market-capitalism-as-usual than the steel industry. Steel has enjoyed some import limitation since the late 1950s, initially through informal quotas. The industry is oligopolistic; it was very slow to modernize. By the mid-1970s, world demand for steel was leveling off just as aggressive new producers such as Japan, Korea, and Brazil were flooding world markets with cheap, state-of-the-art steel.

Antidumping Policy

As the Carter Administration took office, the American steel industry was pursuing antidumping suits against foreign producers—an avenue that creates problems for American diplomacy. The new Administration had a better idea, more consistent with open markets and neighborly economic relations. It devised a "trigger price mechanism," a kind of floor price for foreign steel entering American markets. This was supposed to limit import penetration. The steelmakers withdrew their suits. Imports continued to increase.

So the Carter Administration moved with characteristic caution toward a minimalist industrial policy. Officials invented a kind of near-beer called the Steel Tripartite. Together, industry, labor, and government would devise a strategy for a competitive American steel industry. The eventual steel policy accepted the industry's own agenda: more production, a softening of pollution control requirements, wage restraint, new tax incentives, and a gentlemen's agreement to phase out excess capacity. What the policy did not include was either an enforceable commitment or adequate capital to modernize the industry. By market standards, massive retooling was not a rational course, because the return on steel investment was well below prevailing yields on other investments. Moreover, government officials had neither the ideological mandate nor adequate information to tell the steel industry how to invest. "We would sit around and talk about rods versus plate versus specialty steel, and none of us in government had any knowledge of how the steel industry actually operates," confesses C. Fred Bergsten, who served as Treasury's top trade official under Carter. "There has never been a government study of what size and shape steel industry the country needs. If we're going to go down this road, we should do it right, rather than simply preserving the status quo."

That view, of course, was heresy to most of the Carter Administration (not even Bergsten is quite comfortable with it). It is even clearer heresy to the Reagan Administration. The steel story has an intriguing epilogue. The Reagan Administration put a stop to the government's mild flirtation with industrial policy. U.S. Steel repaid the Tripartite by purchasing Marathon Oil. The industry continued to hemorrhage. And in 1982, under pressure from the now comatose steel industry, the Administration negotiated new, tougher import quotas. There was, of course, no talk of quid pro quos. Reagan believes in free markets.

Dying Steel Industries

Well, we have all read that steel is just a dying smokestack industry. In the new information age, we won't really miss it anyway. All right, take semiconductors, the basic building block of advanced electronic technology. We invented them. Did you know that Japan, Inc., successfully leapfrogged over the last generation of semiconductor technology, and now has 56 percent of the U.S. market in advanced computer memories? The Japanese accomplished this feat through the usual methods. They kept out direct U.S. investment while insisting that American manufacturers wishing to sell in the Japanese market share their technology with Japan. Texas Instruments was permitted to set up a joint venture with Sony, but had to limit its market share to 10 percent and license its patents to Sony, Hitachi, Toshiba, and Mitsubishi. In the early 1960s, MITI organized a consortium of Japanese firms into the Japan Electronic Computer Company, which got loans from the Japan Development Bank.

This, in turn, provided a market for the infant semiconductor industry.

Or consider the important machine tool industry. The future belongs to computerized machine tools, which can be reprogrammed to perform a wide variety of industrial tasks—another natural target of MITI. In 1976 Japanese suppliers held just 3.7 percent of the U.S. computer-controlled machine tool market. Last year the Japanese share was 60 percent. The Reagan Administration is nervously weighing an unusual petition from a major U.S. maker of computerized machine tools, Houdaille Industries; the case captures all the elements of the free-trade trap.

Investment Tax Credit

In early 1982, Houdaille's president, Phillip O'Reilly, stumbled on a little noticed provision of U.S. law. Under the 1971 tax act, the President of the United States may disqualify foreign products from the 10 percent investment tax credit if he finds that they originate in a country that violates trade norms. O'Reilly set out to document that the Japanese machine tool industry systematically engaged in practices that would be illegal in the United States, hiring the prestigious Washington law firm, Covington & Burling. So far the investigation has cost Houdaille a million dollars, and has produced one of the most intimate pictures of Japanese industrial strategy yet available in English.

MITI began by ordering marginal producers out of the Japanese machine tool industry. The remaining big producers then got exemptions from Japanese antitrust laws. The venture got the usual R&D help and the preferential loans. The Japanese also devised an ingenious subsidy to help Japanese manufacturers become customers for the new computerized machine tools. Several hundred million dollars in revenues from the popular spectator sports of motorcycle and bicycle racing are funneled to municipal research centers for the application of advanced technology.

"Americans believe so fervently in free markets, especially in trade, that we shun interventionist measures until an industry is in deep trouble."

Covington lawyer Richard Copaken videotaped Japanese officials proudly describing the process. A Japanese watch manufacturer, for example, asks the Tokyo technology center to evaluate whether he can use numerically controlled machining centers. The center's engineers design software, test it, and use it to produce prototype watch parts. The manufacturer then purchases a state-of-the-art numerically controlled machining center, with the computer program ready to go. Japanese, of course. A smiling official explains, ''These manufacturers cannot afford to do this work themselves and still make a profit. So the center does this work for them.''

GATT Violation

The Reagan Administration wishes that Houdaille would go away. Denying the investment tax credit to purchasers of Japanese machine tools would invite a stampede of similar petitions from other domestic industries. Instead, the Administration hopes to get the Japanese to ''voluntarily'' cut machine tool exports. Using tax policy as a far more targeted instrument of industrial policy runs counter to the ideological embrace of free markets. Houdaille was not an issue during Prime Minister Yasuhiro Nakasone's January [1983] visit. It was mainly about beef, citrus products, and the Administration's campaign to make Japan rearm. Presumably if the Japanese let us sell them more oranges, filet mignons, and mortars, we needn't worry about semiconductors or machine tools. The Japanese, incidentally, in their defense against the Houdaille petition, employ a wonderfully nervy argument. Restriction of the investment tax credit to American capital goods, they contend, would violate the GATT.

''When foreign, state-led competition drives us out of industry after industry, the costs to the economy as a whole can easily outweigh the benefits.''

The argument that we should let ''the market'' ease us out of old-fashioned heavy industry in which newly industrialized countries have a comparative advantage quickly melts away once you realize that precisely the same nonmarket pressures are squeezing us out of the highest-tech industries as well. And the argument that blames the problem on overpaid American labor collapses when one understands that semi-skilled labor overseas in several Asian nations is producing advanced products for the U.S. market at less than a dollar an hour. Who really thinks that we should lower American wages to that level in order to compete?

In theory, other nations' willingness to exploit their work forces in order to provide Americans with good, cheap products offers a deal we shouldn't refuse. But the fallacy in that logic is to measure the costs and benefits of a trade transaction only in terms of that transaction itself. Classical free-trade theory assumes full employment. When foreign, state-led competition drives us out of industry after industry, the costs to the economy as a whole can easily outweigh the benefits. As Wolfgang Hager, a

consultant to the Common Market, has written, ''The cheap [imported] shirt is paid for several times: once at the counter, then again in unemployment benefits. Secondary losses involve input industries . . . machinery, fibers, chemicals for dyeing and finishing products.''

Protected Textile Industry

As it happens, Hager's metaphor, the textile industry, is a fairly successful example of managed trade, which combines a dose of protection with a dose of modernization. Essentially, textiles have been removed from the free-trade regime by an international market-sharing agreement. In the late 1950s, the American textile industry began suffering insurmountable competition from cheap imports. The United States first imposed quotas on imports of cotton fibers, then on synthetics, and eventually on most textiles and apparel as well. A so-called Multi-Fiber Arrangement eventually was negotiated with other nations, which shelters the textile industries of Europe and the United States from wholesale import penetration. Under M.F.A., import growth in textiles was limited to an average of 6 percent per year.

The consequences of this, in theory, should have been stagnation. But the result has been exactly the opposite. The degree of protection, and a climate of cooperation with the two major labor unions, encouraged the American textile industry to invest heavily in modernization. During the 1960s and 1970s, the average annual productivity growth in textiles has been about twice the U.S. industrial average, second only to electronics. According to a study done for the Common Market, productivity in the most efficient American weaving operation is 130,000 stitches per worker per hour—twice as high as France and three times as high as Britain. Textiles, surprisingly enough, have remained an export winner for the United States, with net exports regularly exceeding imports. (In 1982, a depressed year that saw renewed competition from China, Hong Kong, Korea, and Taiwan, exports just about equaled imports.)

But surely the American consumer pays the bill when the domestic market is sheltered from open foreign competition. Wrong again. Textile prices have risen at only about half the average rate of the producer price index, both before and after the introduction of the Multi-Fiber Arrangement.

Investment for the Future

Now, it is possible to perform some algebraic manipulations and show how much lower textile prices would have been without any protection. One such computation places the cost of each protected textile job at several hundred thousand dollars. But these static calculations are essentially useless as practical policy guides, for they leave out the value over time of maintaining a textile industry in the

United States. The benefits include not only jobs, but contributions to G.N.P., to the balance of payments, and the fact that investing in this generation's technology is the ticket of admission to the next.

Why didn't the textile industry stagnate? Why didn't protectionism lead to higher prices? Largely because the textile industry is quite competitive domestically. The top five manufacturers have less than 20 percent of the market. The industry still operates under a 1968 Federal Trade Commission consent order prohibiting any company with sales more than $100 million from acquiring one with sales exceeding $10 million. If an industry competes vigorously domestically, it can innovate and keep prices low, despite being sheltered from ultra-low-wage foreign competition—or rather, thanks to the shelter. In fact, students of the nature of modern managed capitalism should hardly be surprised that market stability and new investment go hand in hand.

"We should stop viewing high wages as a liability."

The textile case also suggests that the sunrise industry/sunset industry distinction is so much nonsense. Most of America's major industries can be winners *or* losers, depending on whether they get sufficient capital investment. And it turns out that many U.S. industries such as textiles and shoes, which conventionally seem destined for lower-wage countries, can survive and modernize given a reasonable degree of, well, protection.

Managed Trade

What, then, is to be done? First, we should acknowledge the realities of international trade. Our competitors, increasingly, are not free marketeers in our own mold. It is absurd to let foreign mercantilist enterprise overrun U.S. industry in the name of free trade. The alternative is not jingoist-protectionism. It is managed trade, on the model of the Multi-Fiber Arrangement. If domestic industries are assured some limits to import growth, then it becomes rational for them to keep retooling and modernizing.

It is not necessary to protect every industry, nor do we want an American MITI. But surely it is reasonable to fashion plans for particular key sectors like steel, autos, machine tools, and semiconductors. The idea is not to close U.S. markets, but to limit the rate of import growth in key industries. In exchange, the domestic industry must invest heavily in modernization. And as part of the bargain, workers deserve a degree of job security and job retraining opportunities.

Far from being another euphemism for beggar-thy-

neighbor, a more stable trade system generally can be in the interest of producing countries. Universal excess capacity does no country much of a favor. When rapid penetration of the U.S. color TV market by Korean suppliers became intolerable, we slammed shut an open door. Overnight, Korean color TV production shrank to 20 percent of capacity. Predictable, if more gradual, growth in sales would have been preferable for us and for the Koreans.

Economic Recovery

Second, we should understand the interrelationship of managed trade, industrial policies, and economic recovery. Without a degree of industrial planning, limiting imports leads indeed to stagnation. Without restored world economic growth, managed trade becomes a nasty battle over shares of a shrinking pie, instead of allocation of a growing one. And without some limitations on imports, the Keynesian pump leaks. One reason big deficits fail to ignite recoveries is that so much of the growth in demand goes to purchase imported goods.

Third, we should train more economists to study industries in the particular. Most economists dwell in the best of all possible worlds, where markets equilibrate, firms optimize, and idle resources re-employ themselves. "Microeconomics" is seldom the study of actual industries; it is most often a branch of arcane mathematics. The issue of *whether* governments can sometimes improve on markets is not a fit subject for empirical inquiry, for the paradigm begins with the assumption they cannot. The highly practical question of *when* a little protection is justified is ruled out *ex ante*, since neoclassical economics assumes that less protection is always better than more. . . .

Fourth, we should stop viewing high wages as a liability. After World War II, Western Europe and North America evolved a social contract unique in the history of industrial capitalism. Unionism was encouraged, workers got a fair share in the fruits of production, and a measure of job security. The transformation of a crude industrial production machine into something approximating social citizenship is an immense achievement, not to be sacrificed lightly on the altar of "free trade." It took one depression to show that wage cuts are no route to recovery. Will it take another to show they are a poor formula for competitiveness? Well-paid workers, after all, are consumers.

Robert Kuttner is economics correspondent for The New Republic *and writes frequently for other newspapers and magazines.*

"Protectionism to preserve wage levels is just a redistribution of national wealth: it creates no new wealth."

Protecting Industry Harms the US Economy

Michael Kinsley

Editor's note: This viewpoint is written in reply to the previous viewpoint by Robert Kuttner.

Free trade is not a religion—it has no spiritual value—and Bob Kuttner is right to insist that if it is no longer good for America in practical terms, it is not a sensible policy for liberals anymore. He and I would also agree that a liberal trade policy ought to be good for working people in particular (including people who would like to be working but aren't). The question is whether free trade is just a relic from two happier eras—the period of liberal clarity two centuries ago when Adam Smith and David Ricardo devised the theories of free enterprise and free trade, and the period of American hegemony after World War II when we could dominate world markets—or whether it is still a key to prosperity.

Ridiculous Theories

Kuttner argues that Ricardo's theory of "comparative advantage"—that all nations are better off if each produces and exports what it can make most efficiently—no longer applies. Local factors such as climate and natural resources don't matter much anymore. As a result, "most basic products . . . can be manufactured almost anywhere" with equal efficiency. This means, Kuttner says, that the only ways one nation (e.g., Japan) gains comparative advantage over another (e.g., us) these days are through low wages or "governmental action." Either of these, he says, makes nonsense of Ricardo's theory. In addition, Kuttner says, Ricardo didn't account for the problem of "idle capacity"—expensive factories sitting unused.

"Idle capacity" is an argument against any competition at all, not just from abroad, and has a long history of being carted out whenever

Michael Kinsley, "Keep Trade Free," *The New Republic*, April 11, 1983. Reprinted by permission of THE NEW REPUBLIC, © 1983, The New Republic, 1983.

established companies (the airlines, for example) want the government to prevent newcomers from horning in on their turf. If you believe in capitalism at all, you have to believe that the temporary waste of capital that can result from the turmoil of competition in keeping all the competitors on their toes. A capitalist who builds a plant knowing (or even not knowing) that it is less efficient than a rival abroad deserves whatever he gets. As for older plants that are already built—that capital is sunk. If the cost of running those plants is higher than the cost of buying the same output from abroad, keeping them running is more wasteful than letting them sit idle.

This brings us to the real problem: not sunk capital but sunk lives. The middle-class living standard achieved by much of the United States working class is one of the glories of American civilization. Yet Kuttner says, "semi-skilled labor overseas is producing advanced products for the U.S. market at less than a dollar an hour. Who really thinks that we should lower American wages to that level in order to compete?"

We shouldn't, of course. But importing the products of cheap foreign labor cannot lower American living standards as a whole, and trade barriers cannot raise living standards. This is not a matter of morality: it is a matter of mathematics. If widgets can be imported from Asia for a price reflecting labor costs of $1 an hour, then an hour spent making widgets adds a dollar of value to the economy. This is true no matter what American widget makers are being paid. If foreign widgets are excluded in order to protect the jobs of American widget makers getting $10 an hour, $1 of that $10 reflects their contribution to the economy and $9 is coming out of the pockets of other workers who have to pay more for widgets. Nice for widget makers, but perfectly futile from the perspective of net social welfare.

After all, if this economic alchemy really worked, we could shut our borders to all imports, pay one another $1,000 an hour, and we'd all be rich. It doesn't work that way. In fact, as a society we're clearly better off taking advantage of the $1 widgets. The "comparative advantage" of cheap Asian labor is an advantage to *us* too. That's why trade is good.

But what about the poor widget makers? And what about the social cost of unemployment? If former widget makers aren't working at all, they aren't even adding a dollar's worth to the economy. Protectionism is, in effect, a "make work" jobs program—but a ridiculously expensive one, both directly and indirectly. The direct cost, in this example, is $9 an hour. The indirect cost is in reducing the efficiency of the economy by preventing international specialization.

If the disparity between American and foreign wages is really that great, Americans just shouldn't be making widgets. We could pay widget workers at $8 an hour to do nothing, and still be better off. We could put them to work at their current wage doing anything worth more than a dollar an hour. We could spend the equivalent of $9 an hour on retraining. And we owe it to widget workers to try all these things if necessary, because they are the victims of a change that has benefited all the rest of us by bringing us cheaper widgets (and because, as Lester Thurow points out, doing these things will discourage them from blocking the needed change). To protect them while they keep on making widgets, though, is insane.

These suggestions are, of course, overt tax-and-spend government programs, compared to the covert tax-and-spend program of protectionism. In a period of political reaction, the covert approach is tempting. But hypocrisy is not a sensible long-term strategy for liberals, nor is willfully ignoring the importance of economic productivity.

American Wages Competitive

In many basic industries, American wages are not all that far out of line, as Bob Kuttner seems to acknowledge in the case of autos. Modest wage adjustments can save these jobs and these industries for America. It is uncomfortable for a well-paid journalist to be urging pay cuts for blue-collar workers. On the other hand, steelworkers (when they are working) make more than the median American income. Protectionism to preserve wage levels is just a redistribution of national wealth; it creates no new wealth. Nothing is wrong with redistribution, but in any radical socialist redistribution of wealth, the pay of steelworkers would go down, not up. So it's hard to see why the government should intervene to protect steelworkers' wages at the expense of general national prosperity. This is especially true when millions are unemployed who would happily work for much less,

and there is no jobs program for them.

But Bob Kuttner believes that protection can be good for general national prosperity even apart from the wage question, in an age when other nations' "comparative advantage" comes from government policies that include protectionism. It is important to separate different strands in the common protectionist argument that we have to do it because Japan does it. Many politicians of various stripes, and William Safire in a recent column, argue (on an implicit analogy between trade war and real war) that only by threatening or building trade barriers of our own can we persuade the Japanese to dismantle theirs and restore free trade. Kuttner, by contrast, thinks that the idea of free trade is outmoded; that the Japanese are *smart* to restrict imports and we would be smart to do the same as part of an "industrial policy."

Mutual Free Trade

Both Safire and Kuttner assume incorrectly that free trade needs to be mutual. In fact, the theory of free trade is that nations benefit from their own open borders as well as the other guy's. This may be right or wrong, but the mere fact that Japan is protectionist does not settle the question of what our policy should be.

"The comparative advantage of cheap Asian labor is an advantage to us *too."*

Certainly, it's worth looking at Japan for clues about how to succeed in the world economy, and certainly one key to Japan's success seems to be a government-coordinated industrial policy. But why must such a policy include trade barriers? One reason Japan thwarts imports is a conscious decision to reduce workers' living standards in order to concentrate national resources on industrial investment. I presume this isn't what Kuttner and other liberal trade revisionists have in mind. Kuttner and others include protectionism in their "industrial policy" for two other reasons. First, as a sort of bribe to get unions to go along with sterner measures—possibly necessary, but not a case for protection on its own merits. Second, to give promising industries a captive market in which to incubate and gather strength before taking on the world.

The trouble with this "nurture" argument is that there's no end to it. Kuttner himself says that it's "not unreasonable" to "treat every emerging technology" this way, and also says that "most of American's major industries can be winners" with the right treatment. After you add the few hopeless loser industries where we must allegedly create barriers to save American wages, you've got the whole economy locked up, and whether this will actually encourage efficiency or the opposite is, at the very least, an open question. And if every major country protects every major industry, there will be no world market for any of them to conquer.

Managed Trade

Kuttner's model for "managed trade" is the Multi-Fiber Arrangement, an international agreement that restricts imports of textiles. This, according to Kuttner, permitted the American textile industry to modernize and become productive, to the point where exports exceeded imports—a less impressive accomplishment if you recall that the M.F.A. *restricts* imports.

Kuttner concedes that, despite the productivity gains, textile prices are higher than they would be without protection from cheap foreign labor. (Indeed, the current situation in the textile industry, as Bob Kuttner describes it, seems to vindicate Luddites, who got their start in textiles: human beings could do the work more efficiently, but machines are doing it anyway.) So what's the point? According to Kuttner, "The benefits include not only jobs, but contributions to G.N.P., to the balance of payments, and the fact that investing in this generation's technology is the ticket to admission to the next." Yet Kuttner does not challenge the "algebraic manipulations" he cites that show how each job saved costs the nation "several hundred thousand dollars" in higher textile prices. The only "contribution to G.N.P" from willful inefficiency like this can be the false contribution of inflation. The balance of payments is a measure of economic health, not a cause of it; restricting imports to reduce that deficit is like sticking the thermometer in ice water to bring down a feverish temperature. As for the suggestion that the *next* generation of technology will bring the *real* payoff—well, they were probably promising the same thing two decades ago when the Multi-Fiber Arrangement began.

"The mere fact that Japan is protectionist does not settle the question of what our policy should be."

Kuttner also worries that "without some limitation on imports," Keynesian fiscal policies won't work. This is like the monetarists who worry that financial advances such as money market funds will weaken the connection between inflation and the money supply. Unable to make their theory accord with life, they want the government to make life accord with their theory. There *is* a world economy—which Bob Kuttner seems to recognize as a good thing—and this means Keynesian techniques will increasingly have to be applied internationally.

As for the automobile "domestic content" bill, which would require companies selling cars and trucks in the United States to build part of them here, Kuttner says it will preserve competition "because it places no limits on the number of Toyotas and VWs Americans may buy." It simply requires those Toyotas to be made in America, which must be a competitive disadvantage or you wouldn't need a law forcing Toyota to do it.

There can be no pretense that domestic content legislation has anything to do with "industrial policy"—improving the competitive ability of American industry. It is protectionism, pure and unadorned, and each job "saved" will cost other American workers far more than it will bring the lucky beneficiary. Like more protectionist measures, far from aiding America's adjustment to world competition, it just helps put off the day of reckoning.

Michael Kinsley is on the staff of The New Republic *magazine.*

"There is no economic advantage of exports over imports."

The US Trade Deficit Does Not Damage the Economy

Richard W. Wilcke

My topic is economics, which emerged as a scholarly discipline in France in the early 17th Century. For certain, there had been global trade for 3,000 years, ever since the Greeks and Phoenicians carried goods around their portion of the world. Later, but still long before the rise of nations in Europe, merchant caravans crossed Asia and northern Africa. But there was no subject matter properly called economics until the 17th Century when the French developed *mercantilism*. This economic theory was nationalistic in the sense that these early advisors were focused on the territory controlled by their kings. (They were also focused exclusively on supply which, I suppose, makes them the first "supply-siders" in history.)

Because they mistakenly believed that Spain's strength was due solely to its gold, and because France needed hard money to pay its soldiers, their trade policy was aimed at the largest possible export surplus. In their view, the sole purpose of trade was competition to gain gold or minerals. The essence of their theory is contained in the famous phrase, "sell more to strangers yearly than we consume of theirs."

Incidentally, this economic theory, for obvious reasons, has always appealed to those in government and business. The idea is that exports are inherently superior to imports. Wouldn't most businessmen tend to agree?

Refuting Mercantilism

Adam Smith, the Scottish philosopher, earned the title, "father of modern economics," by his devastating refutation of these mercantilist theories in his 1776 book, *The Wealth of Nations*. He argued, as has most every respectable economist since, that the wealth of a nation rests not with its supply of gold, but with its individual citizens, its division of

labor and its voluntary exchange. Smith observed that people prospered through specialization. When a town's best shoemaker devoted all his time and energy to making shoes (improving his skills even more in the process) and traded for the other things he and his family required, *everyone* was far better off. This was, to Smith, both sensible and efficient.

He wrote: "It is the maxim of every prudent master of a family never to attempt to make at home what it will cost him more to make than to buy." Since it was clear that this kind of specialization and trade are what made civilization and economic progress possible *within* nations, Smith argued for roughly 1,000 pages that national borders neither repudiated the theory nor altered the process. Keeping yourself inefficiently busy could never be a valid reason for restricting or foregoing imported goods, he argued. A simple story will illustrate that point.

Everyone who ever studied economics is familiar with Robinson Crusoe, the shipwrecked sailor who, in Daniel Defoe's novel, lived alone on an island, or with only a servant. In the book, it took Crusoe two full weeks to cut down a large tree and trim it by hand into a needed plank. During this time, he was fully occupied and unable to fish or gather food. As a result, he was forced to live on his stored provisions. He also dulled his tools in the process of chopping and hewing the log.

Now, suppose that on the first morning he was to begin his work, a plank exactly like the one he was planning to make washed up onto the shore. Free traders, and almost any rational person, would urge Crusoe to retrieve the plank and save himself lots of time and trouble. But, as it turns out, Robinson Crusoe was apparently dedicated to the 1982-style, "neo-mercantilist" school of economics. He reasoned with himself that the productivity of his island economy depended upon the amount of work that had to be done.

Richard W. Wilcke, speech delivered before the Japan Trade Center, January 28, 1982.

"If I pick up this plank," he thought, "not only will I lose two full weeks of productive employment, but also the overtime it will take to resharpen my tools and replenish my store of provisions."

As a result of his "modern" economic analysis of the situation, Crusoe heaved the plank back into the ocean lest it destroy his island's economy.

This would be an amusing story except for the fact that many people seem to be convinced that lower-priced goods from other nations harm their own economies and cause unemployment. They are harmful, according to popular belief, precisely because they are offered for less than they can be produced domestically. Adam Smith would be incredulous.

Of course, we can easily see that Crusoe's rejection of the free plank makes no sense whatsoever. But neither does the less-obvious, but very mercantilist belief that lower-priced goods will harm the economy of any importing nation. This reasoning could lead to the conclusion that Japan, for example, by providing all its consumer goods for free, could totally destroy the U.S. economy.

I must share the observation that the fact an idea is nonsense never prevents it from having an impact on government policy. Politicians rarely judge ideas on their intellectual merits; ideas are usually judged on their perceived support among important constituencies, or among those in the news media with the capability of influencing important constituencies. These nonsensical ideas on trade currently have the support of key politicians everywhere in the world for that very reason.

Changing Answers

Interestingly, as I mentioned earlier, most Western economists agree that mercantilism is unworkable and that free trade benefits all parties. In this area, however, their influence is practically nil. It reminds me of the man who visited his old college economics professor. Noting that a scheduled exam was exactly the same as one he'd taken many years before, he cried, "Professor! You should change the questions on this exam. Don't you realize that the fraternities and dormitories keep files on these things?" The professor smiled at him and said, "Don't worry, my boy. In economics, we don't change the questions. We just change the answers."

The great mystery of a market economy is how things can get accomplished without someone, somewhere pulling all the strings. Because the free market's coordinating function is not widely understood, or even acknowledged, it is not difficult to convince most politicians that government action is required.

With regard to international trade, politicians in Europe and in the U.S. are currently being told that their governments should take positive steps to assure that trade is kept "in balance." This means

only that the level of exports must be *equal to or greater than* the level of imports. I say that because I hear no outcry in this country, for example, about the fact that we have a substantial trade surplus with the European Economic Community, while I hear a great deal about the trade surplus Japan has with the U.S. Obviously, "balance" is not required when exports exceed imports, only the other way around.

Trade Is Mutual

The fact is, bilateral trade statistics are insignificant and dangerous. Trade is mutual, but not just bilateral. There is no economic advantage of exports over imports. The original French mercantilists discovered in the 17th Century that England, with neither an official trade policy nor an economics profession, grew rapidly as gold and everything else flowed in and out. France—which even had export bans on gold—suffered a continual productivity crisis.

"Trade-balance obsessions lead nations to force their taxpayers to subsidize exports."

The U.S. trade surplus with Europe is no panacea, and I suspect that Japanese economists would agree that your current trade surplus with the U.S. is not, by itself, the solution to every economic problem. Trade is cyclical. It includes currency adjustments, flows of capital and trade in non-recorded services. It is also multi-national and circuitous. Bilateral trade statistics have no more significance than would trade-flow calculations between New York and New Jersey. Believe me, I am deeply grateful that we don't keep track of trade between our states.

Trade-balance obsessions lead nations to force their taxpayers to subsidize exports while penalizing, restricting, or raising the price of the imports these same taxpayers want to buy. It's the wrong policy for a large, resource-rich nation like the U.S. and it's the wrong policy for a smaller nation like Japan with fewer resources. It is basing trade policy on mercantilist theory to favor exports while treating imports as a problem.

Improving Trade Balance

This is also illustrated by the fact that a recession in your own country may "improve" your trade balance. A year or so ago, I read an economics story in *Newsweek* that said there was good news and bad news on the U.S. economy. While the past year—I believe it referred to 1980—was a "bad year" insofar as economic growth was concerned, especially as compared to the rest of the world, at least the balance-of-trade picture "improved" over the year before.

Now, what *Newsweek's* writers meant was that the U.S. economy had been sluggish and therefore Americans were not willing or able to buy many foreign products. But because other industrialized economies were booming by comparison, their citizens were buying a great deal, including many American products.

A calculation that looks "favorable" when our economy is depressed and others are doing well should be questioned. Well, the fact is, the very words used to describe trade balances indicate a mercantilist perspective.

Frederic Bastiat, the 19th Century French essayist, once suggested satirically that the solution to the alleged "problem" of trade balance would be shipwrecks. Every time a French ship left its home port loaded with French *exports*, it came sailing back, sooner or later, loaded with foreign *imports*.

Said Bastiat, if these ships would only sink after leaving France, there would be no chance of them returning with imports. A few timely shipwrecks, he said, would much "improve" the balance of trade, according to the mercantilists. But who in France, other than the government and the exporters, would be served?

Trade Restrictions

One of the most common arguments for trade restrictions in the U.S. is national security. But from an economic standpoint, it makes no sense to say, as many do, that our policy should restrict the flow of certain goods into the United States in order to make this country *stronger* and *better-prepared* in case of war. It is a rationalization. Ironically, many of these same people also argue that we should restrict the flow of goods into communist countries in order to make them *weaker* and *less-prepared* in case of war.

Leaving military strategy aside, one economic policy cannot serve contradictory ends. That is, to restrict the flow of goods into a country will have one effect or the other, it can't have both. The restricted nation's economy will either get stronger or weaker.

"Restricting the flow of goods into a country will make it weaker."

Well, as Adam Smith knew, restricting the flow of goods into a country will make it weaker by lowering its productivity, reducing its living standards, and rendering its economy less flexible and less efficient. If the *military* objective is to prevent communist economies from gaining strength through trade with the West, as some people argue it should be, sanctions or an embargo will have that effect.

But there is no reasonable or sensible national-security argument for import protection (what might well be termed "a self-inflicted embargo") since even limited restrictions tend to weaken, not strengthen, an economy. Why should a nation do to itself in time of peace what its enemies would surely do to it in time of war? If national security is really the goal, there are other ways to handle strategic goods. In no way can security be *increased* by actions which weaken an economy.

Besides, trade wars have historically led to military wars. Trade is voluntary and peaceful. Trade makes for a mutuality of interests. Trade builds bridges between people. And trade promotes peace.

The term "dumping," in practical use refers to sales of foreign goods sold *both* below their cost of production *and* below the market price of competing domestic goods. Those who oppose dumping never seem to complain unless the prices of foreign products are below their own. In other words, if a foreign manufacturer is not competitive with domestic manufacturers, who cares if he sells below his costs?

Benefit of Subsidies

This whole area is believed by many to represent a significant exception to the theory of free trade. They ask: What about the case of goods being sold below the cost of production or goods sold with the benefit of government subsidy? As you will have guessed by this point, we also reject this as a valid argument for trade interference. Let me give you three reasons.

First, the buyers of subsidized or dumped goods are never harmed. Imports are not forced on people, they are offered to them. The fact that American, or Japanese, or European, or any other country's consumers have a choice of buying goods on the marketplace for less than these goods cost their countrymen to manufacture cannot be said to harm them. It can only help their individual situation.

Granted, those who manage, own, or who work for a company that is unable to meet this kind of competition may feel that the costs to them personally will outweigh the benefits of cheaper goods. But that is only true in the smallest sample. The larger the sample, the less true this will be. That is why, incidentally, there tends to be more sympathy for protection in the U.S. House of Representatives than in the Senate. A Congressman or mayor will want protection for plants in his area, but a man who represents a whole state or a whole nation will be, or should be, much more aware of the benefits of lower-priced goods.

Besides, we have no objection to domestic merchants selling below their costs, say, in a fire or a closeout sale. Why should our attitudes change because of national borders?

Second, the fact that governments around the

world subsidize their exports cannot be changed by citizens of other countries. Therefore, it should not be denied. As market factors, these subsidies should be reflected in world-market prices. No business was ever made more competitive by being insulated from the many factors that impact supply and demand.

If massive forest fires were to suddenly reduce the world supply of lumber, the firms exposed to world prices (sure to soar immediately in response) would make far more rational decisions than the firms operating in countries where prices were controlled. Likewise, the subsidization of steel, or broilers, or lamb, or airplanes, is least troublesome and harmful in the long run when reflected in market prices. *I firmly believe that the protected industries themselves are the primary victims of protection.*

"In no way can security be increased by actions which weaken an economy."

This is confirmed by U.S. business history. Protected industries and firms have never become *more* competitive in world markets as a result of "temporary" protection. The "infant-industry" or retooling-adjustment rationale for protection goes on endlessly. In 1956, the U.S. textile industry gained "voluntary" restraints of cotton imports from Japan. The reason given at that time was that the U.S. industry needed time to adjust to world markets. Last month, more than 25 years after the original "temporary" protection, a new multi-fiber agreement was negotiated which was stricter than ever.

Infant-Industry Argument

This infant-industry argument was made 200 years ago by Alexander Hamilton at the birth of the United States. In the 1880s, a full century after Hamilton's time, the industries he protected were still requiring protection. This led William Graham Sumner to remark that Hamilton's "infants" had grown but never matured . . . sort of like "hydrocephalic babies." The fact is, whether firms in another country sell below cost or at taxpayer expense, protection can only raise prices. It cannot make domestic industries more competitive.

And third, if there is any "unfairness" in the subsidization of goods for export, it is to the taxpayers of the country doing the subsidizing. In my view, it is a gross injustice to the French people that the French government subsidizes the manufacture and export of steel and broilers. However, it cannot be said to be unfair to consumers who are gaining a windfall.

Neither can it properly be said to be "unfair" to competing businesses. Economic production is neither a business-school project nor a sporting event. Of course, it makes sense to equalize

conditions in a horse race because the whole purpose of the sport is to see which horse is fastest. There is no other reason for the competition.

But, to quote Adam Smith, "the sole end and purpose of production is consumption," or the serving of consumers. If several horses were running side-by-side to deliver medicine or important news or for any other purpose other than simply a race, it would make no sense to handicap one or demand that it carry extra weight for "fairness." The competition in this case is incidental to the delivery of the message or medicine.

In other words, free trade *is* fair trade. Regardless of what other nations do, there is simply no other useful criterion.

Acceptance of Imports

If one accepts the mercantilist view that exports are superior to imports, political control of the access to a market becomes very valuable indeed. This access becomes an important bargaining tool whereby imports are *accepted* by one government solely as a condition of getting another country to *accept* its exports.

But if you reject mercantilism, and have as your goal that of having the strongest possible economy, the freest people, and a peaceful, harmonious world—if you wish to liberalize world trade—reciprocity does not matter. You will advocate unilateral dropping of barriers. Under no circumstances will you threaten new or increased barriers into your own market in retaliation for barriers into the market of another nation.

Bargaining Chips

Many trade barriers around the world are clearly bargaining chips aimed at gaining access to the U.S. market. When the Smoot-Hawley tariff of 1930 was passed in the United States, other countries around the world immediately put up barriers of their own. Some nations blindly followed the U.S. in the belief that this was smart economic policy. But many others were simply attempts by America's trading partners to gain a bargaining wedge into the U.S. . . .

Faced with the prospect of losing access to the largest consumer market on earth (some 25 percent of the world GNP), trade negotiators in other countries want chips with which to bargain. They looked at the goods the U.S. was sending to their country and then slapped stiff tariffs on them. Unfortunately, retaliation of this kind has the wrong effect. Instead of opening up things, it further restricts them.

In 1929, the U.S. exported $5.5 billion in goods; by 1932 the total had fallen to one-fourth $1.7 billion. The Smoot-Hawley tariff was the worst possible response to the stock-market crash in 1929. Likewise, trade restrictions today will be the worst possible step the Reagan Administration can take if it truly hopes for economic recovery.

Because of our world leadership role and the primacy of the U.S. market, I contend that many trade barriers faced by U.S. exporters would fall if this country unilaterally dropped its barriers. The tradeoffs under bilateral negotiations work both ways, as you know, and we could discuss for hours the history of U.S. tariffs on trucks as a prime example.

Retaliatory Threats

Threats of retaliation are useful for government negotiators but they are not meaningful from the viewpoint of the American people. There is simply no way to "counter" or "make up for" the barriers or the subsidies of other countries. Denying access to domestic markets is nothing more than denying the rights of citizens to buy imports. There is no way, for example, that a denial of the rights of U.S. citizens can *neutralize* a similar denial of the rights of Japanese citizens.

If Japan or the EEC protects certain industries, or subsidizes them, no similar action by the U.S. is thereby justified. Even if it were not immoral to retaliate, which I believe it is, it would still be a poor idea on practical, economic grounds.

The only ones served by retaliation are those who gain in the short-term by being protected . . . in other words, those industries chosen for retaliation. If, for example, the U.S. demanded that Japan buy more U.S. beef or else imports of Japanese automobiles would be severely limited, the only beneficiaries would be U.S. automobile companies, unions and politicians. It would not benefit U.S. consumers.

The Reciprocity Issue

The old saying, *qui bono?* (who benefits), is a good question to ask when trying to discover who is pressuring politicians on the reciprocity issue. I don't say it is automobile companies, and I have no evidence that it is. But I would be willing to wager that there are some who hope to be used as retaliation who are pushing the idea. . . .

There are other groups working on this problem in one way or another, and I don't mean to imply that there aren't. But for real impact, there is nothing to compare with the credibility of businessmen who stand on principle, especially if such a stance means the possible foregoing of short-term gain.

Our organization has on its board of directors an American tanner who opposes restrictions on leather imports; an American Ford dealer who opposes restrictions on foreign cars; an American roofing manufacturer who opposes restrictions on Canadian competition; an American steelmaker who opposes export quotas on scrap, "Buy-American" laws and the Trigger Price Mechanism; the owner of an independent refinery who opposes special refinery privileges, and others.

Within our general membership there are many more examples of principled businessmen, from dairy farmers who oppose subsidies and protection to a ski-resort operator who refused subsidized loans after a winter without snow. Needless to say, these men are too few, but we believe there are many more who are unknown to us . . . not only in this country, but around the world.

We plan to continue gathering businessmen of this kind so that together we can stand up for true economic freedom. We are not "pro-business," we are "pro-market" which means just as much, perhaps more, to the consumers of the world. And we are non-political, preferring to uphold principle alone.

"We are not 'pro-business,' we are 'pro-market.' "

A few have accused our organization of being idealistic and unreasonable. However, George Bernard Shaw once wrote that all progress depends on men who are unwilling to simply adapt to the world as it is. We want to stand up with, and for, the ideals of economic freedom. Our members ask from government only the opportunity to compete in serving consumers; an opportunity they willingly extend to foreign businessmen as well.

There is a clear choice. Free trade and economic freedom and prosperity *and* peace, or protectionism in all its forms with all its results.

Richard W. Wilcke is president of the Council for a Competitive Economy.

"Imports are a serious problem for many United States industries and workers."

The US Trade Deficit Damages the Economy

Alfred E. Eckes

It is a special privilege for me to discuss import trends. My message is a somber one. Almost every day you report that an American firm has closed its doors, or moved its operations off shore, or replaced experienced workers with machinery. Behind these events is what *Business Week* has called "America's hidden problem. The big trade deficit is slashing growth and exporting jobs."

In that cover story *Business Week* asks: "Does anyone care?" Based on my experiences at the Commission, where more and more firms are seeking relief from imports, I am compelled to respond: "We had better care."

In my judgment the growing challenge of imports to domestic industry is a major story. It is a story critical to an understanding of America in the 1980s. It is a story as important to this decade as energy was to the 1970s.

As you know, the International Trade Commission is a non-partisan, independent agency. We have no policy mission. Instead, we have a factfinding responsibility to advise Congress and the Executive on trade matters. We also have a quasi-judicial role, to collect evidence, hear testimony, and render a determination about whether relief from imports is warranted.

Imports Are a Problem

I want to offer some personal observations about the import challenge. In my view, imports are a serious problem for many United States industries and workers. This problem is not a passing phenomena. Rather it is a chronic one and has enormous consequences for our nation. To survive in the global market of the 1980s, American business and labor will have to beat vigorous foreign competition.

Alfred E. Eckes, speech delivered to the National Press Club, August 31, 1983.

A good place to begin our discussion is with the trade deficit and its implications for American industry. Last year, the deficit was about $43 billion. This year it could be $65-70 billion. Some published estimates warn of a $174 billion deficit by 1990. Our economists tell me that each $1 billion change in the trade balance affects 25,000 jobs. Thus, an increase in the deficit of $60 billion could mean 1.5 million lost job opportunities for American workers.

Many of these lost job opportunities are likely to be in manufacturing, where the deficit is widening rapidly. As you know, United States exports are down, especially to less developed countries which cannot afford both to buy American manufacturing goods and meet debt repayment schedules. United States imports are soaring, partly because of the dollar's strength and partly because many times imported goods are lower in price and even superior in quality to domestic goods.

Disturbing Trend

To a historian, such as myself, there is something disturbing about the shifting composition of our trade. We are exporting more and more primary products and importing more and more manufactured goods. This, incidentally, is the traditional definition of a less developed country. Our trade with East Asia illustrates the pattern. Last year our five leading exports to Japan were corn, soybeans, wheat, cotton and coal. Our five leading imports from Japan were automobiles, trucks, video recorders, oil well casing and motorcycles. The same pattern of trade is now developing with Taiwan and Korea as well. Some might describe the emerging relationship as reminiscent of the colonial trade pattern this country had with Great Britain in the 18th century.

To what extent is the ballooning trade deficit a temporary problem, the result of high interest rates and an overvalued dollar? Undoubtedly, there is some truth to the widespread belief that a strong dollar handicaps our exports and attracts imports. However, we should not conclude that when the dollar falls, our trade deficit will vanish. In fact, there is now reason to question the conventional wisdom that exchange rates alone dictate trade flows.

The Commission [has released] a unique study which explores in detail how changes in the dollar have affected trade in selected commodities. The study integrates the analytical techniques of econometrics and industry analysis. It concludes that while changes in exchange rates do influence trade, other trade factors are often equally as important. These include variations in the competitors' prices, product demand, local production, and manufacturing costs. The study also points out that there is often very little correlation between exchange rate fluctuation and bilateral trade balances.

Altering the Economy

From this analysis I conclude that a decline in the dollar will undoubtedly provide some relief to beleaguered American industry, but a falling dollar will not end the import challenge. There are significant structural forces at work, altering the global economy, and intensifying competition. These include the gradual reduction of barriers since World War II, the gradual diffusion of technology and spread in industry to under-developed nations, and the rapid emergence of new industrial countries, like Taiwan, Korea, and Brazil. With low labor costs and access to sophisticated technology, they have established export industries capable of competing on a global scale.

Another important, and often unnoticed factor, is the general reduction in international transportation costs. Supertankers, large bulk ocean carriers, and wide-bodied aircraft have produced sizable cost savings. A Commission study shows that freight rates as a percent of value for manufactured imports have fallen nearly 25 percent in the last 6 years. Our economists estimate that from 1976 to 1981 declining transportation costs accounted for 27 percent of the total real growth in imports.

In particular, this trend has assisted sales of foreign steel and automobiles in our huge consumer market. Import penetration in these industries is highest in states farthest from centers of domestic production.

Why Imports Grow

The ordinary citizen must wonder how imported products have established such a strong position in the American market. From many import investigations, I can suggest three answers:

First, we must admit the obvious: In many cases, foreign producers, taking advantage of cost differences, have simply proven that they can produce certain standard goods more cheaply than United States producers. At one time it seemed imports were cheap in price but low in quality. That is changing. In some industries imports are both cheaper and qualitatively competitive with domestic products. Producing and marketing a less expensive mouse trap, or one of better quality, is a legitimate market penetration strategy. Many foreign producers have taken advantage of our open borders and declining shipping costs to do exactly that. I should add that in some areas foreign producers seem to have displayed considerable imagination in anticipating consumer wants with new products at affordable prices. One such example is the Sony Walkman, a portable stereo used by joggers.

"More and more firms are seeking relief from imports."

Second, fortuitous disruptions have enabled some foreign suppliers to build market share at the expense of United States producers. For instance, back-to-back freezes in Florida during 1981 and 1982 enabled Brazil to triple exports of frozen concentrated orange juice and gain a significant market share in only two years. The energy crisis of the 1970s benefited Japanese automobile producers, who were makers of fuel-efficient small cars. A steel strike in 1959 enabled foreign producers to gain a foothold in the United States market as steel users sought to diversify their sources of supply.

Finally, there are other instances, I regret to say, where unfair tactics were used to build market share. Over the last several years the Commission has investigated more than 300 complaints alleging unfair trade practices, like foreign subsidies, dumping, or infringement of United States patents and copyrights. In 57 percent of the cases the Commission ruled in favor of the domestic petitioners. The products varied widely in sophistication—from mushrooms and steel to commuter aircraft and space satellite amplifers. Pacman may have gobbled up Inky, Blinky, Pinky and Clyde, but when Pucman nibbled his copyright, Pacman's makers rushed to the ITC and successfully argued their case for an exclusion order. So did makers of Rubik's Cube to protect their trademark rights. Before the Commission this year have been such novel items as fuzz busters, pacemakers, and brain scanners.

From these investigations I have also observed how American firms react to import competition. At first, some industries chose to ignore the challenge. This was possible when imports were often inferior in quality. Even today, an industry occasionally comes before us, having underestimated imports until it is too late to recover market share with the benefit of remedies available in our trade laws.

More and more industries are seeking to adapt to the realities of intense competition with imports for the American consumer dollar. They seek to cut production costs, perhaps by automating their factories or relocating to states with lower labor costs. Or they move to slash overhead. The bicycle industry is a good example. It faced waves of foreign competition in the 1950s, and 1970s, and now in the 1980s. At first the industry obtained import relief, then it began to automate and move South to low-cost labor states. Now there is another adaptive strategy: Some of the old-line American producers are shifting their sourcing offshore, and importing bicycles from Taiwan. They seem to be saying: If you can't beat importers, join them.

This trend to offshore production, assembly and upstream sourcing abroad is widespread. It promises to expand, as firms seek to allocate resources efficiently in the global economy. Recently, for example, the Commission heard a radio pager's case in which Motorola, the domestic petitioner, assembled radio pagers in Malaysia and Korea, while the Japanese respondents were beginning to assemble pagers in the United States from imported components. As you know, firms in the steel industry are discussing whether to import semi-finished steel from Britain and Brazil so as to make domestic finishing operations more competitive. In the nonrubber footwear industry some of the most successful United States firms, like Florsheim, are importing shoes from a dozen countries. The auto industry is also turning off shore for parts and supplies. Over the last year there has been a 30 percent increase in imports of motor vehicle parts and accessories and a 38 percent increase in imports of motor vehicle engines and parts. In particular, Mexico is emerging as a major supplier of these items.

"Even today, an industry occasionally comes before us, having underestimated imports until it is too late."

While some industries are shifting operations abroad to cut costs and compete, an increasing number are turning to the United States government for relief. Of course, when dumping and subsidized merchandise are actually injuring the domestic industry, it is entirely appropriate to seek legal redress. Countervailing duties can offset the unfair practice and level the playing field for free competition. United States industries are also filing an increasing number of complex complaints involving patents, copyrights, and trademarks. Many of these complaints seem to involve respondents in East Asia.

Many domestic industries have petitioned for duties to offset foreign unfair trade practices. But in some instances I sense what they actually need is not simply a level playing field but temporary shelter from all forms of import competition to restructure and retool.

The Import Challenge

Let me offer two concluding predictions. Since we are not a policymaking agency, I have deliberately avoided prescriptions. First, imports will continue to challenge United States firms at home and abroad. No industry is immune. Problems that have hit footwear, apparel, steel and autos may soon impact the chemical industry, pharmaceuticals, and other high technology sectors. It is true, that foreign market share may decline as the world economy improves and the dollar weakens, but do not expect the import challenge to go away. The American market is too large and too lucrative.

Second, I predict that more and more industries will turn to government for assistance. Undoubtedly, some will seek special remedies from Congress and from the Executive. If the trade deficit spirals, as we have reason to expect, there will be more and more resort to quasi-judicial proceedings, such as the steel industry has done. I expect, too, that there will be more requests for escape clause relief. . . .

Looking ahead, it seems to me that rising imports make it imperative for American industry and labor to become internationally competitive again. Only in this way can we maintain a viable manufacturing sector. We as a nation have not yet proven that we can meet that challenge. As we search for solutions, I would hope that the ITC, which has gained much experience studying competitive conditions, could be of considerable assistance in this important endeavor.

Alfred E. Eckes is chairman of the United States International Trade Commission.

"The Japanese are on the move again in one of history's most brilliant commercial offensives, as they go about dismantling American industry."

viewpoint **53**

Japan's Trade Practices May Destroy the US

Theodore H. White

Today, 40 years after the end of World War II, the Japanese are on the move again in one of history's most brillant commercial offensives, as they go about dismantling American industry. Whether they are still only smart, or have finally learned to be wiser than we, will be tested in the next 10 years. Only then will we know who finally won the war 50 years before.

So we must go back to Japan . . . and see what we made of it. . . .

Our first challenge in those early weeks was, of course, the simple mechanics of occupation. But then we faced the problem of how to govern the now-abject nation—above all, how to feed it. Japan's hospitals were full of the diseases of malnutrition. MacArthur ordered at once that our occupying forces distribute their rations to Japanese civilians from Army kitchens. He then ordered that all the 3½ million tons of food stockpiled for our own armies for the projected landings of October and November be rushed in. Yet still there was not enough. He himself described it best in a cable to the War Department in the spring of 1946—a spring of imminent starvation. We must either feed the Japanese or starve them; he wrote, and then we must face the consequences. "Starvation breeds mass unrest, disorder, violence. Give me bread or give me bullets," he finished in a grandiloquent MacArthurian flourish.

The next paragraph of MacArthur's reminiscences is a single sentence: "I got bread."

MacArthur had, almost immediately after moving his headquarters from Yokohama to Tokyo, set about creating a new Japan. Of the Emperor, he demanded that a new prime minister be immediately named. By October, the Emperor had replaced his uncle, the

nominal prime minister at the time of surrender, with Baron Shidehara, to whom, on his first visit, MacArthur explained America's wishes for the new Japan.

MacArthur's directives were cut from the cloth of American good will. Japan (so ran his first directive) must completely emancipate Japanese women; must let workers organize in unions; ban abuse of child labor; abolish secret police. Further, Japan must reorganize its education system and "democratize" its industrial system. He left it to Shidehara to work out the details.

It was this broad grant of latitude that was most important. The Japanese could pick and choose their way through MacArthur's directives. The way they chose to implement them allowed their industry, their universities, their ingenuity to flourish. And the rebirth of Japan since its defeat is a parable of history. If one speeds up the interaction of ideas and drive, it becomes a drama. . . .

Japan Is a Giant

In the 40 years since defeat, Japan has grown to be a giant. Japan has passed the Soviet Union in industrial production and stands as world class No. 2 to our No. 1. If the present Japanese expansion of production continues, it will be, in 20 years, a greater industrial power than the United States. . . .

What the Japanese have done . . . in remodeling the American model is no less than spectacular. They have devised a system of government-industry partnership that is a paradigm for directing a modern industrial state for national purposes—and one designed for action in the new world of global commerce that the United States blueprinted. . . .

The Japanese are far ahead in the race for world trade markets. . . . They hover over the Draper Laboratories in Massachusetts—the national laboratories that devise the guidance system of our missiles—and acquire what patents security lets free

Theodore H. White, "The Danger From Japan," *The New York Times Magazine,* July 28, 1985. Reprinted by permission of The Julian Bach Literary Agency. Copyright © 1985 by Theodore H. White.

to the public. In the Los Angeles area alone, the Japanese have installed or acquired 1,500 firms. Their acquisitions in our banking system have grown significantly; contrarywise, Americans are all but excluded from Japanese capital markets. And, by the doctrine of GATT [General Agreement on Tariffs and Trade], all this is entirely legal.

Unfair Barriers

Yet what is legal may also be unfair. While Japan's tariff rates are, in broad economic terms, roughly equal to those of other industrial nations, they are spiked with special tariffs in industries that are considered vulnerable to foreign competition. In addition, Japanese markets are protected by a maze of so-called nontariff barriers to trade—many of which fall outside the reach of GATT regulations. We cannot sell our exports freely in Japan, whether beef, tobacco, citrus fruits, or leather goods. Consumer markets, too, are closed by regulations that the Japanese attribute to "cultural differences."

"The Japanese, as Government policy, are undermining one American industry after another."

What Japan does import from us are, chiefly, those raw materials always taken by master nations from colonial nations—grain, cotton, ores, fuel. We still ship to Japan a few remaining high-technology items, like aircraft, and some telecommunications and high-powered computers in which we hold a narrowing lead. But the Japanese continue to squeeze that lead, because their infant-industry-protection laws are planned to give them time to catch up. They will not buy American satellites until they learn to make their own. Corning Glass Works has had a fiber-optics patent pending in Japan for 12 years; in this time, the Japanese have learned to make fiber optics of their own that they now sell to America. Crude oil may be sold to Japan; but the Japanese will not buy our refined oil. American products certified here must go through slow, tedious re-testing in Japan before entering the Japanese market, while Japanese technology catches up.

Open Invitation

American markets for Japanese goods are not only open but come with an invitation. The United States Census makes its marketing information open to all; for a fee anyone can buy its tapes that define, area by area, county by county, income group by income group, where Toyota, Sony, Hitachi, Honda can best space their distributorships; and American advertising agencies will, for a fee, translate consumer appetite into market conquest. No nation that thinks of itself as an assembly of consumers can

resist Japanese penetration. But a nation that thinks of itself as a community has reason for alarm.

Not a single consumer radio is made in America, although Americans invented the modern radio; not a single black-and-white television set is made here, although America invented television. The few companies that assemble color television sets in the United States could not exist without imported parts made in Asia, although color television was originally developed in America. Almost all our video-cassette recorders are made in Japan; so are most hand-held calculators, watches, a huge share of our office machinery, and most high-fidelity audio equipment. Only one American motorcycle manufacturer remains (Harley-Davidson); the Japanese hold 95 percent of our market. Only one American piano manufacturer remains (Steinway). The Brooklyn Navy Yard, where the conquering U.S.S. Missouri was launched in 1943, no longer exists.

Vulnerable Industries

The American automobile and steel industries were the first to be hit by Japan's trade offensive—they were vulnerable. Emerging from the war fat, stuffy and complacent, content largely with obsolescent equipment and practices, shortsighted American management let its technologies fall well behind those developing elsewhere. In 1966, the Japanese shipped only 63,000 automobiles to America; by 1970, MITI [Ministry of International Trade and Industry] had stimulated the shipment of 415,000. Americans found Japanese cars to be good cars; they consumed little gasoline, they were cheaper; their fit-and-finish were splendid, and with the rise in gasoline prices, the American appetite for Japanese automobiles soared. But when the Reagan Administration this spring released Japan from negotiated voluntary quotas on car exports to the United States, Japan announced that it would raise its shipments to 2.3 million autos to America, as if we were a controlled colonial market. It was too much. By a vote of 92 to 0, the Senate declared Japanese trade practice unfair. But it was a belated revolt; this summer, American consumers are gobbling up Japanese automobiles faster than the Japanese can gear up to ship them.

This year, apparently, MITI's chief target is the American electronic industry. Last year, the trade deficit with Japan in electronics surpassed our trade deficit in automobiles—reaching $15.4 billion of our total adverse balance with Japan of $37 billion. The American semiconductor industry is reeling from assault. The Japanese, without mercy, propose to wipe out our supremacy in this industry, based on our own research and invention. . . .

A benign prosperity temporarily soothes the American economy. In the six years since 1979, America has added 6,000,000 jobs to its total work force. But these are mostly service jobs. In the skill-and-brawn base of American production, not only have real wages fallen, but the job base is shriveling. In machinery production, in these six years, the United States has lost 288,000 jobs; in primary metal-making (such as steel) we have lost 439,000 jobs; in fabricated metals, 241,000 jobs; in motor-vehicle production, 118,000 jobs; in textiles, 186,000 jobs. All in all, on the line, in the old shops, where Americans make things, we have lost 1,834,000 jobs.

No industry in America has been harder hit by Asian competition than the American garment industry, which has lost 155,000 jobs in the last six years alone. One should listen to Sol Chaikin, an air corps veteran of the China war theater against Japan.

Chaikin is now the president of the International Ladies Garment Workers Union. Once, in the early 1950s, his union counted 230,000 workers in New York City alone. Today he counts only 100,000 and they work at the lowest-paying union jobs in the city.

A Cheap Industry

"Ours," says Chaikin, "is the most competitive industry in America. It's a cheap industry to get into and we have 15,000 ladies-garment manufacturers in the U.S.A. They all have the most modern machinery, but the Asians have the same machinery and they work for less and for longer hours. The Japanese once were our chief competitors, but Japanese wage rates have now risen to levels comparable to ours. The Japanese now buy American designs, open factories with new machinery in Singapore and Hong Kong, ship the fabrics from Japan, and export from offshore. In Korea and Taiwan, they pay 57 cents an hour; in Hong Kong, $1.08 an hour; and in Sri Lanka they pay $5.00 a week. In New York, our workers get only $175.00 a week take-home pay—and they pay almost $1 for a subway fare each way."

Chaikin knows that his workers in New York cannot compete with Asian standards of living. "It's as if we were being poured into a Mixmaster with China, India, Japan, Taiwan; they've homogenized the international labor market and are squeezing us out like toothpaste." Chaikin insists that some garment jobs, at least, must be preserved for American working people, that the American market should be shared with Americans. But there is no high-technology ladder to leap over cheap Asian wages when it comes to handwork. Of blue-collar jobs in America, one in seven is held by a textile-garment-apparel worker. The National Academy of Engineering estimated in 1983 that, of 2,000,000 jobs in the garment-textile industry, only 750,000 would be left in 10 years. Chaikin's back is up against the wall.

Less than a mile from Chaikin's union

headquarters is the elegant executive suite of the Radio Corporation of America. Chairman of the Board Thornton F. Bradshaw is another combat veteran, whose destroyer was put out of action by the Japanese Navy in the last months of the war. Bradshaw, if anyone, is an authentic statesmen of American industry. He is unworried about RCA, which is happy and prosperous. His view is entirely different from Chaikin's, for his company has adjusted to the world market. But RCA long ago gave up on penetrating Japan. Its creator, Gen. David Sarnoff, thought the American market was enough, and licensed to Japan and the rest of the world the technologies RCA has patented—technologies that underlie much of modern electronics production. RCA prospers from its lead in advanced electronics—from its satellites, from its arms contracts (like the Aegis guided missile cruiser) from its broadcast net, NBC, from its marketing of imported parts and products, from manufacturing television sets. But, despite RCA's prosperity, Bradshaw is deeply worried—about America as an industrial community where both work ethic and practice have decayed.

"Americans are all but excluded from Japanese capital markets."

Bradshaw is concerned for America's economy as a whole, Chaikin for his working people—both equally honorable concerns. But neither believes that any reasonable persuasion can slow the Asian trade surge unless the American Government acts—sooner rather than later. What is needed is a structural change in American life and thinking, as sweeping as Japan's in 1945-1950—from factory floor to research labs and universities, from reduction of the Federal budget deficit, to a total review of our trading policies.

So the story moves to Washington.

Trade Crisis

Washington is always in crisis—small crises, acute crises, lurking crises. But the trade crisis is quite extraordinary for the anarchy of ideas that prevails. Ideas clash in perception of a world that has totally changed since the days of victory. Trade, as we designed it, has become completely global, and America has become the last open gaming table for world adventurers. Within the confusion of Washington's thinking, however, at least three truths are taken as paramount.

The first truth, the starting point of all thoughtful conversations, is the overwhelming burden of the overvalued dollar.

"When I was dealing with Japan the problem was different," says Robert S. Strauss, Jimmy Carter's trade representative from 1977 to 1979. "I talked in a universe of tariffs . . . of trade . . . nontrade . . . cultural barriers . . . political difficulties." . . .

"The Japanese don't adjust the yen every day. But you don't have to be a genius to know that when the Bank of Japan coughs, everyone gets the sniffles. But we have no policy. Even if we started now, we couldn't work things out in a year, or five. We need a strategy."

There comes next the second truth: Japan's "unfair" trading practices, its regulations, rules, restrictions, quotas. Says Secretary of Commerce Baldridge: "Japanese export policy has as its objective not participation in, but dominance of, world markets. Japanese trade policies assume as a *right* protection of their industries that are emerging. . . .

"In 1983, we took 30 percent of Japan's overseas exports, in 1984, 35 percent. In practical terms, this means that all the net increase in Japanese domestic employment in recent years is attributable to sale to the United States . . . . America's pursuit of free trade is like Sir Galahad's quest for the Holy Grail."

US on the Edge

From the National Association of Manufacturers to the AFL-CIO, one catches the alarm in vivid language. "There are six to eight main interacting trade-and-production groups, or 'keiretsu,' " says one association official, who asked not to be identified. "They buy and sell chiefly to their own subsidiaries, and they divide Japan's market up. When we squeeze, they'll allot, say, 11 percent of a particular market to all importers. They are opaque, insensitive people, who don't know that they have brought us to the edge."

Says Lane Kirkland, president of the AFL-CIO, the man most concerned for the fate of American workingmen, who last visited Japan this winter, "To hear the Japanese plead for free trade is like hearing the word 'love' on the lips of a harlot."

The last body of truths comes from the engineering community. . . . John Gibbons is the head of Congress's Office of Technology Assessment—he is a physicist, who comes to Congress from the Oak Ridge Labs of the Atomic Energy Commission. He starts the story of Japan's renaissance with the occupation:

"The most important thing we did after the war was to reorganize it; we democratized it; we lifted the burden of arms from it, and they poured resources into education. We helped them. We gave free doctorates in nuclear science to their students and brought them to Oak Ridge. But you have to realize that the Japanese already had traditional skills and techniques; they were superb in alloying metals, in ceramics, in fermentation—out of the broths they knew how to brew came the fermentation know-how vital to biotechnologies.

"They are ahead of us in productivity in automobiles, in steel, in robotics. We are ahead in fundamental research, but they get all our science papers and research, and they add to that their mastery of 'process technology,' translating fundamental research into the making of things. They recruit their managers from the factory floor; we get ours out of law schools." . . .

A Protectionist Nation

At the State Department with middle-level officers who deal daily with the Japanese—and one hears language almost unheard elsewhere in that labyrinth of quiet diplomats. "Japan," said one, who asked not to be identified, "is a protectionist nation: They have no sense of moderation; they are aggressive. They are an island nation looking out on the rest of the world as plunder from a protected bastion. Negotiations are tedious, painful—oh, so painful— and, when they yield, they yield with no grace. It's not only quotas on beef, citrus fruits, leather, but even on our catsup and peanut butter.

"In 1981, they banned American metal baseball bats. We had the technology for making a safe cap for metal bats. The Japanese made a metal bat with a plastic plug top; a plug flew off at a baseball game and struck a spectator. So all metal bats, safe and dangerous, were banned. We negotiated for three years, we had to get them to change 18 laws and regulations; we had to get the consent of the Japanese Softball Association. Then, when the Japanese learned to make safe metal caps, they reopened the market. Last year, we finally managed to export 350 metal bats to Japan!"

This is the voice of a working diplomat in the State Department. The bureaucracy bows to political leadership. . . .

At the supreme level, President Reagan deals with Premier Yasuhiro Nakasone of Japan, who yields and, with exquisite courtesy, goes on television to urge his people to sample American and foreign imports. But at the working level, each negotiation is a tormented, ad hoc, item-by-item bargaining.

"Japanese markets are protected by a maze of so-called nontariff barriers to trade."

A shawl of self-restraint drapes over most official American spokesmen; to be accused of "Japan-bashing" is considered "protectionist" or, worse, "racist." Foremost among those who thus speak for the old free-trade tradition, one finds Secretary of State George P. Shultz. "There is great sentiment for protection around the country," he told a gathering of the American Stock Exchange recently, "but in my opinion it's wrong . . . it's bad . . . this is a matter of deep conviction on my part." But no such restraint binds Congress, or the unions who influence so many constituencies. Congress is entertaining half-a-dozen bills right now sponsored by afflicted Congressmen; it is even considering a 25 percent tariff on all imported goods.

Congress is where one can best see the deadlock of ideas, as shoe workers, garment workers, steel workers, auto workers demand protection.

Strategy Needed

But Senator Christopher Dodd of Connecticut is typical of a Congressman in the middle; he is a young, liberal, thoughtful Democrat, and knows that foreign trade is essential to America. . . .

"Japanese export policy has as its objective not participation in, but dominance of, world markets."

Dodd is worried not about his state, but about the lack of an American strategy for dealing with the nature of the new trading world. He says: "We can't make a strategy by assembling a majority in the House to protect shoes, or automobiles, or tool-and-die makers. We need an overall trade policy and we need it now before the whole thing explodes." . . .

"Who won the war?," an official State Department spokesman repeated my question and answered: "We won the war. What did we get from the victory? We expanded the area of freedom. We made a democratic Japan. Our bases in the Pacific and Japan are essential to our defense. There's peace in the Pacific now, Japan is our ally, it's stable. Peace is our reward."

Peace, of course, is primordial. But the Japanese share the same peace, and under our protection, paying little for it, reserve the right to press American livelihoods to the wall. How far or how deeply they can press their trade strategy before Congress explodes in anger is unknown. But it would be well for the Japanese to remember that if peace is paramount, they need us to keep the peace more than we need them. And if a ripple of depression forces Congress to act, a lockup of the open American market would wound Japan more than it would wound us. The superlative execution of their trade tactics may provoke an incalculable reaction—as the Japanese might well remember of the course that ran from Pearl Harbor to the deck of the U.S.S. Missouri in Tokyo Bay just 40 years ago.

Theodore H. White was a prolific author and Pulitzer Prize winner and wrote primarily on political subjects.

"Myths about Japan are contributing to a tidal wave of anti-Japanese feeling and protectionist sentiment in America that could eventually prove . . . dangerous."

viewpoint **54**

Blaming Japan for US Trade Problems Is Not Justified

Robert J. Samuelson, *National Review*, and John F. Copper

Editor's note: The following viewpoint is taken from three editorials. Part I is by Robert J. Samuelson for Newsweek, *part II is by a staff writer for* National Review *and Part III is by John F. Copper for* Human Events.

I

Between 1960 and 1980, the proportion of Japanese homes with telephones rose from 2 percent to 77 percent. Grasp that one remarkable statistic and you can fathom the gathering crisis in American-Japanese relations. Societies need time to adapt to change, and the rapidity of Japan's economic rise has been too fast for both countries. The Japanese have acquired global responsibilities before being capable, psychologically and politically, of discharging them. And Americans cannot live with the idea that a nation we defeated in war now challenges us economically.

It's difficult to be optimistic. The irresistible force of American prejudice and the immovable object of Japanese inertia seem bent on colliding. In Congress, protectionism—shortsighted and self-defeating—is in the air. In Japan, tardy and insufficient "action programs" to overhaul its economy fan American anger. At best, these efforts will take time to produce the higher Japanese imports and higher Japanese economic growth that Americans want; at worst, the results may be meager. Japan asks for time to change, but time is not what it's got.

Both sides are prisoners of their pasts. Japan's huge trade surpluses are commonly blamed on lingering Japanese protectionism; this is a half-truth. The central cause of those excessive trade surpluses is an archaic financial system geared to an earlier

Robert J. Samuelson, "Our Japan Obsession," *Newsweek*, August 12, 1985. Copyright 1985, by Newsweek, Inc. All Rights Reserved. Reprinted by Permission.

"Three Myths About Japan," *National Review*, September 6, 1985. © 1985 by National Review, Inc., 150 East 35 Street, New York, NY 10016. Reprinted with permission.

John F. Copper, "Why Do Leftists Deplore Japan's Economic Success?" *Human Events*, February 8, 1986. Reprinted with permission.

era of underdevelopment. Perpetuated into the present, it perversely restrains Japan's domestic expansion and spurs its search for export markets. On our side, resentment of Japan's success has mushroomed into an obsession that grossly exaggerates Japan's role in our own economic problems.

Writing in *The New York Times Magazine*, for example, Theodore H. White—author of "The Making of the President" series—accuses Japan of "dismantling American industry." If it continues, he broods, Japan will have "finally won the war." The war? Wasn't it fought for something greater than global market shares? Never mind, for White reflects America's raw mood: he dislikes the Japanese. As a young reporter in China, the "Japanese had shot at me." His Japanese are still soldiers, not people, They're "on the offensive," "wiping out" our industries. You sense he wants our B-29s to wipe out their factories.

Facts About Japan

His story is less important for its content—which is unoriginal—than for who he is. As one of our premier journalists, White legitimizes economic scapegoating. But his powerful polemic is sloppy reporting. It excludes facts that put Japan's performance in a larger context. Facts like these:

• Japan is not the major cause of our trade deficit, and the deficit is not eliminating our industry. The strong dollar and rapid American growth are critical causes. Between 1981 and 1984, an $8.7 billion trade surplus with Europe became a $13.3 billion deficit. The deficit with Japan, though rising in dollar terms, dropped from 45 to 30 percent of the total during that period. And, despite the deficit, American industrial production in 1984 reached new records.

• Trade is not the only problem of distressed industries. In steel, the use of plastics, aluminum and reinforced concrete has cut demand; steel use

(including imports) was about a fifth less in 1984 than the 1973 peak. And Japanese steel imports are only a quarter of all imports. The distress in the semiconductor industry mainly reflects disappointing personal-computer sales.
• Despite recent advances, Japanese living standards remain more than a fifth below ours. Its efficient global industries coexist with far less efficient service and retail sectors. Many Japanese still work 5½ or 6 days a week. New American homes are a third larger than new Japanese homes.

Japanese Economics

So Japan is not quite the economic juggernaut of our fantasies. But it still harms the world economy. Since 1980, it has grown slowly at home and relied on exports for stimulus. It needs to grow faster domestically so it will import more. But internal growth is retarded because its outmoded financial system encourages Japanese consumers to save too much. Interest rates on consumer deposits have long been held down by law. Paradoxically, this stimulated saving because consumers—earning less on their deposits—had to save more to meet their personal objectives: to buy a home, send children to college or enjoy retirement. Saving was also spurred by restricted consumer lending. In the 1960s and early 1970s, when business investment absorbed these vast savings, Japan grew rapidly. Indeed, high investment was crucial in ending Japan's economic backwardness.

"Japan is not the major cause of our trade deficit."

But now the high savings policy is backfiring. Consumer-deposit rates are still artificially low, but domestic investment isn't absorbing all the savings. The excess is invested in higher-yielding foreign— mainly dollar—securities. Domestic growth suffers because demand is drained away. And the yen is depressed, making Japanese exports more competitive. Low growth and high exports abet protectionism and create an antigrowth cycle. Breaking this cycle requires Japan to deregulate interest rates and liberalize consumer borrowing; it's doing so at a snail's pace.

Global Economic Growth

We are right to press Japan for more open markets, and Japan could do more. But the paramount issue is global economic growth. Growth lubricates open markets and resists protectionism; it makes change easier. Unfortunately, in an interdependent world, growth is hostage to rigid national policies—and how they interact. We are no model. Our budget deficits and tax code (which

subsidizes borrowing through interest deductions) prop up interest rates and, thereby, draw foreign currencies into dollar securities. Our errors compound Japan's.

The central problem is the paralysis of old identities. Japan cannot move energetically and independently. It retains the protective mentality of a poor nation. It acts selfishly and invites resentment. For Americans, Japan is only a symptom of deeper change. Our industries do face global competition, and the world economy is unsettling. But we are too wounded by our lost economic primacy to grasp interdependence. Our imagery is increasingly savage. The vision of refighting World War II is mindless jingoism. When men of Teddy White's stature exploit this sleazy rhetoric, you know we're on a slippery slope.

II

Theodore White . . . writes of a resurgent Japan waging vicious economic warfare on the rest of the world. In ominous tones, White portrays the Japanese as conducting "one of history's most brilliant commercial offensives, as they go about dismantling American industry," and suggests that Japan's spectacular success in export trade calls into question whether or not the United States really won World War II.

While he tries to be fair, White nevertheless makes Japan look like some new kind of enemy power that poses an unprecedented threat to U.S. prosperity— which is how Congress and many U.S. trade unions have come to regard the Land of the Rising Yen. Three prevalent myths about Japan are contributing to a tidal wave of anti-Japanese feeling and protectionist sentiment in America that could eventually prove more dangerous than any number of imported Toyotas and Sony VCRs.

Myth of Protectionist Barriers

Myth Number One is that Japan's massive trade surplus is the result of protectionist barriers thrown up by Tokyo. In fact, even if Japan slashed its tariffs and dismantled every trace of "non-tariff barriers," it would still run a healthy trade surplus with America. Japan's export success derives largely from a labor force willing to work fifty hours a week at wages far below those paid here. The trade surplus has grown dramatically in the past few years partly for that reason and partly because of the dollar's climb in world currency markets. Neither factor is affected by Japan's import restrictions, which, though not exactly liberal, are no worse than those, say, of France or Brazil.

Myth of Oriental Ethos

The second myth is that Japan's productivity derives from a mysterious Oriental ethos, reflected in factory-sponsored group exercises, meditation seminars, what have you. Books abound seeking the inscrutable secret; but in vain. Japan's economic prosperity is the result of a constitutional government and free society imported from America by General MacArthur, to which the Japanese have added the time-honored virtues of hard work, frugality, and sacrifice. Japan's taxation system encourages savings, not consumption; and its government works cooperatively with industry rather than treating it like an enemy best conquered with red tape.

The final myth is that our Japanese problem could be solved by pressuring Japan vastly to increase its defense spending, thus presumably draining its civilian sector of resources while enabling us to stop devoting so much of our own scarce military assests to defending the Pacific. This is, charitably put, balderdash. To begin with, Japan's restraint in defense spending is a consequence of conditions imposed by Washington in 1945 and is the solidest proof of who did win the war. As a geopolitical matter, no U.S. ally in the Far East would welcome a rearmed Japan; hence, the long-term result of Japanese rearmament would probably be to force the U.S. to commit more forces to the Pacific so as to ensure our continuing primacy there. Japan would make a greater contribution to Western security by massively increasing not its army, navy, and air force, but its development assistance to friendly countries in the Far East. Rather than hobgoblinizing Japan, America should try repatriating the formula we exported to Tokyo in 1945.

III

One thing that is very noticeable when listening to the plethora of anti-Japanese rhetoric over the last several years—which has increased due to the protectionist issue—is that most of it comes from the left—labor unions, Democratic congressmen, opponents of the Reagan Administration. Conservatives are less critical of Japan and are less strident in their talk about Japanese.

Two-thirds of the recent spate of protectionist bills proposed in Congress originated from Democratic congressmen and most of them are liberals. Name-calling—"Jap," "yellow people," etc.—is heard from Democratic congressmen, not Republicans.

Why is this true? The left has long stood for free trade, an open foreign policy, internationalism. Liberals have long been critics of racism.

Japan Bashing

Clearly the left cannot—and does not—make an intellectual argument for Japan-bashing. In fact, emotional criticism has supplanted academic discourse.

For example, you have heard that Japan is not buying American goods. Japan is the second-largest purchaser of U.S.-made products in the world (more than Britain, France and West Germany combined).

And it is buying more than it ever has.

Japan is hurting the U.S. by earning too many dollars and keeping them! The truth is that Japan is investing more in this country than any other nation in the world and its investment is more job-producing than most foreign investment—especially oil dollars. It is even more job-producing than America's own investment (which is incidentally insufficient to create enough jobs in the future).

"Even if Japan slashed its tariffs and dismantled every trace of 'non-tariff barriers,' it would still run a healthy trade surplus with America."

Imports of Japanese goods hurt American companies! Industries hurt by Japanese imports have been hurt by imports from a host of countries, not just Japan. Furthermore, if one looks at the industries protected, they are doing much worse generally than those that aren't. We seem to hear only about the exception.

The trade deficit (Japan accounts for more of it than anyone else) causes unemployment in the U.S.! This is a simple bromide that the facts don't support. The U.S. trade deficit is now worse than at any time in history—yet the U.S. economy is in very good shape. It is breaking new records for creating new jobs. Europe has prevented a trade deficit with protectionist legislation and has created virtually no new jobs in recent years.

Japan doesn't spend enough on defense! America gives Japan a free ride on security! Japan has the seventh-largest defense budget in the world. True, it spends only one-fifth what the U.S. spends relative to its gross national product, but it makes up for this in considerable part by paying (out of Ministry of Interior funds because public opinion overwhelmingly opposes a bigger defense budget) much of the costs of U.S. forces stationed in Japan—about $20,000 per soldier, or almost all of his or her salary.

In addition, Japan spends a much larger share of its budget on foreign aid than the United States and most of its aid goes to countries (at the "suggestion" of the United States) that have security problems Washington is worried about—South Korea, Thailand, Turkey and others.

Japan as a Model

The real reasons for Japan-bashing from the political left in the United States must lie elsewhere. It can be traced to the fact that Japan is increasingly seen as a model for the United States in terms of how to change things and do things right—not only economically, but politically and socially.

In fact, there is no other good model for the United States at a juncture when America is ready and needs to revamp its political and economic system: Japan is the only other large, developed, capitalist nation—plus it is eminently successful.

But that is threatening. Here is why:

• Japan is basically a conservative country. Its conservative party—the Liberal-Democratic party—has been in power, without challenge, for 30 years. The left is regarded as representing special interests without an agenda, particularly an agenda that can maintain growth, economic dynamism, social stability, crime-free streets, good labor-management relations, a realistic foreign policy, peace, and most other good things the Japanese population wants. God forbid if this should happen in the U.S. . . . and it seems it is.

• Japan's economy works on the basis of Reaganomics. In fact, Japan knew about Reaganomics before Reagan did. Keynes was never as popular in Japan as among American liberal economists. Productive forces have made the Japanese economy successful; not consumerism. Now Japan's economy is not doing so well, what does Japan do? More supply-sided economics!

Japan and Reaganomics

In short, the Japan example proves the validity, or at least the effectiveness, of Reaganomics. Few know this (and liberals would prefer they didn't).

• Taxes are lower in Japan; so is social spending. In fact, one might wonder if the capitalist nations that are doing better in terms of economic growth and employment resemble Japan in these respects. They do! But even worse in Japan's case, i.e., embarrassing, Japan has lower taxes than the U.S.—yet income disparity is less. This is a contradiction to the left—and a nightmare.

According to liberal dictum, you get income equality (of which social equality is built) with high and progressive taxes. That Japan has done it another way is tantamount to heresy.

So is the fact that Japan spends less on social security and health care—much less—than the U.S., yet its elderly population is better off than ours and life expectancy is higher in Japan than in the United States (and other Western countries as well; in fact, is the highest in the entire world).

Robert J. Samuelson is an economics editorial writer for Newsweek. The National Review *is a bi-weekly conservative magazine published by William F. Buckley Jr. John F. Copper is a professor of International Studies at Rhodes College in Memphis, Tennessee, as well as director of the Pacific Area Project at the Ethics and Public Policy Center.*

Japan's Domestic Problems Are Responsible for the Trade Imbalance

W. Allen Wallis

For years there have been problems about our trade with Japan. What is new and dangerous today is the intensity and emotion with which trade problems are viewed by many Americans. Concern about our trade relationship comes at a time when our bilateral deficit with Japan and our global trade deficit both are at record levels.

Even though we have a number of legitimate grievances about restrictions on or access to Japanese markets, I believe that it is the size of our deficit with Japan, more than any specific problem, that is driving the debate on Capitol Hill today. If that is correct, opening access to Japan's markets will not be sufficient to lower the temperature on the Hill, because opening access to markets will have little effect on our balance of trade with Japan. At best, opening access will simply redistribute our trade deficit among countries and among products. Our total payments deficit is essentially equal to the amount by which total investment in the United States exceeds our domestic savings. Similarly, Japan's payments surplus equals the amount by which her domestic savings exceed total investment. That is why the Japanese Government is taking steps to expand the demand for investment in Japan, something which we enthusiastically endorse.

Open Access to Markets

Even though opening access to markets will do little to redress the balance of payments, it nevertheless is extremely important. One reason is economic; another is political.

Economically, opening access to Japan's markets will make trade between the two countries more beneficial to both. It will enable each to specialize in those goods and services where its comparative advantage lies and trade them for the goods and services in which the other country has a comparative advantage. By this specialization and trade, each country gets more of all the traded commodities than if it had produced them only at home.

For political reasons, also, we must work to open foreign markets to our goods and services, not just Japanese markets but all markets, if we are to succeed in keeping our markets open. The protectionist mood in the United States is at its strongest point in years. When a company has a product that foreigners would like to buy if they could, but they can't buy it because of barriers erected by the government of those potential buyers, the would-be exporters are irritated, if not downright infuriated. And the reaction is intensified if exporters from other countries have far freer access to our markets than we have to theirs. Over 300 protectionist measures have been introduced in the Congress this year, many aimed at Japan.

Bilateral Trade Deficit

Opening Japanese markets has been a primary goal of U.S. trade policy for years. Indeed, there are many people on both sides of the Pacific—government officials, lawyers, lobbyists, and journalists—who have made careers out of our trade problems. But Japan is a special focus of congressional and public attention today because our bilateral trade deficit with it is the largest we have ever had with any country and because Japanese consumer products are so visible in our streets and homes. The demands for protection from foreign imports, therefore, usually include specific calls for action to "get tough" or "retaliate" against Japan.

The most frequently cited statistic in U.S.-Japan trade relations is the size of our bilateral trade deficit—$37 billion [in 1984] and a . . . $50 billion [in 1985]. As the doomsayers like to point out in ominous tones, this is the largest trade deficit we

W. Allen Wallis, "The Relation of Japan's Economic Inefficiencies to Its Balance of Trade," *Department of State Bulletin*, December 1985.

have ever had with any country in history. There are many other figures, of course, that also are the highest in our history—our GNP [gross national product], the number of Americans with jobs, and our exports to Japan.

Less noted is the growing imbalance in the ratio of trade between our two countries. In 1981, Japan exported twice as much to us as we exported to them, but today Japan sends us nearly three times as much as we send them. Japan has grown more dependent on the United States as an export market. While we received only 25% of Japan's exports in 1981, today over one-third of Japanese exports come here.

Japan Had to Export

[I] remember when "made in Japan" was a synonym for "shoddy" and Japan had difficulty selling its products abroad.

In 1958, the *Economist* in London published the first of its periodic surveys of Japan. The *Economist* was concerned about the viability of Japan's economy, "Japan has to find a way of paying for a 10% rise in imports every year, in order to keep the economy expanding at the required speed," the *Economist* said. But to do so, Japan "will have to export roughly twice as much as it does now, to a world that appears increasingly unwilling to help it to do so."

This, of course, was the thesis that was drummed into the head of every Japanese above kindergarten age: Japan had to export to live. It had to earn foreign exchange to buy food, oil, raw materials, and capital equipment. In the same year, 1958, the U.S. Tariff Commission said:

> Japan's ability to maintain a viable economy is, of necessity, dependent on maintenance of an expanding volume of foreign trade, and its choice of trading partners will largely govern the composition of that trade. The choice, however, will be circumscribed by the willingness of various countries to receive the kinds of goods that Japan can profitably make. These countries, in turn, must consider the impact on their respective economies of receiving such goods.

Japan Turns to America

In those days, the Japanese were running a trade deficit with us. John Foster Dulles had warned them just a few years earlier that, if they wanted to expand exports to correct that imbalance, they would have to look elsewhere in Asia because Japan did not make anything that Americans wanted.

As the *Economist* points out, however, most of the countries in Asia to which Japan's chief hopes were pinned were still suspicious of Japanese intentions so soon after the war, and, anyway, the Asian countries were too poor to buy much. Japan was forced, therefore, to turn to America for an opportunity to earn the foreign exchange that it needed to survive.

So, notwithstanding John Foster Dulles' well-intentioned advice, the Japanese tried to make

products that Americans would buy. It was difficult for Japanese companies at first. In 1957, when Japan was still famous for dishes, stainless steel tableware, and $1 blouses, Toyota shipped its first cars to the United States—288 of them—and sold them through five dealers. They cost $2,300 each, compared to $1,600 for a Volkswagen beetle. Toyota's own president says that the quality of his cars was so bad that they broke down frequently on American highways. I can testify from personal observation that they also broke down in droves on the Japanese mountain roads from Tokyo to Nikko. Toyota retrenched, let go half of its U.S. staff of 65 people, and waited nearly 8 years before it reentered the U.S. market in a major way. The rest is history—and current events.

The Export Machine

It was during the 1960s that Japan transformed its domestic economy and became the great export machine that it is today. That story is well known and needs no elaboration. There is no denying Japan's success as an exporting nation. Japan produces many products of high quality that the world wants and at prices that it is willing to pay. The Japanese "economic miracle" is praised as a model for others to emulate. Many have emulated it: witness the rise of the "four tigers"—Korea, Hong Kong, Singapore, and Taiwan.

"Opening access to [Japan's] markets will have little effect on our balance of trade with Japan."

Japan has developed a very efficient export sector within its economy. Moreover, that sector has shown a remarkable ability to adapt to change. In the 1970s, Japan faced higher wage rates, higher prices for energy and other inputs, a more expensive yen, and new competition in low-wage goods from the "four tigers" and others. All of this meant the end of the economic and foreign trade structure that Japan had developed in the 1960s. Japan had developed what many called a "bicycle economy": it had to keep riding or fall off. To survive, Japan had to transform itself again, just as it had in the 1960s. Japan produced a new "industrial vision" of its future, and it moved from labor-intensive, low-wage industries to knowledge-intensive, high-technology fields such as computers, semiconductors, and telecommunications. In addition, its companies also made major investments and paid higher wages through productivity. Rather than watch its steel, automobile, shipbuilding, and consumer electronics industries migrate to lower wage countries, Japan tried to stay in the game by innovating and by producing products of better quality with high value added.

Today, Japan's large trade surplus with us and the rest of the world leads some people to say that Japan has not only succeeded but exceeded; the "bicycle economy" has become a roaring motorcycle—even a jet airplane.

"Much of the Japanese economy is astonishingly backward and inefficient."

But what is the cost of this to Japan? Japan's trading relationships with many countries are endangered today. How stable are the economic and foreign trade structures that Japan has developed when they depend on consistent trade and financial surpluses and the good will of the rest of the world?

Japanese Economy Is Inefficient

Japan's success in its export sector has created the appearance of a miraculously efficient economy. Notwithstanding that popular image, however, much of the Japanese economy is astonishingly backward and inefficient. It is ironic that Japan, which in its foreign trade has been so effective in directing its resources and talents into the most productive areas, has not allowed the same kind of efficiencies to operate in its domestic sector. A few examples:

Agriculture. America's farmers are five times as productive as Japan's and could provide food to Japanese consumers at a much lower cost. Yet they are prevented from doing so in many cases because of quotas and high tariffs. Many of the products that we are interested in selling—for example, wine, beef, citrus, and fruit juices—are marginal to the Japanese diet, and the economic impact on Japan's farmers of a more open market for these products would not be great. Rice is a bulwark of the Japanese diet, especially at the lower income levels, yet it sells for about seven times the world price. Soybeans also sell for about seven times the world price. Because an inefficient sector is protected, the Japanese consumer pays the price, as does the Japanese economy as a whole.

Forestry and Paper Products. Japan has no problem buying logs from us—in fact, they go in duty free—but if our sawmills, which are much more efficient than Japan's, cut those logs and process them into plywood or paper, Japan levies a high tariff on them. The result? Japanese houses and furniture are more expensive than they need to be. Every time anyone in Japan puts pen to paper or remodels his house, he is subsidizing an inefficient industry. A lumberman told me that he has seen many mills in Japan that are more primitive than any that have ever operated in this country in this century.

Retailing and Distribution. Japan's cumbersome distribution system raises the price of goods, especially imported goods, and also restricts their availability. Japan's retailing law limits the size of stores, so even though a larger retailer could provide a greater variety of goods at a lower price, he can be prevented from doing so.

Depressed Industries. When industries in Japan become depressed, Japan moves to subsidize them by providing specific tax benefits and loan guarantees; it also protects a number of them by organizing cartels that bar lower priced imports. Industrial users, therefore, are forced to buy the more expensive products of an inefficient domestic industry. Today, 22 industries in Japan—most of them in such basic materials as petrochemicals, fertilizers, paper, textiles, and aluminum—are classified as depressed.

Buying Practices. Many Japanese companies prefer to buy products made by companies in their own "group" or with which they have been doing business for many years. I recognize that part of the reason for this has to do with the nature of the Japanese society. But the result is that outsiders, whether foreigners or Japanese, are excluded, and this prevents the end-user from obtaining the best product at the best price. I recognize, also, that this practice has not been unknown in our own country, though deregulation, intensified competition and foreign imports have reduced it to insignificance.

Financial Markets. Japan's postwar financial structure has taken the savings of the Japanese people and diverted them primarily into industrial investment. Today, Japan's companies are financing much of their investment from new stock issues and corporate profits. Yet Japan's high rate of savings continues, so the surplus has been moving overseas, lowering the value of the yen and expanding Japan's exports. Japan could put more of its savings to work at home. Yet its financial system does not effectively channel Japan's large savings into their most productive uses where they would bring most benefit to the Japanese people. We believe, for example, that there is an unfilled demand in Japan for consumer credit and housing loans—and, indeed, just this week the Japanese Government announced proposals to meet this demand.

Japanese Inefficiencies

As I said earlier, the surplus in Japan's balance of payments is essentially equal to the excess of its domestic savings over its investment. Its savings are large, but because its economy, except for export industries, is generally inefficient, only part of those savings is invested in Japan. A large part of the savings is invested abroad, thus lowering the exchange rate of the yen against the currencies of those countries in which the savings are invested. Chief among the countries receiving the investments is the United States, because of the excellent returns and the prospects here. An important step toward reducing Japan's payments surplus is to raise the value of the yen, and an essential requirement for this is to increase the attractiveness of Japan to investors—both Japanese and non-Japanese investors. Increasing the attractiveness of investment in Japan requires drastic measures to reduce the inefficiencies that characterize much of the Japanese economy except for those conspicuously successful export industries.

This is the kind of "demand expansion," not fiscal deficits or public works, that will benefit the Japanese people and also reduce the trade imbalance—that is, expansion of the demand for investment in Japan.

Reducing Japan's Import Barriers

Many of the inefficiencies in the Japanese economy that I have described are in the areas that we have under discussion in our current intensive trade talks with Japan.

The basis of international trade is comparative advantage. A country should export what it is more efficient at making and import what it is less efficient at making. Japan is good at making cameras and consumer electronics and watches and cars; so we buy them, and so does the rest of the world. We are better than Japan at making satellites and wine and plywood and telecommunications switching gear. We believe that we should be selling more of these products in Japan. Japan enjoys essentially open markets here for products in which it has a comparative advantage, and this openness benefits both us and Japan. But Japan's home market has been excessively closed to those products and services in which our comparative advantage lies, and this closure reduces the economic welfare of both the United States and Japan.

"Many Japanese companies prefer to buy products made by companies in their own group."

We have been engaged since January in intensive trade discussions with Japan called MOSS—that stands for market-oriented, sector-selective. Prime Minister Nakasone and President Reagan agreed . . .[in] January [1985] that, instead of approaching our trade problems in a piecemeal, barrier-by-barrier fashion, we should look at all barriers in an entire sector. We chose four sectors to start with—telecommunications, electronics, medical equipment and pharmaceuticals, and forest products.

Our goal in the MOSS discussions has been to identify and remove impediments to imports into Japan. We chose carefully four sectors in which we are competitive, in which we have good products, and in which we could sell more to Japan.

We have made important progress already, but both Japan and the United States recognize that much more needs to be done. We have done very well in the hard-wired telecommunications sector, though not yet in wireless telecommunications. We have made good strides in medical equipment and pharmaceuticals also, and we are moving forward in electronics. Progress in forest products, so far, consists only of enhanced hope.

Preserving the World Trading System

There is a clear link between the inefficiencies in Japan's domestic economy and our trade imbalance. If we achieve open markets in Japan in these four MOSS sectors, as well as in the other sectors that we have under discussion, it will not be the United States alone that benefits. Japan will benefit, too. Its consumers will benefit from lower prices and greater choice. Its companies will be able to buy products with better technology at more reasonable prices. Its economy as a whole would be more efficient if regulatory processes and approval procedures were reduced, and this would attract investments and would reduce the trade imbalance.

The benefits to Japan of a more open and internationalized economy will not be within its domestic economy alone. Japan's relations with the rest of the world surely would improve, and calls for restrictions on Japanese imports would lessen.

Finally, Japan would make a major contribution to preserving the world trading system from which it has benefited so greatly and on which its own economic survival depends.

All of this is something that Prime Minister Nakasone, Foreign Minister Abe, Finance Minister Takeshita, and other leaders of the Japanese Government recognize fully. We applaud their vision and courage in working for the internationalization and liberalization of Japan's markets.

Today, the United States is at the most important crossroad in trade policy since 1930. The decisions to be made in the next few months can shape our economic destiny for decades to come.

Japan stands at that crossroad, too. Together, we must work to ensure that both our countries continue to take the right path—the path that for the past 40 years has taken both our nations into an era of peace and unprecedented prosperity.

W. Allen Wallis is US Undersecretary for Economic Affairs.

"None of [the United State's] problems was imported from Japan, and none of them will go away by weakening the dollar [or] blocking imports from Japan."

viewpoint 56

US Domestic Problems Are Responsible for the Trade Imbalance

Sam Jameson

The storm of protest from Washington about Japan's allegedly unfair trade practices has quieted again, but the prospects for significantly more-balanced trade appear to be little brighter than before.

Thanks to an appreciation in the value of the yen in the past two months, hopes that the cost of Japanese products sold in the United States will rise while the cost of American products sold in Japan go down, appear to be the main reason for what probably will be no more than a pause in the storm of protest.

The challenge of Japan has in no way lessened.

If the yen continues to strengthen, chances are good that eventually there will be some improvement in the U.S. trade imbalance with Japan.

History of Trade

But the history of 21 consecutive years of U.S. trade deficits with Japan shows that neither yen appreciation nor a further opening of the Japanese market is likely to make a significant impact on the deficit.

In August, 1971, two weeks after then-President Richard M. Nixon suspended the convertibility of the dollar for gold, Japan abandoned a costly attempt to hold the yen's value at the fixed rate of 360 yen to the dollar that had prevailed for 22 years. The move was hailed as a victory for the United States.

That was a year in which the United States recorded a $4.1-billion trade deficit with Japan.

When the oil crisis struck in 1973 and 1974, years in which the U.S. deficit with Japan has fallen to only $1.7 billion, American leaders—among them Secretary of State Henry A. Kissinger—wrote off Japan in the belief that its heavy dependency on imported oil would impair Japanese competitiveness.

But by 1976, the bilateral deficit with Japan had risen to a record $5.37 billion. Every year since, with the single exception of 1979, it has risen to another record level. It has snowballed even as Japan's market has become far more open, and is heading toward $50 billion for this year.

The big change was that Japanese manufacturers adjusted to the new exchange rates and made their operations more efficient. There was a shift away from energy-consuming industries and, at the same time, massive investment for the purpose of conserving energy.

Resource-saving investments reduced the need for imported raw materials, and a stronger yen also cut the bill for imported raw materials. Tariffs and other obstacles to imports were lowered, and imports, including manufactured products, increased. Exports, however, increased more rapidly.

Closed Market?

The perception of Japan as a closed market stems mainly from the fact that most Japanese businessmen are inclined to be sellers, not buyers. And too few U.S. businessmen have come to Japan to try to sell, though the few who have come tend to report profits that exceed those in other foreign countries.

The most tightly closed doors in Japan today—or doors that are just beginning to open—are in the field of services, not products.

Foreigners are still banned from practicing law here [in Japan], and even foreign newsmen are prohibited from attending most of the press conferences given by government officials and private businessmen.

The first foreign trust banks opened here just last month. There are still restrictions on the activities of foreign banks and insurance companies. And foreign data communications and other "information industry" firms are just setting up shop in the wake of . . . deregulation of the telecommunications industry.

More freedom to operate in Japan's services area would most likely give the United States a better balance in its bilateral current accounts, which include nontrade transactions. (In the United States, services now account for the greater part of the gross national product.) But in manufacturing, which produces the goods that go into the trade statistics, the United States continues to be on the outside.

The doors that Japan still keeps closed on manufactured or agricultural products account for such a small proportion of the U.S. trade deficit with Japan that they are statistically insignificant in relation to the size of the deficit. By the wildest estimate, they account for no more than a fourth of this year's expected bilateral deficit of $50 billion.

Manufacture at Home

Most of Japan's surplus with the United States is accounted for in two broad areas: The automotive industry and electronics. In both, U.S. manufacturers have yet to show that they can compete against Japanese products being sold in the United States, much less in Japan.

In some major product lines, there is no competition at all. The United States, where the idea for the video cassette recorder originated, does not produce VCRs. Japan supplies 99% of the VCRs sold in America.

U.S. manufacturers, complaining about the strength of the dollar, have increasingly closed factories in the United States and turned to foreign sources. Japanese firms, however, continue to depend on manufacturing at home for the great part of their production, although they too suffered from a strengthening of their currency's value.

"Neither yen appreciation nor a further opening of the Japanese market is likely to make a significant impact on the deficit."

Compared with the 1971 rate of 360-to-1, the yen has gained 43% in value—a gap that should have, but has not, made American products that much more competitive against Japanese goods.

Japanese manufacturing investments in the United States have been carried out largely in reaction to U.S. protectionism, such as government-imposed quotas, and usually have not replaced production in Japan.

Widespread Japanese investment in U.S. color TV factories and Nissan's truck production in Tennessee did replace exports from Japan. But every one of the six Japanese investments in passenger car manufacturing in the United States, planned or already carried out, represents an addition to, not a substitute for, existing exports.

The money-game approach to management, which has become a way of life in the United States but not in Japan, has taken a noticeable toll, too.

Selling Out

On Oct. 18, for example, Sony of America bought out its 50-50 partner, CBS, and took over 100% ownership of the only factory in the United States producing compact audio discs, widely regarded as the records of the future. In announcing the move, Sony said it plans to increase production from 12 million to 25 million discs annually within a year.

Why did CBS sell out? The announcement did not say, but it was reported that CBS was short of capital and was trying to reduce the debt it incurred in fighting off last summer's hostile takeover bid by Ted Turner, owner of Cable News Network.

Similarly, Dow Chemical, after years of a highly successful joint venture here, sold out its 50% equity to bolster its capital position.

Such examples of major U.S. corporate decisions based on considerations stretching no further into the future than next quarter's earnings report have become commonplace.

Without an overtly political limit being imposed on the trade imbalance, prospects for a major reduction of the red ink appear very dim. And a political limit will not solve the troubles in the United States that allow Japan to continue becoming ever more competitive.

US Domestic Problems

In addition to management problems, those causes run deep. Fundamentally, the United States is falling behind Japan in education. More than 90% of Japanese youths earn a high school diploma, compared with fewer than 75% in the United States.

Since 1980, Japan has graduated at least the same percentage (24%) of its youths from four-year colleges as the United States, and it has already exceeded the United States in the number of students obtaining engineering degrees.

The sluggishness in U.S. productivity gains, America's inability to save, a decline in the quality of American education through high school, a slackening in commitment to product quality, a lack of teamwork between labor and management and such socially destabilizing factors as a high crime rate all contribute to making the United States more vulnerable to Japanese competition.

None of these problems was imported from Japan, and none of them will go away by weakening the dollar, blocking imports from Japan—or opening up Japan's remaining closed doors.

Mr. Jameson is the Tokyo correspondent for the Los Angeles Times.

"The question is not really whether the new Americans can be assimilated—they must be—but rather how the U.S. will be changed by that process."

Immigration: An Overview

Otto Friedrich

Reina came from El Salvador because of "horrible things." She says simply, "I got scared." When she finally reached Los Angeles and found a job as a housekeeper at $125 a week, her new employer pointed to the vacuum cleaner. Vacuum cleaner? Reina, 24, had never seen such a thing before. "She gave me a maid book and a dictionary," says Reina, who now writes down and looks up every new word she hears. "That's how I learn English. I don't have time to go to school, but when I don't speak English, I feel stupid, so I must learn."

Manuel Martins Simoes had been a truck driver in Lisbon, but when he got to Newark in 1974, he worked on a construction gang during the week and waited on tables weekends. Eventually, he saved enough money to buy a restaurant. "The building was really broken down and dirty," Simoes says, "but my wife and I rebuilt the whole thing and put in a private dining room and a barbecue in the back." After seven years, he sold the place for a $185,000 profit and returned to Lisbon to set himself and his brother up in business and live like a lord. But Simoes was miserable. "All business in Portugal now is bad," he says, "and the kids are a headache, always wanting to go back to the U.S." Next week the family is emigrating all over again. "The first thing we will do," says Simoes, "is become American citizens."

Lam Ton, from Viet Nam, is already a U.S. citizen, and he too did well with a restaurant, the Mekong, at the intersection of Broadway and Argyle Street in Chicago. "When I first moved in here, I swept the sidewalk after we closed," he recalls. "People thought I was strange, but now everyone does the same." Lam Ton's newest project is to build an arch over Argyle Street in honor of the immigrants who

live and work there. "I will call it Freedom Gate," he says, "and it will have ocean waves with hands holding a freedom torch on top. It will represent not just the Vietnamese but all the minorities who have come here. Just look down Broadway. That guy is Indian, next to him is a Greek, next to him is a Thai, and next to him is a Mexican."

The Secret of America

They seem to come from everywhere, for all kinds of reasons, as indeed they always have. "What Alexis de Tocqueville saw in America," John F. Kennedy once wrote, "was a society of immigrants, each of whom had begun life anew, on an equal footing. This was the secret of America: a nation of people with the fresh memory of old traditions who dared to explore new frontiers. . . ." It was in memory of Kennedy's urging that the U.S. in 1965 abandoned the quota system that for nearly half a century had preserved the overwhelmingly European character of the nation. The new law invited the largest wave of immigration since the turn of the century, only this time the newcomers have arrived not from the Old World but from the Third World, especially Asia and Latin America. Of the 544,000 legal immigrants who came in fiscal 1984, the largest numbers were from Mexico (57,000, or more than 10%), followed by the Philippines (42,000) and Viet Nam (37,000). Britain came in ninth, with only 14,000.

This enormous migration is rapidly and permanently changing the face of America. It is altering its racial makeup, its landscapes and cityscapes, its taste in food and clothes and music, its entire perception of itself and its way of life. There have long been Chinatowns in American cities, but now there is Little Havana in Miami, Koreatown in Los Angeles, Little Saigon in Orange County, Calif., Little Odessa in Brooklyn, N.Y. Monterey Park, Calif., was the first U.S. city to have a Chinese-born woman as mayor, and the five-member city council includes two Hispanics and a Filipino American: Hialeah, Fla., has a Cuban-born mayor; Delaware, a Chinese-born Lieutenant Governor.

"It's fascinating," says New York Governor Mario Cuomo, the son of Italian immigrants. "For those of us who have been in the city for 50 years, it's wonderful to see the faces on the street now. Our diversity level has gone up." The new immigrants' contribution to America, Cuomo says, is "plus, plus, plus."

Waves of Illegal Immigrants

In addition to the half-million immigrants who are allowed to come to the U.S. each year, a substantial number arrive illegally. Estimates of the total vary widely. The Immigration and Naturalization Service apprehended 1.3 million illegal immigrants last year (many of them more than once) and guessed that several times that many have slipped through its net. The Census Bureau, however, estimated the total of illegal immigrants in the U.S. at between 3.5 million and 6 million in 1978. A National Academy of Sciences study . . . denounced the INS statistics as "woefully inadequate" and put the total of illegals at no more than 2 million to 4 million. These include anyone from German students who deliberately overstay their visas to Haitian boat people who scramble ashore in South Florida, but roughly 60% of the illegals are Hispanics, and about two-thirds of these are Mexicans driven by poverty and unemployment across the highly porous 2,000-mile southern frontier.

"How many immigrants can the country absorb and at what rate?"

The newest wave raises many questions: How many immigrants can the country absorb and at what rate? How much unskilled labor does a high-tech society need? Do illegals drain the economy or enrich it? Do newcomers gain their foothold at the expense of the poor and the black? Is it either possible or desirable to assimilate large numbers of immigrants from different races, languages and cultures? Will the advantages of diversity be outweighed by the dangers of separatism and conflict?

When asked about such issues, Americans sound troubled; their answers are ambiguous and sometimes contradictory. In a *Time* poll taken by Yankelovich, Skelly & White, Inc., only 27% agreed with the idea that "America should keep its doors open to people who wish to immigrate to the U.S. because that is what our heritage is all about." Two-thirds agreed that "this philosophy is no longer reasonable, and we should strictly limit the number." Some 56% said the number of legal immigrants was too high, and 75% wanted illegal immigrants to be tracked down. On the other hand, 66% approved of taking in people being persecuted in their homelands.

"One of the conditions of being an American," says Arthur Mann, professor of history at the University of Chicago, "is to be aware of the fact that a whole lot of people around are different, different in their origins, their religions, their life-styles." Yet most Americans do not know exactly what to make of those differences. Of those polled by Yankelovich, 59% believe that immigrants generally end up on welfare (the best estimate is that less than 20% do), and 54% feel that immigrants are basically good, honest people, and 67% think they are productive citizens once they become established. One out of every two knows someone who came to the U.S. in the past few years; of them, a majority says this knowledge has changed their views for the better.

Illegals Take Jobs

"Such a mess," says Roger Conner, director of the Federation for American Immigration Reform (FAIR), which advocates stronger restrictions. "We imagine ourselves as responsible for the whole world's problems, but immigration over the next 40 years will mean 50 million more people, and once they get here, they have children." "Our kids can't get jobs because the illegals take them," says Harold Ezell, Western commissioner of the INS. "If we don't control this border, we're going to lose control of this country." Says Conner: "The politicians don't want to talk about what is happening and what will happen."

But they do. "Every house needs a door, and every country needs a border," says Colorado's Democratic Governor Richard Lamm. If the U.S. fails to stop illegal immigration, he warns, "we shall have a legacy of strife, violence and joblessness for our children." Florida's Senator Lawton Chiles is equally alarmist. "If we do not regain control of our borders . . . I think that within ten years, we will not recognize the United States as the United States we see today."

Much of the concern comes from people who favor continued immigration, but who fear the consequences if a slowdown in the economy were to heighten the sense that immigrants, especially illegal ones, take jobs away from Americans. "We could have a terrible backlash, a terrible period of repression," warns the Rev. Theodore Hesburgh, president of Notre Dame and chairman of the Select Commission on Immigration that was established by Congress in 1978. "People tend to forget that twice in our lifetime, this country has rounded up hundreds of thousands of Mexicans and pushed them back over the border. That was a terrible thing . . . but it could very well go on. Police sweeps from house to house, rounding up millions of people, pushing them back over the border, turning that border into a kind of armed camp."

Gumption, Courage, and Ambition

Senator Alan Simpson, the Wyoming Republican who joined with Kentucky Democrat Romano Mazzoli to turn the Select Commission's findings into an immigration reform bill, estimates that Mexico would have to generate 700,000 new jobs every year (200,000 more than it is currently creating) just to keep its unemployment from getting worse. Simpson and Mazzoli have failed three times to get their bill passed, but Simpson, undaunted, presented yet another bill in May.

Xenophobia is not the force behind today's serious efforts to reform immigration. Simpson and other proponents recognize that most new immigrants, like the generations who came before them, work long and hard, and as much as possible on their own. Says Melvin Holli, professor of history at the University of Illinois, Chicago: "This work ethic serves them well, and its serves us well. In a sense, they are refurbishing our work ethic." The new immigrants, says Lawrence H. Fuchs, chairman of American Studies at Brandeis, "have gumption, courage, ambition. They want to make it." This quality, which Fuchs has dubbed the "X-factor," is evident also among the children of immigrants. "They have a double X-factor: they are unencumbered by homesickness, alienation or the psychology of exile.". . .

The number of newcomers is large in itself (an amazing two-thirds of all the immigration in the world consists of people entering the U.S.), but their effect is heightened because they have converged on the main cities of half a dozen states. Nowhere is the change more evident than in California, which has become home to 64% of the country's Asians and 35% of its Hispanics. Next comes New York, followed by Texas, Florida, Illinois and New Jersey. Miami is 64% Hispanic, San Antonio 55%. Los Angeles has more Mexicans (2 million) than any other city except metropolitan Mexico City, and nearly half as many Salvadorans (300,000) as San Salvador.

These population shifts change all the bric-a-brac of life. A car in Los Angeles carries a custom license plate that says SIE SIE LI, meaning in Chinese, "thank you." Graffiti sprayed in a nearby park send their obscure signals in Farsi. A suburban supermarket specializes in such Vietnamese delicacies as pork snouts and pickled banana buds. The Spanish-language soap opera *Tu o Nadie* gets the top ratings among independent stations every night at 8.

Such changes require adaptation not only in the schools and the marketplace but thoughout society. The Los Angeles County court system now provides interpreters for 80 different languages from Albanian and Amharic to Turkish and Tongan. One judge estimates that nearly half his cases require an interpreter. Sometimes the results are freakish. A police officer testifed that he had read a Chinese suspect his Miranda rights in Chinese, in the Taishan dialect. The suspect only understood Cantonese. The judge thereupon ruled out his confession.

Valuable Skills

These changes do not represent social decline or breakdown. The newcomers bring valuable skills and personal qualities: hope, energy, fresh perspectives. But the success stories should not blot out the fact that many aliens face considerable hardships with little immediate chance of advancement. Avan Wong, 20, came from Hong Kong in 1983 and hoped to go to college. She lives in the Bronx with her aged father, commutes two hours by bus to a job of up to twelve hours a day in a suburban restaurant. "I don't even read the newspapers," she says. "You don't have time. Once you go home, you go to sleep. Once you get up, you have to go to work. The only thing I'm happy about is that I can earn money and send it back to my mother. Nothing else. You feel so lonely here." College is not in sight. . . .

"An amazing two-thirds of all the immigration in the world consists of people entering the U.S."

Many immigrants are still the tired, the poor, the huddled masses whom the Statue of Liberty traditionally welcomed to New York Harbor. But the newcomers disembarking at Kennedy Airport or Miami or Los Angeles also include the successful. Baron Guy de Rothschild, for example, recently took refuge in New York City from the vagaries of French Socialism. Australia's publishing tycoon Rupert Murdoch, who has made a deal to buy several television stations in the U.S., announced in May that he would become a U.S. citizen. The roster of Soviet immigrants includes not only the black-garbed babushkas huddled over their knitting in Brooklyn's Little Odessa but such artists as Alexander Solzhenitsyn and Mikhail Baryshnikov.

In greeting them with a mixture of sympathy and anxiety (lighly flavored with hypocrisy), Americans express one of their oldest national traditions. Thomas Jefferson, who proclaimed it self-evident that all men are created equal, felt considerable doubts about whether they were all equally well suited to be U.S. citizens. He complained of "the unbounded licentiousness" some of the newcomers displayed, and he warned that they would turn the nation into "a heterogeneous, incoherent, distracted mass." This at a time when the U.S. population was only 2 million, and still 80% from the British Isles.

A History of Want

Early in the 19th century came the great flood of Irish (2 million between 1815 and 1860) and Germans (1.5 million), some driven westward by political persecution, more by hunger and hardship. Philip Hone, mayor of New York in the 1820s, regarded both the Irish and the Germans as "filthy, intemperate, unused to the comforts of life and regardless of its proprieties." "Nativists" in Philadelphia raided Irish Catholic churches and burned Irish homes.

The next wave was more than twice as large—10 million from 1860 to 1890—but these were still mostly Northern Europeans: English, Dutch, Swedes, Norwegians. The third wave was even bigger: 16 million from 1890 to 1914, including a still unmatched record of 1.3 million in 1907 (when the total U.S. population was only 87 million). And to the dismay of the now established Irish and Germans, more than 80% of the newcomers were Eastern and Southern Europeans: Sicilians, Bulgarians, Greeks, Russian Jews fleeing the Czar's pogroms. This was the era in which Emma Lazarus wrote the Statue of Liberty's welcome to the huddled masses yearning to breathe free, but it was also the era in which the eminent Thomas Bailey Aldrich, editor of the *Atlantic Monthly*, composed a poem entitled "Unguarded Gates":

> Wide open and unguarded stand our gates,
> And through them presses a wild motley throng—
> Men from the Volga and the Tartar steppes,
> Featureless figures of the Hoang-Ho
> Malayan, Scythian, Teuton, Kelt, and Slav . . .
> These bringing with them unknown gods and rites,
> Those, tiger passions, here to stretch their claws . . .
> Accents of menace alien to our air,
> Voices that once the Tower of Babel knew!

Even with the best intentions on all sides, the question of how to fit all these varieties of strangers into a relatively coherent American society remains difficult. Linda Wong, a Chinese-American official of the Mexican-American Legal Defense and Education Fund, sees trouble in the racial differences. "There is concern among whites that the new immigrants may be unassimilable," says Wong. "Hispanics and Asians cannot melt in as easily, and the U.S. has always had an ambivalent attitude toward newcomers. Ambivalent at best, racist at worst."

Many historians disagree. Hispanics, says Sheldon Maram, a professor of history at California State University at Fullerton, "are moving at about the

same level of acculturation as the Poles and Italians earlier in the century. Once they've made it, they tend to move out of the ghetto and melt into the rest of society." Asians often have it easier because they come from urban middle-class backgrounds. "They are the most highly skilled of any immigrant group our country has ever had," says Kevin McCarthy, a demographer at the Rand Corp. in Santa Monica, Calif. . . .

Changing Genes

The genes change too. Statistically, according to one study, about 80% of European immigrants marry outside their own ethnic groups by the time they reach the third generation. Among Japanese Americans, at least in the Chicago area, the comparable figure is 15% in the second generation, 50% in the third.

How long, how complete and how painful the process of Americanization will be remains unclear. It is true that ethnic elitists have bewailed each succeeding wave of Irish or Germans or Greeks, but it is also true that the disparities among Korean merchants, Soviet Jews, Hmong tribesmen, French socialites and Haitian boat people are greater than any the U.S. or any other country has ever confronted. On the other hand, Americans are probably more tolerant of diversity than they once were. "America is much more of a pluralistic society now," says Peter Rose, professor of sociology at Smith College. "You don't hear so much talk about the melting pot today. The old ideology, the concerted effort to make people the same, has been overtaken by reality."

"Many immigrants are still the tired, the poor, the huddled masses whom the Statue of Liberty traditionally welcomed to New York Harbor."

The question is not really whether the new Americans can be assimilated—they must be—but rather how the U.S. will be changed by that process. Economically, there will inevitably be strains, but most evidence indicates that the immigrants create more wealth than they consume. Socially and culturally, the diversity can hardly help benefiting the U.S. by acting as an antidote to everything that is bland and homogenized. The sad fact, indeed, is that uniformity is exactly what the immigrants' children will probably strive for, and their grandchildren achieve.

Politically, the prospects are uncertain. A large majority of immigrants—some illegal, some ineligible, some anxious, some apathetic—do not vote at all. Hispanic registration drives are trying to change that, but even in Los Angeles only 12% of the voters (vs. nearly 33% of the population) are Hispanic. Asians appear even more wary of political activism, though some are beginning to seek clout through financial contributions. By one estimate, they provided 25% of Los Angeles Mayor Tom Bradley's last campaign fund.

"There is nowhere else to run. We have to stick to this country and help it do better."

Historically, immigrants have tended to vote Democratic, but this is no longer so predictable. Many Cubans, Koreans, Taiwanese and Vietnamese came with strong anti-Communist fervor, and President Reagan's appeal has broken open many traditionally Democratic groups. In Miami there was a bizarre confrontation over the Memorial Day weekend as exiled Cubans and Nicaraguans waved U.S. flags to welcome Reagan, while native-born Americans brandished placards denouncing his Latin American policies. "Go back to Russia," one Nicaraguan shouted at an Anglo demonstrator. "Y'all go back to Cuba," came the answer.

The new wave of immigrants, says former California Governor Jerry Brown, is gradually changing the country's angle of vision. "The Pacific Rim is becoming the focal point for economic and political concerns," he says. "This immigration will eventually move Europe to a lower priority in the way we look at the world." It is a mistake, though, to think of immigrants as an undifferentiated clump, politically or otherwise. Not only do they differ by national origin and social class and ideology but also according to whether they plan to stay permanently or eventually return home. "What binds Americans to one another, regardless of ethnicity or religion, is an American civic culture," says Brandeis Professor Fuchs. "It is the basis for the *unum* in *E pluribus unum*. It is a complex of ideals, behaviors, institutions, symbols and heroes connected by American history and its great documents, the Declaration of Independence, the Bill of Rights, the Gettysburg Address. It is backed by a civil religion giving transcendent significance to those ideals. And it is the basis for accepting ethnic diversity while protecting individual rights. An American can be as ethnic as he or she wishes in private actions, but in public actions, the rules of the civic culture are binding."

Nowhere Else to Run

Lam Ton, the Vietnamese restauranteur who wants to build a freedom arch in Chicago, says these things differently because he is not a professor at Brandeis,

but he feels very strongly about the civic culture. "This is the last stand," he says. "There is nowhere else to run. We have to stick to this country and help it do better."

Otto Friedrich is a staff reporter for Time *magazine. This article was written as a cover story for* Time.

Immigration Raises the Living Standards of Americans

Julian Simon

Wherever it may lead, a debate on U.S. immigration policy ought to be based on facts. Regrettably, a number of myths about immigration work against a reasoned debate. The sum of these myths is that immigrants lower the standard of living of U.S. natives. This simply is not supported by the evidence. In the interests of an informed debate on immigration, these myths must be examined.

Myth #1: Immigrants Are Welfare Abusers

It is frequently alleged that immigrants no sooner arrive in the U.S. than they become public charges; draining welfare money from the U.S. taxpayers and paying no taxes. Solid evidence gives the lie to this charge. . . .

The services that most often catch the public eye are welfare and supplemental security, unemployment compensation, aid to dependent children, and food stamps. The average native-born U.S. family received $498 from these programs in 1975 (calculations include families getting no assistance). The average for immigrant families that arrived between 1950 and 1974 was $548. Not much difference. For immigrant and native families of similar education and age, there is no difference. . . .

When public retirement programs are included—such as Social Security, Medicare, and Medicaid—immigrant families on average are seen to receive much less in welfare payments and services than do average native families. Immigrants in fact lessen the Social Security burden upon native workers by contributing to the fund while not drawing from it. And if there is any single factor that cramps government economic policies right now, it is payments through Social Security, other pension plans, and other assistance to the elderly.

Immigrants typically arrive young and strong. Native U.S. families received in 1975 on average $735 for Social Security, $167 for Medicare and $20 for Medicaid, a total of $922. Immigrant families received a total of $92 during the first five years in the U.S., $227 in the second five years, $435 in the third five years, and $520 in fourth and fifth five-year periods. The difference in favor of natives is large. Immigrants thereby benefit the natives.

But what about Social Security when immigrants reach retirement age? The answer depends not on entitlements or legal obligations, but on the flow of real resources from workers to retirees. In this way, the children of retired immigrants support their parents with their taxes, as in the case of natives. Hence the immigrant retirees do not increase the burden on natives.

Natives and Immigrants Compared

In summing the figures for all the transfers and services, the average immigrant family is found to receive $1,404 in welfare services in years 1 to 5, $1,941 in years 6 to 10, $2,247 in years 11 to 15, and $2,279 in years 16 to 25. Native families overall average the same, $2,279, considerably more than the immigrants receive during their early years in the U.S. Figures for these early years are more relevant because in making rational policy decisions the distant future is weighted less heavily than the near future.

Myth #2: Illegals Make Especially Heavy Use of Welfare Services

Contrary to common belief, illegal immigrants from Mexico and elsewhere receive little in welfare services because of their illegal status. Labor researchers David North and Marion Houston of the New Trans Century Foundation found the following proportions of illegals using services: Free medical, 5 percent; unemployment insurance, 4 percent; food

Julian Simon, "Nine Myths About Immigration," *Backgrounder*, February 1, 1984. Reprinted with permission from The Heritage Foundation.

stamps, 1 percent; welfare payments, 1 percent; child schooling, 4 percent. Practically no illegals receive the costliest service of all—Social Security. But 77 percent of illegal workers paid Social Security taxes, and 73 percent had federal income tax withheld. Several other studies using a variety of research methods reveal similar results. The low use of social services is largely because the illegals are afraid of being apprehended. And among the illegal Mexicans, more than 80 percent are male, half are single (most of the married men leave their wives and children in Mexico), and most are youthful (less than 10 percent of the workers are over 35) and need few services.

Immigrants As Taxpayers

Myth #3: Immigrants Pay Less Than Their Share of Taxes

If immigrants paid relatively little in taxes, it could be argued that they still burden natives, even with fewer welfare services for immigrants than for natives. While there is no direct information on taxes paid, data on family earnings allow a reliable estimate.

Within three to five years after entry, immigrant family earnings reach and pass those of the average native family, because of the variance in age composition of native and immigrant families. The average native family paid $3,008 in taxes in 1975. In comparison, immigrant families here 10 years paid $3,359, those here 11 to 15 years paid $3,564 and those here 16 to 25 years paid $3,592. Such substantial differences benefit natives. . . .

Myth #4: Immigrants Cause Natives to Lose Jobs

The most politically powerful argument against admitting immigrants has been that they take jobs held by natives and thereby increase native unemployment. The logic is simple: If the number of jobs is fixed, and immigrants occupy some jobs, then there are fewer jobs available for natives.

"In the few sectors . . . where immigrants concentrate, there tends not to be a deleterious effect on natives because natives do not want these jobs."

In the immediate present, the demand for any particular sort of worker is indeed inflexible. And, therefore, additional immigrants in a given occupation, in theory, must have some negative impact on wages and/or employment among people in that occupation. For example, the large recent influx of foreign physicians means additional competition for U.S. physicians. There is good reason

to believe that U.S. physicians will earn less because of immigrant physicians. Such negative effects upon particular occupations could be avoided only if immigrants were to come into all occupations in proportion to the size of those occupations. Workers whose occupations immigrants enter disproportionately can therefore be expected to complain.

Theory says that there must be some unemployment in some sectors. But theory does not say whether the effect will be huge or trivial. For this, empirical research is needed. The effect is difficult to measure, because natives move away from areas with high unemployment to areas where it is lower, and immigrants move there, too, thereby obscuring the impact of immigration. Nevertheless, if immigrants were to cause large amounts of unemployment in particular industries, the phenomenon would surely be noticeable. Yet no empirical study has found such unemployment in noticeable amounts.

Even in the few sectors, such as the restaurant and hotel industries, where immigrants concentrate, there tends not to be a deleterious effect on natives because natives do not want these jobs. Evidence comes from experiments conducted by the Immigration and Naturalization Service together with San Diego County. In one case, 2,154 illegal aliens were removed from jobs, and the California State Human Resources Agency tried without success to fill the jobs with U.S. citizens. The County of San Diego Human Resources Agency reported:

> Some of the reasons for the failure were: (1) most employers paid less than the minimum wage rate, (2) the job categories were not appealing to the local resident (a matter of prestige), and (3) applicants were discouraged by not only the low wages but also the difficulty of some jobs, and the long hours demanded by the employers.

No Noticeable Effect

Research also does not show across-the-board unemployment caused by immigrants, either in the U.S. as a whole or in particular areas of relatively high immigration. Heretofore such studies have been rather casual. Therefore, research assistant Stephen Moore and the author recently mounted a systematic attempt to detect whether such immigrant-caused unemployment exists in a significant amount. Still no such effect is observable. It seems fair to conclude therefore that, while in theory immigration ought to produce some unemployment in the short run, the amount is in fact negligible. And in the long run, when there is not even a theoretical reason to believe that immigration causes unemployment, there is no reason at all to think that it does.

One reason that unemployment is not caused is that potential immigrants have considerable awareness of labor-market conditions in the U.S. and tend not to come if there is little demand for their skills. Also, immigrants tend to be varied in their skills and therefore do not have a disproportionate impact on a few industries. At the same time—this point is crucial, but too little understood—immigrants increase demand for labor across the range of occupations, because immigrants consume goods as well as produce them.

They Make Jobs

Another reason, then, for the absence of unemployment caused by immigrants is that they not only take jobs, they make jobs. Immigrants not only create new jobs indirectly with their spending, they create new jobs directly with new businesses, which they are more likely than natives to start. A Canadian government survey, which should be similar to U.S. experience, finds that almost five percent of the 2,037 immigrants surveyed had started their own businesses within the first three years in Canada. Not only did they employ themselves, they employed others, "creating" a total of 606 jobs. Expressed as a proportion of the 2,037 total immigrants, roughly 30 percent as many jobs were created from scratch as total jobs were held by immigrants. Furthermore, these numbers rose rapidly after the three-year study period; after one year there were 71 self-employed immigrants creating 264 jobs, compared with the 91 and 606 respectively after three years.

The businesses immigrants start are small at first, but small businesses are the most important source of new jobs, according to a MIT study. . . .

Myth #5: Immigrants Push Wages Way Down

The impact of immigration is likely to be greater on wages than on unemployment rates, because potential immigrants with skills that are in low demand choose not to migrate, and those with saleable skills gravitate to industries where there are jobs. This will have some downward pressure on wages. For example, immigrant physicians are more likely to reduce a native physician's yearly income than to throw him or her out of work.

Economists Barton Smith and Robert Newman of the University of Houston found that adjusted wages are just 8 percent lower in the Texas border cities, where the proportion of Mexicans is relatively high, compared to Texas cities away from the border where the proportion of Mexicans is much lower, a considerably smaller difference than they had expected to find. Much of the apparent difference is accounted for by a lower cost of living in the border cities.

Myth #6: Immigrants Are "Huddled Masses"

The belief that immigrants arrive now, as they did in the past, with little or no education, few marketable skills, and in a generally tired and depressed condition is one of the most powerful, least accurate, and most persevering myths about immigration. This description is found in many books and articles including Oscar Handlin's famous *The Uprooted.*

"Immigrants not only create new jobs indirectly with their spending, they create new jobs directly with new businesses, which they are more likely than natives to start."

The central fact about immigrants now, as throughout U.S. history and in almost all places at almost all times, is that immigrants are just entering into the prime of work life. This is the very best time to make a maximum contribution in all ways to the country receiving them. In contrast, the U.S. resident population is rapidly aging. But the immigrants are concentrated in their twenties and thirties, when they are flexible about job and geographical location, and therefore contribute importantly to the constant adjustment of the economy to changing conditions. They are of the age of greatest physical and mental vigor. And in this age bracket they contribute heavily to old-age support while requiring relatively little welfare service from the public coffers. . . .

Self-Reliant and Innovative

Along with youth and skill, immigrants tend to bring an unusually high degree of self-reliance, initiative, and innovative flair. Again, it makes sense that it is such people, rather than the dull and frightened, who have the courage and the belief in themselves necessary to the commitment to the awesome change that international migration represents.

Myth #7: Immigrants Increase Pressure Upon Resources and Environment

Still another unfounded charge is that immigrants create a squeeze in natural resources for natives. For example, Zero Population Growth's honorary president, Paul R. Ehrlich, talks about the effect of additional people on the "perilously shrinking water supply in this country. And our food supply. Think of the competition they'll cause for housing and jobs." The basis is the assertion that "The United States in less than 50 years will be more crowded, more polluted, more ecologically unstable, more prone to political unrest, more burdened with social stress, and far, far more precarious than we can possibly imagine."

These predictions are without foundation. The water and food supplies consumed in the U.S. have been improving in past decades by every reasonable measure of quantity and purity, though this appears to be little known. The air, moreover, is becoming less polluted, according to the official Pollutant Standard Index prepared by the U.S. Environmental Protection Agency. And over the long run, natural resources are becoming less scarce rather than more scarce, as indicated by the fundamental economic measure of cost. . . .

Myth #8: The U.S. Is Flooded by Mexican Illegals

The number of aliens illegally residing and working in the United States is an issue that enters into the discussion of immigration in many ways. It is the main focus of the writings of those who oppose immigration, and it is used to generate strong feelings on the grounds that it causes a breakdown in the law and order of the country and corrupts attitudes toward the law. The issue also is used to suggest that the United States is rendered vulnerable to invasion or other unnamed dangers because it has "lost control of its borders." The Federation for American Immigration Reform (FAIR) and The Environmental Fund (TEF), the two organizations most active in fighting against immigration, dwell upon the word "control." This plays upon a fear of chaos and social breakdown. And the supposed large-scale loss of jobs by natives due to illegals is a major objection to immigration generally, including that by labor unions.

Evidence Is Flimsy

Are such arguments justified by the data? Clearly not. The evidence for the largest and most frightening estimates of illegals is flimsy or nonexistent. In general there is a strong negative relationship between the quality of the research and the size of the estimate.

The Immigration and Naturalization Service frightened many with its 1970s estimates that there were 4 to 12 million illegals in the U.S. But a study by the Bureau of the Census staff at the request of the Select Commission on Immigration and Refugee Policy noted that this estimate was based on nothing more than an impression derived from the data on the number of apprehensions of illegals either crossing the border or on the job. The INS gave no evidence in support of its estimate. And apprehension records are obviously a fallacious basis for any such estimate. For example, the same person might be apprehended several times during a single week.

Later the INS shifted its estimate to 8.2 million persons, as of mid-1975, deriving the figure from a Lesko Associates study it commissioned. The basis for the estimate was the "Delphi technique." This technique may be appropriate for such tasks as forecasting technological developments. But it is an absolutely unreliable and inappropriate estimation method for a subject such as the number of illegals

in the U.S. Even Lesko called the estimate "not analytically defensible." Yet for a long time these figures were the basis for much of the the political debate on the subject.

"Along with youth and skill, immigrants tend to bring an unusually high degree of self-reliance, initiative, and innovative flair."

The INS then offered an estimate of 6 million illegals as of 1976. This was derived by asking INS District Directors to estimate the number of illegals residing in their districts. According to the Bureau of the Census description

> The district officers were asked to provide, in addition to estimates of illegals for their districts, a description of the methodology used to generate the estimates. None gave specific procedures. Rather, all but one referred to the 'experience' of officials as the basis for the estimate; the other claimed no 'scientific' basis at all for his estimate. Thus, the overall estimate may be characterized as 'synthetic speculation.' . . .

Immigration's Costs Are Minimal

Just about all the individual economic objections to immigrants are without factual foundation. No mention has been made, moreover, of the benefits from immigration. And there are very large benefits. Improved productivity, as a result of the increased production volume that flows from immigrant purchasing power as well as from the additional supply of ingenious inventive minds that immigrants bring, is one of the most important such benefits. It quickly dominates all the short-run costs.

Exactly how beneficial immigrants are to the U.S. society and economy may be debated. What is certain, however, is that many of the alleged costs of immigrants are simply unfounded, hollow myths.

Julian Simon is a senior research fellow at The Heritage Foundation, a conservative thinktank. A professor at the University of Maryland, Mr. Simon writes frequently on the issue of immigration.

"Large-scale legal and illegal immigration lowers the standard of living for disadvantaged Americans."

Immigration Lowers the Living Standards of Americans

Roger Conner

Editor's Note: This viewpoint is taken from a debate sponsored by The Heritage Foundation between Mr. Conner and Julian Simon, author of the previous viewpoint. Because this article is taken from a debate, Mr. Conner frequently quotes and addresses Mr. Simon.

It is FAIR's [Federation for American Immigration Reform] position that immigration to the United States is out of control. FAIR believes that a "prudent, responsible policy" would include (1) vigorous steps to stop illegal immigration; (2) a reasonable ceiling on legal immigration of 350,000 to 400,000—that level of legal immigration which prevailed from 1965 until the surge in legal immigration in the mid-1970s; and (3) a periodic review of the ceiling on legal immigration in light of changing circumstances. . . .

The Productivty Myth

A) The Productivity Myth: Immigration Is the Mainspring of U.S. Technological Progress

Julian Simon's productivity myth is based on "a crucial historical cycle" which goes like this:

> (a) an immigrant-swelled population leads to greater use of natural resources; (b) prices of raw materials then rise; (c) the price and the resultant fear about scarcity impels individuals to seek new sources of raw materials, new production technologies, and new substitutes for the resources; and (d) eventually the price of the service provided by the resource in question . . . falls lower than it was before.

Simon actually believes that population growth "has been the mainspring of all economic advance for the past 5,000 years"; "more immigrants mean a faster growing population and thus even more progress.". . .

Economic historians have identified many factors driving economic advance in the last 5,000 years: the

Roger Conner, "How Immigrants Affect Americans' Living Standard," *Heritage Lecture #39*, May 30, 1984. Reprinted with permission from The Heritage Foundation.

birth of reason, discovery of the scientific method, capitalism, democracy, individual freedom, natural resources, the thirst for knowledge that drives inventors, war, the desire for individual advancement, and so on. The notion that immigration is vastly more important than all of these is preposterous. . . .

Dr. Michael Teitlebaum, in a review of available literature prepared for the U.S. Chamber Foundation, argues that precisely the opposite is likely to result from today's illegal immigration.

> . . .the low educational levels of many undocumented immigrants may be significant impediments to creativity and high productivity in an economic setting in which high skill levels are important. Certainly the fact that there has been almost no immigration to Japan in recent years does not appear to have limited productivity growth in that country. . . . It is worth noting that those sectors of the economy that become dependent on undocumented labor are typically under-capitalized, and hence their productivity tends to be low. . . .

Unlimited and illegal immigration to the United States creates an environment that actively discourages automation and innovation. Why should a farmer invest in a mechanical harvester when illegal aliens are cheap, docile, and available? Why should a company invest in the development of a computerized sewing machine when an unlimited labor pool guarantees that there will be little market for such a capital-intensive machine? As long as the United States continues to ignore massive illegal immigration, many of America's oldest industries will have little incentive to modernize their means of production. Instead, these industries will remain content to plod down the easy path leading to economic obsolescence and protectionist tariffs.

Another way to look at Simon's theory is to ask what would happen if the flow of illegal immigrants were to be cut off. The economists who have investigated this question are in agreement: to replace the immigrant workers with American workers, employers would have to offer higher wages. Higher labor costs would, in turn, act as an incentive to increase productivity through improvements in management and labor-saving technology.

In short, Simon has yet to produce any serious evidence for his claim that without immigration "the mainspring of all economic advance" will wind down. The evidence indicates that just the opposite is true.

Immigrants and Welfare

B] The Myth That Illegal Aliens Don't Use Social Security

The second leg of Julian Simon's theory relates only to illegal aliens: even if they do not benefit the economy, they benefit us as taxpayers since they "receive little in welfare services because of their illegal status."

In support of his conclusion, Simon has repeatedly maintained that only 1-4 percent of illegal aliens receive welfare, unemployment compensation, or food stamps.

His authority is a 1976 study by David North and Marion Houston. Simon surely knows, but never acknowledges, that this study was not a survey of welfare use or tax payments by illegal aliens in the United States, but simply a profile of a small group of illegal aliens apprehended by the U.S. Immigration and Naturalization Service. North and Houstoun have cautioned researchers not to use this study as evidence of welfare use by illegal aliens. The reason: 46 percent of those sampled had been in the U.S. for less than a year, and 90 percent were apprehended males—the very group least likely to make use of U.S. social service programs. This discrepancy has been called to Simon's attention, and yet he continues to cite the North/Houstoun survey as "proof" that illegal aliens do not use welfare.

More Representative Studies

Recent, more representative studies show quite another pattern of social service use by illegal aliens:

- A 1980 study by David North of apprehended illegal aliens with fraudulent Social Security numbers showed that a full 49 percent applied for (and 35 percent received) unemployment insurance benefits.
- The Los Angeles County Department of Public Service Social Services has found that illegal aliens in Los Angeles County alone apply for over $36 million worth of benefits a year.
- A study by David Heer found that 18.5 percent of illegal alien mothers in Los Angeles County General Hospital have used either AFDC, Food Stamps, or MediCal since arrival in the United States.
- A May 1983 study by the Arizona Hospital Association estimated that providing health care to illegal aliens cost $4.4 million a year. To recoup this loss, Arizona hospitals charged regular patients an average surcharge of $10.10 per patient per day.

- A 1982 study by the Illinois Attorney General's office found that 50 percent of non-citizen unemployment insurance applicants were illegal aliens using fraudulent documents. The estimated loss to Illinois taxpayers: $50 million a year.

Julian Simon consistently failed to note these studies in any of his work. Instead, he repeatedly returns to the North-Houstoun report, which is not a study of welfare use at all. It is time to look at the facts. The evidence is in: illegal aliens make average to heavy use of the American social service system. Julian Simon's assertion that illegal aliens do not use welfare is an outdated myth.

How Much Taxes?

C] The "Free Lunch" Myth: Illegals Pay More in Taxes Than They Receive in Benefits

During the debate, when challenged on his assertion that "illegal aliens use little welfare," Julian Simon fell back to argue a different position: that aliens pay more in taxes than they receive in benefits. In short, immigrants—both legal and illegal—are a "free lunch."

Simon's primary support for his argument is an analysis of Census bureau data on immigrants who arrived in the United States between 1950 and 1975. Oddly, when David North (the same expert Simon relies on in other contexts) went back to the same Census Bureau data, and using Simon's formulation, recalculated the "costs" and "benefits" from immigrants, he came to precisely the opposite conclusion. . . .

Even if you accept Simon's study, it cannot predict the "costs and benefits" of today's immigrants (illegal aliens, legal immigrants, and refugees) unless you assume today's immigrants will be as productive and earn as much money as the legal immigrants who entered the United States between 1950 and 1975—a group dominated by skilled professionals from Eastern Europe and Cuba.

"[The] assertion that illegal aliens do not use welfare is an outdated myth."

Simon offers no evidence to support this assumption. All available data indicate that illegal aliens are significantly less productive and earn less money, and according to economist Barry Chiswick, recently arrived refugees, legal Hispanics, and Filipinos have all been less successful than the group Simon studied. This is a significant finding in light of the fact that these three immigrant groups represent a large percentage of the immigrants coming to the United States today.

Simon's cost-benefit argument discounts at least one significant costs: Social Security. He ignores this cost when discussing illegal aliens, assuming that they pay into but make no use of this costly federal program. Yet current law permits both legal and illegal aliens to receive Social Security benefits, and increasing numbers are doing so. A recent study by the General Accounting Office found that, of the 312,000 non-citizen Social Security recipients residing overseas, as many as 194,000 may be illegal aliens. On average, these Social Security recipients are receiving $23 in benefits for every $1 they paid into the system prior to retirement.

"Illegal immigrants do not take jobs Americans will not fill; they make jobs Americans will not fill."

As the alien population of the United States grows older, we can expect more legal immigrants to file for (and receive) Social Security benefits. It is important to note here that these claims will increase rapidly at the very time American "baby boomers" begin to come of age and make claims. The effect of adding additional numbers to this sizeable bulge in the U.S. age structure can only accentuate what will be a significant problem in years ahead. . . .

Disadvantaged Americans Affected

D) The Myth That Poor Workers Own American Industry

On one subject Simon and we are in agreement: today's immigration has the result of driving down wages for American workers. The reason is that immigration increases the supply of labor, and increasing the supply of any factor of production tends to lower the price.

Since today's immigrants tend to concentrate in low skilled jobs, the Americans who face lower incomes because of competition from immigrants tend to be disadvantaged American workers—the young, minorities, handicapped, and women.

Simon actually cites a study which found wages depressed by 8 percent by the pressure of illegals. Other studies indicate the effect is three times as great in areas of heavy concentrations of illegals.

Nonetheless, Simon dismisses this loss of earnings by American workers. The reason is that any loss of wages is offset by an increase in profits to the owners of capital. And, he states matter of factly,

> Much of America's private capital is owned directly by "workers" through pension funds and by way of taxes paid on interest and dividends. Hence the loss to the "worker" is unclear.

It is hard to believe that Julian Simon really believes this unique version of the trickle down theory: that American workers at the bottom of the economic ladder are not affected by illegal

immigration because of the dividends they receive from employers who hire illegal aliens. It is worth noting that Simon does not supply any data to support his remarkable assertion.

There is not a single scholarly dissent from the proposition that large-scale legal and illegal immigration lowers the standard of living for disadvantaged Americans.

Stealing Jobs

E) The Myth That Americans Will Not Do Jobs Held by Illegals

Millions of immigrants have joined the workforce of the United States over the last ten years. Former Secretary of Labor Ray Marshall has observed that unemployment could be 2 percent lower than it is today if illegals were not taking so many jobs from Americans.

Simon disagrees. He asserts that "there tends not to be a deleterious effect on natives because natives do not want these jobs."

Yet in every major occupation in which aliens are found, the majority of the labor force are American citizens. In every single occupation where illegal aliens are employed, they toil side by side with citizen and legal resident alien workers. In other words, the assertion that American workers would not do those jobs now held by illegals is absurd. Americans workers as now doing those jobs—as long as they are paid a decent wage under reasonable conditions.

Yet employers continue to hire illegal workers. The reason: illegal aliens are willing to work for less than the prevailing wage in occupations where they concentrate.

Though Julian Simon suggests that Americans are unwilling to do difficult or "stoop" labor, a moment's reflection reveals this to be untrue. American workers have always been willing to do boring, dirty, and dangerous work. American workers actively seek jobs mining coal, resurfacing roads, and laying hot tar roofs. Every sidewalk in America was built by someone who stooped.

What Simon fails to grasp is the very important relationship between depressed wages and working conditions brought about by illegal immigration (which he acknowledges) and the displacement of American workers. Illegal immigrants do not take jobs Americans will not fill; they make jobs Americans will not fill.

The presence of illegal aliens create a vicious labor market cycle. Large numbers of illegal aliens depress wages and working conditions in these industries. At some point the wages are so low, the working conditions so bad, that American workers are unwilling to accept them. The "unavailability" of American workers is used as an excuse to justify more illegal immigration, which drives wages and working conditions even lower, resulting in even fewer Americans applying for such jobs. The reemergence of the sweatshops in New York and Los Angeles in the past ten years is an example.

Now consider what would happen if illegal immigration were cut off. Some sweatshops might be moved abroad. But the restaurants, hotels, and construction companies would have to stay and attract unemployed Americans with better wages and working conditions, thereby reducing unemployment.

America Has Limits

F) The Myth That There Is No Limit to America's Carrying Capacity

Immigration will add more than fifty million people to the population of the United States by the year 2025 if today's levels continue and do not increase. Many scientists believe that such population growth will result in severe strains on our natural resources and a significant reduction in the quality of life in this country.

Simon concedes that such population growth will create real strains on our natural resources and a significant reduction in the quality of life in this country.

Simon concedes that such population growth will create real strains on the carrying capacity of our country. He predicts "prices of raw materials [will] rise," and that there will be "fear of scarcity."

Why is he so willing to bring about this reduction in the standard of living? Because the scarcity will trigger technological progress "in the long run."

His faith in technology is based on what he asserts to be a historical fact: "natural resources are in the long run getting increasingly more available rather than increasingly scarce."

"More and more of the world's displeased and dispossessed will seek to improve their lot through migration."

The reader should be aware that this assertion is hotly contested by most of the experts in the field he cites. For example:

Fisheries: Simon has frequently said that the total world fisheries catch has increased in recent years. But population has grown even faster, so the per capita world fisheries catch has declined. It is per capita availability of a resource that determines its overall scarcity.

Land: To show that land resources are not getting scarcer, Simon claims that the ratio of acres per farmer has increased. But the number of acres per person has decreased in recent years.

Forestry: In discussing forest resources, Julian Simon points out that the United States has more

forests than ever before. Yet he ignores readily available national and global data that indicate per capita forest resources are decreasing. . . .

Regain Control of Immigration

In recent years, public figures as divergent as Attorney General William French Smith and Father Theodore Hesburgh have all reached the same conclusion: America has lost control of its borders. The consensus is that legal and illegal immigration to the United States is high and is growing with each passing year. Yet Julian Simon suggests that this is not so; that illegal immigration is not increasing and that, in fact, we are accepting fewer immigrants than we have in the past.

Simon's Numbers Game: Unrealistic Estimates for Illegal Immigration

Legal immigration has ranged from 600,000 to 800,000 over the past five years. If illegal immigration has ranged from 500,000 to 1,000,000 per year, as many experts believe, immigration is now at the highest levels in American history.

Simon ridicules the experts, claiming that 250,000 per year is the true figure for illegal immigration. Yet he himself cites the Census Bureau's conservative estimate that there were between 3.5 and 6 million illegal aliens in the country in 1978. As most of this stock was accumulated in the 1970s, at least 350,000 to 600,000 per year were coming in to stay in each of the past ten years. . . .

Whatever the precise number of illegal aliens, one thing is clear: it is large enough to cause concern. And it is growing. . . .

Illegal Immigration—Not Growing?

Apprehensions of illegal immigrants have increased 3,000 fold in the past twenty years, even though the number of Immigration Officers has barely increased at all. Apprehensions per hour of Border Patrol time have increased by 250 percent in the past ten years. . . .

Since 1955, apprehensions have been rising. The escalation has been sharper since the late sixties, without significant increases in Border Patrol. Last year over a million persons were apprehended crossing the border. Some are obviously repeat offenders. But Border Patrol officials estimate that for every one they catch two or three simply slip across the border.

Illegal immigration is growing, and has been for twenty years. . . .

Should We Do Nothing?

Even if the reader accepts Simon's argument that the number of immigrants entering today (or a modest increase over that number) is acceptable, there is still an urgent need to take action now to control illegal immigration. Most immigration experts agree: immigration pressures on the United States are going to increase sharply in the coming years. Simon seems unconcerned over the prospect, perhaps because his theories predict that things will get better in the developing world in the coming decades. Consider the evidence:

Africa, hard-pressed to feed 513 million persons today, must somehow find the means to feed a population of 1.39 billion the year 2020. Latin America, with a gross national product one-fifth that of the U.S., must create twice as many jobs as the United States averaged throughout the 1970s, and do it every year for the next 40 years just to maintain current levels of unemployment. It is hard to imagine that the economic growth of these two continents will be able to keep pace with their rapid population growth. . . .

For most of the developing world, the question is not economic prosperity, but economic survival. The most recent World Bank *Developing Report 1984* concludes that rapid population growth endangers, rather than enhances, precarious economic conditions in the developing world.

Even if Third World economies grow as their populations expand, more and more of the world's displeased and dispossessed will seek to improve their lot through migration. Many will seek passage to the United States. Already, nearly everyone in El Salvador, Mexico, and the Philippines knows someone who has come to America—the land of Ivory Snow, Chevrolet, and designer jeans. In Haiti, a popular local myth holds that in America there is a computer on every corner and all you have to do is punch in a few numbers and money comes pouring out—a classic interpretation of computerized banking. Though such stories are amusing, it is a sad and frightening truth that whole generations of children are growing up today with only one thought in mind: to migrate to the United States.

America's Frontier Has Disappeared

Though America has a long immigrant tradition, it cannot afford to accept all who come. We are no longer a nation of frontiers. Our western states are already suffering from a mounting water crisis. And today's natural resource constraints endanger our national security and leave us vulnerable to the whims of unstable foreign governments.

Though the U.S. birth rate has dropped, we continue to have one of the fastest population growth rates in the industrialized world. The reason: legal and illegal immigration, which accounts for 40 to 50 percent of U.S. population growth. Between 1980 and the year 2000, current levels of legal and illegal immigration will add over 20 million people to the population of the United States—a sum equal to the combined 1980 populations of Los Angeles, New York, Philadelphia, Chicago, Phoenix, Houston, and Dallas.

Though some employers may derive short-term economic benefit from hiring cheap, docile, illegal alien labor, society as a whole must bear the burden and pay the price—a price that includes a lower wage for American workers, higher unemployment, and increasing social service costs.

Julian Simon has failed to show that today's uncontrolled immigration is a net benefit to the United States. In fact, careful scrutiny of his sources of authority demonstrates the validity of FAIR's contention that America must regain control of its borders.

Roger Conner is a prominent and outspoken critic of immigration. The executive director of FAIR, the Federation for American Immigration Reform, Conner has also been a leading conservationist and the author of many articles on conservation.

"Whatever we do about the level of immigration shouldn't be done relying on the standard arguments about jobs and resources. They are false to the core."

Immigration Need Not Be Restricted

Joseph P. Martino

Practically every problem we have in the United States is said to be either created or aggravated by immigration. Colorado Governor Richard D. Lamm has probably made the case as eloquently as anyone. Writing in the October 1983 issue of the *Futurist*, he admitted that "when the United States was a vast empty frontier, it needed immigrants to people an empty continent." But he admonished his readers that "those days are gone, never to return. . . . The America of the empty frontier has been replaced by an America of 9.5% unemployment."

The arithmetic seems simple. For every immigrant who enters the country and takes a job, there is one less job for an American who was already here. When the United States has nearly one worker in 10 looking for a job already, it certainly doesn't need to add to the problem. And if the immigrant doesn't displace an existing worker by taking a job, he ends up on welfare and becomes a burden to those who have jobs and pay taxes.

What about America's role as a refuge for those in need elsewhere? What about Emma Lazarus's "golden door"? Lamm argued that the country can no longer afford to play that role. "The United States is no longer a frontier; our humanity can no longer be boundless," he declared. "Our increasingly scarce resources and our own multiple economic problems are already substantial enough without encouraging the entrance of many millions of new immigrants who would compound these problems and diminish our standard of living significantly."

The theme of limited resources is a recurring one in such discussions of immigration's threat. The "limits to growth" school that was prominent a decade ago is still sentient despite the end of "the energy crisis." Its advocates still raise the alarm

about diminishing resources. Paul Ehrlich of *The Population Bomb* (1968) warns that even though the US birth rate has dropped below the replacement level, we're still not home free—immigration, particularly illegal immigration, is still increasing the country's population. And this will inevitably lead to more rapid depletion of the country's natural resources. His prediction is echoed by environmentalist Garrett Hardin and scores of others. . . .

But people who are concerned about immigration often worry that it is a threat not only to our jobs and well-being but to our freedom itself. As Lamm voiced this fear in his 1983 article, "Democracy has always prospered on growth. The pie usually grew and fostered social and political expectations of progress. The legitimacy of government has not been based so much on justice or religious freedom as on material advancement. Everyone could and did have a better tomorrow. If these conditions disappear, perhaps the legitimacy of our governmental structure will also disappear."

Good Reasons?

For all these reasons, the US government is urged to further limit or even end immigration. But are they good reasons?

If a ceiling is to be placed on legal immigration, it ought to be established for the right reasons. Even if a particular level of immigration were appropriate in the short run, setting it for the wrong reasons would mean that we would probably suffer in the long run, since we would be unlikely to change when change is called for by the right reasons. So it's worth examining the reasons being given for limiting or ending immigration. It's also worth looking at some of the reasons we might even want to *increase* the level of legal immigration.

To start with, the concern about immigrants taking jobs and the concern about immigrants accelerating

Joseph P. Martino, "Two Hands, One Mouth." Reprinted, with permission, from the September 1984 issue of REASON magazine. Copyright © 1984 by the Reason Foundation, 2716 Ocean Park Blvd., Suite 1062, Santa Monica, CA 90450.

the depletion of our natural resources contradict each other. They can't both be valid.

Consider that resources such as iron ore and timber can't be used "as is." Before they can be consumed, they must be transformed into products. The transformation inevitably involves human labor, which is to say it provides jobs. So if an immigrant actually takes a job that would have been held by a non-immigrant worker, he cannot at the same time increase the depletion of our resources. An immigrant can speed the depletion of our natural resources only by taking a job that didn't exist before he arrived.

"The fact that America no longer has a frontier has nothing to do with whether we can 'provide jobs' for immigrants today."

But the notion of the displacement of workers itself bears more scrutiny. Abraham Lincoln once remarked that every person is created with two hands and one mouth, and he presumed that the Creator intended those two hands to feed that one mouth. Lincoln was speaking of slavery and objecting to the slaveowner appropriating the product of the slave's labor, but his observation is relevant to the issue of immigrants and unemployment.

Many people look upon jobs as something produced by an economy, in the same way an economy produces steel. This is the idea that underlies Lamm's "forecast" that the world economy will "generate" only 450 million jobs when 700 million will be needed.

We can get a better perspective on the "generation of jobs" if we consider a typical primitive subsistence economy. One of the most prominent features of such an economy is that everyone has a job—even the children and the old folks. For the able-bodied adults, it's a back-breaking, dawn-to-dusk job. "Unemployment" is unheard of. Yet in no sense has the *economy* provided those jobs. Every person in that economy uses his two hands to provide the food for his mouth (and the clothing on his back and the roof over his head). Each person's *existence* generates a demand for sustenance; that demand for sustenance in turn provides work for the person. The match is perfect: two hands producing and one mouth consuming.

What has this to do with immigration? Just as nearly every person comes into the world with two hands and one mouth, nearly every immigrant arrives in the country equipped the same way. The match is still perfect. An immigrant demands

sustenance and is equipped to provide it. Just as in a subsistence economy, the presence of an immigrant creates a new job while simultaneously providing a worker to fill it.

Immigrants Work

This can be seen readily when an immigrant enters the country and homesteads a farm, as millions did during the 19th century. Where did that job come from? The immigrant brought it with him. He ate what he grew, and he grew it because he needed to eat. The economy did not *generate* that job, any more than a subsistence economy generates the jobs in it.

But, the Lamms counter, we no longer have a frontier to absorb millions of immigrants. This agrarian imagery may have been relevant once, but it isn't any longer.

Ironically, their own simple picture of immigrants settling on the frontier never was true. It we check out the history of various immigrant groups in America, as Thomas Sowell did in his book *Ethnic America*, we find a more-revealing picture.

Sowell reports that in 1900, over half of the farmers in America were of German ancestry. That is, the bulk of the immigrants who settled the frontier were Germans. Even so, during colonial times nearly half the German immigrants were craftsmen rather than farmers and worked at their crafts after they immigrated. By the late 19th century, the proportion of farmers among German immigrants had dropped to 25 percent.

Most Jewish immigrants, from colonial times on, were craftsmen and businessmen rather than farmers. In fact, the massive influx of Jews in the late 19th and early 20th centuries (one-third of all Jews in Eastern Europe immigrated to the United States during that period) remained and worked almost exclusively in the large cities of the East.

The vast bulk of Italian immigrants came after the closing of the frontier and took jobs in the port cities where they arrived, despite the fact that most had been peasant farmers in Italy. The Slavs ended up in the coal mines of Pennsylvania and the steel mills of Pittsburgh and Youngstown. Even Japanese immigrants, who are often stereotyped as farmers, followed a similar pattern: only about 40 percent of them worked as farm laborers and the rest worked in industry.

In reality, most of the immigrants to the United States did not settle the frontier. Instead, they crowded into the cities, where they obtained and held jobs supplying their own needs for sustenance in an exchange (not subsistence) economy.

That was the 19th century, but a look at Hong Kong suggests that things are not different today. Hong Kong is a small island. Its area of 1,050 square kilometers holds 5.2 million people, more than the population of any of the smallest 40 members of the

United Nations. In fact, Hong Kong has more people than the smallest 35 UN members put together. Its population density of 4,900 persons per square kilometer is the third highest in the world, following Monaco and Gibraltar and just ahead of Singapore.

How could such a crowded speck of land possibly allow immigration? Yet it has. From 1945 to 1956 alone, Hong Kong accepted a million immigrants, including 700,000 refugees, and has admitted another million immigrants in the years since. By comparison, the United States, 9,246 times the size of Hong Kong, has admitted about 13 million legal immigrants since 1945, including about 1 million refugees. This comes to not quite 6 percent of our population. In Hong Kong, about 40 percent of the current population is immigrants, and many of these were refugees who arrived with literally nothing but the clothing on their backs. Some who swam across from China didn't even have that.

How is Hong Kong doing with all those people crowded in there? Very well, thank you. The death rate is 4.8 per 1,000, the lowest in Asia. The infant mortality rate of 9.8 deaths per 1,000 live births is the second best in Asia, bettered only by Japan's 7.1 and better than any nation in North America, including the United States' 11.7. Life expectancy is 72 years for males and 78 years for females, better than virtually every other nation in the world. The literacy rate is 81 percent for all those over 15, one of Asia's highest.

Hong Kong Compared to US

Nor is Hong Kong's economy in the straits one would expect according to popular worries about immigration. Although Hong Kong's government apparently doesn't bother to compile figures on employment, it would appear that it doesn't need to. The 1984 edition of the *Encyclopedia Britannica Yearbook*, in its entry on unemployment, refers to Hong Kong as an "industrial magnet" that attracts labor. And according to data compiled by the United Nations, Hong Kong's population grew by 12 percent between 1970 and 1976—while during the same time employment in manfacturing grew by 21 percent and wages by 83 percent (compared to a 12 percent increase in consumer prices). Meanwhile, capital formation per capita was growing at 7.5 percent a year. All in all, it doesn't sound as though there was much room for unemployment in immigrant-"burdened" Hong Kong.

In short, the American experience in the 19th and early 20th centuries and the experience of present-day Hong Kong demonstrate that the frontier was largely irrelevant to the absorption of immigrants. The fact that America no longer has a frontier has nothing to do with whether we can "provide jobs" for immigrants today.

If an immigrant brings his job with him, though, why aren't the unemployed creating their own jobs?

Why doesn't their demand for sustenance generate work? What happened to the match between their hands and their mouths?

The answer is complicated, but it includes minimum-wage laws, occupation-licensing laws, legal bias in favor of labor unions, tax laws that encourage consumption and discourage saving, tariffs and import quotas that protect dying industries at the expense of growing ones, and thousands upon thousands of regulations that hinder the growth of business. In a nutshell, those who worry about immigration torpedoing our freedom have it backwards. It is not that freedom prospers only under economic growth. It is that economic growth occurs only under freedom.

The number of workers in the United States doubled between 1874 and 1900, with most of the increase coming from immigration. Despite the increase, real wages rose over 40 percent during that same period. That's what freedom can do to foster prosperity. In today's Hong Kong, under conditions of freedom comparable to those of 19th-century America, economic growth is creating room for the immigrants. In today's America, with our economic freedoms considerably diminished since 1900, the economy is staggering along and nearly 1 out of 10 workers either can't find work or is unwilling to take an available job because the alternative (often, government assistance) is more attractive.

"The immigrant . . . brings with him the job of providing his sustenance, and he brings with him the hands to produce the resources he consumes."

We've really done it to ourselves, and what's worse, at one time we knew better. The original settlers of the United States came to an unknown land to get away from government restrictions, confident that they could prosper if only the government would get out of the way. The signers of the Declaration of Independence would have been horrified to hear Governor Lamm aver that the legitimacy of a government depends on whether people prosper under it. To them, the legitimacy of a government depended on whether the people consented to it rather than having it imposed on them. They knew that prosperity is individuals' own responsibility, and they realized that governments don't create prosperity—at best governments can only refrain from destroying it. In 200 years, the accepted wisdom has changed radically.

Despite the restrictions that hinder growth in our economy, immigrants still manage to find room in it. Julian Simon in *The Ultimate Resource* notes that within three months of their arrival in the United

States, 47 percent of Vietnamese males aged 14 or older had obtained jobs. Simon also points out that when illegal Mexican aliens were removed by the Immigration and Naturalization Service (INS) from jobs they held in California, no native Americans could be found to fill those jobs.

This is a graphic example of aliens creating their own jobs, not displacing native workers. They were taking jobs that native workers, *including the unemployed*, refused to take. As Tom Bethell put it, writing in *National Review*, "Illegal aliens are good at lubricating an economy because they . . . slip into all sorts of economic nooks and crannies, sometimes taking two or three part-time jobs. In properly planned, bureaucratically approved economies, this kind of voluntary activity is against the rules and nothing works very well as a result."

So "jobs" are clearly not a sensible reason for limiting immigration. Instead, unemployment would probably end overnight if we simply abolished the rules that prevent or discourage law-abiding citizens from acting on the fact that they come equipped with both mouths and hands.

"The payoff from illegal immigrants is even higher, since they pay taxes but don't get social security."

Yet it may still seem that those immigrants getting jobs converting raw materials into finished products will hasten the day we run out of natural resources. This supposed linkage of natural resources and wealth is behind the paradox that Lamm finds in the inability of Mexico, even with its great oil wealth, to provide jobs for its citizens. Since an economy doesn't "provide" jobs, the paradox really doesn't exist. Still, the resource worry warrants another look at wealth.

Is oil in the ground "wealth"? That depends on the calendar. In 1800, the answer was no. In 2100, the answer will probably again be no. Oil in the ground is wealth only so long as someone wants it badly enough to trade something for it. It is then worth exactly what people are willing to give in exchange for it. In 1800 no one would have given anything in exchange for it; therefore it was worthless.

Lack of Resources Irrelevant

This applies not just to oil but to *everything*. The economic value of anything at all is precisely what people are willing to exchange for it. So if you have something people want, you can gain access to raw materials that you want. Consider Hong Kong again. It not only doesn't have a frontier to absorb immigrants, it has no natural resources to speak

of—not even a supply of fresh water. Hong Kong's drinking water comes from reservoirs that are filled during the rainy season and last the rest of the year. Yet with virtually no natural resources at all, the people there still generate wealth, *importing* the raw materials they need.

But there's a deeper issue yet. People do not exchange what they have for products made of natural resources simply because they want something made of iron or of wood. People want products for the services that they can perform, not for the products themselves. As someone has put it, the real reason you buy a quarter-inch drill is that you want a quarter-inch hole. So the issue is not natural resources themselves but how we can continue to get the services we want when there are more and more people to share an earth of fixed size—or, for that matter, to share a United States of fixed size.

By and large, technology is a way of getting more and more services out of a given amount of material. That may mean extracting specific materials out of leaner and leaner ores, or it may mean doing with a given amount of refined material. Consider the amount of material that goes into a transistor radio of today compared with the amount of material that went into a vacuum-tube radio of a generation ago. The difference is one measure of the progress of technology since then. If technology advances rapidly enough, we can continue to get the services we want even though we have to divide a fixed amount of iron, copper, and so on among a larger number of people.

People Create Resources

So the question is put one step back—can we be sure technology will advance rapidly enough to keep pace with population? If not, it seems that population growth, including immigration, must be limited to a rate with which technology can keep pace. But this is to misconceive why technological developments occur. As Julian Simon emphasizes in *The Ultimate Resource*, "the development of new methods that prevent scarcity is *not fortuitous*." Drawing from history, Simon shows that "to a large extent new methods are invented and developed *in response to* the signals of impending scarcity." Thus his ultimate conclusion, that "an increase of human beings constitutes an addition to the crucial stock of resources along with causing additional consumption of resources." In short, people *create* resources by finding ways to do more with less.

This makes it sound as though population increase, including immigration, might even benefit a nation, particularly if that nation allows the increased population the freedom to use their hands to feed their mouths. Simon has documented this possibility, showing that people begin to produce net economic benefits to society about 30 years after they are born. In the case of immigrants, the payoff usually comes even sooner. Simon's calculations show that the "return on investment" legal immigrants make to the rest of society is about 20 percent per annum, certainly one of the best payoffs around today. The payoff from illegal immigrants is even higher, since they pay taxes but don't get Social Security and other benefits.

So those who worry about economic harm from immigration are "dismembering" the immigrants: those who worry about immigrants taking jobs are looking at their hands but forgetting about their mouths; those who worry about immigrants consuming resources are looking at their mouths but forgetting their hands. If fact, the immigrant is a whole person. He has two hands and one mouth. He brings with him the job of providing his sustenance, and he brings with him the hands to produce the resources he consumes.

Does this mean that we ought to throw open the gates and let anyone enter who wants to? The American experience of a century ago and the experience of Hong Kong today suggest that we might very well be better off for doing so. However, that's another subject entirely. The point here is simply that whatever we do about the level of immigration shouldn't be done relying on the standard arguments about jobs and resources. They are false to the core.

Joseph P. Martino is a technology forecaster at the Research Institute of the University of Dayton. He has degrees in physics, electrical engineering, and mathematics and is an associate editor of Technological Forecasting and Social Change.

"American immigration policies are in a shambles."

Immigration Must Be Restricted

Richard D. Lamm

Let me begin with a metaphor. The U.S. fleet was on the high seas. All of a sudden a blip appeared on the radar screen. "Tell that ship to change its course 15 degrees!" said the Admiral. The radio man did and the word came back on the radio, "*You* change *your* course 15 degrees." "Tell that ship that we're the U.S. Navy and to change its course 15 degrees," said the Admiral. The radio man did and the word came back again, "You change your course 15 degrees." This time the Admiral himself got on the radio and said, "I am an Admiral in the U.S. Navy. Change your course 15 degrees." The word came back over the radio. "You change your course 15 degrees, I am a lighthouse!"

We often expect the world to adjust to our course, but alas, we find we must adjust to the realities around us. I would go further—I believe it is the duty and the obligation of each generation to perceive the realities of their times. It is easy to be wise in retrospect. Anyone can tell you yesterday's issues, yesterday's realities. But our challenge, and certainly the challenge of every generation of policy makers, is to confront today's and tomorrow's realities. Lincoln said it so well: "As our case is new, so must we think and act anew. We must disenthrall ourselves and then we shall save the country." Out of my youth comes an old Presbyterian hymn: "New occasions teach new duties. Time makes ancient good uncouth."

It is my thesis that our immigration laws are one example where "time has made ancient good uncouth."

I want to make five points:

I. The world has gone through a demographic revolution that is hard for us to conceive.

Throughout most of human history death rates,

especially the young, have been very high. High birth rates were essential to survival.

We cut the death rates around the world dramatically with modern medicine and the green revolution. For example, we sprayed to eliminate mosquitoes in Sri Lanka in the 1950's. In one twelve month period, the life expectancy of everyone in Sri Lanka was extended by eight years as the incidence of malaria suddenly declined.

Population Is Soaring

There were magnificent human achievements. But we cut the death rate without cutting the birth rate. Now population is soaring. There were approximately one billion people living in the world when the Statue of Liberty was built. There are 4.5 billion today.

Planetary population growth is projected to be of enormous magnitude. The world is going to add a billion people in the next 11 years, 224,000 every day. Demographers project at least 1.6 billion people in the next 20 years.

We must understand the implications of those numbers. Let's look at the question of jobs. The International Labor Organization projects a 20-year increase of 600 to 700 million people who will be seeking jobs. To put that into perspective, this anticipated unemployed labor force of 600-700 million is larger than the present labor forces of all the industrialized countries taken together.

Eighty-eight percent of the world's population growth takes place in the Third World. More than a billion people today have an annual per capita income of $150.00, which is less than the average American earns in a week. The developing countries have 70 percent of the world's people but only 17 percent of the world's income. And many of them, in growing, significant numbers, want to come to the United States.

In the 1970s virtually all other receiving countries,

Richard D. Lamm, speech delivered in Chautauqua, New York, on August 19, 1985.

other than the United States, restricted their admissions, thereby deflecting future flows to the United States.

The numbers, themselves, are staggering. The potential for human suffering they represent—nightmarish.

Latin America's population is now 390 million people. It will be 800 million in the year 2025. Mexico's population has tripled since the Second World War. The present work force in Mexico is 19 million people, it will be 45 million people by the year 2000. Mexico, with 76 million people, had more babies born last year than the U.S. did with 236 million people. One third of the population of Mexico is under ten years of age.

"The city of Los Angeles estimates that one out of ten people in the city is an illegal immigrant."

Latin America's labor force amounted to 55 million in 1950, 99 million in 1975, and will be 197 million by the year 2000. That is *not* a projection: these people have already been born.

For Latin America to maintain an unemployment rate of 40 percent, 4 million jobs must be created annually from an industrial base one-fifth the size of the United States. The United States only creates 2 million new jobs every year.

Infants do not migrate, by and large. So we really need to look not at population growth, but the growth in the working age population. These numbers give a sense of acceleration:

The world added 22 million new workers per year in 1950-75. It will add 36 million per year during the rest of this century. In the 25 years between 1975 and 2000, there will be 118 million job seekers in the developed world. There will be 782 million for the less developed world. *Most will come in the next 15 years.*

In 1980 Latin America had a labor force of 117 million. By the year 2000, it will have a labor force of 207 million. To underscore, I repeat—these are not projections. These people have already been born.

Geometry of Chaos

These are not abstract numbers. This is the geometry of chaos. It is the algebra of discontent—the mathematics of despair.

These people look to the United States. Man is a migratory species. We learned in school "All roads lead to Rome." This reminds us that Italy is a nation of immigrants—all nations are. Human populations have moved, like a demographic wave, to fresh lands throughout human history. But "as our situation is new, we must think and act anew." We must realize that, for the first time in human history, there are no fresh lands, no new continents.

The world is going through a demographic revolution. And we will have to think and decide with great care what our public policy will be.

II. My second point is that the pressures for immigration are growing.

As a result of the communications revolution, America has colonized the consciousness of much of the rest of the world through the media. Its impact cannot be measured, and it cannot be underestimated. Accounts of the Shiite hostage crisis reported on relationships between the captors and the captives. What did one of the Shiites guarding the hostages want to talk about? Shiite theology? No. He wanted to know the latest on "Dynasty," his favorite TV program.

The idea, the image of America is a powerful magnet:

In 1984 the Spanish International Network conducted exit polls during the El Salvadoran elections. *More than 80 percent* said they would come to the U.S. if they could.

Dong Al Ilbo, the leading newspaper of Seoul, South Korea found that a third of South Koreans would emigrate if allowed.

My wife and I were in a refugee camp in Thailand in 1979. News arrived that one of the people we were talking with had been accepted to go to Switzerland. The person said no. When told that his refusal could mean his going to "the back of the line," he responded, "No problem, I'm going to America. I can wait five more years."

I would like to quote to you from the *U.S. News and World Report*:

> America has become a destination for an enormous part of the world. If you say to someone in the north of Thailand or in Sri Lanka that you're an American, the reaction is: 'I'd like to go there.' Usually that's because life is so much thinner for people in Third World countries. In the 1960's they didn't speak that way; they thought something positive might happen in their land. In Nigeria they thought the country might get rich. Then Nigeria went bankrupt. Now there are Nigerian taxi drivers all over Houston.

Miami as Heaven

There is a joke heard in the Cuban underground. When a good Cuban dies, he doesn't go to heaven. He goes to Miami.

To sum up this point—the population revolution combined with our unique history means that immigration pressures are building rapidly. The economic growth north of the border can never keep up with the population growth south of the border.

III. At this critical point in history, American immigration policies are in a shambles.

Our borders are totally out of control. Our border patrol apprehends 3,000 illegal immigrants per day, 1.2 million per year. *And two get in for every one caught; those caught just try again.*

There has been a 3,000 percent increase in apprehensions since 1965 with only a 50 percent increase in manpower.

Not just our borders, but our whole immigration apparatus is out of control:

400,000 more people fly in to the U.S. than fly out every year.

INS believes that 30 percent of the persons granted permanent residence each year on the basis of family ties are making fraudulent claims. They don't have the manpower to investigate. One U.S. citizen was recently caught after marrying 700 different foreigners for money.

The Miami Herald reports that:

> Luis Antonio Carmona's wedding march began last July when he exchanged vows in an austere Miami courtroom with a 29-year-old Colombian woman named Clara.
>
> Later, records show he married Ester of Ecuador; Ana Maria of Argentina; Clelia of Colombia; Hsiu-Lan of China; Altagracia of the Dominican Republic; and Emma, Flor and Marianella of Peru.
>
> Scores of people in South Florida have accepted money and risked bigamy charges to wed immigrants and refugees seeking a permanent home in the United States.
>
> Some have received as much as $1,800 a wedding. Others have married as many as 11 times without getting a divorce, an investigation by *The Miami Herald* has found.

This story illustrates how brazen the fraud can be. And it's just the tip of the iceberg. It is exceptional because the INS found out about this case.

Our immigration laws themselves breed disrespect. It is, for example, illegal for an illegal immigrant to work here. It is a felony to harbor an illegal immigrant. But a provision, put in at the behest of Texas employers in 1952, says, quote, "employment, including the normal incidents thereof, shall not be deemed to constitute harboring," i.e., you can go to jail for hiding an illegal in your basement, but if you hire him, there is no penalty at all. It is, thus, illegal to be an illegal immigrant, but it is not illegal to hire an illegal immigrant.

This situation has led to an explosion in the number of illegal immigants. How many? The government has no idea. 5 . . . . 12 million. The city of Los Angeles estimates that one out of ten people in the city is an illegal immigrant. 67 percent of all births at LA County General Hospital are to illegal immigrants.

Demography Is Destiny

Adding the numbers of legal and illegal immigrants, fifty percent of all net U.S. population growth comes from immigration. We are taking more than all of the rest of the world combined. A very basic assumption upon which the existence of a sovereign nation rests is the right to control one's borders. As every house needs a door, so every country needs a border. And yet, our borders are a virtual sieve. The numbers of people who daily pass through our borders for unknown destinations will have a tremendous impact. Demography is destiny, and we have clearly lost control over our future.

IV. The fourth issue I would like to raise is the fact that inevitably, our children will pay the price of uncontrolled immigration.

The United States is no longer an empty continent. When the Statue of Liberty was built, there were 58 million people in the United States or 17.8 persons per square mile. In 1984 there were 240 million people or 64 per square mile.

We have witnessed an increase in the number of people who are structurally unemployed. Clearly, we are not doing a good job with our own poor. We cannot persist in the illusion that the U.S. can and should be the home of last resort for all the world's dispossessed.

"Our immigration policies are sorely in need of restoration."

As Georges Fauriol stated in the May/June 1984 issue of *The Humanist*, "We should be asking ourselves certain important questions about illegal immigration."

> First, what portion of the 800 to 900 million new job seekers in the developing world between 1980 and 2000 will the United States be forced to accept as a result of porous borders?
>
> Second, will the 15 million Americans earning minimum wages, who compete directly with many illegal aliens for employment, be better or worse off if the system of illegal immigration continues and worsens?
>
> Third, will respect for the laws of the United States, for the integrity of its natural sovereignty, be strengthened by perpetuating a weak system of immigration law enforcement?
>
> Fourth, will creation of enclaves of often second-class citizens, speaking only their native tongue, contribute to the political and linguistic cohesion of the country?
>
> Fifth, will the blurring of the distinction between citizen and non-citizen, between lawful and unlawful resident, undermine the integrity of the electoral process and the legal fabric that holds the nation together?
>
> Sixth, will immigration at current levels (nearly 1.5 million annually) contribute to the energy security of the United States when projections indicate that the growth from legal immigration alone from 1982 to 1992 could consume an amount of energy costing $88 billion annually?
>
> Seventh, will the addition of tens of millions of immigrants to the country over the next few generations improve our chances to conserve our natural resources, reduce our foreign oil dependence, and secure a high standard of living at a sustainable resource use rate?
>
> Finally, will U.S. foreign policy remain coherent and

independent and able to best serve the national interest if the decisions concerning who enters this country and uses its resources are strongly influenced by other governments and their populations?

Disturbing Facts on Immigration

Let us examine certain justifications that the opponents of immigration reform have perpetuated:

Illegal immigrants take jobs no Americans want. The fact is that the average illegal immigrant picked up in Denver makes more than $7.00 an hour. Many were making over $100 per day. We identified 43 illegal aliens making $100 a day as roofers, and we have 438 people registered in our employment services who would love those jobs. The average illegal immigrant apprehended in Chicago makes $5.65 an hour. More than 30 million American workers make less than that.

"We must have a ceiling on legal immigration."

Another myth is that illegal immigrants work hard, pay taxes, and don't go on welfare. The sad truth is that these folks seem to learn the ropes of the welfare system with incredible speed, partly owing to effective work of our own advocacy groups.

Governors complain to me at national meetings.

—Illinois discovered illegals with fake green cards getting 67 million dollars in unemployment compensation per year. How many go undiscovered?

—Some employers don't pay taxes. And now the word is out that illegals who claim large numbers of dependents won't have any money withheld.

Illegal immigration has its own particular set of consequences.

Brutalizing People

The same people who smuggle drugs also smuggle illegal aliens. Our present system brutalizes people. One farmer held a woman's children when she went back to Mexico so she would have to return. Recently, a group of illegal immigrants died when their escort ditched the truck in the hot desert—locked. Welcome to America.

A recent Chicago TV expose discovered thousands of illegals have voted in recent elections. So many illegals have voter registration cards that the INS will no longer accept them as proof of citizenship for reentering the country from Mexico.

This pressure is well summed up by the Select Commission on Immigration and Refugee Policy, which in its final report said:

> If it is a truism to say that the United States is a nation of immigrants, it is also a truism that it is no longer, nor can it become, a land of unlimited immigration. As important as immigration has been and remains to our country, it is no longer possible

to say as George Washington did that we welcome all of the oppressed of the world, or as the poet Emma Lazarus, that we should take all the huddled masses yearning to be free. The United States of America—no matter how powerful and idealistic—cannot by itself solve the problems of world immigration. The nation must continue to have some limits on immigration.

V. My final point should be clear by now. Our immigration policies are sorely in need of restoration, much like the Statue of Liberty.

The "five C's" of immigration reform provide us with a good blueprint for this restoration:

—Cut the magnet of jobs that draws illegals here.

—Close the loopholes in welfare and entitlement programs, for this too is an attraction.

—Cap legal immigration, which is growing every year.

—Control the border and ports of entry.

—Contribute to population control and economic development in source countries. . . .

Taking Safeguards

We must enact safeguards to make sure that illegal immigrants do not have access to our social services. Today's illegal immigrants apply for and receive scarce social service benefits from the government. Illinois recently did a study showing that it paid $66 million in unemployment compensation to illegal immigrants in one year, despite a law making illegal immigrants ineligible for unemployment compensation. Los Angeles estimates it spends $269 million in social services on illegal immigrants each year.

We must have a ceiling on legal immigration that would stop its growth without affecting the admission of refugees or immediate relatives of United States citizens. The United States is not trying to stop immigration, we are merely trying to control it and make sure that the United States decides who comes into our country and on what terms.

The task of controlling our border and ports of entry is not as impossible as it seems. 60 percent of all illegal crossing takes place in 60 miles of border. Machine readable passports and visas can give us speed and control at airports. There is much we can do to create a deterrent to illegal crossers.

To the extent that is both possible and helpful, we should contribute to population control and economic development in source countries. I am no pollyanna. The problems of countries such as Mexico can only be addressed by Mexicans. We should support the agents of change when we can—as with population assistance—and avoid imposing trade barriers that will hurt their development.

In conclusion, I would like to tell you why I should be a pessimist and why I am an optimist. I should be a pessimist because:

—Legislation has twice passed in the Senate, only

to be killed by the worst kind of political maneuvering.

—There has been no Presidental leadership.

—Powerful and persuasive special interest groups want the status quo.

But let me tell you why I am a determined optimist:

—First, in a cosmic sense, as Churchill said, the only causes worth fighting are the impossible ones. But I really do not think that immigration reform is impossible.

—The program of reform I have outlined has public support. 91 percent want an all out campaign to stop illegal immigration. The Roper poll showed that 80 percent want reductions in legal immigration.

—A powerful national organization has emerged, Federation for American Immigation Reform, FAIR. FAIR is armed with the facts, fighting for the public interest in courts and in the Congress, and taking the issue to the people. The chairman of that group, John Tanton, is here with us today.

—Real reason to be an optimist—Oscar Wilde once said ''Basis of all optimism is sheer terror.''

But ultimately this issue will not go away. Previous generations of Americans sacrificed so that we today could enjoy the freedom, the quality of life, the standard of living that we have. When I think of what uncontrolled immigration will do to the dreams of my parents and grandparents sacrificed for, what it will mean to the future my children will have, I realize that we will find a way to control immigration. Because we must.

Richard D. Lamm is governor of Colorado and an outspoken critic of immigration policy.

"The massive wave of immigrants may actually have strengthened the economy . . . by providing a large pool of low-skill, low-wage workers."

viewpoint **62**

Illegal Immigrants Have Little Impact on the Economy

Robert Walters and Karen E. Klein

Editor's Note: The following viewpoint consists of two articles. Part I is by Robert Walters and part II is by Karen E. Klein.

I

Conventional wisdom holds that immigrants, especially those who come into the country illegally, deprive native workers of their jobs, drive down wages, and otherwise disrupt the nation's economy.

The principal victims, according to that popular theory, are those Americans—many of whom are black—holding low-skill, low-wage jobs, because they must compete with recent arrivals willing to work harder, longer, and for less money.

If that's true, during the past 15 years, economic dislocation on a massive scale should have affected native workers holding unskilled and semi-skilled jobs in California generally and in the Los Angeles area specifically.

That's because this state and metropolitan area have become by far the most popular destination for millions of immigrants from Latin America (especially Mexico) and, to a lesser extent, Asia.

The more than 1.8 million legal immigrants who settled in California during the 1970s exceeded the total of foreign arrivals in all previous years throughout the state's history. Between 1980 and 1983, another 810,000 immigrants arrived.

As a result, a quarter of the country's foreign-born population now resides in California. More than half of that group lives in the Los Angeles area, with large concentrations in middle-income communities such as Gardena.

The influx of more than 600,000 Mexicans into the Los Angeles metropolitan area has radically altered the region's character—and that includes only legal immigrants.

Robert Walters, "Are Jobs Being Stolen?" *The Washington Times*, October 28, 1985. Reprinted by permission of Newspaper Enterprise Association, Inc.
Karen E. Klein, "Citizens in all but Name," *Newsweek*, May 31, 1982

According to one recent study, there are more than 2 million "undocumented" aliens in the country, half of whom live in California. About three-fourths of the state's illegal residents are believed to be Mexicans.

Two-thirds of all the Mexican immigrants have no high school education whatsoever, while fewer than 3 percent are college graduates. Nevertheless, about half of all recently arrived Mexicans have found employment, primarily in the garment and apparel industry, as well as in other forms of labor-intensive manufacturing.

(A popular myth holds that Los Angeles is populated almost exclusively by television producers, movie stars, and other members of the entertainment industry. In fact, it provides manufacturing employment for more workers than the states of Oregon, Washington, Idaho, Nevada, Arizona, and Colorado combined.)

The Urban Institute, a Washington-based organization specializing in public policy research, has launched an ambitious effort to identify the impact of those immigrants here—and the preliminary results have been surprising.

No Job Competition

"We found no evidence for the existence of job competition between Mexican immigrants and native black workers in Southern California," one Urban Institute report says.

"The recent influx of Mexican immigrants to Southern California has not resulted in any significant adverse consequences for unemployment rates," another study concludes.

The federal government's unemployment statistics support those findings. During the 1970s and early 1980s, jobless rates for all workers (blacks and whites, adults and teen-agers) rose somewhat statewide and in the Los Angeles area—but the rate of increase was substantially lower than it was nationwide.

The Urban Institute studies also conclude that Mexican immigrants may have slightly depressed the wages of other unskilled workers, but have had virtually no impact upon the earnings of semi-skilled and skilled employees.

Finally, the studies suggest—and others agree—that the massive wave of immigrants may actually have strengthened the economy here by providing a large pool of low-skill, low-wage workers needed by industries that might otherwise have fled to other nations in search of such employees.

II

The dusty blue Dodge pulled up to the curb. I wrestled with the heavy door, swinging it creakily open, and picked up the nurse's two tattered black bags—one filled with supplies and the other with measuring tape, scales, charts and bandages. The nurse, Kathy, glanced at the closely written yellow sheet of paper containing her day's schedule. "It's No. 126B," she said, "in the back." We lugged the bags up the oil-stained driveway and past the small green house we had stopped in front of. Kathy, a non-Spanish-speaking public-health nurse from Orange County, Calif., and I, her part-time interpreter, had come to make a postpartum home visit to a family who had immigrated to the United States illegally from Mexico.

It was the summer of 1979. The house number, given Kathy by a local hospital, was in the heart of the Spanish district of Santa Ana, Calif. Gang *placas*, or graffiti, covered the tiny houses. The front yards were littered with old cars and ancient, decaying dolls and rusting toys. We walked to the back of the house. Behind it stood an even smaller one, hardly a house at all. It had been painted light blue, but now it was more of a faded gray.

We stepped up to the sagging porch. I knocked. As usual, though we had made dozens of home visits that summer, I felt my apprehension rising. I rocked back and forth on my heels. The door swung open. A young girl, barely 18, stood on the threshold, surprised to see two anglo women on her porch. "Hello," she said, the brow-wrinkling confusion on her face turning slowly to fear when she spotted our charts and bags. *"Mucho gusto,"* I said, smiling. I explained that we were from the Public Health Department and wanted to check on her and her baby. *"Oh si,"* she said. *"Pase, por favor."* She stepped back, timidly inviting us to enter.

A Familiar Story

The house was sparse, but neat. Refried beans simmered on the secondhand stove in the kitchen. There was a narrow sagging bed in the bedroom and a bassinet made out of an old scaled-down crib for Jesus, the woman's four-day-old son. Kathy and I took down the woman's family history. The story

was a familiar one. Her father had died when she was 12 and her mother was left with seven children. The woman and her husband had not applied for welfare or Medi-Cal for fear they would be deported by the immigration authorities, *La Migra*. Maria's two brothers and her mother lived with them in the one-bedroom house. They had come to Santa Ana from their village near Sonora, Mexico, to work in the fields—picking carrots, strawberries, corn, bell peppers—whatever they could do. They were the best people their country had to offer: the most courageous, the most disciplined, the hardest-working. They had serious dreams.

"Most of the undocumented workers I met and talked to . . . . bothered no one and asked only to be left in peace."

The situation was typical of what I encountered all over Orange County that summer. Gentle, simple people—few had received high-school-level education—trying to better their lives, had risked everything they had to come to the United States. They lived better than they had in their own country, but humbly and often in fear. They were afraid to make trouble, and often would be afraid to look me in the eye when I spoke to them. They asked little of the government, received little, yet they paid sales tax every time they bought groceries. They went to free clinics for medical care, if they knew about them, or ignored their health problems. They bought clothes and what furniture they could from thrift shops. They survived.

Clearing Out the Fields

This summer the area will change. The undocumented workers, once deliberately ignored by local immigration officials, are being hustled into vans from the strawberry fields and sweatshops this spring and deported. The Reagan Administration's tougher stance on illegals is clearing out the fields, putting heavy burdens on the growers as well as the produce distributors and retailers. Meanwhile the berries ripen in the sun.

When the widely publicized raids left the country's strawberry growers desperate for workers to pick the harvest, some out-of-work Americans showed up in the fields. Many left before noon. Those who made it though the day declared they would never be back. The back-breaking labor left them with a new respect for the Mexicans. Sore legs and aching fingers had earned the best of them only $30 or $40 for ten hours' work. An experienced picker can gather $90 worth of berries in the same amount of time.

Most of the undocumented workers I met and

talked to lived quietly on the money, when they could get it. The neighbors banded together and many of the women worked, leaving their children at one house during the day. They sent money home to family members still living in Mexico, always hoping they could save enough to buy the expensive passage across the border. They bothered no one and asked only to be left in peace.

Jesus will be close to 3 years old now. "My son," his mother told me that day in her brisk Spanish, "is different. He is American, a citizen. My little boy's life will be better than ours." If his parents are not crowded into a van this spring, it will.

Robert Walters is a nationally syndicated columnist.
Karen E. Klein is a freelance writer.

Illegal Immigrants Hurt the US Economy

Donald L. Huddle

A widely circulated thesis—bordering on a myth—holds that most illegal workers in the United States are a blessing in disguise. Since the mid-1970s, some advocate scholars have maintained that illegal aliens from Mexico and other Third World regions do not displace U.S. workers, but rather take physically demanding and low-paying jobs that U.S. residents, cushioned by the welfare state, do not want.

Essentially, windfall advocates see Mexico's undocumented entrants as a manifestation of a symbiotic relationship between the two countries: Mexico finds an outlet for its surplus labor, while the United States finds a never-failing source of cheap, mobile labor.

This thesis of migrants is badly in need of revision. Since the 1960s, Mexico has faced an overwhelming population problem. Increasingly, undocumented migrants either remain in the United States and bring in families, or they gravitate to Mexico's slum-ridden cities. In turn, Mexico's urban workers often move on to U.S. cities in search of higher wages and a better life for their families.

Meanwhile, a significant new pattern of illegal immigration and settlement has emerged. Growing numbers of illegal aliens come from urban backgrounds. These urban workers generally possess specific occupational skills and seek out jobs in industry, construction, and services. They are more likely to bring in families and to stay three times longer. Plainly, we have in them a more competitive threat to U.S. urban workers.

In a 1983 survey in Houston, we found that urban immigrants, mostly Mexican nationals, were 38 percent of the 200 illegals interviewed. About 53 percent of the sample earned an hourly wage in excess of $5 an hour, and 12 percent earned more

than $6 an hour. Only 38 percent of the respondents were working as common laborers. The others were distributed among 14 trades, including foremen, cement layers, carpenters, ironmen, plumbers, and roofers. In a 1982 field study of highway and commercial construction, we found that illegals commonly earned between $8 and $9 an hour.

Informed legislators, public officials, and immigration experts no longer hold that most undocumented aliens are migrant workers who for the most part seasonally return to their home countries. Rather, they accept as a fact that illegal immigrants from Mexico and other Third World countries are here by the millions. Not only are they settling in U.S. cities, but scores of immigrant-aid and civil-rights groups are now dedicated to keeping them here and bringing in their dependents. Little wonder that Congress feels pressed to grant amnesty-rights for what has commonly been known as America's third-largest minority—disadvantaged aliens.

The two leading questions are now:

1. Do undocumented Third World immigrants in urban job-markets pay more in taxes than they consume in tax-funded services?

2. Do they displace U.S. workers, causing social assistance expenditures for the unemployed?

Snatching Government Benefits

A good part of the consumer-subsidy money in circulation in Third World colonies comes from federal and state funding for social assistance, food stamps, public education, bilingual programs, and health services for low-income households.

Many of the recipient households are mixed families consisting of legal and illegal residents, often organized as large, extended families. In the case of Mexicans, these include countless U.S.-born-citizen-children of undocumented parents. Since such children, like other legal family members, are

Donald L. Huddle, "Immigration: Debt or Credit," *The Washington Times,* July 12, 1985. Reprinted with the author's permission.

entitled to social assistance and food stamps, they provide legal access to such programs and thus subsidize the mixed household.

In America's "Third World" counties along the open border of Texas, the income of Mexican-origin settlers was barely half the U.S. poverty line—around $10,600 for a family of four. In fact, since the war to abolish poverty began in 1965, government subsidies and entitlements have been the principal economic base of most U.S.-Mexico border counties.

In Texas, Mexican-origin people were, according to the 1980 census, 21 percent of the population, but made up 40 percent of AFDC recipients and 51 percent of the food-stamp recipients.

These data suggest that the heavy influx of Hispanic immigrant labor, legal and illegal, into pre-existing, Spanish-speaking communities, contributes to high levels of unemployment and socio-economic dependency among the nation's Hispanic minorities. And since U.S.-born Hispanics readily make use of welfare programs, the data also suggest what might be some of the long-range costs of a generous amnesty for undocumented workers.

The U.S. Immigration and Naturalization Service calculated in 1983 that there is a probable net loss to federal, state, and local governments of $1.26 billion annually for each 1 million illegal aliens.

Based on our surveys of job displacement in the Houston area, we estimated that for every 100 undocumented workers, at least 65 U.S. workers are displaced or remain unemployed.

Illegals Displace Workers

The concept of job displacement should be understood in its several dimensions.

It means, first, that U.S. workers are replaced by undocumented workers and thrown out of work.

Second, U.S. workers remain unemployed because they are not informed of job openings dominated by immigrant labor.

Third, because of the presence of immigrant labor, U.S. job-seekers, particularly minority teen-agers, cannot find entry-level jobs in motels, restaurants, car washes, assembly lines, cleanup crews, and construction.

Displacement also has a fourth manifestation. U.S. workers and job applicants, facing competition from cheap alien labor, often migrate elsewhere in search of jobs and better labor standards. In the depressed, Mexicanized border counties of the Southwest, this displacement has been going on for years.

Many of the displaced border-area Hispanics move to cities in the interior, such as Houston, Dallas, even Detroit, where they compete directly with earlier immigrants.

Why is it that so many unemployed U.S. workers who want to work at a wage comparable to that paid illegal aliens in metropolitan areas have such difficulty finding a job in the same labor market?

During the severe recession of 1982 through 1983, our field studies followed unemployed American workers in their frustrating search for jobs in sectors of the secondary labor market in the Houston area. All the while, undocumented workers were continually hired at better than the minimum wage.

Employers' Advantages

We concluded that in three ways employers have an advantage in hiring illegal aliens in common labor and some semiskilled jobs. First, illegal aliens work harder under less favorable conditions than do U.S. workers. Second, undocumented employees are frequently paid less than the prevailing wage. Third, the employer has a net advantage in hiring illegals even if he pays them the equivalent of the prevailing wage.

About half of the employers and contractors who employ illegals in Texas do not deduct taxes from the worker's gross pay. We found that illegal aliens commonly received a tax-free wage that is around one-third lower than the going wage in the industry. Yet this wage, with no tax deductions, is roughly equal to the net wages paid U.S. workers for the same job. What matters to the undocumented worker is the take-home pay, not the gross pay. In this sense, illegals are obviously cheaper to hire.

"About half of the employers and contractors who employ illegals in Texas do not deduct taxes from the worker's gross pay."

Aside from under-the-table cash payments, employers of undocumented workers use at least three cover-ups for dodging tax payments. First, the illegal is hired as a casual laborer. Under IRS rules, one may work for up to 30 days with no with-holding of income or Social Security taxes. Many illegals in Texas work continuously in this guise for the same employer.

Second, there is the independent contractor ruse. By treating illegals as independent contractors, who are themselves responsible for payment of all taxes, the employer avoids FICA and workman's compensation. In Houston, this ruse is much used in subcontracting construction jobs and in the service trades.

Third, an undocumented worker who has taxes deducted from his wages commonly declares a large number of dependents, who may be fictitious. This greatly reduces income tax withheld from his pay.

A work week for non-union illegals is frequently between 50 and 60 hours at straight time wages. Moreover, about half the illegals injured on the job are not covered by medical insurance or workman's compensation. They are immediately replaced from huge reserves of illegal aliens on call here and in the home country.

Hospitals Pick Up the Bills

One result of the foregoing is that while employers and contractors profit from cheap alien labor, tax-supported county and city hospitals usually pick up the bills for treating low-income or jobless illegals—and their dependents. The Los Angeles County Board of Supervisors determined that for fiscal 1983, unpaid medical bills for undocumented aliens reached $145 million. In fact, in all Southwestern states such unpaid bills have become a hand-wringing problem involving compassion vs. deficits.

In brief, because they are so abundant, illegal aliens in common-labor jobs are treated by employers as a disposable commodity. It is little wonder that U.S. workers either often can't or won't compete in such a labor market.

As former U.S. Commissioner of Immigration Leonel Castillo said: "All our successes in dealing with poverty and other problems are wiped out by the new arrivals. The bottom of the barrel is always filling up."

Donald L. Huddle is professor of economics at Rice University, Houston, and a member of the Task Force on Immigration in Texas.

"Unionism's future will depend to a great degree on its ability to organize the new and expanding areas of the economy."

viewpoint 64

The Future of Unions in America's Economy

A.H. Raskin

The time of reckoning is at hand. . . . [Unions'] losing bet on the Presidential campaign of Walter F. Mondale was the most intense and costly political drive in union history. It was also a fateful warning that, unless organized labor begins to change its ways, and soon, the union movement may not be able to halt its three-decade-long downhill slide, becoming ever more irrelevant to its membership and to the political leadership of the nation.

The disenchantment with labor and with its early and massive king-making effort lost Mondale many independent votes in the primary and general elections. Worse still, running against a conservative Republican President whom the A.F.L.-C.I.O. denounced throughout the campaign as a champion of "scab-hearders and union-busters," the liberal, pro-union Democrat was able to win only 55 percent of the vote in union households. Support for President Reagan was particularly strong among the younger, well-paid, white unionists from whose ranks labor has traditionally drawn its leaders.

Unions' Feebleness

Inside the Democratic Party, influential leaders are clamoring for decisive action to persuade the electorate that the party is not a prisoner of organized labor. And the greatest binge of mergers in union history underscores the feebleness of many unions whose membership and treasuries have been shrunk by the triple squeeze of import competition, deregulation and sophisticated assaults by employers on every aspect of contract negotiations. . . .

Self-righteousness is so pervasive in organized labor's upper reaches that even the danger flags flapping all around may not be sufficient to make the leadership acknowledge either inadequacy or error.

At the bargaining table and on the picket line, labor's political defeat has encouraged increased aggressiveness by management. "A lot of businessmen feel they can forget the trade-union movement," says Prof. Herbert R. Northrup, chairman of the Labor Relations Council at the University of Pennsylvania's Wharton School. In Congress, a stalemate is the best labor can hope for, as unions and employers vie for a leg up on labor legislation. At the White House, labor expects the worst. The President is already in the process of solidifying a pro-employer majority on the National Labor Relations Board, the key Government agency for enforcing the labor laws. Says Murray Seeger, the A.F.L.-C.I.O.'s information director, "The union busters are in hog heaven now."

The robust industrial recovery that contributed so substantially to the Reagan sweep has brought no respite from management pressure to cut union benefits and hold down labor costs. Union wage gains are running at the lowest level since such records have been kept, and many contracts still call for pay freezes or outright cuts. Two-tier wage, systems, which condemn younger workers to entering jobs at rates 25 to 50 percent below those received by senior employees, are becoming increasingly common, a time bomb waiting to explode into generational conflict.

[Unions] will have before [them] some arresting new ideas for reversing labor's plunge, but [their] readiness to accept them is problematic. The ideas have been volunteered by sympathetic advisers invited in from academe, a source of inspiration rarely turned to in the lush years of double-digit wage increases and fat benefit packages.

One set of recommendations envisions a much more enterprise-oriented brand of unionism that would involve workers deeply in corporate decision making and make profit-sharing a key element in wage determination. Another professorial prescription calls for unions to recognize that their present image is so repellent to millions of unorganized workers that the unions' best hope for getting them on their side lies in a flanking maneuver—providing seed money to encourage the formation, outside the labor establishment, of nonunion employee associations that over the years might ripen into full-fledged unions.

Questions about how receptive the A.F.L.-C.I.O. chieftains will be to such fundamental reforms have been sharpened ever since Election Day by their disposition to claim a kind of victory in the disastrous Presidential contest. They have lost no opportunity to boast that if all Americans had voted as did A.F.L.-C.I.O. cardholders, labor's chosen candidate would have been carried into the White House by a landslide.

"Two-tier wage systems . . . are becoming increasingly common."

When John Perkins, director of the A.F.L.-C.I.O. committee on political education, made a euphoric presentation along these lines at a Virgin Islands meeting of ranking Democratic officials a fortnight after the election, David Nagle, the party's Iowa state chairman, caustically suggested that all Democrats rush home and demand a recount.

"A state of auto-hypnotism seems to have set in," says Dr. Arnold R. Weber, president of Northwestern University and an assistant secretary of labor in the Nixon Administration. "They cannot afford to fall into the trap of self-delusion when the need is to recognize that many of their problems arise out of the changing attitudes of workers and long-term trends affecting industry and the work force."

Where Unions Must Organize

Unionism's future will depend to a great degree on its ability to organize the new and expanding areas of the economy in the high-technology and service industries. So far, it has pretty much struck out in "Silicon Valley," the California home of hundreds of computer and electronics companies.

The day after the Reagan election triumph, I spent some hours talking to workers at the California valley's biggest unionized plant, the Sunnyvale works of the Lockheed Missiles and Space Corporation. Built 27 years ago, Sunnyvale has operated from the outset under a master contract with the International Association of Machinists and Aerospace Workers, under which 6,000 of the plant's current 20,000 employees must either be union members or pay union dues to hold their jobs.

But it quickly became evident that this seeming bastion of space-age unionism was no model of solidarity. All but one of the first dozen unionists to

whom I talked had voted for Reagan. Most of them expressed resentment that their parent union had made a political choice before anyone knew for sure who was running, and few had kind words to say for the union in any connection.

Anticipating that union activists would put the previous day's election results on their agenda, I went to the regular monthly meeting of the lodge, which represents 1,433 day-shift workers in blue-collar operations. Only 40 persons attended, virtually all officers or shop stewards. Not a single person uttered a word about the defeat of the candidate whose success the union's convention last September had unanimously declared imperative to the survival of free unionism and collective bargaining.

After the meeting, when I asked the lodge's president, Mac N. Goff, why there had been no discussion of the election, he grinned, "Oh, they don't want to talk about that," he said. Ken Benda, head of the district council that embraces all six union lodges at the Lockheed plant, later supplied a footnote. "They don't see Reagan's name on their paycheck," he said, "but they feel he's the guy they're working for."

The sentiments of the missile makers at Lockheed are hardly representative of those of the great mass of trade unionists, but the width of the political chasm that separates them from their leaders helps explain the misleading nature of the all-for-one ballots by which, months before the first primary or state caucus, a relative handful of top unionists sealed the Mondale endorsement in the name of 90 percent of the federation's 13.7 million members.

In support of that position, organized labor enrolled 150,000 volunteers, spurred registration through phone banks in 500 large cities and mobilized its computerized membership files to inundate union households with Mondale literature keyed to their particular jobs. Contributions to union political action committees rose 21 percent over 1982, despite a drop of a million in A.F.L.-C.I.O. membership. Yet when November rolled around, Ronald Reagan's share of the vote in union households was almost exactly the 45 percent it had been four years earlier, when labor campaigned half-heartedly for Jimmy Carter.

Enthusiasm for Reagan was strongest among white male unionists under 40 and among those who had climbed highest on the income ladder, their $25,000 to $50,000 wages testimonials to the struggles of union pioneers.

"Each generation has to learn the hard lessons for itself," says William W. Winpisinger, the machinists' international president. But the breaking of ranks by so many youthful mainstream unionists—college-educated and impatient with institutional constraints—makes such appeals to tradition a dubious safe-guard for the 1990's and beyond.

Where the labor establishment has the most

reason for feeling good about its political efforts is in the Congressional and gubernatorial races. Nearly two-thirds of those whom labor endorsed, the great bulk of them Democrats, were elected: 72 percent of A.F.L.-C.I.O. members voted for Democratic Senate candidates and 69 percent for Democratic House candidates.

Reason for Optimism

Another reason for optimism stems from federation polls limited to the A.F.L.-C.I.O.'s own members, and leaving out such unaffiliated organizations as the pro-Reagan International Brotherhood of Teamsters. A 61-39 margin for Mondale was reported—20 percentage points above his vote in the general population.

Unfortunately, painful experience has taught labor that its favorites must get at least 65 percent of all the votes in union familes—not just members' votes—to counter the conservative tilt in the general electorate.

The disparity between the size of the union vote for President and for members of Congress suggests a basic weakness of the A.F.L.-C.I.O. as a national political force. In the Congressional and gubernatiorial races, labor's endorsements traditionally emanate from local and state unions and are viewed by both union members and most voters as a standard expression of local civic involvement, akin to the endorsements of local business and professional groups. At the national level, the demonology of American politics takes over.

In the public mind, the image of big labor today is still stereotyped in the cartoonists' version of longtime A.F.L.-C.I.O. leader George Meany: a baleful-looking figure with a bulging belly and a clenched cigar, hurling monkey wrenches at the White House and the Capitol. Neither the atrophy in labor's muscle in recent years nor the gentility of Meany's successor, Lane Kirkland, a soft-spoken technocrat, has done much to erase that image of a boss-led monopoly that uses its enormous resources for selfish purposes.

When the union nabobs sought to turn the 1984 primaries into a stampede that would allow Mondale to clinch the nomination in the first two months, Senator Gary Hart fastened on this widespread perception to impugn Mondale's independence. Once raised, the issue never went away. Even union stalwart Douglas A. Fraser, former president of the United Automobile Workers, says of the special-interest tag, "It became an albatross, and a most unfair one."

In the recent scramble for selection of a new Democratic national chairman, all the candidates used code words to make clear their desire to have labor stay in the party in 1988 but to lower its profile lest independent voters conclude once again that the party's Presidential nominee is in labor's hip pocket.

Yet Democrats already being mentioned as possible aspirants for the 1988 Presidental nomination show little sign of shrinking from labor's support. In the primaries, the A.F.L.-C.I.O. clearly has enormous power—power it demonstrated convincingly in the key industrial states to deliver the nomination for Mondale after his early stumble in New England. As for the general campaign, New York's Governor Cuomo, for one, recalls his gubernatorial victory in 1982, despite "all the geniuses who told me it would hurt to take labor's backing." The idea that any significant number of people would reject a candidate on that ground, he says, represents "a naive view of the American voter."

Labor and Democrats

The Democrats' tip-toe search for ways to lessen the appearance of party subservience to labor without chilling union zeal in getting out the vote has reinforced union chiefs' confidence about the correctness of their decision to go in early and hard for Mondale. . . . It represented the fullest flower of the process of collegiality and consensus that is the hallmark of Kirkland's leadership style.

In five years at the helm, Kirkland has won solid respect or reasonableness and sharpness of mind, not solely among his associates on the executive council but from virtually all the tycoons and political leaders with whom he has dealt at close range. The missing ingredient in his makeup is magnetism, a major deficiency for unionism in this telegenic age.

But something beyond charisma or the repackaging of outworn practices and programs will be necessary to recoup the political and economic strength of organized labor.

"Contributions to union political action committees rose 21 percent over 1982, despite a drop of a million in A.F.L.-C.I.O. membership."

Three decades ago, nearly one-third of the nation's employed work force was unionized. According to a new study by Leo Troy of Rutgers University, the country's foremost expert on union membership trends, that ratio dipped in 1983 to an all-time low of 20.6 percent, and is still dropping. How damaging this slump has been in sharpening management interest in getting rid of unions altogether is starkly reflected in a five-year report soon to be published by Audrey Freedman, a labor economist for the Conference Board, a business research group. The data show a steep decline in the proportion of union members in 500 companies, large and small, chiefly the result of the opening of new plants or divisions. Whenever the proportion fell below half of the total work force, Mrs. Freedman reports, employer priority tended to shift from collective bargaining to avoiding unions.

Another sign of the diminished union power detected in the Conference Board report is a "startling change" since 1978 in the standards employers apply to determine the upper limits of settlements they will accept at the bargaining table. Considerations of efficiency and cost-containment based on the company's own profit-and-loss statement are now uppermost. In determining all their personnel policies, union pressures rank at the top in only 30 of the 499 enterprises surveyed.

In years gone by, corporate managements bowed to regional or nationwide wage patterns. Individual companies' distinctive needs and ability to pay were blandly disregarded on the comforting assumption that big pay increases could be passed on to the consumer in even bigger price increases.

Hard-Line Employers

Now competitors at home and abroad have banished that easy out and so-called "pattern bargaining," a bedrock element in union efforts to stabilize wage rates and thus eliminate intercompany rivalry at the expense of workers, is perceived to be a formula for industrial suicide. The hard-line employers succeeded last year in holding down the average annual increase in major contracts covering 2.3 million workers to a record low of 2.3 percent, less than enough to offset even the sharply reduced inflation rate. In unionism's black book, much of this toughness is rooted in the pattern of management resistance President Reagan set in 1981 when he dismissed striking air-traffic controllers and put their union out of business.

Out of recognition that the survival of their unions and the jobs of their members depend on substituting new forms of teamwork for atavistic tests of strength, unionists are making long strides in many once-turbulent industries toward a genuine involvement in corporate governance at every level, from workbench to board room.

Not all these experiments in industrial democracy have worked, but where both sides have tried hardest to modify authoritarian command systems and enlist the creative talents and brain power of the work force, the benefits have been remarkable in terms of raised efficiency and job satisfaction. Profit-sharing, employee stock ownership and other devices for giving workers a "piece of the action" have muted the battle for the buck at some negotiating tables. Elsewhere, unions have joined employers in mutual ventures to develop advanced technology or expand product lines and markets as a means of promoting the economic well-being of American business and labor.

The Bricklayers Union, for example, under its Harvard-trained president, John T. Joyce, has contracted with its employers to put money that would otherwise go to its members as wages into a jointly administered fund to devise strategies for long-term growth of its branch of construction through research and development, improved apprenticeship training and more stable labor-management relations. Even more sweeping types of social inventiveness are being exhibited by unions and management in industries forced into a survival mode by the hammer blows of overseas competition. The United Automobile Workers and the Big Three auto companies have been in the forefront of these transformatons. Thus the union is in on every aspect of the design and marketing of General Motors' challenge to Japanese supremacy in the small-car market, its projected Saturn subcompact.

At the joint General Motors and Toyota venture at Fremont, Calif., the assembly line, since Henry Ford's day the symbol of machine's mastery over man, can now be stopped by any factory worker in the event of a production defect or a safety hazard.

"In the public mind, the image of big labor today is still stereotyped in the cartoonists' version of longtime A.F.L.-C.I.O. leader George Meany."

Time clocks have been banished. And job classifications have been cut from 80 to 4 to make operations more flexible and to give workers added responsibility.

The United Auto Workers

Changes of equal magnitude are likely in many other major auto plants as a result of the trailblazing master agreements signed in Detroit last fall. The contracts enable the companies to move full speed ahead on introducing robots and flexible business practices in exchange for establishment of a jointly run job-opportunity bank designed to insulate displaced workers against layoffs by providing them with retraining, transfer to other plants or even assignment to nontraditional jobs outside the auto industry. But the slim margin by which the accord won membership ratification at G.M. suggests that it is too early to be sure the new cordiality will continue when the union finds it necessary to line up alongside management in decisions that require sacrifice by some employees to protect the jobs of many more.

Suspicions of bad faith are slow to die on both sides. For unionists, they revive every time National

Guardsmen are mobilized to run scabs through a picket line or a sophisticated unionbuster is hired to frustrate an organizing drive. In recent months, unionists have hauled out the bloody shirt afresh in alarm over union setbacks at Greyhound, Continental Airlines, Phelps Dodge and dozens of lesser battlefields. Even Lane Kirkland, normally the most civilized of communicators with industry, talks darkly of a return to the "law of the jungle" in industrial relations.

"Three decades ago, nearly one-third of the nation's work force was unionized."

With union ranks thinning and union revenues melting, the A.F.L.-C.I.O. has been moving into a matchmaker role to encourage more of its weaker affiliates to merge and thus better equip themselves to stave off management challenges. The Bureau of Labor Statistics has recorded 29 union mergers in the last six years, fully a third of all that have occurred since the A.F.L. and C.I.O. set the pattern in 1955 by uniting after 20 years of civil war. The hope of the founders was that affiliates with overlapping jurisdictions would swiftly follow suit, but few took the hint until adversity began hammering at the door.

Paying Union Bills

Most of today's marriages have less to do with rationalizing union structure than with making it easier for unions to pay their bills. A conspicuous exception is the prospective merger . . . of the International Typographical Union, hard hit by the automation of the composing rooms of America's newspapers and publishing houses, with the Graphic Communications International Union, itself an amalgamation of four pre-existing printing unions, all shrunk by new technology. The I.T.U., one of the oldest of America's unions, was on the verge of merger with the International Brotherhood of Teamsters last spring, but a palace revolt inside the printers' union killed that project in favor of one that would wed the organization to the other publishing crafts.

[Unions] have a few things to cheer about. . . . One is the agreement concluded . . . after a 10-week strike at Yale University, under which 2,500 clerical and technical employees, 80 percent of them women, will receive salary increases averaging as much as 35 percent over the next three and a half years. Two aspects of the pact were especially significant—the ingenuity and solidarity the strikers showed in their long battle with Yale and the start that the 17-step pay structure created under the contract makes toward evening out a few of the

inequities women have traditionally labored under.

Another bit of good news was a Government analysis . . . showing that the average full-time worker represented by a union earned $101 a week more in 1984 than the average nonunion worker. The union average was $404, as against $303 for the four-fifths of the work force outside unions. The edge was even higher for members of minority groups, with blacks under union contracts averaging $352 a week compared with $236 for blacks lacking union protection. Among Hispanic workers, the union average was $346 against $236 for non-union employees.

A Greater Voice Needed

In the estimation of James L. Medoff, a Harvard economist whose ideas were among those solicited by the A.F.L.-C.I.O.'s committee on the future of work, the road to more victories lies in greater stress in the function unions fulfill in helping workers to gain a greater voice in the work place and in public affairs. A Harris poll commissioned by the A.F.L.-C.I.O. indicated that a near-majority of nonunion workers applauded these aspects of unionism, while refusing to join because they see unions as "self-serving monopolies."

Medoff believes many of these workers can be successfully wooed if unions concentrate on employees in small businesses, traditionally neglected by unions because turnover is high, as are organizing costs. A special receptivity to unionization, the Harris poll indicates, exists among women, blacks and younger workers in companies with fewer than 100 employees, particularly in such growing service areas as finance, insurance, real estate and retail trade.

Partially because of the low standing of labor in the eyes of most other unorganized workers, and because of strong management opposition, Medoff sees real problems in inducing appreciable numbers of the unorganized to enroll under the A.F.L.-C.I.O. banner. Instead, he proposes that the unions foster the creation of nonunion, independent employee associations. Organized according to geography or trade, the associations would offer vocational and work-place counseling, provide retirement, health and dental insurance, and arrange volume discounts on purchases of consumer goods. By helping to form such associations, Medoff believes, unions could demonstrate that their interest in doing things for working people extends beyond collecting union dues. They might also set in motion a process out of which orthodox unions could arise—as has happened in the conversion over the last 20 years of associations representing teachers, civil-service workers and nurses.

From Thomas A. Kochan of the Massachusetts Institute of Technology comes the suggestion tht the high mobility of younger workers makes it desirable for organizers to focus on services to youths starting their work careers by skipping from one part-time job to another in such places as supermarkets, construction sites and hospitals. Kochan was impressed by the seriousness with which union leaders listened to his presentation. "They seemed willing to entertain more ideas and take more risks than in the past," he says.

The "Young Turks"

Nevertheless, the pervasive stand-pat attitude of the federation makes young turks in labor skeptical that anything fundamental is going to change. Small stirrings of impatience find occasional expression at the grass roots. For example, 40 young unionists, from the federation's headquarters in Washington and others from out in the field, formed a loose, unofficial network a year and a half ago to exchange ideas on programs for rebuilding the labor movement from the ground up.

As one member, Martin Manley, political action director for the Santa Clara County Central Labor Council, in San Jose, Calif., explains: "When you have a generation of workers who are better educated and not ready to settle for eight hours of mindless work they don't have to think about, the labor movement is not going to fly if all we have to offer is the highest buck."

Manley complains that the parent federation is "not putting out any sort of message to our members on what we stand for." His own conviction is that such a message must center on a larger voice for workers and unions in corporate management, with a distinct agenda for each company or facility. He concedes, however, that this focus is not popular with some in the group, who consider it too collaborationist.

Manley, a 32-year-old graduate of the University of California at Santa Cruz, who used to be a representative for the machinists in the West, declines to disclose the names of the other members of the group: "The A.F.L.-C.I.O. would flip out and so would some international unions."

The limitations of labor's tolerance for dissent have been made plain in recent months to Ray Rogers, who organized the campaign of financial pressure on big banks and insurance companies that was instrumental in forcing the J.P. Stevens & Company textile empire to call off its long war against unionization in 1980. Rogers, now a New York union consultant, has been openly critical of union leaders for excessive timidity and over-chumminess with management. Top-level retaliatory moves aimed at freezing him out of projects he has begun have failed, he says, only because "embattled local leaders refuse to be intimidated." . . .

Kirkland has not taken Ronald Reagan's victory in stride. Traditionally, the A.F.L.-C.I.O. president sends a congratulatory telegram to incoming Presidents,

friends or foes. Not this time. And Kirkland also let it be known that he would accept no more appointments to bipartisan Presidental commissions on such critical issues as Social Security and Central America. "We are not going to answer the problems these people have created for themselves," is the word from Murray Seeger, Kirkland's spokesman. . . .

The Lesson of 1984

There has not been even a momentary let-up in the denunciations of Reagan policies from the federation's executive suite in Washington. A typical Kirkland comment came at a post-election conference of A.F.L.-C.I.O. shipbuilding unions: "There is an international trade war under way, a war to capture the American market at home and abroad. It is a war in which we have no allies, only adversaries. We are losing that war because this Administration has not only surrendered, it has unilaterally disarmed America and is collaborating with our enemies."

The least likely thing to expect from the executive council is a turnaround in political approach. Labor leaders are not going to join Republican ranks, despite the large union vote racked up by the President.

"The average full-time worker represented by a union earned $101 a week more in 1984 than the average nonunion worker."

The unions are firmly within the Democratic camp. And, notwithstanding the concern of some Democrats about the baneful effects of the union embrace, their party is not likely to be overly harsh with its best-heeled, best-disciplined, best-organized source of campaign support. That leaves both party and unions with a problem to solve: How can they avert a future bind in which heavy-handedness on the part of labor imperils the victory chances of the candidate it most wants to see in the White House?

One useful hint is volunteered by a longtime observer of the labor scene, Jay S. Siegel of Hartford, past chairman of the labor-law section of the American Bar Association: "The lesson labor ought to learn from the 1984 election is that they will have to settle for people who don't see eye-to-eye with them on every issue, but who can win."

Yet for all such advice, labor's stance today—not only in the political arena but in terms of its basic failures to gain new members and find new ways to meet old members' needs—is mainly defensive. The leadership is seeking ways to rationalize defeats and maintain the status quo. Some in the union movement predict it will take an earthquake to bring reform.

"If we hurt more, we'll do more," says Murray H. Finley, president of the Amalgamated Clothing and Textile Workers Union. "We'd better do it before it's too late."

A.H. Raskin is the former chief labor correspondent for The New York Times. *He is currently writing a book about the labor movement since the New Deal.*

Unions Do Not Benefit the Economy

Morgan O. Reynolds

Labor unions remain the most controversial private organizations in our society despite more than 150 years of experience with them. As Douglass Brown and Charles Meyers put it, "Basically, we are impressed by what seems to have been before 1930, and what seems to exist today, a feeling of 'unease' in the presence of unions on the part of large segments of the population." Why? It cannot be general contempt for self-interest or greed per se that creates unease over labor unions. Americans have no general objection to groups of people who seek to enhance their own prosperity. In fact, almost all economic activity would fit under such a broad rubric. Nor are Americans opposed to the announced objective of labor unions, namely, raising the standard of living for all wage earners.

I think the answer ultimately lies not in the goals toward which unions work, but in the *means*, the *tactics* that they use to pursue their economic gains. The use of intimidation, coercion, and violence by unionists is a continuing issue for public policy. Strikes, picketing, and boycotts create potentially violent confrontations and help to explain the multitude of laws, regulations, and rulings directed at union tactics. There are other issues, too. There is ample room for concern over some of the objectives that unionists pursue, from pushing up wages and benefits and enforcing closed shops, to demanding the dismissal of nonunion employees. The economic side effects of union actions are important too. How, for example, do union wage rates, fringe benefits, work rules, and strikes affect employment, unemployment output, inflation, income inequality, investment and the amount of competition in our economy? What are the *political effects* of union pressures for more government spending, protective tariffs, building codes, welfare programs, and so on? . . .

Many writers emphasize that unions are complex creatures with political, social, and economic aspects. Unfortunately, though, pointing out that the world is complicated is not really helpful from a scientific point of view. In approaching unionism and other observable phenomena, it is useful to have a simple, coherent idea about what is going on. Truly useful theories are compact, yet they explain or predict a wide variety of observed and yet-to-be noticed behavior.

Defining the Union

The monopoly theory of unionism is just such a vehicle. Although, like all theories, it has limitations, none is fatal, and we can get a tremendous amount of mileage from a handful of correct statements about unions. A labor union can be defined as a group of labor suppliers who individually have little or no market control over wages and working conditions but who want to control (raise) compensation as a group. Expressed this way, there is nothing different in principle between combinations of workers and combinations of sellers in other markets (businessmen, farmers, oil producers, physicians) who attempt to restrict supply and push up the prices of their services. As Edward H. Chamberlin wrote, "It is fundamental to distinguish between the labor market and the product market, but it is also common to place far too much emphasis on the distinction." Unions are fundamentally cartels—groups of producers with sectional interests diametrically opposed to those of consumers. Unions are labor OPECs.

This states the main economic purpose of unions, albeit in unflattering terms. Trade unionists never really spend much effort concealing their main objective anyway, because a classic union slogan has been to "take competition out of wages" and to "take labor out of competition," results that could hardly redound to the benefit of consumers. Imagine if other sellers vowed to "take competition out of prices" or take their services out of competition. Arthur J. Goldberg, former general counsel of the AFL-CIO, wrote a grudging acknowledgement of the anticompetitive nature of unions in an article defending union exemptions from antitrust laws:

> Technically speaking, of course, any labor union is a monopoly in the limited sense that it eliminates competition between employees for the available jobs in a particular plant or industry. By concerted economic action, these workers attempt to increase the wage at which the employer will be able to purchase their labor.

Although Goldberg attempted to denigrate the importance of this bit of truth by saying that he was speaking only "technically," he was stating the precise truth: *a union is a monopoly.* Unions are the primary anticompetitive ingredient in labor markets. . . .

Unions' Controlling Tactics

If we suspend the question of who pays for union gains, we can ask *how* unions might deliver on their promises to raise compensation above the market prices that otherwise would prevail. The key is that unionists must restrict the available supply of labor services *or* directly impose higher wage rates on enterprises. Analytically, this same proposition is at work in the theory of cartels and monopolies, where either price or quantity can be viewed as the decision variable. A monopoly must restrict production to enhance profits *or* directly fix a higher price and then reduce production in accord with the lower rate of sales. In the case of trade unions, as Henry Simons wrote in 1944, "control of wages *is* control over entry."

"Unions are the primary anticompetitive ingredient in labor markets."

For a trade union, the closed-shop arrangement corresponds rather closely to a business monopoly that restricts production. Both are instances of an "artificial scarcity" that produces artificial abundance elsewhere in the economy. Under an effective closed shop, buyers of labor services are compelled to hire only union members, and, of course, union membership is rationed among favored individuals in order to limit the supply of labor. Obviously this arrangement depends on the use of force or threat of force to prevent enterprises from dealing with nonunion workers or members of other unions, because employers might be unhappy about the cost, quality, or availability of the labor services allowed by the union. Employment and outputs are

smaller, wage rates higher in the closed-shop sector, and employment and outputs are larger and wage rates lower in the nonunion sector as a result of these union restrictions.

Strikes and wage negotiations are nearly superfluous if a union can enforce a closed-shop arrangement since competition among independent, noncolluding employers would bid up the price of artificially scarce labor to the desired level. The closed shop is generally associated with a union hiring hall and still can be found in the building trades, longshoring, and the hotel-restaurant industries. However, the literal closed shop is *not* the common means the unionists use to raise labor costs because it is relatively difficult to impose on enterprises (which want control over the exact individuals hired), and the tactic has been illegal since the 1947 Taft-Hartley amendments to the National Labor Relations Act.

The most popular union device is to try to fix wages above market rates via wage negotiations, popularly called collective bargaining. Although the term "collective bargaining" is widely accepted and used, it is basically a misleading phrase. It conveys that the notion that labor representatives are simply expert negotiators and bargainers for their members' services, much like attorneys who represent clients in legal disputes. If it were as simple as that, few could object to the arrangement, because if unionists only bargained for members' services *and* abstained from the threat of using organized force against those who disagreed with their demands, wage rates and working conditions would be no higher than the market for their members' skills would allow. But there is more to union bargaining than simply informing employers of their employees' wishes and discussing the nature of current and prospective labor market conditions.

The Use of Coercion

The strike or threat of strike is the principal tactic that unionists use to impose higher wage rates and superior working conditions on buyers of labor services. A great deal of confusion deliberately has been spawned about the right to strike. Most writers leave the impression that strikes are nothing more than a peaceable withholding of labor services by unhappy employees. If so, relatively few would object to a strike, provided that strikers did not breach legal contracts with owners of the enterprise. Strikers, in other words, would be exercising their basic right to refuse to deal on unsatisfactory terms. Two conditions would be necessary for a *noncoercive work interruption* to achieve economic gains for strikers: (1) an employer would have to offer substandard wages and working conditions—in other words, wages and conditions that are below prevailing market rates and (2) employees would have to be dissatisfied enough to regard an organized walkout as the best means of voicing their displeasure. Under these conditions, an employer would quickly discover that his offer is substandard because he could not attract enough replacements of comparable quality without raising the ante.

Most strikes, however, are not simple denials of striking employees' labor services to the enterprise. If they were, picket lines would not be used at all, because striking employees could stay home or work elsewhere until the enterprise realized the wisdom of their demands and some mutually agreeable pact was consummated between the enterprise and its experienced work force. Ordinarily when a strike is called by union officials, some employees prefer to continue working, including members of the union who are unsympathetic with the particulars of the specific strike. Other people, currently unemployed or employed elsewhere at less attractive terms, seek the work abandoned by the strikers. Also, during the course of a strike, some strikers become discouraged or find that their employer offers a better package than they can hope for elsewhere, and they gradually return to work. A union's problem is painfully obvious: organized strikers must shut down the enterprise, close the market to everyone else—uncooperative workers, union members, disenchanted former strikers, and employers—in order to force wages and working conditions above free-market rates. If too many individuals defy the strikers, if they go their own way, if they are happy to accept the work the strikers abandoned, then unionists often resort to force. Unionists ultimately cannot impose noncompetitive wage rates (monopoly wage rates) unless they can prevent employers from hiring consenting adults on terms that are mutually satisfactory. Unions must actively interfere with freedom of trade in labor markets in order to deliver on their promises. . . .

Employer Power Myth

"Unions protect workers from employers' superior bargaining power."

This is the most important argument for unionism. Its adherents range from devout believers to lukewarm adherents who talk about the "obsolete concept of individual bargaining" in an economy of a "few corporate giants." In the jargon of economics, they believe that buyers (employers) of labor services have an immense amount of power to dictate the terms of trade in labor markets *and* that the appropriate policy to offset this monopoly power on the demand side is to monopolize the supply side. Even if we accept the assertion about the degree of market power among buyers, the policy recommendation does not necessarily follow because it must be weighed against competing remedies—for example, promoting more competitive, independent behavior among buyers of labor services, say, through antitrust policy.

Unionists, intellectuals, and a substantial share of the general public believe that employers have superior bargaining power that they can employ to abuse the wages, hours, and working conditions of employees who lack union protection. Unionists especially point to the real and imagined evils of the nineteenth century and claim that unions partially offset the excesses of capitalism, thus acting as correctives in an unjust society by promoting an equitable sharing in the decision-making power and the fruits of production. In sum, actual labor markets depart so much from the competitive model of economics that unions are an inevitable and desirable by-product of a real-world market economy.

Union Propaganda

The belief in employer power over wages and working conditions is almost entirely without basis. It is largely a result of union propaganda, the distortions emanating from the intellectual community, and public gullibility and lack of interest. Professional economists never offered much support for the doctrine, although they are far from blameless in the matter.

"The belief in employer power over wages and working conditions is . . . . largely a result of union propaganda."

Generally, enterprises are forced by competition among businesses to pay competitive prices for *all* scarce, productive commodities, including labor services. Individual enterprises are not free to fix wages wherever they want because, if they choose to offer very low wages, they cannot attract the quality of labor services in the quantity they want; if they choose to pay very high wages, employment must be rationed among an excess supply of eager, qualified applicants. Also, if wages are too high, a firm necessarily overpays its labor suppliers, and the equity value of a private enterprise plummets. Inefficient managers would be displaced because the firm would go under or be taken over by more efficient managers via proxy battles, tender offers, or other capital-market techniques.

Supply and Demand

Wage rates are determined by the interaction of supply and demand among large numbers of potential buyers and sellers for each type of labor. Individual employers, no matter how large, cannot depress wages and working conditions for any significant period of time, because they must compete for productive labor by paying wages at least at the level paid by the next highest bidders.

It is easy to mistake the caution of employers in bidding up the price of labor as "superior bargaining power," but, in truth, it is the real groping process by which actual markets converge on prices that "clear markets," a vivid phrase to describe pricing that maximizes trade volume and avoids both shortages and surpluses. The facts clearly do not support the idea of immobile employees exploited by employers. More than 4.5 million enterprises hire labor; more than 500,000 new ones appear each year (a smaller number expire each year); and more than 2 million people quit their jobs each month. Dynamic competition and mobility are the rule in the labor market. Moreover, if conspiracies among employers to depress wages below competitive rates ever were an important phenomenon, it is hard to explain why there were no prosecutions or civil suits under our antitrust laws, especially prior to 1914, the year Congress tried to redefine labor services as no longer commodities.

Individual employers, no matter how large, have negligible ability to exploit labor by depressing a worker's wage below the market rate for his skills. The only prominent exceptions are buyer combinations in some professional sports and among NCAA colleges to depress wages for athletes. Monopoly on the buyer's side is call *monopsony* Although it has occurred, there is an exaggerated belief in its power and ubiquity. Union leaders naturally are interested in promoting an exaggerated view of the scope of industrial monopoly and monopsony because such a view encourages the public to accept unions as a desirable countervailing power.

Changing Jobs Costly

True, there is immobility among employees because it is costly to change jobs. Older employees who invested in skills specific to a particular firm might be cited—a senior administrative secretary, for example, who knows the ropes. In theory, an employer can lower wages of such employees, to some extent, without fear of losing them if—and I emphasize the word "if"—their firm-specific skills are significantly less valuable to other employers. By the same reasoning, however, such an employee can withhold his individual services in order to exploit his monopoly skills. The employer's alternative to accepting the employee's offer is costly firm-specific training of another employee. Each party can try to exploit this temporary immobility in the bargaining process, but we can make no general statement about the outcome, because it is a bilateral monopoly situation. There is no reason to expect that employees consistently suffer the worse end of deals that offer some scope for bargaining, especially since large employers have an incentive to maintain a reputation for fair dealing in the labor market. . . .

"High living standards in the United States are due to a strong union movement."

Union leaders are eager to take credit for the long, historical advance in the standard of living in the United States. Not only is it immodest for union officials constantly to repeat this boast, it is also demonstrably wrong. As a historical matter, real wages rose about 2% per capita each year in America on average long before the advent of powerful unions, and wages rose at a comparable rate after the formation of big unions. The 1970s had zero growth in real wages and pulled the post-1930s big-union era down to the historic average.

"The sad fact is that unions, tough bargaining, and political pressure do not create real wealth."

If high wages could be achieved on an economy-wide scale by union wage pressure (or wage legislation), it would be easy for even the poorest nations of the world to get rich quick. The government of Sri Lanka or Sierra Leone or Egypt could simply encourage powerful labor unions and watch poverty disappear, or issue a decree simply declaring high wages for everyone (rather like presidential candidate George McGovern's "$1,000 for everybody" in 1972). The idea, of course, is preposterous. It reverses the essential line of causation: High productivity of labor causes high wages, not vice versa.

The United Kingdom provides another easy instance of the fallacy. If unions cause high wages for all, we should expect to find real wages higher in more highly unionized countries. Yet the U.K. is much more unionized than the United States—55% versus 20% of the labor force—yet real wages are at least 40% lower in England. And British unions are as militant as any. The same could be said of some other European countries and of Australia, but their situations are not quite so clear-cut as the British example because union membership figures are unreliable. European unions also tend to be political and religious associations besides being economic-interest groups. Also, more wage-setting and income policies occur at the level of the central government in these economies.

The sad fact is that unions, tough bargaining, and political pressure do not create real wealth. A highly productive economy, with its accompanying high real wages, depends on abundant physical capital, educated and skilled people, and an institutional framework that allows individuals to work to improve their lives. Governmental policies, in other words, must avoid destroying people's incentives to work, save, and invest.

Material output can be divided into two

components: (1) the number of people working, and (2) the output produced per person, or "productivity." Union actions, rhetoric aside, do nothing to increase either, and they often do a great deal to harm both the employment situation and productivity. Union actions frequently destroy employment opportunities in the high-productivity sectors of the economy through strike actions, high wage rates, and so on. Unions also hobble measures to raise productivity by imposing restrictive work rules, opposing the installation of new equipment and techniques of production and fostering a depression mentality that encourages members to save some work for the next guy. It is much more correct to argue that wages—real wages, that is—are lower in our society because of labor unions rather than the reverse, because unions discourage investment in high-productivity, unionized sectors, they restrict employment there, restrict ouput on the job, prevent efficient deployments of labor at the work place, and thereby depress real demand for goods produced by noncompeting labor, increase the supply of labor in less productive employments, and raise the level of unemployment in the economy.

The true source of our prosperity is capital plus efficient management and efficient labor, not unions. If we were to arrange these factors in order of importance, we must rank capital first, because even the most ambitious managers and employees, without capital assets, are much less productive than are unenthusiatic people with machinery to work with. "We are better off than earlier generations," as Ludwig von Mises said, "because we are equipped with the capital goods they have accumulated for us."

"A competitive labor market is the ultimate protection for employees, not union grievance procedures."

Unionists point to two things in support of their claim to be the main source of workers' prosperity: (1) Union workers are generally well paid, and (2) employers resist union wage demands in collective bargaining and, therefore, would not grant raises without union threats. Both of these are factually true, more or less, but the explanation (theory) of unionists is wrong. Union workers ordinarily would be well paid, with or without unions. People in plumbing, construction, long-haul trucking, mining, railroads, and printing were well paid before unionism and will continue to be well paid after unions disappear (which they will, I suspect). In addition, if unions do raise wages for their members, this does not imply higher wages for *all* workers, or even necessarily higher earnings for union members.

Since more labor is forced into the nonunion sector by high union wage rates, the greater supply reduces wage rates there, with the net result that unionism does not raise wages for all workers. . . .

Union Rivalry

"The enemy is the company."
This is completely false. Unions do not compete against employers, despite superficial appearances to the contrary. Sellers compete with sellers and buyers with buyers. When people ask, "What's the competition got?" they mean, "What do other sellers have to offer?" Unions compete with those who sell substitutes for their members' services, which means other forms of labor—members of rival unions, foreign workers, strikebreakers, nonunion workers— as well as machinery and other nonlabor commodities that can substitute for direct labor, or, in effect, the labor of those who produce and service machinery that can substitute for the services of organized workers.

Union control of labor markets has always been incomplete, in spite of the substantial governmental machinery supporting unionization since the 1930s. As a result, organized workers must prevent competing workers, who want to improve themselves, from entering a unionized labor market and thereby restoring open-market conditions.

Bitter jurisdictional disputes among unions dramatically illustrate the fact that the main "enemy" is competing labor. Unions assert exclusive jurisdiction (properly speaking, monopoly jurisdiction) over particular kinds of work and workers, much as national governments claim suzerainty over people and territory. Interunion disputes break out at times, accompanied by strikes, picketing, boycotts, and violence. Two craft unions, for example, can claim the same work, especially if a new technique or material is introduced, and the employer often is caught in the middle of a union battlefield.

As Woodruff Randolph, who ruled the International Typographical Union from 1944 to 1958, said, "The ITU is a craft union exercising jurisdiction over all composing room work. Our jobs are dependent on that work. The life of our trade is dependent upon that jurisdiction. Whatever weakens or destroys our jurisdiction destroys our union." William L. Hutcheson's Carpenters' Union claimed to cover everything from the growing tree to the finished product: "Once wood, it is always the right of the carpenter to install it." Unionists are not much interested in other unionists' welfare despite all the cant about "the labor movement," "solidarity," and "brotherhood."

One of the venerable cliches of the union movement is that "labor is not a commodity," a phrase that has served as an all-purpose response whenever anyone raises difficult questions about whether unionists are monopolists, where they interfere with commerce or use strong-arm tactics. Supposedly, people who ask such graceless questions are callous propagandists in comparison with union leaders who have such deep concern for the less fortunate. This high-minded cry that labor is not a commodity is even enshrined in the Clayton Act of 1914 in order to justify union exemption from antitrust laws. Congress, by declaration, attempted to exempt pricing of labor services from the same economic laws that govern pricing of tires, kumquats, and Lionel trains. The hypocrisy is that unionists know that labor services are commodities and that people trade their labor services in markets every day. Unionists' livelihoods depend on bargaining for the sale of other individuals' labor services.

"Unionism is a rejection of free markets, open competition, and individual freedom in favor of their opposites."

Unions battle one another over jurisdiction essentially because they treat people as commodities, as pawns in labor empires. An examination of any union constitution confirms the validity of the charge. The documents begin by solemnly identifying a group of people who "belong" to the union. The UAW, for example, declares that it takes in and holds jurisdiction over all employees in automobile, farm implement, and aircraft plants "and such other branches of industry as the International Executive Board shall decide." In other words, workers are the property of the union organization. And woe to any other sectionalist labor group that fails to recognize this. . . .

Protection Myth

"Unions protect workers against the abuse of managerial authority."

This notion is a variant of the first myth and cannot withstand scrutiny either. Workers are not captives. In a competitive labor market employers are forced by competition for productive labor to offer wages and working conditions that cater to the preferences of workers. This includes equitable treatment of workers' grievances by management, because failure to supply attractive working conditions implies that an employer must pay higher wages in order to attract and retain workers. It pays companies to develop reputations for dealing fairly with employees because this keeps labor costs lower than they would otherwise be. A competitive labor market is the ultimate protection for employees, not union grievance procedures.

Three additional points should be made about this issue. First, the value of grievance procedures, whether union or nonunion, depends on how easy it is to change jobs. Employees place no value on a complaint system if mobility among employers is without cost, but they value it highly if there is only one available employer (the socialist state?). Most real cases lie somewhere between these two extremes of costless mobility and prohibitive cost mobility. Second, managerial abuse can occur in situations where union-imposed pay scales are higher than pay in the competitive sector because so many employees are eager to retain their high-paying jobs. Managers can demand more productivity from workers and still attract a plentiful labor supply. Naturally, unionists contest managerial authority over working conditions in such cases, although if a union succeeds in controlling most of the grievance process, it is unclear which employees will be helped and which harmed by the change. Third, empirical studies by L.F. Dunn and George J. Borjas suggest that the nonpecuniary effects of unionism are virtually zero or even negative in the minds of employees, although the question is far from resolved as a matter of empirical study.

The more general problem is that unionism eliminates free labor markets and substitutes controlled (unfree?) markets, controlled by union officials. Consider the testimony of Walter Reuther, president of the United Auto Workers, before the House Committee on Education and Labor in 1953:

> Reuther: We [UAW] do not control the workers at all, and I do not control a single worker in America. . . . no one has control over anybody. I don't contol a single General Motors worker. They have much more control over me than I have over them. . . . He [the employer] surely is free, and he is free to say no and they often say no.
>
> Rep. Gwinn: Well, he certainly is not free to go into the market and find other workers, is he?
>
> Reuther: Well, you see, labor is not a commodity which you go and shop for in the free marketplace. . . . We are trying to develop collective bargaining, to advance.
>
> Gwinn: No, it seems to me it is quite offensive to have a monopoly of human flesh, and I think that they are different.
>
> Reuther: . . . The whole concept of monopoly is where you get into a field where you are carrying out practices which are unethical and which are deliberately directed toward the restraint of free trade and free competition. We are not doing that.
>
> Gwinn: . . . and where is the free competition in this whole business?
>
> Reuther: The competition is between General Motors Corporation and its workers at the collective bargaining table. That is where the competition is. You just treat labor as a commodity, and labor is not a commodity. Labor is people.
>
> Gwinn: I know. That is an old story, and I do not treat it as a commodity. I want to make it free, and I am talking about free men and not a commodity.

Unionism is a rejection of free markets, open

competition, and individual freedom in favor of their opposites: monopoly power, private coercion, and aggrandizement of personal rule. In a perverse way unions fit our age, so intent are they on forcibly designing pleasing outcomes, constructing restrictions, harassing successful businesses, impeding the accumulation of productive capital, and subverting the pricing mechanism in its task of coordinating human activity. Despite the brilliant success of free markets on both logical and empirical grounds, there is a widespread bias against them that is hard to explain. George Gilder has puzzled over it: "Evidently, there is something in the human mind, even when honed at Oxford or the Sorbonne, that hesitates to believe in capitalism: in the enriching mysteries of inequality, the inexhaustible mines of the division of labor, the multiplying miracles of market economics, the compounding gains from trade and prosperity."

Fortunately, we need not solve this mystery to understand what sorts of public policies will restore individual freedom in the labor market and drastically diminish the union problem. Outlawing unions or strikes or repressing unions in any special way would be the wrong thing to do. Taft-Hartley and Landrum-Griffin offer rich testimony about the likelihood of further federal intervention to tame these organizations.

Try Freedom for a Change

Instead, the right thing to do is to deregulate. Try freedom for a change. Repeal, abolish, rescind, revoke, and do away with the Railway Labor Act, the Norris-La Guardia Act, and the National Labor Relations Act. Also abolish the commissions, executive orders, state laws, rulings, administrative orders, and regulations derived from the three major statutes. Restore the rule of law in labor relations by treating unions in a manner consistent with the way everyone else is treated under contract and tort law. Treat workers and worker organizations as responsible adults, not as children who are exempt from the rules of peaceable conduct. . . .

The logical and empirical case for free trade, domestic and foreign, rather than "free trade" unions, must continue to be made. Inflation, unemployment, and union tyranny will plague us until people learn the true nature of unionism. Maybe it will take more impoverishment, more industrial welfare, and more suffering to teach people what so-called collective bargaining is all about. They are very close to that state in Britain, where even a Labour member of Parliament recently admitted that trade unions are destroying the living standards of workingmen in the country. I hope that we do not sink to the British standard of living, or impose "industrial democracy," or look to our false idols to alleviate our union and industrial problems. We took a wrong turn in 1947 by trying to patch a

bad law, and we have been patching it ever since. Repeal is the answer. . . .

We should immediately restore the right of every American to raise his or her income by accepting any remuneration a prospective employer may offer, free from union threat and intimidation, no matter how much these trades supposedly harm the interest of those with higher incomes. The time for dissembling is over.

Morgan O. Reynolds is an associate professor of economics at Texas A&M University. His articles have appeared in Fortune *and* The Freeman, *as well as in* American Economic Review, Journal of Political Economy, Journal of Labor Research, *and other specialized journals.*

"Union leaders at all levels must . . . place renewed emphasis on bringing the benefits of trade unionism to the unorganized as a prime function of every labor organization."

Union Leaders Support Organizing Efforts

AFL-CIO Committee on the Evolution of Work

The nature of work, the organization of the workplace, and the size, location, composition and background of the workforce have been changing at an especially rapid rate in recent years and that process of change is continuing unabated.

Given the magnitude and velocity of these destabilizing changes, the labor movement has demonstrated a notable resiliency. Unions represent over 20,000,000 working men and women in the United States. Organized labor remains a vital force for progress in this nation; no serious observer denies that unions have played and continue to play a civilizing, humanizing and democratizing role in American life.

The Changing Situation

But despite their accomplishments, unions find themselves behind the pace of change. During the 1960s and 1970s, the American workforce grew in an unprecedented way—adding 1.3 million new workers per year in the 1960s and 2.1 million new workers per year in the 1970s—whereas the labor movement's membership remained static as gains made in organizing were offset due to job losses in basic industries. In the 1980s, union membership has shown a decline in absolute numbers as well as in percentage terms. The proportion of workers who are eligible to join a union and who in fact belong to a union has fallen from close to 45 percent to under 28 percent since 1954; using the measure of percentage of the entire workforce, the decline has been from 35 percent to under 19 percent. . . .

To begin with, it is important to recognize that the decline in union membership that occurred in recent years has *not* been the result of dissatisfaction of union members with their unions but was, instead, a function of the economic recession which hit with

American Federation of Labor and Congress of Industrial Organizations, "The Changing Situation of Workers and Their Unions," published by an AFL-CIO Committee on the Evolution of Work, 1985. Reprinted by permission.

particular force in those sectors of the economy that are heavily unionized. . . .

Second, despite all the changes that have occurred and are occurring in the workforce, the value of organization for workers remains as great today as when unions began. Our own experience shows that to be true and the data confirm it; unionized workers earn on average 33 percent more than their non-union counterparts. . . .

Third, workers who already are organized appreciate the benefits of unionization. Over 90 percent of organized workers believe that unions improve the wages and working conditions of members; 67 percent reject the proposition that unions are unnecessary to assure fair treatment; and over 60 percent of unionized workers believe that if their own employer were not unionized, wages and fringe benefits would be lower. . . .

Seeds of a Resurgence

Fourth, unions are increasingly successful in enrolling the types of workers who are forming an increasingly large share of the workforce. Labor union members are better educated than the general population, with a higher proportion of both high school and college graduates. . . .

Fifth, the opinion survey data show that non-union workers accept the fundamental premise on which the trade union movement has been and is based: that workers are more effective in insuring democracy in the workplace and in obtaining redress for their grievances when they act in concert than when they act alone. . . .

Sixth, and finally—and, in our view, most important of all—experience demonstrates that the current generation of workers, when given a fair chance to form a union at their workplace, elects to do so in large numbers. . . .

In sum, a period of resurgence—of sustained growth—is within our grasp. The recommendations that follow are designed to spur such a resurgence.

Our recommendations are based upon the fundamental premises stated at the start of the report: that the labor movement exists to advance the interests of workers as workers see their interests, and that to continue to perform their role, unions must come to grips with the current and changed realities workers face. Our aims—achieving decent wages and conditions, democracy in the workplace, a full voice for working people in the society, and the more equitable sharing of the wealth of the nation—remain unchanged. The means of securing those aims, while grounded in experience, must meet today's needs and anticipate tomorrow's aspirations.

"The labor movement exists to advance the interests of workers as workers see their interests."

There are, we believe, steps that can be taken to improve the efficacy of our traditional programs, and. . . we begin with recommendations for new approaches that we believe worthy of examination.

Unions should experiment with new approaches to represent workers and should address new issues of concern to workers. The diversity of approaches different unions have developed to meet the myriad of interests and desires of a diverse workforce in workplaces scattered throughout this country is an essential part of the genius of the American labor movement. . . .

First, unions must develop and put into effect multiple models for representing workers tailored to the needs and concerns of different groups. . . .

Second, and equally important, unions must continually seek out and address new issues of concern to workers. . . . Collective action through labor unions can develop constructive steps to meet these concerns.

In this regard, the survey data suggest, and our experience indicates, that there is a particular insistence voiced by workers, union and non-union alike, to have a say in the "how, why and wherefore" of their work. . . .

New Methods

It is the special responsibility of the individual unions that make up the labor movement to make creative use of the collective bargaining concept and to adapt bargaining to these times and to the present circumstances.

Consideration should be given to establishing new categories of membership for workers not employed in an organized bargaining unit. The polling data indicate that approximately 28 percent of all non-union employees—27,000,000 workers in all—are former union members; most of those individuals left their union only because they left their unionized jobs. . . . New categories of membership should be created by individual unions or on a Federation-wide basis to accommodate individuals who are not part of organized bargaining units, and affiliates should consider dropping any existing barriers to an individual's retaining his membership after leaving an organized unit. . . .

Coordinated-comprehensive corporate campaigns and the pressure of public opinion should be used to secure the neutrality of employers whose employees seek to organize a union and to assure good faith bargaining. In the past, organizing has often proceeded on the assumption that the law could be relied upon both to assure employees a fair and free choice on whether to form a union and also to require the employer to bargain with a union chosen by a majority of the employees. Members of the general public assume that such a law is in place and is scrupulously observed by employers. This assumption is fanciful; an employer bent upon opposing unionization is not even inconvenienced by the present law in carrying out his anti-union activities. Accordingly, neutralizing employer opposition and compelling good faith bargaining should be considered an essential part of organizing. . . .

Union's First Priority

The AFL-CIO should establish a pilot project of experimental organizing committees. The experience gained in earlier periods of union growth suggests the potential usefulness of organizing committees. That experience suggests that an entity single-mindedly devoted to the task of assisting unorganized workers in forming unions may be more successful than an ongoing entity whose first priority must be to provide service to its present members. . . .

Interferences with the right of workers to form a union should be forcefully brought to the attention of the general public to develop public support for labor law reform. The survey data indicate that over 80 percent of the American public agree with the proposition that workers should have the right to join unions. But the American public does not realize that under existing labor law that right exists only in theory and not in practice—that employers can, in fact, intimidate and coerce their employees and that the law's remedies are too little and too late. The public needs to be informed of these facts, through exposés of particular cases, in order to develop a constituency for real labor law reform in private employment and for the passing of legislation legalizing collective bargaining for public employees at the state and local levels.

There must be a renewed emphasis on organizing.

The large increase in the workforce and in the extent of employer opposition requires an equal increase in the emphasis placed on, and the resources devoted to, organizing. All of the destabilizing changes we have detailed above have had the effect of decreasing the time and effort put into organizing. This trend must be reversed if any of the recommendations made below are to have any effect.

Organizers should be carefully chosen and trained. Organizing is a skill; it is not something that everyone can do and is not something that can be taught in a one-week training session. There should be broad recruitment effort within and outside the labor movement for organizers, and organizers should be extensively trained. . . .

Union leaders and rank-and-file members should be more involved in organizing efforts. In organizing, personal contacts both with union leaders and with rank-and-file members who have formed a union can be of critical importance. Union leaders at all levels must continue to be directly involved in organizing and must place renewed emphasis on bringing the benefits of trade unionism to the unorganized as a prime function of every labor organization. Greater use also should be made of rank-and-file members in campaigns because they are the best witnesses of trade union effectiveness. . . .

Organizing targets should be carefully chosen to maximize the chance for success. From the national polling data, it is possible to identify particular types of employers or employment conditions which are conducive both to organizing and, of equal importance, to obtaining a first contract, and it is also possible to identify particular groups which are more likely to want union representation; for example, former union members and younger workers tend to be more favorably inclined to unionization than are older workers who have never been in a union. . . .

Small units should not be overlooked as organizing targets. Thirty-five percent of the national workforce is employed in companies with less than 25 employees. Labor conditions in smaller companies tend to be inferior to conditions in larger companies, and employers in these companies are less likely to resist their employees' desire to form a union; not surprisingly, therefore, unions have been more successful in representation elections in small bargaining units than in elections in larger bargaining units. . . .

More Coordination

When a unit is organized, unions representing other units of the same employer should coordinate assistance to the new unit to obtain a first contract. Coordinated bargaining and, where necessary, coordinated pressure maximizes labor's strength. Such strength is especially important in attempting to obtain a first contract in a newly-organized unit. . . . The AFL-CIO and the trade and industrial departments should facilitate such coordination.

Unions should make special efforts to attract those who belong to organized bargaining units but have not joined their union. By most estimates, 2,000,000 of the employees who are covered by AFL-CIO union contracts are not union members. These workers are known by the local leadership and are a natural audience for the union's message, and every effort should be made to turn them from free riders to full and enthusiastic members. . . .

"Neutralizing employer opposition and compelling good faith bargaining should be considered an essential part of organizing."

The preceding recommendations result from a searching self-examination and honest appraisal of our strengths and weaknesses and encompass a wide range of proposed actions to strengthen our unions and our movements and to enhance our ability to serve present and future members. This process of examination and appraisal must be continued within the Federation and within every affiliate as the basis for planning realistically for the future.

The AFL-CIO Committee on the Evolution of Work was established in August 1982 by the Executive Council of the AFL-CIO to review and evaluate the changes taking place in America in the labor force, occupations, industries, and technology. The committee issued its initial report, The Future of Work, *in August 1983.*

Union Leaders Undermine Organizing Efforts

Suzanne Gordon

At the beginning of [1986], many of the nation's newspapers featured stories about what appeared to be an unusual labor dispute. In many ways the dispute was no different from countless others: the executive officers of a major national organization had arrived at their headquarters in Washington and found a group of picketers blocking the entrance. The picketers were protesting their employer's refusal to agree to a salary increase and had—in traditional union style—gone on strike. In traditional corporate fashion, the managers brushed by the strikers and went into the building and, when the employees refused to call off the picket line, filed an unfair labor charge with the National Labor Relations Board (NLRB).

What distinguished this case was that the managers in question were not traditional managers but were top officials of the AFL-CIO, including Secretary-Treasurer Thomas Donahue, the organization's second-highest official. And the picket line they crossed—thus committing the cardinal sin of the labor movement—had been set up by employees of the AFL-CIO's Food and Allied Service Trades department, a research and organizing unit represented by the AFL-CIO-affiliated Newspaper Guild.

Myriad of Difficulties

The myriad difficulties unions face today make the labor movement particularly vulnerable to public criticism. And on top of charges of corruption, discrimination, coziness with employers, and other real and imagined wrongdoings, the last thing union officials need is to be accused themselves of being anti-union.

But as union-busting has become the norm, rather than the exception, in U.S. labor relations, it has also

Suzanne Gordon, "Unions: Unfair to Worker," *Mother Jones*, April/May 1986. Reprinted with the author's permission.

become increasingly commonplace when staff members of major unions organize to improve their wages, hours, and working conditions. Instead of quickly and voluntarily recognizing a staff union, officials often insist that there be a formal recognition election conducted by the notoriously slow-moving NLRB. Instead of agreeing on who should be represented in the staff bargaining unit, they will often haggle endlessly about the eligibility of particular staff members. Rather than respecting and accepting union activists, they may try to buy them off with promises of raises and promotions, or intimidate them with threats of tranfers or terminations. In the most extreme cases, a few unions have driven staff organizations out of existence by a combination of all these tactics, about which they are very quick to complain when utilized by other employers.

Unions as Employers

Officially, of course, unions are all in favor of organizing the unorganized, particularly the millions of clerical, administrative, and professional employees who have never been strong union adherents. And while a few unions, like the Teamsters, have succeeded in maintaining a 100 percent union-free environment among clerical workers as well as professional staff, most union leaders admit that their clerical and maintenance staffs need unions to represent them with management. The Office and Professional Employees International Union (OPEIU) represents thousands of bargaining units of clerical workers and maintenance staff at local unions around the country and about 50 bargaining units at union national headquarters. Although OPEIU negotiators say union employers can be as difficult to deal with as their corporate counterparts, far more clerical and maintenance staffers at union offices are organized than in the private sector.

And at some unions—such as the United Auto Workers, the United Food and Commercial Workers International Union, and International Association of Machinists and Aerospace Workers, the National Education Association, and the United Steelworkers of America—professional staffers have been organized for years and report generally harmonious labor-management relations.

Union Resistance

But a number of other unions have resisted unionization by the salaried employees who make up their professional staffs: lawyers, researchers, organizers, lobbyists, and labor educators. Lance Compa of the Electrical Workers union, a small Left-led union that left the CIO during the anticommunist witchhunts of the late 1940s, has articulated the most compelling argument against professional staff unions. "You're working to serve the membership," he says, "so it's inherently a conflict of interest to act in an adversarial manner that involves the use of strikes or pressure tactics to . . . interfere with the workings of the union." An even more important issue, Compa adds, is "whether [your work is] just a job or whether you consider yourself as belonging to a movement that has a broader social meaning. Our union believes that the labor movement is part of a broader movement to change society. And that kind of movement requires dedication and the ability to resolve conflicts as colleagues and comrades, not as adversaries or enemies."

"As union-busting has become the norm . . . in U.S. labor relations, it has also become increasingly commonplace when staff members of major unions organize to improve their wages, hours, and working conditions."

Compa acknowledges that "not all . . . labor leaders see the labor movement as a movement for social change. They run business unions that provide services in return for dues, and they often run them like companies run their businesses. It's understandable that their staffs would respond . . . by organizing to improve wages, hours, and working conditions."

When these staffers do organize, their fears often echo those of workers in the corporate world. Many of the union employees interviewed for this story were afraid to allow their names to be used, and even those who no longer work for a union would not speak for attribution for fear of being blacklisted. "These union officials don't like staff unions," one young man says, "and they don't want to hire anyone who's been involved with one."

History of Organizing Efforts

Such reluctance is not surprising, considering the history of union staff organizing efforts. In 1961, for example, organizers at the International Ladies' Garment Workers Union (ILGWU)—recognized as one of the more progressive unions in the United States—decided that they could no longer live on commitment alone. To bargain for increases in their $65-a-week salaries and to reduce their long hours, they formed the Federation of Union Representatives (FOUR) and approached ILGWU president David Dubinsky with their demands.

Dubinsky denounced them for having "lost their idealism" and succumbing to the "materialistic age," refused to recognize FOUR, and fired its leaders.

More than a decade later, professional staffers of the United Mine Workers (UMW) formed a union to protect themselves from bitter infighting in the national union leadership. Reform candidate Arnold Miller had recently ousted the murderous Tony Boyle as president, but Boyle loyalists on the UMW executive board fought back with attacks on Miller's staff appointees. To make matters worse, Miller's own supporters began squabbling, and he was soon at odds with two fellow officers and many staff members.

Ellen Chapnick, who worked in the UMW general counsel's office, says that situation got so bad that "Miller decided we weren't allowed to work after five or on weekends because he didn't think we were actually working—he thought we were conspiring against him."

Volatile and Hostile Environment

In such a volatile and hostile environment, where rational personnel policies were virtually nonexistent, Chapnick and others on the staff had no trouble forming an independent union. They petitioned for and won an NLRB election by a large majority, and the UMW then appointed a three-member committee to negotiate a first contract. But rather than accept the tentative agreement reached by his own representatives, Miller and the rest of the board claimed that negotiations had never been authorized. At the union's 1976 convention, Sam Church—who was then Miller's executive assistant and would soon be his successor—proposed a resolution instructing the officers and executive board never to sign a contract with the staff union. It passed unanimously.

"It's a clear violation of federal labor law for an employer to refuse to bargain with an NLRB-certified employee organization," says Steve Early, a labor lawyer then working on the *Mineworkers Journal*, under Miller. "Even the most rabidly anti-union employer would refrain from having its annual stockholders meeting publicly repudiate its legal duty to bargain in good faith. Yet here were 1,900 union delegates voting in favor of no bargaining with the staff union at all. It was outrageous: probably the largest mass unfair labor practice ever committed, and a union was responsible.". . .

After the convention, the union leadership also began firing pro-union employees and replacing them with followers of Miller and Church. "The UMW," Ellen Chapnick recalls, "finally got a bunch of loyalists to initiate decertification proceedings." A formal decertification election was never held; the staff union simply died of attrition, and to this day the UMW headquarters staff—except for clerical workers—remains unorganized.

Hiring and Firing at Will

Another major player in the history of staff union organizing was the late Jerry Wurf, longtime president of the American Federation of State, County, and Municipal Employees (AFSCME). "To his credit, Wurf told us to our faces that he did not believe that professional staff should have a union," says Paul Rosenstein, former AFSCME education department employee and chief steward of the headquarter's professional staff union. "He felt that clerical workers needed a union, but that professional staff were supposed to serve the members and should be hired and fired at the will of union officials."

By December 1977 the staff union had spent six months working without a contract while union negotiators and Wurf's representatives haggled over AFSCME's attempt to eliminate the staff's cost-of-living escalator clause. (At the time, the executive board was considering raising members' dues to keep up with inflation.) Frustrated and upset by management's intransigence, the union members decided to take the issue directly to AFSCME's executive board by engaging in information picketing at the national headquarters in Washington. "When Wurf drove up to the building with his lawyer and saw us picketing," a member of the union remembers, "he was furious. He flew into a rage, ordered the building locked, took our names, and informed us we were all fired. 'If this is the way you feel about *my* union,' he said, 'then I'm not going to let you into *my* building.'

"When we met with him later that day, he told us he knew what he was doing was against the law, but added that if he'd worried about the law he wouldn't have built the union the way he did. Then he told us sarcastically that we could certainly take our case to the NLRB. Maybe, he laughed snidely, we could have our jobs back in five or ten years."

The intimidation worked. "We finally settled into a long heart-to-heart bargaining session where Wurf promised he'd let bygones be bygones, if we accepted his original contract proposal," the union member says. "We accepted and he rehired us." Fortunately, union staff members say, labor relations have improved dramatically under Wurf's successor, Gerald McEntee.

Attempts to Form a Staff Union

A recent and perhaps more typical tale reveals how more sophisticated managers handle labor relations with their staff. After Service Employees International Union (SEIU) President John Joseph Sweeney was elected in 1980, the union hired a number of new organizers and field reps and expanded its research staff. "Most of us were very glad to be working for a progressive union," says one SEIU staff member. "That's why people with extensive labor experience were willing to work for $13,000—$16,000 a year. But soon we learned that the union was being very arbitrary about salaries, benefits, and workloads. So we decided to form an independent staff union."

"OPEIU negotiators say union employers can be as difficult to deal with as their corporate counterparts."

Like rank-and-file organizers at any private firm, the SEIU staff was concerned that the employer might discourage organizing activity as it had in the past: George Hardy has openly declared his opposition to staff unions when he was the SEIU president. Organizers kept the campaign a closely guarded secret until 85 percent of the staff had signed on. Then they approached Sweeney through an influential third party.

"The good news was that he said he'd be willing to recognize us voluntarily," another participant in the union recalls. "The bad news was that he had no intention of recognizing the unit we thought appropriate. The process of just bargaining over an agreement of voluntary recognition took eight months," the organizer continues. "Then we began to discuss the actual contract terms. We were very careful not to jeopardize the union's fluid, progressive character. Some union staffers make $30,000 or $40,000 a year, travel first class, and have all kinds of perks, and we weren't interested in that. But we at least wanted to make as much as the union's secretaries, who earn from $19,000—$24,000 and we wanted to have uniform benefits and conditions of work."

Notwithstanding the apparent modesty of the SEIU demands, the negotiations dragged on for over a year before being settled in April 1985. Staffers won some improvement in wages, but remained vulnerable to layoffs and report continuing problems with some middle managers. "They made nasty remarks impugning our loyalty to the institution," says one organizer. "They felt that working for a union was different than working for any ordinary employer, and that by unionizing and demanding decent salaries and working conditions we were, in effect, ripping off the members."

Institutional Disloyalty

The charges of institutional disloyalty can be emotionally draining. Union staffers, says one organizer, "get discouraged, their sense of accomplishment evaporates, and many of them wish they had never heard of labor unions." And the more sweeping insinuations that staff union activists are disloyal to the very spirit and ideals of the labor movement often give union managers an effective weapon their private-sector counterparts don't have. "It's like fighting with one hand tied behind your back," says an organizer at an international union who's been involved in a three-year battle for union recognition. "If workers we organized or represented were in the private sector, we'd be a whole lot more aggressive. We'd immediately advise them to go on strike or take their case to the public. But most of us are loath to do that because we really don't want to give the labor movement a worse name than it already has."

"They felt that working for a union was different than working for any ordinary employer."

Organizers may be reluctant to further taint labor's image, but union officials don't always share that concern. Perhaps the richest irony of the recent Food and Allied Service Trades strike was AFL-CIO Secretary-Treasurer Thomas Donahue's attempt to get the National Labor Relations Board to limit picket lines that were being honored by other unionized employees at AFL-CIO headquarters. Donahue's argument was based on cases in which the labor board and the courts have outlawed *common situs* picketing by building and construction trade unions. The restrictions on *common situs* are designed to prevent strikers against one constractor on a construction site from setting up pickets that would encourage union members working for other contractors on the site to walk off the job. The legal precedent cited by Donahue is one that the AFL-CIO's building and construction trade unions have been trying to overturn for years.

Within the movement for social change, union officials are not alone in resisting the formation of staff unions: Two of Ralph Nader's Public Citizen groups, the NOW Women's Legal Defense Fund, the

San Francisco Bay Guardian, and the Eighth Street Bookstore in New York have all been involved in messy disputes in recent years over employee attempts to unionize. Officials of such groups may be quite comfortable challenging other people's arbitrary authority, but they have not always responded well when employees challenged theirs.

For both unions and other progressive organizations that function as employers, the litmus test of their real commitment to official institutional values and goals ought to be the handling of their own labor relations. To their credit, many trade unions have lived up to their principles. But when trade union leaders fail the test of good-faith bargaining and observance of federal labor law, it undermines the very principles unions are supposed to uphold and defend. In these difficult days for organized labor, when the union gospel appears to be increasingly unpopular, unions can hardly afford not to practice what they preach.

Suzanne Gordon is a free-lance writer living in Arlington, MA. She is the author of several books and frequently writes about trade unions.

Worker Ownership Can Benefit Labor

Dan Swinney

A profound change has taken place in the economy, a change which requires an equally profound change in labor. In the mid-1970s, the American economy began to reflect dramatic symptoms of a period of sustained decline. The United States entered a period of sharp international competition with a real loss of American market share in most areas of production; a sharper and more intense scramble for profits; and a general lowering of the real and social wages of the American people.

As a result, there is increasing unemployment and attacks on union strength and organization, increasing the divisions between workers. Most important, there is a corporate willingness to discard whole industries, communities, people and productive capacity not because they aren't profitable but because they aren't profitable enough.

Within this deepening long-term crisis is the emergence of a political and economic vacuum in major urban and industrial areas. Companies which provided job creation and economic development in an expanding economy are now exporting capital and casting off assets in traditional industrial areas. Traditional defenders of the people's livelihood—like the civic machinery, political parties, the church, and organized labor—have been unable to fill the vacuum created by the change in corporate strategy.

Labor's Ineffectiveness

Labor's inability to lead effectively in this period is rooted in its training during the years following World War II. During the expanding post-war period a social contract generally defined the role of organized labor: Capital would generally increase the real wages of labor, and labor would provide a stable workforce and keep out of the management of

Dan Swinney, "Worker Ownership: A Tactic for Labor." Reprinted with permission from the November 30, 1985 issue of *Multinational Monitor*, a monthly news magazine published by Essential Information, Inc.

business. Because of this social contract, labor did not develop a sophisticated understanding of the companies and industries for which they worked. The debate between the left and right was frequently around "more" or "less," with no real difference in the depth of understanding of the company, the market or the industry. Strong relationships were not built among the various elements in the working community, the unemployed and unorganized, churches, community groups and local government.

Given this experience, the labor movement was unprepared for the depth of the current economic crisis. Unions were left without tactics or strategies. Unemployment is permanently high, deeply undermining the strength of organized labor. It is being used to break strikes and force concessions. With the cutting of social programs, many of the unemployed are hungry and desperate and willing to break ranks to replace workers on a picket line or to accept substandard wages and benefits. Benefits and important contract provisions that protect seniority in the jobs that remain are perceived as unfair by women, youth, Blacks, Hispanics and other minorities who have been laid off first and have no chance of being recalled. This leaves labor in an adversarial position with its most important allies at a time when it is under the most determined type of corporate attack.

Organized labor is becoming a smaller and smaller percentage of labor. The dwindling percentage of organized vs. unorganized occurred gradually during the post-war period. Now the decline is increasing along with the decline in real wages, and labor is losing its base when it needs it most. Under current conditions, a major loss in a major battle such as steel or auto could result in a decisive and qualitative set back for organized labor. A union could be literally destroyed.

This crisis requires innovation. Union organizing

efforts must have a much more sophisticated and substantial understanding of economics in order to develop effective tactics and strategy.

Worker Ownership and Union Power

Worker ownership is a tactic that can and should be used by unions in confronting the new realities. When the term "worker ownership" is used today, it can mean any of a thousand different combinations of how a company is financed and managed. On one end of the spectrum are corporate tax and financing strategies which are designed to neutralize worker solidarity, union strength and militance. These programs create the illusion of "profit sharing," give workers no real role in management, no power to make critical decisions, and very little share in the profits. Frequently, the only role workers have in this situation is to give concessions in wages and benefits to keep "their" company rolling.

On the other end of the "worker ownership" spectrum are companies that are worker-owned, worker-managed, unionized, and a real asset to the labor movement and the community. Examples include the O & O Supermarkets in Philadelphia, Franklin Forge in Michigan, Atlas Chain in Pennsylvania, and Seymour Specialty Wire in Connecticut. The examples are few, but the potential for many more exists.

"Used effectively, [worker ownership] strengthens the union, its members and the labor movement."

Within these extremes, there are hundreds of possible combinations. Workers must ask who is initiating worker ownership and why, what leverage and plan do the workers have, how is worker authority and dignity protected and promoted, and so forth. Based on an evaluation of these factors, a plan for worker ownership should be rejected or supported. Where the plan is not developed, negotiations can give it substance. Effective and aggressive negotiators with some kind of leverage— the potential to close the company down, the capacity to strike or cripple production, a strong community backing—can transform a general concept into a constructive working plan. Uninformed and passive negotiators, with or without leverage, can transform even a good situation into a scam for the workers and, despite good intentions, end up benefiting only the original owners.

A Tactic, Not a Strategy

Worker ownership is a tactic not a strategy. It is just like any other tactic, such as a strike, a retreat, a picket line or a demonstration. It can be used effectively or ineffectively. Used effectively, it

strengthens the union, its members and the labor movement.

Worker ownership is part of the general struggle for economic reform. Like any reform struggle, it can be consumed with narrow details. If elevated to more than what it is, it can perpetuate illusions. And, it can be co-opted. These are dangers for any struggle for reform.

Pursuing the option of worker ownership exhausts the marketplace limits and can serve as a springboard for effectively raising consciousness about the necessity for national change and reform. It does this by taking advantage of viable opportunities that aren't recognized or aren't profitable enough for traditional entrepreneurs. The fact remains that worker- and community-owned enterprises combined with enterprises run by traditional parties won't meet all the needs of the American people. Worker ownership will not create full employment. On the other hand, the experience of worker ownership will train the labor movement in workplace democracy and in effective leadership and management. These skills will profoundly complement any major progressive change in the character of the U.S. economy.

The pre-condition for the effective use of worker ownership is a detailed and full understanding of the company, its markets and its industry. Worker ownership is not a good tactic when: proposed by a company as an effort to get the workers to finance the closing of a plant which has been milked dry and would have no viable future under any owner; proposed by a company as an effort to liquidate or neutralize the union; the company is not capable of surviving in the marketplace; the workers are not capable of running the plant.

Worker ownership is a tactic to consider when: there is a viable company that is being closed and could be operated profitably; wage and benefit concessions are the only option to maintain a viable company—worker ownership becomes the quid pro quo in bargaining with the company as the cost for cash; or where there is a viable company that is available for worker ownership for any reason.

Excluding the Unemployed

Any discussion of the strategy and tactics of the working class movement must include those who don't work as well as those who do. Even for those who do work, the threat of not working, the threat of a shutdown, frequently dominates and sets the stage for the demand for concessions. This means that we must take the issue of jobs very seriously to forge unity with the unemployed. By discussing the labor movement in terms of just those who are organized into unions, the unemployed are excluded as are the vast majority of those who are working.

The labor movement has generally failed in this challenge and still operates within the understanding of the earlier period of economic expansion. Even within organized shops, union members are losing confidence in the capacity of unions to protect their jobs. That confidence can be sustained by leadership that has a very precise understanding of what actually causes job loss and what are legitimate options for preventing job loss. Worker ownership is a tactical option for those situations where jobs could be saved or created; and it identifies a commitment to create jobs and fill the vacuum created by traditional market forces.

A Last Resort Tactic

It is argued that worker ownership has been and necessarily will continue to be restricted to the "crumbs" of the economy, the "financially troubled" companies that are thrown to workers to avoid the cost of their closing. Many of the efforts at worker ownership to this point have involved some of these crumbs, but this is not an inherent aspect of worker ownership. Some plants are exhausted and beyond recovery because of being completely milked or being in an industry sector that has been wiped out because of competition, changes in technology, changes in critical costs or declines in market demand. Others close because:

• they are profitable but not profitable enough for a parent company or private investors who can make more in the short term in other areas.

• there isn't an owner to succeed the current owner. The family interest dies and there isn't a successor capable of taking over.

• there is mismanagement. The company is run by those who simply can't utilize its assets.

There is a common assumption that traditional capitalists are the most efficient and capable managers and initiators of companies. If they don't do it, it can't be done. If they don't want to do it, it must not be worth doing. In a declining economy, this narrow vision of traditional market forces often comes into conflict with the long-term needs and capacity of particular firms and industry sectors. The requirement of a big return in the short run excludes the possibility of experimenting with new technology or processes that are required for the health of an industry. Under the pressure of a declining economy, many valuable and productive assets, companies and opportunities for job creation simply fall through the cracks.

In this context, the ability and willingness to take over the management of productive capacity including owning and operating a particular company which is being ruined, ignored or discarded by traditional market forces is an important complement to the other tactics the labor movement uses in defending its interests and expanding its power. It preserves jobs, union or potential union membership, and enhances the

union's reputation for leadership capacity.

A major reason for the labor movement to include worker ownership in its arsenal is to strengthen its ties with the aspirations of a much broader movement that is committed to job retention and job creation. This movement includes community organizations, urban political organizations, religious organizations, unemployed organizations, and others who are responding to the reality of very high levels of unemployment accompanied by the Reagan onslaught on the welfare state.

"The effective use of worker ownership can strengthen labor's role among the unorganized, the unemployed, and in society in general."

The labor movement can play a critical role in leading this effort because of its closeness to production, its familiarity with all the issues, and its strategic position. It can bring into negotiations a commitment to the social obligations of production to workers and the community; a defense of worker and union interests in the organization of production; and aggressively exhaust what potential remains in a diverse market atmosphere. Labor, by utilizing the tactic of worker ownership at the proper times, can create a choice for the growing number of people becoming aware of the limits of capital, and it can provide some models of creativity and broadened social vision. To effectively choose the opportunities and to broadly expose how the narrowness of traditional market forces holds back our country's development, while demonstrating a willingness to fill the void when it is possible, can have a tremendous internal and external impact on the labor movement.

If the labor movement is aggressive in encouraging working people and organizations from working-class communities to take advantage of opportunities for worker ownership, even if the workers aren't initially organized, it can enhance its own organizing of the unorganized. It has a greater capacity than most to provide technical assistance and orientation as well as a national network that could service these efforts in important ways.

One Important Option Among Many

Despite the numerous negative examples that exist, worker ownership belongs in the tool box of the labor movement as one option among many to pursue its efforts to defend the interests of those who work and the unemployed. It's a tactic that in some situations meets the issues of job loss and capital flight head on.

The effective use of worker ownership can

strengthen labor's role among the unorganized, the unemployed, and in society in general by helping to fill the political and economic vacuum created by traditional market forces. Finally, use of this tactic will immensely broaden the scope of the labor movement, deepen its level of sophistication, and train it for leadership in the critically important trend toward economic reform and democracy.

Worker ownership is a concept and an option that we can no longer afford to avoid. To be willing to rise to the challenge of this and other new approaches like the use of eminent domain, nationalization, and popular control of investment funds, will bring the labor movement into a position of prestige and strength that will exceed that of earlier periods in American history.

Dan Swinney is the director of the Midwest Center for Labor Research in Chicago.

"Worker ownership is not only economically unfeasible, its overall impact on the labor movement is negative."

Worker Ownership Can Only Harm Labor

Mike Slott

American employers may not have a solution to the long-term crisis of the world economy, but they have developed a coherent strategy to weaken the labor movement. Through a combination of concessions bargaining, plant shutdowns, and shifting capital, corporations have succeeded in intimidating unions and dividing workers. As a result, the labor movement grows weaker, and workers lose what little protection they now have for their standard of living and basic rights.

Unions will become a marginal force in society unless the labor movement develops a viable strategy for responding to these employer attacks. The current program and policies of most sections of the trade union leadership are clearly inadequate. The labor movement urgently needs a new strategy.

Clearly, worker ownership merits serious consideration as an alternative to the current strategy of union leaders. But a strategy should be supported only if it has the overall effect of strengthening the labor movement—increasing the power, unity, and self-confidence of rank-and-file workers. A strategy which strengthens one group of workers while hurting the rest can only be harmful to labor.

Many people support worker ownership not as a means of strengthening labor, but as a way to foster labor-management cooperation and give workers a greater stake in the capitalist system so that they will be more productive and more concerned about the profitability of companies.

Limitations of Worker Ownership

The potential for worker ownership is severely limited by the structure of capitalist economies. All of the vital sectors of the economy are already owned and controlled by the capitalist class; in the

absence of a mass political movement, they can block any attempt by workers to make significant economic inroads on their power. Workers simply lack the financial resources to challenge employer domination of the "commanding heights" of the economy.

Given this lack of resources, worker ownership will be limited to the "crumbs" of the economy: either to certain labor-intensive industries (the traditional co-op sector) or to financially-troubled companies. In either context, worker-owned companies face serious problems. Many are bound to fail economically due to a lack of capital and/or poor market conditions. The ones that survive may be taken over by investors looking for a profitable place to put their money. A final scenario is one in which worker ownership survives, but as a non-threatening, marginal part of the economy.

Negative Impact on Labor Movement

Worker ownership is not only economically unfeasible, its overall impact on the labor movement is negative. The precarious positions of employee-owned companies in the economy requires workers to put most of their effort into two basic tasks: raising the capital to buy the company and start it up; and, competing successfully against other businesses. The whole orientation of workers is shifted from militant confrontation with their employers to survival in the marketplace.

When worker-ownership consists of isolated employee-owned companies, as it does in this country, this approach does even worse damage to unions. One of the basic components of trade unionism is the idea that workers achieve strength through unity, that solidarity is the basis upon which unions can fight effectively for their demands. In the current economic and political context, worker-ownership strikes at the heart of union solidarity.

Workers who gain ownership of a company tend,

Mike Slott, "The Case Against Worker Ownership." Reprinted with permission from the November 30, 1985 issue of *Multinational Monitor,* a monthly news magazine published by Essential Information, Inc.

over a period of time, to identify less with workers employed by other companies than with the company they now own.

Worker ownership is also divisive because it undermines union standards. Most employee buy-outs have occurred as part of a concessions deal. In order to save jobs and prevent a plant closing, workers agree to major wage-and-benefit reduction and a weakening of traditional work rules. In exchange, the workers buy out the owners and gain employee ownership. This seems like a perfectly reasonable deal: concessions for ownership. Yet, while the concessions save jobs in the short-run, they hurt workers in the rest of the labor movement. Lower wages and benefits at the employee-owned company put pressure on other employers (or give them the excuse) to seek wage reductions at their companies. Workers end up competing with each other to offer employers the lowest labor costs.

Industry-wide contracts aim to prevent such competition by creating uniform wages, benefits and working conditions. Unfortunately, uniform standards have already been seriously eroded in several industries because of concessions bargaining union leaders. When worker ownership is achieved in exchange for concessions, it further erodes industry standards.

"A strategy [such as worker ownership] which strengthens one group of workers while hurting the rest can only be harmful to labor."

The pitfalls of worker ownership are evident when one examines several employee owned businesses which were recently established in the United States. Advocates of worker ownership have sometimes pointed to these companies as examples of the potential of worker ownership. In reality, they show that worker ownership is not a viable strategy for the labor movement.

Worker Ownership as Management Ploy

Worker ownership is primarily used in this country not as a means of saving workers' jobs but as a management ploy to increase profits. In the vast majority of the estimated 6,000 companies which have some degree of employee ownership, management has initiated ESOPs [Employee Stock Ownership Plans] to improve employee motivation and gain certain tax advantages. Typically, workers own only a small percentage of the company's stock and have no control over the company's policies.

Workers have more significant ownership and control in some companies, although the extent of workplace democracy varies widely. Several ESOPs

including those at Weirton Steel and Hyatt-Clark Industries (HCI), give workers majority or full ownership, but severely limit their ability to vote their stock shares and control management.

The employee buy-out at Weirton Steel was promoted by the previous owner, National Steel. For a number of reasons, the conglomerate wanted to unload the Weirton plant and opted for employee ownership when it couldn't find a corporate buyer. Desperate to save their jobs, the workers agreed to a 20 percent wage-and-benefit reduction in return for gaining ownership of the plant. Beyond the formal transfer of ownership, however, little has changed. Management retains control of the Board of Directors and the company's daily operations. Workers can't even vote their own shares.

The structure of the ESOP and a six-year labor contract which prohibits strikes and wage increases insure management control in the years ahead. Furthermore, by agreeing to such major wage-and-benefit cutbacks, the workers have set a precedent for additional wage concessions in the steel industry. The bosses can now point to Weirton's labor costs in the next six years as the "competitive" rate for all employers.

Hyatt Clark Industries (HCI), a tapered bearing plant in Clark, New Jersey, has an ESOP similar to Weirton's. The HCI ESOP was shaped to a large extent by General Motors, the former owner of the plant, and the banks who loaned the money for the buy-out. In a letter distributed to HCI employees in April 1984, Alan Lowenstein, chairperson of the Board of Directors, noted that ". . . the business and financial leaders who were in a position to decide whether the company [i.e., the employees] could purchase the plant . . . insisted that the company be controlled by an independent board of directors as a condition of the purchase of the plant." HCI workers, represented by UAW [United Auto Workers] local 736, now have three people out of thirteen on the board. They will not gain equal representation until 1991.

Forcing Concessions

Despite the undemocratic ESOP, worker morale was high when the ESOP was initiated in October 1981. But, tension between management and the workers has grown considerably. The demand for HCI's product, tapered bearings, is declining as auto manufacturers switch from rear- to front-wheel drive cars. Management has responded to the company's shaky economic prospects with demands for greater productivity and sacrifices by the workers. The UAW is caught between management's push for more production and the worker's growing dissatisfaction. Contract negotiations in the fall of 1984 reflected the high level of worker discontent and General Motors' dominant influence. GM demanded that the union agree to a no-strike guarantee and threatened to cancel its purchases of the company's bearings if an agreement was not reached on the issue. Since GM purchases nearly 90 percent of HCI's output, Local 736 and HCI management worked feverishly to come up with an agreement that would satisfy GM.

GM's support for the buy-out was motivated less by concern for the workers' jobs than its calculation that the ESOP was a way of forcing concessions in the plant, which, in turn, could be used to pressure workers in other plants to make concessions. (In exchange for ownership, the workers accepted a 30 percent reduction in wages and benefits.) In fact, GM threatened to shut down the Fisher Body Division hardware factory in nearby Trenton, New Jersey, only three months after the HCI ESOP was finalized. The Trenton UAW Local agreed to changes in shift assignments and job classifications to prevent the plant from closing.

Of course, the HCI ESOP didn't start the concessions trend in the auto industry and cannot be seen as the basic cause of disunity in the UAW. Still, to the extent that the ESOP contributes to the dynamic of concessions, it is harmful to the labor movement.

In the context of employer domination of the economy and a weak labor movement, worker ownership is not a solution to labor's problems. It diverts workers' activity into projects which will either fall economically or be coopted by the system. Worse, they can be an additional source of disunity for the working class already hampered by sexual, racial and occupational divisions.

Needed: Grass-Roots Revitalization

At the heart of an alternative strategy to fight plant closings is the notion that the union's most effective weapon is the organized power of rank-and-file workers. In contrast to the AFL-CIO's emphasis on gaining influence with "labor's friends" in the political arena, what's needed is a grass-roots revitalization of the labor movement, from the union local up to the level of the international union and the AFL-CIO.

Effective resistance at the local level requires the union to have an active and informed membership which is prepared, in advance, to respond to the company's action. It's a sad commentary on the current state of the labor movement that the basics of democratic trade unionism—a strong shop steward system, elected and accountable leadership, education and training for members, a lively and relevant newsletter—have to be emphasized over and over again. But it's absolutely necessary to do so, for in the absence of an active membership, the union's response is bound to be half-hearted and ineffectual.

A democratic local will be better able to respond with an array of militant tactics which put economic and political pressure on the employer. Depending on the circumstances, the local can initiate work-to-

rule actions, demonstrations, sit-down strikes, or any number of other responses. In addition to its own militant activities, the local needs to solicit support from other local unions and from community organizations—to bring together the largest and most cohesive force opposed to lay-offs and plant shutdowns.

"Workers who gain ownership of a company tend . . . to identify less with workers employed by other companies than with the company they now own."

As a result of such militant tactics and the local's thorough research of the company's financial situation, the employer will be more likely to deal seriously with the union. If this can't keep the firm afloat, the local can demand that management eliminate waste and inefficiency in their own ranks before asking workers to make sacrifices. The union can also suggest ways of improving productivity which don't worsen working conditions or weaken work rules.

At a later stage, assuming that the corporate concessions approach hasn't solved the problem, the local can wage a campaign for government aid to keep the plant in operation or for conversion of the company's product line from, for example, obsolete military hardware to socially useful domestic products. Given the reluctance of government to subsidize businesses—unless substantial corporate interests are at stake—this approach requires the union to mobilize massive outside support to get the funds. United Electrical Workers (UE) Local 277, which represents workers at the Morse Cutting Tool plant in New Bedford, Massachusetts, asked the city to use its right of eminent domain to take over the plant after Gulf & Western threatened to shut it down. Municipal and regional ownership established through eminent domain has also been proposed by the Tri-State conference on Steel to salvage the steel industry in the Monongahela Valley. These new approaches need to be developed as part of an overall response to plant closings.

Local Focus Not Enough

Finally, if, despite all these efforts, the plant is still going to shut down, the local should get the maximum level of health, pension, severance, and retraining benefits.

While militant tactics and innovative proposals at the local level are crucial, the union's response cannot just be a local one. A union local fighting a conglomerate or a large corporation often lacks the resources to win against an adversary who can shift production to different locations or invest in other industries. An effective response to plant closings requires that all levels of the labor movement develop an alternative strategy.

Furthermore, union solidarity and coordination allow labor to gain greater collective control of the economy. The solution to plant closings and unemployment lies not in making individual plants profitable through wage cuts and employee buy-outs, but in changing the basic patterns of capital investment and economic power. When each level of the union movement—local, international union, federation—is part of an overall strategy, labor has the potential to exert some control over the general direction of the economy.

International unions have a key role to play in an alternative strategy. They can provide assistance to locals fighting plant closings, and they can help to create a contractual framework in which plant shutdowns, when they do occur, are less painful for workers. Such a strategy would include: pushing for industry-wide standards, industry-wide job security, public works projects for the unemployed, control of pensions funds and restrictions on capital investment; encouraging government aid for product conversions and to prevent plants from closing; and promoting international solidarity by resisting the attempts of multinational companies and governments to divide workers by nationality.

Even though some of these are not feasible today, innovative programs to deal with plant closings can become a part of labor's agenda. Labor activists have begun to propose specific ideas for limiting employer prerogatives as part of a broader strategy to empower rank-and-file workers. It is through these admittedly exceptional efforts, and not through employee ownership ventures which play into the concessions dynamic, that the labor movement can regain its strength and become a progressive, social force.

Mike Slott is a field organizer in the Philadelphia area for the United Electrical, Radio & Machine Workers of America.

Minimum Wage Laws Cause Teenage Unemployment

Raymond J. Donovan and Orrin G. Hatch

Editors note: The following viewpoint has two parts, both taken from congressional testimony. Part I is by Raymond J. Donovan; Part II is by Orrin G. Hatch.

I

I think we can all agree that youth unemployment is not a temporary or a recent problem resulting simply from cyclical fluctuations in our economy. Unemployment rates for 16- to 19-year-olds have increased steadily over the past 30 years from 12.6 percent in 1954 to 17.8 percent in 1980 and to 19 percent in May of [1984]. . . .

During this same period, unemployment rates among black teens have soared from 17 percent to 38 percent in 1980 and to about 44 percent in May [1984].

These dismal statistics for black teens are compounded by a significant deterioration in their ratio of employment to population, a decrease from 38 percent in 1954 to 24 percent in 1980 and to about 20 percent in May [1984]. . . .

The problem also exists with Hispanic youth. During the last 10 years, their employment as a percentage of population has declined by 5 percentage points to 32.5 percent in 1983.

Lost Opportunities

Clearly, these statistics are unacceptable. They signify opportunities lost to our youth, opportunities for obtaining early and valuable employment experience as well as income and the intangible benefits associated with work, such as enhanced pride, self-esteem, and self-discipline.

These statistics also prove, however, that we as a nation can do better. And of course, we must. We can do far better if we are willing to critically examine long-held biases, if we are able to fashion

Raymond J. Donovan, testimony presented June 18, 1984 before the Senate Committee on Labor and Human Resources.
Orrin G. Hatch, address delivered on the floor of the U.S. Senate on May 17, 1984.

initiatives which generate broad-based support, and if we are prepared to construct and try solutions which will increase the long-term skills and quality of our work force.

This Administration shares with the Congress and the people an enduring and deeply held commitment to successfully solving the youth unemployment problem, which often leads to adult structural unemployment. . . .

We realize that young people are the Nation's next generation of workers, and we know, too, that they need a wide variety of training and work experience. And we recognize that no single initiative is appropriate for all youth. That is why we are committed to maintaining a complementary package of effective youth employment and training programs.

Accordingly, this Administration supported targeting the basic-training funds available under Title II of the Job Training and Partnership Act to economically disadvantaged persons under the age of 22. This is why we continue to provide jobs for disadvantaged youth under the Summer Youth Employment Program and residential training under the Job Corps. It is why the President proposes to extend the authority for the targeted-jobs tax credit. In total, about $2 billion of JTPA's resources are targeted for youth.

New Approach Needed

Despite these and similar prior efforts, a new approach is needed. We have examined various proposed explanations and solutions, and we believe lowering the minimum wage barrier is crucial to increasing the number of meaningful work opportunities available for youth.

Consequently, this Administration is proposing an initiative that permits firms to create summer jobs at wages which make it worth hiring youth who lack experience. . . .

Young people need employment and work experience to secure adult employment. Youth programs exist, in part, because many teenagers lack the basic skills that are required to even earn the current minimum wage. There are some aspects of work that are learned best on the job and cannot be taught in a classroom or in a job training program. The private sector can and will provide valuable employment experience for more young people, especially those with fewer skills, if the artificial barrier of the minimum wage is lowered. . . .

Our proposal offers the potential for providing summertime employment experiences and training for youth on a large scale. Under our proposal, jobs would be created in the private sector. This would ensure the integrity of the work experience; that is, these would be real jobs, jobs with genuine work experience, work experience that will help youth later when they seek adult employment.

President's Proposal

The President's proposal applies to youth aged 19 and under, from May 1 through September 30. It would allow employers to hire such youth at $2.50 per hour, or about 75 percent of the current $3.35 per hour minimum wage. No special paperwork requirements would be imposed on employers beyond normal payroll recordkeeping, and no new Government bureaucracy would be needed to administer and market the program.

Some people argue that a youth employment opportunity wage would be used by employers to replace adults with youth. We believe these claims are unwarranted. Limiting the proposal to the summer months makes it unlikely that employers would discharge current workers and then rehire them later. Moreover, because the intent of the bill is to create new jobs, employers are prohibited from discharging, demoting, or transferring current employees and replacing them with youth hired at the opportunity wage.

We have also included a provision prohibiting reductions in pay below the basic $3.35 minimum wage for any youth age 19 or under who is employed at any time during the 90 days prior to May 1 each year.

The stringent Fair Labor Standards Act penalties of fines up to $10,000 and prison terms up to 6 months would also be applied to those who violate the law.

If the youth employment opportunity wage is enacted as proposed, we estimate that about 400,000 new summertime jobs would be created for teenagers. And if those States with minimum wage laws inconsistent with this bill were to undertake similar revisions to their codes, as many as 640,000 jobs could be provided.

We firmly believe these jobs that would be created do not exist, and would not exist otherwise. We appreciate that the youth employment opportunity

wage is an innovative and untried concept with possible important social consequences. But at the same time, it must be conceded that there is some uncertainty associated with the size of our employment estimates. The effect could be much greater than the 400,000 new jobs we estimate. It is simply not possible to be more precise at this time. . . .

I think the country is prepared to try this concept. I am confident of that because of the broad-based support the measure has received from interested and affected groups throughout this Nation. With forthright leadership we can come together in the interest of achieving larger shared objectives.

II

We currently have a youth unemployment rate of 19 percent and almost 50 percent for blacks. I find this situation reprehensible. It is time we recognized that the minimum wage is in large part responsible for diminishing youth employment opportunities. We should ask ourselves just how these young people are supposed to get the on-the-job training and experience they desire and which they need to be successful in life if we deny them the flexibility to negotiate a beginning wage with a potential employer. The minimum wage ties the hands of both the employer and the young job seeker. We have removed the bottom rungs from the ladder of employment by making it economically unfeasible for an employer to hire anyone without the skills, experience, or maturity to immediately earn the minimum wage in terms of productivity. How do young people get jobs without experience and how do they get experience without jobs?

"The private sector can and will provide valuable employment experience for more young people, especially those with fewer skills, if the artificial barrier of the minimum wage is lowered."

Economic evidence bears this out. Study after study has shown that increases in the minimum wage lead to decreases in teenage employment. It is obvious that the minimum wage is pricing young people out of the job market. Even with all other factors being equal, a teenager, simply by virtue of his or her age, cannot compete with the age advantage held by adults.

Effect on Adult Workers

It has been alleged that a youth opportunity wage would displace older, adult workers from employment. We can consider this argument only so long as we believe there are a finite number of jobs in America. For displacement to be a significant, negative ramification of a youth opportunity wage, the situation would have to exist whereby first, for every person who obtained employment, another person lost it, and second, a youth was a perfect substitute for an experienced adult worker. This argument reflects unsubstantiated pessimism as well as misunderstanding of the way our economy responds to incentives. Given the positive correlation between increases in the minimum wage and decreases in youth employment, there is no reason to believe that, if employers were given the incentive to hire and train young people they would not take advantage of the opportunity to improve their customer service or their production capability. . . .

"The minimum wage is pricing young people out of the job market."

As an enthusiastic supporter of the Job Training Partnership Act (JTPA), I recognize the efforts that are being made through that program to provide valuable training opportunities for our Nation's disadvantaged youth. I fully appreciate JTPA's potential and will continue to support that program wholeheartedly. However, we cannot rely on JTPA, or any other Federal initiative, to fully address the alarming problem of youth unemployment. The National Conference of Black Mayors, a national organization with a firsthand view of the tragedy of youth unemployment in our cities, has endorsed the experimental program proposed in this legislation. They endorsed it because they are unwilling to overlook a youth differential as a solution to a problem deeply felt by the young people in their cities. The National Conference of Black Mayors, one of America's oldest Hispanic organizations, the American G.I. Forum, the Opportunities Industrialization Centers, Inc., and the National Federation of Independent Business are the current members of a growing coalition of Americans in support of the youth employment opportunity wage. I am grateful for their efforts and support and will do all I can as chairman of the Labor and Human Resources Committee to work with them toward enactment of this legislation.

Greater Opportunities

It is disheartening to see young people become discouraged and cynical of our free enterprise system when they are unable to find jobs. It is disturbing to think that these teenagers may become the hard-core unemployed of the future unless we do something about it. We cannot afford to sacrifice the talents and ambition of our young people in this way. The youth employment opportunity wage will provide greater opportunities and incentives for employment and training as well as a chance for young people to start up the ladder to economic self-sufficiency and personal self-esteem.

Raymond J. Donovan was Secretary of Labor in the Reagan administration from 1981 to 1984. Orrin G. Hatch is a Republican Senator from Utah.

Minimum Wage Laws Do Not Cause Teenage Unemployment

Augustus F. Hawkins

The phenomenon of unemployed youth in today's labor force will carry forward to higher rates of adult unemployment. In order to secure the future of this great Nation, we must successfully solve the problem of youth unemployment.

Current statistical data indicate that this problem is, indeed, a serious one. During January [1984], for example, 1,479,000, or 20.5 percent of the teenage labor force was unemployed. In other words, approximately one out of every five teenagers who actively searched for employment was unsuccessful. For the black community, the problem is much worse, 47.9 percent, or approximately one out of every two teenagers who actively searched for employment was unable to find it. With respect to the overall teenage jobless rate, not only is it twice the rate of the total civilian labor force, but also, jobless teens accounted for over 17 percent of the unemployed. Undeniably, a serious, painful problem in employing young Americans does exist.

Steadily Increasing Jobless Rates

Youth unemployment cannot be dismissed as a result of normal cyclical fluctuations in our economy. By no means an ephemeral phenomenon, jobless rates for youth have been steadily increasing since the early 1950's. Overall youth unemployment has risen from 11 percent in 1954 to 20.5 percent in 1984. For the white teenage jobless, the rate has climbed from 13 percent to 16 percent during this period. For black teens, the unemployment rate has skyrocketed from 16 percent in 1954 to a dismal 47.9 percent 30 years later. Consequently, finding a solution to youth unemployment will be dependent largely on explaining why such a rapidly diverging gap between white and black youth unemployment occurred during the past three decades.

Augustus F. Hawkins, remarks to the U.S. House of Representatives on March 7, 1984.

In addition to the argument, refuted above, that the youth unemployment problem is a temporary one produced by cyclical fluctuations in our economy, there are four other widely held explanations or causes for the problem of youth unemployment. Two deal with the demand side of the economic argument: minimum wage coverage and a decrease in unskilled or low skill entry level jobs. The other two causes are supply related: an increase in the youth age population and inadequate skills, education, and motivation possessed by youth. While all of these factors may have some impact on the dimensions of the problem, only one can adequately explain the diverging unemployment rates of white and minority youths.

Baby Boomers' Impact

Much has been written about the baby boom cohort and its impact on the economy. The argument, simply stated, is that as the baby boom generation enters the job market, its large number creates an oversupply of labor and, as a result, higher unemployment. While this may partially explain the situation of the late 1960's and early 1970's when the baby boom cohort reached teen age, it does not explain the current continually rising rates of teenage joblessness. But most importantly, this interpretation does not explain why the black to white youth unemployment gap widened by 31 percentage points from 1954 to 1984.

A similar argument on the demand side suggests that a steady decline in the availability of unskilled or low skill entry level jobs can explain much of the youth unemployment. With the advent of self-service gas stations, for example, and more capital intensive manufacturing methods, youth are no longer able to find traditional low skill, entry level jobs. However, existing data suggests that as the traditional areas decline, other areas, most notably the service sector of our economy, are increasing. The fast food industry, to name one example, is a major employer of youth which continues to expand. Also, it is important to point out that youth were never employed in large numbers in those basic industries which are currently in decline. Thus, while the lack of jobs is a problem, it is not the sole explanation for the youth unemployment problem.

The more important aspect of the lack of jobs for youth is the fact that the employment opportunities that do exist are not readily accessible to a young person searching for work. These employment opportunities may exist outside the community in which many youth reside, and thus are impossible for them to reach. This factor is of particular significance to youth in low-income families, who are most likely not to have access to personal transportation.

Subminimum Wage Proposal

A third explanation of the youth unemployment problem is the use of federally imposed minimum wage standards. According to this view, rising minimum wage standards have made it unattractive to hire youth who possess no skills and, therefore, must be trained while on the job. Creating a subminimum wage, it is concluded, would entice employers to offer job opportunities and training to youth because of the perceived lower cost.

In "Youth Employment and Public Policy," Richard Freeman, noted Harvard economist, argues that the impact of any subminimum wage would be significantly less than its proponents suggest. According to Freeman, most studies have found that a 10 percent increase in minimum wage would likely reduce youth employment by 1 to 4 percentage points. While this does imply that a reduction in the minimum wage would modestly lower youth unemployment rates, it would also raise the level of youth labor market participation. Because the overall effect on youth unemployment would be greatly offset, Freeman concluded that recent increases in the minimum wage have probably increased the youth unemployment rate by no more than 3 percentage points. Given the steadily increasing rate of youth joblessness over the past three decades and the current 48 percent black youth unemployment rate, lowering the minimum wage would have an insignificant effect on youth joblessness.

Furthermore, there are several other problems with the subminimum wage proposal. First, the concept does not address the important factor of job availability. If a subminimum wage exists but there are no available jobs in the area, youth still will be unemployed. Second, there is no evidence to suggest that employers will provide training to improve the long-term employment prospects of youth. Two programs currently on the books, the Targeted Jobs Tax Credit, and section 14b of the Fair Labor Standards Act, which allows payment of lower than minimum wages for certain youth activities, have not been utilized extensively since their enactment. If employers have not used these mechanisms to offset the cost of employing unskilled youths, then why would a subminimum wage, which is premised on the same assumptions, be more effective? Finally, and most importantly, the entire concept of microeconomic incentives to hire youth does not explain the immense divergence in jobless rates between white and minority youth.

Inadequate Skills and Motivation

The fourth and most frequently cited explanation of youth unemployment, inadequate skills, education and motivation possessed by youths, is widely considered to be the key to the youth employment problem. In fact, it is the only explanation that begins to explain the 30-year divergence in jobless rates of white and minority youth. According to this view, high youth unemployment is a direct result of the unwillingness of employers to hire inadequately trained and educated youth who do not possess the proper level of motivation. Today's youth, it is asserted, do not possess the communicative or computational skills necessary to succeed in the workplace.

"The more important aspect of the lack of jobs for youth is the fact that the employment opportunities that do exist are not readily accessible to a young person searching for work."

A variety of sources support this contention. The National Commission on Excellence in Education found that 13 percent of all 17-year-olds are functionally illiterate. In another study conducted by the Department of Defense, 7.2 million young adults, or 28 percent of the young adult population, are reading below the eighth grade level. According to Ellwood and Wise in "Youth Employment in the Seventies: Changing Circumstances of Young Adults," once a youngster leaves school, the highest level of education reached is strongly associated with employment, regardless of sex or age. Notably, less than 20 percent of the 17-year-old black male dropouts work, and virtually none of the comparable females work. With dropout rates for all youth, and minorities in particular, increasing over the past few years, it is no wonder that youth employment rates are rising.

Not Ready for Work

The strongest evidence for this hypothesis, however, comes from the employers themselves. In a survey conducted by the Center for Public

Resources, employers cited the inadequacy of entry academic and work readiness skills as the primary problem of new workers. Companies indicated that they were spending millions of dollars for remedial training that should have been spent in high school. In another survey conducted in 1978 by the Vice President's Task Force on Youth Employment, one respondent lamented:

"Yes, I have vacancies, and sometimes I give a kid who looks mature a break. But frankly, I just can't take the risk. I can't find enough kids who can read or write. Preposterous as that sounds, it's true. . . . We can train people, but we can't teach them reading or writing."

This clear, undeniable link between success in school and success in the labor market holds the key to the youth unemployment problem facing our Nation today. . . .

Making Job Opportunities Accessible

While some existing programs provide training opportunities for youth, they are unable to address the youth employment problem in a comprehensive manner. The Job Training Partnership Act, for example, severely restricts use of funds for work experience, which is essential to developing the requisite skills necessary to succeed in the job market. Although the vocational education program does provide some work experience, it only affects in-school youth. Consequently, dropouts cannot benefit. Also, because all students are eligible, there is no guarantee that those who need the experience most will get it. Finally, neither program addresses the problem of the lack of jobs in specific areas. In destitute urban areas and depressed rural areas, jobs are scarcely available for adults, much less youth. Without accessible employment opportunities, work experience is impossible.

"With dropout rates for all youth, and minorities in particular, increasing over the past few years, it is no wonder that youth unemployment rates are rising."

I am confident that as the chosen leaders of contemporary America, we have not forgotten that in each and every young American resides the future of this great Nation. Without the benefit of experience as a responsible, productive member of our society during their youth, our future could be in serious peril.

California Democratic Representative Augustus F. Hawkins is a member of the House Committee on Education and Labor.

Women and the Economy: An Overview

Doris Byron Fuller

When a woman's work was defined as what she did in the kitchen, a woman's own money often was referred to as "pin money" because it was reserved for buying minor household items, like pins. Today, a woman's work is more likely to be done in an office or a factory than at home, and her labor and her money are anything but incidental.

"If women didn't work, the economy would grind to a halt," said Linda Waite, a sociologist and researcher for the Rand Corp. in Santa Monica. "Women are such a fundamental part of the labor force that, without them, the economy would not exist as we know it."

Working women now number 50.1 million and make up 44% of the work force. Since 1979, working women have outnumbered those who stay at home, and the percentage of adult women holding full-time jobs has continued to rise every year. Women now earn about $500 billion a year—nearly one-third of all the wages and self-employed income earned annually in this country.

Economists say working women have become an enormous factor in the growth of U.S. family income. In the last 10 years, average hourly wages for all workers declined 6% after adjustment for inflation. The addition of a wife's income has been one of the few ways a family could get ahead during that time. "They have been an incredible engine for national income growth," said economist Michael Wachter of the Wharton School of Business.

Improving Living Standards

With all that income has come an improvement in the standard of living for countless families, who are able to live in bigger and better homes, drive more luxurious automobiles, travel in style and otherwise enjoy greater material comfort because of the wife's

Doris Byron Fuller, "Working Women Reshaping Economy," *Los Angeles Times*, September 12, 1986. Copyright, 1984, Los Angeles Times. Reprinted by permission.

paycheck.

The paychecks of working wives make it possible for families who otherwise could not qualify for a loan to purchase homes. The National Assn. of Homebuilders says that the income of a working wife is essential to most home buyers; to buy the average new single-family home, which costs $101,000, a family needs an annual income of at least $54,321 to qualify for a 15% loan after a 10% down payment. In 1983, two-income families accounted for 57% of all home sales, up from 45% in 1976.

Single women, too, are becoming homeowners in record numbers; they bought nearly one out of every four new condominiums sold in the United States in 1983.

Moreover, women are making money in an ever-growing universe of pursuits. In 1972, women owned 468,000 companies with gross receipts of $23.5 billion, according to the U.S. Census Bureau. Just five years later (the last year for which there are official figures), the number had jumped to 631,000 firms with gross receipts at a time when the total number of private enterprises rose barely 10%.

Causing Changes in Business

Women who work have prompted changes in the hours that department stores keep and in the menus that fast-food restaurants offer. They have spawned whole new industries, such as for-profit child care, and have nourished the growth of others, such as the microwave oven business.

Even more profoundly, experts say, the influx of women into the work force during the last decade is modifying the U.S. economy in basic ways—making recessions and high unemployment rates more tolerable and transforming American society into a market economy where services of all kinds are bought rather than provided without charge by a family member.

"The economic impact of women is beyond belief," said Peter Francese, publisher of *American Demographics*, an Ithaca, N.Y.-based research magazine.

Economists and social scientists agree that there is a price to be paid for these gains, but they say that the toll must be measured in social terms, such as the effect on the divorce rate or the impact on leisure time.

"On the economic side, it's hard to say there's anything that's a disaster," said Lester C. Thurow, an economist and professor at the Massachusetts Institute of Technology.

If there are any economic losers, experts say, they are the families that do not have a second worker. Increasingly, the one-income family is being left behind in the economic sweepstakes—outdistanced at every level by two-worker households.

"What the data suggests is that the economic welfare of a family is increasingly dependent on whether the family can field two wage earners," said Wachter of the Wharton business school. "Any family, no matter how badly skilled, will do all right if they have two wage earners. As long as they can stay married, their income situation can remain pretty good."

"The time limitations of the working woman have made the fortunes of industries with convenience products and services."

The case of Kinder-Care Learning Centers, Inc. demonstrates the economic ripples that working women have generated.

In July, 1969—when private, profit-making child-care companies were virtually non-existent—businessman Perry Mendel opened a private day-care center in Montgomery, Ala., to meet the child care needs of Montgomery's growing population of working mothers.

Over the next 15 years, the company grew into the nation's largest private child-care provider, with more than 850 company-operated centers caring for 75,000 children 6 weeks through 12 years of age in 40 states and Canada.

In the process, Kinder-Care became the employer of 11,000 mostly female workers and grew into a company that in the first nine-months of its current fiscal year generated $123 million in revenues, paid $4 million in corporate income taxes, earned $13.6 million in after-tax profits and sent $1.2 million in dividends to approximately 35,000 shareholders.

Despite such examples, there persists a popular misconception that the working woman is an economic spoiler who takes jobs that otherwise would go to unemployed men. No less than President Reagan in an April, 1982, meeting with journalists from the Southeast said that the unemployment rate would not be so high if there were not so many women entering the job market.

"Part of the unemployment is not as much recession as it is the great increase in the people going into the job market and . . . because of the increase in women who are working today," the President told the editors and broadcasters.

However, although the jobless rate of women historically has been higher than that of men—thus boosting the overall rate, as the President said—economists and other experts almost universally dismiss the idea that women take jobs away from men. "There's just not a question of women displacing men," said Elizabeth Waldman, senior economist with the Bureau of Labor Statistics in Washington.

Men and Women Don't Compete

With a few exceptions, men and women simply do not compete for the same jobs, the experts say. Although women have made significant inroads into some non-traditional professions such as medicine and law and taking a more visible place on America's fire and police forces, their actual numbers in these fields are small.

More than half of working women remain concentrated in what labor leader Joyce Miller calls "female job ghettos," performing secretarial, bookkeeping, nursing, typing and teaching jobs. Men typically do not want those jobs, and women typically do not seek the blue-collar manufacturing jobs where men dominate.

Indeed, as Miller, vice president of the Amalgamated Clothing and Textile Workers and president of the Coalition of Labor Union Women, pointed out, "As wages go up, men are taking jobs traditionally held by women."

For example, at United Airlines, the nation's largest commerical airline, about 12% of the flight attendants today are men. In 1970, there were none. In the same period, annual wages for flight attendants at major U.S. airlines rose 40% after adjustment for inflation (compared to a decline for all workers) and 259% in nominal terms, according to the Air Transport Assn. in Washington.

In the male-dominated occupations in which women have made inroads, the gains have been miniscule. The percentage of women employed in construction work, for example, rose from 0.7% in 1970 to 0.9% in 1983. And, although 25% of medical school graduates were women, they still account for only 13% of practicing doctors.

Equally important, it is working women who have created countless new jobs. When a woman goes to work, she may hire someone—probably another women—to clean her house, do her laundry and care for her children. She needs more clothing, buys more meals away from home, maybe even purchases a new car—all of which generate jobs.

"A lot of 'women's work' is work that was once done unpaid in the home—teaching, nursing, interior decorating, the counseling of children," said Audrey Freedman, a labor economist for the Conference Board, a business research organization. In the 1980s, "we have to pay each other to take care of each other."

Economist June O'Neill said that this wholesale move by women into the job market ultimately is transforming the U.S. economy into a giant marketplace where people buy what once was provided in exchange for non-monetary compensation.

A New Market Economy

"Instead of a lot more being produced in the home, women work more and buy things," said O'Neill, director of policy research on women and families at the Urban Institute in Washington. Even something like child care is a commodity you purchase. We've become more of a market economy . . . . People purchase things in place of expending time. They buy the child a home computer instead of playing with him."

If anybody is being displaced by the trend, she says, it's the housewife, who finds herself surrounded by labor-saving devices that have made keeping house less than a full-time job and who constantly faces the allure of paying work outside the home. "The same thing happened in agriculture," O'Neill said. "The workers were lured to other jobs."

Whatever social ramifications the shift from home to workplace may have, it is good for the business where women are spending their new-found funds.

Data Resources, Inc. estimates that expenditures for women's apparel for the first five years of this decade will have grown an average of 5.48% a year compared with men's apparel. "Obviously, the reason is women's growing income and needs," said Melinda Skaar, an economist and consumer affairs expert at the Lexington, Mass., research firm.

The time limitations of the working woman have made the fortunes of industries with convenience products and services: Shipments of fast-cooking microwave ovens zoomed from just over 1 million in 1975 to an estimated 6.8 million this year; fast-food restaurant sales tripled from $13.6 billion to an estimated $41.2 billion and sales for the rest of the restaurant business roughly doubled; mail-order catalogue sales doubled between 1975 and 1983 and are growing at 15% a year, twice as fast as over-the-counter sales.

"The growth in the restaurant industry owes its entire existence to working women," said Francese

of *American Demographics*. "The percentage of meals eaten away from home has risen tremendously. It's the time element. When people work long hours, there really isn't time or inclination to cook. Microwave ovens were around for decades, and they basically went nowhere . . . until vast numbers of women went to work. Mail order clearly is doing a gangbuster business because people don't have time to shop anymore."

Working Woman Is the Norm

Beyond boosting the sales of selected industries, manufacturers and marketing experts say, the buying power of the female work population now permeates the thinking of manufacturers and marketers who promote everything from beer to briefcases.

"The working woman is a phenomenon you don't treat as an exception but as a norm," said Steven Regur, vice president of marketing for J.W. Robinson's, the department store chain. Regur said that Robinson's has changed the way it staffs its stores largely because of the working woman. Training has been intensified, staffing has been increased in the evening and on weekends when busy women are likely to shop and management staffing in those hours is not voluntary, as it once was, but mandatory.

"The working wife's paycheck does moderate the impact of recessions on the American family."

"Most everything we do is oriented toward (the working woman)," he said.

Restaurant industry executives say that the movement toward light food and salad bars in fast-food restaurants can be traced to the female customer, for whom nutrition seems to be a major concern. Home builders say that the trend toward smaller, low-maintenance homes is partly a reflection of the growing number of two-worker families and of women buyers. Sarah Worman, Robinson's vice president of fashion merchandising, sees the busy woman behind the popularity of labels.

"The working woman, because she doesn't have time to try on 75 things, tends to stay with one label that fits her life style, her pocketbook, her figure," Worman said.

Dudley McIlhenny, regional manager of strategy services at Kurt Salmon Associates Inc., an Atlanta-based management consulting firm, said that the working woman's need to save time has led to the proliferation of factory outlet malls and the trend toward clustering stores. The working woman, he said, has dictated the hours that stores operate and the personnel they hire to staff them when she's shopping.

Although all this buying power may not be enough to keep America's factories running at full capacity during downturns such as the 1981-82 recession, economists say that the working wife's paycheck does moderate the impact of recessions on the American family by providing economic insulation when unemployment hits.

Janet L. Norwood, the commissioner of labor statistics, noted in a recent speech that, when unemployment hit its peak of 11 million-plus at the end of 1982, two out of three unemployed persons lived in a family with another working member."

"Working women act as a cushion," said Waldman of the Bureau of Labor Statistics. "They act as a major factor in family well-being. We know that, on the average, women contribute a fourth of family income. Women who work year-round, full-time, contribute 40% of family income. That's quite a contribution—nothing to sneeze at—despite the fact that women are earning less than men."

Doris Byron Fuller is a Los Angeles Times *staff writer. This article was part of a series on working women written for the* Times.

"The sexual division of labor has been a permanent feature of society because it expresses innate psychological differences between the sexes."

viewpoint **73**

The Male/Female Wage Gap Is Biological

Michael Levin

We live in an age which tends to treat the most innocent phenomenon as a "problem" to be "solved" by "public policy," which means the intrusive machinery of the state. So it has proven with the "wage gap" separating men and women—it is touted by feminists as one more proof of the oppressiveness of Western society and the inequitability of the free market.

The factual basis of the feminist case is that the income of the average full-time working female is approximately 59% of that of the average full-time working male. Indeed, the gap has actually widened slightly over the last 30 years despite the passage in 1963 of the Equal Pay Act, which mandates equal pay for men and women doing the same jobs. (The failure of the Equal Pay Act to collapse the wage gap is taken by feminists to show, not that discrimination is not and never was primarily responsible for the wage gap, but that discrimination is even more insidious and subtle than they thought.)

Of course, once this is stipulated to be a "problem," the range of "solutions" becomes limited to measures for making the average wages of full-time working men and women numerically equal. What is more, a number of sub-problems arise which invite their own sub-solutions. The clear tendency for jobs to segregate by sex, for example, must be met by attempts to "integrate" women into "non-traditional" jobs. Feminists see this as critical because, they claim, the percentage of women in an occupation correlates negatively with the wages that occupation pays. This claim, which in effect has the market penalizing women for being women, is based on statistical studies of jobs which agree with respect to some fixed set of variables controlling job characteristics and "human capital," but differ with

respect to the proportion of women performing them—a technique which obviously ignores the possibility of unidentified variables which affect wages and correlate with sex.

However the "wage gap" is construed, it becomes a "problem," an occasion for action, only given some antecedent presumption favoring numerical equality. And, indeed, the view that numerical equality is somehow the "natural" state, with deviations therefrom requiring special justification, is very common. Its proponents characteristically describe any such deviation as "inequitable," "a failure of parity," or the like.

Working Women Are Not Equivalent

Yet even in these terms it would seem that there is far less to the wage gap than meets the eye fixed on slogans, for the average full-time working woman is not the economic equivalent of the average full-time working man. She works on average 35.7 hours a week, for example, while he works on average 44 hours/week. There are marked differences in job tenure—a reasonable proxy for experience. In 1978 the average male had spent 4.5 years with his current employer, the average female 2.6 years. June O'Neill has, in fact, assembled variables which correlate differentially with males and females, and which explain 90% of the wage gap. Since the wage gap is not a case of equals getting unequal returns, it is absurd to describe it as an inequity: it is explainable on reasonable economic grounds not involving invidious discrimination.

Most economists I have consulted agree that the difference between male and female labor force participation is due largely (not entirely) to the fact that women see themselves as more responsible for household chores than men, for much of the male/female difference disappears when men are compared to single women. In 1971, for example, the wage ratio for strictly single Canadian women to

Michael Levin, *Equal Pay for Unequal Work*, published by Eagle Forum Education and Legal Defense Fund, Washington, DC: 1984. Reprinted with permission.

Canadian men in the age cohort of 30 and up was 99.2%. Women, most especially married women, are less willing to put out the energy needed to work their way up the career ladder, and tend to see their income as supplementing that of their husband, the breadwinner. As a side effect, women seem more prepared to gravitate toward jobs, such as those in the clerical area, which permit repeated entry and exit without exacting a great economic toll.

Indeed, it is simply a mistake to say that women are thereby crowded into occupations lacking prestige (and thereby suffer the economic consequences of holding unprestigious jobs), since on average female sex-typed jobs are slightly more prestigious than male sex-typed jobs. Men may go after the most prestigious jobs, but they also settle for the least prestigious, while most "female" jobs, like typist or manicurist, have middling prestige. The consequences of the different expectations men and women bring to marriage and their relation to careers are virtually limitless.

> "Since the woman making 59 cents may be married to the man making $1, she will gain nothing if some government exertion raises her income at the expense of his."

To take a final example, the oft-cited average difference in salary between male and female college instructors can be explained by assuming (a) that the husband's career preferences are determinative in a two-instructor household, and (b) that, since female instructors like females generally tend to marry up, a greater proportion of female instructors marry male instructors than vice-versa. Female instructors must thus compromise their career ambitions more often in deference to their mates than must male instructors.

Mothers Sustain Society

To say that women sacrifice market earnings to household activities is of course not to say that female energy devoted to the family is less valuable than energy spent earning wages. The manifold activities of mothers sustain society, yet these activities cannot register as high-priced market commodities because they lack exchange value. The price attached to anything, labor included, is the measure of its capacity to secure other goods and services in barter. From an econometric point of view, mother love has the disadvantage of being fixed on a small number of unique objects, and therefore is not exchangeable. I would pay a young mother handsomely if for five mornings a week she would transfer her love of her own infant to my

children. Unfortunately, she does not regard children as fungible, so the routine services she is willing and able to provide for others are worth perhaps $5/hr to a stranger like me. Mother love falls outside the GNP not because society undervalues it—only feminists undervalue mother love—but because mother love cannot figure in exchange.

If the wage gap is a product of preference, how can it be construed as discriminatory? True, when women gravitate to secretarial work they depress its wage, in the sense that secretarial wages would rise if there were fewer female secretaries and males did not take up the slack—but this is only to observe that supply and demand is at work in this situation as elsewhere. So long as nobody forces women to be secretaries, so long as what brings women to the "pink collar ghetto" are their own life choices and skills (such as the greater female knack for repetitive tasks), just where is the inequity?

Brainwashed Women

I would let these rhetorical questions rest except that the feminists take them so seriously and even supply what they think is a compelling answer. Feminists occasionally speculate about actual conspiracies to "herd" women into pink-collar jobs and "keep women's wages down," but the preferred feminist explanation of the wage gap is a straightforward application of the general feminist indictment of society: sex-role conditioning has handicapped women by pursuading them that their main task in life is not wage labor but childrearing, and that the best jobs are not "for them" even should they decide to work. Thus brainwashed, women of course subordinate career aspirations to family, tend to leave work when their children are young, and so on. Unmarried women, for their part, are conditioned to see the office as a hunting ground for husbands.

In short, according to feminists, the choices women make merely perpetuate the evil of "sexism." Even an observer as shrewd as June O'Neill writes: "One could also classify as discrimination the pervasive cultural factors that have led to different roles for men and women and that shape the extent to which women are able to devote themselves to a career outside the home." In the words of Nancy Barrett,

"Economic gender roles in the traditional family work against economic parity in several ways. First, of course, they perpetuate gender-based stereotypes and stereotypical self-images. . . .Second, women's household responsibilities compete for time and energy with labor force activities; while for men, household (financial support) responsibilities are complementary to labor force activities. . . . The relative positions of men and women in the labor force are not the outcomes of supply and demand in the conventional sense. Rather, they are the outcomes of a complicated set of traditional expectations that have to be analyzed in a model in which gender confers a set of distinct property rights on certain activities.

Both citations—drawn, incidentally, from writers who so far as I know do *not* unambiguously endorse characteristic feminist policy demands—deploy the two central feminist assumptions: (a) that economic gender roles are the result of *socially induced* expectations, and (b) that action based upon such "stereotyping" is discriminatory. I will consider these assumptions presently, but I would note now that "second-stage" feminists—*arrivistes* who claim to acknowledge gender differences without abandoning feminism—tend to agree with standard feminists that present economic gender roles are discriminatory, even while admitting that these roles reflect biologically programmed preferences.

Women's Hormones a Handicap

Thus Betty Friedan speaks of the female's lower testosterone level as a "handicap" and, in *The Second Stage*, elaborates plans for communal living so that women will be able to pursue careers more easily despite their need to raise children. Benjamin Barber, a self-styled third-stager, insists that the great challenge posed by innate sex differences is that of finding ways "to preserve (or create) political and economic equality in the face of different sex roles." Those few progressives who have faced the evidence for innate sex differences still do not want to let these differences run their course. They do not like the social order which results from behavior motivated by innate impulses. Neofeminists see these impulses as no more than the occasion for tinkering, generally by the state.

Yet even before turning to the origin and justification of the sexual division of labor, it is worth stressing the senselessness of virtually all talk of the economic disparity of men and women, and of all comparisons between women and blacks or other isolable social groups. Despite the feminist representation of men and women as hostile camps in a war for the world's goods, the simple fact is that *men and women marry*. The battle of the sexes is distinguished chiefly by the degree of collaboration.

That the world's men and women share a common fate puts that 59¢ figure in a quite new light; since the woman making 59¢ may be married to the man making $1, she will gain nothing if some government exertion raises her income at the expense of his. Their joint income will remain the same at best and probably fall, since state intervention exacts a cost from everybody.

Gender Quotas Harm Husbands

Note, too, that job quotas conceived as compensation for discrimination allegedly suffered by women are absurd for the same reason. Even if contemporary statistical gender disparities are the legacy of past discrimination, you cannot make up

for that discrimination to today's generation of women by giving a woman of today a job over a man of today, for that simultaneously worsens the situation of another of today's women, namely the man's wife. Gender quotas harm virtually as many women as they help—more, if one includes daughters of men passed over for jobs—and thus leaves the average position of the world's contemporary women unchanged and very probably lower. This elementary point tends to be overlooked as a result of feminism's quite successful propaganda campaign to portray the sexes as competitors. This absurd model applies only to career women who do not intend to marry and see not only men, but also married women and children, as competing for resources and opportunities she desires.

But the main trouble with the feminists' diagnosis of the economic division of labor is its disregard of biology. The sexual division of labor has been a permanent feature of society because it expresses innate psychological differences between the sexes. It is sometimes suggested that the home/work division of labor, and even the "nuclear family," were created by the Industrial Revolution, but this suggestion is misleading at best. In every society of which there is any record, men and women have paired off (sometimes polygamously, to be sure) to rear children in a family unit. Granted, fewer people live with their grandparents and aunts and uncles in industrialized urban settings than in pastoral, rural settings—which may seem like an indictment of urban society until one remembers that a staple of literature of two centuries ago was the young man who wanted nothing more than to escape the confinement of his "extended family" and make his way by himself in the big city.

> *"Any such cultural universal as the sexual division of labor suggests a non-social, biological cause."*

Moreover, in every society of which there is any record, men have carved a distinctive niche for male activities. If women have gathered berries, then men have hunted. Women in every culture have been the ones responsible for childcare and allied domestic tasks, while men have pursued extrafamiliar activities. Wage labor may be a recent invention, but not his division of responsibilities. What was introduced by the Industrial Revolution, and more particularly the railroad and later the automobile, was commuting. Never before had men daily travelled tens of miles away from their homes to do productive work. Never before had the locus of productive work been so disconnected from the home. Yet whether or not commuting has changed the psychosocial character of work, it has not changed the basic sexual division of social tasks.

Any such cultural universal as the sexual division of labor suggests a non-social, biological cause, and indeed it is as certain as anything in science can be that men and women do differ in the abilities and, more importantly, the motivations they bring to paid labor and everything else. Neurologists are now reasonably sure that females are born with a greater capacity for fine motor coordination and tolerance for repetitive tasks. These innate capacities translate in adulthood into measurable differences in skills highly prized by a highly "technical" society. According to a . . . study commissioned by the Department of Defense, men score considerably better than women in mechanical ability.

But much more important than any innate difference in abilities is the difference in competitiveness which men and women bring to the labor market. Men are more competitive than women, which is to say more apt to do whatever is needed to get ahead, whatever "getting ahead" happens to be under the circumstances. This disposition, called "dominance aggression" by physiologist John Money, is perhaps the determinative factor in economic sexual differentiation. Men, more willing to put out the energy required to dominate in extrafamiliar pursuits—success in the world of work is such a pursuit—tend to go further in such pursuits. Not all men are prepared to make such efforts, but most of those so prepared are men, which is why most of those who excel in the hierarchical, competitive, rationalized world of the free market are men. For better or worse, money is a symbolic measure of others' estimate of one's worth to them, so that the impulse to compete and dominate will manifest itself as an impulse to seek activities for which remuneration is highest.

What is more, the mesh of this difference in competitiveness with the Law of the Margin magnifies the difference between male and female performance in the market. The Law of the Margin, most simply put, is that small differences can make a big difference. If one salesman is 5% more highly motivated than another—which is to say that he spends 5% longer at the office and makes 5% more telephone calls—he is likely to outdo his rival by far more than 5%. That extra 5% may be spent closing deals that his rival leaves open. After all, a mousetrap only 5% better than its competition will monopolize the mousetrap market.

Women Are Nurturers

It would be a gross error to suppose that women are simply less competitive than men but like men in every other motivational respect. Women have their own nurturant and cooperative drives which deflect energy away from the sort of competition favored by the economic marketplace. Greater female concern with nurturing one's young has an obvious adaptive advantage, since a woman can reproduce only a few dozen times at most to a man's thousands. Liberated female mammals, as heedless of their offspring as male mammals tend to be and as feminists would like human females to be, went extinct a long time ago. The care of young children puts a premium on patience and above all empathy—and, given the helplessness of human children for the first few years of their life, a complete absorption in the child to the exclusion of extrafamilial pursuits. Once again, there will be women who do not experience these impulses, but they will remain in the minority and the basic institutions of human society will continue to coalesce around the impulses felt by the majority of women.

"The wage gap does not mean a denial of 'equal opportunity' in any reasonable sense that can be attached to that much abused slogan."

It may seem a long step from these general motivational differences between the sexes to the particulars of "sex role stereotyping." There may be a gene for nurturance, not for washing the dishes. In fact, however, "sex roles" as we know them are just consequences of underlying general sex differences, given unavoidable environmental contingencies. As Steven Goldberg has noted, there is a feedback loop between biologically given sex differences and the social roles they create. People, particularly parents, notice that on the whole boys and girls act differently. This perception is frozen in the more categorical maxim "boys do one sort of thing, girls another," which maxim then informs parental expectations about boys and girls.

Since boys and girls are expected to act differently, they are socialized to act differently, and when this socialization *takes*—socialization which emphasizes the differences in gender behavior—the original maxim is confirmed, and is deployed in another round of socialization. In this way, biological sex differences are magnified. It will not do to call this process "oppressive," since people are simply exercising their perfect right to form generalizations on the basis of experience, and if the object of the feminist exercise is to prevent the formation of "stereotypes," it will once again involve massive interference with the socialization of children by parents.

Role differentiation is, in any case, a rational solution to the problems of day-to-day life that most couples adopt spontaneously. Since the mother is taking care of the children at home while the father is at work, it stands to reason—to the reason of the people actually involved, if not to the reason of feminists—that Mom be responsible for keeping the home clean and preparing the meals. Somebody must do these things, after all. As children do not dematerialize after a year or two on Earth to let Mom "return to her career and fulfill herself," this modus vivendi crystallizes over time. I would add that, in my view, it is not out of the question that some innate female nest-building drive plays a role in the development of the sexual division of labor as well.

"I am skeptical about 'solutions' to the wage gap problem because I do not see it as a problem at all."

In saying that the wage gap—if not the precise figure of 59%—is justified because it arises out of the free choices of individuals following biologically-given impulses, it is crucial that we be clear about the kind of justification this is. I am not arguing that people ought to follow their biological impulses. In themselves, biological impulses are not good or bad; they are simply there. Nor am I arguing that the sexual division of labor works better than any other. I have no idea whether this is so, although it would be amazing if nature were so inefficient as to make each sex best at what the other sex prefers to do. Nor, finally, am I arguing that men deserve economic preeminence because they want it. Wanting something creates no title to it at all.

Rather, I see the sexual division of labor and its broad statistical contours justified not by its intrinsic character, but precisely because it is the result of uncoerced, free human choice. Left to their own devices, responding to the contingencies of the environment and the unalterable constraints of the human condition, which tend to be exchangeable in a ratio of roughly 6:10. In other societies the ratio might be different. There is nothing intrinsically admirable about this figure. It is perfectly all right, not a "problem," because it came about in a perfectly proper way.

Women Have Equal Opportunity

The wage gap does not mean a denial of "equal opportunity" in any reasonable sense that can be attached to that much abused slogan. Women certainly have opportunities equal to those of men in the sense that there are *no laws preventing* women from undertaking any activity available to men. Women certainly have opportunities equal to those of men in the sense that even private discrimination against women is now expressly forbidden by

Federal law. The average woman may not have the training of some hypothetical male counterpart, but training and like advantages are *means* that one uses to exploit an opportunity, not opportunity itself. Equality of opportunity must never be confused with equality of means. Few of us have the financial means to purchase a ticket for the Concorde, yet we all have the opportunity to do so.

Nor will it do to say that women have less opportunity than men in light of their family responsibilities. A woman who sacrifices a career for her children has *chosen* one of many paths that she might take, in much the way that a man who gives up a career in sports to join the military has chosen to forgo one path open to him. In neither case has any external force foreclosed any choices.

Finally, it borders on the idiotic to say that women lack equal opportunity because they are less interested than men in pursuing careers. Only feminists are so uncomfortable with feminine impulses as to regard these impulses as alien impositions on women. I have spoken to feminist-mothers (generally in the academic world) who do profess that "society made me have children" to the detriment of their careers, and demand some sort of social recompense for their sacrifice, quite forgetting that having a child is a joint decision with one's husband. (Possibly these women were talked into having children against their will, but most women are not that extraordinarily weak-minded.)

This strange view that children are something that happens to women out of the blue (at society's behest) usually prefaces a demand that "society" let women climb the career ladder just like men while also having children. This is not a demand for equal opportunity at all but a demand to be protected from the consequences of one's choices, in this case the effects on one's wage-earning power of devoting a crucial portion of one's life to children. This is a request for special privileges. A man who takes a few years off to follow his guru to the Himalayas does not and cannot expect society to guarantee him academic tenure upon his return.

The Road Not Taken

The incessant feminist message that a career is as vital (perhaps more vital) to mental health as a family has created a generation of women ever regretting the road not taken. This message has made women who spend full time with their children think they have cheated themselves. This message has burdened women who sacrifice children for work with deeply unsatisfied biological drives. No matter which way they turn, these women feel cheated and discontented.

So, I am skeptical about "solutions" to the wage gap problem because I do not see it as a problem at all. Of course, if private parties perceive wage-gap and career problems for women, I am all for these parties attempting private solutions. More power to the firm that wants to provide a day-care center for its female employees, and—as some firms actually do—require its male executives to put in a stint at such facilities. More power to the firm which disregards the messages from the marketplace and adjusts its salaries to the "social value" of the work done by female employees. Let them try such schemes and bear the consequences when their efficiency-minded competitors fail to follow suit. If the female employees retained by provision of day-care are really so much more valuable than male employees available without comparable expenditures, the market will have declared day-care an appropriate "solution" to childbirth. But if firms can do better in retaining men costlessly, day-care is not a market "solution."

Michael Levin is a professor of philosophy at the City College of New York. His articles have appeared in Newsweek, Commentary, Fortune, *and the* Washington Post.

"Whatever women do, from seed gathering to skilled crafts, is valued less than those same tasks are when performed by men."

The Male/Female Wage Gap Is Societal

Sharon Toffey Shepela and Ann T. Viviano

We believe there is a significant psychological component to the relationship between occupational segregation and wage differentials. The hypothesis we offer is the following: Women are paid less because they are in women's jobs, and women's jobs are paid less because they are done by women. The reason is that women's work—in fact, virtually anything done by women—is characterized as less valuable. In addition, the characteristics attributed to women are those our society values less. In the workplace, the reward (wage) is based on the characteristics the worker is perceived as bringing to the task as well as on the "pure" value of the task to the employer. The lower the value of those characteristics, the lower the associated wage.

The situation is cyclical and interwoven because the factors themselves may not be independent. It may be that "female" characteristics are valued less precisely because they are considered female. The same may be said of the lower value placed on female activities. There are considerable anthropological and sociological data to indicate that the value of an activity or characteristic can be lowered simply through its association with women. Margaret Mead has said that in all cultures, without any known exception, male activity is seen as achievement. Whatever women do, from seed gathering to skilled crafts, is valued less than those same tasks are when performed by men in a different culture: "When men cook, cooking is viewed as an important activity; when women cook it is just a household chore. And correspondingly, if an activity once performed by women becomes more important in a society, it may be taken over by men. For example, midwifery, once a profession in which the female practitioners were both constricted and

feared, has been taken over by male obstetricians," [writes J. Williams in *Psychology of Women's Selected Readings*, 1979.]

A Sequence of Arguments

The following is the sequence of arguments that has lead us to our hypothesis.

1. People view the sexes differently from birth on.
2. Part of that different view involves differential evaluation of characteristics and work, with male work and characteristics more highly valued.
3. The different view includes differential attributions regarding the reasons for success and failure for women and men.
4. Studies on rewards allocation in a stimulated business setting show that differential rewards are based more on attributions than on gender, although the two are separated only with some difficulty.
5. The attributions that are more highly rewarded are those associated with males.
6. Gender-based occupational segregation may be related in part to these perceived attributes.
7. Therefore, if a job is perceived as a woman's job, associated with female attributes, it will be paid less, and if a woman is doing a neutral or male-dominated job, she will be seen as bringing to that job her female attributes, and the tendency will be to want to pay her less for the same job.

Seeing What We Expect to See

That the sexes are viewed differently from birth has been well documented. [J.Z.] Rubin, [F.J.] Provenzano, and [Z.] Luria demonstrated parents' differential perception of female and male first-borns. They asked thirty pairs of parents (parents of fifteen girls and fifteen boys) to describe their infants before leaving the hospital, using an adjective checklist. The parents of the girls rated their infants as significantly smaller, finer-featured, softer, and

From Sharon Toffey Shepela and Ann T. Viviano, "Some Psychological Factors Affecting Job Segregation and Wages." In *Comparable Worth and Wage Discrimination*, edited by Helen Remick. © 1984 by Temple University. Reprinted by permission of Temple University Press.

less attentive than did the parents of the boys, despite the fact that there were no significant differences in length, weight, or physical condition between the babies at birth. The fathers' sex-typed ratings of both sons and daughters were more extreme than the mothers', although both mothers and fathers agreed on the direction of the difference. We see what we expect to see.

In another experiment, women who were themselves mothers were asked to interact with the same six-month-old child, who was identified to half of them as a male and to the rest of them as a female. The "girl" child was offered different toys than was the "boy" child, and the women described the child as typical of the sex they thought it to be. . . .

[John] Condry and [Sandra] Condry videotaped an eighteen-month-old child and showed the same tape to adults. The same behavior was interpreted as "angry" if the adult subjects thought the child was a boy and "afraid" if they thought the child was a girl.

While adults' perception of children is influenced by the gender of the child, there appear to be few consistent gender-dependent patterns in parents' actual interaction with children, except that parents provide gender-typed toys and discourage children, especially boys, from engaging in activities they believe appropriate only for the opposite sex.

"In a recent organizational analysis . . . women managers who perceive themselves to be equal to their male cohorts in a large, integrated organization were shown to have significantly less power."

The schools take up the message. Studies of textbooks show extremes of stereotyping. In a context analysis of 2,760 stories in 134 elementary school readers, [an organization named] Women on Words and Images discovered that males were shown in 147 different occupations and females in 26. The study found only three working mothers. Girls were found rehearsing their domestic roles 166 times to boys' 50. Passivity, docility, and dependence were attributed to girls six times as often as to boys: Tommy builds a playhouse; Sally stands and admires it. The positively valued characteristics of courage, exploration, and imagination were overwhelmingly attributed to males (216 to 68 instances), while industry, problem solving, courage, and strength were attributed selectively to males with similar ratios. As the grade level increased from first to sixth grade, the difference increased. Not only were the girls perceived differently, but girls and women tended to disappear altogether from textbooks and this was especially true for science and math books. In the original 1972 study of 134 textbooks, the ratio of male-centered to female-centered stories was five to two; in 1975 it was seven to two. [Another study] found that the representation of women in illustrations in science textbooks dropped from 36 percent in the second grade to 18 percent in the sixth grade. One second-grade science series had no adult women in 99 of 100 pictures. [Further study] summarizing over a dozen studies on this topic, reports that the findings are remarkably similar. While some positive changes have been made, and both male and female characters are more human, considerable stereotyping is still evident in textbooks. Whereas Mark once commented about Janet: "Look at her. She is just like a girl, she gives up," Pedro now makes the same comment about Nina, and our children learn that bias knows no cultural bounds.

In addition to presenting children with stereotypical images, the schools view and treat girls and boys differently. [One study] found that nursery school teachers' differential responses to good and bad behavior by girls and boys actually resulted in more misbehavior by the boys. [Another] found similar differences in teachers' perceptions of and reactions to boys and girls.

[I. Broverman, S. Vogel, D. Broverman, F. Clarkson, and P. Rosenkrantz,] in a now classic study on sex role stereotypes, found widespread agreement across age, sex, educational level, and marital status on the reality and desirability of different characteristics for women and men.

Evaluating the Sexes Differently

"Different" does not necessarily imply "better" or "worse"; yet perhaps one of the most consistent findings in the research on sex differences is that males and females are evaluated differently. Both men and women tend to value men and male attributes more highly than women and female attributes. There is research indicating that male products are rated more highly than female products, even when the quality of the actual product is constant. . . . An identical piece of work— article, abstract, even art object—is attributed to John T. McKay with one group of subjects and to Joan T. McKay with another. Each group is asked to evaluate the work on a number of dimensions. The standard, replicable result is that any work by a man is evaluated more favorably than the identical work by a woman. This prediction fails only when the woman's work has been independently highly rated, as when it has won an award.

In a work setting, the performance and credentials of women are rated less favorably than those of an equivalent man. In [one] study, 184 female and 184 male college students read a completed job application and an article written by a "person recently hired as a newswriter for a local paper." Subjects were told that the study concerned the prediction of job success and were asked to answer eight evaluative questions regarding the competence of the applicant and the merits of the article. The manipulated factors were the sex and the marital and parental status of the applicant. On all eight questions females were significantly devalued by both male and female subjects, but particularly by males. Male applicants were rated as more professionally competent and dedicated to the journalistic profession, had a higher professional status, and greater job success was predicted for them. The article, when ostensibly written by a male, was more highly valued by the reader, was more influential in changing subjects' opinions, was judged better written, and got a higher overall grade. Each subject rated only one applicant, so these data do not result from a conscious comparison of men and women job applicants, although they do represent a strong bias against women. [The study] suggest[s] that the differences in the salaries of women and men may be due in part to these differences in perceived competence, and that this effect may be exacerbated by the fact that the vast majority of managers and administrators in the United States work force are male, the sex that in this study showed the greatest tendency to devalue women.

The pervasiveness of this sex bias appears even in situations in which equality between sexes in a work environment seems to have been realized. In a recent organizational analysis of several large eastern corporations, women managers who perceive themselves to be equal to their male cohorts in a large, integrated organization were shown to have significantly less power (defined in terms of budget and personnel responsibilities), even when their salaries were equivalent.

Giving Credit Where Credit Isn't Due

Attributional bias is yet another manifestation of the phenomenon that men and women are viewed differently. The differential perceptions of males and females persist even when success and failure are to be explained. That is, the reasons offered for the success and failure of a male are different from the reasons offered for the success and failure of a female.

The research of [G.] Pheterson, Sara B. Kiesler, and Phillip A. Goldberg demonstrated that specific information regarding the quality of performance eliminates sex-linked biases in the evaluation of that performance. This research has generated additional questions about whether observers attribute identical causes to identical performances. According to [Kay] Deaux and [T.] Emsweller, they do not. In their study, males' performance was more likely to be attributed to ability, whereas females' performance was more likely to be attributed to luck. This difference in attribution of cause was particularly evident when the task performed was masculine in nature. Subsequent research in this area showed that male success, which is expected, is attributed to ability, a stable explanation, whereas female success, which is unexpected, is attributed to the unstable explanation of luck.

"Women, because they are women, are less likely to be hired or promoted and more likely to receive lower starting salaries."

[Kay] Deaux suggests that the choice of these attributions reflects the stereotypical assumption that men are more competent and women incompetent. That is, competence or success is explained differently in men and women because it is expected in men but unexpected in women. When failure is to be explained, the findings continue to show the same pattern. In [further] research, failure by a man was attributed to unstable, external causes such as bad luck, whereas the failure of a woman was attributed to stable, internal causes such as lack of ability. According to [another study], we attribute performance to stable factors when we expected that performance and expect it to recur in the future and to unstable factors when it was unexpected and we do not expect it to recur. Therefore, the consistent attribution of women's success to luck reflects the unexpectedness of that success to the evaluators and their anticipation that it will not recur.

Results of recent research has shed further light on these findings. [H.] Garland and [T.] Price gave male subjects descriptions of a successful or unsuccessful female manager and asked them to rate each of four possible causes for the success or failure: two internal variables (ability and effort, or the lack of them) and two external variables (luck and the easiness or difficulty of the job). Effort received the highest rating for explaining success and lack of effort received the highest rating for explaining failure.

[G.] Stevens and [A.] DeNisi replicated the Garland and Price study and included both male and female subjects. In their study, men attributed a woman's success to the internal but unstable factor of effort, whereas women attributed it to either the internal stable factor of ability or the internal unstable factor of effort. Men attributed women's failures to either lack of ability, which is internal and stable *or* task difficulty, which is external and unstable; women attributed failure primarily to the internal, stable factor of lack of ability. Men's attributions are thus similar to those found by Garland and Price. However, an interesting difference emerged: women added the possibility that women succeed because of a stable factor, and men added the possibility that women fail because of an unstable factor.

The trend of all the results reported above is that people explain the success and failure of men and women differently. Men's success is internal and stable; it was expected, and it will occur again. Women's success is external and unstable; it was unexpected, and it will not recur.

The Consequences of Societal Sexism

[G.] Rose and [T.] Stone suggest that widely shared sex role stereotypes may result in performance decisions based on unwarranted performance inferences. Hence, employees, despite good performance records, risk being discriminated against and having their careers disrupted when organizational rewards are distributed.

Indeed, several studies have shown that identical performances by males and females result in different rewards. In an early study of the consequence of sex role stereotypes, [researchers] asked ninety-five male bank managers to assume the role of a personnel manager and to make four decisions. The results were as follows: a male applicant was recommended for promotion to branch manager significantly more often than a female; the male applicant received significantly higher ratings for both customer and employee relations; and, when an employee was chosen to attend a conference, a highly promotable female was preferred only slightly more than an employee with less potential, whereas a highly promotable male was strongly preferred over an employee with less potential.

"Women earn less money than men because women are culturally devalued and their work is devalued as a result."

A later study asked subjects to take the role of a consultant to a clothing manufacturer who had to fill four executive positions. Female applicants were selected significantly less often; males received significantly higher ratings for technical potential, potential for long service to the organization, and potential for fitting in; and females were rejected for the most demanding job significantly more often than the males. . . . The pattern that this research has identified is, as Rose and Stone suggest, that organizational rewards are distributed inequitably on the basis of gender alone.

[James R.] Terborg and [Daniel R.] Ilgen, in an attempt to understand this phenomenon more thoroughly, examined the effects of sex role stereotypes on two types of discrimination: access and treatment. Access discrimination refers to pre-job-related limitations and rejection based on these reasons: for example, discrimination involving the decision to hire and starting salary. Treatment discrimination refers to invalid differential treatment once a person has been hired—discrimination in, for example, employee development, employee evaluation, delegation of assignments, and promotion.

In their study, personnel administration undergraduates were asked to complete an in-basket exercise that included rating the resumes of three applicants for an engineer's job. They were asked which, if any, of the applicants were unacceptable, to set a starting salary, and to evaluate the applicants' past performance. The results indicated that the woman's performance was seen as due to luck more than was the man's. Furthermore, perhaps as a result of this differential evaluation, the female applicant was assigned a significantly lower starting salary and second-year salary than the identical male applicant. Analysis of the treatment variables reveals that the likelihood of being sent to training programs correlates with how lucky a woman is viewed to be, rather than her ability or effort, whereas both task assignment and size of bonus correlate with how much ability a man is seen to possess. The authors suggest that a less ostentatious form of discrimination occurs when the applicant is rated as acceptable but, because of sex or minority group status is offered a lower starting salary.

Some research has focused on the sex context of the situation, which includes the sex of both the evaluatee and his or her subordinates. Rose and Stone asked business students to make career decisions about four managers. Male managers managing females received significantly higher salaries than male managers managing males, but female managers' salaries did not depend on their subordinates' sex. In addition, male managers were expected to remain with the organization longer than female ones.

The pattern that these studies reveal is that women, because they are women, are less likely to be hired or promoted and more likely to receive lower starting salaries. Thus, the devaluation of women and their products discussed above has been shown to have practical consequences in terms of hiring, salaries, and promotion.

Expecting Less from Women

Some recent research has illustrated that it is not gender per se that causes these differential perceptions, attributions, and rewards, but rather expectations about men and women and responses to the traits, behaviors and characteristics associated with them. A study that provides evidence supporting this view was conducted by [Madeline E.] Heilman and [Lois R.] Souivatari. They suggest that physical attractiveness exaggerates perceptions of gender-related attributes, thus enhancing sex bias in reward. In their study, attractiveness in a male always led to higher evaluations and stronger recommendations to hire than unattractiveness. But attractiveness benefited females only when they were applying for nonmanagerial jobs. Unattractive female applicants for managerial jobs received higher evaluations of their qualifications and stronger recommendations to hire than attractive applicants. The authors conclude that the more attractive a woman is, the less suitable she will be judged for a job that is thought to require male characteristics. That is, since a female is already seen as possessing fewer managerial traits, the more attractive she is, the greater the incongruity between her gender and the job.

[Madeline E.] Heilman and [R.A.] Guzzo suggest that it is the causal attributions made about the success of men and women that result in discriminatory behavior. In their study, male and female MBA students were given "supervisors'" evaluations of subordinates. These evaluations were varied along the luck/ability continuum for both males and females. The subjects were asked to make salary and promotion decisions about four employees, all identified as either male or female. Their results indicate that success attributed to ability or effort received higher pay in both males and females than success attributed to luck. In addition, promotions were more strongly favored for able employees than for those exhibiting either effort or luck. Since ability is typically attributed to males, it appears likely that they will receive higher rewards than females, whose performance, though comparable, is attributed to luck when its cause is left to inference.

Ability Unexpected in Females

Probably the most interesting finding of this study was that females were preferred significantly more often for promotion than were males when ability as the cause of performance was held constant. Perhaps ability is so unexpected in females that it is highly rewarded when found. This interpretation is partly supported by Heilman and Guzzo's further finding that subjects were more likely to attribute characteristics typically considered requisite for high-quality management to employees whose success derived from ability. Since a vast body of research has indicated that these managerial traits are identical to traits attributed to men, ability in a woman is considered highly unusual.

A recent study confirmed the results obtained by Heilman and Guzzo. Subjects awarded a significantly greater proportion of a reward to themselves when the experimenter attributed their performance to

effort rather than to luck.

[R.R.] Mai-Dalton [S. Feldman-Summers, and T.R. Mitchell] compared the effects on perceived effectiveness and likelihood of promotion of behavior consistent or inconsistent with female stereotypes. They gave male and female banking executives of equal rank a scenario describing a male and female manager dealing with an incident in an emotional (angry) or unemotional (calm) manner. Calm and unemotional behavior was rated significantly more effective and appropriate. Furthermore, the calm manager was seen as significantly more likely to be promoted, regardless of gender, than the angry manager. As in the Heilman and Guzzo study, the behavior expected of women received poorer responses than the behavior expected of men, and women who behaved as the men did received the same reward.

"Women earn less money than men because women are culturally devalued and their work is devalued as a result."

That we do still expect men and women to act differently was confirmed by [Anne] Locksley [Eugene Borgida, Nancy Brekke, and Christine Hepburn], who found that a target's behavior (assertive or passive), and not his or her gender, determined whether he or she was viewed as masculine or feminine. Furthermore, in the absence of any other information, significantly more assertiveness was attributed to males than females, and subjects believed that a significantly greater proportion of males than females were assertive. Finally, they found that prior beliefs about the proportion of assertive males and females correlated with judgments of the probable assertiveness of subjects when no behavioral information about assertiveness was given.

The studies reported in this section indicate that we still have expectations of men and women that are consistent with traditional stereotypes and that the behavior consistent with the female stereotype receives lower rewards than that consistent with the male stereotype, regardless of the gender of the person exhibiting the behavior.

Summary: The Wage Gap

We have proposed that women earn less money than men because women are culturally devalued and their work is devalued as a result. Some of the alternative arguments are that women lack certain key credentials, such as tenure; they have interrupted their careers; they have different qualifications; and they tend to work part-time. If these variables were truly the explanation for lower pay, then we would predict that women who had the same tenure, had not interrupted their careers, had worked full-time, and so on should make the same money as a comparable man. However, studies show this not to be the case, and even when individual women *do* make the same money as a comparable man, their power and control are not the same.

Our review has clearly indicated that women earn less because they are in women's jobs, because the attributions made about women in general are extended to what they do on their jobs, and, finally, because anything associated with women is worth less in our society than things associated with men.

What are the implications of this research for policy decisions regarding compensation systems? We have shown that there are deeply ingrained, pervasive psychological biases that affect decisions made about the competence and work of women. Women's work is everywhere devalued. The subtle forces that we hypothesize to be in part responsible for continued gender-based wage discrimination will be difficult to eradicate, but their effects have been well documented. Those trying to develop equitable compensation systems must assume that bias will be in operation and control its effects as best they can.

Sharon Toffey Shepela is professor of psychology, director of research at the Counseling Center, and director of the Women's Research Institute at Hartford College. Ann T. Viviano is a supervising psychologist and administrator at Shield Institute in New York. She is currently president of the academic division of the New York State Psychological Association.

"Women are not being victimized in the labour market by the discriminatory practices of employers."

viewpoint 75

Discrimination Does Not Cause the Wage Gap Between Men and Women

Walter Block

Editor's Note: The author is addressing the Economic Council of Canada and so refers specifically to Canada in several places. The viewpoint, however, remains a universal one.

There are many Canadians who now support equal pay legislation. As one indication of the popularity of this idea, the three major political parties in this nation seem to have adopted for themselves several of the major planks of this program.

But there are problems. If legislation incorporating EPFEW [Equal Pay for Equal Work] and EPFWOEV [Equal Pay for Work of Equal Value] is enacted, the present (mainly) marketplace determination of wages will inevitably tend to be replaced by the arbitrary edicts of civil servants, bureaucrats, consultants, judges and/or human rights boards. In contrast, one of the important functions of wages in the market system is to allocate labour to its most needed and productive locations. If this process is short-circuited by EPFEW and EPFWOEV legislation, then labour mobility to that extent will be reduced. But it is important that workers locate themselves in accord with changing consumer demands. Unless they can be induced to act in this manner by market signals in the form of wage changes, the flexibility of the economy will be diminished. As well, equal pay enactments function so as to "protect males' jobs from low-wage female competition."

Things would be bad enough if EPFEW and EPFWOEV were required to right wrongs now existing in the labour market. Then, we would have to face a trade off between the injustice of discriminatory behavior imposed on women by employers, and the risks of economic inefficiency. But a drawback of equal pay legislation is that women are not being victimized in the labour market by the discriminatory practices of employers. Thus, such legislation will not be effective in its main objective: it is a cure for which there is no disease.

According to the most recent statistics available, the ratio of female to male earnings in Canada is .64. At first glance, this might appear *prima facie* evidence of the existence of employer discrimination against women. But, while superficially plausible, such an explanation is highly untenable. In order to see this, let us assume that male and female productivity in the marketplace is exactly equal. If so, successful discriminatory employer behaviour would entail that women, not men, were being paid less than their marginal productivity levels. Should this state of affairs ever occur in the first place, it would be very unstable. For large profit opportunities could be gained by those willing to employ women. Sex-neutral entrepreneurs could drive to the wall those who insist upon indulging in their "male chauvinistic" tastes for discrimination. And in the process of "exploiting" the poorly paid women (by hiring them, and bidding up their wages), these profit oriented businessmen would act so as to equate male and female incomes.

The Gap: A Statistical Artifact

But the facts are clear. Women do earn far less than men. If this is not due to employer discrimination, how then can we account for it? There are several alternative explanations. The first and most basic is that the supposed male/female income gap is really nothing more than a statistical artifact. Consider married women first. One problem is that a "family's income is recorded in the official statistics under the husband's name," alone. But most marriages, at least in their economic aspects, are like a business partnership. The husband may earn all or most of the income in a superficial legalistic or accounting sense, but it is due, in great

Walter Block, speech made at the Economic Council of Canada's Coloquium on the Economic Status of Women in the Labour Market, November 26, 1985.

part, to her efforts that his salary is as high as it is. It is therefore highly misleading to credit the husband with all or most of his "own" income. It would be much more nearly accurate to divide the total family earnings by two, and credit each marriage partner with a full-half share.

Suppose there were two attorneys in a partnership who agreed to split the proceeds of the firm equally. A, the "outside" partner, deals with clients, conducts the trials, and brings in new business. B, the "inside" partner, looks up the precedents, does the research, and manages the office. To credit A with all or most of the profits, a ludicrous supposition, makes exactly as much sense as assuming, as does Statistics Canada, that the typical Canadian husband really earns all or most of his "own" income.

In point of fact, husband and wife act in many ways to enhance the registered income of the former, and reduce the registered income of the latter. This is done in order to maximize family earnings, given other family desires, such as raising children. Examples of such behavior are legion. While this may be changing slowly, at present the married couple will typically choose a geographical location to enhance his earnings, despite what it does to hers. As well, there is almost always an unequal division of child care and house work. There are differing labour force participation rates, education and training, and advanced degrees. One indication of the strong asymmetrical effects of marriage on registered earnings (increasing the male, reducing the female) is that the female-male earnings ratio for those who have never been married is a startling .992.

Women's Choices

A third explanation for the female-male wage gap is occupational choice: women tend to enter lower paying occupations than men. Here, human capital obsolescence—due to time off for child rearing—will not occur to as great a degree, and will not penalize part time work as stiffly. Occupational choices toward low income careers ("pink collar ghettos"), are also made by non married women. Partially, this may reflect anticipated married status in the future. According to some analysts, this choice may be due to women's lower self esteem, or self image, or fear of success. In their view, young girls are socialized into believing that they are inferior to boys, and that they must at all costs avoid competing with males. If true, this phenomenon could account for lowered expectations and ambitions. On this basis, wives might reject raises or promotions, and avoid entering higher paying occupations in the first place, for fear of making themselves unattractive to their husbands, present or future. To the degree that such behavior occurs, it is a personal tragedy to the women involved, psychologically, socially, and personally, in terms of the human potential destroyed. But the

explanation for this must be complex and deep seated; it can hardly be blamed on employer discrimination in the labour market.

There is a reason the phenomenon of unequal wages between males and females seems to be in need of explanation. It is because of a basic assumption that absent discrimination, male and female earnings would be equal. And underlying this is the view that men and women have equal productivity in the labour market. (With unequal economic productivity, unequal wages would not be in need of any explanation.) But this is more of a pious hope than it is a conclusion based on evidence. That it should be taken as an article of faith that male and female productivities must always and ever be equal has more to do with political ideology than with the realm of economic reality.

"The supposed male/female income gap is really nothing more than a statistical artifact."

So deeply entrenched is this view that it even spills over into methodology. In much economic and empirical work, any male-female income differential which cannot be accounted for on the basis of variables such as age, education, labour force participation, etc., is *assumed* to be the result of employer discrimination. Discrimination, that is, is seen to be a "residual"; if gender differentials cannot be explained any other way, they are accounted for on an *a priori* basis by discrimination.

But there are grave problems with such a view. First, "it would seem evident that the failure to explain the wage gap by a given set of variables is consistent with the operation of undiscovered variables having nothing to do with discrimination." Secondly, the "human capital" variables employed in most regression analyses of this type are only highly imperfect approximations of what really accounts for productivity. Years of schooling, for example, admits of great differences in quality. Their correlation with productivity is far less than exact. Third, this imparts a bias toward that which can be quantified, as an explanation of the gender pay gap. Ruled out of court as unquantifiable are such things as ambition, perseverance, motivation, pride in being a breadwinner, reliability, competitiveness, attitude toward risk, and, dare we suggest it, possible innate biological sex-linked differences.

Let us now return to EPFEW and EPFWOEV. We have already seen that one drawback of such enactments, as with all legislation interfering with the market process, is the tendency to retard the ability of the economic system to allocate labour to its (continually changing) most optimal employments. In the case of EPFWOEV, third party "experts" will be called upon to determine whether mainly male occupations, such as truck driver, are "really" of equal value to jobs held mostly by females, such as secretary. A spurious scientific objectivity will be imparted by numerically rating such aspects of these callings as training, responsibility, working conditions, education, etc., and then adding them together to derive a total point score. Say what you will about such a scheme, at least it has one undoubted advantage; it will serve as a full employment measure for lawyers; for the values assigned to each dimension can only be arbitrary. The procedure will thus open society up to a spate of contentious lawsuits, as the various newly-created pressure groups endlessly strive for more favourable ratings.

The point is, there is no such thing as an intrinsic or objective "worth" of a job. (Nor of goods and services such as paper clips, music lessons, etc.) On the market, crucial in the evaluation of employment slots is the subjective rank ordering of the consumers—the willingness of people to pay for things. The job of whip-maker, horse-trainer or carriage-wright might have required tremendous investments in skill, and great responsibility. But with the invention of the horseless carriage, and fickle consumer preferences, all this goes for naught. Were there such, the expert job evaluators at the turn of the century might have given these tasks high point totals. But on the market, that is, in reality, these jobs were suddenly rendered obsolete and valueless.

"Any male-female income differential which cannot be accounted for on the basis of variables such as age, education, labour force participation, etc., is assumed to be the result of employer discrimination."

Presently, the jobs of dentists, dental hygienists, teeth x-ray technicians, all require much intelligence, years of intensive training, great diagnostic skills and a high level of professionalism. Were the evaluators unleashed upon these jobs to work their magic, there is no doubt at all that a high point total would ensue. But if and when a cure for tooth decay is found, these skills will go the way of the dodo bird, as far as value is concerned. Consumers will no longer be willing to purchase their services, and the returns to human capital invested in these lines will fall precipitously.

Let us consider one more example. Suppose that female prison guards do exactly the same quality and kind of work as done by male prison guards. We assume, in other words, that male and female prison guards do "equal work." But let us suppose that for some reason women are far more reluctant to enter this profession than are men. Under such conditions, in the marketplace, female prison guards will receive higher salaries than their male colleagues. This, according to the logic of the EPFEW philosophy, is obviously "unfair."

What can be done? If the female wage rate is lowered to that of the male, there will not be a great enough supply of women prison guards to satisfy the demand. If the male wage rate is increased to match that of the female, there will be an over supply of male prison guards. If the wage rate of both is set at some intermediate point, there will be an excess supply of men prison guards and a shortage of women prison guards. If the expert evaluators take into account this phenomenon too in their evaluations of male and female prison guard jobs (as well as all other unquantifiable factors which determine wage rates), they will escape the quandry of creating either a shortage and/or surplus of prison guards, but two anomalies will obtain. First, the results will be incompatible with equal pay notions of fairness. If the unequal reluctance of males and females to enter this profession is considered by the evaluators, they still will have to award more points to the female guards. Since by stipulation they do the "same work," this would be "unfair." Secondly, and more basically, if the evaluators take into account *all* phenomena that determine wages in the economy, of what possible use can they be? At best, they will no more than replicate the pattern of wages established on the marketplace. More likely, they will only imperfectly succeed in achieving this goal. After all, entrepreneurs succeed or fail in business to a great degree based on how closely they can tailor wage rates to productivity level. The compensation of the "experts," in contrast, will depend more on how well they satisfy their political constituencies. If there is, at best, only imperfect success in duplicating the market pattern of wages, this process will misallocate labour throughout the economy.

The implications for future research are clear. More attention should be paid to marital status as an explanation of female-male income differentials. Statistics should be published in a manner that more easily facilitates such research. Attempts should be made at an independent definition and measurement of discrimination. The residual method—especially in the facts of non-employer discrimination—should be rejected. In comparing private and public sector discrimination, wage variances, not wage rates, should be considered.

Walter Block is a senior economist at The Fraser Institute.

Discrimination Causes the Wage Gap Between Men and Women

Paula England

Between 1950 and 1980 the proportion of women in the paid labor force rose dramatically, from 28 percent to 51 percent. In the 1950s the increase came mostly from women over thirty-five returning to jobs when their children were older. The 1960s and 1970s brought unabated increases for women of all ages, but especially for married women with children. By 1980, 45 percent of married women with children under six and 41 percent of those with children under three were in the labor force. Yet most women still work in female-dominated jobs. Associated with this segregation has been a nearly constant sex gap in wages. Women who work full time all year earn about 60 percent of what is earned by men who work full time. . . .

Female occupations average lower earnings than male occupations at every educational level and stage of the life cycle. Female occupations offer women neither higher starting wages nor less wage depreciation than male occupations. So women pay a price in lifetime earnings for choosing female occupations. To the extent that the supply-side choices of women explain segregation, sex role norms must motivate these choices, since women have no pecuniary motive to choose female occupations.

Employers' "Tastes"

Why would employers engage in discrimination in allocating men and women to jobs? The major theories of discrimination emphasize tastes, error, or statistical generalization as inducing discrimination. The sex-role socialization discussed not only affects job choices on the supply side, it also produces employers with discriminatory attitudes. Employers may simply deem it inappropriate to place women in traditionally male-dominated jobs. Economists think

of these norms as "tastes" that people indulge for nonpecuniary reward. Thus Gary Becker, in *The Economics of Discrimination*, coined the term "taste discrimination" to refer to preferences for not hiring members of some group. He pointed out that since tastes provide nonpecuniary satisfaction, employers are willing to pay some price to indulge them. "Error discrimination" occurs when employers do not have discriminatory tastes, but they erroneously underestimate the potential productivities of women in men's jobs and therefore hesitate to hire women in these jobs.

A more subtle notion is the concept of statistical sex discrimination. This occurs when hiring decisions are based on differences between male and female averages on predictors of productivity. For example, if employers correctly observe that women have less mechanical knowledge than men, on average, they may hesitate to hire women in positions requiring mechanical knowledge, screening out even women who are atypical for their sex in having extensive mechanical knowledge. Or, if women have slightly higher turnover rates than men, employers will hesitate to hire women in jobs in which they will provide expensive training, screening out even those women who would have stayed for decades. Since men and women have overlapping distributions on virtually all characteristics, using sex-group means to estimate applicants' productivities results in mistaken predictions for individuals above or below the mean for their sex. Statistical discrimination comes about because employers have limited information about employees' productivity when they hire them, and getting more information (for example, through testing, a trial period, or by contacting references for each applicant) is costly. For example, how is an employer to predict how long an applicant will stay with the firm, or how successful a managerial style he or she has? Because of this uncertainty and the

Paula England, "The Sex Gap in Work and Wages," *Society*, July/August 1985. Published by permission of Transaction, Inc., from SOCIETY, Vol. 22, No. 5, copyright © 1985 by Transaction, Inc.

cost of information, basing predictions on averages for easily recognizable groups (defined by race, sex, age, or education) may save more in screening costs than is lost by the nonoptimal work force that results. Actually, all hiring decisions rely on group averages of some sort, even those decisions we do not usually label "discrimination." For example, requiring a high school diploma may be based on the observation that workers who dropped out of high school are less disciplined on average. The use of group averages makes us call the process "statistical," but when the proximate cause of a personnel decision is an ascriptive characteristic that one has no way of changing, like race or sex, we call the process "discrimination."

> *"Women who work full time all year earn about 60 percent of what is earned by men who work full time."*

It is virtually impossible to estimate how much of the segregation of men and women into different jobs result from employers' discrimination and how much results from the differential socialization and, hence, occupational choices of men and women. The reason it is so difficult to estimate the magnitudes of these two factors is that we seldom have data sets containing information on the qualifications of applicants and employees, their preferences for job placements and promotions, and the resultant occupational distributions.

Surveying Managers

Given these limitations in available data, how can we tell what role discrimination has played in the allocation of men and women to jobs? One approach has been to survey managers for their opinions on the appropriateness of men and women in various jobs. Such studies often unearth discriminatory attitudes and actions. For example, Milton Hakel and Marvin Dunnette, for *Checklists Describing Job Applicants*, asked managers who interview job applicants to rank a number of applicant characteristics on a scale from unfavorable to favorable. The average manager saw female gender as favorable for clerical applicants but saw male gender as favorable for managers, management trainees, and engineers. Summers et al., in *Industrial Invasion of Nonmetropolitan America*, report on interviews with managers who decided a priori which gender to hire for production jobs in new factories in nonmetropolitan areas on the basis of which sex they predicted to be more productive at the job. Richard Levinson, in an article in *Social Problems* in 1975, documented discrimination by having people make bogus phone calls in response to

job advertisements. He found that 28 percent of the females inquiring about traditionally male jobs and 44 percent of the males asking about typically female jobs received responses stating that persons of their sex would not like or be good at the job.

An interesting research project on discrimination was begun in 1972 at the School of Business Administration at the University of North Carolina. Benson Rosen and T.H. Jerdee conducted a national survey of 884 male managers and administrators across 66 establishments. Participants anonymously completed a questionnaire that asked for a comparison of men and women on numerous traits relevant for managerial effectiveness. For each trait, participants could choose from a five-point scale with "men much more than women" on one end and "women much more than men" on the other end. Averaging across all those who answered, men were evaluated more highly on understanding the "big picture" of the organization, approaching problems rationally, getting people to work together, understanding financial matters, sizing up situations accurately, administrative capability, leadership potential, setting long-range goals and working toward them, wanting to get ahead, standing up under fire, keeping cool in emergencies, independence and self-sufficiency, and aggressiveness. Characteristics attributed to women more than men included clerical aptitude, being good at detail work, enjoyment of routine tasks, crying easily, sensitivity to criticism, timidity, jealousy, excessive emotionality regarding their jobs, absenteeism, likelihood of quitting, and putting family matters ahead of their job. . . .

Discrimination Persists

This research suggests discrimination on the basis of tastes, error, or statistical generalization. What is striking about the research by Rosen and Jerdee is that it was all done after 1972—when the women's movement was in full swing and fully eight years after sex discrimination in employment became illegal. This evidence does not refute the notion that discrimination has declined in the last decade, but it does suggest that substantial discrimination persists.

Given this evidence of discrimination, what arguments are offered by those who think very little sex discrimination in hiring, placement, or promotion persists in the economy? Some economists base such arguments on a theoretical notion that discrimination should erode in competitive markets without government intervention. This is their reasoning: Employers who will not hire women in certain jobs force women who want these jobs to offer their labor to other employers at a lower wage. The employers who will hire women in "men's jobs"—those who have no discriminatory taste or erroneous estimates of women's average productivity or those who find a better predictor of productivity than sex-group averages—reap the benefits of the discriminators' acts in lowered labor costs. Since nondiscriminators will have a cost advantage, many economists predict that discrimination will eventually lose market shares or go out of business.

Making Discrimination Disappear

I agree that market forces erode discrimination, but I think discrimination often brings countervailing forces into existence, so that discrimination may not disappear without intervention. Economists have failed to recognize feedback effects between household and labor markets that create discrimination anew before it has a chance to erode completely, creating a vicious circle. The direction of causation runs both ways between labor-market discrimination and household behavior. Consider discrimination at some hypothetical starting point. How will such discrimination affect behavior in the household? If women are discriminated against, fewer females will aspire to train for male jobs (knowing that they are unlikely to get them), more couples will specialize with the wife doing household work and the husband doing paid work, more educational and geographical investments will be made in male careers, and traditional socialization will seem more rational to parents. These developments will reinforce stereotypical notions about women, tastes for discrimination, and will allow correct statistical calculations suggesting that fewer women than men are suited for male-dominated jobs. New discrimination may be created before market forces have had time to erode the discrimination that existed at the starting point. These feedback effects operate at cross-purposes with market mechanisms that erode discrimination. Given the empirical evidence of managers' discriminatory attitudes and behavior, and the theoretical argument regarding feedback from discrimination, I conclude that discrimination has been an important, though declining, force in occupational segregation. . . .

Women in Lower Paying Jobs

A large part of the male/female earnings gap among full-time, year-round workers results because of the concentration of women in lower paying jobs, not because men and women in the same job are paid different amounts. When male and female earnings are compared within occupational categories, the income difference is much smaller than that in the labor force at large. Men and women in the same occupation are often segregated by firm. It is clear that the finer the job classification, the smaller the differential between men's and women's incomes within jobs. At the same time, the finer the classification, the more segregation is revealed and thus the greater earnings difference between the sexes is a consequence of

between-job differences. To the extent that segregation "explains" the sex gap in pay in that women are segregated into lower paying jobs, all the explanations of segregation I discuss are explanations of the sex gap in pay as well. These factors of sex-role socialization; discrimination in hiring, placement, and promotions . . . have their effects on the sex gap in pay via their effects on segregation. There are two other factors that affect the sex gap in pay more directly—human capital and the type of wage discrimination at issue in comparable worth.

"Segregation in jobs among adults provides the data for children to learn how roles should be, and this is said to explain job segregation when the children become adults."

Since men and women in the labor force have completed the same average number of years of schooling, there are no sex differences in this aspect of human capital to explain the sex gap in earnings. Employment experience and firm seniority are the kinds of human capital that are related to the sex gap in pay. Early work by Polachek and Mincer argued that about half of the gap could be explained by differences in the amount of time men and women had been employed versus their working at home as homemakers. Steven H. Sandell and David Shapiro, in the *Journal of Human Resources* in 1978, disputed some earlier procedures and estimated that sex differences in years of experience explained only about a quarter of the gap in pay. Research using data with a fuller age range and a more complete list of measures of human capital and labor force attachment finds less than half of the gap explained. In the same journal, in 1979, Mary Corcoran and Greg Duncan decompose sex differences in wage into portions attributable to sex differences in years out of the labor force since completing school, years of work experience before present employer, years with current employer (broken into those years involving training and those not involving training), the proportion of working years that were full-time, absences from work due to illness of self or others, limits placed on job hours or location, and plans to stop work for nontraining reasons. All these variables, plus education, explained 44 percent of the earnings differences between white men and white women and 32 percent of the earnings differences between white men and black women. For both black and white women, the factor explaining most of the sex gap in pay was years with current employer, especially the years during which the employer provides training. To the extent that employers discriminate in not providing as much training to women as men, some of the pay gap explained by this factor may reflect demand-side discrimination rather than supply-side choices.

I have argued that sex differences in human capital (job experience) explain up to 44 percent of the sex gap in earnings among whites, and much of the sex gap in earnings is explained by segregation. We might infer from this that human capital differences explain the segregation of women into lower paying jobs which, in turn, explains the sex gap in earnings. This is not the case. Instead, human capital differences and segregation are independent components of the sex gap in earnings. Women who have more experience earn more than other women, but they are just as apt to be in female occupations. Concomitantly, women in male occupations earn more than women in female occupations, but they have no more experience, on average.

Comparable Worth Doctrine

Discrimination in hiring, placement, and promotion are demand-side phenomena affecting segregation. There is a second type of discrimination operating on the demand side of labor markets. It is the type of discrimination identified by the doctrine of comparable worth. The first type of discrimination involves taking sex into account in hiring or assigning people to positions. The second type, the wage discrimination at issue in comparable worth, involves taking the sex of a job's typical incumbent into account in setting wage levels. . . .

"Female occupations average lower earnings than male occupations at every educational level and stage of the life cycle."

Some economists reject the existence of comparable worth discrimination by invoking crowding in female occupations, rather than pay discrimination, to explain the low wages of female-dominated jobs. Barbara Bergmann's crowding thesis holds that the low wages in women's jobs result from the exclusion of women from men's jobs. It is irrelevant to the main contention of the thesis whether the exclusion of women from some jobs results from hiring discrimination or premarket sex-role socialization. The consequence is an inflation in the supply curve. In contrast, if employers discriminatorily take the sex composition of jobs into account when they set wages, they are shifting the demand curve for labor in female jobs inward. I agree that crowding will lower wages, but I see little evidence that women's occupations, such as clerical work, are more crowded than men's jobs. Sex

segregation does not necessarily imply that women's jobs are more crowded than men's. The fact that women are concentrated into fewer job categories than men is not necessarily indicative of greater crowding since occupational categories differ greatly in size.

The main evidence against the contention that women's jobs are more crowded than men's comes from evidence that women's jobs have had unusually large increases in labor demand in this century. The service industries and many sex-typed jobs such as secretary, nurse, and waitress have grown tremendously since World War II. If we accept the thesis that economies tend to grow in agricultural, manufacturing, and service sectors, in that order, then recent growth in service jobs that were female dominated even before this surge of growth must be viewed as a change in labor demand rather than an escalation of crowding. Given this, we have little reason to believe that a net coefficient on jobs' sex composition in an earnings function will reflect crowding in females' jobs rather than the sort of wage discrimination at issue in comparable worth.

Conclusion

Occupational sex segregation and the sex gap in pay have multiple causes. Segregation persists because of sex-role socialization affecting job choices; discrimination in hiring, placement, and promotion; and structured mobility ladders that perpetuate much of the segregation that occurs in entry-level jobs. Since the jobs in which women are concentrated have lower pay than male jobs, these factors explaining segregation have indirect effects on the sex gap in pay. The sex gap in pay is also affected by the fact that women have less job experience than men. Finally, the sex gap in pay results in part because employers pay lower wages in female-dominated jobs than in male-dominated jobs requiring comparable amounts of skill and experience. This last factor is the type of pay discrimination at issue in the debate over comparable worth.

Paula England is associate professor of sociology at the University of Texas, Dallas. She has been an expert witness concerning discrimination litigation and is the author of several articles on occupational segregation and comparable worth.

Comparable Worth Would Mean Economic Disaster

Clarence M. Pendleton Jr.

Editor's Note: The following viewpoint was taken from a speech given before Phyllis Schlafly's Eagle Forum.

I will admit to you that I am the person David Brinkley accused of "straight talking." This compliment was paid to me after I said comparable worth was the looniest idea since "Loony Tunes" came on the scene. Somewhere in that simple phrase I mentioned the tooth fairy. I believe I asked a rhetorical question about the dollars necessary to pay for comparable worth legislation. I wondered if these dollars, some $320 billion per year needed if a national comparable worth policy were enacted, would come from the tooth fairy. My assistant, who is here this evening, is still shaking her head—Loony Tunes and the tooth fairy in one paragraph! . . .

I make a personal appeal to each of you. . . to make it a point to correct public inaccuracies about comparable worth. Unfortunately, it masquerades as pay equity; it is not. I support pay equity; equal pay for equal work is the law. It is government's role to enforce the law.

In 1963, Congress enacted the Equal Pay Act, requiring that employers pay equal wages for equal work, and specifically rejected a comparable worth standard. The next year, Congress passed Title VII, which bans employer discrimination on the basis of race, religion, sex, or national origin in hiring, job classification, promotion, compensation, fringe benefits. . . ."

Title VII, like the Equal Pay Act, requires equal pay for equal work. It also forbids intentional discrimination by employers in wage setting on the basis of sex. For example, I cannot tell my secretary, "I'd pay you another $2.00 per hour if you were a man." The courts have not, with few exceptions, accepted the idea that you can compare two different jobs based on some job evaluation study and on that basis find discrimination.

I implore you to end the masquerade, and expose comparable worth for the wolf in sheep's clothing that it is. You may ask why I am so anxious to enlist your support in this endeavor. Just pick up any newspaper and read about comparable worth issues. The newspaper 9 times out of 10 will report that most Americans support pay equity; therefore, comparable worth is a great idea. I cringe each time I read one of these articles.

Feminists blame lack of progress on lack of enforcement of the Pay Equity Act. They claim that the segregation of men's and women's jobs has been a barrier to successful litigation and bargaining for equal pay for women. They tell us that because jobs are not identical, it is difficult to demonstrate the discriminatory basis of women's wages.

Women Don't Want to Be Plumbers

I believe that this is not quite the true story. I am sure you each remember that a few years ago the rage was non-traditional careers for women. I remember it well. At the time I was the President of the San Diego Urban League and successfully, on a voluntary basis, created thousands of jobs and trained thousands of women in construction industry trades. I did this as a joint project with the trade unions. I learned something very important from this project. I believe it is the something that most feminists learned. Most women do not want non-traditional careers. They do not *want* to be plumbers! Most women prefer traditional women's jobs. They want to be secretaries, school teachers or nurses. These professions allow women to have families. In these professions, they can more easily enter and exit the market place. However, the feminists are not willing to admit this lesson. But they do want to reevaluate these "women's" jobs, compare them to men's jobs, and set an administered wage scale

Clarence M. Pendleton Jr., speech delivered at the Eagle Forum in Orange, California on February 15, 1985.

based on this subjective comparison.

Comparable worth focuses on paying an entire profession or occupation the same wage rate as a second profession or occupation both of which are determined by some outside impartial authority to be of the same value or worth to an employer.

How would this impartial third party determine worth or value? The answer we are told is in a job evaluation point system (this used to be called task analysis a decade ago). Points are advanced based on four different job criteria:

—Skill
—Effort
—Responsibility required on the job and
—Working conditions under which the job is performed.

Now, I hope you begin to see why I have called this "Loony Tunes." Once the number of points are assigned, wages are administered based on the point scale. A secretary, we are told, who records and types outside orders from customers may be as valuable to the employer as the truck driver who delivers the product to the customer. What ever happened to supply and demand? High wages indicate that consumers value the job and the small supply of workers relative to the demand for the job keeps those wages high.

Upsetting the Market

Comparable worth, if implemented, would lead to capricious wage differentials, resulting in unintended shortages and surpluses of workers in different occupations with accompanying unemployment. Moreover, it would encourage women to remain in traditional occupations. Not only do wage differentials between jobs reflect the values consumers place on the contributions workers make to the final product, but they also depend upon the scarcity of qualified workers relative to the demand for their contributions. Employees who have skills, experience, abilities, and contributions needed by an entrepreneur and who are also scarce relative to demand will be paid higher wages.

Wage differentials between men and women are not the consequence of women being inherently less productive than men. The differentials exist because women, in comparison, generally have less education and fewer skills and are higher risks for employers. For example, those women who entered the work force in the 1950's were generally more educated than their male counterparts. Since then, however, as more and more women have entered the work force, the average level of education for working women has fallen behind the average level for men.

Men do not leave their jobs to have children and are less likely than women to leave jobs to care for their children. In addition, men are less likely to move if their spouses are forced to relocate for professional purposes. All of these are reasons why

turnover rates for men are lower than for women. One study using Department of Labor statistics estimates that the number of years men stay on their jobs exceeds that for women by 77 to 100 percent.

Differences in wages between men and women can also be explained by other factors. Men are usually physically stronger than women, and they tend to work in jobs that have a higher probability of physical harm. Because of this increased risk to the employee, these jobs command higher wages.

With a comparable worth policy, what would happen if supply and demand conditions were to drive up wages in one particular occupation? For example, with regard to the *AFSCME v. State of Washington* decision, if there is a sudden shortage (relative to demand) of warehouse workers in Washington state, causing wages to increase at a greater-than-normal rate, should clerk-typists automatically receive the increased wage simply because their occupation is determined to be of comparable worth?

The Value of Workers

Through the use of prices, the competitive process enables market participants to learn about opportunities. As consumers' tastes and preferences change, prices change to reflect the new choices the consumers are making. As the prices of consumer products change, wages in the labor market change. Workers, like entrepreneurs, are always at the mercy of consumers, and prices are the signals that tell all market participants how products, services, and ultimately workers are valued in the market.

A national comparable worth policy would institute an administered wage system. The sole aim of this policy would be to eliminate differences in wages between men and women. This will not eliminate discrimination. It is just one of countless cosmetic, political solutions, remedies if you will, which promises change without changing anything. Enforcement of the pay equity laws is the answer.

"Workers, like entrepreneurs, are always at the mercy of consumers, and prices are the signals that tell all market participants how products, services, and ultimately workers are valued."

There are more reasons than just upsetting the delicate balance of market forces that should motivate you to advocate against comparable worth. I would like to share the reasons that, to me, are the most invidious. Instituting a comparable worth policy would be like instituting a system of preferential treatment. The group being protected and getting preferences would be upper middle class white women.

Many of you are in that group. I do not mean to offend you. I am just being honest. I am on record against preferential treatment for any group. Upper middle class white women are no more deserving of preferential treatement than blacks, Hispanics, American Indians, handicapped, older Americans and the list goes on. I do not support reparations for anyone. In order to confer benefits on one group one must take benefits from another. We will not end sex discrimination by instituting a policy that would favor a particular group.

Robbing from the Poor

I travel extensively. Recently, I spoke on the campus of the University of Mississippi. That in itself is quite an experience. Adding to this historic occasion was a conversation with a woman that I will never forget. The woman was black and old. She works in the cafeteria of Old Miss. Her hands are swollen and scarred. Years of hard work show on these hands. This women has sent 9 children to college on a salary earned from serving food in Old Miss' cafeteria. She is a proud old woman, and so she should be. What do you think a policy of comparable worth would do to her occupation? The answer is obvious—eliminate it.

"Repealing the practice of wages determined by supply and demand and replacing it with an administered wage scale will ruin the current economic recovery."

The rating systems associated with comparable worth are inherently biased. Far more so than the market. These rating systems favor credentials over experience and mental activity and responsibility over manual effort. There is not much hope for that old woman in the Old Miss cafeteria.

Is there sex discrimination in the market? Yes! I have never met a working woman who had not experienced at least a taste of it. What should be done about it? Forgive me for being redundant, but I will repeat again. We must enforce the Equal Pay Act and Title VII. Additionally, we should continue to encourage non-traditional options for those women who want them.

Women As Entrepreneurs

One non-traditional option I have not mentioned, I would like to suggest. That is, the entrepreneurial alternative. In his 1981 book, *Markets and Minorities*, economist Thomas Sowell pointed out that

"Discrimination in labor markets . . . creates additional incentives for self-employment, including owner-operated businesses" self-employment offers a way to use talents that are underutilized in a discriminatory job situation and to get as many rewards as the market will allow. In large numbers, groups that have traditionally faced some discrimination in the marketplace are choosing the entrepreneurial option.

This option can offer women greater flexibility in work schedules and wider opportunities to utilize their skills. These advantages are becoming apparent to women. The small business administration estimates that there are over three million women business owners in the United States.

If I may quote Jennifer Roback, a Labor Economist at Yale, "The number of self-employed women has nearly doubled since 1965, keeping up with their increase in labor-force participation, while the number of self-employed men has scarcely risen at all in the same period, despite a 28 percent rise in the size of the male labor force."

Even if these figures are off, and it is likely that the number of sole proprietorships and professional corporations are under-counted by as much as twenty-five percent, it is clear that the increase in women owned businesses is significant. This is definitely an alternative to be considered.

Finally, I feel compelled to tell women and men as I speak on comparable worth that we must respect the decision of those women who place family as a priority over career. Many people have forgotten to do this. Strong families are the backbone of this nation.

Worth Its Weight in Taxes

The Eagle Forum and Mrs. Schlafly deserve the praises of sensible right thinking Americans for taking a leadership role in the debate. And for the forthright, reasonable stand against this unwarranted intrusion of government into the lives of its citizens. And it *is* an intrusion. The costs to the taxpayer, if a national comparable worth policy is instituted, would be enormous. I told you the number for the first year, $320 billion dollars, in the opening part of my remarks. I forgot to mention that the United States Chamber of Commerce estimates that in addition to the cost the inflation rate would rise to a minimum of 9.7 percent. Repealing the practice of wages determined by supply and demand and replacing it with an administered wage scale will ruin the current economic recovery. Comparable worth will lead to more real or imagined injustices, more litigation, and of all things, more politics—and that, too, is loony. Right now—I don't get all the government I pay for—and thank heaven!

I would like to close my remarks by stating that I believe the Civil Rights position of this administration reflects the attitudes and opinions of

the American people. What clearer indication that
this is true can one have than the results of the last
election. I am proud to be on President Reagan's
team. It is an honor to develop Civil Rights Policy
with other distinguished Americans, gentlemen like
Brad Reynolds, Clarence Thomas and Edwin Meese.
This is truly a team of men and women who believe
in opportunity for all Americans and special
preferences for none.

*Clarence M. Pendleton Jr. is the chairman of the United
States Commission on Civil Rights.*

Comparable Worth Is Affordable

Jan Rosenberg

Comparable worth is the latest collective effort to raise the wages of working women in the labor force. It grows out of the dying embers of the old political demand, "Equal Pay for Equal Work," the success of which depends on the elusive, unlikely integration of jobs by men and women.

Even today, more than twenty years after the Equal Pay Act of 1963, women's average pay is only 59 percent of men's and most women continue to work in the same "pink collar ghettos" that their mothers and grandmothers worked in. Some of the particulars are instructive: in 1983 the occupations of secretary, registered nurse, and child-care worker were each more than 95 percent female; billing clerks, librarians, waiters and waitresses, and health technicians all had well over 80 percent female employees. In 1980 about 80 percent of all women were still concentrated in "women's jobs" (typically defined as 70 percent or more of the work force).

The undisputed facts, then, are that most women and men continue to work at different jobs, and that women's jobs are paid less than men's and frequently offer fewer opportunities for advancement. The question is: Are women underpaid, or are their jobs simply worth less than men's?

The proponents of comparable worth emphasize both overt and institutional occupational and wage discrimination against women, as well as the deeper structures of sex role socialization, cultural attitudes about women, the family, and the value of women's work in which discrimination is embedded. They conclude that the work women do is paid less simply because it is done by women, not because of intrinsic characteristics or value of the job to the employer. To eliminate the discriminatory, ascriptive,

sexist attitudes and assumptions which still determine and justify wages, they urge that employers adopt job evaluation studies to explicate the value (or "worth") of each job to an employer in terms of its level of skill, effort, responsibility, and working conditions. Such studies, long used by management but now refined to eliminate biases against women, compare actual male and female wages to what they "should" be (according to the statistical regression model) if the jobs were all filled by *white men*. Ironically, management consultants urgently warn companies of the new dangers introduced by job evaluation studies, the fifty-year-old management technique recently taken over by dissatisfied employees.

The question of race, though built into the model and recognized on some level by the advocates and evaluators, does not figure explicitly in the abstract discussions of comparable worth. Empirically, however, female government workers (the main group likely to be strongly affected by comparable worth) include a high proportion of black women.

Discrimination: A Historical Reality

Opponents of comparable worth claim that women workers choose from a small range of traditionally earmarked "women's jobs" in spite of their low pay because they offer other compensations; easy exit and reentry, for example, mesh with women's primary family roles, allowing them to take time off for childbearing and rearing, to piece together a good fit between their work and family roles. These jobs are paid less than men's jobs because of "The Market," say the foes of comparable worth. Wages, they claim, are set according to laws of marginal productivity or by laws of supply and demand, and women, by crowding into fewer occupations that fit best with their essential family roles and responsibilities, reduce the market value of their wages. Their free market analysis denies such

Jan Rosenberg, "Judging on the Merits," *Commonweal*, May 31, 1985. Reprinted with permission from the Commonweal Foundation.

irrational but historical factors as outright discrimination (by workers, by employers, or both), and the existence, extent, and efficacy of unionization. The complex historical, social, and political conditions in which work and workers are evaluated, and wages are set, cannot be reduced to ahistorical equations.

While in the past female work patterns and wages more closely reflected social norms and family-work relationships, today many women and their families suffer severely from the continuation of these patterns. Numerous contemporary women (from those living alone to those heading their own families or co-heading families with husbands) are increasingly reluctant to accept wages they have come to see as inadequate and unfair, whatever the historical-cultural patterns in which they were once embedded.

"Comparable worth offers unions an important bargaining chip in their current efforts to organize new women workers."

In 1950, 70 percent of American households were headed by men whose income was the sole income for their family; by 1984 less than 15 percent of American families fit this traditional model. Women are no longer temporary and peripheral participants ("intermittent," in economic parlance) in the labor force. High divorce and illegitimacy rates and the enormous increase in female-headed households, record numbers of women (particularly those with pre-school children) in the labor force, and the concentration of female workers in women's jobs have converged into a complex dubbed the "feminization of poverty." While this concept masks some key internal distinctions and contradictions among women who are poor at a given moment, the fact remains that families headed by women continue to grow by leaps and bounds and are far more likely to be impoverished than those headed by men or by male-female couples. Many of these women and children would be helped considerably by the implementation of comparable worth. In addition to the issue of equity, comparable worth directly confronts the snowballing issues of need and adequacy.

Making Comparable Worth Affordable

But can we afford it? Isn't comparable worth, no matter how just, an impossibly expensive objective, likely to bankrupt the already unproductive, inefficient public sector toward which it's primarily directed? Or perhaps to impose an impossibly heavy financial burden on the taxpayers? In fact the cost is

closely related to the strategy used in pursuing comparable worth. There are three basic strategies: on the government side, legislation and litigation, and on the non-government side, collective bargaining. A great deal of opposition focuses on the dangers of government-imposed settlements, whether new laws or judicial decisions. This criticism should be taken seriously. The costs of comparable worth are much higher when litigation has dragged on, job evaluation studies have to be updated, and back pay awarded. Most settlements, so far, particularly those reached through collective bargaining, involve very small percentage increases (less than 5 percent) to a city's or state's overall budget. (This is true in San Jose, Minnesota, and now in Los Angeles.) The lesson is not that comparable worth is too expensive, but that comparable worth won through the courts is too expensive. The *threat* of litigation is likely to be more helpful than the litigation itself. Trade union leadership avoids the problems of bureaucratic regulation in which judges and lawyers arbitrarily define pay levels.

Unions stand the best chance to head off the dangers of polarization (between men and women workers, and between industrial and white-collar workers) that many skeptics fear. Union leaders, of course, must be (somewhat) responsive to the support this policy has among their diverse members. Internal education in key unions has aimed at increasing support among members, just as lobbying and some public education has aimed at drumming up support among politicans and the public. The AFL-CIO has officially endorsed comparable worth since 1979, while the Coalition of Labor Union Women (CLUW) and several of its more heavily female affiliates (AFSCME, SEIU, IUE and CWA) have actually led the fight. Finally, given the overlapping and contradictory interests of union members, and the overall orientation of American unions, comparable worth is not likely to become ideologically abstracted from the workplace. Fair wages for women is one goal among others, and unionists will have to weigh it against these other issues (e.g. safety, job protection, and so forth) in each concrete instance.

More specifically, comparable worth offers unions an important bargaining chip in their current efforts to organize new women workers and, perhaps more importantly, to solidify the support of their female membership. This is particularly the case for heavily female public employee unions like the American Federation of State, County, and Municipal Employees (AFSCME), the undisputed leader of the nationwide movement for comparable worth. (Nationally, 40 percent of AFSCME members are women while 60 percent of all government workers are women.) Involved in comparable worth since 1974 when they supported an employee-initiated job evaluation study in the state of Washington,

AFSCME gained wider attention during its 1981 strike in San Jose, California. That settlement included $130 million (more than 30 percent of the total dollar settlement) targeted to raise the wages of underpaid, mostly women workers in "women's jobs." But only after AFSCME's 1983 Washington state victory, in which the union won a federal district court judgment (now being appealed) against the state for discriminating against its female employees in terms of their jobs and wages, did the union and the issue of comparable worth gain national attention.

Not all predominantly female unions in the private sector actively support comparable worth. ILGWU represents garment workers (including many women) in an industry that is intensely competitive, requires low capital investment, and operates on a very low margin of profit. It cannot afford comparable worth, according to union leaders (and industry spokesmen, of course). Garment workers and their representatives have been far more concerned with enforcement of labor laws and regulations than with comparable worth.

Support for Equal Pay

Comparable worth draws support far beyond the union movement. As Eleanor Holmes Norton, then chair of the U.S. Equal Employment Opportunity Commission predicted in the late 1970s, it has snowballed into one of the biggest issues of the decade. The Democratic party first endorsed the idea at its National Convention in 1972, and has continued to endorse it ever since. Countless government officials at all levels—from Carol Bellamy and Andrew Stein in New York City to U.S. congressional representatives Mary Rose Oakar, Patsy Schroeder, Geraldine Ferraro, to Senators Dan Evans, Alan Cranston, and Bill Bradley—have jumped on the bandwagon by holding hearings, commissioning studies, and sponsoring legislation. A bill mandating comparable worth pay scales just sailed through the House of Representatives by a vote of 413 to 6, indicating surprisingly wide Republican as well as Democratic support. In addition, 23 House Republicans issued a report recommending the early adoption of comparable worth policies as well as stepped-up federal investigation of discrimination against women in the workplace.

Activity in the states is even more dramatic. Legislatures in thirty-three states have passed measures concerning comparable worth, while those in many others (eighteen at last count) have called for job evaluation studies to examine the extent of pay discrimination against women. New laws and studies roll in so fast that it is difficult to keep up with the latest score! These studies, as both advocates and opponents are quick to point out, typically provide evidence for collective bargaining,

grievance, or law suits on behalf of aggrieved female employees, a large and increasing proportion of all government workers. (Government workers are, in turn, an increasingly large proportion of a state's total work force.)

Feminist leaders, organizations, and journals (including but not limited to NOW, the League of Women Voters, Women's Action Alliance, and *MS*) support comparable worth but, with the exception of social scientists, they are clearly not at the center of the political mobilization around this issue. (This may well be because most feminist activists are not in predominantly female jobs in the "pink collar ghetto"; for others, welfare reform has seemed far more urgent than the workplace problems around comparable worth.) Feminist economists and sociologists, however, have contributed heavily to the mountain of data, analyses, and policy proposals pouring forth from the comparable worth movement. These social scientists are prominent among the "usual suspects" rounded up repeatedly for hearings in Washington D.C. as well as state capitals and cities around the country.

Perhaps most surprising of all, *Business Week* and the *New York Times*, hardly the vanguards of trade unionism or feminism, have both endorsed comparable worth in their respective editorial pages.

Promising a Bright Future

There are two main reasons for the wide support that comparable worth has achieved. First, fear of its inevitability (a plausible fear continually reasserted by its advocates) has pressed government agencies and some large corporations to consider initiating comparable worth studies and policies, thus avoiding polarization and increased costs resulting from protracted legal suits. Second, comparable worth promises to expand individual equity, to fulfill the bourgeois promise to reward people's work and achievements on their merits, not in terms of ascribed characteristics of the worker.

"Comparable worth promises to expand individual equity, to fulfill the bourgeois promise to reward people's work and achievements on their merits."

In addition to the wide support given comparable worth, a number of leading business journals and organizations (including *Fortune,* the *Wall Street Journal, Commentary,* and the U.S. Chamber of Commerce) as well as conservative intellectuals and politicos (from sociologist Brigitte Berger and economist June O'Neill to the indefatigable Phyllis Schlafly), staunchly oppose the movement, convinced that it is neither good nor inevitable. In the words of Reagan-appointee Clarence Pendleton, ". . . this is probably the looniest idea since Looney Tunes came on the screen." The critics offer a concerted opposition, repeatedly emphasizing the efficacy of the "free market" (my quotes), the dangers of imperious "new class" experts and judges dictating wage levels in accord with their anti-market, utopian assumptions, and the credentialist, meritocratic justifications on which the movement rests. In addition, some critics from both left and right fear that comparable worth will sound the death knell to the goal of intregrating men and women in the work force.

The fear of "new class" experts is especially ironic. Many of the pro-business opponents have conveniently forgotten the long history of wage-setting by expert job evaluations in the U.S., and write of them as though they are a trick designed by greedy, pushy women and their representatives. Their fears in interventionist, activist judges imposing costly and impractical judgments is more firmly grounded in recent experience; at its best this fear creates a climate in which intransigent firms and governments are more likely to reach an agreement with their workers. Both workers and managers share an interest in their company's economic viability, which may seem far less urgent to a judge.

The fear of radical, utopian changes pitting "pink-collar" women against blue-collar men, wrought in the name of comparable worth, is overdone. As the movement has developed in the United States, it promises to fulfill the individualist, bourgeois promise to judge people's work and achievements on their merits, not in terms of ascribed characteristics of the worker. We are once again asked to stretch our values, to incorporate a new group, women workers, and to reward them in terms of the work they do in the labor market, not in terms of their femaleness.

Jan Rosenberg teaches sociology at Long Island University and has written on issues concerning women, work, and family structures.

Jobs Cannot Be Evaluated by Their Comparable Value

Geoffrey Cowley

[In] November [1983] a federal judge in Tacoma, Washington, made national news by ruling that the state had discriminated against women. Sex discrimination lawsuits are hardly new to American life, but the issue in Washington was not whether the state was willing to hire women, or whether it offered equal pay for equal work. Rather, it was whether the 15,000 state workers holding traditionally female jobs—nurses and secretaries, for example—should be paid the same as those holding "comparable," male-dominated jobs in different trades, like plumbing or carpentry. In deciding against the state of Washington, Judge Jack Tanner declared that Title VII of the 1964 Civil Rights Act "was designed to bar not only overt employment discrimination, but also practices that are fair in form but discriminatory in operation," among which he counted the state's failure to grant equal pay for work of comparable worth. Tanner found the state guilty of "pervasive and intentional" discrimination, and promptly awarded the plaintiffs a projected $1 billion in back pay and wages.

No one missed the opportunity to hail the ruling as a major turning point in the battle against sexism. "The state of Washington was the defendant in this case," said a local spokesman for the American Federation of State, County, and Municipal Employees, the union that brought the suit, "but all of society was on trial. This ruling gives us great cause for hope, because it will provide a model for other suits across the country." Dan Evans, the Republican ex-governor recently elected to fill Henry Jackson's Senate seat, proposed that Congress create a commission to "study how the federal government . . . can root out gender bias" within its own workforce. And Gary Hart, who along with

Walter Mondale, John Glenn, and Alan Cranston has jumped on the comparable worth bandwagon, was so overcome with enthusiasm that he hopped a plane to Seattle to hold a press conference where he called Tanner's decision "a national example of how women's organizations and unions can use existing laws to destroy wage discrimination."

Support for the notion of comparable worth has come to be expected of anyone who claims to care about the equality of women in our society. Proponents of the doctrine rightly argue that "equal pay for equal work" is only a partial solution to the problem women face in the workforce. The average working woman earns only 62 cents for every dollar a man earns. Women's groups correctly point out that the real problem isn't that female professionals are paid less than their male counterparts; if half of all lawyers were women who received the same salaries as their male colleagues, a wide income gap would still exist. The real problem, they say, is that secretaries and other women who toil in traditionally "female occupations" are making considerably less than men who possess the same, or lower, levels of skill, intelligence, and responsibility.

Comparable Worth Destructive

The egalitarian appeal of the comparable worth principle is obvious: why *shouldn't* a female secretary with an M.A. in English literature and responsibility for managing the office's accounts get paid the same as a Teamsters truck driver who hauls frozen chickens? But when it comes to larger problems of inequality faced by both women and society at large, comparable worth is a principle that will ultimately prove not merely inadequate, but destructive. Its greatest asset is that it affords politicians a way to demonstrate their solidarity in the battle for sexual equality, while leaving all the necessary little details that the "comparable worth" standard implies—like deciding who is worth what, and exactly how one

Geoffrey Cowley, "Comparable Worth: A Terrible Idea," *The Washington Monthly*, January 1984. Reprinted with permission from *The Washington Monthly*. © by the Washington Monthly Company, 1711 Connecticut Avenue, NW, Washington, DC 20009   202-462-0128.

goes about comparing the job of a deputy assistant to the administrator to that of a cleaning woman—to somebody else. And it isn't hard to figure out who that "someone else" is going to be. When Tanner's decision was handed down, lawyers and consultants everywhere no doubt experienced something akin to the thrill felt by Cortez when he first gazed upon the shimmering Aztec temples of Tenochtitlan.

Worth on the Willis Scale

The state of Washington first began to toy with the idea of comparable worth back in 1973, when then-Governor Dan Evans hired the Seattle consulting firm of Norman D. Willis & Associates to figure out whether the state was paying women as much as it was paying men at "a comparable level" of skill and responsibility. The study found a 20 percent wage gap. For example, laundry workers, who were mostly women, were estimated to be worth the same as low-level truck drivers, who were mostly men, but the laundry workers were making 41 percent less than the truck drivers.

Perhaps you're wondering how to figure out how much a laundry worker is worth. After all, such questions have perplexed philosophers and theologians for centuries. (They have even been known to give personal-injury lawyers some difficulty.) The answer is to develop "point-factor job evaluation systems" to do the job for you.

Each system works on a slightly different conception of "worth," of course, but all share a cheerfully mathematical view of qualities that you would think would be hard to quantify. Let's take a closer look at the Willis scale, which Judge Tanner relied on in making his decision. It assumes that the worth of any job, from circus clown to key-punch operator, varies in relation to the "knowledge and skills," "mental demands," "accountability," and "working conditions" it entails. Each of these components is further broken down into two or three subcomponents, and points are awarded on the basis of each one. Under "accountability," for instance, you can win points for your "freedom to take action" as well as for the nature and size of your "impact." Admittedly, the guidelines the instruction manual for the system offers are somewhat informal; for example, on "impact," the consultants instruct, "The simplest way to look at Size is to say the job most clearly impacts on something BIG, or on something LITTLE, or on something IN BETWEEN."

The "knowledge and skills" component breaks down into "managerial," "interpersonal," and "technical" dimensions, each of which carries its own rating. To top out on the "managerial" scale, you have to manage "subfunctions that have significantly different natures, or where the end results of the subordinate subfunctions tend to be conflicting or competitive with each other and

require special harmonizing." Got that? In English, "you have to know how to do different things and how to play your assistants against one another." There are two kinds of "mental demands"—"judgment" and "problem solving"—and three kinds of "working conditions"—"uncomfortable," "strenuous," and "hazardous."

A "C1N 106 C2-f 23 C1N 23 L1A 0"

To calculate all these factors, Willis assembled a group of people from within the state civil service. These civil servants reviewed job descriptions, interviewed their fellow workers and then, after much solemn mutual consultation, assigned each job a score. Thus a clerk-typist became a "152," or, to be more precise, a "C1N 106 C2-f 23 C1N 23 L1A 0." Broken down, this meant a clerk-typist scored 106 on "knowledge and skills," 23 on "mental demands," 23 on "accountability," and 0 on "working conditions." (A score of 0 on "working conditions" is the Willis method's understated way of saying either that the employee has nothing to complain about or that he or she is working in embarrassingly plush surroundings. Because there are no negative points on the Willis scale, access to excessive perks does not lower anybody's score.) Broken down still further, the clerk-typist rating on "knowledge and skills" is level C on a "technical" scale from A to G, level 1 on a "managerial skills" scale of one to three, and level N on an "interpersonal skills" scale that is too complicated to explain without the aid of an astrolabe and a mood ring.

"If the courts are going to define 'discrimination' so broadly that it applies to people who do different things and earn different salaries, they can't just go around measuring it on any scale they like."

With the help of Willis's team of metaphysicians, Washington state calculated the worth of every civil service job category on the payroll. These were unveiled in 1974, revealing the awkward 20 percent gap between what women were earning and what their male "comparability" counterparts were earning. True to a long-standing tradition of how to respond to consultants bearing bad tidings, Evans ordered a second, more detailed Willis study. This study, published in 1976, estimated that the wage gap between "comparable" men and women could be closed by paying the women $38 million more a year. (What? Lower the wages for the men instead, you say? You must be kidding.) The $38 million gap struck the legislature as a problem warranting still further study. By July 1982 AFSCME had run out of patience, and filed suit.

The decision that resulted will be a serious blow to the finances of Washington state. The state will now have to cough up not $38 million, as the second Willis study showed, but an estimated $1 billion over the next 18 months. When Winn Newman, the lawyer who argued AFSCME's case, was asked about this he answered, "Congress didn't put a price tag on ending discrimination when it passed the Civil Rights Act. It didn't say to employers, 'Stop underpaying women and minorities when you think it's convenient.' The only ones saying we can't *afford* to stop discrimination are bigots—bigots and people with an interest in perpetuating it."

"If the administrative and judicial aspects of comparable worth are messy, the economics could be even messier."

Surprisingly, the decision was disowned by none other than Norman Willis, who, despite the hubris of his worth-measuring enterprise, recoils at the thought that his or anybody else's scorecard should become law. Even some of those who support the decision seem hard-pressed to find a sound legal basis for Tanner's reasoning. When I asked Gary Hart about this, for example, he said, "I don't think it's appropriate for legislators to run around commenting on judicial rulings," even though that's exactly what he had come to Seattle to do.

All Scales Being Equal

Hart and Newman have their hearts in the right place; we *do* want to pay people what they deserve, rather than what society's petty prejudices dictate. But if the courts are going to define "discrimination" so broadly that it applies to people who do different things and earn different salaries, they can't just go around measuring it on any scale they like—there will have to be state and federal laws saying there shall always be, say, three kinds of occupational adversity, as opposed to two or 20, and just two kinds of mental demands. Otherwise, employers will start defining worth any way they please. Truck drivers could end up being paid entirely on the basis of their familiarity with *Finnegan's Wake*.

Getting the nation to unite behind the Willis or the Hay or the Jones system of worth detection will be tricky, for we all have direct, and conflicting, interests in how the scale is calibrated. A ditchdigger could argue that the Willis system favors mental over physical exertion, a typist that it doesn't adequately register boredom. And anyone could claim, rightfully, that it gives more weight to

meaningless job requirements—for instance, why should a probation officer need a master's degree—than it does to individual initiative and resourcefulness.

But even if we agree on a scale, we'll have to accept the possibility that it will produce widely different results when applied in different environments. Unless we take the next step, which is to treat the whole economy as a single firm and determine the proper salary for every position in it, we'll have no way of knowing that secretaries are keeping up with each other, let alone staying ahead of the nation's janitors.

Imagine the nightmarish society that might result. A waitress down at Uncle Bob's House of Ribs might sue her boss because her sister-in-law was getting twice as much (and better tips) waiting tables at the diner across the street. Executives would knock back martinis after coming home on the five-forty-eight and torment themselves about their prospects for ever making F1Y 380 E4-k 122 E1D 160 L1A 0. Children would have new ways to taunt one another in the sandbox:

"My daddy's a 634!"

"Oh yeah? Well, *my* daddy's a 723, and he says if he can harmonize subordinate subfunctions three more times this week we can go to Bermuda!"

More Trouble than It's Worth

AFSCME isn't proposing anything as ambitious as a planned economy, of course; it is simply claiming that individual employers have an obligation to rise above the sexism inherent in the marketplace. Once employers have done away with the wage gap between men's and women's professions, a spokesman for the union says, the problem will have been solved and everything will return to normal.

But will it? Many civil servants in Washington state who hold jobs as "worthy" as other, higher paying jobs are men. But unless they can prove that they're being discriminated against for performing "women's work"—legally defined as any job where women comprise more than 70 percent of the workforce—they won't get the raise that the nurses and the secretaries will get. It isn't hard to imagine the next step: a lawsuit by the men, arguing that they deserve "comparable worth" raises, too.

Then there are the inevitable adjustments that will have to be made to keep the worth scale up-to-date. Maintaining a standard as vague as "worth" could make quantum mechanics look simple. It's fairly easy for the Equal Employment Opportunity Commission to spot a disparity in the wages an employer pays men and women to perform "equal work"; all it takes is a glance at the payroll. But checking out a comparable-worth complaint would be quite another matter. In order to determine whether a Lockheed audit-machine operator II was legally entitled to the same pay as a senior stem-dryer maintainer, the EEOC would have to haul in a committee to perform a company-wide worth analysis.

The courts, too, would have to evaluate the working of an entire industry every time they heard a discrimination suit. Major civil rights battles would turn on such questions as whether error-free typing is a greater corporate asset than leak-free plumbing, or whether sitting at a VDT places greater strain on Betty's eyes than pipefitting places on Jack's back. And does Doris, the floor manager at Sears, "most clearly impact on something IN-BETWEEN" as opposed to "something LITTLE"?

"Comparable worth . . . . will enshrine [inequality], while fine-tuning lesser inequalities through the use of questionably 'scientific' means."

If the administrative and judicial aspects of comparable worth are messy, the economics could be even messier. In the marketplace, people are paid in part according to the availability of labor. At Weyerhaeuser, for example, where a Willis comparable worth survey rated the job of personnel manager at 916 and that of pulp mill superintendent at 760, pulp mill superintendents make more money than personnel managers—because good ones are harder to find. Under a comparable worth standard, Weyerhaeuser could end up with two choices: pay the pulp mill superintendents less, thereby making good ones even harder to find, or give the deskbound manager a big raise.

Comparable worth also creates problems for labor-management relations. Subjected to the worth standard, many existing collective-bargaining agreements could be shown to have disparate impacts on men and women in different jobs. And if the unions that negotiated those agreements didn't move fast enough to pin the blame on the employers, as AFSCME did in its claim against Washington state, they could face massive lawsuits from their own members. (In fact, the AFSCME local that brought the suit against Washington pays its own employees not on the basis of comparable worth but by the same allegedly sexist pay scales used by the state.)

Putting a Price Tag on Justice

Advocates of the worth standard insist that this is all beside the point; as Newman says, you can't put a price tag on discrimination. But if anyone's putting a price tag on justice, it's the worth proponents themselves. Just take a look at the Willis scale. A beginning licensed practical nurse scores 158 comparable worth points, while an "Information

Specialist III"—an experienced PR flack—scores 324. Or look at a janitor, who scores 101, while "Advisory Sanitarian II"— someone who doesn't actually clean anything himself, but makes sure local hospitals and nursing homes do—scores 395. Why on earth should our society value people who issue press releases or fill out reports all day long more than people who save lives and do the dirty work?

This is the most pernicious aspect of comparable worth—it would do nothing to endanger the larger inefficiencies and inequalities that are built into the present heirarchy. In fact, it would solidify them by giving them the force of law. Whereas today we overpay lawyers regardless of their need, skill, and general value to society, because we are irrationally adversarial, credential-loving snobs who hope someday to behave more sensibly, in a world governed by comparable worth we would do so because it is the law. The purpose of comparable worth is not to balance the earnings of lawyers and secretaries who make equal contributions to the common good, but to make fine distinctions about the "worth" of jobs already accorded roughly the same status within society.

Advocates Don't Want Equality

The comparable worth scale reflects the same credentialism that corrupts the society it is designed to mirror. Why is an advisory sanitarian any worthier than a janitor? Because it is suggested that advisory sanitarians have "an M.A. in public health, environmental health, or a closely allied field," and you must be registered as a sanitarian—an affiliation whose only advantage might be that its monthly four-color newsletter, *Sanitarians Today*, advertises cheap charters to Luxembourg. AFSCME doesn't have any problem with unequal arrangements that result from society's obsession with credentialism; to the contrary, one official of the union was quoted a couple of years ago as complaining, "When a person whose job requires a college education makes less than what is basically a common laborer, there's something wrong." Advocates of comparable worth don't want to achieve equality or a system of rewards based on true merit. They want a merit-blind system of inequality.

Willis insists that his scale doesn't pretend to measure a person's contribution to the social good. Instead, it is a "bias-free instrument." But what does this bias-free instrument measure? It measures the biases of society. That's the problem. When a lawyer calls in his secretary to ask her to type up a brief on comparable worth, he isn't demonstrating to her his willingness to flatten the income curve; he's demonstrating to her the inevitability of her inferior status. Even if she's the best secretary in the world, and he the worst lawyer, comparable worth dictates that the lawyer will always be worth more than the secretary.

There are far better ways to fight sexual discrimination in the workplace. Where sexism obviously exists in hiring decisions, an anti-discrimination lawsuit is just one way to apply pressure. Another is to combat the deep-seated cultural prejudices that funnel women into jobs like that of secretary and nurse to begin with. And a final remedy is to fight the rigid rules that exist to keep women—and men—who occupy the lower status rungs in their place. Nurses and midwives, for instance, should have more freedom to perform essential medical services. And legal secretaries ought to have the authority to prepare wills and other documents that they now draw up for their bosses.

Obviously, the problem of sexual discrimination runs deep in our society. At least for a while, there will still be bosses who look upon their underpaid—and more intelligent—secretaries with condescension and perhaps lust. But comparable worth, appealing as the idea might sound, won't help end that inequality. Instead, it will enshrine it, while fine-tuning lesser inequalities through the use of questionably "scientific" means to measure what is ultimately unmeasurable.

Geoffrey Cowley is a staff writer for the Seattle Weekly.

"Different jobs can be compared through job evaluation just as nutritionists compare apples and oranges."

Job Evaluation for Comparable Worth Is Possible

Ronnie J. Steinberg

The primary goal of equal pay for work of comparable worth is to correct the wage discrimination that is a by-product of occupational segregation. The link between segregation and the wage gap is now undeniable. The National Research Council of the National Academy of Sciences (NAS) succinctly describes the pattern: "Not only do women do different work than men, but the work women do is paid less and the more an occupation is dominated by women the less it pays." The NAS committee concludes from this that "Women are systematically underpaid . . . on the basis of the review of the evidence, our judgment is that there is substantial discrimination in pay."

Viewed from a policy perspective, comparable worth broadens the earlier policy of equal pay for equal work that prohibited wage discrimination if women and men were doing the same or similar work. It requires, instead, that dissimilar jobs of equivalent worth to the employer be paid the same wages. Conceptually, the policy goal of equal pay for work of comparable worth concerns the issue of whether work done primarily by women and minorities is systematically undervalued because the work has been and continues to be done primarily by women and minorities. Systematic undervaluation means that the wages paid to women and men engaged in historically female or minority work are artificially depressed relative to what those wages would be if these jobs had been and were being performed by white males. Operationally, pay equity involves correcting the practice of paying women and minorities less than white men for work that requires equivalent skills, responsibilities, stresses, personal contacts, and working conditions.

Comparable worth is the most controversial of the

equal employment opportunity policies to evolve since the enactment of Title VII of the 1964 Civil Rights Act. The revaluation of women's work is regarded as costly to employers. It raises questions about cultural attitudes toward women and about the distribution of power in the labor market. . . .

Debate Shifts on Technical Aspects

Over the last five years, the terms of debate between advocates and opponents has shifted. Whereas formerly the dialogue focused on whether or not there would be a comparable worth policy, differences now hinge on the technical underpinnings of problem identification and policy implementation. These include the nature, scope, and extent of wage discrimination; the appropriateness of techniques for measuring wage discrimination; the standards of worth to be used as a guide to estimating undervaluation; and the strategies and procedures for achieving pay equity adjustments in a fair and fiscally responsible fashion. . . .

Comparable worth is not just a white middle-class reform but one that will help assure fair pay for a broad spectrum of jobs including the working poor. Given the policy goals of comparable worth it could hardly be just a middle-class reform since women and minorities are disproportionately concentrated in low status, low paying jobs. Comparable worth studies examine potential wage discrimination in jobs such as garment worker, launderer, food service worker, institutional caretaker, retail salesworker, and entry-level clerk-typist. In the New York State Comparable Pay Study, for example, estimates of undervaluation will be made for such job titles as youth division aide, window washer, elevator operator, janitor, cook, barber, and bus driver. This is because processes perpetuating undervaluation are the same, whether the source of differential treatment is race or sex or ethnicity.

Ronnie J. Steinberg, "Evaluating Jobs," *Society*, July/August 1985. Published by permission of Transaction, Inc. from SOCIETY, Vol. 22, No. 5, copyright © 1985 by Transaction, Inc.

Legitimate job worth differences exist. Comparable worth policy is directed at closing only that portion of the wage gap between women and men due to systematic undervaluation; not all of the wage gap is a function of this undervaluation. Some differences are legitimately derived from differences in job prerequisites, requirements, and responsibilities. Women have also been segregated into lower paying jobs that require the equivalent amount of skill, effort, and responsibility as traditionally male jobs. The policy of comparable worth is concerned with salary differences between women and men that cannot be justified in terms of productivity-related job-content characteristics. The final report of the NAS declared:

> Paying jobs according to their worth requires only that whatever characteristics of jobs are regarded as worthy of compensation by an employer should be equally so regarded irrespective of the sex, race or ethnicity of job incumbents.

Job Evaluation Possible

Different jobs can be compared through job evaluation just as nutritionists compare apples and oranges. This apples and oranges analogy has recently been transformed into we cannot compare poets and plumbers. Although the example of the poet is farfetched, we can conceive of comparing plumbers to parking lot attendants or physicians, because employers have been comparing such jobs for decades as well as translating these comparisons into wage rates. Even the federal goverment has been involved in evaluating dissimilar jobs for purposes of setting salaries. The *Dictionary of Occupational Titles*, published by the U.S. Department of Labor, is a ranking of jobs from the most important and valuable to the least important and valuable according to three general categories. This ranking has been offered to and used by thousands of firms as an aid in setting salaries.

"The way job evaluations have been designed in most firms have had the effect of creating a two-tiered pay policy."

Well over two-thirds of all employees work in firms where there is some form of job evaluation underlying the wage structure. Some of the same employers who for years have been using classification techniques to compare dissimilar jobs now say that job evaluation systems cannot be used to compare male-dominated and female-dominated jobs. And yet, the National Research Council of the National Academy of Sciences did conclude that such comparisons could be made with caution. One

chapter of their report recommends formulas for correction of point-factor systems to remove the impact of femaleness and minorityness. . . .

Job evaluation techniques used in comparable worth research incorporate market considerations such as supply and demand in the weighting of job-content factors. Resulting wages are based on the productive contribution of jobs to the firm. The point factors provided in these approaches have been developed by management consultants most frequently on the basis of what the market pays for a given job-content characteristic. These general point values are further grounded in the labor market by finding out what the wages of a set of so-called benchmark jobs are in other nearby firms in order to develop a pay policy line in which the wage rate is plotted against evaluation points. It is nothing more than the institutionalization of the invisible hand of the market. Ray Marshall has recently concluded that one source of the difference between comparable worth proponents and opponents is over the nature and functioning of the labor market. Proponents regard the market in terms of the dynamic functioning of firms as social institutions; opponents describe the market in terms of the consequences of the dynamic forces of supply and demand and maximization of economic self-interest.

Policy-Capturing

More statistically based approaches called *policy-capturing* also capture the actual wage policy of a firm by developing a compensation model using regression analysis. To the extent that the firm has been basing its wage structure on the external market, the compensation model will reflect market wages. Since comparable worth is concerned only with eliminating those differences in wage rates that cannot be accounted for by productivity-related job-content characteristics, the standard of worth can similarly be partially based on market wages.

Because comparable worth addresses wage discrimination that is a by-product of occupational segregation, it is necessary to understand what institutional mechanisms reinforce and perpetuate the fact that those engaged in historically female or significantly minority work are not compensated equivalently for their productivity-related contribution to a firm. This draws on the framework of internal labor market analysis. These markets differ from competitive markets in that employees are protected from direct competition with the external market as well as constrained by specified routes of promotion and by highly articulated and rigidly fixed wage structures. . . .

In practice, the way job evaluations have been designed in most firms have had the effect of creating a two-tiered pay policy, in which sex- and race-type . . . [depress] the rate of pay. The likelihood that current job evaluation approaches embed broader cultural assumptions about the value of activities performed by women and minorities should not be surprising. Shepela and Viviano report in an article surveying the research literature addressing this issue, in [Helen] Remick's *Comparable Worth and Wage Discrimination*, "there is considerable anthropological and sociological data to indicate that the value of an activity or characteristic can be lowered simply through its association with women [or minorities]." In a more cautiously worded statement, the NAS committee arrived at the same conclusion, "it is possible that the process of describing and evaluating jobs reflects pervasive cultural stereotypes regarding the relative worth of work traditionally done by men and work traditionally done by women. . . .

The Case of AT&T

Negotiations between American Telephone and Telegraph (AT&T) and the Communication Workers of America over the classification of telephone operators offers a[n] . . . example. AT&T uses separate job evaluation schemes for its nonmanagerial and managerial employees. The managerial job evaluation system assigns a high point value to customer contact; telephone operators were given almost no points for customer contact, even though the company randomly screens the operators' calls to assess quality of assistance. The job of telephone operator was upgraded to take into account the importance AT&T places on customer contact.

This multiple plan problem has recently been identified more broadly by [Heidi] Hartmann and [Donald] Treiman:

> It is often the case that one plan is used for clerical workers, another plan for managerial level workers and yet a third plan for manual workers. When multiple plans are used, it is difficult to compare jobs across sectors of the firm. Since a major source of the wage differential between men and women stems from the fact that men tend to be concentrated in manual and managerial jobs which both tend to pay better than clerical jobs, the inability to compare jobs across sectors makes an assessment of the possibility of wage discrimination very difficult.

Interestingly enough, job specifications in New York State and no doubt elsewhere essentially use the same job-content characteristics to describe work in all families. Thus, the lack of comparison across sex-segregated job families is less a function of technical capability than of cultural oversight. Until women point out the possibility of making such comparisons across sex-segregated occupational groups, no one thought to make them. Comparing women's jobs to men's jobs was a culturally irrelevant activity with obvious financial benefits to employers who could pay incumbents of some jobs less for doing equivalent work. It is in this way that the inconsistent application of standards of worth translates into wage discrimination.

A second way in which cultural assumptions embed wage discrimination into classification systems involves the differential description of jobs. This occurs when compensable job-content characteristics of female-dominated and significantly minority jobs are not obtained, overlooked, or ignored. To examine concretely how this occurs, I draw examples from outside of New York State. The first is from a University of Wisconsin extension school study of the third edition of the *Dictionary of Occupational Titles*. The dictionary compiled by the U.S. Department of Labor, contains a list of almost every job title along with a rating of the job in terms of a skill-complexity code. The skill-complexity code is built on the assumption that "every job requires a worker to function at some definable level with regard to Data, People and Things." These researchers were disturbed by the ratings given to certain types of predominately female jobs compared to certain predominately male jobs. For instance, dog pound attendant and zookeeper were rated more highly than nursery school teacher or day-care worker. The researchers carried out an independent assessment of the predominately female jobs. Their ratings differed substantially from those of the Labor Department evaluators.

"Dog pound attendant and zookeeper were rated more highly than nursery school teacher or day-care worker."

When examining why the differences emerged, they found that the Labor Department evaluators had overlooked important characteristics of the female-dominated jobs, especially those associated with taking care of children. The evaluators did not regard these as job-related skills but rather as qualities intrinsic to being a woman. The job evaluators were confusing the content and responsibilities of a paid job with stereotypic notions about the characteristics of the jobholders. This is often done with respect to fine motor coordination and rapid finger dexterity in female-dominated blue-collar and clerical work.

Job Experience and Salary

Donald J. Treiman, in *Job Evaluation: An Analytic Review*, provides a second example in the Interim Report to the NAS Committee:

> . . . two factors in traditional job evaluation systems have been suggested as areas particularly subject to sex stereotyping: "experience," and "physical effort." Women's jobs are often thought of as requiring little experience mainly because the experience required to perform them is gained outside the labor market, in school or at home. But the same assumption is not usually made regarding men's jobs, even when

experience is gained independently of the job. A comparison of the ratings of "truck driver" and "typist" in a job evaluation plan . . . is a striking example.

On the "job knowledge factor," which calls for consideration of the length of "recognized training which is specialized, previous experience judged as an essential prerequisite, and on-the-job training necessary to learn and perform the job duties with normal supervision," "typist" is scored as requiring one month of training time while "truck driver" is scored as requiring 12 months of training time. It is easy to speculate that this difference may result from cultural stereotypes since both positions involve skills usually learned prior to entry into the labor force, sometimes by means of formal instruction and sometimes by quite informal means. Were typists judged to require the same training time as truck drivers it would mean an increase to two full pay grades. . . .

Making the Invisible Visible

Job evaluation studies that identify wage discrimination under an evolving policy of comparable worth seek, in a sense, to make the invisible visible for the purpose of removing these discriminatory components in the setting of salaries. To use these methodologies to meet these objectives, we must build on and adjust job evaluation methodologies to minimize the impact of cultural biases on the salaries paid for historically female and minority work. According to Remick:

> Job evaluation and comparable worth differ in very few ways . . . they differ in intent. The traditional use of job evaluation is to justify existing salary practice or simplify salary setting, whereas comparable worth is used to remedy sex discrimination. . . .Initially, only comparable worth applications looked for and corrected sex bias in the evaluation systems, although good traditional applications now also look for this source of bias.

Conceptually, comparable worth studies add a third dimension of equity to conventional classification analyses. Existing job evaluation methodologies attempt to balance a certain kind of *internal equity*, or "the value of one job to another within a firm," and *external equity*, or "the value of each job with respect to prevailing labor market practices." Comparable pay studies introduce *gender equity* as a new kind of internal equity. By this we mean that a female job and a male job of equivalent value to a firm should be paid equally. . . .

How Expensive Is Comparable Worth?

Rumors abound as to the great cost that will be incurred if comparable worth policy is implemented. Dire consequences have been predicted as a result of costly litigation or expensive wage adjustments or both. These myths have escalated since the *AFSCME v. Washington* decision, which was reported by some newspapers as costing the state $900 million. These economic chaos scenarios do not stand up in light of the voluntary wage adjustments that have taken

place. Alice Cook documents several cases of voluntary implementation, through legislation in Minnesota, through collective bargaining in San Jose, California, and Connecticut.

A comparison of the Washington State and Minnesota implementation experiences can both redress opponents' concerns and suggest appropriate implementation strategies. Washington State commissioned a comparable worth study in 1974, the results of which showed that state employees in traditionally female jobs received about 20 percent less on average than state employees in traditionally male jobs of comparable value. In 1975, Governor Dan Evans appropriated $7 million to begin implementing comparable worth. In 1977, Evan's successor, Dixie Lee Ray, removed these appropriations. In this same year, the state legislature amended the compensation statutes to instruct state officials to provide it with separate supplemental comparable worth salary schedules in addition to recommended salary schedules. The express purpose was to provide the legislature with specific costs of eliminating past wage discrimination and ongoing disparities in pay. Despite receiving these estimates the legislature took no action from 1978 through 1982. After the AFSCME law suit was filed in 1983, the legislature appropriated $1.5 million to implement the elimination of pay disparity.

"A female job and a male job of equivalent value to a firm should be paid equally."

In September, 1983, Federal District Court Judge Jack Tanner ruled that Washington State had intentionally violated Title VII of the 1964 Civil Rights Act by practicing "direct, overt, and institutionalized discrimination" by paying lower wages for jobs traditionally held by women than for jobs traditionally held by men. Under this ruling the plaintiffs are entitled to back pay since 1979. It is the back pay award, and not simply the correction of the undervaluation of women's jobs which has created the high price of the Washington State ruling.

Four Percent of the Payroll

According to estimates provided by the Manager of Standards and Surveys in Washington State, Tanner's order will cost about $325 million in back pay and $75 million per year in the future. With back pay this amounts to over 25 percent of the payroll but without back pay it amounts to roughly 5 percent of the annual payroll if all adjustments were corrected in one year. In contrast to Washington State, the

Minnesota legislature moved quickly to make comparable worth adjustments. A legislative advisory body, the Council on the Economic Status of Women, established a Task Force on Pay Equity in October, 1981. Using the job-point evaluation system already in place in Minnesota, the task force put together a pay equity report estimating the undervaluation of traditionally female jobs. By March, 1982, a pay equity bill was passed which provided for a phased-in equalization over four years. The cost over this four period was:

- Seven million dollars in the first year correcting 25 percent of the undervaluation;
- Fourteen million dollars in the second year correcting an additional 25 percent of the problem while still covering the first 25 percent;
- Twenty-one million dollars in the third year correcting 75 percent of the undervaluation;
- Twenty-eight million dollars in the fourth year completing the correction for undervaluation.

"The very emergence of the issue of comparable worth can be regarded as both a cause and a consequence of the change in the power position of women in the labor market."

The total wage adjustments come to 4 percent of the annual payroll, or 1 percent a year over a four-year period.

The political morals of the story appear to be: not to put off for a decade what can be done in the next legislative session, and voluntary corrections are much cheaper than after-the-fact litigation based corrections. In addition to being cheaper, voluntary corrections allow flexibility in phasing-in implementations of comparable worth. For instance, the New York State Comparable Pay Study includes an economic forecasting piece to assess potential costs of closing any gap in wages and to provide several options for carrying out phased-in pay equity adjustments in a voluntary and efficient fashion. We expect that the results of this cost estimation exercise will provide labor and management with the information necessary to implement change in a fair and fiscally responsible fashion.

I believe that the parameters of a national comparable worth policy are presently being formulated at the state and municipal level. Studies are still needed because, while there is growing acceptance of wage discrimination in general, there is no political consensus over which jobs are undervalued and by how much. Interest groups must combine strategies to bring about equity adjustments because the affected employees are relatively powerless, and the nature of comparable worth goes against the grain of the theoretical operating principles of the United States political economy.

Comparable Worth's Success

In its short history, comparable worth success has stimulated further success. For example, collectively bargained agreements implementing pay equity adjustments have not only been significant to the employees they cover, they have also been powerful models for other employees seeking to eliminate wage discrimination in their employment contracts. Firm level studies of the parameters of wage discrimination not only provide information to correct a specific wage structure, but also provide important material for educating women workers and the general public about the contours of wage discrimination. Similarly, court cases establish precedents for eliminating the most flagrant instances of intentional sex discrimination in compensation. Once these precedents are in place, they serve as a resource for employee groups to pressure for change in their workplace. They provide, as well, a foundation for further legal precedents making illegal more subtle forms of wage discrimination.

As proponents of comparable worth build up a body of scientific evidence, establish legal precedents, and introduce pay equity adjustments into contracts, they negate the arguments of critics of comparable worth. Criticisms are best addressed when the policy is effectively implemented and without deleterious consequences. . . .These concrete actions transform a highly charged and controversial political demand into what no doubt eventually will become a routine and institutionalized feature of equal employment.

A Political Issue

Comparable worth is less a technical than a political issue. The very emergence of the issue of comparable worth can be regarded as both a cause and a consequence of the change in the power position of women in the labor market. The considerable progress that has been made on comparable worth since 1977 demonstrates the power women and minorities are able to command when they organize and press for legal and political change. Moreover, what most women and minorities might have considered as a fair relative wage even twenty years ago, is now proving unacceptable to them. Fundamentally, comparable worth is an issue of fairness. As Eleanor Holmes Norton said, it is the equal employment issue of the decade.

Ronnie J. Steinberg is director of the Program on Comparable Worth at the Center for Women in Government, State University of New York. She has testified before Congress and several state legislatures on comparable worth.

viewpoint 81

The Poor Need More Government Help

Joseph Lelyveld

It is hard even to think the word hunger while sitting in a typical American kitchen with a freezer and other appliances gleaming as they do in the pages of a Sears catalogue, but in just such a kitchen, in Peoria, Ill., the wife of a laid-off worker at the slumping Caterpillar Corporation described how she sometimes takes only a little food on her plate at dinner, then plays with it as if she isn't really interested in eating. The point of the strategem, Sally Sawatzki explained, was to get her children to eat more without letting them guess she was denying herself for their sake. And what, I asked, did she do after they left the table?

"You eat a lot of popcorn," Mrs. Sawatzki replied. "I can get by with popcorn for a night. It's tacky but true."

Having said that much, she flushed and looked away in embarrassment. At the urging of the minister of the Baptist church she attends, she had agreed to speak to me so that people in need would understand that they must not be too proud to accept help in the form of food stamps or charity food, and so people not in need would know that not all those on food stamps were cheats. But finding words for her predicament was visibly painful. "Gosh, I can't believe I'm saying these things," she said.

Food Emergencies

Losing their home because they couldn't meet their mortgage payments was certainly hard. Applying for food stamps may have been harder, but the worst moment for Don and Sally Sawatzki was probably when the youngest of their two sons, Brock, now 9 years old, had to be told the reason there wasn't any milk in the refrigerator. "He went digging in his drawer and found 32 cents, which was

Joseph Lelyveld, "Hunger in America: The Safety Net Has Shrunk But It's Still in Place," *The New York Times*, June 16, 1985. Copyright © 1985 by The New York Times Company. Reprinted by permission.

all he had, and told me I could use it to buy food," Mrs. Sawatzki said. "And that just done me in."

The Sawatzkis are one of many families I visited that had recently experienced food emergencies. My aim was to see, after five years of the "Reagan revolution," what remained of the social safety net that was supposed to save Americans from hunger, and that now, so the President's critics constantly charge, is full of gaping holes.

The number of poor people in America has increased by about 10 million since 1978, according to Census figures, and the poor are generally further below the poverty line—now calculated by the Census Bureau to be $10,610 for a family of four—than they were then. It follows that, like the Sawatzkis, they are probably eating less well. Yet those who try to be heard on behalf of the poor as a moral obligation or political cause are often met with skepticism when they draw this deduction. When they go a step further, to contend that hunger is a central experience in the lives of millions of Americans—many of them children—they are met with downright disbelief. Nevertheless, when the country is not supposed to be in a recession, there are more soup kitchens serving more meals to more people than at any time since the Great Depression. There has been a steep annual rise in the 1980s in the tonnage of outdated, unsalable or surplus food that is channeled by food companies to the needy through private "food banks" serving thousands of "food pantries" in churches and charitable agencies. But Congress has generally held the line against proposed cuts in food and nutrition programs since bowing in 1981 to Ronald Reagan's original mandate at the polls, by tightening up on access to the Federal larder. About a million Americans were cut off food stamps then, but 20 million still get them. Federal outlays on food and child nutrition are significantly lower than they would have been had the basic laws not been changed, but $18.5 billion—

in absolute numbers, if not in real terms, the highest amount ever appropriated for these programs—still buys a lot of food.

The Hunger Debate

Such figures, however, are as remote from the lives of the poor as a satellite weather photo, and the debate over the subject of hunger is as amorphous as a bank of clouds. To some, the emergence of food banks is something to celebrate, a healthy private-sector initiative that redresses overdependence on public welfare programs and preserves a reasonably comprehensive social safety net. To others, budget cuts and the ever-growing demand for charity food signify a "growing hunger crisis" (to quote the New York City Coalition Against Hunger, one of the many public-interest lobbying groups that have sprung into being on the issue). Latter-day social Darwinists, while not exactly denying the possibility of hunger in America, imply that those who fail to eat adequately are themselves to blame for their own ignorance or indifference to the nutritional needs of their families. The counterargument—bristling with statistics on the shrinkage in the real value of welfare payments and the paltry disposable incomes of the underclass—is that it has become virtually impossible to sustain an adequate diet if you are poor.

"Hunger is a central experience in the lives of millions of Americans."

The debate has its unseemly side, for inevitably it involves the well-fed seeking to determine what degree of nutritional deprivation is unavoidable for the poor in existing economic and political circumstances. It is a hard political fact, if not exactly a moral axiom, that they cannot be seen to eat better than those who are nearly poor, who are expected to get by without direct food aid. Throughout, the word "hunger" is used in different senses by those who deny its existence as a wide-spread and worsening phenomenon in America and those who insist it is there, "silent" and "invisible"—a far cry, obviously, from Ethiopia, but spreading insidiously, nonetheless, in a bountiful land that habitually discards about one-fifth of its food.

Missing Meals

Even in inner-city emergency rooms and soup kitchens, it is far from an everyday experience to see a child or adult who is *visibly* malnourished. A pediatrician at Boston City Hospital, Dr. Deborah A. Frank, said she had seen three cases in three years of kwashiorkor, the protein-deficiency disease, and a handful of cases of marasmus, the disease that gives Ethiopian children their spectral look. "But you can come here any day and there will be something like this," she said, holding up a sweet infant who appeared normal, except that at the age of 1 she weighed only 15 pounds and could barely sit up. "She looks like a brilliant 6-month-old," she said, adding that social workers had found no evidence of neglect, only poverty, in the home from which that baby came.

Sometimes what is called "hunger" in America means "going hungry," in the sense of frequently missing meals. More often it means being chronically anxious about food because you are eating less than you believe you should and, episodically, perhaps every few weeks, don't know where your next meal is coming from. Malnutrition is a clinical state, readily gauged by physicians. Hunger is described by health experts as "subclinical"—that is, subjective, necessarily gauged in the first instance by the hungry.

When do hungry Americans acknowledge to themselves and others, "I am hungry"? Far less often, I found in the course of visits in six states to families that had recently experienced food emergencies, than one would expect from talking to those who attempt to be heard on their behalf. Least of all, however spare the diets of their families, were they ready, by calling their children hungry, to acknowledge that they had failed in the basic duty of a parent to nurture and provide.

Instead of quibbling over the word "hunger," it often seemed better to say that they had severe food problems. What that means, in everyday terms, can be seen in the following verbal snapshots of families I visited across the country:

"Oh, I've missed a lot of meals," said Gerelene Gibbs, who had taken refuge with two grandchildren in a shelter for homeless mothers and children on Chicago's South Side after having been cut off food stamps for failing to find her way through recertification formalities. Before she came to the shelter, the children sometimes got only oatmeal for dinner. As for herself, "You drink a lot of water," she said. "Water or black tea. It's not a meal, but it's better than nothing."

Hungry Children

Farther down the shore of Lake Michigan, in a neighborhood called South Chicago that has been hard hit by steel-mill closings, Ricardo and Hilda Escotto told me how the youngest of their nine children, 2-year-old Veronica, kicks the refrigerator and cries when she can't find any bologna inside. The Escotto children mainly subsist on rice and beans at home and free school lunches. . . .

'They get full off rice and butter and sugar," a welfare mother in Houston named Joyce Wiltz replied when I asked her how she kept her children from going hungry after she has used up her monthly allotment of food stamps. The staples she was mentioning, I realized, come in the distribution of commodities from surplus Federal food stocks. Her friend Ernestine Coleman was appealing a ruling of the local branch of the Texas Department of Human Resources, which had terminated her food stamps, forcing her to use the rent money for her apartment in a row of dingy so-called "efficiencies" to buy food. Mrs. Coleman allowed me to peer into the fetid interior of her refrigerator, which hadn't worked since the power company turned off the electricity several days earlier. There I found a package of grits, the remains of a box of powdered mashed potatoes, three onions, a half-used container of Parmesan cheese, some milk that had long since turned sour and a little Coffee-Mate.

If I had arrived in Albuquerque, N.M., on a Thursday, I might have found even less in the refrigerator of Bobby and Julie Stembridge, a young couple of 22 and 21, respectively, who had headed west from Amarillo, Tex., with four small sons and wound up destitute on the doorstep of the Salvation Army. Instead, I visited them on a Saturday, the day after they had collected their monthly allotment of food stamps, and there wasn't room for another frozen tuna casserole, chicken pie or packet of hamburger meat in their refrigerator. The cupboard was crowded with canned green beans, 40 jars of baby food, Mr. T cereal, instant strawberry-and-cream oatmeal, a large cylinder of regular oatmeal and 20 boxes of America's favorite low-budget, dollar-stretching staple, macaroni and cheese. The Stembridges' idea, being tested for the first time, was that if they spent all their food stamps at once, they would be able to budget their provisions for the month.

Twice in recent months the Stembridges had gone to an Albuquerque food pantry for a box of emergency groceries. The boxes are designed to last a family in need for at least a few days. The Stembridges said they made them last seven. Their children had missed meals, but never for a whole day, Bobby said. But 15-month old Joseph, called Jo-Jo, weighed only 18 pounds, just 4 pounds more than cherubic Christopher, who is 10 months his junior. Plainly, Jo-Jo was what pediatricians call a "failure to thrive" infant.

Negotiating for Help

Back in New York, I met Celia Rosado, who lives with her two sons, ages 8 and 4, in an East Harlem tenement. Her last welfare check had been stolen from her mailbox and she was still three days from getting her next allotment of food stamps. Celia said she took her older boy, Jose, to Public School 72 every morning and returned there for his lunch period, to watch over him in the cafeteria, just to be sure he finished his subsidized lunch. Jose was a picky eater, she explained. She had no money, but

her mother, who was also on food stamps, had managed to feed her and the boys the night before. St. Cecilia's Parish Services on East 105th Street had given her enough food to tide her over the coming weekend and, being a responsible mother, she had already made arrangements to be driven to the Bronx when her stamps finally came through to buy a large economy packet of meat at a cut-rate market called Tops.

" 'They get full off rice and butter and sugar,' a welfare mother . . . replied when I asked her how she kept her children from going hungry after she had used up her . . . food stamps."

She had negotiated with the corner grocer for a little more credit, with the landlord for an extension on the rent, with the welfare system for a new check. It was an arduous business, taking days, but she could now feel that her crisis management in the case of the burgled mailbox had been effective— except for the small detail that she herself had skipped breakfast and lunch that day and had tasted only coffee. If somebody said that her family was suffering from hunger, I asked, what would she reply?

"It's not true," Celia Rosado said proudly.

I dwell on the particulars in order to make the point that what is called "hunger" in America is not everywhere the same. And yet everywhere there are families for whom food is an abiding problem. I visited many more of them, for I was trying to view that problem through the opposite end of the telescope from the one that is usually used by Congressmen and budget-makers, to understand the dietary strategies and choices people are forced to improvise when they are hard-pressed. But, of course, I could only skim the surface. Each of these stories was a saga, with its own distinct causes and context and possible outcomes. You could choose your stereotype in order to score a political point by blaming either the needy or the system. They were all there—families that grew up on welfare, families that were trapped into it by sudden economic reversals or bureaucratic Catch-22's that seemed to penalize them for going to work or observing the rules, and families that were nonetheless fighting their way out. All of them seemed to know what it was to run out of food as a regular, recurring experience in their lives.

Shrinking Welfare

It was clearly possible to know hunger on public assistance, at least episodically. Advocates on behalf of the poor regularly stress the constant shrinkage in the value of welfare checks, which vary hugely from state to state. Often their calculations neglect the value of food stamps, which are supposed to rise with the cost of living. Yet even when the food stamps are counted, there is no question that the poor are poorer than they were only a few years ago. For those who got them without interruption, the combined value of food stamps and welfare payments declined by 8 to 9.7 percent in real terms in the four years starting in 1980, according to a study done last year for the House Ways and Means Committee; in 18 states, for families with no other income, their value is now only two-thirds of the poverty threshold—or less. . . .

Those who debunk the existence of a hunger crisis tend to assume that private food and feeding schemes are mainly for the incompetent, persons unable to clear the many procedural hurdles established for public aid. "A far-gone alcoholic or a borderline schizophrenic may not be able, and certainly isn't often inclined, to go through that sort of hassle if he knows of a church-supported soup kitchen nearby that will feed him without asking any questions whatever," William A. Rusher, the conservative commentator, observed last year.

Feeding Women and Children

That is true as far as it goes, but it doesn't explain the growing number of soup kitchens that find themselves feeding families with children, or the proliferation of food pantries. The St. Martin de Porres House of Hope, a shelter for homeless mothers and children in the Woodlawn section of Chicago, reports that it had to turn away 14,192 mothers and children for lack of space and funds in its first 20 months of operation. . . .

Far from matching the stereotype of social deadbeats and down-and-outers, more than two-thirds of the recipients of private food aid in the New York survey were children, which is not altogether surprising, considering the point underscored by Senator Daniel Patrick Moynihan in his Godkin Lectures at Harvard that children account for an increasing proportion—39 percent as of 1983—of all Americans living in poverty. . . .

Inevitably, most food-stamp families live on a nutritional cycle that starts off reasonably well, then deteriorates as the month wears on, becoming marginal if not desperate in the final week or 10 days, depending on how frugal they were earlier. "The first part of the month I always cook us a good meal," said Patricia Roberts, who is raising three children in Houston on a Social Security widow's pension and food stamps. "Something we don't get and something we like. Fish usually." There are ample portions and fresh vegetables and all the milk the children can drink, and Mrs. Roberts tries for one night not to worry about her unpaid bills. "I just say at that point, 'I don't care what happens,'"

she said. "'I'm going to take care of myself.'"

The splurge is over almost as soon as it begins. By the end of the month, the Roberts family is sometimes reduced to eating potatoes as a staple and Mrs. Roberts has to borrow from relatives. She is the head of a single-parent household and black, so she conforms to another kind of stereotype. But she was laid off two and a half years ago from a job as a machinist at the Hughes Tool Company, where she had earned $13.62 an hour. Since then she has taken any work she could get, for as little as $3.35 an hour. The idea that she is now classed with women who have never found their way into the job market incenses her. "There seems to be a mix-up as to who's who," she said.

"In the case of 585 families turning to welfare centers in food emergencies, only five—fewer than 1 percent—reported receiving any kind of tangible assistance."

The food problems of the so-called "new poor"—industrial workers like Mrs. Roberts who have fallen into dependence on public assistance—shed light on the nutritional problems of the old poor, undercutting the easy, middle-class assumption that the impoverished diets of the poor are traceable to ignorance and a dependence on junk food, rather than lack of money. . . .

Often when I left the homes of people who had experienced food emergencies, I found myself reflecting that hunger was not really their central problem. It was the whole poverty cycle—the demeaning encounters with the welfare system, squalid housing, lack of preparation for a changing job market and the high level of stress, anger or self-doubt that come with all these burdens and are nightly reinforced by a cascade of television commercials showing the kinds of cars Americans are supposed to drive, the kinds of kitchens they're supposed to have, the kinds of meals they are supposed to serve their families, and the kinds of planes they are supposed to fly in to far-off lands. . . .

The puzzle is why, if there are more hungry people living below the poverty line, there are not now more people receiving food stamps. Robert Greenstein, who ran the Food and Nutrition Service in the Carter years and now heads the Center on Budget and Policy Priorities, a research group in Washington, calculates on the basis of current poverty estimates that the number of food stamp recipients should be 2 million higher than it was in 1980, even after taking into account the 1981 tightening of eligibility requirements that knocked a million working poor out of the program. Instead, there are 300,000 fewer recipients. The reason, he speculated, must have something to do with difficulty of access to the system, its nightmarish qualities as experienced by the poor. It might even, he theorized, have something to do with a deeper sense of social disapproval.

Teen Pregnancy

It isn't just whites new to food stamps who feel or express that judgment. I met Barbara Davis in a public housing project in Peoria called Harrison Homes that is overwhelmingly tenanted by black families on public assistance. A welfare mother of 5 who became a mother at 16 and a grandmother at 32 and now has 2 daughters and 5 grandchildren who are on welfare themselves, Mrs. Davis was as unsparing in her judgment of what was happening to her community as any suburbanite.

"My daddy worked every day," she said. "He was a meat cutter at the Armour packing house. My daughters are doing pretty good, they all right, but I didn't want them to wind up like this. They don't care. They figure the more babies they have, the more money they get from A.F.D.C. [Aid to Families With Dependent Children, as the main welfare program is formally known]."

"Far from matching the stereotype of social deadbeats . . . more than two-thirds of the recipients of private food aid in the New York survey were children."

Social scientists who have studied the subject contend that there is little evidence that the prospect of welfare benefits has anything to do with the pregnancy rate among teenagers. But as Mrs. Davis's judgment showed, popular attitudes on what the system is doing to those it is supposed to benefit are not necessarily determined by which side of the poverty line a person stands on.

Crusade Against Fraud

The sense of judgment is even stronger inside the welfare centers, where case workers are under constant and increasing pressure to uncover fraud and repel cheats. Under an "error rate reduction system" implemented by the Reagan Administration, a state that can be shown to have an error rate of more than 5 percent on food-stamp cases loses out on a portion of the funds it would otherwise have received from Washington. Underpayment to an eligible recipient, or the failure to serve an eligible person altogether, doesn't count as an error for the

purpose of that calculation. Only overpayment is penalized.

The pressure is logical from the standpoint of legal draftsmen trying to freeze social "entitlement" programs as part of a crusade against budget deficits. It may even be necessary as a political fact to save food and nutrition programs from more drastic cutbacks. But the level of suspicion a genuinely needy person meets as a consequence on venturing into a government office to apply for help is suggested by two findings in the report of the East Harlem Interfaith Welfare Committee: in the cases of 585 families turning to welfare centers in food emergencies, only five—fewer than 1 percent—reported receiving any kind of tangible assistance. . . .

Insensible Donations

However the poor spend their food money—nutrition surveys indicate they are no less prudent or more foolish than everyone else—it is hard to imagine families that would be quite as erratic in their choices as food pantries are forced to be in what they distribute as a result of the unplanned, helter-skelter pattern of the donations that flow in from food companies. One day they are rolling in doughnuts, the next they are drowning in pink lemonade. In Peoria, at the Central Illinois Food Bank, I saw crates and crates of cast-off marketing ideas that had gathered dust on supermarket shelves—peaches-and-cream instant oatmeal, cherry Pop-Tarts, apple-cinnamon cream cheese, caramel candy bars, fruit sticks and Dijon mustard. Most of these items would come in handy somewhere, but they were hardly building blocks of a sensible diet.

Then there is the problem of getting the poor—especially poor children—to the food. On a Saturday afternoon in Albuquerque, a Jewish congregation, Nahalat Shalom, had taken responsibility for serving meals to the needy at the Salvation Army. These were not "almost fresh" groceries saved from supermarket dumpsters or the pallid institutional fare that is the best most soup kitchens can manage. There was roast chicken done to a turn, enough for seconds, even thirds, fresh vegetables, salad, cake, fruit, brownies and ice cream—a feast, by any standard.

That day, I had been in homes of needy families whose children had seldom, if ever, seen a meal as succulent. But they were miles away on the north side of town, while the missions were in a downtown area that looked semideserted and a little on the rough side on a Saturday afternoon. A single mother with three or four children would think twice before taking them there, unless she was desperate.

Joseph Lelyveld is an author and staff writer at The New York Times Magazine.

"They run the whole program all wrong. . . . They ought to be telling people to find jobs and take care of themselves. Instead they're just trying to put everybody on welfare."

viewpoint 82

The Poor Do Not Need More Government Help

William Tucker

"Help the Homeless," said a button pinned to the woman's beret. She was black, about 30, and standing in front of a table of trinkets being sold by a sidewalk vendor on 33rd Street in Manhattan.

"What do you think New York City ought to do for the homeless?" I asked her.

"Well, you know, they could give us a little more money. I've only got $325 a month to live on. I've got my four kids to feed, and it's hard to do."

Her name was Carmen. She was not unattractive, intelligent, and spoke with a trace of an accent that she finally told me was Puerto Rican. Her home was the Martinique, a beautiful old tourist hotel facing Herald Square that used to have three luxurious restaurants, and now teems with 2,000 welfare tenants—500 women and 1,500 children.

"I was in Section 8 housing down on West Third Street," she told me. "We got burned out. I've been here about two months. We're waiting until something opens up in the projects."

Burning Down the House

For years, getting into the projects—city-sponsored housing—has been one of the most coveted goals of New York's poor. Waiting periods were once two years, but for the last decade the city has given immediate priority to people whose apartments burned down. As a result, tenants often burned down their buildings in order to move to the top of the list. Add this to a landlord's incentive to burn down his own building to rid himself of rent-controlled tenants, and you have the South Bronx.

Now, however, the waiting periods have swelled to ten years. Even arson can't get you into a city housing project. Consequently, there is a new category of "homeless."

I spent two weeks floating among New York City's

William Tucker, "Visits with the Homeless," *The American Spectator*, May 1985. Reprinted by permission of King Features Syndicate.

population of 50,000 homeless people. I visited the Men's Shelter, where I ended up posing as just another homeless resident. I did volunteer duty in a synagogue that has been temporarily converted into a makeshift shelter. I visited the Coalition for the Homeless, headquarters of the legal attack for "homeless rights," and spent another afternoon talking with people in front of the Martinique, one of New York's largest "welfare hotels."

Defining the Homeless

It is difficult to sum up except perhaps to say four things: 1) There is a hard core of homeless people, most of them refugees from mental hospitals, who are incapable of taking care of themselves; 2) there is a down-and-out population of homeless men who could probably take care of themselves; 3) the "homeless families" that are now surging into the system are really the familiar black-woman-and-her-illegitimate-children welfare families in a new guise; and 4) the people who are most emotionally involved in helping the homeless haven't the slightest idea what they're doing.

Lumping the first three categories together as "the homeless" seems useful only to the fourth category, i.e., those who patronize the homeless. First, it makes for a classification that is racially and ethnically neutral. Second, it obscures the fact that we are only dealing with problems that liberal programs have created. And third, it fends off public opinion that is probably getting tired of dealing with "welfare families."

Welfare Women

What I encountered in several hours at the Martinique, for example, had little to do with "homelessness." It was simply the sociological debris from the catastrophic upheaval that has occurred in the black family over the last twenty years.

Thomasina was typical. A black woman, age 28,

she had been living in two rooms at the Martinique for the last three months with her six children. She wore a red beret and sunglasses, and her two bottom teeth were missing. She could have been 50.

"I had my own apartment and my own job six months ago," she said. "I was living in Columbus, Ohio. I came to visit my sister here, and while we were staying her apartment burned down. So they put me in here."

What happened to her job and apartment? "I don't know—they're gone now. That's the way it goes sometimes, you know." Thomasina didn't seem terribly concerned about getting in or out of the Martinique. "They put you on a bus every week and take you around to show you apartments, and tell you you have to take something. I didn't like anything they showed me yet, so I'm staying right here."

"What I encountered . . . had little to do with 'homelessness.' It was simply the sociological debris from the . . . upheaval that has occurred in the black family."

Carmen was the same way. She had four children. Had she ever had a husband? I asked.

"Are you kidding? Get beat up all the time? No sir, not me."

She actually seemed fairly responsible. She had worked as a store clerk, and was now tending one end of the trinket table for the elderly Oriental who was operating the sidewalk stand. He was paying her $3.00 an hour.

"The only thing I don't like about it here at the hotel are the fights," she told me. "A lot of women beat their children. You know, they get mad at 'em and whip 'em or lock 'em outside. Or else they spend their welfare money on a nickel bag instead of feeding their kids. A six-year-old got raped in there a couple weeks ago, too."

She said she wasn't particularly looking for another place to live. Her room at the Martinique wasn't all that bad. After we finished talking, she urged me to come up and visit her, and wanted to give me her phone number.

Welfare Men

Where were the men in this world? A lot of them were standing right outside, their noses almost literally pressed against the glass.

Cloyd was a 29-year-old black who paced back and forth in front of the hotel like a caged fox. He was thin and wiry, with a strung-out look. A fresh two-inch scar ran down his left nostril, the stitch-marks still clearly visible.

"They won't let me in," he said. "These bastards won't let me past the door. I'm trying to get in to see my old lady."

It emerged that he had had "a little fight" with his old lady a week ago, and was now banned from the hotel. He lived in Queens with a relative and spent his days "doing nothing." I had the feeling his old lady wasn't terribly anxious to see him.

Cloyd was nervous and didn't want to talk, so I struck up another conversation with Carlton, an older, much more respectable-looking man with a Jamaican lilt in his voice.

Baby-Mothers

"My baby-mother lives in here," he told me. "She has five other kids. The last one's mine. I'm 39, she's 38. We were living together in the Bronx, but the Spanish moved in. They're the ones that are ruining New York. They think us black people are nothing, so they stole everything from us. Then they wrecked the building. It was too crowded for me to live in here, so I'm staying at a hotel on East 23rd Street. The city is paying my rent."

I was curious about that term "baby-mother." What did it mean?

"It means the mother of your baby," he explained patiently. "You know, if she has your baby, that makes you the father, and she's the baby-mother."

But didn't that make her your girlfriend, or your common-law wife or something?

"No, mon, that's the baby-mother."

Cloyd had drifted back, and was listening intently to our conversation.

"I've never heard that term, 'baby-mother,' before," I said.

For the first time all afternoon, Cloyd's face dissolved in a smile. "You never heard of a 'baby-mother' before?" he said. "Shee-it man, where you been?"

Shelter Dwellers

The day before, I had been down to the Men's Shelter on West Third Street. Originally a city-sponsored sleeping quarters for Bowery Bums, it has recently become the central clearing house for New York City's homeless men.

I originally walked in looking for a supervisor to ask about some interviews. The place was so busy, though, and everyone seemed so indifferent to my presence, that I finally just fell into the routine of acting like another homeless individual.

About 300 men crowded into the Shelter's first-floor recreation and intake rooms, with perhaps another 300 scattered among the three upper floors.

The crowd was mostly black and Spanish, probably a little older than younger. It was a boisterous group.

There were few places to sit. Card games occupied one whole side of the large recreation room. On the other, a group of black transvestites carried on an endless melodrama about someone's borrowed shoes. In the middle of the room, two men played a furious game of ping-pong. It took me a while to realize there was an old drunk asleep under the ping-pong table.

One thing obviously marked the few white men in the crowd. All of them seemed at least a little disturbed. One wild-haired Jewish-looking guy in his thirties, who looked like a shipwreck from the 1960s, marched up and down the room spouting loudly about Marx and revolution. When I asked him if he had grown up in New York, he said: "I'm from the USA, one nation under God—one, one, one, one." He jabbed his arms and legs out in a fair imitation of a swastika. Then he marched off again.

Down on Their Luck

If I had to characterize the majority of men I talked to, I would say they were "down on their luck." One very kind black man in his forties, named Ken, said he had been running a small video parlor in the Bronx only a few months before. "I had to go to North Carolina to take care of my mother. She got sick, and didn't have any insurance. I used all my money to pay her hospital bills. She finally died.

"Then when I came back, some kids had broken into the game parlor and wrecked everything. We didn't have any insurance. My partner and I went bankrupt. I couldn't pay my rent, so I ended up here. I'm trying to scrape a little money together so I can get started again."

One kid was sitting on a bench selling individual cigarettes for ten cents apiece. He was 23 years old. "I've been in here about four months," he said. "I make about $10 a day. I do it because I'm not the kind of person who'll rob or steal from people. I wasn't raised like that." Did he have any plans for the future? "Just get out of here and try to get a job, I guess."

It was an institutional setting, not unlike a jail or mental hospital. (In fact, many of these people undoubtedly would have been in mental hospitals twenty years ago.) In an upstairs pool room, two older guys spent fifteen minutes doing a clumsy Harlem Globetrotters imitation. In another room where garbage details were being handed out for $12 a week, one man fell down and had an epileptic seizure right in front of me.

Jazz Musicians and Surgeons

I went through intake, told a social worker I had left my wife and children and was issued a 30-day meal card. When I told him I had spent a year in college, he didn't blink an eye. The guy just ahead of me, a jazz musician, had claimed to have a Ph.D. "It's the economy," Ken told me earlier. "The guy I slept next to last night said he was a surgeon."

Finally, as we lined up for a meal, I ended up next

to an Irish-looking guy, graying, with pointy shoes, pegged pants, and a funny, cross-eyed look. Even to my untutored eye, he had "jail" written all over him.

"What've they got you in here for?" I asked.

He laughed, and told me all about his days in prison. "You've got a much tougher bunch of guys in there," he said. "In jail, you've got to protect yourself all the time. I saw a guy get stabbed 39 times once just like that. When it was over, nobody seen nothing. Here everybody just minds their own business. But don't get drunk. They'll roll you in a minute.

"You've got to make plans," he advised me. "You've got to think of something to do on the outside. A lot of these guys in here have given up. They're just living day to day. They'll stay here as long as the city lets them."

The requirement for staying at the Men's Shelter is that you take a shower. After you're through, the shelter gives you a clean T-shirt. The shirts are color-coded to make sure everyone washes every day. Some residents of the men's shelter are opposed to bathing on principle.

The cleanest, brightest, and most acceptable of the homeless are farmed out to the dozens and dozens of armories, churches, synagogues, and former mental hospitals that have been mobilized to deal with the state court settlement that created the "right to a place to sleep" for everyone in New York City.

"A lot of these guys [in shelters for the homeless] have given up . . . . They'll stay here as long as the city lets them."

A few nights later, I spent an evening at the Congregation Rodef Shalom on West 86th Street. The temple was putting up twelve homeless men, but eight of them had already retired to their cots when I arrived at nine o'clock. (No shelter can take more than nineteen people. Otherwise, it must secure a city license, which requires an impossible amount of refurbishing and paperwork.)

Three Homeless Men

Gary, Rodney, and Vinnie, three homeless men, were sitting at a card table playing a wicked game of pinochle. The two other volunteers—a middle-aged man and woman from the neighborhood—were watching television. There was supposed to be some "counseling" going on, but the card players were having such a good time and the volunteers seemed so intimidated that the whole idea of "rehabilitation" seemed inappropriate.

I sat down at the table for a while and tried to

learn the game. Then gradually, I started asking the players about themselves, telling them I was doing a newspaper story. They were cautious at first, but eventually opened up.

Gary was 35, although I would have guessed 28. He was black, had a small mustache, and a well-educated manner. An accountant by trade, he had just come back from six months in London.

"I sublet my apartment and was living over there," he said. (In New York City, subletting a rent-controlled apartment at double or triple the rent allowable to the landlord is a major source of income for tens of thousands of people.) "But my sub-tenant moved out and didn't even tell me. The landlord took it over again, and when I got back I didn't have anyplace to live. So I had to come here. I haven't been able to land a job in six weeks, but I just got something with Bank of New York. I start Monday. It's almost impossible to look for an apartment and a job at the same time in New York."

Rodney was 38, black, and extremely pleasant. He owns a liquor store in Los Angeles, where he lives with his common-law wife and five children. His eldest daughter is attending the University of Southern California.

"I came back here to settle the estate with my mother and stepfather," he said. They had died under mysterious circumstances that he didn't want to elaborate. "We don't think they were murdered, but we're not sure. I was staying with my sisters and brothers while the house is in probate, but things got too crowded, so I moved here. I sent my kids back to L.A. My wife and I aren't legally married, but we've been together for 18 years."

He was extraordinarily sensitive to the nuances of the situation. "My mother was the first black woman CPA in this country," he said. "We've always been accountants in our family. My mother and father were the only liquor store owners in our neighborhood to survive the New York liquor strike in the 1970s. It's much easier to run a liquor store in Los Angeles, though. You don't have so many regulations out there."

Vinnie was the youngest of the three, 24, Italian, and probably the least savvy of the group (he was also losing the card game). He was willing to talk about things that left the other two a little embarrassed.

"I'm married with two kids," he said. "I'm a construction worker. My wife and I live with her brother in Queens. He's a real bastard. He's a cop, about 38 years old. We don't get along. He's retiring and moving to Florida in the spring, though, so we'll have the whole house to ourselves."

What was he doing among the homeless? "I got hurt on the job a month ago," he said. "I got some glass in my feet, and then it got all diseased." He showed me the soles of his feet, which were damp and peeling, and indeed looked painfully infected.

"I'm collecting disability and unemployment for a while. I came down here because we're telling the disability people we're separated. We collect a bigger check that way." He told me all this without a trace of embarrassment.

Was he sure he wasn't having a little fight with his wife, and just telling this story as an excuse? "Oh, no," he said, "I go out there every day. I'm just sleeping down here at night so we can get more money."

Get a Job

After an hour-and-a-half of this, I finally had to admit I felt a little strange. "I feel like I'm sitting with a group of impostors here," I said. "I came down looking for an interview with the unfortunate homeless, and here I find intelligent, grown men, all with jobs and families." (Gary had a teenage daughter, but was separated from his wife.)

"I came . . . looking for an interview with the unfortunate homeless, and [found] . . . three intelligent, grown men, all with jobs and families."

They ignored my comment for a bit. Then Gary finally pursed his lips and formulated a response. "I think you have to differentiate us from those people down at the Men's Shelter," he said. "All those people are really institutionalized. Even a lot of the staff started out as homeless. All they think about is getting you on some kind of social-services program. They're always trying to send you to Camp LaGuardia." (Indeed, during my interview, the social worker had immediately suggested I go to this large state-run compound in the Catskills.)

"I think they run the whole program all wrong down there," he concluded. "They ought to be telling people to find jobs and take care of themselves. Instead, they're just trying to put everybody on welfare."

New York City's Homeless

New York City now has an estimated 50,000 "homeless" people. The numbers have grown in the past few years, although the phenomenon is not new. In 1978, Kim Hopper and Ellen Baxter, of the Community Service Society, published a paper estimating there were 35,000 homeless in New York. (They now claim 60,000.) The real change seems to have been that the issue has become politicized.

In 1979, Robert Hayes, a young Wall Street attorney, brought a class-action suit that eventually determined every person in New York City had a "legal right" to shelter at city expense. At the time there were 2,000 men in the Men's Shelter and 50 women in the Women's Shelter. The City was spending $14 million per year on the program....

"Slumlords"

The inevitable accusation, of course, is that some mysterious "slumlords" are making millions off these welfare payments. But when I talked with Sal Tuccelli, the owner of the Martinique, sitting in his mezzanine offices overlooking the lobby, he didn't seem like a man getting rich.

"If you'd told me I'd end up like this ten years ago, I'd have thought you were crazy," he said. "This used to be a beautiful place. We had an off-Broadway theater in here. I was the first hotel owner in New York to win the Silver Award for Fine Restaurants. That's a hand-painted ceiling out there."

Tuccelli said he leased out the Martinique for ten years, and his leaseholder converted to welfare without telling him. "Even then he couldn't make it, so we had to take it back," he said. "I've got 1,500 kids in here. Can you imagine the vandalism? Four months ago we spent half-a-million dollars on five new elevators. Now all of them have been destroyed. I'd sell this place in a minute, but there isn't a person on earth who would buy it."

New York City's complicated tenant-protection laws forbid any welfare hotel owner from evicting a tenant who has lived with him for more than 29 days. In New York, once you've accepted a tenant, you're stuck with him for life. This is another reason no one builds rental housing anymore.

The only way Tuccelli could empty his building now is if the hotel burned down.

"Almost every homeless person I had encountered so far was a black who had split up his or her family—or never bothered forming one—making it necessary to find two apartments instead of one."

Fred Griesbach is director of the Coalition for the Homeless. He doesn't think New York City is spending nearly enough. "Each year's peak of homelessness is next year's average," he said, sitting in his cramped office. (The Coalition for the Homeless receives no city funds.) "The numbers just keep going up. There's no end in sight.

"Studies have shown that about 25-30 percent of the homeless are mentally ill," he said. "That figure is probably about right. There's a hard core out there who just can't take care of themselves."

Most of these people were dumped out of mental hospitals in the 1960s and '70s when another "civil rights" crusade decided they should be "free" to

refuse treatment. Nationwide, the population of state mental hospitals has fallen from 559,000 to 132,000 over that period. Thousands of these "bag ladies" and "vent people" now live in railway and bus stations, in bank lobbies, on sidewalks, under bridges, and in makeshift "tent cities."

Many of these people are obviously irrational. When New York City officials began forcing them to go to shelters on sub-freezing nights, however, the ACLU objected loudly that their "civil rights" were being violated. In very cold weather, the pick-up van from the Department of Human Resources now carries two psychiatrists who make on-the-spot diagnoses designed to stand up in court.

This winter, Grand Central Station began staying open all night to accomodate the homeless. Within days there were rumors that Human Resources vans were dumping people off at Grand Central, rather than putting them into the city's overcrowded shelters. Soon, Grand Central travelers were stepping over indigents to get to their trains. One supposedly "harmless" vagrant attacked a Connecticut commuter and bit his finger off. Grand Central officials started closing the station at one a.m. again once the cold weather eased.

Intact Families

But this hard core of shamefully abandoned drunks and incompetents has only served as a wedge to drag thousands of other people into the social services network. A survey of the men's shelters in 1983 found that a significant number of shelter residents were younger men who had come in for economic reasons, and 60 percent of the homeless had lived with close relatives or friends in their last three sleeping arrangements. That was long before the city started processing welfare mothers and their children into the system as well.

"How many of these families are intact?" I asked Fred Griesbach, after he told me that homeless families represented "the biggest growth area."

"What do you mean, 'intact'?"

"I mean a father, mother, and children."

"Very few," he said. "They are almost all minorities. You know what it's like for black people in this society, especially black women. They can't find jobs, they don't get adequate day care, there are no training programs available. It makes very little difference whether a family is quote-unquote intact."

Affordable Housing

Griesbach was bearded and young, a nice-looking guy. I thought he looked 27, but he was 34. He was a school-teacher before becoming involved in the homeless. His office was decorated with political posters ("Help Angola Win Independence—Boycott Gulf").

What is the city supposed to do about the homeless? I asked.

"Housing. We've got to have more public housing. There's just no place for anyone to live. We're a rich society, we can afford it."

Can New York City afford it?

"Well, probably not. We've got to have the federal government come in here and build housing for us."

Wouldn't getting rid of rent control help, since New York City's housing regulations have driven every private developer of rental housing out of business?

"No," he replied. "The private developers only build housing for the rich."

Attractive System

Well look, I said. I admit it's hard to find a place to live in New York. (John F. Kennedy, Jr. recently spent two months trying to find an apartment.) But didn't he think that people had to provide something for themselves? Almost every homeless person I had encountered so far was a black who had split up his or her family—or never bothered forming one— making it necessary to find two apartments instead of one. By going to court and trying to force the city to spend hundreds of millions or more dollars in building shelters, wasn't he just making the whole system more attractive?

Griesbach stared at me in disbelief. "Almost anything is attractive to a person who doesn't have a place to live," he said. "All we're talking about here is shelter. We're talking about having a bed to lie on and a roof over your head to protect you from the rain. The people in these shelters don't even have a place to cook. Some of them don't have a private bathroom. We're talking about things every human being is entitled to."

As I jotted in my notes, I could feel his voice rising with emotion. When I finally looked up, his face was glowing with righteous indignation. He looked like a candidate for sainthood.

William Tucker is a contributing editor at Harper's.

"In 1980, one in fifteen Americans faced . . . poverty, compared with about one in five Americans just a generation earlier. This was accomplished, almost entirely, by the government."

viewpoint **83**

The War on Poverty Helped the Poor

John E. Schwarz

Imagine all the people living today in the industrial states of Massachusetts and Michigan, with such cities as Boston and Detroit. Then add all the people living in the states of Minnesota, Colorado, Oregon, Arizona, Maryland, and Kentucky. These states contain Minneapolis, St. Paul, Denver, Portland, Pheonix, Tucson, Baltimore, Louisville. To complete the picture, include some of the more rural states such as New Hampshire, South Carolina, and Iowa. Then imagine every person in every one of these states living in poverty. That describes the number of people and the breadth of the poverty existing in America in 1960 at the end of the Eisenhower era.

Another point must be understood. Many Americans living in poverty either had jobs or had worked for their entire adult life. During the early 1960s, the heads of about half the families living in poverty held jobs, and one out of every four impoverished family heads had full-time employment all year long. Even in the last half of the 1970s, about 1 million heads of poor families in America who were employed full time were still living below the poverty line. They and their dependents numbered almost 5 million Americans. The size of the problem is made real enough by these figures. As head of a family of four, could a worker earn his or her way out of poverty? Possibly, but for many Americans—bookkeepers, laborers, janitors, secretaries, household workers, library aids, small farmers, cashiers, receptionists, nurse's aides—not easily. . . .

Substantial Progress

Perhaps the best overall indicator of the substantial progress made by the nation in the battle against poverty after 1960 is that by the second half of the

1970s only 4 to 8 percent of the American public remained beneath the poverty level compared with about 18 percent in 1960. These figures take into account the income Americans received from every source, including income from all private economic activities and the private sector as well as from governmental programs. In the space of one generation, the economic growth of the times combined with the government's programs had reduced poverty among Americans by about 60 percent. . . .

Surely one would anticipate that a period of such robust economic growth—growth that was very strong after inflation and taxes—would lower the percentage of impoverished Americans. The validity of this presumption can be examined by considering what the private economy accomplished in reducing poverty. Let us compare 1965 and 1972. When one takes all income except that transferred to individuals through governmental programs, census evidence for 1965 indicates that about 21.3 percent of the public would have been living in poverty; in 1972, again considering all sources of income except that received from governmental programs, census figures show that about 19.2 percent of the public would have been living in poverty, about one-tenth less than in 1965. Thus, the private sector, in these times of substantial economic growth, reduced the percentage of Americans living in poverty by about one in every ten Americans; and exclusive of governmental programs, even by 1972 almost one in five Americans would still have been living in poverty.

Obviously, the economy's growth during these highly prosperous years alleviated poverty only marginally. In contrast to private economic performance, consider the performance of the programs of government. As a result of the govenment's programs, more than half of the remaining 19 percent of impoverished Americans rose above the poverty line, leaving about 9 percent of the American people below the poverty line by 1972; and by the late 1970s that figure was further reduced to between 7 and 8 percent, and possibly even lower. . . .

Shortfalls of Economic Growth

In certain crucial circumstances, economic growth does not help the very weak. Several major groups of Americans—groups that comprised millions upon millions of people across the nation—were almost completely excluded from the benefits of the private economic growth that occurred over these years.

The expanding economy did not directly touch, at least not very much, the impoverished elderly, for example. Most of our elderly are retired. Senior citizens who try to find jobs after retirement soon learn—if they can locate new employment at all— that the private sector is often unwilling to pay more than a marginal wage to people over 65 who reenter the labor market. . . .

A prosperously growing economy in the nation at large did little, directly, for the impoverished elderly.

"Exclusive of governmental programs, . . . one in five Americans would still have been living in poverty."

A second important group of Americans bypassed by the expanding economy included white and nonwhite families headed by women under the age of 65. Although more than one in seven families are headed by women, the average earnings of women in the private economy are about 60 percent that of males. In addition, the jobs available to women are often dead end, with little possibility for advancement. Again, when the labor markets teem and the competition for jobs is severe, opportunities for women are particularly limited.

In this light, consider the plight of white female family heads under the age of 65. The period from 1965 through 1972 produced a remarkable result with respect to this group. Exclusive of the government's programs, a slightly *higher* proportion of these female-headed families found themselves in poverty in 1972 than in 1965: Forty percent of these families lived in poverty in 1972, an increase of .4 percent over 1965. And the figures for nonwhite female family heads under the age of 65 are no more encouraging. The nation's substantial economic growth made little dent in the levels of poverty experienced by these families, for, aside from the government's programs, poverty within this group dropped only 3 percent, from 69 percent in 1965 to 66 percent in 1972.

The situation encountered by women in the private sector of the economy has always been difficult. Even after very high rates of growth, the private economy left millions of women and their families in poverty, as great a percentage after the economic expansion as before. . . .Had it not been for the government's presence, hardly any change in the rate of poverty facing this very large group of Americans would have been realized over the whole of this prosperous period.

The plight of a third group, really a subgroup of females, the families headed by females under the age of 25, is similarly desperate. For the young, who are just beginning their work careers, are highly vulnerable in a labor market full to overflowing and an economy undergoing change. The rate of poverty among these families in 1965 was 62 percent; by 1972, although personal income growth in real terms had risen by more than one-fifth per American in the nation at large, the percentage of these families living beneath the poverty level remained the same. Seven years of vigorous economic growth has not alleviated their situation by even one percentage point.

Competitive Economic Groups

On its own, above-average economic expansion reduced the overall rate of poverty among American people marginally, from 21.3 percent (exclusive of governmental programs) in 1965 to 19.2 percent in 1972. Whereas economic growth reduced the poverty of one in ten Americans, governmental intervention reduced that of more than one in two Americans over the same period, a rate five to six times greater than that of the private economy. Economic growth did help some segments of the population, particularly families headed by males (white and nonwhite) under the age of 65. Among these families, rates of poverty declined sharply, by one-third or more, exclusive of governmental intervention. Yet, these were the strongest and most competitive economic groups, groups that entered the era of economic expansion already with, comparatively, the lowest rates of poverty. By way of contrast, economic expansion made little or no difference to the poverty rates of many other groups, particularly the elderly, white and minority women, and the youngest of the economically weak. In light of this experience, it would be nothing less than blind faith to argue that vigorous economic growth alone would have effectively reduced poverty in America within a reasonable time span. The circumstances of the 1960s and early 1970s demonstrate that while a prosperous economy may benefit the stronger economic groups, its impact on weaker groups can equally be nonexistent, reducing some to even more dire situations. *The government's programs were vital in fighting poverty precisely because the private sector was itself incapable of making more than a marginal dent in poverty among the many millions of Americans who remained trapped within the weaker economic groups,* either too old to get work or channeled into dead-end jobs that often paid little more than half-time wages for full-time work. Including their dependents, more than 30 million Americans lived in such families.

Work Incentive

The economic experience of the 1960s and 1970s equally belies a second familiar belief, that is, that welfare programs substantially reduce the incentive to work. True, some effect is possible; it is most likely to be experienced by those Americans who remain at or near the poverty level even when holding down full-time jobs. Nevertheless, neither the expansion of the poverty programs in the 1960s and 1970s, nor the decisive contribution they made to reducing poverty, seems to have come at the cost of much reduction in the incentive of Americans to become a part of the work force and earn a living. To help set the context, consider that the numbers of people seeking work and taking jobs increased at historically high rates during these years, by 35 percent in 1965-80 alone. Employment climbed at a far faster pace during and after the great acceleration of the poverty and welfare programs in 1965-80 than during the preceding fifteen-year period (employment during 1950-65 rose by 21 percent). . . .

The work ethic continues to prevail in the United States. For the majority of AFDC recipients, the use of the federal government's major welfare program has been transitory, except when family heads are disabled. There exist few better indicators of the survival of the work ethic than to note the special kinds of situations that have commonly led families to turn to AFDC assistance and the relatively high turnover of the majority of families on welfare. Moreover, as a way of placing all this in context, it is relevant that even as such assistance became more widely available, the number of Americans who became employed grew at an unprecedented rate, one barely diminished by the programs' existence, and the rate of unemployment grew comparatively little. Even among the families living in poverty, the percentage of family heads who were employed in the late 1970s was almost as high as in the early 1960s, before the programs' rapid expansion. Something else was going on in America; it was not a denial of the work ethic. . . .

Quality of Life

In addition to reducing poverty, another crucial goal of the attack on poverty was to raise the quality of people's lives, specifically with respect to essential human needs. Well into our times, devastating situations faced many low-income families in America concerning basic nutritional, health, and housing needs. . . .

Dr. Gordon Harper [a] member of the Field Foundation team, observed that since 1967 there had been "a striking decrease in the number of grossly visible signs of malnutrition." Food stamps have made a critical difference.

It is disturbing that wide sections of the public are generally unaware of this improvement. It is an achievement that should bring at least a degree of pride in what the nation has done. But there is instead hardly any sense of accomplishment, almost as if nothing at all had taken place.

"The percentage of [poor] family heads who were employed in the late 1970s was almost as high as in the early 1960s, before the [welfare] programs' rapid expansion."

A similar conclusion pertains to the results of governmental programs in the medical sphere. In 1963, before the implementation of Medicare and Medicaid, fully one in five of those Americans living beneath the poverty level *had never been examined by a physician,* at least not within their memory. In many respects, use of medical care was significantly lower among low-income people as compared with middle- and high-income groups, despite the higher incidence of illness and disease among the impoverished persons.

Inequality describes the situation encountered by the medical programs and the programs for the elderly that were enacted in the middle of the 1960s. By 1970, only five years later, notable changes had already taken place, positive changes that were to continue into the 1970s. By 1970, the percentage of people living in poverty who had never visited a physician was reduced from 19 percent in 1963 to 8 percent. The percentage of impoverished persons seeing a doctor at least once a year approached that of high-income persons. . . .

Infant Mortality

The best single index of a community's general health is reputed to be its infant mortality rate. From 1965 to 1975, the overall infant mortality rate among the poor fell by fully 33 percent. Gains among blacks were particularly evident. Between 1950 and 1965, before the great expansion in the federal medical and nutritional programs, the infant mortality rate among blacks barely fell, from 44.5 per 1,000 births in 1950 to 40.3 in 1965. Following the expansion of the programs, the rate of black infant mortality declined quickly, from 40.3 in 1965 to 30.9 in 1970, and to 24.2 in 1975. . . .

Apart from the goal of improving nutritional and medical conditions, a third basic need governmental programs sought to serve centered on housing.

Among the programs directed to basic needs, federal housing programs alone enjoy a continuous history, dating back to Arthurdale in 1933. By the 1970s about 3 million low-income families resided in housing subsidized partly or wholly by public funds. In addition, the government had long fostered a broader approach in the area of housing, an approach that employed tax incentives and guaranteed loans to stimulate the building and private purchase of new middle- and upper-income housing, thereby opening vacancies in existing housing for low-income buyers and renters. Tax relief for middle- and upper-income persons who purchase homes typically amounts to billions of dollars a year, and significant numbers of mortgage loans to purchase private homes are guaranteed by the government.

Clearly, these various governmental programs operated in conjunction with the private housing industry and the private housing market, in combination with increased real income, to affect housing conditions. Although the government played only a part, the combination of these forces accomplished much. In 1940, 20.2 percent of American households lived in overcrowded housing conditions (housing occupied by more than one person per room); twice as many, or 40 percent of black and other minority households, lived in overcrowded housing. Gradually, overcrowded housing has been reduced. In 1950, 16 percent of American households lived in overcrowded housing; by 1960 the figure was about 12 percent, by 1970 about 9 percent, and by 1976 less than 5 percent of all American households lived in overcrowded housing. The figure for black and minority families residing in overcrowded housing was reduced by more than 50 percent between 1940 and 1970.

Improved Programs

A similar reduction occurred in the percentage of Americans living in substandard housing. "Substandard" defines housing that lacks hot running water, or some or all other plumbing, or is in great physical disrepair. The percentage of American households living in such housing stood at almost 49 percent in 1940 and was slightly above 35 percent even in 1950. The figure declined to about 20 percent in 1960, 11 percent in 1970, and about 8 percent in 1976.

That some of the massive buildings of public housing constructed before and during the 1960s are now viewed as eyesores is not denied; indeed, some are tragic failures. During the process, however, the government learned from its mistakes and the programs changed course. Alternatives to the construction of huge housing complexes were increasingly emphasized in the housing programs of the 1960s and 1970s: far smaller projects, public purchase of privately built housing, subsidies to

builders of low-income housing, income supplements to help impoverished persons rent private housing, subsidies on mortgages to help low-income persons purchase housing, and other programs to enable low-income people to obtain decent housing through the private sector. These and earlier government housing programs, combined with the private market, have served since 1940 to reduce the percentage of Americans living in overcrowded and substandard housing by three-quarters or more.

"From 1965 to 1975, the overall infant mortality rate among the poor fell by fully 33 percent."

In the view of some, each of the programs discussed to this point lacked an essential element. However much progress took place along the nutritional, health, and housing fronts, many Americans thought that the various income and in-kind transfer programs failed to strike at the core of the poverty problem. There was only one real solution to poverty, according to this view, only one solution that could substantially end the need for programs involving massive subsidies and transfers of income. This solution, simply, was to provide people with the skills needed to obtain a self-sustaining livelihood through full-time employment. The manpower programs of government (job training and job creation) were established with this objective in mind.

Job Programs

Sometimes we forget, however, that full-time employment is not always feasible for large numbers of people: for the elderly, for the permanently ill or disabled, and possibly also for most single heads of families with very young children. Many millions of impoverished Americans are members of these groups. The manpower programs were relevant to comparatively few of these people. To enable these Americans to rise out of poverty, the various direct assistance and in-kind programs of government constitute the only realistic help that could have been made available. Nothing else would substitute.

Yet there remain outside these groups hundreds of thousands of other Americans with very low levels of education, many not having finished high school or perhaps even the eighth grade and many with virtually no job skills. Job-training programs might help them. In 1970, one in five males in the American labor force had not gone beyond the eighth grade. Many of these people were unemployed. Others, though employed, earned only a subsistence living. Consequently, more than a million American families headed by a fully employed person continued to live in poverty.

The objective of the government's job-training and job-creation programs was to speak to the situations of these people as well as the many other Americans who confronted an intensely crowded labor market in the onrush of the postwar baby boom. . . .

CETA's Success

How successful were these programs? The most thorough study on the results of governmental programs over the long term concerns the effects of job training and job creation under the Comprehensive Employment and Training Act. This study, the first of its kind, examined the employment careers of people for the five years subsequent to their CETA employment, covering the histories of 1,136 workers in and around the Baltimore area from 1973 through 1978. Most of the CETA participants were members of groups traditionally hard hit by unemployment; 60 percent were black. The study, carried out by Johns Hopkins University, took seven years to complete.

The Johns Hopkins team discovered that the employment of CETA participants jumped significantly following participation in the CETA program and that it continued to improve over the long term. Of those participants who had not been employed at all during the entire year preceding entry into CETA, 40 percent became employed immediately upon terminating the program, and 56 percent were employed within six months. Of all program participants, 48 percent found jobs immediately after leaving the program, 59 percent within one month and 66 percent after six months. The employment rates of the CETA participants continued to climb thereafter, despite the rise in unemployment in the Baltimore area for the labor force as a whole. After five years, only 6 percent of the former CETA participants were looking for jobs.

"We forget, . . . that full-time employment is not always feasible for large numbers of people: for the elderly, for the permanently ill or disabled, and possibly also for most single heads of families with very young children."

The findings of the Baltimore study also shows a significant increase in the wage levels of the CETA participants. Comparing the wages of the participants employed before entering CETA with the real wages (after discounting for inflation) earned by the same participants after completing the program indicates an increase of 15 percent. Starting at 70 percent of the average wage in the Baltimore area, CETA participants had advanced to 89 percent of the average wage by 1978. . . .

Head Start's Success

Standing at the other end of the spectrum from the adult job-training and job-creation programs is the concept of Head Start. The Head Start program was devised to provide superior early education for lower-income children to prepare them for the school environment and subsequent employment without need for later training. On the average, Head Start has reached about 300,000 children a year, or about 20 percent of all eligible low-income children.

The foremost study on the effects of Head Start, undertaken during the 1970s, analyzed the impact of fourteen Head Start programs across the nation. A majority of the children examined by the study had been randomly selected for the programs from among all low-income children in the community. Thus, most of the children who entered these Head Start programs were similar to other low-income children in the same community.

In comparing children who participated in Head Start with those who did not, the study found that children who participated before the age of 6 were about 60 percent less likely to be assigned to special education classes in grade school or high school (thereby producing a savings for their school systems); were about 45 percent less likely to be held back a grade (again producing a substantial savings to the schools); exhibited a 7-point increase in their IQ scores as an immediate result of the program, with a long-term increase on average of about half that; had more favorable perceptions of the quality of their schoolwork when in high school than did their non-Head Start cohorts; and were more likely to want to pursue higher education at a college or university. Needless to say, the parents of the Head Start children were practically unanimous in their enthusiasm for the program, a feeling that remained even among those parents who were interviewed almost a decade later.

Did the benefits exceed the costs? In reducing the number of children who otherwise would have been held back in grade or who would have required special education later and other such benefits, one study estimates that the benefits of Head Start have amounted to approximately double the costs. . . .

Attack on Poverty

A most basic goal of the attack on poverty was to assure that all Americans benefited from the nation's economic expansion. The programs generated little change in the distribution of incomes in the nation during the whole of the post-Eisenhower era. In line with the objective just mentioned, however, the attack on poverty did assure that the benefits brought by the nation's rapidly expanding economy would be shared by both the stronger and the weaker groups. In 1980, one in fifteen Americans faced the desperation of poverty, compared with about one in five Americans just a generation earlier. This was accomplished, almost entirely, by the government.

John E. Schwarz received his Ph.D. from Indiana University and is a political science professor at the University of Arizona.

"A higher percentage of the American population was officially poor in 1980 than at any time since 1967."

The War on Poverty Harmed the Poor

Charles Murray

During the 1970s, the poor receded from public attention. Their plight was invoked when it had to be, as the justification for new and expanded social programs. But they were at the periphery of our national concerns, presumably taken care of, more or less.

Within three months of Ronald Reagan's inauguration on 20 January 1981 the poor were once more at center stage. A budget crisis was upon us, and something had to give. In the administration's view, the social welfare programs were prime targets for budget cuts. An intense debate began over what could be done without ripping the "social safety net." Conservatives wanted to save money without causing pain and argued that only "fat" was being excised from overgrown programs. Liberals insisted that this was wishful thinking. . . .

Nothing Changed

Both sides proceeded from a tacit, common premise: that the important progress of recent years should be preserved. Few asked the questions it would seem natural to start with: How much progress in fact has been made? How have the poor been doing?

The unadorned statistic gives pause. In 1968, as Lyndon Johnson left office, 13 percent of Americans were poor, using the official definition. Over the next twelve years, our expenditures on social welfare quadrupled. And, in 1980, the percentage of poor Americans was—13 percent. Can it be that nothing had changed?

What *really* has been happening to the poor? To the disadvantaged? Not just since the Great Society, but since mid-century? What are the facts about poverty and the phenomena we have come to associate with being poor—crime and family

disintegration and illiteracy and chronic unemployment? What are the facts about inequalities between blacks and whites? Are things better or worse or the same? What have been the trends?

The answers are complicated by the fact that our goals kept changing. Americans in 1950 were not simply blind to the existence of poverty and discrimination (although that was part of it). They also had very different perceptions from those of Americans in 1981 about the nature of "poverty" and "inequality," about their causes and cures. Indeed, our policy toward the poor and blacks was by 1981 almost the opposite of our policy in 1950. What happened to them is inextricably linked with what the large society decided to do for them—or with them, or to them, depending on one's view. . . .

The complex story . . . comes down to this:

Basic indicators of well-being took a turn for the worse in the 1960s, most consistently and most drastically for the poor. In some cases, earlier progress slowed: in other cases mild deterioration accelerated; in a few instances advance turned into retreat. The trendlines on many of the indicators are—literally—unbelievable to people who do not make a profession of following them.

Strategic Error

The question is why. Why at that moment in history did so many basic trends in the quality of life *for the poor* go sour? Why did progress slow, stop, reverse?

The easy hypotheses—the economy, changes in demographics, the effects of Vietnam or Watergate or racism—fail as explanations. As often as not, taking them into account only increases the mystery.

Nor does the explanation lie in idiosyncratic failures of craft. It is not just that we sometimes administered good programs improperly, or that sound concepts sometimes were converted to operations incorrectly. It is not that a specific program, or a specific court ruling or act of Congress, was especially destructive. The error was strategic.

A government's social policy helps set the rules of the game—the stakes, the risks, the payoffs, the tradeoffs, and the strategies for making a living, raising a family, having fun, defining what "winning" and "success" mean. The more vulnerable a population and the fewer its independent resources, the more decisive is the effect of the rules imposed from above. The most compelling explanation for the marked shift in the fortunes of the poor is that they continued to respond, as they always had, to the world as they found it, but that we—meaning the not-poor and un-disadvantaged—had changed the rules of their world. Not of our world, just of theirs. The first effect of the new rules was to make it profitable for the poor to behave in the short term in ways that were destructive in the long term. Their second effect was to mask these long-term losses—to subsidize irretrievable mistakes. We tried to provide more for the poor and produced more poor instead. We tried to remove the barriers to escape from poverty, and inadvertently built a trap. . . .

"We tried to provide more for the poor and produced more poor instead. We tried to remove the barriers to escape from poverty, and. . .built a trap."

A moral dilemma underlies the history of social policy from 1950 to 1980, an anciently recognized dilemma that in the enthusiasm of the 1960s we dismissed as fusty and confuted. It is indeed possible that steps to relieve misery can create misery. The most troubling aspect of social policy toward the poor in late twentieth-century America is not how much it costs, but what it has bought. . . .

Great Society Goals

Reducing poverty was the central objective of federal social programs during the reform period. Policymakers and legislatures hoped for a variety of good things from the War on Poverty. . .the entitlements, and the widening population of eligible recipients. But, whatever else the programs were to accomplish, they were to put more money in the hands of the poor people. They were to reduce poverty. . . .

The popular conception about poverty is that, at least on this one fundamental goal, the Great Society brought progress. The most widely shared view of history has it that the United States entered the 1960s with a large population of poor people. . .who had been bypassed by the prosperity of the

Eisenhower years. The rich and the middle class had gained, but the poor had not. Then, after fits and starts during the Kennedy years, came the explosion of programs under Johnson. These programs were perhaps too ambitious, it is widely conceded, and perhaps the efforts were too helter-skelter. But most people seem to envision a plot in which dramatic improvement did not really get started until the programs of the Great Society took effect.

The reality is that improvement was stopping, not starting, during that time. . . . Poverty did fall during the five Johnson years, from 18 percent of the population in 1964 to 13 percent in 1968, his last year in office, and the slope of the decrease was the steepest during this period. But the . . . poverty before 1964 and after 1968 reveals the fallacy in the popular conception of historical cause and effect.

More Poor People

In the first place, . . .the Great Society reforms had very limited budgets through the Johnson administration. The real annual expenditures of the 1970s were far larger—by many orders of magnitude, for some of the programs—than expenditures in the sixties. Yet progress against poverty stopped in the seventies. The steep declines in poverty from 1964 to 1968 cannot glibly be linked with government antipoverty dollar expenditures.

Secondly, the declines in poverty *prior* to 1964 were substantial. In 1950,. . . poverty had stood at approximately 30 percent of the population. From there it declined to the 18 percent of Johnson's first year. The size of the officially "impoverished" population dropped by about 17 percentage points in the years from 1950 to 1968, of which the Johnson years accounted for five: about their fair share.

Then, after two decades of reasonably steady progress, improvement slowed in the late sixties and stopped altogether in the seventies. The proportion dipped to its low point, 11 percent, in 1973. A higher proportion of the American population was officially poor in 1980 than at any time since 1967. By then it stood at 13 percent and was heading up. The number of people living in poverty stopped declining just as the public-assistance programs budgets and the rate of increase in those budgets were highest. The question is why this should be.

If we were asking about progress in reducing a problem like chronic unemployment, explanations would be easier. Fixing the last 10 percent of a problem is often more difficult than fixing the first 90 percent of it. But poverty as officially defined is a matter of cash in hand from whatever source. The recipient of the benefits does not have to "do" anything—does not have to change behavior or values, does not have to "qualify" in any way except to be a recipient. To eliminate such poverty, all we need do is mail enough checks with enough money to enough people. In the late sixties, still more in the seventies, the number of checks, the size of the checks, and the number of beneficiaries all increased. Yet, perversely, poverty chose those years to halt a decline that had been underway for two decades.

Trickle-Down Effect

The explanation that comes first to mind is that the bright hopes of the sixties dimmed in the seventies as the economy slowed. According to this view, inflation and the dislocations brought on by the Vietnam War, along with the revolution in energy prices, hobbled the economy. As the expansionist environment of the sixties vanished, strategies and programs of the War on Poverty had to be put aside.

What, if anything, do the data suggest about the merits of their economic explanation? Let us take the simplest, most widely used measure of the state of the economy, growth in GNP, and examine its relation to changes in the number of people living in poverty. The answer, despite the ridicule heaped on "trickle-down" as a way to help the poor, is that changes in GNP have a very strong inverse relation to changes in poverty. As GNP increases, poverty decreases. But we cannot use this relationship to explain why we stopped making progress against poverty in the 1970s. Economic growth during the 1970s was actually *greater* than during the peacetime 1950s, memories of Eisenhower prosperity notwithstanding. The average annual growth rate from 1953 to 1959 was 2.7 percent, noticeably lower than the average annual growth of 3.2 percent from 1970 to 1979. Moreover, the lower growth of the seventies took the form of a few very bad years. During those years that had growth rates as high as those of the palmy days of the 1960s, the trendlines on poverty "should" have behaved as they did during the comparable growth years of the fifties and sixties. But they did not.

Upon consideration, it will be apparent that in important ways the 1970s were even richer than the percentage increases in GNP indicate, because the base for calculating the percentage increase kept getting larger. The real dollar increase in GNP during the 1970s was half again as large as in the 1950s. This sizable increase holds up when we also control for population change. . . . Even after holding both population change and inflation constant, per capita GNP increased only a little less rapidly in the seventies than it had in the booming sixties, and much faster than during the fifties. Growth did not stop. But, for some reason, the benefits of economic growth stopped trickling down to the poor. . . .

Even if poverty has stopped decreasing among the population as a whole, there is reason, given the logic of the structuralist school of poverty, that poverty among blacks might have continued to drop nonetheless. Suppose that racial discrimination had

created a segmented labor market and otherwise kept poor blacks from sharing in the bounty of a growing economy. If so, then the black population as of the late 1960s would have included a large proportion of poor people who were trapped in poverty despite the economic boom. In that case, white reduction in poverty might track with economic growth, but black reductions would be contingent on the income transfers, jobs programs, and other special measures that moved into higher gear in the seventies. Let us compare this possibility with what actually happened to working-aged blacks (persons under 65). . . .

"Economic independence—standing on one's own abilities and accomplishments —is of paramount importance in determining the quality of a family's life."

Black progress did not continue into the seventies. It stopped very much as white progress stopped. . . . In 1959, 58 percent of working-aged blacks were below the poverty line. A single decade later, the percentage was 30 percent—a precipitous drop of 28 percentage points in ten years. Blacks did indeed make economic progress in the sixties, huge progress for such a short period of time.

With the experience of the seventies tacked on, . . . our perspective on the sixties has changed accordingly. We know that in 1969 funding of the programs that were then being given credit for the progress was still relatively low compared with later years (when progress did not continue). We are more aware that greatest progress occurred in 1963, 1964, 1965, and 1966, when the reforms were little more than rhetoric. We are more aware of the pump that the Vietnam War was giving to the economy from 1966 through the end of the decade. . . .

During the period following 1959, black progress against poverty among the working-aged coincided with the civil rights movement and with the general economic boom that began in the early 1960s. Progress *stopped* coincidentally with the implementation of the Great Society's social welfare reforms. . . .

Latent Poor

What is the number of poor *before* the governmental transfers are taken into acount? This population constitutes the "latent poor." It has been determined by subtracting all government payments (AFDC, Social Security, Disability Payments, SSI) from total reported income in the March Current Population Survey of the Bureau of the Census, then comparing the remaining income with the poverty level. Thus the "latent poor" include those who show up below the poverty level in the official measure, plus those who are above the poverty line in the official measure, only by virtue of government support. . . .

Latent poverty decreased during the 1950s from approximately a third of the population to 21 percent by 1965. Put another way, economic dependency decreased by about a third during the years 1950-65, up to the beginning of Johnson's War on Poverty. Increasing numbers of people had been able to make a living that put them above the poverty line.

The proportion of latent poor continued to drop through 1968, when the percentage was calculated at 18.2. This proved to be the limit of progress. At some point during 1968-70, the percentage began to grow, reaching 19 percent in 1972, 21 percent in 1976, and 22 percent by 1980.

The reason for calling this the most damning of the statistics is that economic independence—standing on one's own abilities and accomplishments—is of paramount importance in determining the quality of a family's life. Hardly anyone, from whatever part of the political spectrum, will disagree. For this independence to have *decreased* would be an indictment of the American system whenever in our history it might have occurred. For it to begin decreasing in 1968-70 was odd but perhaps attributable to the slowing of the boom. For it to have continued to decrease throughout the seventies was extraordinary.

Labor Market

Once we have accepted that progress against poverty did in fact stop during the 1970s and, in the case of latent poverty, reversed, might there not be reason for thinking that things would have been much worse if the antipoverty transfers had not been enacted? We may consider, for example, the huge influx of women and baby-boom youths into the labor force during that period. From 1970 to 1980, the size of the total labor force increased by 24 percent, compared with a 13 percent increase from 1950 to 1960 and a 19 percent increase from 1960 to 1970. Even a strong economy could not possibly absorb so many people, we hypothesize. The antipoverty budget made up for those who were left out. This logic is coordinate with a variety of other hypotheses about the effects of changes in the economy (a shift away from unskilled labor, for example) that made it more difficult for people at the bottom of the ladder to get a start.

There is surely some truth to such arguments. On the other hand, employers for the millions of new jobs that were created during the 1970s did not hang out signs reading "Poor people need not apply." What happened, then, to the acquisition of jobs by the poor and disadvantaged? We begin with

unemployment and labor force participation, and some events of the 1960s that confounded traditional expectations of the job market. . . .

Let us consider the role of status in fostering the escape from poverty. We are [not]. . .discussing. . .the average man of average ambition whose realistic hope is for no more than a secure job at a decent wage. We are envisioning a potential Horatio Alger. By taking away responsibility—by saying, "Because the system is to blame, it's not your fault that. . . ."—society also takes away the credit that is an essential part of the reward structure that has fostered social and economic mobility in the United States.

Socioeconomic mobility has been America's stock in trade. Immigrants arrive penniless and work their way up. The sharecropper's son becomes an assembly-line worker and his granddaughter goes to college. The immigrant who speaks no English has a son who goes to night school for nine years and finally gets a law degree. These are the personal triumphs that constitute the American epic. . . .

The black ghetto. . .forms the archetypal example of characteristics found (not only in America, but world-wide) wherever some members of society have been segregated and told they are inferior. Virtually every commentator on what it is like to grow up black in America, whether novelist or sociologist or memoirist, has reflected on the devastating effects of racism on self-confidence. Inside the ghetto, the rules and rule-setters are known. Moving outside, competing on white terms for what have traditionally been white prerequisites, is objectively difficult. When the real difficulties are compounded by the fears engendered by centuries of white propagandizing that white is smarter (and by elements of self-denigration by blacks), the result can be immobilization of even the most able and ambitious.

"Black progress against poverty. . . . stopped coincidentally with the implementation of the Great Society's social welfare reforms."

This debilitating aspect of black socialization is not a recent creation. The problem is that post-1964 social policy fed it. Every assumption that a young black in the ghetto might make about his inability to compete with whites was nourished by a social policy telling him, through the way it treated him day to day, that he was an un-responsible victim. Society's actions were at odds with society's rhetoric telling him to be proud and to believe in himself.

Day to day, going to a typical inner-city high school, such a young person saw that most of the special programs were directed at the most conspicuous failures. There were likely to be special programs for the mentally retarded, for the learning-disabled, and for the emotionally disturbed. The rules of school conduct placated the trouble-makers. Special tracks for the gifted were attacked as elitist. Where programs for the gifted (or just the hardest-working) did exist, they fell into the magnet-schools trap—to avoid trouble, the course materials were watered down and the demands (and sense of reward) were low. The ambitious and hard-working students were passed along with A's and with the teachers' gratitude for not contributing to the discipline problem, but without an education that enabled them to compete in a good university.

"In the day-to-day experience of a youth growing up in a black ghetto, there was no evidence whatsoever that working within the system paid off."

Outside of school, the rules of the game argued against the proposition that hard work pays off. The network of social service agencies—the most visible (legitimate) resources bank—existed to help the least provident and least able. The most conspicuous local success stories were drug dealers, pimps, and fences. Friends who were arrested by the police went free or were assigned to educational or counseling programs for which the youth who went straight were not eligible. And when the hard-working student did get into a government-sponsored job program, his first lesson was that the ones who did no work were treated exactly the same as he was, except that he was likely to come under attack from his coworkers for threatening to get the others in trouble.

This experience contained only one kind of lesson: In the day-to-day experience of a youth growing up in a black ghetto, there was no evidence whatsoever that working within the system paid off. The way to get something from the system was to be sufficiently a failure to qualify for help, or to con the system. What a racially segregated society once taught the young black about living with his inferiority was now taught by a benevolent social welfare system. The difference was that in an earlier age, a black parent could fight the competing influences. The parent could drum into the child's head the belief that he could make it—that the people who said otherwise were racists who obviously *wanted* him to fail. How did a parent in the aftermath of the reform period compete with a system that proclaimed its devotion to equality, but whose purpose was to minister to a black population, that it tacitly assumed had proved its inability to compete in the straight, white system? . . .

The moral imperative to do something to correct the situation of poor people and especially the minority poor is at least as powerful now as when Lyndon Johnson took office. I have for the most part used the data to make a case that the reforms flowing from the new wisdom of the 1960s were a blunder on purely pragmatic grounds. But another theme of the discussion has been what we did was wrong on moral grounds, however admirable our intentions may have been.

It was wrong to take from the most industrious, most responsible poor—take safety, education, justice, status—so that we could cater to the least industrious, least responsible poor. It was wrong to impose rules that made it rational for adolescents to behave in ways that destroyed their futures. The changes we made were not just policy errors, not just inexpedient, but unjust. The injustice of the policies was compounded by the almost complete immunity of the elite from the price they demanded of the poor. . . .

If the behaviors of members of the underclass are founded on a rational appreciation of the rules of the game, and as long as the rules encourage dysfunctional values and behaviors, the future cannot look bright. Behaviors that work will tend to persist until they stop working. The rules will have to be changed. . . .

Scrap the Entire Program

I begin with the proposition that it is within our resources to do enormous good for some people quickly. We have available to us a program that would convert a large proportion of the younger generation of hardcore unemployed into steady workers making a living wage. The same program would drastically reduce births to single teenage girls. It would reverse the treadline in the breakup of poor families. It would measurably increase the upward socioeconomic mobility of poor families. These improvements would affect some millions of persons.

All these are results that have eluded the efforts of the social programs installed since 1965, yet, from everything we know, there is no real question about whether they would occur under the program I propose. A wide variety of persuasive evidence from our own culture and around the world, from experimental data and longitudinal studies, from theory and practice, suggests that the program would achieve such results.

The proposed program, our final and most ambitious thought experiment, consists of scrapping the entire federal welfare and income-support structure for working-aged persons, including AFDC, Medicaid, Food Stamps, Unemployment Insurance, Worker's Compensation, subsidized housing, disability insurance, and the rest. It would leave the working-aged person with no recourse whatsoever except the job market, family members, friends, and public or private locally funded services. It is the Alexandrian solution: cut the knot, for there is no way to untie it. . . .

"It was wrong to take from the most industrious, most responsible poor. . .so that we could cater to the least industrious, least responsible poor."

Let me step outside the persona I have employed and put the issue in terms of one last intensely personal hypothetical example. Let us suppose that you, a parent, could know that tomorrow your own child would be made an orphan. You have a choice. You may put your child with an extremely poor family, so poor that your child will be badly clothed and will indeed sometimes be hungry. But you also know that the parents have worked hard all their lives, will make sure your child goes to school and studies, and will teach your child that independence is a primary value. Or you may put your child with a family with parents who have never worked, who will be incapable of overseeing your child's education—but who have plenty of food and good clothes, provided by others. If the choice about where one would put one's own child is as clear to you as it is to me, on what grounds does one justify support of a system that, indirectly but without doubt, makes the other choice for other children? The answer that "What we really want is a world where that choice is not forced upon us" is no answer. We have tried to have it that way. We failed. Everything we know about why we failed tells us that more of the same will not make the dilemma go away.

Charles Murray has written several books and articles and is Senior Research Fellow at the Manhattan Institute for Policy Research.

"A properly administered [workfare] program could. . .[help] many of the poor overcome the 'poverty wall' created by America's current welfare and tax systems."

viewpoint **85**

The Poor Should Work for Welfare Benefits

Peter G. Germanis

Expenditures on welfare programs have been rising at an alarming rate over the last two decades. A principal cause of this enormous expansion is the work disincentive created by continual benefit liberalizations. Rather than paving the way for a higher standard of living, however, many of these government programs have tended to foster permanent dependency on welfare by providing benefits of greater value than the income an individual could earn by working. In effect, the American welfare system allows an able-bodied individual to ask himself: "Will I be better off if I work or if I allow myself and my family to become dependent upon the work of other individuals?" A system permitting this question to be posed is a system desperately in need of review and reform.

Still on the Dole

Encouraging welfare recipients to become self-supporting is supposed to be a major objective of many government programs. Most of these programs provide recipients cash incentives to work their way off the dole. In many cases, however, the result has been that individuals with relatively high incomes continue to receive welfare benefits. Office of Management and Budget Director David Stockman has voiced skepticism concerning such a system: "I just don't accept the assumption that the federal government has a responsibility to supplement the income of the working poor through a whole series of transfer payments. We believe that the guy who takes two jobs and makes $26,000 a year shouldn't be obligated to transfer part of his income and taxes to the guy who's making $10,000." Moreover, although these programs may be designed to aid the poor, in the long run they may actually lower their living standard by discouraging them from entering

the labor market where they could acquire the job skills that eventually could lift many from poverty's depths.

There is an alternative to the self-defeating, degrading system of the dole which long has characterized the U.S. welfare system. This alternative is widely known as Community Work Experience Programs (CWEP), or more commonly as "workfare," in which employable recipients of public assistance—primarily able-bodied male and mothers of school age children—must perform some public service without pay in return to their welfare benefits. Robert Carleson, who was Governor Reagan's welfare director in California, and who as Special Assistant to the President for Policy Development helped draft the Administration's current workfare proposals, maintains: "Anyone who is capable of working should expect to earn their own welfare benefit." As such, workfare reflects the American work ethic. Its objective is to promote financial independence by giving people greater incentives to seek out unsubsidized employment. This work requirement is crucial for successful welfare reform because it is the most effective way to offset the work disincentives now created by the welfare system.

As part of an overall welfare reform package, the Reagan Administration [proposed]. . . "workfare" for beneficiaries of the Aid to Families with Dependent Children program (AFDC). This would replace the Work Incentive Program (WIN), which was established in 1967 to provide eligible recipients with training and job placement services. While the Omnibus Reconciliation Act of 1981 gave states the option of requiring AFDC recipients to work in exchange for their benefits, the Administration's new proposals would make this mandatory. . . .

The primary purpose of the Administration's strict job search requirements is to assure that employable adults applying for AFDC actively will pursue

Peter G. Germanis, "Workfare: Breaking the Poverty Cycle," *Backgrounder*, July 9, 1982. Reprinted with permission from The Heritage Foundation.

unsubsidized employment. By diverting potential recipients into employment, the cost of the program eventually could be cut. Several existing job search programs already are cost-effective.

Example: Oregon's Coordinated Job Placement Program. About 10 percent of the applicant pool was kept off the rolls in fiscal 1981 because the applicants had found employment. Oregon's AFDC caseload has declined by 25 percent since the job search program began in August 1980, despite a 40 percent rise in the unemployment rate.

Example: In Kent County, Michigan, the job search demonstration program for unemployed parents cut the caseload by 60 percent. Of that, one-third found jobs before collecting benefits and the remainder either withdrew their applications or were dropped from consideration for refusing to participate.

The program thus tends to discourage those unwilling to work from viewing welfare as an alternative. Other states and localities also report that job search is an effective tool in placing welfare recipients in jobs, even in areas plagued by high unemployment. The Administration projects that the AFDC caseload will be reduced by over 150,000 through a national mandatory job search program.

Benefits of Workfare

There are several inherent advantages to the *quid pro quo* concept of workfare.

I. The community receives something in exchange for its assistance. All communities surely have work that needs doing but has been ignored because of budgetary constraints. Admittedly, workfare participants' contributions may be small, but since the welfare grants would be paid whether or not work is performed, the community's gain nevertheless is real. Among the jobs created by workfare in some of the optional CWEP programs are maintenance, custodial, day care and library services and assistance to police and emergency medical personnel. Existing workers are not displaced since workfare project tasks would not otherwise have been performed. In fact, federal requirements prohibit any CWEP assignments from replacing paid positions.

II. Participants in the program may find that their attractiveness to potential employers has been enhanced through their exposure to a working environment. Even if the jobs provided give little in the way of training, they introduce work disciplines. Such informal training encourages development of crucial work habits—punctuality, dependability and good working relations with fellow workers. The work experience also gives participants a chance to gain the kind of references, such as a letter of recommendation, which will help them in future job searches. The workfare experience thus may very well enhance the value of participants as productive members of the workforce and ease their transition

into unsubsidized employment.

III. A workfare program may reduce welfare costs by deterring some persons who should be self-supporting from remaining on the dole. Though not intended as a primary objective, workfare has a "deterrent effect" that eliminates welfare recipients who either refuse to participate or have another source of employment which prevents them from doing so. Establishing a work requirement would give employable recipients an incentive to seek other, more attractive means of support when they realize that their benefits no longer are free. Workfare has proved an effective means of sizeably reducing the fraud and abuse so prevalent in our current system by encouraging the departure of undeserving recipients, thereby reducing the burden on the taxpayer and making more money available for those in genuine need.

"Anyone who is capable of working should expect to earn their own welfare benefits."

The record of other current and past experiences in mandatory work programs is mixed. Careful analysis, however, indicates that these programs can work if they are properly administered.

One of the most efficiently administered workfare programs in Cincinnati, which has been part of the General Relief welfare program for over 40 years. Most of the work has little skill content, with heavy emphasis placed on having the participants put in their time. The program appears to have been cost-effective. Notes one evaluation:

> There is a very high initial attrition rate, when people realize they have to work for their benefits. It is sometimes necessary to assign 200 people to get 50 to show up at the work site. The average no show rate may run as high as 60-75 percent. . .although the deterrent effect and the reduction in the caseload is not an explicit objective, it is an obvious reality.
> Although no formal cost/benefit assessments have been made, the amount of GR grant money saved from case closings and the deterrent effect, appear to be far more than the costs of administering the program. On that score alone the program has won general support and agency endorsement.

Critics of the Administration's workfare proposals contend that, unlike the General Relief population, most AFDC recipients are mothers with small children and, therefore, are not able to work. The 1980 Census Report, however, reveals that over half of America's mothers, in fact, do work. Moreover, because of the flexibility that states are given in setting up their programs, some workfare participants could be employed as day care center aides, thereby alleviating child care problems for mothers.

A second workfare program, and one which very likely will receive a great deal of attention because it is part of the AFDC program, is the Utah Work Experience and Training Program (WEAT). For many years, Utah was the only state with a statewide mandatory work program that included AFDC recipients, although it exempted mothers with children under the age of six. Utah's WEAT program, established in 1974, requires employable recipients to work three days a week and to participate in job search for two days. This approach assures work-site sponsors a stable work schedule. A twelve-week limit on workfare participation ensures that workfare participants do not become permanently dependent on workfare in place of regular employment.

"Workfare has proved an effective means of sizeably reducing the fraud and abuse so prevalent in our current system by encouraging the departure of undeserving recipients."

Of those assigned to projects, 27 percent were removed because they failed to perform. Usher West, who heads the Utah program, acknowledges that "WEAT had a general housecleaning effect." In addition, the program also helped many of those assigned work by enhancing their employability. The *Wall Street Journal* reported:

> One of those who benefited is Dennis Wickert, a 42-year-old Marine Corps veteran with a ninth-grade education. A combination of inadequate training and absences caused by problems with bad gums, plus relentless bill collectors, bounced him from the last of several service-station jobs and back onto AFDC several years ago, Mr. Wickert recalls. Indeed, he was feeling like a loser, until the WEAT program assigned him to a neighborhood maintenance crew working out of a local community-action office.
>
> After that "I could walk up to my neighbor and say I earn my welfare money, it's honest," he says with conviction. Mr. Wickert's performance persuaded his employer to hire him as a crew chief. Today he is off AFDC, earning $800 a month plus some extra cash from odd hauling jobs done with his own truck. . . .

Job Creation

West Virginia began its CWEP and job search program for AFDC recipients on January 4, 1982. . . . Among the jobs created are meter maids, police helpers, ambulance assistants, library and park aides, clerical workers and laborers. These jobs did not exist before the workfare program because there were no revenues to fund them. The work performed by these individuals would not otherwise be done, thereby providing the taxpayer with public services and the program participants with on-the-

job training. By integrating the CEWP's with existing work programs, West Virginia has not had to expand its administrative staff. The success of the program among the public and the participants thus far has evoked the praise of the state's Welfare Commissioner, Dr. Leon Ginsberg:

> There is enthusiasm on the part of many of these individuals to work, and many are regularly engaged in looking for jobs. We think that the Community Work Experience Program will both assist non-profit organizations and local government in carrying out some of their responsibilities and will also help the clients maintain their work skills and motivation to be employed.

Reducing Dependency

The concept of workfare should be expanded to other welfare programs, such as food stamps. Preliminary review of seven pilot workfare projects run for the food stamp program indicates that savings in this program could also be achieved by reducing dependency. The first-year results of the program show that 28 percent of the 3,515 individuals eligible to participate lost their benefits because they did not meet the program requirements. John Flynn, county supervisor in Berkley County, South Carolina, attributed the success of their food stamp demonstration program to several factors: "They either didn't need food stamps or they went out and got gainful employment. Either way it takes the people off the food stamp program because if they don't show up to work they don't get the food stamps obviously.". . .

Although not all experiences in workfare have met expectations, it does appear that a properly administered program could reduce significantly burgeoning welfare costs while helping many of the poor overcome the "poverty wall" created by America's current welfare and tax systems.

It is quite possible that the recent immigrants to this country who speak no English are better off than many of the poor because the newcomers do not know how to take advantage of the welfare programs. Social analyst Tom Bethell has characterized their plight: "The newcomers are compelled to take those demeaning jobs at the bottom, but they soon work their way up, as immigrants always have in the past, and eventually rise above those on the isolated welfare platform." The purpose of workfare is not to put the poor to work on workfare projects, but to get them into the productive and rewarding labor force by improving the incentives for serious job search.

Peter G. Germanis is a Policy Analyst at the Heritage Foundation, a conservative think tank in Washington, DC.

"The group most associated with the underclass—young, 'unemployable' males—are least likely to gain in any way from workfare."

viewpoint 86

Working for Benefits Will Not Solve the Poor's Problems

Morton Sklar and *Commonweal*

Editor's note: The following viewpoint consists of two articles. Part I is an article by Morton Sklar in America *and Part II is an editorial in* Commonweal.

I

Workfare is a system that requires recipients of government assistance to "work off" the value of their benefits in assignments with government agencies or non-profit groups. As a concept that seems in line with the work ethic, it has considerable appeal and growing popular support. But there are also increasing concerns that workfare may have serious negative effects on the poor, and most especially on children and families. . . . Congress . . . authorized it's use in major Federal assistance programs such as Aid to Families with Dependent Children (A.F.D.C.) and food stamps [in 1982]. Prior to that time workfare requirements had been applied on a much smaller scale under 20 state-supported welfare programs (called general assistance or home relief), but not under Federal grants except on a rare, demonstration project basis.

As a result of this change in Congressional policy, 22 states have quickly moved to require workfare for at least some portion of A.F.D.C. recipients, and 12 states have operated food stamp workfare projects on a limited (one or two-site) pilot basis. Under most of these workfare programs, recipients who are deemed employable (without disabilities or infant children) are assigned to work at government or nonprofit service agencies for the number of hours, computed at the state or Federal minimum wage level, that equal the value of their grant. On the average, this comes to between two and six days per month.

Part of the popularity of workfare stems from the public's conception that, especially at a time when many are suffering economic hardships, all able-bodied people should work, and no one is entitled to a "free lunch." But this folk wisdom may not be based on an accurate reading of who the recipients of public assistance are, and why they are on welfare. The great majority of A.F.D.C. recipients are women and children, many of whom are below elementary school age, and most of them recent victims of harsh family crises, such as abandonment or battering. For these women and children, the application of work requirements comes at the worst time, when practical problems such as housing and child-care arrangements may not be fully resolved and the need to maintain close family supervision and presence is greatest.

The view that the majority of welfare recipients are on the dole by choice, and seek to avoid work, is also undercut by the fact that a high percentage (about a quarter) hold part-time jobs while still receiving aid, which is legal if earned income is low. An even higher percentage have held a job some time during the two-year period prior to their application for A.F.D.C. When it is understood that the reason for welfare dependence is more related to legitimate social and economic hardship and to the difficulty of finding jobs in a severely depressed economy, the rationale behind workfare begins to make less sense.

Unskilled Work

Another justification for the program is the claim that participation helps provide a "first step up the ladder" by honing job skills and good work habits, and by providing a beginning work history for those without job experience for many years. But critics in most workfare jurisdictions doubt the training potential of workfare assignments. As one Ohio welfare recipient testified at recent hearings on a proposed workfare plan, "You don't learn much by cutting grass in summer, shoveling snow in winter and raking leaves in the fall." Unfortunately, too many workfare assignments tend to fall in this make-work or unskilled category. As important, the likelihood of a workfare assignment leading to a regular job remains slim during a deep recession when unemployment is high and new job openings are not being created. A placement from workfare in these circumstances does little but move another worker onto the public benefit rolls.

Actual experiences with workfare in a number of jurisdictions where it has been tried have raised several more specific concerns among recipients, government officials and unions as to the effectiveness of the program and its potential negative impacts.

The recent General Accounting Office [G.A.O.] analysis of 14 food stamp demonstration sites came to similar conclusions. Costs under the program came to $50 per recipient, while reductions in benefit payments averaged out to $21 to $29 per person, even without a careful system for verifying claims for recipients that they had good cause for not participating. A more effective verification system, G.A.O. found, "would create additional and possibly excessive administrative burden and cost."

In many circumstances, workfare participants are assigned to jobs that ordinarily would be performed by regular civil service personnel. Unions have been especially critical of this type of worker "displacement," because it means the undercutting of collective bargaining agreements they have won. Workfare participants are not paid amounts equivalent to what they would earn as regular employees, and they do not receive worker benefits and protections such as sick leave, holidays or health plan coverage.

Of primary concern to government officials are the substantial expenses associated with administering a workfare program. They include work-expense reimbursements (such as day care), the costs of locating and monitoring the large number of part-time assignments and expenses in processing cases of no-shows or inadequate performance.

Cut-Rate Hiring

Because of these factors, every objective assessment of workfare that has been done, including some carried out by state governments themselves, have found that workfare costs more than it saves in reduced benefit payments. California's own assessment found that "workfare did not prove to be administratively feasible or practical." The comparison of counties applying workfare with nonworkfare jurisdictions found no savings through reductions in the average size of grants or in the number of participants leaving welfare. A Brandeis University study of

Massachusetts workfare also found no significant reductions in welfare payments. Costs of $445 per client to run the program were not offset, "either in terms of increased work or reduced welfare costs," the Brandeis study concluded.

"As one Ohio welfare recipient testified . . . on a proposed workfare plan, 'You don't learn much by cutting grass in summer, shoveling snow in winter and raking leaves in the fall.' "

Jim Butler, president of a hospital workers local of the American Federation of State, County and Municipal Employees Union in New York, has been especially vocal. "We have lists of [workfare] people," he said, "doing the jobs of hospital aids, dieticians and maintenance workers, all of them doing civil service jobs but not getting paid wages or benefits." He called workfare a "back-door system of cut-rate hiring that amounts to union busting."

Mr. Butler's parent union, A.F.S.C.M.E. Local Council 37, recently filed suit against New York City, claiming widespread displacement in violation of state civil service laws. Federal law also prohibits displacement, not only where regular workers are dismissed specifically to make room for workfare participants but also where workfare is being used to fill gaps created by economically motivated layoffs.

Child Care Problem

Because the large majority of A.F.D.C. recipients are single mothers, child care is a special problem under workfare. Organizations like Catholic Charities, Family Services, the National Women's Law Center and others focusing on the needs of women and families have been very critical of the potential negative impacts of workfare on child rearing.

All workfare programs include some protections for child-care needs. Most exclude mothers of children under three entirely and require participation of mothers of older children only when "adequate child care is available." The problem comes when judgments are made as to what is adequate, with a tendency to assume that the ability of a mother to leave the home for any other purposes indicates that child care is available.

With a view to costs, workfare does not usually provide government-supported child-care facilities. About all that is done is to provide reimbursement for up to $25 per month in child-care costs and other work expenses and to establish a system where some workfare mothers are used to provide child care in their homes for other participants. Welfare advocates are critical of both approaches. The reimbursable amounts are seen as too low to provide decent care. The use of workfare mothers as providers is considered a problem since little training or support services are provided, and facilities are often inadequate and downright dangerous for larger numbers of children.

Opening the Door to Abuse

Janet Diamond and Mary Ann Martorana are leaders of the Coalition for Basic Human Needs in Boston, a group that has successfully challenged workfare proposals in Massachusetts. Miss Martorana is especially concerned about the problem of mothers "under the pressure of losing their grants, who may be forced to settle for child-care arrangements that are not in the best interests of their kids." She cited a case of a handicapped teen-age youngster who was assaulted when left at home because her mother was with workfare. No reasonably priced facility that could meet her needs was available after school.

"Low-income neighborhoods," said Miss Diamond, "are no place to take chances with children, but that is just what is forced on mothers because of workfare. Placing children, all day, in the homes of other workfare women who are untrained, unpaid, unlicensed and who are reluctant day-care providers is opening the door to increased abuse and neglect."

"Workfare participants are not paid amounts equivalent to what they would earn as regular employees, and they do not receive worker benefits and protections, such as sick leave, holidays, or health plan coverage."

A key element that has been relied upon by workfare opponents in Massachusetts, Minnesota and other states has been Pope John Paul II's recent encyclical *Laborem Exercens (On Human Work)*. The encyclical supports several themes that seem in basic opposition to workfare. It calls for "just remuneration for work" and supports the right to work-related benefits such as holidays, pensions, insurance and health care, rights and protections that are denied the workfare participant. Most important, it stresses the necessity of protecting the family environment and providing adequate care of children, a value that may be endangered by many workfare programs without effective day-care guarantees. . . .

More communities are beginning to organize against workfare, and more concrete documentation

of problems and shortcomings are beginning to come to light as the program is extended to larger A.F.D.C. and food-stamp populations. With these developments, it should become increasingly difficult for workfare proposals to be adopted at both Federal and state levels. In the meantime, however, the dangers and problems of workfare are going to become more and more real for poor and unemployed single mothers and their families.

II

Americans have always been hostile to public assistance provided without any apparent reciprocal effort by the recipients. There is in this attitude a great deal of common sense mixed with self-righteousness and suspicion of the poor. The public demands assurance that the rules of the game by which most people must live are not, in some way, being violated by tax-supported programs. At a time when government provision of benefits is under pressure on all fronts, it may be a strategic concession by advocates of the poor that employment-for-benefits is a necessary condition if funds are to go from the public coffers for those in need. . . . Yet the fact remains that many traditional worries about workfare retain their validity.

Degrading Burden

What are those worries? First, that the real purpose of workfare is not to better the condition of welfare recipients but simply to deter those in need from receiving public aid. Second, that workfare can foster a whole set of illusions about those in need and the programs they require.

Consider the first problem—the deterrent, punitive function of workfare. Historically, workfare has often been used to provide cheap labor for undesirable tasks at seasonally opportune moments, or to keep the poor off the welfare rolls whenever there was need to swell the labor pool at the bottom of the wage scale. More narrowly, workfare has usually been nothing but another hurdle to discourage the needy from applying for the assistance for which they qualify, or another meaningless but degrading burden to encourage those on welfare to drop out. These motives are very much alive among some supporters of workfare currently, and it is hard to imagine that programs may not be influenced by them.

Too Much Work Ethic

Advocates of workfare have also argued that it exposes individuals who collect public benefits while earning more on the side than is legally allowed. It is an ironic argument, of course, since these individuals seem, if anything, to be guilty of too much of the work ethic. Certainly they've exhibited the ability to find and hold employment, and in many cases, their resort to fraud reflects the reality that wages for many jobs are too low and welfare benefits too meager to suffice. In short, even a positive work ethic has not led these individuals to financial independence without (fraudulent) subsidy. Of course, no one can argue for the toleration of fraud; but it is worth pointing out that measures aimed at rooting it out are apt to very different, and carried out in a different spirit, than measures aimed at promoting the work ethic. The latter are meant to bolster those lacking skills and ambition; the former are meant to catch out those with all too much skill and ambition.

It is, to be sure, mandatory workfare that threatens to function largely in a deterrent, punitive way. Voluntary programs—offering options of job placement, education, or job training—pose few of these problems in principle. But these programs, too, should be carefully assessed so as to learn from their successes, failures, and regional idiosyncrasies. Both voluntary and compulsory workfare, moreover, may foster illusions about the poor and their needs. It is worth asking a few further questions.

Who Needs Workfare?

1. Who really needs workfare? Workfare purports to develop a positive attitude toward work and values associated with employment—self-confidence, discipline, ability to plan ahead, etc.—by extending on-the-job experiences to a group of individuals with limited employment histories. But who really needs this help? The hard core, long-term welfare recipients who constitute only a fraction of the whole? Or the more fluid majority who find themselves on welfare because they are caught in a temporary crisis? The emphasis on workfare may do little (except, perhaps, strengthen the public acceptability of welfare) for the latter group, who basically need *income*, not new skills or work habits, while they get themselves back on their feet.

"Workfare has usually been nothing but another hurdle to discourage the needy from applying for the assistance for which they qualify, or another meaningless but degrading burden to encourage those on welfare to drop out."

2. What really builds the work ethic? Would *any* work experience produce the desired results? Is the exercise of choice itself—whether to work or not—a formative factor in developing self-esteem? A case could be made, based on studies by the Brookings Institute of women in the Work Incentive Program (WIN) in the 1970s, that it is not work per se that contributes to a positive work ethic. Non-working mothers in the study showed a strong work ethic

which they, in turn, passed on to their children. Furthermore, women who participated in the WIN program without being placed in an expected job at the end perceived the project as a failure. After a negative work experience, these women looked upon welfare much more positively than before. In sum, for them the program backfired. Which leads to the next question.

No Poverty Panacea

3. Can workfare really succeed except in an environment of high employment? What jobs will unskilled, semi-skilled, or newly skilled laborers find given the high unemployment rate? Will these workfare participants be in direct competition for jobs with displaced workers receiving unemployment compensation? Or will workfare participants only find part-time, dead-end employment for low wages and few job benefits? There is a real danger of ending up with the worst of both the welfare and the working worlds—mothers separated from children, anxious about undependable day care, and yet still not independent of public money, which may ultimately function as a subsidy for low-wage labor.

4. Is workfare really the answer to the problem of poverty—or, more specifically, of the underclass? The facts are that many of the poor already work, that many others (such as the elderly) are out of the job market, and that the group most associated with the underclass—young, "unemployable" males—are least likely to gain in any way from workfare. In brief, it's no panacea.

None of these questions provides sufficient reason not to try workfare. But they indicate why programs should be flexible and closely monitored; why the emphasis must be on opportunity and not punitiveness; why decent child care is the key to the whole process; and why participants must receive the tools and the wages to live adequately and get ahead. If workfare is to be fair, its limitations and risks should be fully acknowledged. Else the old soldier should be finally laid to rest.

Morton Sklar is director of the Jobs Watch Project, a public interest group at the Catholic University Law School. Commonweal is a national Catholic magazine.

"Welfare policies have been artificially rewarding the feminine mystique, long after it has been abandoned as false by the rest of society."

Government Support Harms Welfare Mothers

Joan Kennedy Taylor

The Reagan administration's effort to reduce federal social spending has sparked a debate over the proper role and level of the "social safety net." One aspect of the issue that is receiving increasing attention is the so-called feminization of poverty: the fact, long identified by feminists, that the most visible of the national welfare programs is Aid to Families with Dependent Children (AFDC), with most of these families headed by women. . . .

[In 1982] two quite different sources took up the issue. Ken Auletta's book, *The Underclass*, has an entire chapter on "Single Mothers: 'The Feminization of Poverty.' " And a long article by Barbara Ehrenreich and Karin Stallard in the tenth-anniversary issue of *Ms.*, "The Nouveau Poor," uses the same phrase, which originated in an article by Dr. Diana Pearce in 1978. Both sources also quote the same grim sentence from the thirteenth annual report of the president's national advisory council on economic opportunity, issued in September 1981: "All other things being equal, if the proportion of the poor in female-householder families were to continue to increase at the same rate as it did from 1967 to 1978, the poverty population would be composed solely of women and their children before the year 2000."

Growing Poverty

Of course, no matter how many poor women there are and how fast their number increases, we will never get to the point where there are no poor *men*, whatever extrapolation the figures seem to show. But the fact remains that ever larger numbers of women and children continue to swell the welfare rolls and, in Ken Auletta's words, "threaten to become, perhaps for the first time in American life, an intergenerational underclass."

The figures are startling and upsetting. While the number of poor families headed by men declined by 25 percent between 1970 and 1977, the number of poor families headed by women increased by 38.7 percent. One-third of all families in the United States headed by a woman are classified as poor, compared to only one-tenth of those headed by men. The *Ms.* article summarizes: "Two out of three adults who fall into the federal definition of poverty are women, and more than half the families defined as poor are maintained by single women." Add to this Auletta's figure, that in some urban ghettos over 70 percent of all the babies born are illegitimate.

Even more alarming than the feminization of poverty is that, in absolute terms, poverty is growing. It is time to consider a relationship that for most people has been unthinkable: government welfare policies are directly acting to create and perpetuate this permanent, intergenerational underclass.

Socially Unjust Policies

Charles A. Murray, who for seven years was a senior scientist at the American Institute for Research, has presented some compelling arguments for the thesis that "social welfare policy in the last couple of decades has not simply been too costly, but has also been socially unjust." Murray points out that the official number of poor declined in the period 1949-68, from about 33 percent of the population in 1949 to about 12.8 percent in 1968. This decline in poverty was correlated with a growth in the GNP over these years, but seemed to have *no* correlation with the growth or shrinkage of poverty programs. But then the proportion of the poor surprisingly leveled out, fluctuating somewhere between 11 and 13 percent throughout the seventies. In 1980 we had a slightly *higher* percentage of poor people than we had in 1968.

These official figures include income from

Joan Kennedy Taylor, "The Welfare Mystique," *Inquiry*, November 1982. Reprinted with the author's permission.

government transfer payments—that is, even after these have been paid out, between 11 and 13 percent of the population is poor. The trend remains the same even if this income is not counted: There was a steady decline in poverty until 1968, but then a steady *increase*.

Thus, we had a steady decline in poverty from the end of World War II until 1968, both in the proportion of people who could not provide for themselves without government help and in the proportion of people below the poverty level. Then, as the welfare budget more than doubled in constant dollars between 1970 and 1980, dependency increased. Despite the huge sums of money spent there was no further decrease in absolute poverty. What happened in 1968?

Subsidized Poverty

Some people have argued that the increase is related to the deteriorating economy and the lowering of everyone's real income. But Murray goes further, pointing out that the War on Poverty's "big" programs started to take effect in 1968: "For the first time in American history—and I mean literally the first time in American history—it was widely suggested and then acted upon that welfare benefits be extended to working-age people who already held jobs." Across the political spectrum, people viewed this as a measure that was fair and just, perhaps because times were *not* hard—in 1968 unemployment was less than 4 percent. It looked as though a little more help from the government actually might eradicate poverty.

"Government welfare policies are directly acting to create and perpetuate this permanent, intergenerational underclass."

Instead, apparently, the government subsidized it. According to Murray, the new programs were supposed to encourage people to get off welfare by allowing them to earn a little money and still receive aid. "We changed the policy," he says, "for what seemed at the time to be a very commonsensical reason—let's provide some incentive to get off welfare." But, he goes on, "the other half of the equation which was not considered at the time is—it works both ways. You not only have an incentive to get a job, which involves a cost. There is also an incentive from the other direction, whereby if you are working at a low-paying job, there are now advantages to getting on welfare. . . . I think what happened was this—we miscalculated the relative force of the fairly small incentive pushing up. The fairly large incentive turned out to be pushing

down." . . .

Perhaps even worse has been the effect on values. Again for the first time in American history, "it became socially acceptable within the poor community to be unemployed *because the working poor were on welfare too*. Before, the working poor had a way to distinguish themselves from the non-working poor. They were better. They were productive members of the community while the others were not." The understandable desire not to blame poor people for being poor, says Murray, has nearly destroyed the incentive for getting off welfare and getting out of poverty. "By taking away blame, society also took away credit, credit that has been an essential part of the reward structure that has fostered economic mobility in this country."

By itself Murray's analysis doesn't explain why young women with children are particular victims of this policy. Nor does that of Barbara Ehrenreich and Karin Stallard, authors of the *Ms.* examination of the problem. Their figures clearly show a correlation between the feminization of poverty and the growth of government programs, but they don't tackle the analytic problems that this data represents. They seem rather to assume that more of the same will be an adequate response. They recommend government efforts to provide day care, income support, job training, and minimum-wage law enforcement—the standard welfare-establishment, big-government menu.

Women and Children Last

What is it about our approach to welfare that is putting women and children last? Can it be that the consequence of our programs to eradicate poverty is not only more poverty in general, but specifically female poverty? Virtually everyone who has tackled this issue acknowledges that government programs have tended to break up families by making it easier for broken families to receive aid and thus encouraging male heads of households to leave. Conservatives such as George Gilder take this observation even further by claiming that government programs wrongly interfere with traditional male/female roles: that of the man as breadwinner and the woman as dependent and mother.

But his criticism completely misses what has happened in American society. As a whole, our society has been moving away from such traditional male/female economic roles, with a massive movement of women into the workplace; in fact, the *Ms.* article argues that "an estimated 85 percent of American women can expect to have to support themselves (if not themselves and their children) at some time in their lives." Not only are half of the jobs in the country now held by women, but the two-paycheck family seems here to stay. John Cogan, David Henderson, and John Raisian, economists with the Department of Labor, have analyzed annual unemployment figures with this trend in mind. They found that "over the last 50 years a safety net, not created by the government, has emerged. By far the most important safety net in our society is the multiearner family." Because of this trend, the worst effects of unemployment fall on that percentage of the unemployed who are both in poverty and either have no family or are female heads of families—less than 1 percent of the labor force. Most of the unemployed are living in families with employed members.

The Ghetto's "Feminine Mystique"

As women have moved into the work force, the power of what Betty Friedan in 1963 called "the feminine mystique" has radically decreased in American society. Friedan's famous book of that name explored a milieu where women no longer were content with defining themselves solely as wives and mothers, in the absence of other meaningful and productive activity. To the extent that suburban ideals in the 1950s defined masculine success by the ability to keep a woman in comparative idleness (which meant that the work she did at home was devalued) and defined feminine success by the subordination of personal interests to the care of husband and children, a malaise developed, "the problem that has no name." Since then, our society has changed. Women as well as men take it for granted that the ability to support oneself is part of successful maturity, and the mystique which dictated that outside interests devalued home and family is no longer current. In the 1980s women are working in record numbers—and they are telling pollsters that they intend to continue doing so.

Except in the ghetto. While the rest of American society has moved away from the traditional male/female role models, the ghetto apparently has not. Reading the case studies in Ken Auletta's *The Underclass*, one sees young mothers, most of them teenagers, who are almost totally passive. Indeed, passivity is the defining characteristic of welfare mothers that emerges from his portraits. They have drifted through government schools for a while; they may have taken care of younger brothers and sisters; they want something to love. In the words of a nun who works with such mothers, "lots of girls feel that if they get to be eighteen and they don't have a baby, they're not a woman. A baby is something everyone considers something of worth." But instead of marrying a man who will take care of them, they "marry" welfare.

Auletta also quotes a field report by a team of researchers at the City University of New York:

> Many of the girls' mothers' friends had pregnant daughters, so that it was almost expected for their daughters to get pregnant. There seemed to exist a

peer group of not only young mothers but also a group of grandmothers who were in their early thirties in the neighborhood. It seemed that the daughters continued having the children that their mothers couldn't have.

A 1978 column by Jimmy Breslin, "Pregnant Thoughts—Out of the Mouths of Babes," describes one woman's struggle to keep her fourteen-year-old daughter from going this route. The woman worked as a legal secretary and lived in a housing project where many of the families were on welfare. Most of the other fourteen and fifteen-year-olds were becoming pregnant. "Then her daughter began to talk about it openly. 'I want to have a baby,' she said one night. 'Why?' the mother asked. 'I want something of my own,' the daughter said. 'Well, who's going to pay for this? I'm a working woman. You don't get a cent from me.' 'I'll get on welfare when I have the baby and get my own pad,' her daughter said."

"While the rest of American society has moved away from the traditional male/female role models, the ghetto apparently has not . . . . Passivity is the defining characteristic of welfare mothers."

Breslin goes on to summarize: "In many places today, the daughters of the poor regard pregnancy as the way to welfare, and welfare as the way to lives of their own." Young women in the 1950s regarded marriage as the way to lives of their own; today a new version of the feminine mystique is alive and well in the ghetto.

Dependency

Our perspective on welfare might change if we considered the relationship between a welfare mother's dependency on the government with the kind of dependency the women's movement was talking about in the late sixties and early seventies. Take current discussions of the Reagan budget cuts as an example. A study by the Washington-based Center for the Study of Social Policy in February 1982 criticized the notion that welfare is a "safety net" rather than an income-supplement program. The study concluded that welfare cuts increased the likelihood that those poor who were working while receiving some form of public assistance would stop working and go on welfare full time. In New York State, for example, the analysis showed that a mother of two children earning nearly $4.00 per hour would net $12.00 less per month than if she were not working at all, whereas, before the cuts, she would have earned $166 more per month while working. The inescapable question is: why should she work? Absent the perspective of the women's movement, the implied answer is: she would have no reason to work.

Yet this question can be asked with equal validity of a nonwelfare wife who is entering the job market for the first time, and whose job-related expenditures for clothing and child care leave her with little or no net earnings. Why should *she* work?

Reasons to Work

The reasons she works are both economic and psychological. She works as a form of job training, to better herself in the expectation that she can use the job to advance to a point where she does have significant net earnings. And psychologically, she works because she feels more productive. She knows that her choice between earning a living or being supported by her husband is not accurately described as a choice between working and not working, for she is doing some sort of work in both instances. But she feels more independent if she is working out of the home, and she probably also feels that both her family and society in general value and respect her work more.

"Where people used to be aware of their interdependence, now they assume that it is the government's job alone to take care of people who have problems."

Do the same factors operate in the life of the welfare mother? They could, but often they don't. As Charles Murray's analysis stresses, policies that reward failure in life cannot at the same time reward success. "The central error of existing social welfare policy," Murray argues, "is that it insists on homogenizing the poor. In the rest of society, we continue as always to differentiate the clever from the dull, the virtuous from the criminal, the industrious from the indolent. But when it comes to the poor, all must be victims. They are not permitted to be superior to one another."

Most of the women interviewed by Ken Auletta hated welfare and wanted to get off it, even if they had gone on welfare as a matter of course as teenage mothers. Many of them were becoming aware that they had alternatives. But Auletta ends his chapter on the feminization of poverty with a visit to a woman with no sense of alternatives—Jean Madison, thirty-nine-years old and pregnant. She has been bearing children since she was eleven. She considers that she devotes herself to them. Her goal? To have a house on Long Island and eat ice cream. "Maybe one day I'll get it—if the right man comes along and I get married," she concludes. "If not, I'll be right here, waiting."

It's a paradox. Jean Madison seems to represent exactly the sort of "feminine" woman that conservatives honor, but it is hard to imagine contemporary society producing her in the absence of the welfare programs, which conservatives criticize, that have supported her since 1968.

Undermining Women's Independence

As for the liberals and liberal feminists, if they believe women should be encouraged to be independent, self-confident, and self-supporting, why aren't they raising these issues in connection with welfare? Sharon Presley, in her now-classic article, "Libertarianism and Feminism," stated the case against the liberals:

> If a woman said to you, "I want to be free from the domination of men," but turned to a tyrannical husband not only for financial support but for decisions about her own personal and social life, you would undoubtedly consider her inconsistent. Yet that is what many feminists are doing on a political level. They say they want to be free of the domination of men but ask for favors and handouts from a government. . . .

The so-called liberal vision that our policy makers have accepted has at its heart an image of the poor, especially the ghetto poor, as permanent dependents. This in turn has seemed to give plausibility to the "public good" argument for welfare—the argument that individuals would be willing to pay a proportion of their income to care for these dependents only if they knew that all other members of the society were forced to pay a similar proportion. But this argument, as well-entrenched as it is, overlooks the reality of how individuals behave in a free society. No one would argue that since all the infants in the world are a dependent class, therefore, "if the state didn't pay for the nurturing of these children, who would? Surely no individual would want to take on such a responsibility unless assured that everyone else in the society would take on an equal share." The answer to the question, of course, is obvious; we still live in a society in which, despite pressures from government in the opposite direction, individuals do take responsibility for the welfare of others.

Many liberals justify the present big-government approach to social problems, for all its failings, in the name of compassion. But a close look at the programs show that compassion is exactly what they are devoid of. Government has replaced community and tradition with the impersonal hand of the bureaucrat dispensing laws and regulations. Where people used to be aware of their interdependence, now they assume that it is the government's job alone to take care of people who have problems— and thousands of people, both the elderly and the very young, are literally dying of loneliness as a consequence.

Feminists, in particular, should accept the full implications of welfare as a woman's issue and apply some of the techniques that have resulted in the successes of the women's movement, the techniques of self-help. Small-town grass-roots consciousness raising in the 1970s was *about* dependency: about the assumptions that women in differing life situations had accepted unquestioningly—that they couldn't or shouldn't make decisions, that they couldn't or shouldn't travel alone, that they weren't smart enough or organized enough to enter the workplace. Why aren't more feminists starting similar consciousness raising in the ghettos? There are already surrogate-mother programs (mostly run by religious groups) for ghetto teenage mothers. Why not augment them with Big Sister-type programs that pair teenage mothers with working women? Surely the women who have organized community day care, feminist health clinics, networks of business women, and support groups for people with every conceivable problem would have valuable ideas for ghetto mothers, too—if they weren't blinded by the assumption that these are things that government *ought* to be doing. That is, if they really understood welfare as a psychological woman's issue.

Rewarded behavior increases, and welfare policies have been artificially rewarding the feminine mystique, long after it has been abandoned as false by the rest of society. The physical act of having a baby is not, in and of itself, a productive activity. It is time to reward something else.

Joan Kennedy Taylor is the publications director of the Manhattan Institute for Policy Research.

Welfare Mothers Deserve Government Support

Theresa Funiciello

"Every mother is a working mother." By extension, every poor mother is a member of the working poor. These contentions contrast sharply with the prevalent notion that a welfare mother is, by definition, an unproductive human being who is suffering from a nearly terminal disease, dependency, which can be cured only by repeated application of one specific medicine known, generically, as a JOB.

My intention here is to demonstrate that targeting the notion of dependency as the key problem facing welfare mothers is to so distort reality as to render proposed solutions virtually meaningless. It does nothing to unravel the complexity of the "welfare mess" vis-a-vis the state and only adds to the burdens welfare mothers must carry in their struggle for social equity. "Dependency theory" ignores the severely restricted life chances available to poor women; it does not adequately address or even identify those limitations that are self-imposed. It is only by understanding the character of choices available to poor women that we can begin to discern the kinds of policies that may help make a decent existence possible for poor people.

"Choosing" Welfare

For some period of time, particularly when infants and toddlers are at home, most single mothers who have access to neither a well-paying job nor any other form of adequate income (like a trust fund) find themselves "choosing" welfare (Aid to Families with Dependent Children, or AFDC) out of concern for the well-being of their children. "The best interests of the child" is, in theory, the key principle governing AFDC, but in making their decision welfare mothers become disenfranchised workers: They perform what is supposed to be a socially

Theresa Funiciello, "Countering the Myth of Dependency: Welfare Mothers Earn Their Way," *Christianity & Crisis*, December 10, 1984. Reprinted with permission. Copyright 1984, Christianity & Crisis, 537 West 121st Street, New York, NY 10027.

valued service, but they receive neither adequate compensation nor respect. Instead of having their labor viewed as "mothering" they are labeled as dependent. The result is often defeating: The women become increasingly more insecure, and their lower self-esteem makes the transition out of welfare an even greater hurdle.

In fact, most of us are dependent on others for our survival. Employers expect tasks to be performed. Workers expect to be paid for them. Husbands expect the kids to be looked after, dinner on the table, and so on. The government has similar expectations. If the tasks are not performed, or inadequately performed, the type of dependency may be altered (job loss, strikes, kids taken away), but the fact of dependency—the necessity that others contribute to our material needs—is not altered. We are a truly symbiotic species.

Middle-Class Dependence

The issue with respect to welfare mothers is not dependency, but dependency on the state. Or is it? Large numbers of people are dependent on the state, with little or no stigma attached to their status. At the top of the heap, in terms of per capita income, are the elected officials and policymakers who order much of social life. Then there are the beneficiaries of the social programs: the aged, the blind, the disabled. In addition, middle-class widowed mothers and their children often receive "survivors" benefits that tend to be at least double those of the AFDC family. Social Security recipients can also have substantial outside income, earned or unearned, without incurring reductions in their government checks. To my knowledge, no movement to save these people from dependency on the state currently exists.

There are others still for whom efforts are underway to acquire state benefits. Many feminists who bemoan the "dependency" of the AFDC mother are now promoting the notion of the "displaced homemaker" as a special category deserving state dependency status. They seek to acquire social security benefits for abandoned housewives. The abandoned housewife, in this reading, is a woman who sacrificed her career in order to stay home, raise the children and "keep house" while her husband sped along in the market. When he leaves her for a younger woman, or whatever, she becomes a displaced homemaker—often a woman with children but no income. She is not eligible for social security, because she is not old enough or because he did not die while they were still married. The significant difference between her and the AFDC mother is one of class. In most cases, if a displaced homemaker has no money in the bank and still has minor children, she would be eligible for public assistance. However, since being a welfare recipient carries with it greater stigma and less income than social security, the displaced homemaker's interests are being promoted in a way different from her AFDC sister whose male partner was more likely to be less affluent in the first place. The upshot of all this is a delineation of needs and rights determined not by a universal standard but by the nature and duration of the prior relationship to the man. Brava.

A Matter of Degree?

The issue, then, is not dependency on the state per se, but the type and degree of such dependency. Or is it? According to a report published in 1981 by New York City's Human Resources Administration, by the end of the 1970's, "AFDC recipients spent an average of only 2.6 years on assistance."

While 80 percent of all AFDC families are headed by women, an even greater proportion of long-term recipients are drawn from female-headed households. And, among those families, a disproportionately higher number are black or Hispanic. Nevertheless, researchers involved in a 10-year longitudinal study of income dynamics in the United States found that even for the majority of black women who have headed welfare families, "long-term dependency was the exception rather than the rule."

There is no comparable data that measures the long term dependency of either the "successfully" married housewife (he has a job, she doesn't), or the "successfully" widowed one (she receives some combination of social security benefits, insurance, or pension funds). An educated guess would suggest that the latter two are longer term dependents than welfare mothers.

The Least Dependent

They might also be described as more fully dependent than the welfare mother if we consider the amount of resources upon which they depend. The welfare mother must raise her children without

most of the modern conveniences her more affluent counterparts take for granted. She is less likely to have a washing machine, or a car. She is less likely to have heat in the winter and certainly almost never has air conditioning. She is far more likely to have her utilities shut off at least one or two months every year or so. It is not unusual to see welfare babies sleeping in cardboard boxes or dresser drawers because a crib cannot be found or purchased. The welfare mother is even less likely to have a conveniently accessible supermarket at which to buy food. She is all-too-often called upon to raise her kids in a high-crime neighborhood teeming with drug abuse and other life-defeating modes of survival. *If she gets a job, the chances are high that none of the above will change.*

> *"Large numbers of people are dependent on the state, with little or no stigma attached to their status."*

Unlike the middle and upper class mother, then, the poor mother is constantly called upon to improvise in order to provide many of those things that have become "necessities" by other people's standards. So, if dependency is measured by degrees, she is among the least dependent, surviving with the least material benefit and the most deprivation. Any achievement is testimony to inner resources that others are rarely called upon to display.

It may be, therefore, that what is at issue is not dependency at all, but rather a historical shipment of ideological baggage that informs and confuses our notion of dependency.

An "Immoral Lot"

In 1967 [Louisiana Senator] Russell Long publicly referred to welfare mothers as "brood mares." There was no sustained protest from leaders of either the women's movement or the civil rights movement. The judgment that welfare mothers are an immoral lot was and still is bone and sinew of many people's beliefs. According to this belief, welfare mothers spend their nights making babies and their days watching TV. They readily commit fraud and squander tax dollars on the lottery. If they were ever married, their inner deficiencies caused them to choose the wrong man. But, I have been a welfare mother and have worked over the years with thousands of other welfare mothers. And the popular view just isn't so. In fact, if there is one generalization about us that remains consistent, it is that as a group we are very much like the rest of society—all different. Many have less education and most a tougher hide, but otherwise we span the gamut as mothers, cooks, thinkers, doers, givers and users, housekeepers and gadabouts.

The problem isn't simply that many people believe the worst about welfare recipients, but also that social policy is based on an equally invalid set of assumptions.

Blaming the Victims

Not long ago, it was a generally held belief that women who were raped somehow "caused" the attack, or that women were battered because they did something to deserve it. Fortunately, thanks in large part to the women's movement, the actual facts of the case were reexamined and our beliefs about rape and family violence have begun to change. As a result, more appropriate social responses are evolving. Woman's "perversity," or her tendency to "victimize" others, is no longer the central issue.

Unfortunately, no comparable evolution in thinking has occurred with respect to the AFDC mother. That the man who fathered her children did not support the family is still viewed as a deficiency in *her* character. As a result, she is either punished or patronized—depending on the point in the political spectrum from which the "help" comes. From all corners, she is portrayed as a deviant—lumped together in studies with junkies, criminals, and the psychologically traumatized. Her individual deviance must be corrected, her behavior modified, in order that she and her children can be removed from our overbooked societal calendar.

Male Deviance

Women's role as mothers has been biologically determined and socially reinforced for centuries. Men, or the other hand, have been socialized as providers (hunters/protectors). If there is deviance to be imputed, then, it can hardly be ascribed to AFDC mothers as a group. Yet, because of our sex-biased (read "patriarchal") culture, it is *their* behavior and biological function that we most often seek to modify.

> "That the man who fathered her children did not support the family is still viewed a deficiency in her character."

The forced sterilization of poor women has been well documented in recent years. Granted, poor women are easy targets, particularly when they have been hospitalized for other reasons. But imprisoned poor men, stripped of many of their rights and found by courts to have transgressed society's rules, are also theoretically easy targets. Unless it has skipped public perception, however, neither forced castration nor any other form of sterilization of poor

men seems to have occurred on any notable scale. The point is, we have defined the problem, and it's female.

When the hunter/protector vanishes from the scene, the provider function must be replaced or the children and the mother will die. At present, a woman with no means of support has several alternatives. She can dump the kids in a foster care institution or put them up for adoption. This option can be torture for both mother and children, and while it is generally more socially acceptable for single fathers, it is highly frowned upon for women.

Lousy Options

She can seek another man, and there is no question that for poor, heterosexual mothers, this is usually preferred option. Alvin Schoor quotes a mother of four:

> If a man has anything and offers to help you out, you don't say to him: But you have to marry me first. . . . You take what he offers right off and you hope that someday he will want to make it legal. But beggars can't be choosers (*Poor Kids*, Basic Books).

But marriage or remarriage in the short-term is unlikely.

So two options are left, and, whatever she chooses, the poor mother is likely to remain poor. The first, and usually the most immediately accessible, is welfare. It does allow a woman to fulfill her role as nurturer, if only in the most meager of ways. Particularly for women with infants, this is no small potatoes decision. The second option, depending upon market conditions, may be to enter the paid labor force. It is in this quandary that we come to a second question: Do the conditions exist to help welfare mothers?

Few people who have ever done it would deny that raising children is a difficult task. Few would deny that raising them alone is even more difficult. Alone and poor tops the charts. Alone, poor, and *employed*, however, is sometimes worse yet.

Consider first the "supermom." Usually defined as married and employed outside the home, she gets up early in the morning, bustles through a job all day, and comes home in the evening to cook and clean and take care of the children. Weekends offer little relief. The supermom, though she lives a life of relative affluence, also lives a life of stress.

Poor Supermoms

The not-so-supermom is not married, gets up just as early in the morning, has a job at Chock-Full-o'-Nuts bustling on her feet all day, and then returns home and bustles some more. While dad isn't there to add to the laundry, neither is he there to defray the cost of a washing machine or to take out the garbage. He also can't help with the kids in even the most minor of ways. The not-so-supermom has an additional problem. Unless she has a trusted relative or friend who will take care of her children, she must entrust her small child to the cheapest alternative, and her slightly older child to the mercy of the neighborhood. While her material condition is not measurably altered, her stress quotient has soared. Her self-respect may be higher than the welfare mother's but that can go down the tubes quickly if the local junkies take an interest in her son, or the bargain babysitter turns out to be a child molester.

The bitter irony of it all is that she has relinquished her much indoctrinated (and, in some cases, highly treasured) role to a total and possibly incompetent stranger in exchange for an opportunity to make little money and influence few people. In addition, she has added 40 or more hours to an already difficult work week—and she is still no more likely to be invited to dinner at the home of a supermom than she was as a welfare mother.

Low Wages

According to a book published in 1981 by the National Advisory Council on Economic Opportunity, "If wives and female heads were paid the wages that similarly qualified men earn, about half the families now living in poverty would not be poor." Female-headed households constitute less than 19 percent of all households, yet they account for more than half the households living below the poverty level. This is true even though the majority of female-headed households are in the paid labor force. In 1977, when the minimum wage would have brought an annual salary of about $4,800, women accounted for 53 percent of those who earned less than $5,000 per year. At that time, they made up only 33 percent of the full-time, year-round work force. . . .

"A black woman hired as a nanny for an upper class white family is a 'worker'; the same woman struggling under adverse conditions to raise her own children is a social parasite."

The upshot is that an employed poor mother can hardly be said to have lifted her family out of poverty in any but the most shallow way. While a return to the supplemental benefits package decimated by the Reagan administration would help, unless labor market options expand for women, progress will be minimal. In a labor market that is contracting its opportunities even for men, however, that likelihood is slim.

Contemporary economists point to two major trends in U.S. employment patterns. At the moment, the most profound is the rise in the proportion of service-sector jobs, with the largest growth occurring

at the bottom end of the wage scale, some growth in the middle, and a somewhat larger growth at the top.

Second, technological advances are producing most of the growth in the production industry (and most of the blue collar job losses), with a similar polarization between workers at the bottom and top. Despite a rapidly growing high tech industry, rapidly growing employment opportunities do not abound. Robotized factories with minimal human labor turn out new robots to perform still other tasks formerly done by workers. Estimates by *Fortune* magazine project a further decline of production jobs by one-third to one-half by the end of the decade.

If the "strongest" workers in the labor force (i.e., white men) continue losing relatively better paying jobs (i.e., steel production, automobile manufacturing, etc.) and continue their downward mobility into lower-paid work, it isn't too difficult to guess which workers will get pushed out altogether. Welfare mothers can expect to face even stiffer competition for the jobs nobody else usually wants.

The Value of Raising Children

Viewed in this context, pushing mothers (by dint of popular mores reinforced with social welfare sanctions) to choose a poverty wage job at Chock-Full-o'Nuts over receiving AFDC and raising their own children can have questionable value. While a move into paid employment can advance the interests of some families, the opposite can be true for others. For those whose skill levels and/or education do not allow *real* potential for job advancement, the promise of wage poverty instead of welfare poverty rings hollow.

Poor women, then, are caught in an ideological trap. Their work is almost never valued in economic terms. It is, however, socially sanctioned as long as it is performed *in exchange for a wage*. A black woman hired as a nanny for an upper class white family is a "worker"; the same woman struggling under adverse conditions to raise her *own* children is a social parasite.

The proliferation of studies in recent years on "the feminization of poverty" shows rather notably that having a job by no means guarantees a single mother will not be poor. The New York State census is a rude reminder. While the welfare rolls remained relatively stable between 1970 and 1980, the incidence of poverty among female-headed households did not. During that decade, the number of female householders with children under 18 years old grew by 50.9 percent. The number of these households who were below the poverty rate increased from 41.2 percent to 48.6 percent.

I do not mean to argue that poor women should be hindered in their attempts to enter the labor force if they should choose to do so. On the contrary, voluntary efforts of poor women to enter the paid labor force should be supported by a whole range of appropriate services, not the least of which are income supplements and child care. I do mean to suggest some other things, however: First, the chances for upward mobility for poor mothers who choose to work outside the home are slim, absent income subsidies. Second, so long as women's work in the home remains "illegitimate" labor, women will continue to occupy the least valued positions in the paid labor force. Third, as we proceed toward increasing degrees of cybernation, there will be decreasing need for laborers in general. Fourth, policies and rhetoric that ignore all of the above do so at great expense to large numbers of people—mostly children, and disproportionately third world children—and divert our attention away from redefining our values and refocusing our efforts toward a more equitable system of income distribution in this country and genuine public education reform.

"The problem is not so much whether we, as a nation, are economically capable of alleviating poverty, but whether we are willing to do so."

There is nothing innately more satisfactory or practical or morally superior about "jobs" as the dominant means of resource distribution. Historically, "jobs" are a fairly recent phenomenon. If we can expect the acceptable definitions of work in our culture (independent of that activity to which a wage is attached), we can more easily expand the political potential to advance the interests of poor women and children in particular. If we can confront directly the sanctimoniousness of a work ethic that defines and values as work only that for which one is paid a wage, we might be able to conceive of and realize a whole new range of programs. Children's allowance, mother's wage, family allowances, negative income tax, guaranteed income are alternative forms of income distribution.

Moving Toward a Fair Income Policy

Most other Western-bloc countries incorporate one or more of these forms in their social support systems. The income alternatives in many of these countries provide vastly better living conditions for vulnerable single-parent families. Most notable among them is Sweden, where a mother of two children who has no outside employment can receive up to 93 percent of the income of the average wage-earner.

Nevertheless, the economy of Sweden is no more unstable than our own (a concern of many opponents of guaranteed annual income). In fact, there is ample reason to assume that a more equitable incomes policy in the United States might even spur a healthier economy by generating more consumption, thereby generating more production, and so on.

In any event, the problem is not so much whether we, as a nation, are economically capable of alleviating poverty, but whether we are willing to do so. There have been two major periods of what Daniel Moynihan referred to as times of "social opportunity" in this century. One, in the 1930's, occurred during economic calamity. The other, during the 1960's, occurred during a period of great prosperity. Such times are dictated not by economic conditions so much as by political ones. If we want to be politically effective in advancing social conditions predicated on sound human and economic principles, we will have to seek to alter the way a wide variety of people think about issues. With a little luck and a great deal of effort, maybe next time around, we won't blow it.

Theresa Funiciello is co-director of Social Agenda, a national organization concerned with US poverty policy.

"As soon as a poor girl learns of her pregnancy, she is immediately eligible to apply for welfare assistance. For many a young woman, this is a boon."

viewpoint 89

Welfare Causes Black Poverty and Family Instability

Elizabeth Wright

The social problem that did not go away in spite of all the good will and well-intentioned programs, and which is more widespread today than ever, is finally finding its place in the nation's news media. From the grim demographic statistics which periodically show the persistently rising black illegitimate birthrate, right through the recent reports in the New York City press on the houses of horror known as welfare hotels, the taboo subject is finally coming into its own in print and on the T.V. screen.

"Welfare Mother Begets 3 Welfare Daughters, Perpetuating Life Style," one newspaper headline reads. "New Orleans Leaders Discuss the Problem of Teen-Age Pregnancies," another informs. Editorials on a subject considered too sensitive to mention just a short while ago are now common. One tells of a ". . . disturbing theory currently floating around that blacks are staying poor despite years of government programs because of their relatively intractable female-headed family structure." Another claims that ". . . an increasing number of unmarried black teenagers are choosing poverty by choosing to become mothers."

Recognizing the Problem

And, after years of hesitancy, even black columnists have taken to frankness and candor on the subject, with one claiming that ". . . the epidemic of teenage pregnancy among blacks will only worsen if the problem is neglected by those who have the most at stake—the black community." And another outspokenly suggests that since black teenage mothers are becoming the majority of black mothers, ". . . they can't help but pass on problems, and that is not exactly a recipe for racial progress."

Even the aloof NAACP has finally acknowledged

that something is sorely wrong within the black community. Belatedly responding to what some of its members call a "social crisis," in May 1984, the organization sponsored a 3-day conference on the poor black family, focusing mainly on said family's "disintegration." The National Urban League has also openly acknowledged the subject. Conceding that blacks in the past may have been "too defensive" to publicly examine certain cultural behavior patterns, the League's president John Jacob admitted to the "disturbing" fact that more than half of all black babies are born to unmarried women.

Is it possible that this could all be leading to where the Moynihan Report tried to take us twenty years ago—to a sober appraisal of what is probably our country's most urgent domestic social problem?

Demoralized Black Women

Throughout the past decade we have watched the poor black community fail in its struggle to free itself from the regressive cycle in which it seemed locked. Coupled with this failure has been the poor black woman's inability to reverse behavior patterns which have dominated the lifestyle of past generations of black women. Caught in a bind, she is a victim of long-conditioned habits and attitudes which restrict her, often to a greater extent than real social barriers. For, unlike the vast numbers of women who are daily discovering to what degree they can shape their own futures, she has little consciousness of the part she can play in arresting, if not preventing, her own personal demoralization. Real social changes now offer her alternatives only dreamed of by her grandmother, yet the pattern of her life is little changed from that of women two generations removed. Like them, she too is caught in a cycle of intermittent lovers, pregnancies and abandonment.

Although it is late, it is nevertheless encouraging that a segment of the black community is finally

Elizabeth Wright, "The Problem That Will Not Go Away," *The Lincoln Review,* Winter 1985. Reprinted with permission from The Lincoln Institute.

responding to the alarming signals issuing from the rising black illegitimate birthrate. Those who still stubbornly continue to minimize the calamity that such births promise tend to call attention to the parallel increase in illegitimate births among whites. Such a tactic is meant to effectively inhibit any discussion on the bleakness of the problem among blacks, since it bans all discussion to the realm of moral judgment. What has been purposely ignored in the past is the fact that it is not illegitimacy per se, but the *nature* of illegitimacy among blacks which makes it a more devastating experience. There is now an illegitimacy rate in our major cities of over half the annual births, which means that children born in fatherless households have actually surpassed the number of children born to married couples. Illegitimacy among this group scarcely resembles illegitimacy among others. For the child of an unmarried middle class woman, whether black or white, may very well be taken into a stable family among its own relatives. In the case of the white child, it might be adopted by a couple who can provide such stability. In either case, a structured, protective home and community environment is the norm to be expected. In a middle class setting, even where the household has but a single parent, the child can still look forward to a certain regularity in his dealings with adults. In addition, the immediate surrounding community provides a model of how he will be expected to behave; the ideals of a stable community are passed on regardless of the nature of the child's family life.

"[The black woman] is caught in a cycle of intermittent lovers, pregnancies and abandonment."

In stark contrast, the poor black child born illegitimately is more likely to enter a household already too disoriented to be supportive or provide anything resembling positive structure for his life. And the same is generally true of his immediate surrounding community or neighborhood. In fact, his household is generally no more than a microcosm of the confusion and chaos of that surrounding community. This child is more likely to be born to a very young woman, herself fresh from an unstable, disordered childhood, who has, most likely, never reached a level of maturity to cope with life's daily trials, much less with the overwhelming predicament in which she now finds herself. Coming from her own disorderly background, there is no way this woman can cope with the nearly impossible task of disciplining and keeping control of her growing sons who become men long before boyhood is over. Her physical and emotional

energies are soon sapped as she learns that it takes a man to handle men. In her attempt to exact some measure of obedience from her increasingly rebellious flock, she is notoriously repressive and punitive. Her own lack of development and her immaturity deny her the most elementary understanding of their childish needs. It is no wonder that such a woman, staggered by the burden of frequent pregnancies, and distraught from the futility of coping alone, ends up incapable of creating a stable home. And it is hardly surprising that she eventually turns her resentment directly onto these unwanted children.

Having known no discipline or regularity in her own brief childhood, she can hardly be expected to pass on to a child even the most elementary restraint required to establish regular habits. Daily preparation for school becomes an ordeal which the child ultimately gives up. For there is no one to direct the ongoing, monotonous routine centered around an activity such as getting off to school every day. In fact, consistency of any kind is something unknown in this household. Uncertain of the events that he might encounter in his home from one day to the next, this humiliated youngster feels he belongs nowhere in particular, and spends much of his time aimlessly searching for other social niches to fit into.

Ruthless, Aimless, and Neglected

When we understand the unstable conditions in which this woman drifts, it becomes all the clearer why we are faced with the bands of aimless, neglected youth who presently roam our urban areas. Youth recently described by black writer Claude Brown as "semi-abandoned" and "ruthless." Brown, on a return trip to Harlem, claimed that for these children, "survival is a matter of fortuity and instinct," and that, consequently, those who manage to survive are usually "more cunning, more devious and often more vicious" than any middle-class counterpart. "These traits," he dismally goes on, "are the essential contents of their survival kit." Alvin Poussaint, prominent black Harvard psychiatrist, long publicly avoided making correlations between the treatment of black children within their families and their hostile behavior patterns. Recently conceding that child abuse on the part of parents "can create a free-floating rage which is later turned on others in brutal and murderous acts," Poussaint claims that many youths see violence as a socially acceptable means of economic and psychological survival.

The recent spate of articles and letters to the editors in the press on the subject all speculate on why, in a social climate which encourages contraception and condones abortion, these women and girls still elect to become mothers under the dreariest conditions. By one camp they are described as victims of social forces beyond their comprehension or control. Others less sympathetic view them as cunning and rational in opting for motherhood, while knowing full well they will be financially rewarded by a welfare system gone berserk. The reasons for having babies they are unfit to cope with are both psychological and practical. We can readily understand the emotional satisfaction of such a woman in possessing a love object which unconditionally belongs to her. As sociologist Egon Mayer puts it, "Why doubt that poor teenage girls become pregnant and have children for the same reason that their more respectable counterparts do: because they believe that with a child they will be happier, more fulfilled, more secure and more worthwhile as human beings than without."

The Welfare Boon

In a practical sphere, as soon as a poor girl learns of her pregnancy, she is immediately eligible to apply for welfare assistance. For many a young woman, this is a boon strictly because she can now afford to establish her own living quarters. Some have openly told of their joy at being able to free themselves from economic dependence on a mother or grandmother. Within the confines of their limited mental vision, this is the only avenue to independence that seems open to them.

Dr. Charles Wright, a black obstetrician whose Detroit practice brings him into direct contact with such women and children, tells of the anguish he experiences over the escalating number of unwed teenage mothers whom he treats. Along with other concerned doctors, he has helped to form a medical organization to assist and counsel these young women. Calling teenage pregnancy a "national disaster," he says, "Physicians tend to limit their concerns to issues that are safe and impersonal. By ignoring subjects that may prove painful or embarrassing, we are able to bypass, or delay, the obligation to deal with them philosophically or otherwise."

In the best of contexts, any examination of social relations between men and women tends to meet with resistance. But in our society, when the factor of race is present, evasion becomes all the more common. Everybody gets defensive—not only blacks, but their white "guardians" as well. Until now, there has been a tacit limit to straight-forward public reporting and discussion of the dismal statistics which show that every month growing numbers of young black girls and women are joining the ranks of unwed mothers who, along with their children, can only look forward to burdened and depressing futures. Yet, a failure to focus on this particular crisis may prove to be the most tragic evasion of our time.

It is easy to became disheartened when speculating on the future of poor blacks. There seems little possibility for change until they have broken free of the insidious shackles which keep them bound to old perceptions and attitudes which they, in turn, pass on to their sons and daughters.

"Some [pregnant teenagers] have openly told of their joy at being able to free themselves from economic dependence on a mother or grandmother."

This problem is especially urgent in the realm of the poor black woman who, in effect, is the solitary model for her young. To them she is a lifeline in a way more critical and immediate than is true for most mothers. Because her influence in the black community is without parallel, there is much at stake if this woman fails to reach an awareness that alternatives to the fate of her mother and grandmother do exist—that defeat and failure are not inevitable. Her shortsighted vision, which is understandably blurred by the scores of dead-end lives surrounding her, must eventually be widened enough to encompass something other than her surrender to the same pointless martyrdom. The key to what happens to blacks in coming generations rests to a great extent on the kind of visions black women hold of themselves and of their place in our society. How narrow or wide those visions are will determine to what degree the race will remain trapped in its cycle of ignorance and despair.

Elizabeth Wright is a regular contributor to the Lincoln Review *and edits the New York newsletter,* Issues and Views.

> *"Even when black children live in two-parent families, they are likely to spend four times as much of their childhood in poverty as the average white child will spend."*

Racism Causes Black Poverty

Greg J. Duncan and James P. Comer

Editor's note: The following viewpoint is taken from two articles about black poverty which appeared in the Los Angeles Times. *Part I is by Greg J. Duncan, Part II is by James P. Comer.*

I

Twenty years ago, Daniel Patrick Moynihan's report, "The Negro Family," identified black family structure as the root cause of black poverty. That report by the assistant secretary of labor (now senator from New York) was greeted with such an outcry that policies directed at black family structure were barely mentioned in the decade that followed. Today, black poverty is once again being blamed primarily, if not exclusively, on the structure and culture of black families. But evidence from an ongoing long-term study of American families shows that even when black children live in two-parent families, they are likely to spend four times as much of their childhood in poverty as the average white child will spend. The solution to black poverty lies less in the family than in the labor market.

The all-too-familiar image of black poverty portrays inner-city black children growing up in fatherless families, dependent on welfare and destined to become the next generation of welfare recipients. Are these vivid impressions of an urban underclass representative of the larger group of poor blacks? And can they be used to justify Draconian cuts in programs inspired by President Lyndon B. Johnson's "Great Society"? The survey evidence reveals that most black poverty does not fit the underclass stereotype, and that the welfare system rarely produces long-term dependency either in its present recipients or in their children's generation.

Greg J. Duncan, "Blame Joblessness, Not the Families for Black Poverty," *Los Angeles Times*, February 10, 1986. Reprinted with the author's permission.

James P. Comer, "Black Americans' Problems Are the Orphans of History," *Los Angeles Times*, February 14, 1985. Reprinted with the author's permission.

This recent and surprising evidence on the weak links between family structure, poverty and welfare comes from the Panel Study of Income Dynamics, conducted at the University of Michigan. For 18 years the study has followed the economic fortunes of a large and representative sample of more than 5,000 American families—white and black, advantaged and disadvantaged, urban and rural. Since this study has tracked the same families year after year, the data provide a unique source of information about the economic fortunes of American families over the long term.

Data from annual government surveys paint a bleak picture of the economic plight of black children, but the results from the Panel Study are even bleaker. Among black children, fewer than one in seven lives above the poverty line during every year of childhood. In contrast, a clear majority of white children enjoy economic security throughout their entire childhood. Despite the safety net of cash welfare programs instituted in the last 20 years, the average black child can expect to spend more than five of his or her first 15 years in poverty. For white children the total time spent in poverty averages nine months.

Family Structure

Differences in family structure account for some, but by no means all or even most, of the differences in childhood poverty between blacks and whites. A black child living with only one parent throughout childhood is likely to spend half of his or her first 15 years in poverty, compared with three years out of 15 for black children with intact families. But the most striking implication of these numbers is that, even given the cash welfare system of the 1970s, the average black child living with both parents throughout his or her first 15 years still could be expected to experience three of those years—about one-fifth of childhood—in poverty. This is the same that could be expected for a white child living with only one parent.

There also are surprising findings on the location and persistence of black poverty. The problems of black children concentrated in inner-city enclaves are both severe and highly visible, but the data suggest that more pervasive and persistent poverty lies outside large urban areas. If we want to develop policies that will be effective in solving problems of childhood poverty nationwide, we must include a much larger and different population than is represented in the stereotype of an urban underclass.

The Panel Study's broader scope also shows that, despite the pervasiveness of poverty among black children, less than half of all those experiencing poverty at least once during childhood will be poor for most of their childhood years. For black and white children, escaping from poverty is more closely tied to the employment of parents and older children than to any other event, including marriage.

No Long-Term Dependency

Frequent movements into and out of poverty produce a great deal of turnover among welfare recipients. Overall, less than one-third of all recipients experience welfare "careers" lasting eight or more years. And while nearly three out of four black children grow up in families where welfare is received at least once, fewer than one in six live in families that count heavily on welfare for more than half of the time.

Among the study's important revelations are its findings of very weak links between welfare dependency of parent and child. Fewer than one in four black women growing up in heavily welfare-dependent homes were found to depend heavily on welfare when they were observed in their own homes 10 to 15 years later.

"Fewer than one in four black women growing up in heavily welfare-dependent homes were found to depend heavily on welfare when they were observed in their own homes 10 to 15 years later."

Taken together, the evidence indicates we must look beyond the black family and the "underclass" to find solutions to black poverty and render judgment about welfare programs. Jobs can and do lift many blacks out of poverty, but we have much to learn about how labor market benefits can be extended to include not only the small group of blacks in the professional elite but also the much larger group of black workers in lower-wage labor markets or outside the job market altogether.

Meanwhile, the plight of black children growing up in impoverished households commands our immediate attention while we continue searching for solutions to the root causes of these problems. Until they are found, we must ensure that the safety net provides a greater measure of opportunity for our nation's children.

II

The problem of black teen-agers having children out of wedlock has been the focus recently of several news stories and a well-publicized CBS documentary. The Moynihan Report on the black family initiated this focus more than 20 years ago. These reports, no matter how well intended, do no more than reinforce racist stereotypes. Enough already!

The problem is that none of these accounts adequately present the American system's role in creating the crisis, or its role in addressing the problem. The media leaves the public with an inaccurate image of the black community as primarily dependent and irresponsible, and the problem as being mainly the result of public welfare and a lack of self-discipline.

Black History

Government-sanctioned racism denied blacks the vote after slavery and until the 1960s in the South—where most of the black population was located. Without political power, blacks could not develop economic power. Without political and economic power, they could not obtain adequate educational and social opportunities.

In the eight states that held more than 80% of the nation's black population, four to eight times as much money was spent on the education of white children well into the 1940s, and as much as 25 times more was spent on whites in states where there was a large black majority. The same disparity existed at the postsecondary level. As late as the mid-1960s two prestigious women's colleges had an endowment more than that of all the 100-plus black colleges combined. In addition, blacks were excluded from labor unions until the 1950s and '60s.

As a result, 90% of the black population was forced to the bottom of the job market as laborers and domestics. Until after World War II, with the organization provided by the black church and related institutions, black families were able to function reasonably well, even with only marginal income. As late as 1965, 79% of them were still two-parent families. Parents were able to serve as role models for their children. And because we were a nation of small towns, rural areas and close-knit urban communities, heads of households could interact with like-minded parents, teachers, religious leaders and others, to transmit desirable values to the children.

After World War II education became the ticket to jobs paying a living wage. Successful blacks began moving out of the inner-city, taking their money, leadership and role models, leaving the poor isolated and alienated. Whites began to move to the suburbs, taking quality education and jobs with them. Those trends left certain parents—black and white—less able to transmit desirable values to their children.

"The rate of out-of-wedlock pregnancy among better-educated black women is no higher than their white counterparts."

Blacks, as a consequence of their history of exclusion, were most vulnerable. Some black families began to experience a downward spiral. More white families are beginning to do the same. Indeed, a recent newspaper story noted the rise of white middle-class youth gangs in Los Angeles; and the rate of increase of teen-age pregnancies among whites is higher than the rate among blacks.

Public policies could have been developed to counter the effects of slavery and to bring black families into the societal mainstream. We developed policies to help Europe overcome the effects of a war we did not start. We spent billions rescuing millions from communism. We assist victims of every natural disaster. But we have not spent much to enable blacks to overcome the adverse effects of slavery and the illegal denial of opportunity that followed.

Blitz of Information

Without a historical perspective and an understanding of how events shape behavior, there is no way to grasp the current blitz of information on the plight of poor urban blacks. The facts: A report by Black Enterprise magazine, based on 1983 census data, shows that 81% of black households pay at least one to all six types of taxes, or about $37 billion, and that blacks earn more than $152 billion annually. More than 1 million black households earn more than $20,000 per year. The rate of out-of-wedlock pregnancy among better-educated black women is no higher than their white counterparts.

The focus on blacks under stress would not be a problem if most Americans received a true picture of the full spectrum of the black experience. But the media constantly skew the picture: Black criminals are almost routinely identified by race—photos of black gang members and other blacks accused of crimes are ubiquitous, while many achievers mentioned in the news are never identified as black, and it does not seem to be nearly as necessary to use their photographs. It's as if when blacks achieve, they stop being black, or they become invisible. Yet when they are victims of social problems, then they are black—and highly visible.

Because we tend to see problems among blacks solely as "black" problems, we don't face up to serious social issues until they have spread to the larger community and are out of hand—drugs and violent crime, for example.

When we stop viewing societal problems largely in racial terms, we will be able to devise policies to effectively combat them. But please, no more analyses of the problem of "those poor blacks" until we are mature enough to examine the whole story. And if we don't do it soon, because of the generation-to-generation transmission of behavior patterns, the quality of life for all of us will deteriorate sharply.

Greg J. Duncan is a program director at the Survey Research Center at the University of Michigan and the author of Years of Poverty, Years of Plenty. *James P. Comer is a psychiatry professor at Yale University's Child Guidance Center.*

viewpoint 91

Social Security Is Unfair to Youth

James Dale Davidson

Social Security is 50 years old. Polls commissioned by the program's proponents show that over 90 percent of the American people support it, and consider it a success. Over 90 percent of us like springtime, too. But spring can't last. Neither can Social Security in its present form, no matter what the polls say.

A young black man in the South Bronx, working sporadically at minimum-wage jobs, earns too little to pay income tax. But he and his employer *do* have to pay a 14.1 percent Social Security tax, starting with his first dollar of earnings. This young black man has roughly a 50-50 chance of dying before he reaches age 65. Since Social Security is not a vested program, chances are he'll never get a penny in benefits from it. Far more likely to live past age 65 is a wealthy widow in an East Side luxury condominium. She gets back many times what she, her late husband, and their employers ever paid in Social Security taxes. The young man needs the money. She doesn't. She gets the welfare. He pays the taxes. There's something out of joint here.

Excessive Taxes

A young woman in college, struggling to pay tuition with a part-time job, also earns too little to pay income tax. But she and her employer also have to pay a 14.1 percent Social Security tax, starting with her first dollar of earnings. In five years this young woman will be working. Maybe she'll be running her own business. If so, starting in 1990, she may have to pay as much as *$8,690.40 per year* in Social Security taxes. That's more than she'll probably pay in federal and state income taxes combined.

A typical recipient of this young woman's money might be her grandfather who lives on a golf course

down in Florida. Suppose her grandfather is 78 years old, and started working when he was 18. For ten years, he paid no Social Security taxes. The next 13 years, he and his employer together paid just $780 over *13* years, or just *$60 per year.* By the time he retired, on January 1, 1972, at the age of 65, he and his employer had together paid a lifetime maximum of $8,234.20. That sum, covering a working span of 45 years and a taxpaying span of 35 years, is less than the young working woman—his grand-daughter—may have to pay in Social Security taxes *every year of her life.* Adjust this for inflation, and we still find this working woman paying *30 times* what her grandfather paid at the same stage of life.

If the government were not doing the taxing and spending, would this family arrange an income transfer of this kind? Would this grandfather ever ask for—would he even accept—14 percent of the earnings of a struggling college student? Or an $8,690 check every year from a 25-year-old grandchild who may be raising small children or saving money to buy a house? Of course not. But that's what his government does.

Wealthy Senior Citizens

This grandfather, like most senior citizens, is probably not aware of how Social Security is changing character over time. For him, it has been a fine program. Like most beneficiaries in their 70s and 80s, he's getting back three, five, ten times what he paid in—even when compound interest is added to what he originally contributed.

This might be fine if these examples were atypical. It might be fine if elderly Americans, taken as a group, needed this much money—and if today's young working people could afford it. The common, media-reinforced impression of a senior citizen is that of a widow living on the edge of poverty, struggling to make ends meet. The common impression of a young person is that of a "yuppie"

James Dale Davidson, "Social Security Ripoff," *The New Republic*, November 11, 1985. Reprinted by permission of THE NEW REPUBLIC, © 1985, The New Republic, Inc.

on the fast track, with big paychecks and expensive tastes.

Yes, there are many low-income elderly who need their Social Security checks to survive. Yes, there are affluent yuppies here and there. But let's talk about these generations as a group. Who is poor? Overwhelmingly, the young are poor. When federal benefits payments are factored in, the poverty rate for children is around 20 percent. Compare that with the poverty rate for senior citizens, which is just three percent. And who has spendable discretionary income (the amount after paying food, housing, taxes, medical expenses, and all other necessities)? Among households with money to spend, senior citizens have more per capita—$4,118—than any other age group. Young people aged 25 to 34 have $1,918, less than half as much, in per capita discretionary income.

Benefits and Taxes

It's time we told senior citizens the truth about Social Security and other retirement programs. It's time we told the widow in the East Side luxury condominium that she's getting what amounts to welfare at the expense of the low-wage worker in the South Bronx. It's time we reminded the grandfather on the Florida golf course that he's getting a far better deal than his granddaughter ever will.

How can we make these facts clear? We could start by printing two notations on every Social Security check: how much the beneficiary and his or her employer paid in Social Security taxes, over a lifetime. And how much the beneficiary has gotten back, to date, in benefits. That might make a few senior citizens thing twice before writing their representative or senator demanding that every penny of their benefits be protected, no matter what is happening elsewhere in the economy.

Elected officials will not say this, but it must be said: the senior citizens' demands on federal taxpayers, on working Americans, their demands on their own children and grandchildren have grown far beyond what is fair and can reasonably be provided. America's elders are burdening their heirs with debts and unfunded liabilities that have reached dangerous proportions. In 1986 America will have a two-trillion-dollar national debt. On top of *that* debt must be piled seven trillion dollars in unfunded liabilities for Social Security and other federal retirement programs.

Another Tax-and-Spend Program

If Congress could muster the courage—which it won't—it would immediately stop the explosive growth in retirement programs. But even if it did, today's young taxpayers have reason to doubt they will ever be offered benefits nearly as generous as senior citizens now enjoy. Social Security is not a vested program. There is no trust fund, in the true sense of the word. This is just another tax-and-spend program, the biggest tax-and-spend program in the history of mankind. All that taxpayers get in return for their taxes is the promise that some future Congress will someday make a future generation of taxpayers pay enough taxes to support them. At some point, the chain will be broken. Taxpayers will reach the straining point. Promises will be violated.

"Today's young taxpayers have reason to doubt they will ever be offered benefits nearly as generous as senior citizens now enjoy."

You don't hear such forecasts coming out of the Social Security Administration, its actuaries, and its many friends in Congress. You don't hear such forecasts coming out of the White House. But take a close look at who the actuaries *are*. They're top Reagan administration officials, who are famous for rosy forecasts. And take a close look at the assumptions underlying the prognoses they make of good health and long life for Social Security.

Consider what the actuaries call their "optimistic" scenario. Under this scenario, today's young people would, on retirement, receive benefits matching present levels. Tomorrow's taxpayers would face only another ten percent increase above the 1990 tax levels. (Remember that the maximum tax in 1990 is already scheduled to be 50 percent above today's maximum.)

Impossible Scenarios

Here are some of the conditions that have to be met to keep taxes from rising further. Productivity has to grow at a rate twice that of the 1970s. Workers' earnings have to increase annually at a rate two-and-a-half times that of the past 30 years. The unemployment rate has to fall by one-third, to five percent, and stay at that level. Interest rates have to fall by more than one-half, to five percent, and stay at that level. The labor force participation rate for women has to rise by 15 percent above the present rate—*and* their fertility rate has to rise by 30 percent above the present rate. Immigration must reach an annual rate matched in only one decade (1901 to 1910) of American history. Annual increases in life expectancy must slow to only one-fourth the rate of the past 50 years. Each of these conditions must not be met in one year, or over five or ten years, but throughout a *60-year* period. That's not just optimistic. It's not just highly unlikely. It's almost impossible.

Now take a look at what the actuaries call their "pessimistic" scenario. Under this scenario, today's young people could only reach benefits matching present levels if tomorrow's taxpayers are willing to endure a doubling of Social Security taxes around the year 2020, and a net tripling of these taxes around the year 2050. That would mean a combined employee-employer tax rate of 41 percent—above and beyond federal income taxes and state and local taxes.

For taxes to rise "only" that much, here are some of the conditions that have to be met over the next 60 years. Productivity has to grow at a rate only 30 percent above that of the past decade. Worker earnings have to increase annually at a rate equaling that of the past 30 years, and greater than the rate of the past 15 years. The unemployment rate has to stay at seven percent. Nominal interest rates have to fall by one-third, to 6.5 percent. Labor force participation, fertility, and immigration rates must remain approximately where they are today. Life expectancy must improve slightly less than it has over the past 50 years.

"All that taxpayers get in return for their [social security] taxes is the promise that some future Congress will someday make a future generation of taxpayers pay enough taxes to support them."

The demographic assumptions seem reasonable—not optimistic, not pessimistic. The economic assumptions seem highly optimistic, but possible. But wait a minute. This isn't the "optimistic" scenario . . . it's supposed to be the "pessimistic" one. And even if these conditions are met, who can imagine that some future Congress would allow Social Security taxes to rise to 20 percent, much less 40 percent, of total payroll costs? That will never happen.

Broken Promises

The official forecast the actuaries make—and the one that prompted the recent press reports of Social Security's "good health"—is midway between the two scenarios described above. That puts it somewhere on the spectrum between optimistic and impossible. And the tax increase it would require lies somewhere on the spectrum between very big and impossible.

So what does this mean? It means that today's young taxpayers—and certainly today's small children—will, at some point in their lives, see some Social Security promises broken. Maybe there will be a means test. Maybe benefits will be denied affluent retirees who, over their working lifetimes, will have paid as much as $300,000 in Social Security taxes. Maybe benefit levels will be cut across-the-board, pushing millions of future retirees below the poverty line.

The longer we wait, the more traumatic and expensive the Social Security crisis will be. The problem is all in the family. It's time we sat down—grandparent, parent, and child—and worked this thing out.

James Dale Davidson is head of the National Taxpayers Union.

Social Security Is Not Unfair to Youth

Cyril F. Brickfield and Barry Sussman

Editor's note: The following viewpoint is taken from two articles. Part I is by Cyril F. Brickfield of the American Association of Retired Persons and Part II is by Barry Sussman of The Washington Post.

I

If ever there was a time for advocacy and action, that time is *now*. If ever there was a need to stand together and speak with one voice, that need is *now*. If ever there was a threat to the independence and security of older citizens, that threat is *now*. . . .

At *no* time in these past 20 years has the progress we've made been so jeopardized. Vital programs like Social Security and Medicare—programs that have brought millions of our fellow citizens out of poverty and kept millions more in good health—are now in danger. Even the basic and cherished belief in our society that retired Americans have earned a measure of respect, dignity and economic security in old age is now under attack. . . .

Our enemies in this struggle are well-known to us. They are the ideological descendents of those who fought the creation of Social Security 50 years ago. They are the same people who condemned the new Medicare program 20 years ago as "socialized medicine." And they are at it again today, trying to turn back the clock.

Today, our enemies are trying to drive a wedge between us and our children. Our children are being told that Social Security is "ripping them off." They are being told that they are unfairly taxed to support a generation of "affluent" older persons. They are being told that older Americans have achieved "economic parity" with the rest of the population and no longer need Social Security and Medicare

Cyril Brickfield, speech delivered at Michigan Senior Power Day, May 15, 1985.

Barry Sussman, "Here's the Latest Criticism of Social Security: It Works," *The Washington Post National Weekly Edition,* January 20, 1986. © The Washington Post.

benefits.

Ladies and gentlemen, that's *baloney*.

Television shows pictures of some wealthy older people in front of their condominiums in Florida, as if they were *typical.* . . .

We hear some rich yuppie complaining on a radio talk show that his generation is facing "downward mobility." He doesn't have any idea of what he is talking about. How many of *you* lived through the Depression? Let me hear you. Now *that's* "downward mobility." *That's* when it took *real* courage just to get married.

It is true that older Americans have made economic progress since the 1960s—before Social Security was expanded and Medicare created. At that time, nearly a third of all older people were living in poverty. We are *proud* of the part we've played in bringing about that progress.

Poor Old People

But today, older Americans *still* have the highest poverty rate of any adult age group and only half the median income of younger persons. *One* in every *three* older single women are living in poverty. And the poverty rate among minority elderly and those of advanced age *exceeds 40 percent.*

What kind of wealth is *that?* What kind of economic parity is *that?* Why can't people understand that it is the *oldest* and the *poorest* among us who will be hurt *most* by any further cuts in Social Security and Medicare?

Ladies and gentlemen, I believe that this myth about the affluent elderly is playing right into the hands of those who seek to *cut* Social Security, *slash* Medicare and *eliminate* many other vital social programs. . . .

We've been told by our political leaders that the huge federal budget deficit is threatening the welfare of every citizen.

And we agree.

We've been told by our political leaders that *all* of us must share the burden of reducing the deficit. And we agree, because that's only *fair*.

We've been told by our political leaders that *all* government programs must be on the table in any debate about reducing the deficit. And we agree, because that is the only *effective* way to do it.

We've even been told by *one* political leader that he would *never* stand for *any* cuts in Social Security.

But after all this talk, some things seem to be *missing* from the table.

Congress is . . . considering freezing Social Security COLAs [Cost of Living Adjustment]. Congress is willing to force more than a half million of us into poverty. But the defense budget is exempt from any freeze.

Ladies and gentlemen, let me ask you, is it *fair* that older Americans must lose their inflation protection while the Pentagon doesn't?

And while Congress preaches about *sharing* the burden, one group of Americans is *absent*. I'm talking about those who get their welfare checks in the form of investment tax credits, accelerated depreciation, and business entertainment expenses.

I ask you again, is it *fair* to force older Americans to sacrifice still more to help reduce the deficit, while many of the nation's most profitable corporations and wealthiest individuals aren't sharing the burden?

Is it *fair* to cut back on Social Security, Medicare, Medicaid, job training, housing and student loans, while ignoring massive tax giveaways to the rich?

Is it *fair* that major corporations with billions of dollars in profits are paying little or no taxes, while everyone else must pay higher interest rates or suffer benefit cuts because of the budget deficit? . . .

You know it's *not* fair. And we intend to do something about it. . . .

With your help we can *keep* fairness, equity and justice in our budget process and throughout our government. And we can continue to build the kind of *decent, compassionate* society we want to leave to our children and grandchildren.

II

Over the years most criticism of the Social Security system has been on practical or ideological grounds: that the program is too costly, or that it is regressive, or that government should not be involved in forcing people to save.

Such arguments have been roundly smashed time after time by the force of public opinion. Most Americans love Social Security—and its companion, Medicare, as well. Polls by this newspaper and other organizations show people of all ages to be concerned about the solvency of both programs, yes, but much more upset about attempts to weaken them.

Now there is a fashionable new attack, unlike the

others. . . . The charge is being made that old people are too well off, compared to the rest of us—better off as a group than other adults and much better off than children.

The criticism, in other words, is that Social Security works. . . .

[Recently] *The Wall Street Journal* noted that "perceptions have begun changing among what political scientists call the elite media. Articles in serious journals and influential newspapers are attacking the common view that the elderly are feeble, vulnerable and financially strapped. Supporters of this revisionist line say the articles mark the beginning of an overhaul of how the nation looks at the elderly."

"Many [senior citizens] who now live with a modicum of dignity would go under if not for their old age benefits."

The Journal cited reports in *Scientific American* magazine, *The New Republic*, *The Atlantic*, *The New York Times* and *American Demographics* magazine. The articles tended to focus on the lack of a means test for Social Security: Typically, the one in *New Republic* castigated the East Side widow in a luxury apartment for getting "what amounts to welfare at the expense of the low-wage worker in the South Bronx."

No Right to Delicacies

The new assault is very much like the decades-old criticism of public welfare, which has focused on a relatively small number of abuses as a means of damning the entire program.

Little by little, we are being asked to view the elderly much the way Sigmund Freud, in "Jokes and Their Relation to The Unconscious," viewed a poor soul with a taste for luxury. A wealthy man, Freud wrote, lent 25 florins to an impoverished acquaintance, only to see him in a restaurant the same day, dining on smoked salmon.

"What? You borrowed from me and that's how you spend the money?"

"I don't understand you," the poor man responded. "If I haven't any money I can't eat smoked salmon, and if I have some money I mustn't eat smoked salmon? Well, when am I going to eat smoked salmon?"

The benefactor was not reproaching the borrower for eating smoked salmon that day, but for eating it at any time. "He is reminding him," Freud wrote, "that in his circumstances he has no right to think of such delicacies at all."

For the new attack on Social Security to succeed,

Americans will have to begin thinking of lots of the elderly, not just a small number, as dining on smoked salmon, or living in East Side condos. Not many are in a position to do either.

Depending on Social Security

Government figures portray the elderly in a quite different light, showing that many who now live with a modicum of dignity would go under if not for their old age benefits.

According to the Census Bureau, the median income for a man between the ages of 25 and 64 in 1984 was $20,934; for one 65 or older it was $10,450. Take away Social Security and the older man's fortunes plummet.

For women between 25 and 64, the median income in 1984 was $8,886; for women older than that, $6,020, a much smaller difference. But 41 percent of the older women live by themselves, according to the Census Bureau, compared to only 9 percent of the younger ones. Thus, far more younger women benefit from having additional incomes in their households.

There is no denying the inequities and other problems that exist in Social Security. The tax is high and getting higher and it may well be the most regressive one in existence. There is a natural resentment toward the inclusion of well-to-do people in the program.

"Young people were as much against cuts as older ones, perhaps partly because without these programs they themselves would have far greater individual burdens in helping their parents."

Nevertheless, Social Security is doubtless the most popular program the government runs, and Medicare, with its own set of problems, probably comes in second. Support for both is bumping against the ceiling.

Public Opinion

Early in the Reagan presidency, at a time when budget-cutting had already been given high priority, 87 percent of all citizens in a *Washington Post*-ABC News survey said there should be no cuts in Medicare. In a Post-ABC News poll last year, 94 percent rejected any reductions in Social Security.

Young people were as much against cuts as older ones, perhaps partly because without these programs they themselves would have far greater individual burdens in helping their parents.

It is not exactly news that the elderly have been made somewhat comfortable through Social Security.

One of the first findings I made as a pollster for the *Washington Post* in the mid-1970s was that people of retirement age were somewhat less concerned about inflation than younger ones. That surprised me at the time, but it was old hat even then to experts in the field, who attributed it both to Social Security and to cost of living adjustments that meant the recipients no longer had to live on fixed incomes as prices rose.

Why the criticism all of a sudden, if the situation is not a new one?

The *Wall Street Journal* has one answer: Many have not noticed how well the elderly are doing until now. I'll provide a second: All the other attacks have failed to budge a public that believes the program is working.

Cyril F. Brickfield is the executive director of the American Association of Retired Persons. Barry Sussman is director of polling for The Washington Post.

"If Social Security didn't exist, some 10 to 15 million additional people would have incomes below the poverty line."

Social Security Should Remain a Universal Government Program

Wilbur J. Cohen

Editor's note: The following viewpoint consists of two articles, both written by Wilbur J. Cohen. Part I is taken from a brochure from the Save Our Social Security Coalition and Part II is taken from the Gray Panther Network.

I

The Social Security program, after more than fifty years, today is well and financially sound. A long range financing plan adopted in 1983 will ensure that the program remains financially sound for another fifty years.

The program is administered very effectively. The administrative cost of the program is only 1¼ percent of the contributions paid by employers, employees and the self-employed. And all of the assets of the system are safely invested in U.S. Government bonds. Where can you get such a combination? Certainly not with private insurance companies, whose administration is normally much more than 1¼ percent of premiums.

Getting Your Money's Worth

The 125 million individuals who are currently contributing to the program get their money's worth. Like any group pension and insurance plan, all individuals who pay into the program and become eligible under the provisions in the law will receive payment of benefits from one of the trust funds.

Just as in the case of fire insurance on one's home, if your house does not burn down, no benefit is paid. If an individual does not live to retirement, and leaves no dependents, no benefit will be payable. If an individual does not become disabled, no disability benefit is paid. But the individual who lives to one hundred years of age (as some do!) will get back many times what he or she paid in.

Wilbur J. Cohen, "IRAs May Be Hazardous to Your Wealth," *Gray Panther Network*, Spring 1985. *Social Security Is Here to Stay,* pamphlet published by Save Our Security, August 14, 1985. Reprinted with permission of the author.

Individuals who become disabled at 35 will get back many times what they paid in. The widow with the dependent children of the man who dies at age 30 will probably receive over $200,000 in the future.

A Family Program

Most people think that only old age retirement is covered by social security. This is a serious misunderstanding. Social security also pays monthly life insurance benefits to persons in midlife (between 20 and 65) and to their families. In addition, it pays Medicare hospital insurance benefits not only to the aged but to younger people who have serious disabilities.

There are beneficiaries receiving social security from the time of birth to other individuals who receive it when over one hundred years of age. It extends to the entire life-span from birth to death for various people. It is not simply an old age program. It is a family program.

Moreover, Social Security provides benefits which are inflation-proof in two major ways which most private plans cannot match. The first is that as wages and salaries increase, the individual is provided benefits with the same replacement proportion of wages as time passes. In other words, an employee's entitlements increase as salaries in general increase.

In addition, when an individual becomes a beneficiary—as a young disabled person or as a widow, a mentally retarded child or adult, or as a retired person, his benefit will be increased annually by the increase in the cost of living (COLA). Very few private plans have this built-in advantage.

Therefore, it is possible to say that individuals under the social security program for old age, survivors', disability insurance and Medicare receive their money's worth in *protection*, just as each of us receive our money's worth from fire insurance protection on our home irrespective of whether we experience a catastrophe. Protection is the key to value; not the exact equivalence between money paid in and benefits received, although many of us will receive much more than we paid.

The Nation's Insurance Program

Social Security is a group insurance plan. It is not a savings plan. It has no salesmen and it requires no medical examination. It covers the rich and the poor, the black, white, and the Hispanic. It not only protects the individual; it protects the nation against the possibility of vast increases in the welfare rolls. If Social Security didn't exist, some 10 to 15 million additional persons would have incomes below the poverty line, and many more persons would be on the welfare rolls.

Many experts, who proclaim that individuals can get a better deal by taking their contribution and investing it privately, overlook the life insurance and disability protection to young persons and the Medicare protection in the program to disabled persons of any age. They also assume that interest rates will continue indefinitely at high levels such as 10% or 8%. The fact of the matter is that these high interest rates are not borne out by long-range historical experience. Over 30 or 40 years, a much lower rate is more realistic.

Social Security is sound and here to stay. It is a social compact with the people. It is a solemn commitment by the Congress. I predict that the young people today will receive their Social Security thirty and forty years from now. Congress, in my opinion, will not repudiate a sound program involving every taxpayer; one that has the overwhelming support of the American people. There are over 200 million persons with developing rights under the program. I feel sure Americans will be joyously celebrating Social Security's 100th birthday 50 years from now in the year 2035. Unlike the private retirement plans that recently went out of business, there is no chance that the United States will go out of business.

II

The existing Social Security system is not perfect. It has been improved a number of times and it should be improved further.

There have been several cuts in the program enacted during the past four years. However, the fundamental basis of the system has not been repealed: a contributory earnings-related benefit structure, without a test of income and resources (the "means test"), and with an entitlement to benefits based upon appeal to the Federal courts for carrying out the promises in the law. The basic idea is a universal safety net, not only for the aged but for survivors (widows, widowers, and dependent children) of the breadwinner, and the disabled. Call it insurance, a safety net, an income guarantee, a national income maintenance program.

I prefer to emphasize that it is an intergenerational compact between the young, the working men and women, and the aged.

It is a family protection program covering specific major hazards during the life-cycle from birth to death.

It is a social compact designed to achieve social justice—not simply a savings bank where people's contributions are returned with interest.

"Social Security is sound and here to stay. It is a social compact with the people."

On several occasions, Ronald Reagan has stated that the system should be voluntary. He believes that rather than *community* responsibility, the law should emphasize *individual* responsibility. His general idea has been developed further by Peter J. Ferrara, who proposes that individuals have the option to assign 20 percent of their Social Security contributions to a personal IRA and take a proportionate reduction in their Social Security benefits. . . .

Ferrara's Idea

The Ferrara proposal is an idea, not a detailed thought-out plan. It is rhetoric, not a precise legislative proposal. Ferrara presents the reason for his proposal, but does not discuss any of the basic problems and difficulties it involves, nor how it would affect different individuals under varying economic and social conditions. He is so convinced of the rightness of his proposal that he observes "it is difficult to imagine why anyone would oppose this reform."

Yet the voluntary IRA proposal has "several serious flaws, both in logic and in fact," according to Robert J. Myers, who was the Chief Actuary of the Social Security Administration from 1947 to 1970.

Ignores the Poor

The proposal assumes a voluntary decision and action by each individual taxpayer. While the highly educated and moderate- and high-income persons may have the sophistication and access to professional advice necessary to invest in an IRA wisely, what about others who don't fall into these categories? How available or feasible will investment options be to the household worker employed in a private home, the migratory workers, the employee who doesn't understand English, the employee who doesn't have a bank or other financial account or the part-time employee? Ferrara's idea may serve the interests and needs of the highly educated, enterprising man or woman, but it does not even consider the millions of people whose incomes are below the poverty level.

In order to finance the "transitory" costs involved in changing or adapting the system, Ferrara proposes to use monies from general revenues. However, he opposes any increase in Federal taxes to raise these funds. Instead, he assumes the money can be raised by selling off certain government assests, restraining the growth of other government expenditures, or by cutting back on some programs, including Social Security.

Investment Return

The actuarial data supplied by Ferrara is at best incomplete, and at worst inaccurate. Ferrara assumes a *real* investment rate of return in perpetuity of 5 to 8 percent. Myers, a respected actuary, says this is "completely unrealistic" over the long run. Moreover, there are no actuarial figures supplied that indicate that the residual Social Security plan would be financially sound. No actuary has supported the idea and it is extremely doubtful that the plan would be supported by responsible actuarial, insurance, or banking representatives.

"While the highly educated and moderate- and high-income persons may have the sophistication and access to professional advice necessary to invest in an IRA wisely, what about others who don't fall into these categories?"

Ferrara also does not grapple with the nuts and bolt of implementing such a complicated system. Ferrara assumes an individual adjustment in the person's Social Security benefits in relation to the variable amount allocated by the employee and the employer to the IRA. Yet he does not consider the vast number of inquiries such a highly individualized plan would create or the administrative impact of these changes on the Social Security system.

A Community Program

But the most basic difficulty I have with the Ferrara plan—and the various versions of his idea—is that it does not accept the community solidarity inherent in the Social Security program. Ferrara assumes the eventual disappearance of Social Security and the basic protection it provides for the old, the young, the disabled, and the sick. He basically believes in the doctrine of "Every man for himself." His idea, he states bluntly, would benefit young people the most, particularly on a monetary

basis."

Ferrara is a young man who has not yet witnessed life's unpredictable hazards. There is not a note of compassion or understanding of risk, failure, or catastrophe in his comprehension of the diverse social needs of millions of Social Security beneficiaries. He judges the program solely in terms of financial gain and the free market. All the important values the Social Security system presently reinforces—community and family solidarity, intergenerational responsibilities, and protection of those who suffer sudden crises—are denied in his plan. The IRA privatization idea is not simply one that would change the way retirement benefits are calculated; it would radically alter our expectations of government and each other.

Wilbur J. Cohen was formerly Secretary of Health, Education, and Welfare and is currently co-chair of Save Our Social Security Coalition and a member of the Gray Panthers' Advisory Committee.

> "One big insurance plan with one particular pattern of coverage and benefit provisions cannot possibly meet the widely varying needs and preferences of different individuals."

Social Security Should Not Be a Universal Government Program

Peter J. Ferrara

Many believe that one of the chief purposes of social security is to help the weakest and most vulnerable groups in our society. Indeed, this is one of the prime reasons for the strong public support of the program in the past.

But the truth is that social security discriminates against some of the nation's most vulnerable minority groups, especially the poor, blacks, and women. Moreover, these groups can least afford the negative effects resulting from the program's other problems. As a result, the program hurts most the very people many of its supporters are trying to help.

It is true that the welfare aspects of social security are quite helpful to some of these groups, but these same welfare benefits can be provided through alternative programs or institutions without the discrimination and negative effects of social security. Social security hurts these groups by preventing them from fully enjoying the benefits they are meant to enjoy.

A Structural Problem

Discrimination against minorities and individuals who follow alternative lifestyles is built into the structure of the program. Social security forces everyone to participate in one big insurance program with one particular pattern of coverage and benefit provisions. This pattern of coverage and benefits is geared to the circumstances and characteristics of the individuals who predominate in society and who, therefore, constitute the politically powerful majority. The program's provisions will deviate from this norm only to provide special accommodation to groups with disproportionate political power.

Members of minority groups, however, tend to have circumstances and characteristics that deviate

from the norm. Also, they do not possess substantial political power. Consequently, they will find that the uniform coverage and benefit provisions of the government's social security program are poorly suited to their needs and preferences. The result is that social security will invariably hurt minority groups by forcing participation in an insurance program that does not serve their true needs. The same problems will plague individuals who pursue alternative lifestyles, who also tend to have special circumstances and characteristics, yet lack unusual political power.

Effects on the Poor

Social security discriminates against the poor in several important respects. Poorer individuals tend to start working earlier in life than those in higher income classes, but social security credits these individuals with few, if any, additional benefits for these additional years of work and tax payments. The poor also tend to die earlier than those in higher income classes, and therefore they receive less in benefits. Social security taxes self-employed individuals at a lower rate, yet the poor are far less likely to be self-employed than those in the higher-paying professions. Single, unattached individuals are much more likely to be poor than married couples, yet social security provides additional benefits for married couples. Finally, social security benefit amounts are based on an average on one's past earnings, but the five years of lowest earnings are deleted from the calculation. This benefits most those whose earnings will increase the most over the course of their lives, which is likely to be those in the higher income brackets.

These discriminatory elements all add up to one result—the poor pay more for less. A study by Henry J. Aaron of the Brookings Institution concluded that because of these factors the poor receive a lower return in retirement benefits on their

Peter J. Ferrara, *Social Security: Averting the Crisis,* published by the Cato Institute, 224 Second St., SE Washington, DC 20002, 1982. Reprinted with permission.

past tax dollars than those with higher incomes, despite the substantial welfare elements in the program that are designed to give them a higher return. The effectiveness of these welfare elements therefore is entirely outweighed by the program's discriminatory elements.

Distribution of Wealth

Social security hurts the poor in several other important ways. The program's payroll tax is regressive, taking a higher percentage of the incomes of those at lower income levels. While a standard fee analogous to the payroll tax is an appropriate way to charge for a service such as insurance protection, the welfare benefits paid through social security are also financed by the program's regressive payroll tax. This method of financing welfare benefits is counterproductive, since the burden of the tax falls most harshly on the very income groups the welfare elements are supposed to help. Social security, then, hurts the poor by coupling welfare benefits meant to help them with an inappropriate regressive means of financing.

Social security also wastes many welfare benefits on those who are not poor. Welfare benefits are not paid on the basis of need as measured by a means test, but instead on the basis of other factors that are very inadequate measures to true need. Thus many who are not in need are nevertheless able to qualify for these generous welfare subsidies. . . .

"Social Security forces everyone to participate in one big insurance program with one particular pattern of coverage and benefit provisions."

It should be noted also that social security causes a far more unequal distribution of wealth than would exist under the alternative, private invested system. This is because under social security's pay-as-you-go system individuals lose the large, accumulated amounts of money each would have in their own individual retirement and insurance accounts under the private, invested system. These accounts would be quite large relative to the total amount of wealth in the economy, and the money in the accounts would be far more equally distributed than other wealth, since individuals would each be saving and accumulating fairly equal amounts in their accounts each year. The result is that, under the private system, total wealth, including the wealth in the accounts, would be far more equally distributed than is currently the case under social security. Economists estimate that if individuals saved and invested in their own retirement and

insurance accounts all that they currently pay in social security taxes, over 40 percent of the nation's wealth would be held in this widely distributed form and the nation's concentration of wealth would be reduced by at least one third.

Effects on Blacks

Since a higher proportion of blacks are poor than of other social groups, all the negative effects of social security on the poor apply particularly to them. Two of these effects are especially pronounced.

First, unemployment is more widespread among blacks, especially teenage blacks, than among other social groups. Social security, by discouraging saving and capital investment, keeps this unemployment much higher than it would otherwise be, given our current economic structures.

Second, . . . life expectancy among blacks is the lowest of any social groups, even lower than the poor in general. The expected retirement benefits for young blacks are therefore much lower than for young whites. These lower benefits represent a much lower return on the taxes paid by blacks than on the taxes paid by whites.

Effects on Women

The benefit provisions of social security are based on a traditional view of the family, with the husband as wage earner, the wife as homemaker, and numerous children. This underlying model is the primary source of the program's pervasive and systematic discrimination against women.

The program in particular discriminates against women who are single, or work, or are childless. The program provides many additional benefits to individuals with spouses and dependent minor children, yet a single or childless individual, who can never receive such benefits, must pay the same taxes. In addition, a married woman is penalized for working, in that she must either forego the benefits she has earned on her own earnings record, and therefore receive nothing for her years of tax payments, or forgo the wife's benefits on her husband's earnings record. In the latter case, she still will receive only the difference between her own benefits and the wife's benefits, in return for her years of tax payments, as compared with the woman who does not work and, therefore, pays no social security taxes. It is clear that the message from the Social Security Administration to women is: Get married, stay home, and have lots of children. Social security works less well for those whose families differ from the traditional model. Those whose lifestyles follow the traditional path receive more in benefits and a greater return on their tax dollars than those who stray from the norm. Those who do not follow traditional lifestyles are penalized and forced to subsidize those who do.

Social security has also discriminated against women by denying benefits for their husbands on their past tax payments and earnings record, while paying benefits on the tax and earnings record of men for their wives. The U.S. Supreme Court has recently struck down some of these discriminatory provisions as unconstitutional, but other, similarly discriminatory provisions remain in the program.

Welfare vs. Insurance

The harmful effects on minority groups again are due to the conflict between welfare and insurance objectives. For example, many of the welfare benefits paid through social security are wasted on the nonpoor because the program does not have a means test. The program lacks such a test because it pays out substantial insurance benefits that are considered earned by everyone who paid for them, regardless of need. Mixing welfare benefits with these insurance benefits means that the welfare benefits cannot be made subject to a means test either. Thus, the insurance elements in social security make it a wasteful welfare program.

Similarly, the program is financed by a regressive payroll tax because it is supposed to be an insurance program. This is an appropriate way to finance insurance because everyone should be charged the same price for a good or service, just as everyone is charged the same price for a loaf of bread. It is only fair that the amount paid for goods and services should depend on their value, regardless of whether the purchaser is rich or poor. But with welfare and insurance mixed in together, the result is welfare benefits financed by a counterproductive, regressive tax. . . .

Forcing Everyone to Participate

Finally, the program discriminates against the poor generally by requiring them to pay more for less. This occurs because the provisions of the program are adapted to the circumstances and characteristics of the politically powerful majority, rather than those of the poor. As we have noted, this naturally results from forcing everyone to participate in one big insurance program with one particular pattern of coverage and benefit provisions. Since this pattern is democratically chosen, it will be best adapted to the politically powerful majority, rather than members of minority groups such as the poor.

But everyone must be forced to accept the one particular pattern of benefit provisions offered by social security because of the welfare elements of the program. Because social security pursues welfare objectives in addition to insurance ones, the program must be universal and compulsory. If it were voluntary, those who were not benefiting from the welfare elements would drop out, leaving no one to pay for them. Thus, it is the welfare elements that cause social security to be a naturally discriminatory

insurance program toward the poor. . . .

It should be clear that one big insurance plan with one particular pattern of coverage and benefit provisions cannot possibly meet the widely varying needs and preferences of different individuals in our society. . . .

A Proposal for Reform

Our analysis. . . suggests that the key principle behind any sensible social security reform is to separate the welfare and insurance elements of the current social security program into two entirely separate programs or sets of institutions. This would allow the insurance function to be entirely privatized—to be performed by private savings, investment, and insurance institutions in the general market. The welfare function of the program would be immediately served by an updated SSI program. A reform along these lines would solve all the major problems of the program as well as providing a number of substantial spinoff benefits. . . .

"Many of the welfare benefits paid through social security are wasted on the nonpoor because the program does not have a means test."

The adoption of this reform would lead to the establishment of an entirely new framework, which would cover all of the contingencies covered by our current social security system. Its key characteristic would be a reliance on voluntary, cooperative, decentralized, market institutions, instead of centralized, bureaucratic, coercive, government institutions.

The retirement insurance function of the current system would be covered by each individual saving in his own IRA the money he would otherwise pay in social security taxes. The money in this retirement account could then be invested in numerous economically productive private investment alternatives, which would earn a rate of return that would allow the account to pay much greater retirement benefits than social security. The individual could make these investments on his own or they could be made on his behalf by banks, insurance companies, trust companies, pension plan managers and other market institutions which have the information and expertise to make such investments wisely.

Once an individual has reached retirement, he will have accumulated a large sum in his retirement account that could then be used to finance his retirement benefits. The individual could simply use the interest on the fund and leave the fund itself to his children, or use the fund to purchase an annuity contract, which would guarantee him a certain income for the rest of his life. The annuity could be adjusted to continue payments for the life of any surviving spouse. The individual could also keep the fund and vary the amount of income he would draw from it over his retirement years. He could use some of the money in the account to give lifetime gifts or as a special reserve in case of emergencies. Each individual would in fact have complete control over the money to spend as he wished. In addition, he would not lose the money through any disqualifying act, such as marriage, divorce, or work, as can happen now under social security. Thus, his life would be freer from government restrictions.

Higher Benefits from Private Plans

The new system emerging from our reform proposal would in effect require that each individual save at least as much for his retirement and insurance contingencies as he would otherwise be required to pay in social security taxes. Individuals must either annually invest such sums in their IRAs or continue to pay them into social security. This feature should eliminate any fear that without social security, individuals will simply not save or provide for their retirement or major, insurable dangers.

"This retirement account . . . would earn a rate of return [on investments] that would allow the account to pay much greater retirement benefits than social security."

Because of the much higher benefits that could be provided by the private alternatives, this requirement should at least be lowered eventually. The amount of benefits which could be purchased through the private system by using all the money that would otherwise be paid in social security taxes is probably higher than that for which most individuals would want to pay. In any event, this amount is more than should be mandated through a savings requirement. At best, only a minimum floor of benefits necessary to keep people out of poverty should be required. Reducing the savings requirements would increase the discretionary, take-home pay of working people above what they would have under the current social security system, if they chose to save less than the amount they would otherwise have had to pay in social security taxes. . . .

The current program's days are numbered. The program as it is now structured is unstable. It will be basically and fundamentally reformed. The only question is whether it will be done in

[a] . . . haphazard, unplanned, unintentional way, which will waste valuable time and unnecessarily drag out several of the program's negative impacts, or whether it will be done through a planned, orderly, phased-in approach in advance.

Peter J. Ferrara chairs the Advisory Committee of the Independent Retirement Alliance. He is an adjunct scholar at the Cato Institute and has published three books on social security. Mr. Ferrara was formerly a senior staff member in the White House Office of Policy Development.

"Five years ago, if we had sold out and paid the taxes, we'd have a half a million in the bank. Now we're considering food stamps."

The Farm Crisis Is Real

Ed Magnuson

American farmers have been crying wolf for so long that their city cousins have mostly stopped listening. But along rural back roads last week, the expressions of anguish seemed genuine. Farmers sometimes differed about the causes of their distress, but they shared a frustration, almost a sense of shame, about their plight.

"You really feel like a failure," says Charles Boehmke, 44, who is clinging to his Minnesota farm after losing his animals and machinery because he could not repay a $136,000 loan. One of his neighbors, David Honsey, 40, filed for bankruptcy and said it made him feel like going into the barn and "doing something you shouldn't do there." He has since rejected thoughts of suicide, deciding "there is a higher power than the Federal Deposit Insurance Corporation. But I think they'll find a few farmers in the barn rafters before this is over." (Actually, there are signs that suicides among farmers are rising. There were 47 in Missouri in 1982, for example, and 59 in 1983.)

"I'm Scared"

Country people are often reluctant to confide in strangers, but their alarm is such that Willard Treu, a wheat, milo and corn grower, rushed up to *Time* Correspondent Barbara Dolan when he heard her asking about farm problems at the John Deere store in Quinter, Kans. "I'm scared," he said. "I'm 61 years old and 41 years a farmer, and this is the worst time I've been through."

Many farmers admit that they plunged too heavily into debt in the heyday of the 1970s, planting their fields from fence post to fence post. But they argue that that was precisely what federal bureaucrats and local bankers urged them to do. They reject the argument of Budget Director David Stockman that

they are to blame for their troubles. "I'd like to get about 15 minutes behind the barn with that dude," says Tom Kersey, 45, a Georgia farmer who helped lead "tractorcade" protests to Washington, D.C., in 1978 and 1979.

Although there have been scattered threats of violence among farmers who feel manipulated and want to strike out at someone or something, most of their protest has been a stolid, dignified resistance to farm foreclosures or forced auctions. Some 40 supporters of Ray Parks, 42, gathered in front of the Worth County courthouse in Sylvester, Ga., last week and joined loudly in song to prevent an auctioneer from hearing the bids on the 595-acre spread. To the tune of *Home on the Range*, they sang, "Oh, give me my farm, and a price that is fair, and a chance to pay all of my debts." The auction was postponed. In Minnesota, Jim Langman's farm won a similar reprieve when 1,000 farmers protested its forced sale. His hopes now rest with the state legislature, which is considering a moratorium on foreclosures.

The heavily subsidized farmers of the Midwest, where prices on such crops as wheat, corn and soybeans have been particularly depressed, seem to be suffering the most. The rural South has also been hard hit. California, with its wide diversity of crops (more than 200 in all) and clement weather, is faring better, but even there growers are worried. Because the large Eastern markets are close, mid-Atlantic farmers have avoided the export crunch that has badly hurt the heartland.

American farmers are hardy survivors, used to contending with the vagaries of weather and blight. But as *Time* correspondents toured agricultural regions last week, they found farmers uncharacteristically frightened by changes in the U.S. economy and impending shifts in Government policy. A sampling of their moods and situations follows:

"I just like to watch things grow," is the way J.O. Cross Jr., 58, explains his decision to follow his father's vocation. He bought his own 360-acre spread in central Georgia's Dooly County in 1953 and planted a variety of crops (soybeans, cotton, peanuts, wheat) to hedge against low prices in any one. Profits were never large, but with his wife Ruth teaching at a high school, they were able to send three children through college. "We were enjoying making a living," the balding, bespectacled Cross recalls. "We used to ride out Sunday evenings and just look at my crops."

The profits were steady enough so that by 1977 Ruth decided to stop teaching. That same year a drought hit much of the South. "We didn't make anything that year," says Cross. "We decided that the only way to hold on was to go into debt for an irrigation system." Cross had no difficulty in getting a $100,000 loan from the local production credit association; his land was valued at up to $1,200 an acre, providing ample collateral. Ruth, a slim, handsome woman, went back to teaching.

The loan Cross had acquired carried an adjustable interest rate, fluctuating from 12% to 13%. He also got another loan, this time from the Small Business Administration. Yearly crop planting loans added to his indebtedness. Much of his small profit went to meeting his interest obligations. "When you have to pay tens of thousands of dollars a year in interest, you can't pay the principal."

By 1982 the production credit association advised Cross to get longer-term financing so that his yearly payments would be lower. He got a loan from the Federal Land Bank. "We had to borrow from here," says Cross, pointing to one of his fingers, "to pay here." He touches another finger. "Then we borrowed from here to pay here." At the same time, the value of his land was dropping to $600 an acre. His two tractors, bought in 1968 and 1973, were wearing out. But he had paid $13,800 for the last one, and it would cost him $39,000 to replace it.

Cross is still committed to the land, but admits some of the joy has gone out of his work. "We don't ride out on Sundays anymore. It isn't here," he says, pointing to his heart, "like it was."

In Texas: A Double Whammy

Most of the fringe rice farmers have stopped trying to scratch a living out of the hardpan topsoil in the Texas Gulf Coast area. Now even Jay Anderson, 57, whose grandfather came to Texas from Illinois 87 years ago to build a highly successful farm operation, has lost money for two years in a row. "I've never seen so much gloom and doom in the rice belt," he says. "There's no light in the tunnel."

The oldest of six brothers and one sister, Anderson grows rice on 1,800 acres in Wharton and Colorado counties. That makes him a big operator, but he has had to retrench. He dropped the lease on 2,200 acres he was renting because "I was losing money on it." Anderson has let some of his field hands go, but wants to keep on a nucleus in case things get better.

Anderson, an avuncular man who is active in Texas Republican politics, is worried because he has been hit by what he calls "two whammies." A few years ago, his land was worth $1,400 an acre. Now he figures it runs at best $1,000 an acre. Where he once could get 14¢ for a pound of rice, he now can expect only 8¢. Each acre, in short, brought $700 when he harvested 5,000 lbs. of rice on it in the mid-'70s; now it brings him just $400.

When Anderson looks about for someone to blame for his troubles, he finds Government farm policies only partly at fault. They force farmers to "do unnatural things that are not efficient farming," he complains. But the chief villain, he says, is competititon from abroad, where costs are lower and exports are subsidized.

"When you have to pay tens of thousands of dollars a year in interest, you can't pay the principal."

Anderson is trying to sell some of his older equipment, including seven tractors, three combines, several planters and cultivators. The equipment, which is parked outside the office of the Prairie Rice Co. in Chesterville, cost $1.4 million. "If we got one-fourth of that," Anderson says, "we'd be happy." His brother Arthur, 53, who farms 1,000 acres near by, is bitter about those who buy at forced sales. "At auctions, farmers pounce on a used tractor like vultures," he complains. "They're just feeding on someone else's misfortune."

In Minnesota: Angry at Uncle Sam

Delbert Kahoun, 57, and his cheery wife Christine, 60, like to tell how their 600-acre dairy farm near the southeastern Minnesota town of Rushford (pop. 1,500) has survived through six generations, beginning in 1864. "All the timber on this farm, every acre here, was cleared by my great-grandfather and my grandfather had tree cutters to feed all winter." Now the white two-story farmhouse, where the Kahouns had lived for 37 years, is occupied by their son Philip, 26, his wife Debbie and their three children. The elder Kahouns have moved into a new trailer home on the property to make room for their son's growing family.

Delbert considered selling the farm twelve years ago, when a buyer from Iowa offered a good price. But he asked his son, "Do you want this farm? If you say yes, I'll tell these men to go." Philip did not want his father to sell, and five years ago the value of the farm reached nearly $900,000. But then came bad times. Father and son ran up a combined debt of about $250,000. The value of the farm dropped to roughly $400,000. Now the Kahouns are struggling just to hold on to the place.

To do so, Philip has taken a job driving a milk truck from Minnesota to Illinois; he travels twelve days out of every 14. Debbie works as a licensed practical nurse. The two jobs contribute about $1,000 a month to keep the dairy operation and a smattering of beef cattle going. The farm's electric bill alone often runs to $600 a month.

The Kahouns feel helpless at what has happened to turn their world upside down. One of the elder Kahoun's daughters, Elizabeth, 38, a nursing-home aide, became so angry that she placed telephone calls to both President Reagan and Agriculture Secretary John Block. She never got past secretaries. One in Block's office told her, "Honey, there's not enough money in the U.S. Treasury to bail out all the country's farmers." Predicts Elizabeth: "If and when the farm goes for sale—and I think it's when—Dad will probably die and Mom will go bonkers, and I am suing the U.S. Government for bringing this evil on this family."

Less bitterly, her father muses about lost opportunities. Says he: "Five years ago, if we had sold out and paid the taxes, we'd have a half a million in the bank. Now we're considering food stamps."

In Iowa: Waiting for the Sheriff

A neighbor emerged from Elmer Steffes' white farmhouse amid the gentle bluffs of southwest Iowa. "You might as well go home—and take your dog with you," said Steffes' 23-year-old daughter Kay, in a bitter undertone that the neighbor did not hear. Inside the house, Elmer, 47, a sturdy, barrel-chested man, explained he is losing his 460-acre farm and suspected that the neighbor might have been snooping around for the bank that will seize his property. "You can't be too sure of anybody these days," Steffes said.

"I came through the '30s and can remember the problems. But back then the whole country was in the same position, not just farmers."

There is an air of mourning around the Steffes farm. Friendlier neighbors drop by, bringing covered dishes of food. The quiet talk centers on the misfortune of Steffes, his wife Pat, 45, and their two surviving children, Kay and Bruce, 19. Without saying so, each visitor is aware that his or her farm could go next. Third-generation farmers, the Steffes had acquired 280 acres by 1966, raising livestock

and planting a variety of crops. In the booming 1970s they added another 180 acres and rented 530 more. Farming began to sour for them in 1979, just as tragedy struck. They lost two sons, 16 and 20, to cancer. Their sons' medical costs came on top of farming setbacks. Still, creditors were patient as the family fell $100,000 in debt. Recalls Steffes: "The people in town really trusted me. The feed dealer carried us along. So did the gas dealer. Everybody helped us out."

The recession of 1981-82 put the Steffes further into debt. When they could not get a new $100,000 loan to tide them over, they filed for bankruptcy, reporting liabilities totaling $800,000. While the proceeding was pending, they kept farming, grossing at least $200,000 each year, but losing money nevertheless. Last week more than 100 of Steffes' friends lent moral support at a court hearing over $168,000 owed to the local bank. The bank won the right to temporarily seize the collateral Steffes had pledged on the loans.

After waiting all week for Sheriff Bill Shaw to carry out the seizure orders, Steffes was surprised when 13 lawmen from several counties arrived at the farm before 8 a.m. on Friday. Pat and Elmer were still in bed. The officers blocked off the access roads to the farm. Pat called some of her neighbors to let them know what was happening, but only a few hiked the half-mile from the nearest intersection in the cold weather. The Steffes did not resist, but cooperated only minimally with the sheriff. Workers hired by the bank loaded many of their pigs, sheep and cows into a cattle trailer. They also hauled away much of Steffes' machinery.

The Steffes do not intend to be on hand when the house is taken later. They do not want to be escorted off their land. Neither is outwardly angry, although Pat wonders why "farmers with debt out of proportion to their assets are told to get out of business, but the Government keeps right on going that way." Her husband has been despondent, but he has come to view his situation philosophically. "I'm still a rich man," he said. "I've got my wife, my kids, my health and some good friends."

In California: A Glimmer of Hope

At mid-morning in Modesto, Calif. (pop 127,700), a group of farmers, some of whom had been in their nearby fields since 5 a.m., gathered around the tables at the Salida Kitchen coffee shop. Farmers with varied interests, from fruits and vegetables to dairy cattle and almonds, depend less on federal subsidies than elsewhere. But they, too, are worried.

Few in the group look to Government to save them. "I kinda got to go along with David Stockman," said Mark Boege, 52, who grows walnuts and almonds. "I don't know why the Government has to bail us out. Besides, it seems like every time Government comes in, it makes things worse." Jim

Vella, 51, an almond raiser whose wife, Clarice, 41, had to take a supermarket check-out job to help out, agrees. "Look at what Government did to those guys in the Midwest. They've been getting subsidies for years and they're in terrible shape." But what should be done? "What we need to do is have all the country's farmers stop shipping their produce for two weeks," suggested Vella. "That would show people how important we really are."

"It's devastating. . . . Every time David goes out to drive the tractor now, he leaves a piece of his heart out there."

As things change, the uncertainty of their futures concerns many California farmers. "This is the worst it's ever been," complained Irwin Effird, 64, who raises mostly grapes on his 2,000-acre spread near Clovis. "I came through the '30s and can remember the problems. But back then the whole country was in the same position, not just farmers." Now there is a glut of domestic raisins and Effird's farm is worth half what it was just three years ago. Pat Ricchioti, 65, a grape and fruit farmer with 3,000 acres near Madera, was also gloomy. "I never thought things would drop this far," he said. "I put away a dollar for a rainy day—and that rainy day is here." "We're pretty close to the bottom," conceded Jan Ennenga, 25, program director for the Modesto Farm Bureau. Reflecting the area's optimism, however, Ennenga predicted, "Things should begin to get better soon."

In Kansas: Losing Heirlooms

When the auction began last Friday, some 150 farmers crowded around the steps of the courthouse in Gove, Kans. (pop. 140). Sheriff Dean Baum began reading off the legal orders under which the personal property of C. David Jensen and his wife Virginia, both 54, would be sold to satisfy an unpaid debt of $180,000 to the Citizens State Bank of nearby Grainfield. Someone threw snowballs at one of the sheriff's deputies, and someone else shouted at the assembled officials: "Why don't you go out and steal them?" That was a reference to the two cars, three trucks, two tractors, a combine and other Jensen possessions.

As their more personal items were read off, Virginia Jensen wept. There was a loveseat, a silver oil lamp, brass candlesticks, a woman's rocker. When Baum cited "an oak bedroom set," she lost control. "These are family heirlooms," she shouted. "They've been in our family for 150 years. They're not for sale." But they were. Under the rules of the auction, the articles could not be split up; all of them would go to the highest single bidder. A lawyer for the Citizens State Bank bid $89,000 for everything, the only bid offered. (The rule was designed to stymie a common practice at other forced sales in which local farmers would bid only token sums for many items and then hand them back to their former owners.) Said the sheriff: "going once, going twice. Sold."

"It's devastating," Virginia Jensen said. "David has farmed all his life. He started milking cows when he was five years old. It's a family-type thing, a way of life. Every time David goes out to drive the tractor now, he leaves a piece of his heart out there." The Jensens owe another $400,000 in mortgages on their land. Their 1,120 acres, on which they have raised mostly wheat for the past 27 years, will be sold at a similar involuntary auction this week.

Ed Magnuson, staff writer for Time *magazine, wrote this article with the reporting assistance of several other* Time *staffers.*

"Farm families as a group are not poor."

The Farm Crisis Is Exaggerated

Gregg Easterbrook

Few economic endeavors have any aura of romance and tradition. We don't get misty at the sight of a chain store framed against a prairie landscape or take comfort in knowing that each morning thousands of lawyers head out into the predawn darkness to tend their lawsuits. Farming, though, occupies an honored place in our culture. Even big-city sophisticates who would sooner die than attend a Grange Hall dance find it reassuring to know that somewhere out there honest folk are working the earth much as it has been worked for centuries.

Agricultural industries, from farming itself to the retailing of farm products, constitute the largest sector of the American economy, accounting for 20 percent of the GNP and employing more people than the steel and automobile industries combined. Yet many people find it heartless and somehow unfair for anyone to speak of farming as an industry subject to the logic of supply and demand. To this sentimental faction the thought that any farmer should have to go out of business seems intolerable. As the cost of federal agricultural subsidies has risen, there has come into being an opposing faction, which dismisses farmers as spoiled welfare dependents who bilk the public on an unprecedented scale. Last winter's campaign for an emergency farm-credit bill seemed to divide politicians and the press into two camps: those who would "give 'em whatever they want" and those who would "let 'em fry."

Popular Misconceptions

The actual circumstances of modern farming conform to few if any of the assumptions that underlie the public debate. In order to see what condition American agriculture is in, one must first dispatch a number of widely held misconceptions.

—Farm families as a group are not poor. Their average income in 1983, one of the worst years in memory for agriculture, was $21,907. The average income for all families was $24,580. If one takes into account the lower cost of living in rural areas, farmers live about as well as other Americans. In fact, in some recent years farmers earned more than the national average.

—Farmers are not being driven from the land. From October of 1984 through January of 1985—when what was said to be a dire emergency for farmers was making news—the Farmers Home Administration actually foreclosed on forty-two farms nationwide. The FmHA provides loans to farmers who can't get credit elsewhere. Over the same four-month period its borrowers who "discontinued farming due to financial difficulties"—a broad category that reflects foreclosures by lienholders, bankruptcies, and voluntary liquidations to avert bankruptcy—totaled 1,249, or 0.5 percent of the FmHA's 264,000 clients.

From January to September of 1984 production-credit associations and federal land banks under the aegis of the Farm Credit Administration (which is much larger than the FmHA, handling about a third of U.S. agricultural debt) actually foreclosed on 2,908 loans nationwide. If one includes bankruptcies and loans in the process of liquidation, a total of 1.6 percent of FCA-aided farmers were in trouble.

Debt problems are real: early this year the FmHA, FCA-backed institutions, and rural farm banks saw delinquency rates reach record highs. But the incidence of dispossessions has been vastly exaggerated. The number of delinquent loans usually peaks early in the year, because most FmHA loans come due in January. Newspapers rarely follow up their winter reports of a "dramatic increase" in the number of farms in trouble with summer reports of a dramatic decline.

Gregg Easterbrook, "Making Sense Out of Agriculture," *The Atlantic*, July 1985. Reprinted with the author's permission.

—Farming is not a disastrous investment. Farm lobbyists don't like to talk about disposable income, preferring to speak of "profit"—a problematic concept when applied to the self-employed, who can treat as business expenses items like vehicles and real estate, which most others must pay for out of their salaries. In 1983 and 1984 a trillion dollars' worth of farm assets generated a profit of $48 billion—an average return of 2.4 percent a year. But the annual net return on all corporate assets for the same period was only 5.5 percent.

"It is common for farmers . . . to speak as if in a just society virtuous products like food and fiber would only increase in value. Yet we find nothing amiss when the price of computers or eyeglasses falls."

—The "farm exodus" has been over for years. Much is made of the fact that the number of U.S. farms declined by 33,000 in 1982 and by 31,000 in 1983. But the declines were far bigger in the 1950s and 1960s—a period enshrined in political mythology as better for farmers. In 1951 the number of farms declined by 220,000; in 1956 by 140,000; in 1961 by 138,000. . . .

No Burdensome Debt

—Most farmers don't have burdensome debt. President Reagan was wrong to say that "around four percent at best" of farmers need credit help, but the actual figure is not much higher. According to a study by the U.S. Department of Agriculture (USDA) which farm-spending advocates often cite, only 6.5 percent of all farmers are actually insolvent or on the verge of being so. The Federal Reserve System estimates that eight percent of farmers have debt-asset ratios over 70 percent, and another 11 percent have debt-asset ratios of 41 to 70 percent. But nearly 58 percent of all farmers are well in the clear, with debt-asset ratios of 10 percent or less.

From the impersonal standpoint of economies, the 19 percent of farmers who, according to the Federal Reserve, are in credit trouble might be viewed as representing agriculture's excess production capacity. Last year 81 percent of the production capacity of all U.S. industries was in use, leaving 19 percent idle. Looked at this way, the share of borderline cases in farming is not particularly different from that in other industries.

—Debt has hit farmers hard but not that hard. From 1974 to 1984 outstanding agricultural debt rose 193 percent. Through the same period consumer credit rose 172 percent, mortgage debt rose 167 percent, and all commercial bank debt rose 153 percent.

—The embargo on grain sales to the Soviet Union did not clobber wheat farmers. In 1980, the year the embargo was in full effect, agricultural exports jumped from $31 billion to $40 billion—the largest increase ever. Wheat exports increased from 1,375 million bushels in 1979 to 1,514 million in 1980 and increased again in 1981, to 1,771 million bushels. In 1982 and 1983, after the embargo was lifted, wheat exports declined. . . .

Realistic Cost Rises

It is common for farmers—and reporters—to speak as if in a just society virtuous products like food and fiber would only increase in value. Yet we find nothing amiss when the price of computers or eyeglasses falls, and we're upset when the prices of energy and housing climb. A successful economy is supposed to drive down the prices of goods, especially manufactured goods—and the advent of fertilizers, pesticides, self-propelled combines, and large tractors has made agriculture one of the least labor-intensive of industries. Each year the USDA charts farming "inputs" for capital and labor. The 1980 input for farm labor was a fifth that of 1930, while the input for machinery was three times greater, and the input for chemicals was twenty times greater. Farm groups say that there is something wrong with the fact that wheat costs less in real terms today than it did in 1870. There would be something wrong if it *didn't* cost less.

Farm-state congressmen often cite the index of prices for farm products from the Producer Price Index kept by the Bureau of Labor Statistics. The PPI, like the Consumer Price Index, uses 1967 as its base year. Whereas the CPI rose to 311 in 1984, the index of prices for farm products has risen only to 256. The congressmen never mention that the indexes for almost *every* commodity within the PPI are behind, or only equal to, the CPI. Textile products and apparel are at 210, furniture and household appliances at 219, and rubber and plastic products at 247. Only non-metallic mineral products, at 337, and energy, at 657, are significantly ahead of the CPI. For that matter, low producer prices keep the cost of running a farm down. Indeed, according to the USDA, the index of what machines, supplies, interest, taxes, and wages cost farmers runs about ten percent below the rate of inflation.

No one likes to be thought of as being on the federal dole, least of all farmers, who put a premium on self-reliance. Farm groups across the spectrum invariably say, "We don't want subsidies, we just want a price," meaning higher market prices, and they note that higher prices would result in less federal spending, because deficiency payments would decline. The next logical step is usually not taken. Absent increased demand, higher prices can be realized only if excess production is controlled, either by cutting subsidies and letting some farmers fail (anathema to the left) or by imposing fierce restrictions on how much and what a farmer may plant (anathema to the right).

Farmers find it difficult to face the overproduction issue, mainly because of the nature of rural life. One of the salient cultural differences between farmers and city folk is that farmers live in places where everybody is in pretty much the same line of work. Everybody either is a farmer or provides a service that farmers need. Imagine if advertising executives had to live in complexes populated entirely by other advertising executives and could have only advertising executives for friends. Would they be so aggressive about stealing business? To be true capitalists, farmers would have to view their neighbors as their archenemies. So they compensate by viewing farming itself—the act of working the fields, not of selling the finished product—as their purpose and keeping everybody going as their political challenge. This thinking reflects the kindness and communal purpose we admire in rural life. It also makes for too many farmers.

The regular experience of shared achievement and sorrow in a common pursuit is among the most appealing aspects of rural tradition. Indeed, farmer advocates often argue that the communal quality of rural America should be preserved for its own sake, even if economics has passed it by. They say that farm living sets a spiritual example whose worth thus transcends cost-benefit analysis. But when farmers say that their way of life should be preserved for its own sake, inevitably they must argue that all farmers are equally deserving of protection—that farmers have a right to remain farmers. . . .

Dissatisfaction Rules

Dairy, livestock, and poultry farmers still work year-round, because animals must be tended continually, but well-equipped crop farmers have it easier. They face three months of heavy work during planting and two more at harvest. Farm-crisis stories tend to appear in winter partly because it is then that crop farmers, without daily work to do in their fields, do their lobbying. When the American Agricultural Movement staged its tractorcade in 1979, bringing hundreds of farm machines to Washington to block traffic, AAM members made speech after speech about how their backs were to the wall. Yet many had arrived in brand-new Steigers equipped with stereo systems, and some spent several months in the capital, in no apparent hurry to attend to their businesses. William Olmsted, a United Methodist minister in Greenfield, Iowa, has noticed a subtle change in farm sociology. He told me, "Making your rounds in winter, you can knock on doors at five farmhouses in a row and find no one home. They've gone to town, or are on vacation. Farmers used to *always* be home." . . .

Dissatisfaction rules life on the farm today, and the unhappiness farmers vent in the media or at political rallies probably does more to advance the idea of an endless crisis in farming than does the actual incidence of foreclosures. The unhappiness stems in part from raised and then dashed expectations. "Every year for the last fifty years had been a little better than the year before, until the 1980s," Carolyn Erb, a farmer in Ackworth, Iowa, said when I met with her last winter. At some point having a better year begins to seem like a right. That the Washington, D.C., tractorcade was staged in 1979, a year that turned out to be the second best on record for farm profit, shows how consuming a force self-pity can be. . . .

The Annual Crisis

Senate majority leader Robert Dole said recently that in every one of his twenty-five years in Congress there has been a farm problem. . . .

Partly because of the continuous anxiety to which they are subject, farmers have a long history of crying wolf. The agriculture committees, staffed by farm-bloc congressmen, do too. In 1965 a report of the House Agriculture Committee warned, "Hundreds of thousands of our most progressive farmers will find their debt positions intolerable and will be forced into bankruptcy"—language almost identical to that used last winter.

"Farm-crisis stories tend to appear in winter partly because it is then that crop farmers . . . do their lobbying."

Checking old newspapers, I found that farmers have been proclaiming the "worst year since the Depression" regularly since the early 1950s. Reporting that placed the claim in historical perspective was rare, except for the occasional "down with farmers" piece that exaggerated in the other direction. Covering agriculture is a delicate matter for journalists, and especially for television crews. Someone who loses a farm loses his job, his home, and his way of life all on the same day. It would seem heartless of a reporter to mention that dispossessions are the exception or that thousands of other people experience tragedies that are of equal weight but that simply don't fit a news peg.

"They're taking away my land" is a plaintive cry of farmers, and when true, it's terrible to hear. Often it isn't true. A farmer who defaults on his loan is not losing his land so much as some part of his investment in it. The bank is the true owner of the farm, just as ultimately it is the owner of a mortgaged house.

Through the 1970s the farm bloc complained that farmers were being destroyed by inflation. Senator Jesse Helms, of North Carolina, who is the chairman of the Senate Agriculture Committee, said in 1981, "Farmers understand that unless this inflation is cured, they don't stand a chance." Now that the cure has taken effect, the *lack* of inflation is said to be a special hardship for farmers. Similarly, cries of "foul" were heard in response to the escalation in farmland prices while it was taking place, even though it was making holdings more valuable. Four years ago Catherine Lerza, the head of the National Family Farm Coalition, declared that high land prices had created a crisis for farmers. At about the same time Representative Berkley Bedell, of Iowa, proposed a $250 million Beginning Farmers Assistance Act to subsidize purchases of farmland. Now, of course, it is the decline in land prices that is said to pose a crisis for family farmers.

Misleading Figures

Using the Department of Agriculture's parity tables, some farm advocates claim that farmers are worse off today than ever. Parity tables are supposed to show the buying power of farmers; 1910-1914, when farm prices were strong, is taken as the base period and given a value of 100. In 1984 parity hovered around 58—that is, farmers had 58 percent of the buying power of their forerunners decades earlier. Figures like these are extremely misleading, however, because calculations of parity treat the present as if it were 1914. For example, they take into account the fact that tractors cost more but not that they do more. Parity makes an effective round of political ammunition, but it is not a reliable indicator on which to base policy. One farm-state congressional staff member told me, "Any farmer who seriously believes he would be living twice as well if it were 1914 again is crazy."

"There can still be family farms. It's just that not every person who wants a farm can have one."

At a House Agriculture Subcommittee hearing in February, I gave up trying to count the number of times words like *desperate, disaster, unprecedented,* and *dying* were used. Representative Steve Gunderson, of Wisconsin, asserted, "Clearly, within the credit crisis confronting agriculture we are literally facing the fundamental destruction of rural society." Representative E. Thomas Coleman, of Missouri, declared that "farmers are faced with such high interest rates, declining land values, and low return for their products that they are reliving the Great Depression of the 1930's." At this hearing and throughout the battle over emergency aid, farm-bloc congressmen repeatedly predicted that as many as 10 percent of the nation's farmers could go bankrupt by March 1—the traditional deadline of banks for issuing spring planting loans—if substantially more than $650 million was not provided. A bonus-credit-aid bill was passed but Reagan vetoed it. The first of March came and went, the wave of foreclosures that was supposed to sweep the country did not occur, and the story vanished. . . .

Eventually Congress will have to face the fact that there are too many farmers. The farm bill that Reagan has proposed, which in effect would abandon those part of the federal program that subsidize the least successful farmers, may not be perfect, but so far it is the only one to concentrate on the problem of overproduction. The solutions to that problem do not lie solely in the realm of economic abstraction. They will involve a painful human cost. . . .

Early this year Representative E. Kika de la Garza, of Texas, the chairman of the House Agriculture Committee, said he might support changes in federal agriculture programs, but only if they could be achieved "without sacrificing one single farmer." This is like saying, Let's cut back that bloated defense budget—as long as no contractors lose work. There can still be family farms. It's just that not every person who wants a farm can have one, no matter how fervently we might wish he could.

Gregg Easterbrook is an award-winning staff writer for Atlantic Monthly.

"There's something wrong with the two basic precepts of American agriculture: Produce as much as possible and do it by using expensive, energy-intensive technology."

viewpoint 97

Farms Are Failing Because of High Technology

Daniel Zwerdling

After weeks of travel through America's farm country, from the tumbling wheat hills of eastern Washington to the tedious flat cornfields of Indiana, I'm convinced and scared: Convinced that America's farmers are in deep trouble, and scared because most Americans and their politicians don't realize how deep it is.

The moments that frightened me most were not the painful human dramas I encountered—the plight of Washington wheat farmers like Dave Iverson, who's going broke because he can't afford the quadrupling electric bills for his irrigation equipment, or of Nebraska farmers like Bruce Damrow, whose herbicide bills tripled on some fields last year, or of Iowa farmers like Eldon and Linda Starmer, who couldn't pay their debts and auctioned off their farm.

More troubling than these tragedies was what I heard in the antiseptic calm of a small-town bank down the road from an International Harvester dealership in Osceola, Iowa. Bank President Don Wubbena ushered me into his motel-modern office and said, "Most of the farmers we service couldn't pay back their loans this year." Then he began ticking off dull statistics which, like the technical jargon on a hospital chart, tell you the patient is seriously ill and may be dying.

Perhaps 3 to 5 per cent of his client farmers have been trying to sell their farms and go out of business, Wubbena told me, but the economy has been so bad that most of them can't find buyers. About 20 per cent of the farmers have been selling off part of their land and equipment, trying to raise enough cash to save what's left. Another 20 per cent, Wubbena said, have been taking a dangerous gamble: They've given the bank the deeds to their

land in return for new, high-interest loans so they can pay off the old debts that are long overdue. In effect, these farmers are refinancing with a second mortgage to prop up their shaky finances for one more year.

"What will happen," I asked Wubbena, "if the farm economy this year doesn't take a dramatic turn for the better?"

"I would say," Wubbena began in his monotone, "that 25 per cent of the farmers, if we had another bad year, will be forced to sell out."

A Year Away from Great Depression

"But that would be equivalent to the Great Depression."

"I would say that's correct," Wubbena nodded.

"So you're saying this region is only one year away from a situation like the Great Depression?"

"I would say yes. I don't see how we can go through another year like this and actually save the farmer."

America's farmers are only one bad season away from a collapse comparable to the Great Depression. Perhaps it won't happen: The widely publicized "economic recovery" may continue to cut interest rates, and the Reagan Administration's payment-in-kind (PIK) land-set-aside program may continue to push crop prices up. In that case, farmers will be yanked back from the brink. But it would be a grave mistake if the nation's leaders and farmers were to confuse remission for recovery.

The agriculture system in the United States— blessed with the richest farmland on earth, worked by the most sophisticated technology ever invented— is so fragile that it has come close to breaking down. All the farm protection programs crafted over fifty years—subsidies and target prices and deficiency payments and loans—failed to do what they were supposed to. A sound economic system doesn't flirt with collapse just because interest rates and prices temporarily go out of whack, any more than a healthy person hovers near death after a brief bout with the flu.

Farmers will still face fundamental long-term problems that threaten the future of agriculture in America. And the problems are rooted in the ways U.S. farmers grow food.

Unfounded Assumptions

Since World War II and especially since the mid-1960s, the nation's bankers, Government researchers, agribusiness executives, and farmers have built agriculture on four assumptions that have turned out to be unfounded.

The experience of Marvin Woolsey, who lives in a peeling white clapboard house down a gravel road from an Iowa town called Weldon, illustrates how those assumptions have affected many farmers' lives. With 1,400 acres and two new blue silos, Woolsey would seem to be the model of a prosperous cornbelt farmer. But it's all veneer. "We've been foreclosed on," Woolsey told me as we sat sipping coffee at his kitchen table. "The Aetna Life Insurance Company and Farmers Home Admin-istration both have foreclosed on us. It means we're going to lose our farm if we don't make the payment."

Woolsey and his wife started farming almost twenty-five years ago, just after he left military service. Like half the nation's farmers at the time, the Woolseys couldn't afford to buy land, so they started renting. But Woolsey had dreams: He had been raised in a children's home in Omaha and later by foster parents, and he wanted something he could call his own. "I think it was ambition, if you can call it that," he said. "It was a question of me coming from no background—we never had any-thing—and so we wanted to acquire something." Glancing at his wife, who was putting a coffee-cake batter in the oven, Woolsey added, "That's the all-American way, it looked like to me."

The Woolseys finally got their chance in the early 1970s, when U.S. farm exports—and farmers' profits—exploded.

World Demand Not Insatiable

Assumption 1: World demand for American crops was insatiable, and farmers would sell all the crops they could grow.

There is a widespread impression that the United States has always supplied the world with enormous amounts of grain, but exports did not become a major market for farmers until the beginning of the last decade. In fact, you can pinpoint the day the export market boomed—August 15, 1971. That evening, President Nixon announced what he called "the most comprehensive new economic policy to be undertaken by this nation of four decades." He froze wages and prices and, most important for farmers,

he devalued the dollar. Overnight, American corn and wheat, as well as other U.S. products, could be purchased at much lower prices by foreign countries. Coincidentally, the Soviet Union and other nations were suffering major crop failures.

Grain exports, which had been rising gradually since the end of World War II, suddenly skyrocketed, increasing by 70 per cent between 1970 and 1973, according to a General Accounting Office (GAO) report on the structure of agriculture. With this sudden demand for American crops, the price of corn doubled, the price of wheat tripled, and U.S. farmers scored their biggest profits ever. Farmers like Marvin Woolsey, flush with cash, started buying land.

"I bought 430 acres," Woolsey remembers. "Hey, exports looked great. We had every incentive to expand. We were flying high. And we had every expectation of the thing continuing, too."

"America's farmers are only one bad season away from a collapse comparable to the Great Depression."

The boom psychology provoked a major change in Federal farm policy. For two decades, the Govern-ment had been encouraging farmers to curtail production and prevent too much surplus from building up. But now Nixon's Secretary of Agri-culture, Earl Butz, turned public policy upside down: He stumped the nation urging farmers to plant "fence row to fence row." There was no limit, Butz told farmers to what the hungry world wanted to buy and what they could sell. "Now we see the promised land of full production," Butz said. "Now we see the promised land of the dead hand of government coming off our farmers—and letting them farm the way they want to."

Marvin Woolsey was one of the farmers who bought the message. In the first half of the decade, these farmers planted forty-two million more acres. "We started producing the heck out of stuff," Woolsey says.

As farm production expanded, agriculture land prices surged. In Iowa, for example, prices began climbing 15 per cent and more every year. That gave rise to two more assumptions:

Land Prices Fall, Interest Rises

Assumption 2: Land prices would keep rising.
Assumption 3: The cost of borrowing money would keep lagging behind.

These assumptions were critical. Bankers prodded farmers to go heavily into debt to buy land. Simple arithmetic showed why: It paid to borrow. If a farmer asked his local bank to lend him $100,000 to buy 100 acres of land, and he had to pay 8 per cent interest on the loan, he had to earn a profit of $8,000 that year just to pay his interest. But during that same year, the value of his new land would increase by $15,000 or more. From the farmer's point of view, he couldn't lose—and neither could the banker, for if worse came to worst and the farmer couldn't repay his loans, the bank would simply seize the land and sell it at a profit.

"Sure, we encouraged our farmers to expand," says Harold Laures, chief of the Iowa farm loan division for the Farmers Home Administration, the Federal bank that lends money to farmers who can't borrow it anywhere else. "Everything looked really bright for agriculture—like there'd be an endless market and an endless demand for the food that could be produced."

In the mid-1970s, Woolsey bought another 270 acres. "The psychology of the day was you better buy everything you could buy," he recalls. "We had no choice but to get on or stay static and take a chance of being put out of business by another aggressive farmer coming in and buying the land up so we didn't have access to it, to rent it or buy it."

But now the Woolsey farm was so big that the family couldn't handle all the work. "There was too much to do in a single day," Woolsey says. "I couldn't hire outside labor to help me, because around here there wasn't really any labor available. And besides, I couldn't afford it if there was." So Woolsey took the route recommended by agri-business and the U.S. Department of Agriculture: He replaced labor with capital. He went deeper into debt and invested in new machinery—bigger, more powerful, more expensive tractors, planters, and harvesters that could work as many acres in half a day as his old equipment could work in one.

"We've produced, produced, and produced for the world . . . and now we're being punished for producing."

"It's been a dramatic change," says Rick Barrett, who runs the International Harvester dealership in Osceola. "Sure, we've encouraged farmers to get bigger—if the equipment could farm more acres with the same labor, it seemed it should more than pay for itself."

Along with the new machinery came new pesticides. Despite warnings from environmentalists, farmers like Woolsey were using more pesticides than ever, for petroleum-based chemicals, like machinery, made it possible for farmers to expand.

This push toward high-technology farming was, as the GAO report on agriculture said, "a wise choice." After all, the cost of farm labor had risen steadily

for three decades after World War II, but the price of petroleum-based chemicals and fuels had remained almost stable. Thus the basis for the next assumption:

Costs Rise, Profits Fall

Assumption 4: The costs of high-technology farming would stay about the same while crop yields and farm profits would keep rising.

But OPEC, the oil embargo, and the decontrol of oil and some gas prices changed the equation. Within just a few years, the cost of fertilizer and tractor fuel doubled. The cost of some herbicides quadrupled. Marvin Woolsey's cost of drying corn in his soaring silos, using propane gas, shot up 130 per cent. And for the first time since the export boom of the early 1970s, Woolsey's profits *per acre* declined.

Faced with a cost squeeze of this kind, some businesses would simply raise the price of their products, just as the auto makers boost the price of their cars. But individual farmers can't control the price they get for what they grow. Other businesses might try to cut costs by curtailing production, just as a steel company shuts down a factory. But farmers can't claim big tax write-offs for land that isn't growing crops. So Government policymakers, bankers, and agribusiness researchers all agreed: As farmers made less money *per acre,* they should maintain their total income by farming more acres.

In 1978, Marvin Woolsey went still deeper into debt and bought another 550 acres, bringing the size of his farm to 1,250 acres. "It appeared then that the one who would remain in agriculture and be most effective would be growing and enlarging," says Harold Laures at the Farmers Home Administration. "In fact, we thought many times that a successful farmer had to get bigger just to stay even with rising costs and inflation and all those items, ant it worked quite well for them for a number of years."

Agriculture's Collapse

By 1980, the assumptions that had propped up modern U.S. agriculture began collapsing, one by one. First, the export boom went bust. In January 1980, after the Soviets invaded Afghanistan, President Carter embargoed grain sales to the Soviet Union, confirming what many economists had already feared: In a world of volatile international politics, farmers could never count on foreign markets to gobble up their production and support them. Though farmers and Carter's political opponents like to blame the farm crisis on the embargo, the export market was bound to turn sour in any case. The world economy was in decline, and the Third World countries that were supposed to consume all the surplus U.S. grain could no longer afford to buy it. But American farm technology kept working its magic, churning out record harvests.

With supply up and demand down, crop prices

began to fall. At the same time, interest rates were climbing to record levels—21.5 per cent in 1981. Marvin Woolsey and other farmers started losing money, fast.

Farmers' income fell more than 30 per cent between 1979 and 1982, according to Agriculture Department figures, and the value of farmland shriveled with it. Farmers couldn't afford to buy land, just as teachers and steelworkers couldn't afford to buy houses. In only two years, the market value of Woolsey's land plunged 30 per cent. At his bank and others, alarm bells started ringing. In the past, Woolsey had been a good risk; his total worth was always greater than his debts. But now, without the value of his land to prop him up, his liabilities were beginning to outweigh his assets, and that meant Woolsey, once worth a small fortune on paper, was no longer a safe bet. When he went to the Osceola State Bank and asked to borrow $500,000 until harvest time, Woolsey says, "the banker told me 'No.'"

"The basic motives and methods of farmers must be drastically revised."

"Actually, if the decision had been up to me, I might have given him the loan," says banker Don Wubbena. But the Osceloa State Bank, like a growing number of rural banks, has been forced to turn to bigger "correspondent" banks in the cities to back major loans. And Wubbena says the correspondent bank in Des Moines wanted nothing to do with a farmer in trouble.

"I don't believe your correspondent bank is like dealing with your own banker," Wubbena says. "We're familiar with [a farmer's] operation. They don't come to the operation to see what's going on."

With no loans to prop him up, Woolsey couldn't make his $113,000 mortgage payments last year—and the Aetna Life Insurance Company and Farmers Home Administration, which own the mortgage, foreclosed. Woolsey has been trying desperately to raise enough cash to save his farm—he's sold most of his machinery and is now trying to sell some of the land, too. But while lots of farmers are trying to sell, few are buying. "In this firm alone," realtor Don Ramsey of Osceola told me, "we have close to fifty farms for sale right now, and we're just not finding buyers."

Twenty Days To Survive

The story is almost over now, and Woolsey stares blankly at his kitchen table. "We have twenty days to answer this foreclosure," he says. "So that's how close we are to being out of farming."

The oven buzzes, the coffee cake is ready, and his wife takes it out. The room fills with the smell of hot sugar and dough. "What will you do if you lose the farm?" I ask. "I have no idea," Woolsey says. "No idea."

"I'm not bitter against the lenders. I signed that contract," he says. "I'm responsible for it, totally responsible, and I accept that. But I don't feel like I made the wrong decisions. I feel that society itself has made the wrong decisions. We've destroyed the economy, we've produced, produced, and produced for the world—so we were educated to produce and now we're being punished for producing. I resent the dickens out of it," Woolsey says, bitterly now. "I really resent it. And I can't do anything about it. Except go out of business."

Ironically, there are farmers still making a profit today—farmers who ignored what the bankers and Government policymakers and researchers told them. These are the farmers who refused to expand and invest heavily in new machinery and go deep into debt. It's the farmers who followed the official line who are at the brink.

"Yeah, I think every banker has got some guilt," says Ward Kilgore, president of the Decatur County State Bank near Weldon. "Sure I've got some guilt, and got to take a look and say, 'Hey, you know, I encouraged this guy to go a little too far.'"

"Why couldn't you and other bankers back then see what you see now?"

Kilgore raises his eyebrows and smiles. "That," he says, starting to laugh, "is a great question."

Two False Precepts?

Woolsey's experience and that of many other farmers suggests that there's something wrong with the two basic precepts of American agriculture: Produce as much as possible and do it by using expensive, energy-intensive technology. These two credos have dictated most agriculture research, shaped most agribusiness marketing strategies and Federal policies, and dominated the thinking of most farmers for thirty-five years. Once seen as the American farmers' salvation, these commandments are now beginning to be recognized as the cause of chronic surpluses and crippling costs.

The situation is not likely to improve for the rest of this century. The world market won't grow fast enough to gobble up U.S. surplus grains. Exports actually dropped by more than 10 per cent last year, the first decline since 1970. Economist Dennis Steadman of Chase Econometrics predicts that for the next decade, foreign demand for U.S. grain will grow, "but at a sharply reduced rate from the 1970s." The current grain surplus, Steadman says, "is not a short-run problem."

Costs are likely to keep growing. Agriculture Secretary John Block told a Senate committee recently that petrochemical fuel and chemical costs are no longer climbing and "may even show a decline" this year, but few analysts expect that the price of a dwindling resource will remain stable over the next two decades. If the Reagan Administration gets its way and decontrols the price of natural gas, farmers' fertilizer bills could rise 20 per cent after inflation in just the next few years.

As soil erosion saps the productivity of the land, major farmers will be forced to depend even more on energy-intensive technology. Studies at the Universities of Washington and Idaho suggest that eroded soils produce up to 25 per cent smaller wheat yields than soils that have been protected, so farmers use more fertilizer and other chemicals to boost their yields. "Every year we're going to pay a little bit more because the land has been damaged and is not capable of producing quite as efficiently," says erosion researcher Neil Sampson, director of the National Association of Conservation Districts.

Between now and the next election, politicians are sure to debate various proposals for restoring the farm economy. At the Reagan Administration's mid-June agriculture "summit" in Washington, D.C., 100 representatives from farm and agribusiness groups discussed whether the Government should freeze certain crop price subsidies or increase them, whether the Government should extend the crop set-aside program, known as PIK, or take its hands off and let the "free market" control supply and demand.

Some urged Secretary Block to set up a Government-industry task force to act as a traveling salesman, promoting U.S. grain sales overseas. Such proposals might provide a crutch, propping up U.S. agriculture in the short run. But participants in the conference, including Block, recognized that the nation can't write its farm program from year to year any more; it must write long-term agricultural policy. "I'm asking you to look not two or three years ahead," the Secretary told the conference, "but decades ahead."

Farming Must Change Drastically

The proposals you are least likely to hear, however, may be the only ones that can save American agriculture. The basic motives and methods of farmers must be drastically revised. Farmers must use the *least* expensive, *least* energy-intensive methods of growing crops. And they must produce only as many bushels per acre as the soil can support while still sustaining or even increasing its productivity.

These changes would be so sweeping that the consequences are difficult to visualize. Instead of devoting vast acreage to a single crop—a practice that promotes erosion, pest attacks, and overproduction, according to Agriculture Department reports—farmers would plant a variety of crops on a single farm. Regions that have seen only corn and soybeans for twenty years would be covered with a patchwork of corn and soybeans, barley and alfalfa,

wheat and clover, oats, and perhaps even vegetable and fruit crops. As farmers divided their land into smaller parcels planted with diverse crops, they would find little use for their current equipment—tractors, planters, and harvesters that operate economically only on huge stretches of territory. The equipment that would replace them—nimble machinery, powered by renewable fuels, that can plant and harvest a variety of crops—hasn't been developed yet.

This style of farming would take more labor, so the Federal Government might have to devise a national program to encourage people to stay in the rural areas or even settle there, and farmers would have to scale back the size of their operations.

The basic structure of the farm economy would have to change. As the GAO report on agriculture suggests, years of Federal farm programs, tax code provisions, and research have been skewed toward rewarding farmers for specializing in such big cash crops as corn, soybeans, and wheat.

"The Government has essentially controlled American agriculture for fifty years."

The economies of entire regions have become dependent on those crops. If farmers were to shift back toward greater variety in what they plant, existing economic networks would have to be rebuilt. The Federal Government would have to consider shaping subsidies and regulating market prices so that farmers would be penalized, in effect, for producing as much corn and wheat as possible and rewarded for planting crops that promote the national goals of conserving energy, protecting the soil, minimizing the use of pesticides, and providing a stable farm economy.

Such proposals have a utopian ring, and most politicians and farmers would probably dismiss them as unrealistic, naive, or worse. The question that would immediately be asked is whether we want Government control of agriculture. And that, of course, is the irony: *The Government has essentially controlled American agriculture for fifty years*, shaping the kinds of farms we have and the crops that are grown on them. . . .

But there's a simpler argument for abandoning the current structure of agriculture in favor of a bold new approach: The modern American way of farming isn't working any more.

Daniel Zwerdling is a correspondent for National Public Radio.

Farms Are Failing Because of Government Programs

William Tucker

Just about every week the television news carries another story. A farm family is forced off its homestead in the Midwest. A depressed farmer in Georgia shoots himself. A bitter farmer in Minnesota kills the banker who foreclosed on his farm last year. The nation's Farm Belt is in crisis. Inevitably the question is put: Why don't we give farmers more aid?

Then every once in a while the networks will get tough and analytical. Sure, we've done a lot to help farmers, said Dan Rather in a week-long special last March. Farm subsidies have now risen to $20 billion a year. But after all, shouldn't there be a limit? If the old-fashioned family farmers can't compete anymore, should people from other parts of the economy be forced to subsidize them?

Subsidies Hurting Farmers?

Somehow this endless parade of stories never gets around to asking the key questions: Could it be possible that all the government programs are actually *hurting* farmers? Rather than preserving homesteads, could farm subsidies actually be *taking away* the advantages of the family farm? Is it possible that if we only stopped trying to help farmers, everyone—taxpayers and farmers alike—might be better off?

Farming is the only industry still operating under the New Deal. The original National Recovery Administration, which "cartelized" most major American industries, was struck down by the Supreme Court in 1935. By that time everyone—including Franklin Roosevelt—had realized that it wasn't such a great idea. There was no serious effort to revive it.

But agriculture fared differently. Under pressure from Roosevelt's court-packing scheme, the Supreme

Court made its famous "switch in time" in 1937 and upheld the second Agricultural Adjustment Act. Thereafter, agriculture was completely regulated. Every basic farm program that operates today comes out of the New Deal. As a result, there is almost no form of farming today where the government is not the main player.

Start, for example, with the price support program operated by the Commodity Credit Corporation, a quasi-government agency. In a wide variety of field crops—corn, wheat, rice, cotton, barley, sorghum— the government guarantees farmers an artificially high price. If market prices fall below the "target" level, the government makes up the difference to farmers in the form of a "deficiency" payment. The market price of corn, for example, is now around $2.10 a bushel. [The 1986] "target" price is $3 a bushel. As a result, farmers in the program will sell their corn at market value and the government will pay them the difference of 90 cents a bushel. The target price has no relation to wind, weather, or the price of cheese. It is just what the *political* market will bear.

This program is an "entitlement," like Social Security. There is no way of predicting what it is going to cost from year to year. In 1981, the cost to the Treasury was $2 billion. Last year it was $20 billion. Recently the Reagan Administration did succeed in capping the amount of a crop on which an individual farmer can collect. Thus, the program will probably not expand much further than it already has. But it won't cost less than $20 billion for some time, either.

Yet that is only the beginning. A second, almost equally expansive effort within the Commodity Credit Corporation is the non-recourse loan program. At the end of the growing season, farmers of various crops are given Treasury-rate loans. If the price of the crop doesn't reach an arbitrarily selected "loan rate," farmers don't have to repay the loans. They

William Tucker, "Down on the Farm," *The American Spectator*, June 1986. Reprinted with permission.

simply hand the crop over to the CCC. As of September 1985, the CCC was carrying loans of $12.5 billion—*off-budget*. In 1985 they made another $10.2 billion in loans. No one knows how many of these will ever be paid back.

Supply and Demand

To any student of freshman economics, this is all drearily familiar. It has to do with those simple supply-and-demand graphs that appear on page whatever-it-was in Paul Samuelson's textbook, *Economics*. Supply and demand can be represented as two curves that intersect at a point called "market price," or more accurately, "market-clearing price." When prices are left to adjust themselves, the desires of consumers and producers are brought into alignment, allocating resources in the most efficient way.

The problems begin when a coterie of producers or consumers convinces the government to set prices at a "just" or "fair" level. Producers always think "just" prices are quite a bit above market levels, of course, while consumers think they are quite a bit below. In terms of results, it hardly matters. Once prices are legislated, the two curves will no longer intersect. If prices are artificially high, two things will happen: producers will supply more, and consumers will buy less. The result is an economic "surplus"—as in "farm surplus." If prices are fixed artificially low—as we did with oil prices in the 1970s—consumers will consume more and producers supply less. The result will be a "shortage"—as in "oil shortage."

Target prices and all the other government price manipulations are the sole cause of farm surpluses, our chronic agricultural problem. Take milk, for example. Dairy farmers have their own special price support program that sets prices at about 110 to 115 percent above market levels. As a result, dairy farmers constantly produce more milk than the market can absorb. Once such surpluses gush forth, the government must become the "consumer of last resort" and buy up the surpluses. (Inversely, when price controls produce a shortage of a commodity like oil, the cry goes up that the government must become the *producer* of last resort and create its own oil company, or even nationalize the industry.)

The government's efforts to deal with our milk surpluses are legendary. Whole plants have been built just to turn these surpluses into cheese and powdered milk. Huge caves outside Kansas City are now being filled with enough of these products to stuff every man, woman, and child in the United States for the next two years. The stores grow bigger every day.

Similar surpluses have grown up in all the feed grains. For a while we stored our surplus corn and wheat on decommissioned World War II battleships. Then we started dumping them onto underdeveloped countries, until we found this only ruined Third World farming. The government eventually started renting space in Midwestern silos, and since the Payment in Kind (PIK) program it has been handing the surpluses back to the farmers. No one knows when, if ever, any of these supplies will be eaten by man or animal. The game now is who will pay the storage costs.

Below-Market Credit

Outside of vegetable farming, there is not one major agricultural sector in the country where a farmer must put his seed in the ground in October or April without the knowledge that the government will be there to bail him out at the end of the season. But just as significant as government efforts to hold prices above market levels has been another set of programs designed to supply farmers with below-market credit.

"Government price manipulations are the sole cause of farm surpluses, our chronic agricultural problem."

The statistics are stark. Of the $210 billion in loans now held by farmers, exactly half have been extended by government or quasi-government agencies. The Farm Credit System—not to be confused with the Commodity Credit Corporation—holds the largest share at 29 percent. Another 13 percent have been made by the Farmer's Home Administration and 8 percent by the CCC. Commerical banks finance only 23 percent of farmers' debts, while 22 percent come from private lenders (usually the previous landowner) and 6 percent from life-insurance companies.

The Farm Credit System, almost unique to the farm economy, is one of those ambiguously named agencies like Ginny and Fanny Mae that may or may not be a part of the federal government. Originally funded out of the Treasury, it has since been turned over to the private sector. The system's $80 billion in loans have all been raised in Wall Street's private money markets. But because of the agency's history, investors tend to assume that it is still backed by the federal government. This misunderstanding allows the system to borrow at close to Treasury rates. And in fact, now that many of the Farm Credit System's debts have turned bad, Congress is acting to bail it out—proving that investors were right all along.

The Farmer's Home Administration is another lender of last resort. "You have to have been rejected by two other lenders before you can apply to the Administration," said Bob Thompson, assistant secretary of agriculture for economics. "They're always dealing with very marginal people.

Traditionally the FHA is supposed to help young farmers who haven't had the chance to establish credit, but in practice few farmers have ever established themselves through FHA."

"Debt Crisis"

Thus, there is a tremendous amount of easy credit in the agricultural sector that is not available elsewhere in the economy. The result has been the most recent chapter in the on-going farm crisis—the "debt crisis." Although it is little noted, farmers today are actually making more money than ever. "Farm income has been at the highest level in our history over the last three years," said John Lee, director of the Economic Research Bureau of the Department of Agriculture. . . . What we really have is a debt crisis that is concentrated among about 15-20 percent of all farmers."

When inflation started pushing up land prices in the 1970s, many farmers speculated heavily. Skyrocketing land values allowed them to roll over their debts each year by using their land as collateral. But when the Reagan Administration brought inflation under control, the bubble burst. Farmland prices have tumbled 31 percent throughout the country, and over 60 percent in parts of Iowa, Nebraska, and Minnesota. "All this hasn't meant any loss of production, however," said Mike Belongia, of the Federal Reserve Bank in St. Louis. "Two-thirds of all land transactions take place between farmers. When a farmer in Iowa goes under, his land is usually bought by another farmer who puts it right back into production."

"These new people out here aren't really farming the land anymore. They're just farming the government subsidies."

One of the main causes of the "farm crisis," then, has been the unrealistically easy subsidized credit that has been made available to farmers.

Pushing Prices Down

The surplus production and land speculation are the predictable results of government manipulation of the market. What agricultural economists are now beginning to realize, however, is that this may be only the tip of the iceberg. A consensus is now emerging that, just as the oil price controls of the 1970s eventually pushed oil prices *above* their market levels, so the elaborate system of protections for farmers is actually pushing farm prices *below* their market level.

"It all has to do with risk," said the University of Chicago's D. Gale Johnson, a pioneer in the field of risk analysis. "The greater the perceived risk in any investment, the less capital it will attract. Likewise,

the smaller the perceived risk, the more people will invest.

"The difficulty with farming is that so many of the risks have been reduced. All the tax advantages and government programs make investors perceive farming as essentially risk-free. As a result, farming is attracting too much capital. The more extra investment that goes into agriculture, the more surpluses we produce. And the more surpluses we produce, the more prices go down."

One of the most remarkable statistics floating around these days is the aggregate income that farmers declare for tax purposes. For 1983—the latest figures available—the whole agricultural sector reported a net loss of $10 billion, about $3,000 per farm.

"What these figures mean is that people are using farms to offset other sources of income," said Bob Thompson of the Department of Agriculture. "For an ordinary farmer the lowest income worth reporting is zero. That means you don't have to pay taxes. The $10 billion loss is being written off against other income. In fact, if the IRS taxed farmers at a rate of zero, the Treasury would gain $3 billion. American agriculture has essentially become a cornucopia of tax-shelters for people whose main income is in other sectors." . . .

Inviting Tough Competition

In accumulating tax advantages farmers have assumed they were only helping themselves. What they have failed to recognize, however, is that they are inviting other competitors into the industry. "It's very easy for investors to get into farming on a small scale," said D. Gale Johnson. "The local doctor or dentist can usually do it." Of course it might seem foolish to put money into a business that is already overloaded with surpluses—but then, what are government price-support programs for?

As a result, the farm economy has become hugely overcapitalized. "We recently looked at investment trends in farming from 1956 to 1978," said James Hrubovcak of the Department of Agriculture's Economic Research Service. "Our conclusion was that 20 percent of agricultural investment over that period was made solely for tax purposes. Farming is no longer something that is done solely to raise crops. People are crowding into the business because of all its special advantages and protections."

And they keep coming. In 1972, some Southern farmers suffered damage from Hurricane Agnes. Congress responded by setting up the Disaster Payments Program, the DPP. Originally intended to protect against "acts of God," it quickly came to be used to offset the traditional risks of farming land highly prone to erosion. Since the nineteenth century, the scrubby sagebrush lands of West Texas and the High Plains in Colorado and Wyoming were always regarded as too fragile for "sod-busting."

Instead they were put into cattle grazing or left unused. With federal disaster insurance, however, these marginal lands became accessible. Over the last decade more than 10 million acres of highly erodable land in West Texas and the Sand Hills of Nebraska have been plowed under for wheat and corn. The land often gives out in less than five years. Yet with government crop insurance, plus the price supports, plus the tax advantages, it pays off. As one Wyoming rancher recently told the *New York Times*: "These new people out here aren't really farming the land anymore. They're just farming the government subsidies." . . .

Industry Built on Subsidies

So there you have it—America's oldest and largest industry now almost completely rebuilt around government subsidies. What would happen if we scrapped this whole maze of entitlements upon entitlements and went back to some normal pattern of development?

"It's a question a lot of people are beginning to ask," said John Lee of the USDA. "Obviously, there would be some initial dislocation. Production patterns would probably shift around the country to a more economical alignment. But the long-run results would be healthy. Investors would see more risk in farming and production would fall. As a result, farm prices would firm up. There would be fewer oversupplies, although we would probably have more fluctuation from year to year."

Some sectors almost certainly wouldn't survive without protection. Agricultural economists usually point to the domestic sugar industry, which is insulated from a world market where prices are only one-third as high. "We probably wouldn't grow much sugar cane or sugar beets," said Zeke Pasour of North Carolina State University. Dairy products would face similar competition.

"The great irony about the federal orchestration of agriculture has been that nearly all the programs work against family farms and in favor of larger units."

But would it mean the end of American agriculture? Certainly not. We still have enormous economic advantages, both in the domestic and world markets. Food prices would rise, making farming profitable for real farmers. Consumers would pay higher prices in some instances, but would more than make up for it on taxes. Twenty billion dollars in farm subsidies amounts to $100 a year for every man, woman, and child in America.

One other thing is certain. The major beneficiary would be that sacred American institution: the family farm. The great irony about the federal orchestration of agriculture has been that nearly all the programs work against family farms and in favor of larger units. California's agriculture—which has replaced so much Southern and Midwestern farming—has been built almost entirely around large corporate farms. (California farming, by the way, pays almost no income tax.) Most support payments also end up in the hands of large farmers. A recent *New York Times* story included this remarkable quote from a Texas oil executive who was "farming corn subsidies" in a large-scale corporate effort in Nebraska. "We come up here looking for about twelve percent on our investment," he said. "But to tell the truth, without federal programs we couldn't do it. When there's a guy out there who just wants to live on the land and provide all his own labor, and who only wants to make about 4 or 5 percent on his money every year, there's basically no way we can compete against him."

Help Farmers by Not Helping

The way to solve the farm problem, then, is to stop helping farmers. One big step would be to change the tax structure so that it no longer encouraged overinvestment in agriculture. A neutral tax code—which is what the Administration wants in tax reform—would be the best thing. But if that can't be done, the incentives designed to spur capital investment in other industries should at least be eliminated for farming.

The most important thing is to leave farmers alone to do what they do best—grow crops and raise animals on their own land. Agriculture is too complex and important to be managed by Washington. Farming should be left to the farmers.

William Tucker, New York correspondent for The American Spectator, *has also written about farming for* The Atlantic Monthly *and* Barron's.

"Farm subsidies . . . are necessary to keep the economy grinding."

Government Must Support Agriculture

Tom Daschle and Andrew Kopkind

Editor's note: The following viewpoint is taken from two sources: Part I is a newspaper article by Congressman Tom Daschle; Part II is by Andrew Kopkind.

I

The House Agriculture Committee began working on a bill to save the Farm Credit System, the nation's largest source of loan money for farmers. The system, composed of hundreds of member-owned cooperatives is on the verge of collapse because America's troubled family farmers increasingly have been unable to pay back their loans.

Meanwhile, the Senate finished its version of the 1985 farm bill, which will set the nation's agriculture policies for the next four years. The House passed its version of that bill before it took up the farm credit question.

The timing of the two efforts [was] ironic and instructive; in effect, one body of Congress [was] developing a farm policy for the *next* four years, while the other body [was] trying to rescue farmers from the policies of the *last* four. This is typical of how Congress has been forced to develop farm policy under the Reagan Administration.

Some people think that we in Congress spend too much time worrying about farmers and their many problems. But family farmers don't have lots of problems; they have one problem that causes most of their other difficulties—their income is too low. That's why they're defaulting on their loans and going out of business.

For five years the Administration has driven down farm income with a "free-market" policy, ignoring the fact that unfair foreign trade practices, government subsidization of imports and a tax code

Tom Daschle, "Down on the Farm, Chaos," *Los Angeles Times*, November 11, 1985. Reprinted with the author's permission.

Andrew Kopkind, "Editorial: Clearing the Land," *The Nation*, March 9, 1985. Reprinted by permission of *The Nation Magazine*, Nation Associates Incorporated, © 1985.

that benefits investors who use farming as nothing more than a tax shelter have made a mockery of the term *free-market*.

Money-Saving Ag Bill Costs More

The Administration says that its farm policy saves money. But now we're seeing that driving down farm income by letting farmers fend for themselves costs more than it saves.

The collapsing Farm Credit System is just the first of the costs. During the third quarter of 1985, the system reported losses of $522 million. Further losses of at least $6 billion are expected in the next few years. And a recent Chase Econometrics study showed that without federal assistance the system could default.

A default would affect everyone. The Farm Credit System is about the same size as the nation's third-largest bank. According to the Chase study, a Farm Credit System default would drive up private interest rates by three percentage points, cause the loss of 1 million housing starts in the next two years, cost 1.5 million jobs in 1987 and increase the deficit by anywhere between $53 billion and $265 billion.

We who represent ailing farm families understand that the problem of low farm income has many causes and that we need to deal with them one at a time—with a sensible farm policy, a realistic attitude toward our trading partners, comprehensive tax reform and no-nonsense deficit cutting. But that's not what we have done.

The House's version of the 1985 farm bill is a case in point. We could have passed a bill that would have raised income for small wheat and corn farmers—without busting the budget, encouraging overproduction or giving huge government subsidies to those who don't need them. Instead we passed a bill that continues the bad policies of the last five years.

Family farmers rely heavily on federal farm

programs to help determine the prices that they receive for their crops. When prices are high, their incomes are high; when prices fall, so do their incomes. The farm bill just passed by the House will mean low prices for wheat and corn farmers, who make up the bulk of the farm families in trouble.

So, more of them will default on their loans. The banks that made the loans will suffer right along with the farmers and, eventually, with the rest of the public.

To prevent that, Congress has to deal with the farm credit crisis. The Farm Credit System has requested a $6-billion bail-out. Meanwhile, the Administration has proposed restructuring the system, but refuses to guarantee the system's survival. If the system collapses, we will all pay for it through unemployment benefits, welfare payments and lost tax revenues: an estimated 88,300 farms would face foreclosure.

Neither option addresses the real issue—that we will have to pass more legislation to raise prices and increase farm income.

How much would higher farm prices cost consumers? If the House had agreed to give wheat farmers the price increase that they wanted (about $1.75 per bushel), it would have increased the price of a $1 loaf of bread by 2 cents. That's not entirely inconsequential. But it is without a doubt the cheapest *and* the most humane alternative.

Keeping American family farmers in business is the best way to maintain America's ability to produce the best possible food at the lowest possible price.

The Administration says that it can cut the deficit and food prices by slashing agriculture programs. But the real cost of this policy is much higher than the Adminstration thinks it is. A good farm bill would have cost a lot less. Eventually we will have to have one.

II

Taking a leaf from the book of radical agricultural policies compiled by the late Joseph Stalin . . . President Reagan has determined that small, inefficient farms will be liquidated, their inhabitants driven into urban markets or left to earn low wages on the land of others. Family life will be sacrificed and rural politics will be transformed to serve the demands of national economic development.

Turning Farms into Corportions

In postrevolutionary Russia, of course, the process was called forced collectivization. Reagan's brand, appropriately enough, is forced corporatization. More and more land will be concentrated in the hands of fewer and fewer C.E.O.s—many of whom will be permanent absentees. And what with conglomerates multiplying and mergers made easier (especially if Commerce Secretary Malcolm Baldrige repeals

relevant antitrust laws), great tracts of America's farmland will soon belong to Warner Amex, say, or Pepsico. Structurally, at least, it will be hard to tell the difference between an Apple computer and an apple orchard, a dairy farm and a Dairy Queen. Can we expect McDonald's-franchised feedlots?

Reagan's vision of agricultural paradise, like the Russian fellow's, is grounded in ideology. In this case it is the cure-all dogma of the free market. Let prices drop, production lag, rural unemployment soar, banks fail, towns die, dust blow. In time, the market will make it right.

"Keeping American family farmers in business is the best way to maintain America's ability to produce the best possible food at the lowest possible prices."

There are plenty of political problems with that ideology, and a serious logical flaw as well. It in no way reflects the reality of a national economy that never was and never will be free in the Reaganite sense. Farm credit is controlled by legislation, executive action and Federal Reserve policy. Farm equipment is purchased on a noncompetitive market from near-monopoly manufacturers. World sales and supplies of feed, foodstuffs and agricultural raw materials are exquisitely orchestrated for political and economic purposes. By a flip of a few switches in the world market system, for instance, the Administration could cripple the economies of Third World nations, NATO allies or assorted other consumers and suppliers of American agriculture.

Reagan is right when he says that the elaborate structure of farm price supports should be dismantled. He is not the only one saying so, either. Liberal and leftist critics have argued for a long time that the system is unfair, irrational and unable to do what it was designed for: reducing excess agricultural capacity. But neither was the vaunted free market of the 1920s able to absorb the excess production. The result was a catastrophic depression on farms throughout the decade, while business boomed in the cities. New Deal and Fair Deal programs kept some farmers from ruin (although millions more left the land), but they were full of inequities, often did not take consumers' needs into account and did not reverse the trend toward the concentration of land ownership.

Bail Out Countries but Not Farmers?

The farm crisis today is exacerbated by various policies introduced by Reaganomics to serve other ends. Tight money, intended to hold down inflation, and big deficits, tolerated for the sake of tax cuts and military extravagance, have produced the credit crunch. If Reagan's farm program is implemented, farmers could default on as much as $212 billion worth of farm loans. The captains of capitalism are eager to bail out countries—Mexico, Brazil, Poland, Argentina—with only a fraction of that potentially bad debt. We hear few paeans to the free market when big banks, like Continental Illinois, or big corporations, like Chrysler, are in financial danger.

The Reagan solution looks simple, if cruel. Ridding the land of its weakest cultivators is the Administration's latest example of free-market triage, which has already been applied to the smokestack industries of the Northeast and the Midwest, to the urban service sector and to the national welfare system. As Donald Regan advised New Yorkers when he was Treasury Secretary, if you are dissatisfied with the quality of life after the ax falls on the North, move South.

Reagan's do-nothing farm policy will, in fact, do nothing to revitalize agriculture, at least not in the ways the Administration claims. Without serious and sophisticated government intervention, the problems of unemployment, over-production, credit, soil conservation, export/import regulation and community survival cannot be addressed. The billions the government will "save" if farm programs are defunded will not, as Reagan's coterie hopes, be transferred from struggling farmers to corporate coffers. For whether they like it or not, farm subsidies, like military spending, are necessary to keep the economy grinding.

"We hear few paeans to the free market when big banks . . . or big corporations . . . are in financial danger."

Reagan's opponents need to project their own vision of farm life and the way to secure it, beyond the myths in Hollywood's head. The Democrats should seize the present crisis and offer the farmers a better deal, including regional pricing systems, income and property tax reform, production quotas, resource and machinery cooperatives. Finding the middle way between Stalinism and Reaganism should be as easy as hitting the broadside of a barn.

Tom Daschle is a Democratic Representative from South Dakota and a member of the House Agriculture Committee. Andrew Kopkind's viewpoint first appeared in The Nation.

"The most pervasive and harmful myth is that farmers cannot survive without federal welfare."

Government Must Get Out of Agriculture

Henry Eason

W.L. Tatum thinks nothing can keep the American farmer from prospering—except perhaps his own government's agricultural and fiscal policies.

Federal budget deficits, by driving up the dollar's foreign exchange rate, have cost the president of Tatum Farms lucrative markets in Latin America. High federal price supports for the grain he feeds his chickens have knifed into his profit margin. The federal government's policy of granting fewer export subsidies than his European competitors get from their governments has cost him sales abroad.

And yet, even without government welfare, the Dawsonville, Ga., chicken breeder built a modest hatchery into a $20 million-a-year business with customers in 50 countries. Tatum, like two thirds of the country's food producers, gets no direct federal aid. That is the way it should be for *all* American farmers, he says. . . .

Numerous segments of agriculture are challenging the policies that keep wheat, feed grain, sugar, dairy and cotton producers in a public hothouse—at great expense to taxpayers and others in the food chain.

Too Much Government

Critics of the existing price support system say U.S. agriculture is losing world markets because of too much government interference and because it is geared more toward protecting the incomes of a minority of inefficient farmers than toward production. A more market-oriented approach, they say, would harness agriculture's strength as a global competitor and help shrink the nation's trade deficit. President Reagan is leading the fight for deregulation.

Two thirds of all food produced in the United States is not federally subsidized. The meat, vegetable and fruit industries operate without the government programs that prop up the prices of feed grains, dairy and cotton. Soybean farmers receive minimal government backing. . . .

Stimulate Exports

"We need to stop these programs that pay farmers not to produce," says Tatum. "We need to knock down fences and produce and export." Instead of spending billions of federal dollars providing income transfers to a minority of farmers, the government should stimulate exports, eventually giving farmers in these programs a profit on the open market, Tatum argues.

Tatum is a farmer of the kind the Reagan administration says can restore American agriculture to greatness. Looking always beyond the Blue Ridge Mountains, Tatum has traveled from Katmandu to Tokyo to sell his Cornish breeding stock. His export prowess has been commended by the Commerce Department.

A practitioner of high tech farming, Tatum has adapted creative innovations in selective breeding and automated production to his business. He also sells management services to his global clients.

He is even banging on doors in Africa, where the smart money says there is no market. Tatum has heard that before.

"They're selling chickens for $7 a pound in Nigeria," he says. "There are 100 million people there. We could feed them chickens for a dollar a pound."

It has not been easy for Tatum to continue operating in the black. Along with the drought, the Payment-in-Kind program, which paid grain farmers not to produce, sent prices soaring and drove up Tatum Farms' feed costs one third. The billions of dollars all agriculture programs cost the taxpayer contribute to budget deficits that help keep interest rates up and increase the value of the dollar abroad. That cost Tatum his $1.3 million Venezuelan market

Henry Eason, "Farm Problems: The Answer." Excerpted by permission from NATION'S BUSINESS, May 1985. Copyright 1985, U.S. Chamber of Commerce.

an another $1.7 million in sales to other Latin American countries.

Paradoxically, the farmers who are in the worst shape financially are the very ones who were supposed to have benefited from federal agriculture programs. . . .

"I don't think the government can bail out agriculture," [rancher Marshall] Frasier says. "We've just got to get more competitive. Those who know what to do and can control costs will stay in agriculture. Hard as it might sound, 15 to 20 percent more farmers are going out of business. . . .

Like Tatum, Frasier has traveled globally and understands the potential for exports. He also appreciates the impact the budget deficit has had on interest rates and the dollar. Two thirds of the million dollars he lost went for interest rates on operating loans.

"We've had too many years of people thinking that government money is free money," he says. "Now we're paying for it. These farmers produce for the government instead of for the market."

Costly Farm Support Program

The costly, unwieldy government farm support program has been a half century in the making. Back in the 1930s, when dust storms, drought and hard times turned the heartland brown, the Roosevelt administration thrust the government into farming. It was to have been a quick-fix program.

New Deal Agriculture Secretary Henry Wallace implemented the farmer bailout scheme. He said then: "The present program for readjusting production acreage to market requirement is admittedly but a temporary method of dealing with an emergency. It could not be relied upon as a permanent means of keeping farm production in line with market requirements."

"Paradoxically, the farmers who are in the worst shape financially are the very ones who were supposed to have benefited from federal agriculture programs."

Hundreds of billions of tax dollars later, descendants of the Dust Bowl farmers are in trouble again. As many as 200,000 could go broke this year. They are clamoring for one more extension of that perennially temporary program. They will be using all of their considerable political muscle to get what they want. Congress rushed to oblige them this year with credit aid, and only a presidential veto blocked the assistance.

Ironically, an infusion of still more federal dollars could turn agriculture—America's largest economic

sector—into another declining industry.

American agriculture today employs 24 million and has global markets. It is much more than farming. It is chemical companies producing fertilizers, pesticides and herbicides. It is equipment manufacturers. It is trucking companies, shipping lines, textile companies, banks, food processors, supermarkets and countless firms supplying production and consumer needs for the whole food and fiber chain.

It is, in short, a highly complex, integrated industry.

Agriculture is also myth-ridden, and some of its myths, if distilled from political rhetoric into political action, could end up idling far more workers than the comparatively few farmers who now face ruin.

The most pervasive and harmful myth is that farmers cannot survive without federal welfare. Only one third of the nation's food and fiber producers benefit from the array of government support programs. The rest operate in the marketplace.

It is also a myth that the entire farm economy will collapse if heavily debt-ridden farmers are not bailed out. According to the Agriculture Department's Economic Research Service, 83.4 percent of all farms are financially sound.

Normal Debt Range

About 10 percent have debt-to-asset ratios between 40 and 70 percent. That ratio is high, but it is also a normal and profitable range for many kinds of operations, like cattle feedlots, poultry operations, nurseries and sod farms. Such operations often have relatively small amounts tied up in physical assets. Their ownership is more widely spread. Only 6.6 percent of the country's farms face extreme financial problems or are technically insolvent.

Yet another myth is that the family farmer is an endangered species. Over 73 percent have no financial problems. About 17 percent—including those who ably manage higher debt-to-asset ratios—face financial challenges. Only 9.4 percent are in real trouble, according to the ERS survey.

As Congress now turns its attention to proposals to reform the farm economy, many—led by President Reagan—believe it is more appropriate to ask how federal programs have *harmed* American agriculture, rather than helped it.

The damage has already been extensive. Artificially high support prices in recent years, pegged above world prices, have cost agriculture vital foreign sales that could have further offset trade imbalances in manufacturing goods. Exports are not only the last hope for real expansion in agriculture, they are vital to the United States' balance of payments ledger.

Also, massive government spending on agriculture, as Tatum and Frasier have seen, has boosted interest rates and the dollar, further dampening foreign markets. . . .

Tatum and Frasier are representatives of the silent majority in agriculture: the meat producers and fruit and vegetable growers, as well as those prudent, efficient wheat, corn, soybean, cotton and rice producers who till their fields while other farmers march and get headlines. Most farmers want the government out of agriculture.

So do other segments of the agriculture industry—the wholesalers, retailers, food servers, manufacturers, shippers and other businesses that support the food and fiber system. They have a big stake in the outcome of the farm policy debate in Congress.

If, as some farm groups wish, the production system is shrunk to the status of a public utility that services primarily the domestic market—at high support prices—companies dependent on massive food sales for the world market will collapse.

Long silent, these nonfarm segments of the agriculture sector are beginning to raise their voices. Associations representing bakers, food brokers, cracker manufacturers, candy companies, grocers, food processors, equipment producers, chemical companies and ports are swinging behind the Reagan administration's production-oriented approach.

The Fertilizer Institute, for example, is pressing for a farm program that emphasizes growth. When PIK cut production, fertilizer companies went into a tailspin.

"Our major industry effort," says institute President Gary Myers, "will be in working for solid, long-range farm programs which can provide relief from up-again, down-again swings in our farm economy—and resultant industry instability."

The Milk Industry Foundation, representing the middlemen between dairy farmers and consumers, is fighting for lower milk price supports. A consumers' lobby, Public Voice for Food and Health Policy, is joining the foundation's battle. The American Meat Institute is calling for "a fundamental review of agriculture policy" that will reduce federal outlays, stimulate exports and lessen farmers' drain on credit markets.

According to the Agriculture Council of America, the PIK program threw 50,000 farm machinery employees out of work and caused hundreds of dealers to go out of business. "Is there any justification for asking American taxpayers to subsidize the incomes of farmers?" a report by the educational foundation asks. "In the depressed 1930s, the answer was clearer. The American people wanted to guarantee that an abundant, varied and healthful food and fiber supply would be available at reasonable prices."

But since then, it says, "agriculture has changed enormously." Today, "farmers are so productive that, even without full production on our farms and ranches, the U.S. population is able to consume only 61 percent of all the commodities sold. The criterion for abundant, varied supply is being met."

The council is supported by all segments of the food chain.

Government Support and Farm Income

And yet federal support for agriculture has never been more costly than during the past few years. Numerous funding programs, in addition to basic price supports, nurture the farmer. Indeed, the government contribution to agriculture in 1983 was $12 billion greater than net farm income. If current funding policies continue, taxpayers will spend another $52 billion over the next four years supporting the approximately 800,000 farmers who get income support.

"Ironically, an infusion of still more federal dollars could turn agriculture—America's largest economic sector—into another declining industry."

In addition, farmers benefit from government-subsidized interest rates. The government spends another $1 billion annually on farm research programs. Special tax provisions in 1982 totaled $3.6 billion. Agriculture is the most heavily subsidized economic sector relative to its contribution to the gross national product, according to the Congressional Budget Office.

Farming also benefits from price-boosting import tariffs, marketing orders, resource conservation programs, customs revenues and food assistance sent abroad.

Even at this elevated level of government support, segments of farming across rural America are suffering from sluggish sales. Main Streets are really feeling the effects.

In downtown Greeley, Colo., business people have seen the fortunes of food producers rise and fall. They are keenly sensitive to farm trends. They have seen a once-prosperous sugar beet industry decline. Herds of cattle have been pouring into the town's feedlots for more than a century. Fewer and fewer people are required to bring in the crops. Merchants' rural clientele has dwindled. . . .

The latest ill wind over the plains has not shaken the town's faith in the marketplace.

Amos Finch, general manager of the farmers' supply co-op Agland, says trouble on the range has had a "domino effect" on Greeley businesses. But, he adds, "a majority of farmers and ranchers want the government out of agriculture."

Greeley accountant Ken Whitney sees a lot of people's books. "Big is becoming better," he says. "If it's not big, it's not going to make it. If we really believe in free enterprise, then we'll have to let the market work."

"We've got to have aggressive, positive attitudes," insists William R. Farr, president of Farr Farms, a feedlot operation that readies some 25,000 cattle for packing houses yearly. For four generations, the Farrs have handled sheep and cattle around Greeley.

William D. Farr, Farr's father, is a rural banker as well as a cattleman. "Politicians never face up to what they are doing," he says. "The problem has never been severe enough. Now that it is, we should start over and build a healthy agriculture system. Out of it, you're going to have a restructuring of rural America. Our country is maturing, and we can't maintain an artificial system forever." . . .

Move Toward Free Market

Most observers, in Washington and in the hinterland, agree that the agricultural sector must move toward the market. . . .

Current Ag Programs Not Working

Agriculture Secretary Block says flatly: "The current agriculture programs are simply not working. More of the same is not the answer to agriculture's difficulties." Charged by the President with focusing on the big picture, which includes the huge budget deficit, Block says, "Keeping inflation low and reducing the federal deficit could very well have a greater impact on the well-being of farmers over the next several years than farm programs."

"Is there any justification for asking American taxpayers to subsidize the incomes of farmers?"

"Let's be honest with farmers, agri-businesses and consumers," he told the Senate Agriculture Committee. "We cannot afford to keep mortgaging agriculture's future for a temporary quick fix. It is time to face the realities, set the proper course and make the transition as smoothly as possible. The pressures from ineffective acreage programs, rapidly building inventories, declining farm prices and the loss of world markets would force changes in the current legislation after only a few years." He continued:

"Excessive budget outlays that would *not* improve the farmers' long-term financial condition *would* likely give way to mandatory production controls. By then, the United States would have also given away any growth in export markets."

Forty percent of America's cropland is planted for foreign markets. That is a crucial fact in the whole debate. Farm exports peaked in 1981 at $43.3 billion and slid to $37 billion last year. They will dip to

$35.5 billion this year, according to the Agriculture Department. Each $1 billion in exports produces an estimated 25,000 nonfarm jobs.

Meantime, Peruvian researchers are achieving record yields in rice, corn, peanuts and soybeans. China is moving strongly into the export market with soybeans and cotton. Thailand is challenging the United States in rice exports. Latin American honey is pouring into the United States—at the same time that the American government is holding more than 200 million pounds of surplus, domestically produced honey.

Soon plant hormone research will enable Canadians, Russians and Argentinians to grow wheat in extremely cold climates. Other nations are striving for greater food self-sufficiency. Competitors are racing American scientists toward momentous breakthroughs in food science.

Sweeping Reforms Needed

Says Sen. William Armstrong (R. Colo.): "The federal government has often intervened in exactly the worst ways. First, the government creates soaring inflation and allows interest rates under the Carter administration to rise above 20 percent. Then the government subsidizes exports to get rid of the surpluses, causing farm prices to rise above world markets."

What Armstrong calls "this bizarre combination of federal benefits" has seeped down to the roots of American agriculture. Only sweeping reforms can revive to health the nation's most productive industry.

Henry Eason wrote this article for Nation's Business, *a monthly magazine of business news.*

glossary

Terms

aggregate demand all the money spent by people, businesses, and governments

aggregate supply the capacity of a nation's total resources to produce goods and services

AFDC Aid to Families with Dependent Children; main welfare program for poor mothers and their children; established in 1935 as part of the Social Security Act by President Franklin D. Roosevelt

arbitration the referral of **collective bargaining** or grievance disputes to an impartial third party; usually the arbitrator's decision is final and binding, although sometimes advisory arbitration is used: the decision of the arbitrator is taken under advisement by the parties

balance of payments the ratio between a country's income (from exports, loans, etc.) and its outflow of payments (imports, debt repayment, etc.)

bargaining unit a specified group of employees empowered to bargain collectively with their employer

base currency the currency (money) on which a country's money standard is based; e.g., in the United States, the present base currency is the dollar

blue-collar workers those who engage in factory work, manual labor, or the skilled trades and often wear protective clothing

boycott term originating in 1880 when Irish landowner Charles Boycott was denied all services; it now means collective pressure on employers through refusal to buy their goods and services

central bank the bank—sometimes part of the government, sometimes a private bank—used by the government to issue money, determine the value of the country's money, and regulate the amount of money in circulation

collective bargaining the determination of wages and other conditions of employment by direct negotiations between the union and employer

CETA Comprehensive Employment and Training Act; designed to train and employ poor people who have difficulty finding jobs; established in 1973 by President Richard Nixon and repealed in 1982 by President Ronald Reagan

conciliation an attempt by an impartial third party to reconcile differences

COLA cost of living allowance; used for **social security** and other social programs as a way to determine how much money recipients need to live

Cost-of-Living Index the Consumer Price Index prepared by the US Bureau of Labor Statistics; the Index measures changes in the cost of living month by month, year by year

currency used by consumers (e.g., paper money) to buy and sell goods and services, reflecting the value of those products

deficit the amount by which the money spent by a company or country exceeds its income

demand-side economics economic theory stressing the demand side of the **supply-and-demand** equation based on the idea that an increased demand for goods creates markets and the need to supply those markets; according to demand-side theorists, taxing and redistributing big corporate profits and maintaining wage pro-

tections enables a much larger segment of the population to buy goods, thereby stimulating growth on both sides of the equation

economic efficiency vs. economic equity and other social values lovers of the free-market system say it is most efficient—that is, gives the greatest output for a given input of resources; critics contend that markets don't take into account wider social concerns—like pollution or depletion of resources—nor provide for wider social needs—schools for the poor, public parks, etc.

ESOP employee stock ownership plans; many companies offer programs in which employees receive company stock as part of their compensation or offer employees the opportunity to buy stock

Fair Labor Standards Act passed in 1938, this law set minimum wages and overtime rates and prohibited child labor for industry connected with interstate commerce

FDIC Federal Deposit Insurance Corporation; federally established system of insuring bank deposits; i.e., accounts up to $100,000 are guaranteed to be repaid even if the bank holding the account should go bankrupt

"the Fed" Federal Reserve Banking system; the central bank of the United States; the Fed sets interest rates and regulates the money supply

fiat money standard creating money which cannot be exchanged for the same amount in gold or precious metal; for example, the amount of paper money in circulation is not dependent on the amount of gold held by the government

fiscal policy actions taken by the Federal government to stabilize the economy by increasing or decreasing Federal spending, increasing or decreasing taxes, and increasing or decreasing the deficit or surplus in the Federal budget

flat rate tax a tax system in which all persons are taxed the same percentage regardless of earnings

FOMC Federal Open Market Committee; regulates the money supply chiefly by buying or selling **government securities** in the "open market"—that is through security dealers, banks, businesses, and individuals; the money supply is tightened when the committee sells **government securities** and expanded when the committee buys them

food stamps a US government program which enables (income and asset levels vary from state to state) people to buy food with food coupons or "stamps"

fringe benefits negotiated gains for workers other than wages such as vacations, holidays, pensions, insurance, and supplemental unemployment benefits

GATT General Agreement on Tariffs and Trade; established as an agency of the UN in 1948, its members are pledged to work together to reduce tariffs and other barriers to international trade and to eliminate discriminatory treatment in international commerce

government securities similar to stock certificates or bonds, except in this case one buys or sells stock in the government

GDP Gross Domestic Product; the value of all goods and services produced within a country over a given period regardless of who owns the production facilities

GNP Gross National Product; the value of all goods and services produced by an economy over a given period (usually a year); the production facilities must be owned by residents of the nation

gold standard basing a country's money system on the value of gold; i.e., using gold itself as money or using paper money or some other substitute that would be based on the value and amount of gold that is held in reserve by the country; the paper money could be exchanged for gold

Head-Start established in 1964, it is a nationwide program designed to give disadvantaged children a better start in school and life

industrial democracy a phrase once used to describe unions as a humanizing force in the workplace; through the 1970s and 1980s it has meant worker participation in management decision-making

industrial union a union which includes all the workers in an industry regardless of their craft; industrial unions formed the base of the CIO (Congress of Industrial Organizations)

infant industry a new industry, often given special trade protections by the government to encourage its growth

inflated dollar when the dollar is overvalued in the world market US investors can buy more foreign goods with the dollar than they can US goods; this means an influx of more dollars abroad, and more goods in the domestic economy; related to the *strong dollar*, which again means the dollar's purchasing power is valued too highly; too many dollars abroad could bring about a *devaluation* of the dollar, producing **inflation** at home and a **trade deficit** in the world economy

inflation a relatively large increase in the price level of goods and services, usually caused by a shrinking supply of goods or an increase in the amount of currency beyond the needs of trade; usually steep inflation like that of pre-WWII Germany (2500% in one month) leaves money virtually worthless and can lead to economic collapse

interest-rate policy one way the **Federal Reserve** manages the economy is by influencing changes in interest rates; lower interest rates encourage borrowing, higher rates deter it

IMF International Monetary Fund; a specialized consulting agency of the United Nations which encourages international monetary cooperation, facilitates balanced growth of international trade, assists member countries in correcting **balance of payment** deficits, and promotes foreign exchange stability

Keynesian economics named after its major proponent, John Maynard Keynes, this approach called for limited government interference in an essentially capitalist system to insure a healthy economy (high employment, low **inflation**)

LDC less developed country; has relatively poor transportation and communication systems and relies on other countries for refined goods (i.e., technology)

lockout the closing down of a factory by management to coerce workers into meeting management's demands or modifying their own

macroeconomics the part of economics concerned with the operation of a nation's economy as a whole

markets particular goods and services are exchanged at a price, with the traders free to swap or not swap what they have for what they want

MDB Multilateral Development Bank; a bank contributed to by a number of different countries which loans and grants money to member countries to aid in their development; the **World Bank** is one example

mediation attempts by an impartial third party to get labor and management to find agreement during a dispute

microeconomics the part of economics concerned with specific sectors of the economy

minimum wage the lowest rate of pay an employer is allowed to pay under the law or a union contract

monetarism an economic theory which states that stable economic growth can only be achieved by matching the money supply with a country's real productivity

monetary base equal to the total money or money base (e.g. gold) that a country has in reserve plus the total money in the hands of the people

monetary policy regulation by the Federal Reserve System of the nation's money supply and interest rates

monopoly complete control of a product by one seller or producer

national debt the total amount of money a country owes other countries and private investors

National Labor Relations Act of 1935 also known as the Wagner Act after the law's chief sponsor, Senator Robert Wagner of New York; the law created a National Labor Relations Board to carry out its goals of guaranteeing the right of workers to form unions of their own choosing and to bargain collectively with employers

OECD Organization for Economic Cooperation and Development; a primarily European organization whose goals are to promote the economic and social welfare of its members and to coordinate and stimulate member assistance to developing countries

picketing stationing people outside a place of employment to publicly protest the employer and to discourage entry of nonstriking workers or customers; most picketing takes place during strikes although there is also informational picketing conducted against nonunion business establishments

PIK payment-in-kind; a federal program designed to pay farmers for not producing as much as they normally do but still allow them the same profit; designed to reduce surplus and keep prices at reasonable levels; for example, grain farmers are given government stocks of grain (which they may then sell) in exchange for leaving part of their land fallow

political action the expenditure of substantial amounts of effort and money by unions, businesses, and organizations to promote their political causes; their rationale is that what is gained at the bargaining table can be taken away through legislation

private goods and public goods private goods (food, autos, cigarettes) are paid for directly by the buyer, and are sold for profits; the cost of public goods (highways, public beaches) is shared by the taxpayers and the "profits" (good roads, access to the ocean) are more intangible

private sector that part of the economy made up of privately-owned businesses

privatization having the private sector do things currently done by government; e.g., some cities have eliminated city garbage pickup, turning over that service to private companies

progressive tax a tax system in which those who make more money pay a higher percentage of their earnings than those who make less

protectionism policies designed to protect a country's industries from foreign competition; might include import tariffs or quotas, **subsidies** for domestic products, and other kinds of support for domestic industries

public sector the government; that part of the economy made up of federal and other organizations which are the shared responsibility of the public

real wages wages expressed in terms of what today's dollar will buy; a common way of determining buying power is through the Consumer Price Index

refinancing debts new loans granted to help pay off current debts

rescheduling debts changing or postponing the dates on which debt payments are due in order to create additional time to repay a debt

right to work laws the term used by opponents of unions to institute open shop (non-union) laws in the state

Smoot-Hawley Tariff Act passed by Congress in 1930, this brought tariff levels to their highest point in US history; other countries retaliated by raising their tariffs and US foreign trade declined sharply

strike a temporary work stoppage by workers to put pressure on an employer

social security established by President Franklin Roosevelt in 1935, this program called for employers and employees contributing a percentage of their gains to a national pension fund which they could all draw from after retirement

social unionism the theory that unions should look beyond immediate objectives to try to reform social conditions and improve society as well

subsidy a grant by the government to a person or company to support an enterprise deemed advantageous to the public; e.g., farm subsidies are given to farmers to enable them not to plant all their land and still make profits; this is designed to stabilize farm prices by steadying the supply of farm goods and preserve the land by resting it

supply and demand the core concepts of old-style (market) economics; supply is the quantity of a good that would be *offered* at different prices; demand is the quantity of a particular good that would be *purchased* at different prices; the law of **supply and demand** holds that the cost of goods is determined by the ratio of supply to demand

supply-side economics an economic theory claiming that a supply of goods creates demand for them and that the proper role for government is to stimulate production, or the supply side of the **supply and demand** equation; reducing tax rates and proving incentives for corporate development are two things most supply-siders suggest to achieve this

Taft-Hartley Labor Act passed in 1949, this act outlawed the closed shop, jurisdictional **strikes**, and secondary **boycotts**; employers and unions where forbidden to contribute funds out of their treasuries to candidates for federal office and the unions seeking the services of the National Labor Relations Board had to file their constitutions, by-laws, and financial statements with the US Department of Labor

trade credits short-term loans granted to finance the purchase of specific goods

trade deficit when a country imports more goods than it exports

trickle-down an economic theory which postulates that if the wealthy are unimpeded by harsh taxes and other limiting laws, their wealth will "trickle down" to the poor through increased investment, more jobs, and a healthier economy

unfair labor practices defined by the **National Labor Relations Acts** and by the **Taft-Hartley Act** as practices of discrimination, coercion, and intimidation prohibited to labor and management; management cannot form company unions or use coercive tactics to discourage union organization; unions cannot force workers to join organizations

universal programs those programs (like **social security**) which are available to all people of a certain group (e.g. those 65 or older) without regard to need

War on Poverty in response to strong indications that a large segment of America was mired below the poverty line, President Lyndon Johnson declared "an unconditional war on poverty" in 1964; the offensives in this war included the liberalization of unemployment compensation, expansion of the **food stamp** program, and increased youth employment opportunities

white-collar workers those who are in managerial, professional, or other salaried jobs not involving manual labor

World Bank a worldwide banking organization that provides funds for the economic development of member nations

workfare requiring people who get welfare benefits to work at jobs the state welfare agencies designate

organizations

Alliance for Social Security Disability Recipients
P.O. Box 161
Waxhaw, NC 28173
(704) 843-4787

The Alliance for Social Security Disability Recipients is made up of disabled individuals and interested parties. It works to help Social Security Disability recipients and applicants, and to educate the public about Social Security. Newsletters are published by local chapters.

American Federation of Labor/Congress of Industrial Organizations (AFL/CIO)
815 16th St., NW
Washington, DC 20006
(202) 637-5000

The AFL/CIO, made up of 95 labor unions, 51 state federations, and 742 city bodies, is the largest federation of its kind. Its publications include the weekly *AFL/CIO News*.

American Federation of State, County and Municipal Employees (AFSCME)
1625 L St., NW
Washington, DC 20036
(202) 452-4800

The AFSCME is a union with more than a million members which publishes the *Leadership Newsletter* and the *Public Employee Newspaper* monthly.

Cato Institute
224 Second St., SE
Washington, DC 20003
(202) 546-0200

The Institute sponsors programs designed to assist scholars and laymen in analyzing public policy questions. It is dedicated to extending social and economic freedoms. The Institute publishes a variety of publications, including the monthly *Policy Report* and the *Cato Journal*.

Campaign for Economic Democracy
1337 Santa Monica Mall, #301
Santa Monica, CA 90401
(213) 393-3701

The Campaign for Economic Democracy seeks to introduce new issues onto the political scene and to extend democracy into the economic sphere. It is particularly interested in rebuilding the Democratic party, controlling toxic wastes, and promoting alternative investment policies. The *Economic Democrat* is published monthly.

Center for Corporate Public Involvement
1850 K St., NW
Washington, DC 20006
(202) 862-4047

The Center for Corporate Public Involvement encourages social responsibility in life and health insurance companies. It does this by providing assistance, providing a public accounting of insurance companies, and sponsoring health education and promotion programs. Its publications include the bimonthly *Response* and the annual *Social Report*.

Citizens' Committee for Immigration Reform
1424 16th St., NW, 4th Fl.
Washington, DC 20036
(202) 331-1759

This committee of national leaders is interested in the reform of US immigration and refugee policy. The group proposes to legalize a majority of undocumented aliens and distributes immigration information. It publishes a monthly newsletter.

Citizens for a Debt Free America
2550 S. Sunny Slope Rd.
New Berlin, WI 53151
(414) 782-1305

The Citizens for a Debt Free America, founded in 1983, are intent on eliminating the national debt through massive private contributions to the US Department of the Treasury. By doing this, it hopes to ensure hope and opportunity in the US. Its newsletter, *Silver Linings*, is published four times per year.

Citizens for a Sound Economy
122 C St., NW, Suite 700
Washington, DC 20001
(202) 638-1401

Citizens for a Sound Economy is an advocacy group dedicated to returning economic decision making to citizens. It publishes a large number of issue analyses, issue alerts, capitol comments, and news releases on many economic issues.

Committee for Economic Development
477 Madison Ave.
New York, NY 10022
(212) 688-2063

The Committee for Economic Development is a research organization made up of economic experts. Through its studies and reports, it seeks to increase employment, improve living standards, and increase opportunities for all. It provides statements on national policy, digests, discussion guides, reports, films, and filmstrips to interested parties.

Committee for a Responsible Federal Budget
220 1/2 E St., NE
Washington, DC 20002
(202) 547-4484

The Committee for a Responsible Federal Budget is a nonprofit, educational association whose membership is committed to educating the public regarding the budget process, the deficit, and other issues that have significant fiscal policy impact. Among its publications are two booklets on the deficit.

Co-op America
2100 M St., NW, Suite 310
Washington, DC 20063
(202) 872-5307

Co-op America tries to encourage, through its support of cooperative markets now in place and its aid in bringing businesses and consumers together, socially responsible buying habits in consumers and ethical responsiveness in businesses. Co-op America puts out a number of informative materials including a bi-annual catalog, a quarterly magazine, *Building Economic Alternatives*, and a number of special information packets on responsible investment, alternative travel options, etc.

Council on Economic Priorities
84 Fifth Ave.
New York, NY 10011
(212) 420-1133

The Council on Economic Priorities gathers information on the social responsibility of corporations and disseminates it through its monthly newsletter, reports, and studies. The Council also compares different corporations' levels of responsibility. Its recent publications include a book on Hazardous Waste Management, and one called *Good Business* which carefully compares the performance of American corporations in the area of social responsibility.

Eagle Forum
Box 618
Alton, IL 62002
(618) 462-5415

Eagle Forum is a conservative organization headed by anti-feminist Phyllis Schlafly that opposes comparable worth. The organization publishes a monthly newsletter.

Federation for American Immigration Reform
1424 16th St., NW, Suite 701
Washington, DC 20036
(202) 328-7004

The group advocates comprehensive reform of present immigration laws and promotes enforcement of laws against illegal immigration. The Federation seeks to establish a single, stable ceiling for all legal immigration. It sponsors seminars and publishes a monograph series.

Fiber, Fabric, and Apparel Coalition for Trade (FFACT)
1101 Connecticut Ave., NW, Suite 300
Washington, DC 20036
(202) 862-0500

FFACT is a garment industry organization that supports trade restrictions on imports. It sponsors research and position papers on the trade issue.

Foundation for Economic Education (FEE)
30 S. Broadway
Irvington, NY 10533
(914) 591-7230

This organization focuses its research efforts on free market theory and society without government interference. FEE also maintains a speakers bureau, a library with related materials, and publishes *The Freeman* monthly.

Foundation for Rational Economics and Education (FREE)
P.O. Box 1776
Lake Jackson, TX 77566
(409) 265-3034

Made up of individuals who wish to study the Constitution, economic freedom, and personal liberty, the Foundation for Rational Economics and Education conducts seminars for high school and college students and produces a number of publications including the monthly *Freedom Report*.

The Heritage Foundation
214 Massachusetts Ave., NE
Washington, DC 20002
(202) 546-4400

The Heritage Foundation is a conservative public policy research institute. It produces a tremendous number of research and position papers on current policy issues along with publications like the *Backgrounder*.

INFORM
381 Park Ave., S
New York, NY 10016
(212) 689-4040

INFORM studies the effects US industry has on the environment and human health. It tries to discover the extent to which corporations are responsible for these kinds of problems and to specify ways of correcting or alleviating them. INFORM publishes a bimonthly newsletter and in-depth studies.

Institute for Socioeconomic Studies
Airport Rd.
White Plains, NY 10604
(914) 428-7400

The Institute for Socioeconomic Studies focuses its efforts on research, particularly in the areas of quality of life, social motivation, poverty, urban regeneration, and the problems of the elderly. In order to disseminate its findings, it sponsors conferences and seminars, publishes books and monographs, and puts out the bimonthly *Socioeconomic Newsletter* and *The Journal/The Institute for Socioeconomic Studies*.

Interfaith Center on Corporate Responsibility
475 Riverside Dr., Rm. 566
New York, NY 10115
(212) 870-2293

The Interfaith Center on Corporate Responsibility represents fourteen protestant denominations and over 180 Roman Catholic Dioceses and works with the businesses that the member churches invest in to encourage social responsibility. It maintains a library and publishes the *Corporate Examiner* monthly.

International Institute for Economic Research
1100 Glendon Ave., Suite 844
Los Angeles, CA 90024
(203) 208-7735

The International Institute for Economic Research educates students and the general public in the area of economics. It sponsors reports on economic problems, radio and television series on issues, and the monthly publication, *Broadcast*.

Invest-in-America National Council
Architects Bldg.
117 S. 17th St., Suite 906-907
Philadelphia, PA 19103
(215) 568-7311

The Invest-in-America National Council works with teachers, students, and education-oriented organizations to increase understanding and appreciation of the American free-market system. It presents American capitalism as a very positive system and stresses people's personal opportunities in it. It sponsors institutes at universities and circulates films throughout schools.

National Committee on Pay Equity
1201 16th St., NW, Rm. 422
Washington, DC 20036
(202) 822-7304

The National Committee on Pay Equity was organized to examine and educate the general public about wage discrimination and the historical, legal, and economic bases of inequities between women and men and between whites and people of color. The committee provides education, research, and advocacy and serves as a center for publicity and information on these and similar topics.

National Committee to Preserve Social Security and Medicare
1300 19th St., NW, Suite 310
Washington, DC 20036
(202) 822-9459

The National Committee to Preserve Social Security and Medicare is a non-profit organization of over two million members which lobbies in support of the United States' Social Security and Medicare programs. It publishes a newspaper, *Saving Social Security*, and some educational publications.

National Organization for Women (NOW)
425 13th St., NW, Suite 723
Washington, DC 20004
(202) 347-2279

The National Organization for Women seeks to end prejudice and discrimination in all parts of American society. It supports comparable worth and the Equal Rights Amendment. It publishes the newsletter *NOW Times*.

Public Service Research Foundation
8330 Old Courthouse Rd., Suite 600
Vienna, VA 22180
(703) 790-0700

The Public Service Research Foundation is dedicated to the ongoing support of research projects and studies on the issues of public sector labor relations and unionism. The Foundation's program disseminates the results of these studies to the media, public officials, educational organizations and the general public. Its purpose is to enhance understanding and stimulate discussion on controversial events and topics in governmental labor relations. It issues a fortnightly newsletter, the *Government Union Critique*, and the academic quarterly, *Government Union Review*.

Reason Foundation
P.O. Box 40105
Santa Barbara, CA 93103
(805) 963-5993

The Reason Foundation's purpose is to provide a better understanding of the intellectual basis of a free society. It promotes individualist philosophy and free market principles through all its outlets. These include the publications, *Fiscal Watchdog* and *Reason Magazine*.

Rockford Institute
934 N. Main St.
Rockford, IL 61103
(815) 964-5053

The Rockford Institute is a conservative research center which studies capitalism and liberty. It publishes three periodicals, *Chronicles of Culture, The Rockford Papers*, and *Persuasion at Work*. The Institute has also published occasional papers on nuclear freeze and antinuclear activism in the United States.

Save Our Security (SOS)
1201 16th St., NW, Suite 770
Washington, DC 20036
(202) 822-7848

Save Our Security (SOS) is a coalition of organizations that support the present Social Security program or wish to expand it.

SOS lobbies against benefit cuts and has a number of publications supporting Social Security including *Cutting Social Security Benefits is Unnecessary and Wrong*, and *Health Care in the United States*.

Union for Radical Political Economics (URPE)
155 W. 23rd St., 12th Fl.
New York, NY 10011
(212) 691-5722

The Union for Radical Political Economics (URPE) seeks, through political economic analysis, to present a continuing critique of the capitalist system and of all forms of exploitation and oppression while helping to construct a progressive social policy and create socialist alternatives. URPE publishes a quarterly journal, *Review of Radical Political Economics*, and has published a variety of pamphlets for use in teaching and research.

United Farm Workers of America (UFW)
LaPaz
Keene, CA 93570
(805) 822-5571

The United Farm Workers is a labor organization which advocates for the rights of farmworkers and consumers. It seeks to give farm laborers pride in their work by improving working and safety conditions and wages. The UFW's monthly publication is entitled *Food and Justice*.

Wider Opportunities for Women
1325 G St. NW, Lower Level
Washington, DC 20005
(202) 638-3143

The organization's purpose is to expand employment opportunities for women. Its focus is to recognize the need for compensatory training and education to remedy deficiencies resulting from sex discrimination and stereotyping. The organization provides career counseling, access to non-traditional jobs, skills training, job development and placement, and employment advocacy. It publishes a number of newsletters, books and directories.

Women's Equity Action League (WEAL)
1250 Eye St., Suite 305
Washington, DC 20005
(202) 898-1588

The Women's Equity Action League works to advance the legal and economic rights of women through a program of research, public education, litigation, and legislative advocacy. WEAL puts out the bimonthly *Washington Report*, along with reports and action kits.

bibliography

The following bibliography of books, periodicals, and pamphlets is divided into chapter topics for the reader's convenience. The topics are in the same order as in the body of this Opposing Viewpoints *SOURCES*.

Many entries in this bibliography are taken from published materials by The Heritage Foundation. To obtain copies of these publications write to the address listed in the organizations appendix of this volume.

Business Ethics

Patrick M. Boarman	"Business and Ethics: Contemporary Capitalism," *Vital Speeches of the Day,* June 15, 1982.
Commonweal	Special Issue on "Faith & Economics," November 2-16, 1984.
The Corporate Examiner	Available from the Interfaith Center on Corporate Responsibility, Rm. 566, 475 Riverside Dr., New York, NY 10115
John A. Davenport	"Beyond the Market," *The Freeman,* January 1985.
Milton Friedman	"The Social Responsibility of Business to Increase Its Profits," *The New York Times Magazine,* September 13, 1970.
Mark Green and Robert Massie Jr., eds.	*The Big Business Reader: Essays on Corporate America.* New York: The Pilgrim Press, 1980.
Eugene Hillman	"Doing Evil For a Good Cause," *America,* May 10, 1986.
Victor Lasky	"A Deal America Must Refuse," *American Legion Magazine,* April 1986.
Miles W. Lord	"A Plea for Corporate Conscience," Speech published in *Harper's,* June 1984.
Minneapolis Star and Tribune	"Ethical Choices," October 20, 1985.
Morton Mintz	*At Any Cost: Corporate Greed, Women, and the Dalkon Shield.* New York: Pantheon Books, 1985.
Russel Mokhiber	"Criminals By Any Other Name," *The Washington Monthly,* January 1986.
Multinational Monitor	Special Issue on the Dalkon Shield, January 15, 1986.
Charles W. Parry	"My Company—Right or Wrong?" *Vital Speeches of the Day,* August 1, 1985.
Tom Regan, ed.	*Just Business: New Introductory Essays in Business Ethics.* Philadelphia: Temple University Press, 1983.
Donald V. Seibert	"Time to Revive a Commitment to

	Ethics," *New York Times,* December 25, 1983.
Milton Snoeyenbos, Robert Almader and James Humber, eds.	*Business Ethics: Corporate Values and Society.* Buffalo, NY: Prometheus Books, 1983.
Sidney C. Sufrin	"How Moral Can a Business Be?" *The Christian Century,* March 2, 1983.
Amanda Spake	"A New American Nightmare?" *Ms.,* March 1986.

Privatization

James Bovard	"The U.S. Postal Service: The Last Dinosaur," *USA Today,* September 1985.
Harvey Brooks et al., eds.	*Public-Private Partnership: New Opportunities for Meeting Social Needs.* Cambridge, MA: Ballinger Publishing Co., 1984.
Stuart M. Butler, ed.	*The Heritage Lectures: The Privatization Option.* Washington, DC: The Heritage Foundation, 1985.
Stuart M. Butler	*Privatizing Federal Spending: A Strategy to Eliminate the Deficit.* New York: Universe Books, 1985.
Tibor R. Machan	"The Ethics of Privatization," *The Freeman,* July 1986.
Stephen Moore	"How to Privatize Federal Services by 'Contracting Out,'" *The Heritage Foundation Backgrounder,* March 13, 1986.
Lee Smith	"Reagan's Budget: Selling Off the Government," *Fortune,* March 3, 1986.

Deregulation

Stephen Barone	"How Stupid Can They Get?" *Reason,* April 1986.
Black Enterprise	"Taking the Brakes Off Transportation," June 1984.
Andrew S. Carron	"Banking on Change: The Reorganization of Financial Regulation," *The Brookings Review,* Spring 1984.
Robert W. Crandall et al.	*Regulating the Automobile.* Washington, DC: Brookings Institution, 1986.
Martha Derthick and Paul Quirk	*The Politics of Deregulation.* Washington, DC: Brookings Institution, 1985.
Edwin Diamond et al.	*Telecommunications in Crisis: The First Amendment, Technology, and Deregulation.*

Bob Kuttner
Washington, DC: Cato Institute, 1983.
"Ma Bell's Broken Home," *The New Republic*, March 17, 1986.

Robert Linton
"Through the Financial Looking Glass," *USA Today*, May 1984.

Ken Livingston
"All Revved Up and No Place to Go," *Reason*, March 1986.

Thomas K. McCraw
Prophets of Regulation. Cambridge, MA: Harvard University Press, 1984.

John C. Moorhouse
Electric Power. San Francisco: Pacific Research Institute for Public Policy, 1986.

Steven Morrison and Clifford Winston
The Economic Effects of Airline Deregulation. Washington, DC: Brookings Institution, 1986.

Marvin N. Olasky
"Hornswoggled!" *Reason*, February 1986.

Edwin Rothschild and Steven Emerson
"Born Again Cartel," *The New Republic*, November 5, 1984.

Donald R. Wells and L.S. Scruggs
"Toward Free Banking," *The Freeman*, July 1986.

Money

A. Anikin
Gold: The Yellow Devil. New York: International Publishers, 1983.

The Cato Journal
Special Issue on "The Search for Stable Money," Spring 1983. Available from the Cato Institute, 224 Second St. SE, Washington, DC 20003.

Rowland Evans and Robert Novak
"Should the U.S. Dollar Be Backed by Gold?" *Reader's Digest*, April 1983.

David Glasner
"Understanding the Gold Standard," *National Review*, April 5, 1985.

William C. Melton
Inside the Fed: Making Monetary Policy. Homewood, IL: Dow Jones-Irwin, 1985.

Allan Meltzer and Alan Reynolds
Towards a Stable Monetary Policy. Washington, DC: The Heritage Foundation, 1982.

Marc A. Miles
Beyond Monetarism: Finding the Road to Stabler Money. New York: Basic Books, 1984.

Michael Moffitt
The World's Money: International Banking from Bretton Woods to the Brink of Insolvency. New York: Simon and Schuster, 1983.

Maxwell Newton
The Fed: Inside the Federal Reserve, the Secret Power Center that Controls the American Economy. New York: Times Books, 1983.

Ron Paul and Lewis Lehrman
The Case for Gold: A Minority Report of the US Gold Commission. Washington, D.C.: The Cato Institute, 1982.

Lawrence S. Ritter and William L. Sibler
Money. New York: Basic Books, 5th edition, 1984.

Robert J. Samuelson
"The Global Money Game," *Newsweek*, November 5, 1984.

Taxes

Marcus Alexis
"Reaganomics: Who Will Reap the Benefits?" *Black Enterprise*, September 1984.

Bruce Bartlett
"The Case Against a Value-Added Tax," *The Heritage Foundation Backgrounder*, November 5, 1985.

Bruce Bartlett
"The Dangers of a Minium Corporate Tax," *The Heritage Foundation Executive Memorandum*, May 6, 1985.

John Blundell
"Rolls Royces and Canned Carrots," *Reason*, February 1984.

Phillip Briggs
"Taxing Employee Benefits: Fair or Unfair?" *USA Today*, September 1985.

David S. Broder
"It's Not Nice, but Someone Has to Say It: *Raise Taxes*," *Los Angeles Times*, February 10, 1985.

Edgar K. Browning and Jaquelene M. Browning
"Why Not a True Flat Rate Tax?" *The Cato Journal*, Fall 1985.

The Cato Journal
"The Principles and Politics of Tax Reform," Fall 1985.

Emily Card
"Because You Can't Afford to Ignore Tax Policy," *Ms.*, January 1986.

Emily Card
"Good News on Tax Reform," *Ms.*, February 1986.

Kurt Eichenwald
"No New Taxes? Look Closer," *The New York Times*, February 17, 1986.

Martin Feldstein
"How to Get the Deficit Under $100 Billion," *Time*, February 4, 1985.

George Gilder
"Tax-Reform Critics Should Have Second Thoughts," *The Wall Street Journal*, May 29, 1986.

Arthur H. Goldberg
"Tax Shelters," *Vital Speeches of the Day*, November 15, 1984.

C. Lowell Harris
"Fairness in Taxation," *Vital Speeches of the Day*, February 15, 1985.

Floyd K. Haskell
"Retain Tax Indexing," *The New York Times*, March 4, 1984.

Michael Jacobson and Mark Albion
"How to Slash the Deficit and Save Lives in One Easy Step," *The Washington Post National Weekly Edition*, August 26, 1985.

John B. Judis
"All the Current Tax Proposals Will Make the Poor Pay More," *In These Times*, September 12-18, 1984.

Dean M. Kelley
"The Supreme Court Redefines Tax Exemption," *Society*, May/June 1984.

S. Anna Kondrates
"Reagan's Tax Evolution: A Big Boost for Families and the Poor," *The Heritage Foundation Issue Bulletin*, July 25, 1985.

Dwight R. Lee, ed.
Taxation and the Deficit Economy. San Francisco: Pacific Institute for Public Policy Research, 1986.

Joseph Pechman
Who Paid the Taxes, 1966-1985? Washington, DC: Brookings Institution, 1985.

The Progressive
Comment Column: "Beauty and the Beast," March 1986.

Public Agenda Foundation
Taxes: Who Should Pay and Why? Dayton, OH: Domestic Policy Foundation, 1985.

Robert J. Samuelson
"Why Tax Reform Will Fail," *Los Angeles Times*, December 6, 1985.

Budget Deficit

Fred Barnes
"Who's to Blame for the Deficit?" *Reader's Digest*, May 1986.

Robert J. Buckley
"Tax Reform, Trade and the Deficit," *Vital Speeches of the Day*, December 1, 1985.

Center for Popular Economics
Economic Report of the People. Boston: South End Press, 1986.

Richard E. Cohen
"Bright New Chance for a Balanced Budget," *Los Angeles Times*, February 23, 1985.

Robert Eisner
How Real Is the Federal Deficit? New York: Free Press, 1986.

Milton Friedman	"Spending Must Be Cut," *The St. Croix Review*, June/July 1984.
Milton Friedman	"Why Deficits Are Bad," *Newsweek*, January 2, 1984.
Robert E. Hall and Alvin Robushka	*The Flat Tax*. Stanford, CA: Hoover Institution Press, 1985.
Oswald Johnston	"Economists Now Find Deficit Isn't So Bad," *Los Angeles Times*, Februrary 6, 1986.
Monroe W. Karmin	"Where Budget Ax Will Fall," *U.S. News & World Report*, February 17, 1986.
Jack Kemp	"My Plan to Balance the Budget," *Policy Review*, Spring 1986.
Michael Kinsley	"Liberals and Deficits," *The New Republic*, December 31, 1983.
Susan Lee	"Of Course, I'm Sure, I Read It in. . ." *Forbes*, November 19, 1984.
Robert Ortner	"The Deficit Problem Is Exaggerated," *The New York Times*, October 19, 1984.
Richard W. Rahn and Ronald D. Utt	"Federal Budget Deficits: Myths and Reality," *Human Events*, February 11, 1984.
Ronald Reagan	"Spending Is the Problem, Not Taxes," Speech in *The New York Times*, February 6, 1986.
Alice M. Rivlin	"The Need for a Better Budget Process," *The Brookings Review*, Summer 1986.
Paul Craig Roberts	*The Supply-Side Revolution*. Cambridge, MA: Harvard University Press, 1984.
Robert J. Samuelson	"The Budget Masquerade," *Newsweek*, February 20, 1984.
Irwin Schiff	*The Great Income Tax Hoax*. Hamden, CT: Freedom Books, 1985.
Herbert Stein	*Presidential Economics: The Making of Economic Policy from Roosevelt to Reagan and Beyond*. New York: Simon and Schuster, 1984.
Lester C. Thurow	*The Zero-Sum Society*. New York: Basic Books, 1980.
Time	"Ouch! Ouch! Ouch! This Will Hurt," February 24, 1986.

The World Debt Crisis

Michael Adamson	"The International Debt Problem: The Case of Argentina," *The Freeman*, December 1985.
Christine Bagdanowicz	"Debt: Beyond the Quick Fix," *Third World Quarterly*, October 1983.
Tom Bethell	"The Return of the Debt Crisis," *National Review*, August 23, 1985.
Commonweal	"Third-World Debtors' Prison," July 13, 1984.
Dan Dickinson	"Free Enterprise: The Salvation of Many Third World Countries," *Human Events*, January 21, 1984.
Gerald Epstein	"Unshackling the World Economy," *World Policy Journal*, Fall 1985.
Andy Feeney	"Sacrificing the Earth," *Environmental Action*, November/December 1985.
S.C. Gwynne	"Adventures in the Loan Trade," *Harper's*, September 1983.
James S. Henry	"Where the Money Went," *The New Republic*, April 14, 1986.
Mark Hulbert	"Will the US Bail Out the Bankers?" *The Nation*, October 16, 1982.

John H. Makin	*The Global Debt Crisis: America's Growing Involvement*. New York: Basic Books, 1984.
J. William Middendorf	"A Free Market Prescription for Third World Debt," *The Heritage Lectures*, no. 46, 1986.
Felix Rohatyn	"The New Chance for the Economy," *The New York Review of Books*, April 4, 1986.
Stephen Schwartzman	"Banking on Disaster," *Multinational Monitor*, June 15, 1985.
Sara Sleight	"Latin America's Debt," *Report on the Americas*, July/August 1984.
Alexander L. Taylor III	"The Gathering Storm," *Time*, July 2, 1984.
Richard S. Wienert	"Banks & Bankruptcy," *Foreign Policy*, Spring 1983.

Trade

Gilbert F. Amelio	"Danger and Opportunities," *Vital Speeches of the Day*, February 15, 1986.
Deborah Baldwin	"Not So Free Trade," *Common Cause Magazine*, November/December 1984.
Walden Bello et al.	"Comparative (Dis)advantage," *Dollars & Sense*, March 1986.
The Brookings Review	"William E. Brock on International Trade," Spring 1984.
Ernest Conine	"When in Rome, or Tokyo, or . . ." *Los Angeles Times*, October 29, 1985.
Anna DeCormis	"Trade Deficit Brings Calls for No More 'Open Door'," *Guardian*, July 10, 1985.
Pete du Pont	"Kamikaze Economics," *Policy Review*, Fall 1985.
Edmund B. Fitzgerald	"How America Can Compete," *USA Today*, March 1985.
Milton Friedman	"Protectionism Won't Cure U.S. Trade Imbalance," *Human Events*, August 17, 1985.
Eric Gelman	"Tremors of a Trade War," *Newsweek*, September 9, 1985.
David M. Gordon	"Do We Need To Be No. 1?" *The Atlantic*, April 1986.
John C. Griffin Jr. and William Rouse	"Counter-Trade as a Third World Strategy of Development," *Third World Quarterly*, January 1986.
Gary Clyde Hofbauer et al.	*Trade Protection in the United States: 31 Case Studies*. Washington, DC: Institute for International Economics, 1985.
Edward L. Hudgins	"Why Limiting Textile Imports Would Hurt Americans," *The Heritage Foundation Backgrounder*, September 30, 1985.
Lane Kirkland	"Meeting the Challenge of the Future," *Vital Speeches of the Day*, December 15, 1985.
Robert Kuttner	"Blind Faith in Free Trade Doesn't Pay," *Business Week*, October 14, 1985.
Donald Lambro	"Big Business Safety Net," *Inquiry*, June 1984.
Jay Olnek	*The Invisible Hand*. Washington, DC: Liberty Library, 1985.
Herbert Schlossberg	"The Ethics of Protectionism," *Eternity*, November 1985.
Jane Seaberry	"Congress Is Coming Back to an Epidemic of Protectionist Fever," *The Washington Post National Weekly Edition*, September 9, 1985

Jay Stuller — ''Whatever Happened to Made in the U.S.A.?'' *American Legion*, April 1986.

Joan Kennedy Taylor — *Free Trade: The Necessary Foundation for World Peace.* Irvington-on-Hudson, NY: The Foundation for Economic Education, Inc., 1986.

Lester C. Thurow — ''The Hidden Sting of the Trade Deficit,'' *The New York Times*, Janurary 19, 1986.

Robert Trautman — ''The 'Buy American' Drive,'' *The New American*, March 24, 1986.

Raymond E. Walk — ''U.S. Must Dump 'Free Trade','' *The Spotlight*, July 8, 1985.

W. Allen Wallis — ''Open Markets: Key to a Stronger, Richer, and Freer America,'' *Department of State Bulletin*, December 1985.

Case Study in Trade: The US and Japan

Howard H. Baker Jr. — ''Time for a Truce in the Japan Trade War,'' *The New York Times*, August 21, 1985.

Edmund G. Brown Jr. — ''Using U.S. Muscle in World Markets,'' *The New York Times*, November 21, 1985.

Allen C. Brownfeld — ''Japan—the Scapegoat,'' *The St. Croix Review*, June/July 1985. Correspondence: *The St. Croix Review*, Stillwater, MN 55082.

Ernest Conine — ''Can Japan Shift Economic Strategy,'' *Los Angeles Times*, July 29, 1985.

Ernest Conine — ''Japan's About-Face Is Far From Sure,'' *Los Angeles Times*, April 21, 1986.

Kiyohiko Fukushima — ''Japan's Real Trade Policy,'' *Foreign Policy*, Summer 1985.

George Gilder — ''Imports Are Not a Problem But a Cure,'' *The Wall Street Journal*, March 27, 1985.

Thomas M. Hout — ''Trade Barriers Won't Keep Out Japan,'' *The New York Times*, April 29, 1984.

Edward L. Hudgins — ''Tokyo's Trade Plan: A Tiny First Step,'' *The Heritage Foundation Executive Memorandum*, July 11, 1985.

Edward L. Hudgins — ''U.S.—Japan Trade Tension Part 1: What Is at Fault?'' *Asian Studies Center Backgrounder*, November 8, 1985.

Henry A. Kissinger — ''Persuading in Trading Means Knowing a Partner,'' *Los Angeles Times*, October 6, 1985.

Paul H. Kreisberg — ''Japan-Bashing Will Not Solve the Trade Problem,'' *The New York Times*, August 5, 1985.

Robert Kuttner — ''Zen and the Art of Trade Negotiation,'' *The New Republic*, August 12 & 19, 1985.

The New Republic — ''How to Gyp the Japs,'' September 2, 1985.

Hobart Rowen — ''Fears of a Trade Showdown,'' *The Washington Post National Weekly Edition*, July 22, 1985.

Katsuro Sakoh — ''Japan's Secret,'' *Reason*, February 1986.

Katsuro Sakoh — ''U.S. Services Exports: Time for Japan to Lower Barriers,'' *Asian Studies Center Backgrounder*, June 11, 1985.

Katsuro Sakoh — ''U.S.-Japan Trade Tension Part 2: The Sticky Problem of Nontariff Barriers,'' *Asian Studies Center Backgrounder*, December 12, 1985.

Robert J. Samuelson — ''The Japanese Blindness,'' *Newsweek*, May 5, 1986.

Herbert Stein — ''Japan Fills the Gap,'' *The New York Times*, August 9, 1985.

U.S. News & World Report — ''Sometimes a Problem Is Overexaggerated,'' July 29, 1985.

U.S. News & World Report — ''U.S.-Japan Trade 'Will Get Worse Before It Gets Better','' October 28, 1985.

Kim Woo-Choong — ''Building a Third World Multinational,'' *Vital Speeches of the Day*, October 1, 1985.

Clayton Yeutter — ''Improved Market Access to Japan,'' *Economics*, October 1985.

Immigration

America — ''How to Mend a Wall,'' May 31, 1986.

Evan T. Barr — ''Borderline Hypocrisy,'' *The New Republic*, July 14 & 21, 1986.

Congressional Digest — ''Pending Immigration Legislation,'' March 1986.

Jose Cuello — ''Curbing Illegal Immigration from Mexico,'' *USA Today*, March 1986.

Albert Fried — ''Let the Torch Cast True Light on Our Immigrant Story,'' *The New York Times*, July 4, 1986.

K.E. Grubbs Jr. — ''Just Another Wetback,'' *National Review*, February 14, 1986.

Jane Hamilton-Merritt — ''America's Refugee Mess,'' *Reader's Digest*, June 1985.

William F. Jasper — ''The Silent Invasion,'' *The New American*, June 2, 1986.

Terry Johnson — ''Immigrants: New Victims,'' *Newsweek*, May 12, 1986.

Charles B. Keeley — ''Issues in Immigration Since 1965,'' *Social Education*, March 1986.

Kirk Kidwell — ''Peril at the Border,'' *The New American*, June 2, 1986.

Veronica Kot — ''We Will Still Be an Immigrant Nation,'' *In These Times*, April 24-30, 1985.

Chuck Lane — ''Open the Door,'' *The New Republic*,'' April 1, 1985.

Thomas Massey — ''The Wrong Way to Court Ethnics,'' *The Washington Monthly*, May 1986.

Kevin F. McCarthy and R. Burciaga Valdez — *Current and Future Effects of Mexican Immigration in California.* Santa Monica, Ca: Rand Corporation. November 1985.

Frank Moan — ''Immigration Reform: Three Missing Ingredients,'' *America*, March 22, 1986.

Mark Olson — ''Open the Border!'' *The Other Side*, April 1986.

David M. Reimers — *Still the Golden Door: The Third World Comes to America.* New York: Columbia University Press, 1986.

Richard Rodriguez — ''A Minority Scholar Speaks Out,'' *American Education*, November 1982.

John Simon — ''Black and White in Purple,'' *National Review*, February 14, 1986.

Lucia Solorzano — ''Educating the Melting Pot,'' *U.S. News & World Report*, March 31, 1986.

U.S. News & World Report — '''It's the Immigrants Who Can Move Dramatically','' July 4, 1983.

Labor

James Abdnor and William L. Clay — ''Should the Congress Lower the Minimum Wage for Youth,'' *The*

AFL-CIO Committee on the Evolution of Work	*American Legion*, December 1983. "The Future of Work." The initial report issued by the Committee in August 1983. Available from the AFL-CIO, 815 Sixteenth Street NW, Washington, DC 20006.
Stanley Aronowitz	*Working Class Hero: A New Strategy for Labor*. New York: The Pilgrim Press, 1983.
Ken Aulette	*The Underclass*. New York: Random House, 1982.
Clarence B. Carson	*Organized Against Whom?: The Labor Movement in America*. Alexandria, VA: Western Goals, 1983. Available from the Foundation for Economic Education, Irvington-on-Hudson, NY 10533.
William Foot-Whyte et al.	*Worker Participation and Ownership: Cooperative Strategies for Strengthening Local Economies*. Ithaca, NY: Institute for Labor Relations Press, 1985.
Robert W. Haseltine	"Idle Thoughts on Unions," *USA Today*, May 1986.
Dirk Johnson	"Labor Scarcity Is Forcing Up Low-Level Pay," *The New York Times*, March 17, 1986.
Thomas A. Kochan, ed.	*Challenges and Choices Facing American Labor*. Cambridge, MA: The MIT Press, 1985.
Frank Lindenfeld and Joyce Rothschild-Whitt, eds.	*Workplace Democracy and Social Change*. Boston: Porter Sargent, 1985.
Eric Mann	"Union Busting Made Easy," *The New York Times*, March 21, 1986.
Muriel Merkel	*The Labor Union Handbook*. New York: Beaufort Books, Inc., 1983.
Nicolaus Mills	"Why Local P-9 Is Going it Alone," *The Nation*, April 26, 1986.
Daniel J.B. Mitchell	*Union, Wages, and Inflation*. Washington, DC: The Brookings Institution, 1980.
The New Republic	"Subminimum Seduction," June 18, 1984.
President's Commission on Organized Crime	"The Edge: Organized Crime, Business, and Labor Unions." A report to the President and the Attorney General, available from the President's Commission on Organized Crime, Suite 700, 1425 K Street NW, Washington, DC 20005-3468.
Albert Rees	*The Economics of Trade Unions*. Chicago: University of Chicago Press, 1977.
William Serrin	"New Climate for Unions," *The New York Times*, March 18, 1986.
William Somplatsky-Jarman	"The Real Hormel Story," *Christianity and Crisis*, March 3, 1986.
Juan Williams	"A New Debate on the Sub-Minimum Wage," *The Washington Post National Weekly Edition*, May 20, 1985.

Male/Female Economics

Morris B. Abram	"Against 'Comparable Worth'," *The New York Times*, November 4, 1985.
Barbara Bergman	"Pay Equity—How to Argue Back," *Ms.*, November 1985.
engage/social action	Special issue on "Economic Justice for Women," January 1984.
Suzanne Fields	"Why Poverty So Often Wears a Skirt," *The Washington Times*, January 2, 1986.

Ted Guest	"Fair-Pay Drive by Women Hits a Legal Detour," *U.S. News & World Report*, September 16, 1985.
Claudia Goldin	"Understanding the Gender Gap," *New Perspectives*, Fall 1985.
Clifford Hackett	"Women, Work, & the Question of 'Comparable Worth'," *Commonweal*, May 31, 1985.
Blythe Hamer	"Sex, Statistics, and Salaries," *Science 85*, December 1985.
The Humanist	Special issue—"Comparable Worth: What Is *Its* Worth?" May/June 1986.
Kenneth E. John	"Comparable Worth: It's Gaining," *The Washington Post National Weekly Edition*, March 17, 1986.
Kenneth B. Noble	"Low-Paying Jobs Foreseen for Most Working Women," *The New York Times*, December 12, 1985.
Jane M. Orient	"Comparable Worth Versus Civil Liberty: Are Feminists Pro-Choice?" *The Freeman*, June 1985.
Phyllis Schlafly	"Shall I Compare Thee to a Plumber's Pay?" *Policy Review*, Winter 1985.
Harvey Lee Smith	"Women in Economic History," *The Freeman*, September 1984.
Society	Special issue on Comparable Worth, July/August 1985.
Thomas Sowell	"The Fallacy of 'Comparable Worth'," *Washington Inquirer*, March 8, 1985.
George F. Will	"A Doctrine of High Priests," *Newsweek*, September 30, 1985.

Welfare

Nancy Amidei	"Welfare Does *Not* Dictate Child-Bearing," *Los Angeles Times*, August 7, 1985.
Tom Bates	"Our Welfare Recipients Need Jobs, Not Workfare," *Los Angeles Times*, August 19, 1985.
James Bovard	"How Many Federal Programs Are Needed to Cure 'Hunger in America'?" *Conservative Digest*, February 1984.
Allan C. Carlson	"Poverty and Ideology, 1985: Or Why Do We Always Have the Poor with Us?" *Persuasion at Work*, February 1985.
The Cato Journal	"The Political Economy of Poverty," Spring/Summer 1985.
Barbara Ehrenreich	"Welfare is Not the Lap of Luxury," *The New York Times*, February 14, 1985.
Barbara Ehrenreich	"Two, Three, Many Husbands," *Mother Jones*, July/August 1986.
Gregory A. Fossedal	"Corporate Welfare Out of Control," *The New Republic*, February 25, 1985.
Gregory A. Fossedal	"The Second War on Poverty," *The American Spectator*, Feburary 1986.
John Kenneth Galbraith	"The Heartless Society," *The New York Times Magazine*, September 2, 1984.
Pete Hamill	"Toward the Abolition of Welfare," *The Village Voice*, December 24, 1985.
Michael Harrington	*The New American Poverty*. New York: Holt, Rinehart and Winston, 1984.
David L. Kirp	"The California Work/Welfare Scheme," *The Public Interest*, Spring 1986.
S. Anna Kondratas	"A Strategy for Helping America's Homeless," *The Heritage Foundation Backgrounder*, May 6, 1985.
Jacob V. Lamar Jr.	"From Welfare to Workfare," *Time*, February 3, 1986.

Nicholas Lemann	"The Origins of the Underclass," *The Atlantic*, June 1986.
Lawrence M. Mead	*Beyond Entitlement*, New York: The Free Press, 1986.
Richard Meyer and Barry Béarak	"Poverty: Toll Grows Amid Aid Cutbacks," *Los Angeles Times*, July 28, 1985.
Daniel Patrick Moynihan	*Family and Nation*. San Diego: Harcourt, Brace, Jovanovich, 1985.
Charles Murray	"Helping the Poor: A Few Modest Proposals," *Commentary*, May 1985.
Kevin Roderick	"Case History of a 20-Year War on Poverty," *Los Angeles Times*, July 31, 1985.
Barry Sussman	"Welfare Isn't a Life Sentence, and It Has Helped Many," *The Washington Post National Weekly Edition*, February 24, 1986.
Dorothy Wickenden	"Abandoned Americans," *The New Republic*, March 18, 1985.

Social Security

Doug Bandow	"Sun City for Social Security," *The American Spectator*, October 1985.
The Cato Journal	"Social Security: Continuing Crisis or Real Reform," Fall 1983.
The Christian Science Monitor	"Social Security," August 14, 1985.
Barber Conable	"Social Security: the Real Peril," *U.S. News & World Report*, August 19, 1985.
Maura Dolan and Robert A. Rosenblatt	"Senior Citizens Hold Their Own as Aid Remains Largely Unscathed," *Los Angeles Times*, February 3, 1986.
Martin Feldstein	"The Social Security Explosion," *The Public Interest*, Fall 1985.
Peter J. Ferrara	"A Winning Way to Trim Social Security," *Fortune*, January 6, 1986.
Peter J. Ferrara	"For Social Security, the Crisis Continues," *The Heritage Foundation Backgrounder*, November 4, 1985.
Geraldine A. Ferraro	"Older Women and Poverty," *USA Today*, July 1982.
Mark Graven	"If You're Not Part of the Solution, You're Part of the Problem," *Gray Panthers Network*, Spring 1985. Available from Gray Panthers, 311 S. Juniper St., Philadelphia, PA 19107.
Robert Kuttner	"Flawed Fixes," *The New Republic*, January 6 & 13, 1986.
Richard D. Lamm	"A Means Test for Social Security," *Los Angeles Times*, September 4, 1985.
Philip Longman	"Just Between Generations," *The Atlantic*, June 1985.
Ronald Pollack and Thomas S. Blanton	"Why They'd Cut Social Security", *The New York Times*, September 13, 1985.
Spencer Rich	"Social Security at 50: Checks Are Still in the Mail," *The Washington Post National Weekly Edition*, August 26, 1985.
Patricia Scerschel and Richard D. DeLouise	"Social Security at 50 Faces New Crossroads," *U.S. News & World Report*, August 12, 1985.
Paul Taylor	"Remember the Generation Gap? Well, We Ain't Seen Nothin' Yet," *The Washington Post National Weekly Edition*, January 20, 1986.

Agriculture

Heather Ball and Leland Beatty	"Blowing Away the Family Farmer," *The Nation*, November 3, 1986.
Dennis Bechara	"The Continuing Plight of Agriculture," *The Freeman*, May 1986.
Joseph N. Beldon, et al.	*Dirt Rich, Dirt Poor*. London: Routledge & Kegan Paul, 1986.
Evelyn Bence	"Assisting Hard-Hit Farm Families," *Christianity Today*, May 16, 1986.
Wendell Berry	*The Unsettling of America: Culture and Agriculture*. San Francisco: Sierra Club Books, 1977.
Business Week	"How PIK Is Poisoning Farm Policy," August 8, 1983.
Clarence B. Carson	"Farming Is a Business," *The Freeman*, August 1986.
Harlan C. Clifford	"Exploiting a Link Between Farm Debt and Soil Erosion To Aid Farmers," *The Christian Science Monitor*, September 5, 1985.
The Christian Science Monitor	"Rural America at a Crossroads: Is It Really a Depression?" April 24-May 2, 1986. A five part series.
Susan Dentzer et al.	"Bitter Harvest," *Newsweek*, February 18, 1985.
John D. Donahue	"The Political Economy of Milk," *The Atlantic*, October 1983.
Peter Downs	"Seeds of Discontent," *The Progressive*, July 1986.
Aloysius Ehrbar	"Facts vs. the Furor over Farm Policy," *Fortune*, November 11, 1985.
Val Farmer	"Broken Heartland," *Psychology Today*, April 1986.
The Freeman Library	*The Farm Problem*. Irvington-on-Hudson, NY: The Foundation for Economic Education, 1986.
Jim Hightower	*Hard Tomatoes, Hard Times*. Cambridge, MA: Schenkman Press, 1972.
Karolyn Ide	"The Dairy Dilemma," *Country Journal*, January 1985.
Kandice H. Kahl	"Agricultural Options: An Alternative to Federal Farm Programs," *The Heritage Foundation Backgrounder*, March 7, 1985.
Stephen Koepp	"Amber Waves of Grain," *Time* July 21, 1986.
Mark Kramer	*Three Farms: Making Milk, Meat and Money from the American Soil*. Boston: Little, Brown, 1980.
Christopher Larson	"The Problems of Plenty," *Northwest Orient*, March 1986.
Elmer W. Learn, Philip L. Martin, & Alex F. McCalla	"American Farm Subsidies: A Bumper Crop," *Public Interest*, Summer 1986.
William G. Lesher	"Trying To Harvest a Policy To Keep Farm Sector Competitive," *The Christian Science Monitor*, July 14, 1984.
Clifton Luttrell	"Government Crop Programs: High Costs and Few Gains," *USA Today*, July 1986.
Robert McGough	"A Modest Proposal," *Forbes*, September 23, 1985.
David Moberg	"Debating Farm Policy," *In These Times*, August 21-September 3, 1985.
The New Republic	"Stuffing Farmers, Stuffing Peasants," August 11 & 18, 1986.

E.C. Pasour Jr.	"High Cost of Farm Subsidies," *The Heritage Foundation Backgrounder*, October 24, 1984.
E.C. Pasour Jr.	"The Free Market Answer to U.S. Farm Problems," *The Heritage Foundation Backgrounder*, October 30, 1984.
G. Edward Schuh	"US Farming's Global Reach Doesn't for High Profits," *The Christian Science Monitor*, August 15, 1984.
Jim Schwab	"Saving the System, Not the Farmers," *The Nation*, January 18, 1986.
Jim Schwab	"The Shaky Farm Credit System," *The Nation*, May 11, 1985.
U.S. News & World Report	"It Looks Pretty Bleak for a Lot of Farmers," Interview with Secretary of Agriculture, John Block, February 18, 1985.
Ingolf Vogeler	*The Myth of the Family Farm: Agribusiness Dominance of U.S. Agriculture.* Boulder, CO: Westview Press, 1981.
James Wessel	*Trading the Future.* San Francisco: Institute for Food and Development Policy, 1983.

index